The American West

The American West

A NEW INTERPRETIVE HISTORY
SECOND EDITION

Robert V. Hine, John Mack Faragher,
and Jon T. Coleman

Yale UNIVERSITY PRESS   New Haven and London

Published with assistance from the Joan
Patterson Kerr Fund and from the income of
the Frederick John Kingsbury Memorial Fund.

Yale University Press books may be purchased
in quantity for educational, business, or
promotional use. For information, please
e-mail sales.press@yale.edu (U.S. office) or
sales@yaleup.co.uk (U.K. office).

Set in Minion and Egiziano types by Newgen
North America.
Printed in the United States of America.

Library of Congress Control Number:
2016960137

ISBN 978-0-300-18517-1 (paperbound : alk.
paper)

A catalogue record for this book is available
from the British Library.

This paper meets the requirements of ANSI/
NISO z39.48-1992 (Permanence of Paper).

10 9 8 7 6 5 4 3 2 1

FOR BOB AND SHIRLEY HINE

Contents

Preface to the Second Edition: The Re-Boot

The skeletal remains of an industrial city scroll across the windshield of a cruising automobile. Empty highway off-ramps loop overhead while roadside factories spew filth into pallid skies. A guitar strums the opening chords of Eminem's "Lose Yourself," and day blinks to night. A tough voice hails Chrysler's 200, a ridiculously high-end four-door sedan that somehow captures the spirit of hideously lowdown Detroit.

Detroit molders on the fringes of the United States. Parked next to Canada, the city teeters on a geopolitical drop-off. Detroit's actual location, however, meant little to the advertising professionals that chose the city and Eminem to star in their 2011 Super Bowl commercial. Only the ugly weather suggested a true global position. No, the ad makers came to Eminem and Detroit for their exquisite down-and-out-there-ness. Both were damaged icons. Kneecapped by the auto industry's overreliance on truck and SUV sales, hollowed out by thousands of laid-off workers escaping for sunnier climes, and set aflame by the 2008–9 financial meltdown, the city proffered Hollywood its ashes. The rapper knew hard times as well. An addict with a taste for pills, he spent the 2000s coming to terms with the success he achieved the previous decade. The titles of his last three albums—*Encore, Relapse,* and *Recovery*—hinted at his troubles.

Detroit's status as a car-wrecked municipality and Eminem's reputation as a flawed human being make them the ideal opening act for a revised edition of *The American West: A New Interpretive History*. While nowhere near as obsolete as the U.S. auto industry, *The American West* is due for an overhaul. More than a decade has passed since its last refurbishing. A lot has happened: terror attacks and security crackdowns, wars-of-choice and drone campaigns, economic downturns and taxpayer bailouts, tea parties and occupied parks. The planet has continued to heat up while information has flowed in ever quickening streams to manifold devices. The world has turned since 2000, so too has the history of the American West. A new generation of scholars, inspired by an energetic group of (now) senior citizens, the "New Western historians" of the 1980s and 1990s and their critics, has come into their own and filled bookshelves with new research and interpretations.

The rush of work, for all its intelligence and well-deserved accolades, seems timid and scattered when compared to the vintage stuff. The New Western history organized debates around a set of pressure points: region versus frontier; place versus process; progress versus decline. Was the West a distinctive locale, defined by its aridity, its mountainous terrain, or its proximity to the Pacific Ocean, or was it a set of colonial relationships and power struggles that rippled across many landscapes throughout the continent? Did borders and boundaries in time and space define the place and its history or did line-crossing economies, migrant groups, and nation-states explain the past better? Was this history bright and hopeful or criminal and tragic? Scholars picked sides (sometimes in opposition, sometimes at right-angles, many times in parallel—there was a good deal of talking past one another in the 1980s and 1990s) and threw down in public. The ruckus has since died down, and the scrum parted, not so much in peace as indecision. Most western historians have agreed to agree. Western history deals with most everything now: place and process, region and frontier, men and women, whites and racial minorities, queers and heteronormatives, humanity and nature; the good, the bad, and the ambiguous—especially the ambiguous.

It's hard to plant your feet in such a vast and poorly bounded field. But perhaps a foul-mouthed rapper from the Canadian-American hinterlands can supply a fresh orientation.

Born in 1972, Marshal Mathers III moved from Kansas City to Detroit as a teenager. In the city's eastside eight-mile neighborhood, he reinvented himself as Eminem, a rare musical concoction at the time—a white rapper who wasn't a gimmick or a knockoff. Black artists had dominated rap since hip-hop emerged from the urban youth culture of the South Bronx in the late 1970s. Eminem wanted to crash a party that celebrated hyper-masculine black men with impeccably bad credentials. Artists posed as gangsters and hoodlums and policed each other for signs of softness and fakery. Growing up in poor and violent locations boosted rappers' reputations. Eminem's dysfunctional home environment and squalid surroundings turned out to be assets. (He was also verbally dexterous; a witty writer and a fierce improviser.) Stardom, though, waited until he teamed up with a brilliant producer from a tough background no one questioned. Dr. Dre signed Eminem to a record contract in 1998. A founding member of NWA, Dre came from the crack-infested Compton section of Los Angeles. He and his band mates pioneered "gangsta rap," a version of hip-hop dedicated to brutal realism. Cores didn't come any harder.

Eminem's conquest of the globe's airwaves and earphones depended on his connection to two hardscrabble places—Detroit's eastside and LA's Compton neighborhood. His fame transcended geographic, political, and demographic boundaries, yet his persona remained localized. Indeed, his plausibility as a sincere hip-hop artist—a white rapper people of all races and backgrounds could respect—depended on him staying rooted in marginal places. His edginess only intensified with the 2002 release of *8-mile,* the autobiographic film that chronicled his formative years in Detroit. Eminem scored his biggest hit single, "Lose Yourself," from the movie's soundtrack. Chrysler banked on that song's popularity and Eminem's Detroit ghetto lineage to restore its brand. The global corporate entity needed him to drive down some very specific mean streets to recapture its customers' imaginations.

The silliness of the whole setup—extoling luxury with images of "ruin porn" during an international broadcast sporting event—shouldn't detract from its historical import. When placed at the tail end of a narrative history of Americans' relationship with their frontiers, the 200 commercial suggested a break with the past as well as a hold in pattern. The commercial imbibed in the American cultural habit of looking to the margins for inspiration, renewal, and authenticity. While they might abhor and denigrate blighted places and broken people, Americans often staged their comebacks from the fringes. Thus, Eminem and Detroit belonged to a string of down-and-outs or far-and-aways that rebooted the nation.

Yet, despite the fervent wishes of ad agents and auto execs, the gears of American frontier worship never shift smoothly. Nations built on edges tend to fall off them, and Eminem's America balanced on a precipice of global dimensions. Eminem, the 200 sedan, Chrysler, hip-hop, the Super Bowl, even the song "Lose Yourself," weren't contained by one nation. They spilled across an information network that mocked lines on maps. They shot through space and slipped into human minds from Borneo to Buckingham Palace. For successful businessmen-rappers, staying put brought obscurity, and thus poverty. They wanted their products to migrate like a disease, to go viral. Despite its sickly appearance, Detroit languished because it wasn't communicable. The Motor City sat while its workforce retired to Arizona, its factories relocated to China, and its corporate leaders drifted to the Caymans on golden parachutes. In the virtual world of 2011, real places were for losers. And Detroit and Eminem were surely losers, albeit lovable and instructive ones. They embodied the resurgence of frontiers in a globalized United States.

In its own way, the 200 ad scripted a new ending for the American West. "The West" (both as a space between the Pacific Ocean and the Mississippi River and a vague geo-political notion, the obverse to "the East") flourished in a super-powered world where clear lines and boundaries held allies together and kept enemies apart (think Berlin Walls and DMZs). When the Soviet Union crumbled, geographies and ideologies based on cardinal directions collapsed as well. The West, you might argue, won the Cold War and utterly lost itself in the process. The East / West world fragmented politically even as the internet—a Cold War invention—triggered a communication revolution that eroded boundaries of all kinds. The result was a globalized culture in which place mattered a great deal and not at all. The West became a niche among niches, a site in a web of connections.

This is a different ending from the one predicted in the previous edition of *The American West: A New Interpretive History*. In that text, the American West modeled national trends and disappeared into those trends. The region pioneered things like the military-industrial complex, hot tubs, illegal immigrant panics, fast food, energy-based derivatives, big Cabernets, and uni-bombing. It led the nation towards planetary dominance and then withered sometime in the 1980s or 1990s when the United States achieved maximum homogeneity. Basically, the West got Starbucked to death.

With high-end java available on almost every American street corner, it's hard to argue with this conclusion. Western enterprises, politics, and caffeinated beverages have infected the country, muting the differences between regions. Yet the same communications revolution that sped the westernization of the mainstream also strengthened the margins. The internet both linked and fragmented people; it aided globalization and spurred localism at the same time. No event symbolized the clash of these opposing forces better than the 1999 protests against the World Trade Organization in Seattle. Activists of all stripes (and gripes), from sea turtle conservators to antihormone vegans to NAFTA-hating teamsters, coalesced to halt the proceedings. They rejected the neoliberal argument that globalization—symbolized by free trade—represented an unmitigated good. Marginal people, bound to locations, suffered when protections fell, to the benefit of corporations and their first-world government enablers. To underscore this argument, anarchists tossed car batteries through the glass storefronts of the downtown chains. Starbucks's green and white mermaid logo proved an especially inviting target.

Since 1999, regular folks have networked through social media to topple dictators and organize flash mobs. They have spread videos of kittens and leaked classified torture documents. The internet has opened a universe of choices. Confronted with a smorgasbord of information, people satisfy their tastes with preferred delights. Do you enjoy knitting or conspiracy theories? Then you need not consume anything but knitting and conspiracy theories. The end result: a population united and blown to pieces by the same media.

The 200 advertisement cruised in this reality. It linked geographic, social, and cultural margins in a chain of associations that sold over-priced cars to a cash-strapped audience with flashes of industrial decline and a hummable song. The ad celebrated an authentically fringe setting even as it conjured a magical ride out of the Motor City's grime. So diametrically opposed, Detroit and the 200 only synched in a split-screen format that accounted for both the power of place and the joys of dislocation.

Such is America in the twenty-first century. It is our hope that this latest edition of *The American West: A New Interpretive History* will give readers new analytical tools to apply to their present. We contend that western and frontier historians offer a unique vantage point from which to explore the interplay between fragments and wholes, edges and centers, shadows and spotlights.

Our history of the American West reconnoiters the seams of the past, where geographic, social, and cultural margins met, buckled, and subsumed one another. We argue that the tectonic friction along these edges explains some of the most prominent features of the North American historical landscape: the large-scale migration and settlement of peoples, the rise and fall of Native and European empires, the development of a United States of America with continental aspirations, the US's conquest and incorporation of the hunk of space that came to be known as the American West, the growth and dominance of the American West of the late nineteenth and early twentieth centuries, and the near disappearance of the region in the post–World War II era when most of the United States came to look more or less western or Sun-Belted. The narrative ends in the present with a new chapter that considers the West as a site in a globalized, virtual world.

For those of you still unconvinced by the frontier credentials of Eminem, Detroit, and the 200, I offer Chrysler's follow-up 2012 Super Bowl commercial as further proof. In that spot, a whispery voice touted what the city, the company, and the country supposedly represented. Once on its heels, Chrysler was fighting back. Detroit too had regained its feet. If America followed their example, stopped squabbling and took heart, the nation could once again mount a comeback from the margins.

Given the gridiron setting, the ad's "halftime in America" sports metaphor struck a chord. But Chrysler didn't hire a Knute Rockne to deliver its win-one-for-the-Gipper speech. They enlisted a movie star instead, an actor famous for his western roles. Clint Eastwood, the squint-eyed gunslinger, kicked the country out of the doldrums with a boot to the rear, underscoring the connection between frontiers real and imagined, past and present.

Jon T. Coleman
South Bend, Indiana

Acknowledgments

Over the years many friends and colleagues contributed ideas and support for *The American West: A New Interpretive History*. At the Riverside and Irvine campuses of the University of California: Carlos E. Cortes, Edwin Scott Gaustad, Irving G. Hendrick, Spencer C. Olin, and Henry C. Meyer. At Mount Holyoke College: Daniel Czitrom and Joseph J. Ellis. At Yale University: Nancy Cott, Robert Johnston, Howard R. Lamar, Steven B. Stoll, and Robin Winks. At the University of Notre Dame: Patrick Griffin, Annie Gilbert Coleman, and Lindsey Passenger Wieck. In the wider historical world: Kathryn Abbott, Robert Berkhofer, Edwin R. Bingham, Alan Bogue, Elizabeth Fenn, Greg Hise, Paul W. Hirt, Wilbur Jacobs, Elizabeth Jameson, Earl Pomeroy, Rodman Paul, Ruth Sutter, and Eliott West. Several generations of students helped with the research for this book, and we applaud their good work: Laurel Angell, James T. Brown, Robert Campbell, Jack Goldwasser, Jeff Hardwick, Allison Hine-Estes, Jennifer Howe, Benjamin H. Johnson, James Kessenides, Andrew Lewis, J. C. Mutchler, Christina Nunez, Elizabeth Pauley, Robert Perkinson, and Nora Sulzmann. The transformation of manuscript into book was the responsibility of the skilled staff of Yale University Press: we especially want to thank Christopher Rogers, Sarah Miller, and Eva Skewes.

In 2015, as the work on this revised edition was in progress, Robert V. Hine, the book's original author, died at the age of ninety-three. Many years ago, when I was a young graduate student, Bob introduced me to the work of doing history. His joints stiffened by rheumatoid arthritis, his eyes blinded by cataracts, he was not able to browse the stacks and read the documents, and in 1969 he hired me to retrieve the things he needed and read them aloud to him. He was working on the original edition of *The American West,* and he sent me scurrying after monographs and documents of all kinds. For an aspiring historian, this was the opportunity of a lifetime. Bob's eyes had failed him, but the sensitivity of his historical ear was striking. He would sit quietly as I read the things I found, and I knew we'd hit pay dirt the moment he began to punch away on his big brailler. Bob was a master at selecting the telling phrase or quotation that conveys the deep meaning of the evidence. This skill can't be taught by Socratic method but requires an affective process of learning that engages the spirit as well as the mind. His example helped me become a more sensitive reader, always listening for the song in the text. Bob's sight was restored by surgery in 1986—a miraculous event he recounted in his wonderful memoir, *Second Sight* (1993)—and it provided him with renewed opportunity to work during the years of his retirement. It offered us the opportunity to collaborate on a new edition of *The American West*.

For this revision, Bob and I were joined by Jon T. Coleman, a professor of history at the University of Notre Dame. Although Bob's days of doing history were over (in his last years he turned to writing historical novels), he was enthusiastic about passing the torch to a representative of the rising generation. Jon and I join in mourning Bob's passing but also in celebrating his life's work. This book is inspired by his vision of western history. As he wrote in the preface to the previous edition: "In alighting out for the West (that's the way Huck Finn put it) we intend to interpret the story of the American frontier with little pretense of being comprehensive or completely objective. Instead we face with wonder the deep contradictions in our history and try to make sense of them."

John Mack Faragher
Hamden, Connecticut

Introduction: Dreams and Homelands

"The West has been the great word of our history. The Westerner has been the type and master of our American life." When future president Woodrow Wilson wrote these lines in 1895, he infused geography with portent. He was neither the first nor the last to so grandly interpret the American West. An unnamed assemblage of human beings had cultivated a special relationship with a unique space, and Wilson celebrated the mighty people that sprouted there. "The West," a magical utterance, launched an exceptional history that made America what it was.[1]

Wilson was not the first to imagine that power lay in a certain direction. Centuries before they first sailed to the Americas, Europeans were dreaming of unknown lands to the west, places inhabited perhaps by "the fabulous races of mankind," men and women unlike any seen in the known world. The people might be frightening, but their world would surely be a paradise, a golden land somewhere beyond the setting sun. In the words of Horace, the Roman poet,

> See, see before us the distant glow,
> Through the thin dawn-mists of the West,
> Rich sunlit plains and hilltops gemmed with snow,
> The Islands of the Blest!

Such visions dared individuals to bet their lives and fortunes (as well as the lives and fortunes of underlings and investors) on finding pockets of wonderment on the far western horizon. Christopher Columbus longed to see the mythical western isles "of which so many marvels are told," and like Wilson he believed mastery resided there as well. Following the lead of fictional knights who conquered lost islands and ruled them as lords, this Genoese weaver's son foresaw social advantage at the end of his journey. One trip might turn him, a sailor from a modest background, into a "High Admiral of the Ocean Sea and Viceroy and Governor in perpetuity." Columbus sailed to the edge to secure a privileged spot at the center of his world.[2]

Anticipating contact with unknown peoples: the "Fabulous Races of Mankind." From Liber Chronicarum *(Nuremberg, 1493). Beinecke Rare Book and Manuscript Library, Yale University.*

Columbus stood in a line of dreamers that stretched behind and before him. They endowed space with myth, building fantasies of golden cities, fountains of youth, labor-free paradises, Amazonian wonder-women, and empire, always empire, out on the horizon. "Westward the course of empire takes its way," declared Anglo-Irish philosopher George Berkeley in the mid-eighteenth century, and the first generation of American nationalists adopted that rhetoric as their own. "True religion, and in her train, dominion, riches, literature, and art have taken their course in a slow and gradual manner from East to West," the Reverend John Witherspoon preached at Princeton in 1775, and "from thence forebode the future glory of America." As he spoke, settlers and land speculators were carving farms and towns from Indian territory west of the Appalachians. Westward Ho! In the nineteenth century, American expansionists coupled the imagined West to the idea of American greatness and called the result Manifest Destiny.[3]

Dreams motivate history through the men and women they kick into action. Imagination carried Europeans a long way, but accepted without skepticism, those dreams have carried historical inquiry into thickets of delusion. At the end of their fantasies, western adventurers found other people at home, people living in more than two thousand distinct cultures, speaking hundreds of different languages, and making their livings in scores of dissimilar environments. These peoples did not consider themselves at the margins of anything. Most considered their homes to be the center of the universe.

Over the centuries of European colonization, native populations would accumulate an assortment of unwanted and misleading nicknames. Europeans garbled native languages. They heard names wrong, pronounced them weirdly, and applied them inappropriately. The Spanish, for example, labeled all the natives living in agricultural villages along the river that would become the Rio Grande "the Pueblos." They then asked "the Pueblos" to identify their neighbors. "Navajo" and "Apache" grew from these conversions. None of these groups considered these names their own. They called themselves Tewa or Dine or Inde. Native groups' self-identifications often carried the same idea: they meant "the people."

Of course, Columbus pioneered the abuse of proper nouns by labeling all the people he met *los indios,* mistakenly thinking he had landed in the East Indies. Within a half-century "Indian" had passed into English, used to refer to all Native Americans, lumping together urban Aztec militarists with small-town Hopi farmers with roaming Micmac hunters. Just as the term *European* includes dozens of nationalities and ethnic subgroups, so the term *Indian* encompassed a cavalcade of diverse humanity.

The creation of man and woman. Painted pot, Mimbres River culture of southwestern New Mexico, c. 1000. National Museum of the American Indian.

Native peoples' backstory matched Europeans' in grandeur and complexity. The ice brought them. Clad in animal skins, bands of hunters trudged across the frozen tundra, crossing to America from Asia across a Bering land bridge some thirty to forty thousand years ago, about the time migrants elsewhere were settling the British Isles. The ice brought them, and as time passed and temperatures rose, the thaw cut them loose from their ancient moorings. They moved south onto the northern Great Plains, a hunter's paradise teeming with camels, miniature horses, saber-toothed tigers, and wooly mammoths. The humans multiplied with the bounty.

Remarkably, the oral traditions of many Indian people depict a long journey from a distant place of origin to a new homeland. The Pimas of the Southwest sing an "Emergence Song":

> This is the White Land; we arrive singing,
> Head dresses waving in the breeze.
> We have come! We have come!
> The land trembles with our dancing and singing.

The migrants danced, sung, and worked, transforming their natural environments, turning foreign landscapes into homes. They developed a unique tradition of stone tool-making that archaeologists call Clovis, after the New Mexico site where these distinctive artifacts were first discovered in 1932. In the years since Clovis points and choppers have been found in diggings from Montana to Mexico, Nova Scotia to Arizona.[4]

Long-term global warming and a profound (and poorly understood) extinction event altered their natural environment. The giant mammals disappeared, opening the way for alternative subsistence regimes suited to higher average tem-

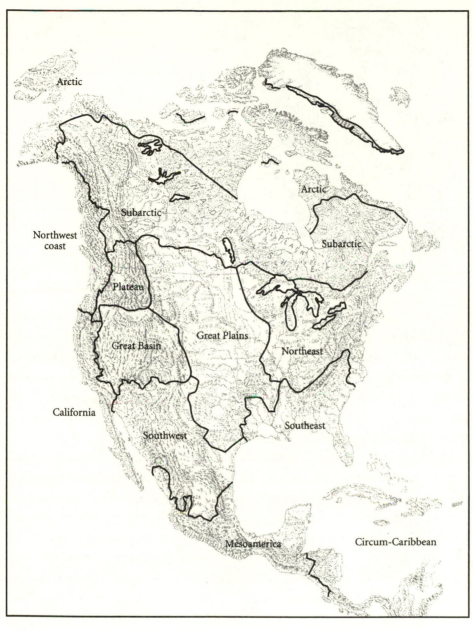

NATIVE CULTURE AREAS

peratures. Groups reinvented themselves as fishers and farmers. An early French
visitor to the Florida coast was amazed at the abundant harvests Timucua fisher-
men took from the sea. They used elaborate weirs, he wrote, "made in the water
with great reeds so well and cunningly set together, after the fashion of a labyrinth
or maze, with so many turns or crooks, as it is impossible to do with more cunning or industry." Across the continent, the peoples of the Northwest Pacific coast
exploited aquatic resources to settle in tightly packed populations, the densest in

An Aztec farmer cultivates his corn. "Floren-tine Codex," c. 1550. World Digital Library.

North America. Salmon, which spawned in numbers so great that they sometimes filled the rivers to overflowing, undergirded these distinct societies. The harvests allowed the Tlingits, Haidas, Kwakiutls, and other coastal peoples the abundance to develop a rich and refined material culture, including grand clan houses with distinctive carved and painted wood, fantastic totem poles, and magnificent blankets woven of wild goat's wool. Powerful clans and families ruled the banks as mighty war canoes patrolled the fisheries.[5]

The ice brought them and fish fed some of them well, but domesticated plants changed huge numbers of them forever. North America counts as one of four world sites where late Stone Age people invented the practice of growing their own food. The uniquely American crop combination of corn, beans, and squash—known by the Iroquois as "the three sisters"—originated in the Mexican highlands some five to ten thousand years ago and gradually spread northward. Maize cultivation fueled population growth and the rise of cities with elaborate social hierarchies and cultural practices. Sun kings rose and claimed spots atop massive earthen pyramids built by conscripted labor. Priests sacrificed captives while warriors punished rivals. Kingdoms rose and fell, and the humans of the Western Hemisphere settled into the ruts in which all agricultural civilizations grooved.

The cultivation of foodstuffs instigated similar flowerings of densely settled human populations on many of the planet's continental landmasses. The same Neolithic revolution, however, produced quite different sets of power relations in Europe and the Americas. When they came together, these farming peoples puzzled over each other's politics. The Europeans sought kings and bosses among

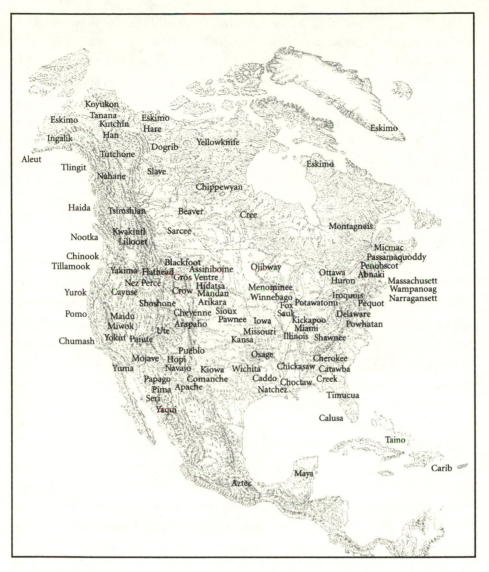

TRIBAL LOCATIONS

the Indians. They expected to find masters like themselves, captains who issued commands that underlings obeyed. The Indians did have leaders, but these chiefs ruled according to principles that seemed bizarre to the newcomers. Headmen in agricultural communities supervised the farming economy. They acted the boss, directing the work of others. Still, they didn't appear to profit from their command of labor. The community judged chiefs not by how much wealth and power they accumulated but rather by how well they distributed resources to clans and families. A good chief was often an impoverished chief, an arrangement that struck Europeans as totally wrong. But Indians found European traditions equally obscure.

In the early seventeenth century a young Huron visited France, and upon his return he reported his shock at the conditions he found there. "Among the French," he told his tribesmen, "men were whipped, hanged and put to death without distinction of innocence or guilt." He had seen a "great number of needy and beggars," and could not understand why the French people tolerated such conditions, "saying that if [they] had some intelligence [they] would set some order in the matter, the remedies being simple."[6]

Indian chiefs weren't saints for their poverty. They gave in order to get. By accepting gifts, followers promised favors and allegiance. Headmen could call on them to fight and work, and to support their leadership in times of trouble. Native politicians exercised their authority differently than their European counterparts, but that doesn't mean that they didn't wield power.

Yet the practice of gift-giving for political advantage kept inequalities in Native America within a narrower range than Europeans' top-heavy distribution of property, and nowhere in North America did natives own land individually. Kinship groups, clans, and whole tribes claimed productive resources. These collective use rights contrasted sharply with the European tradition of private property. The ideology of European settlers mixed individual property rights with individual righteousness, and they doubted the moral fiber of paupers who didn't own land. In their society, the better sort monopolized the best agricultural sites and handed down their privileged locations to their children. Their understandings of real estate and inheritance led many settlers to assault the worthiness of Indians' property systems and personal habits. Deeming the natives to be free-roaming loafers, many settlers denied that the Indians had any rights to the land at all.

Soil embroiled the grain-eaters in contests over rights and calories. But even as they battled fiercely over earth, they struggled just as mightily to comprehend (and alter) each other's supernatural beliefs. Probably the most fundamental distinction between invading Europeans and indigenous Indian cultures came down to religion. In general, Indian peoples didn't recognize a divide between the natural and supernatural. They inhabited a spiritual world in which *persons* of all kinds—humans and nonhumans, the living and the dead—brought order and instigated chaos. Mystical beings strode the earth while normal humans exited reality in dreams and visions. Spirits were neither wholly malevolent nor benign. They were complicated, just like the people they aided and tormented. Native religion addressed the uncertainty and insuperability of life. Native religion connected Indian people with nature and encouraged a strong sense of belonging to their own places, their homelands.

Europeans, by contrast, were less concerned with sacred places than with sacred time, the movement toward a second coming or a new millennium, a way of thinking that encouraged people to belief in progress, to believe that by picking up

"The Arrival of the Englishmen in Virginia" (detail). Engraving by Theodore de Bry, based on a watercolor by John White, from Thomas Harriot, A Briefe and True Report of the New Found Land of Virginia *(Frankfurt, 1590). Beinecke Rare Book and Manuscript Library, Yale University.*

and moving to a new land they might better their future. Christians prayed to one indivisible god, and their monotheism drew their thoughts toward grand designs and single causes. Instead of fluidity, hierarchy governed their reality. The Bible taught them that they were separate and distinct from the rest of nature, granted them dominion over "every living thing that moveth upon the earth." The Christian God revealed himself as a man, not as a coyote or a rock.[7]

Religion is a fitting end to this opening. One might imagine a final scene: a split-screen image of an Aztec priest hacking off a captive's head alongside a Spanish inquisitor disemboweling a heretic. Fade from viscera red to ocean blue as the *Niña, Pinta,* and *Santa Maria* bobbed at anchor somewhere in the Bahamas, and we are on the frontier.

Nothing inspires sorrow like fanatical certainty. On the seams of geography and culture, human beings of many creeds, casts, and colors wreaked much havoc with deadly self-assurance. These attitudes skewed the writing of history long after their originators perished. The American frontier, declared Frederick Jackson Turner at the end of the nineteenth century, was "the meeting point between civilization and savagery." His phrase rang with the arrogance of the victors in the centuries-long campaign of colonial conquest. Frontiers bred violence, as colonizers sought territory and power and Indians struggled to defend their homelands. Turner felt certain that he knew who belonged on which side. But many Americans are no longer sure who exactly was the savage and who the civilized.[8]

Yet, while human ugliness cast dark shadows across North American frontier history, the participants also generated glimmers of optimism. Power carved frontiers, but frontiers created possibilities. The behavior and ideas of frontiersmen and women of all kinds can and should make us wince, but their conduct can also open our eyes to new inventions, arrangements, and opportunities. The colonization of the North American continent fostered a multidimensional world inhabited by peoples of diverse backgrounds, including many of mixed ancestry, the offspring of a process of interaction that spanned many generations. Frontier history tells the story of the creation and defense of communities, the use of land, the development of markets, and the formation of states. It is filled with unexpected twists and turns, sad endings but also grand openings. It is a tale of conquest, but also one of survival, persistence, and the merging of the peoples and the cultures that gave birth and continuing life to America.

Instead of lopped heads and spilled guts, let's end this beginning with a series of images that better capture the blending of power and possibility that fueled history along the seams. Cut to entwined lovers, traders dickering over beaver pelts, diplomats brokering an alliance in a forest clearing, a child of blended parentage planting corn in the sun of springtime. The frontier bred hope as well as hostility. We seek to understand it all.

———

Frontier and *West* are two of the keywords in the American lexicon, and they share an intimate historical relation. From the perspective of the Atlantic coast, the frontier *was* the West, and that could be Kentucky or Indiana. The West moved on with the frontier. Where then is the West? The question has puzzled Americans, for its location has changed over time. A survey of western historians, writers, and editors found that about half believe that the West begins at the Mississippi or the Missouri River, while others propose the eastern edge of the Great Plains or the front range of the Rockies. Most consider the Pacific to be its western boundary, but a sizable minority insist that the states of the "left coast" are not part of the West at all. "I wouldn't let California into the West with a search warrant," the western historian Robert Athearn cracked. East is East and West is West. But consider other perspectives. For Latino settlers moving from Mexico, the frontier was the *North;* for métis people moving onto the northern plains of the Dakotas or Montana, it was the *South;* for Asian migrants headed for California, it was the *East.*[9]

Whatever its boundaries, in American history, the West is not only a modern region somewhere beyond the Mississippi but also the process of getting there. That may make the western story more complicated, but it also makes it more interesting, more relevant. The history of the frontier is a unifying American theme, for every part of the country was once a frontier, every region was once a West.

1

A New World Begins

A dash of outlandishness resides in every human being. No matter their place of birth or their station in life, all individuals function as spinoffs rather than distillations of the larger collectives to which they belong. No single person embodies the entirety of their culture or society. This fact—that all of us are oddballs to a greater or lesser degree—is crucial to an understanding of Spain's attempts to possess and rule the Western Hemisphere. The catchphrases of colonial history exaggerate the unity of the peoples involved. Overblown concepts like New Worlds and Old Worlds, Christians and savages, and Indians and Europeans distort the past. It's impossible to tell the story of the frontier without deploying some of this misleading shorthand, but the uniqueness of the encounters and the quirkiness of the actors carried as much weight.

Europeans did not suddenly appear to overwhelm the Indians. A Genoese captain named Christopher Columbus, sailing under the authority of the Spanish crown and in command of several dozen men on three small vessels, appeared on a string of islands called home by a people known as the Taínos. The Taínos grew corn and yams, made brown pottery and cotton thread, and whittled lethal darts from fish teeth and wood, which they used to fend off their aggressive neighbors, the Caribs (for whom the Caribbean Sea is named). Island dwellers had to be nimble to survive. Columbus, however, ignored the unique human beings in front of him. He measured the Taínos he met against the fantasies he held and found them wanting in nearly everything. The Taínos, he reported, had no weapons, no religion, and no shame. "They are all naked, men and women, as their mother bore them," he condescended in his report to the Spanish monarchs. The Indians' missing clothing symbolized an absence of civilization that destined them for servitude. "All the inhabitants could be made slaves," Columbus wrote, for "they are fitted to

King Ferdinand takes possession of the New World. From Giuliano Dati, Isole *trovate nuovamente per el re di Spagna (Florence, 1495). Beinecke Rare Book and Manuscript Library, Yale University.*

be ruled and to be set to work, to cultivate the land and to do all else that may be necessary, and you may build towns and teach them to go clothed and adopt our customs." His impression of natives as a people vulnerable to conquest is clear in the oddly proportioned image produced to accompany one of the published versions of his report. The fleeing Taínos look like giant, ripe targets. Before he sailed for home Columbus kidnapped a selection of native men and women to display at the Spanish court.[1]

He also carried home delusions of the Taínos' material wealth. "There are many spices and great mines of gold and other metals," he reported. Columbus had promised his backers Far Eastern delights and treasures, but in fact none of the Asian spices familiar to Europeans grew in the Caribbean, and only small quantities of precious metals in the islands' riverbeds. Some of the Taínos wore little gold ornaments, which excited Columbus tremendously. More than anything else, it was the possibility of setting the natives to work mining gold that convinced the monarchs to finance a large return expedition. "The best thing in the world is gold," Columbus confided to his diary, "it can even send souls to heaven." Along with religious conversion, the search for gold and silver would come to define the Spanish mission. "We Spaniards suffer from a disease of the heart," wrote Hernán Cortés, the conqueror of Mexico, "the specific remedy for which is gold."[2]

Many conquistadors came down with gold fever. Yet their desire for precious metals arose from the system used to fund their expeditions rather than from some derangement. European nation-states were puny by modern standards. The newly crowned king and queen of Spain, Ferdinand and Isabella, helped Columbus reach the Taínos, but they couldn't afford much more. To send him and others back to claim territories and subjects, they granted titles and encomiendas—rights to Indian labor—to strongmen who recruited their own armies. These conquistadors funneled private wealth (supplied mainly by Italian merchant investors) into expeditions and expected massive returns for their pains. This method would be employed by virtually all the European states that ventured across the seas. Nation-states envisioned and encouraged the creation of colonial empires, but for the most part private individuals and companies would play the starring roles.

To make colonization pay—and Europeans always believed that it should pay, even though the schemes they launched drained as many coffers as they filled—these men resorted to coercion and expropriation. The invasion of the Americas spurred frightful violence. In the wake of Columbus, conquering armies marched across the islands of the Caribbean, plundering villages, slaughtering men, and capturing and raping women. The strongmen and their armies drew on their experiences fighting so-called infidels in Iberia. In 1492—that most extraordinary year—Granada, the last Muslim territory in Iberia, fell to Christians led by Isabella and Ferdinand of Castile and Aragon. United, Spain's attention turned outward; ambitious upstarts loaded boats with followers and chased after Columbus. They hoped to enrich the home country and spread the true religion even as they empowered themselves. At least that was the plan. In practice, the dreams of monarchical splendor, religious enlightenment, and individual social advancement rarely meshed. The crown, the church, and the conquistadors squabbled endlessly.

To add to the tumult, the pagans they had come to subdue, instruct, and put to work refused to obey. The encomienda system, a feudal arrangement that cast Indians as serfs and conquistadors as lords, placed native labor at the disposal of crown-appointed grandees, who set them to dredging streams for gold, plowing fields, and building new colonial towns. Some natives answered encomienda coer-

Indians pour molten gold down the throats of conquistadors. From Girolamo Benzoni, La historia del mondo nuovo *(Venice, 1565). Beinecke Rare Book and Manuscript Library, Yale University.*

cion with self-destruction. Rumors filtered back to royal authorities of entire villages who took their own lives rather than submit to their Christian lords. Others chose to attack the Spanish. The Caribs—from the more southeasterly islands of the West Indies—successfully defended their homeland until the end of the sixteenth century, ruthlessly killing soldiers and missionaries. One chronicler of the conquest told of a torture that some Indians invented for captured Spaniards with a thirst for gold. They heated the metal to its boiling point and poured it down their prisoners' throats.

The Spanish colonized the Taíno islands in 1493, including one they renamed Hispaniola. After depleting the meager supply of alluvial gold, they invaded Puerto Rico and Jamaica in 1508, then Cuba and Central America in 1511. Over the next few years, several expeditions reached the Yucatán, reporting back that people there lived in splendid towns and even had libraries of handwritten, illustrated books. One mainland native reacted with surprise when he saw a Spaniard reading a European book. "You also have books?" he exclaimed. In 1517 a small group of Spaniards entered a coastal Mayan town, the first European contact with a major agricultural power. The residents offered them many treasures, wrote the chronicler of this expedition, "and begged us kindly to accept all this, since they had no more gold to give us." But pointing westward, "in the direction of the sunset," the Indians insisted that the Spaniards would find plenty. "They kept on repeating: 'Mexico, Mexico, Mexico,'" reads the account, "but we did not know what Mexico meant."[3]

The Spanish conquest of Mexico was a clash of heavyweights. After gathering strength and knowledge in the Caribbean, the Spanish hit the mainland with enough momentum to take down a maize-fed superpower. Unlike the Taínos or the Caribs, the Aztecs resided in cities that rivaled Europe's best efforts at urbanization.

The Spaniards land on the Gulf coast of Mexico, an image produced by an Aztec scribe shortly after the invasion. From "Florentine Codex," c. 1550. World Digital Library.

The rule of their emperor, Moctezuma, stretched from the central valley of Mexico to the coast. His wealth, splendor, and dominion outmatched Ferdinand and Isabella's. He not only served at the pleasure of a god, Moctezuma took pleasure in being one.

The Spaniards' island skirmishes with the Taínos and Caribs looked like preliminaries for the main event. Still, peripheries figured large in the fall of Moctezuma. The Aztecs fell in part because their frontiers turned against them, and the invaders' leader, Hernán Cortés, acted with suicidal (or homicidal, from his men's perspective) daring because he expected his superiors to cancel his conquest and send him home at any moment. A rogue underling, he toppled an empire with the help of rogue underlings.

An officer in Cortés's army, Bernal Díaz, described his commander as handsome and strong, with a broad chest and shoulders, slow to anger but sometimes roused to speechless fury, the veins throbbing in his neck and forehead. He demanded absolute obedience from his men, though he himself had a reputation for bucking authority. A lawyer by training, he had left Spain for the Caribbean to rehabilitate his honor tarnished by an adulterous affair with a powerful man's wife. He participated in the invasion of Cuba and served as the secretary to Diego Velázquez, the island's colonial master. The two had a stormy relationship, with Cortés cycling in and out of Velázquez's favor. When the news of the Yucatán and Mexico reached him, Velázquez appointed his secretary to lead the follow-up voyage. To grasp the ultimate prize, he needed a representative on the ground quickly. Cortés wasn't his first choice, but the need for haste overcame his better judgment.

He may not have been the man of Velázquez's dreams, but Cortés fit another ruler's visions remarkably well. Moctezuma stood at the heart of a civilization made up of several dozen tributary cities under the domination of his Aztecs, the inhabitants of Tenochtitlán in the central highlands. Built on an island in a large lake, the Aztec capital impressed with stepped pyramids, stone temples, golden vessels, and causeways with dams and irrigation canals, built and maintained with the tribute that the Aztecs demanded from the conquered people they governed. Proud and confident, the Aztecs were as full of themselves as the Spanish.

But Cortés appeared at a moment of doubt. For several years Moctezuma and his head priests had witnessed evil omens—strange comets, heavenly lights, monstrous two-headed births, foaming lake waters, an insane woman wailing through the night, "My children, we must flee far away from this city. My children, where shall I take you?" Word of strange invaders from over the waters reached Moctezuma and his priests as they puzzled over these alarming signs. The reports added ominous news to the list of depressing tidings. The strangers looked alien, with bushy beards sprouting crazily from their faces. They rode equally weird creatures, bulked-up deerlike animals with fierce dispositions and thundering hooves. They donned thick helmets and covered their bodies in armor. They carried iron-tipped spears and wielded rods that spit deadly fire. The date of their landing also boded ill. The year 1519 was 1-Reed in the Aztec calendar. In the words of one of their old books: "They knew that, according to the signs, if he comes on 1-Crocodile, he strikes the old men, the old women; if on 1-Jaquar, 1-Deer, 1-Flower, he strikes at children; if on 1-Reed, he strikes at kings." Had Cortés come to fulfill Moctezuma's worst dreams?[4]

He could have crushed the several hundred Spaniards as they struggled to survive amid the sand dunes and mosquitoes of the Gulf coast. But Moctezuma hesitated. Instead of a strike force, he sent emissaries with presents intended to win the strangers over. The items only whet the Spaniards' appetites for more. In the words of the Aztec account: "They gave them ensigns of gold and ensigns of quetzal feathers, and golden necklaces. And when they were given these presents,

Moctezuma observes an evil omen in the form of a comet in an image produced by a native artist soon after the conquest. From Diego Duran, "Historia de las Indias de Nueva España e islas de la tierra firme," c. 1580. Biblioteca Digital Hispánica.

the Spaniards burst into smiles; their eyes shown with pleasure; they were delighted by them. They picked up the gold and fingered it like monkeys. . . . Their bodies swelled with greed, and their hunger was ravenous; they hungered like pigs for that gold. They snatched at the golden ensigns, waved them from side to side and examined every inch of them. They were like one who speaks a barbarous tongue; everything they said was in a barbarous tongue." This remarkable description captures the native perspective of the dramatic encounter between civilizations. To the Aztecs, the Spaniards were outsiders, barbarians, perhaps barely human.[5]

To reach the capital and seize the booty, Cortés needed information and allies. His first assistance came from one of the cleverest—and most mysterious and controversial—women in history, a girl by the name of Malintzin who is best known by the Hispanicized version of her native name, La Malinche. Born in a Nahuatl-speaking village but sold into slavery as a child, Malinche was gifted to Cortés by a local Mexican chief hoping to curry favor. Doubly marginalized by her gender and her captivity, Malinche would seem an unlikely leading actor in the male-dominated pastime of military conquest. But her willingness to aid the Spanish proved crucial, and she anticipated the pivotal role women would play

La Malinche translates for the Spaniards. "Florentine Codex," c. 1550. World Digital Library.

in borderland diplomacy for the next three hundred years. On the frontier, captive women with linguistic skills and interpersonal panache often steered groups toward peace and war.

Possessing an enormous talent for languages—perhaps the heritage of a childhood among strangers—Malinche quickly mastered Spanish and made herself into Cortés's prized interpreter. And she did more than translate other men's words; she advised Cortés, offering him a window into Aztec intentions. According to Bernal Díaz, Malinche was "the great beginning of our conquests." In Aztec images of the conquest, Malinche is nearly always shown by Cortés's side.[6]

Malinche's reputation has proven as dexterous as her mind. The Mexican people have never ceased arguing over her meaning. Her name symbolizes the betrayal of native culture, synonymous with the worst traitor. She shared her body as well as her wisdom with Cortés and bore him a son, before eventually marrying another conquistador. Other Mexicans, however, see Malinche as the mother of *la rasa,* the new people that arose out of the blending of Indian and Spanish, native and European, and ancient gods and new. Thus she symbolizes not only betrayal but also the mixing of cultures and peoples that is the essence of modern Mexico. An ambivalent icon, Malinche stands for the muddled legacy of the frontier. The image of Malinche, at once a slave and a provocateur, a duplicitous whore and a founding mother, whipsaws between the nausea of exploitation and the thrill of possibility. It's hard to know how to feel about her, which makes her an even more fitting symptom for an American history told from the margins.

Though she lent a shove, Malinche certainly didn't cause the fall of the Aztecs by herself. A combination of sheer happenstance, political brinkmanship, ruthless violence, and killer microbes toppled the empire. Cortés pushed into the interior, invading Tlaxcala, a city-state that lived under the heavy heel of Aztec domination. The Tlaxcalans put up a fierce defense, then offered peace. They "prefer slavery amongst us to subjection to the Mexica," Cortés remarked cynically. With the support of the Tlaxcalans he was able to fill his army with native allies sick of Tenochtitlán's domination. Cortés arrived at the capital, appearing more like a radical new addition to the native political scene than an outside conqueror. Moctezuma, still hoping to swing the Spaniards to his side, welcomed them into the city and put them up in plush quarters complete with a shrine to the Aztec gods. The sources describe Cortés's reaction. "I do not understand how such a great lord and wise man as you are," he said to Moctezuma, "has not realized that these idols are not gods, but bad things, called devils." He knocked them to the ground and set up a Catholic altar. Moctezuma was shocked. "We have worshipped our own gods here from the beginning and know them to be good," he replied. "No doubt yours are good for you also. But please do not trouble to tell us any more about them."[7]

Moctezuma's houseguests took him hostage, ambushed his nobles, and finally put him to death. Their god-emperor gone, the residents of Tenochtitlán rose up. The Spaniards fled the city, but not before many were killed, their carcasses left to rot along the roads leading to the city, a warning should the Spaniards think of returning. But return they did, a year later, reinforced by troops from Cuba and thousands of Indian allies who grabbed the opportunity to overthrow their overlords. In the meantime Tenochtitlán was struck by an epidemic of smallpox, spread by the invaders. "They died in heaps, like bedbugs," wrote one Spaniard. An Aztec account underscored the human tragedy: "There came amongst us a great sickness, a general plague. . . . It raged amongst us, killing vast numbers of people. It covered many all over with sores: on the face, on the head, on the chest, everywhere. It was devastating. . . . Nobody could move himself, nor turn his head, nor flex any part of this body. The sores were so terrible that the victims could not lie face down, nor on their backs, nor move from one side to the other. And when they tried to move even a little, they cried out in agony. . . . The worst phase of this pestilence lasted 60 days, 60 days of horror. . . . And when this had happened, the Spaniards returned."[8]

The Aztec capital fell. The Spaniards demolished the temple at the city center and erected a cathedral atop the rubble. Tenochtitlán became Mexico City, the vortex of Spanish colonization. From there the conquistadors radiated out in all directions. In the Andean highlands of South America, Francisco Pizarro encountered a civilization to match the Aztecs. The Incan empire had everything the Spanish

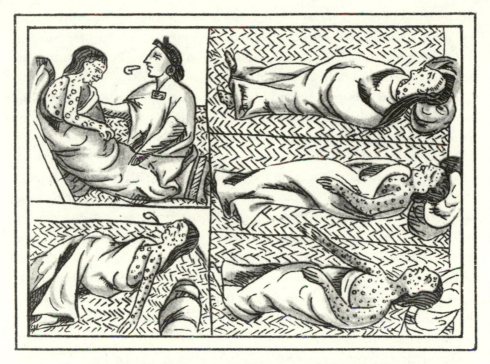

Aztecs suffer with the smallpox. "Florentine Codex," c. 1550. World Digital Library.

desired—a hierarchy to govern, lots of souls to convert, good roads and communication networks, and vaults loaded with precious metals and jewels.

———

Expeditions to North America, however, discovered far less spectacular New Worlds. In 1513 Juan Ponce de León landed on the southern Atlantic coast, which he named in honor of the Easter season—*pascua florida*—making Florida the oldest European place-name in the United States. Native warriors beat back the invasion. Ponce de León made several more attempts to take the peninsula before being killed in battle in 1521.

Several years later, in 1527, a conquistador named Panfilo de Narváez invaded Florida's west coast with an expedition that would set records for miles traveled, miles traveled while naked, and miles traveled in the wrong direction. The Spanish monarch had granted Narváez the right to a huge chunk of North America, stretching from Florida to the Pacific, and he was determined to seize his due. His inexperienced navigator, however, miscalculated the strength of the Gulf's currents, and the treacherous waters wrecked both Narváez and his ambitions. He cut his lifeline by abandoning his ships. The Florida swamps were pitiless and so too the swamp dwellers. Unlike Cortés, Narváez had no talent for building alliances. His men bullied the Indians, stole food and women, and after wearing out their welcome had to endure sniper fire and ambushes. Starving, they ate their horses and melted down their swords to forge axes, implements of rudimentary survival that nobody had thought to pack. They chopped down trees, built rafts, and cast off for Mexico in the swirling waters of the Gulf.

The three rafts coursed westward along the coast, slipping past the gush of the Mississippi River delta. When two of the rafts foundered on a barrier island along the Texas coast, Narváez, in command of the third, refused to assist the stranded men and sailed off into oblivion, never to be seen or heard again. Hungry, cold, and naked, the survivors leaned on the hospitality of the island's native inhabitants, who themselves lived on the edge of starvation during the winter months. They offered what aid they could, but bristled when the strangers demanded more. When the desperate Spaniards began to eat each other, the Indians were horrified. An epidemic of dysentery killed half the island's native population along with most of the castaways. Pushed to the brink, some of the Indians lobbied for the eradication of the strangers. Others thought that they might be remade into slaves. The slavers won the argument, and for the next six years a handful of Spaniards lived as servants in native households.

One of these slaves was Álvar Núñez Cabeza de Vaca, who had been the expedition's royal treasurer. Captivity transformed him. He endured beatings, malnutrition, and existential bewilderment. A man of substance in his former incarnation, he discovered what life was like on the fringe. Knocked off his foundation, he rebuilt his identity from the ground up with empathy and religion. He served his masters well, and they trusted him. They sent him on errands, and he traveled to and traded with neighboring groups, learning the ins and outs of native economies and politics. He cultivated the reputation of a healer, circulating through the countryside with three other survivors of the expedition, visiting tribe after tribe, blessing the sick and healing their wounds. Eventually, traveling in northern Mexico, the survivors encountered a small party of Spaniards who escorted them to Mexico City. Cabeza de Vaca would write an account of his adventures, the first captivity narrative in North American history.

His story thrums with adventure, heartache, and wonder. He constructed it with skill, giving his journey a narrative arc that took him from lackey to faith-healing Pied Piper. He told his story to convince his superiors to give him another crack at conquest. What makes his account remarkable is not that he steered history but rather the guiding philosophy by which he steered it. Humiliation and transformation buoyed his account. A royal appointee from an influential family, Cabeza de Vaca filled his report with instances of woe and suffering. A high-born male from a culture that valued masculine potency, he went out of his way to show his vulnerability, to bear witness to his utter powerlessness.

His years among the Indians had reformed his idea of how Christians should approach them. Instead of frightening them into submission and turning them into laborers and slaves, Cabeza de Vaca argued that the Spaniards should go among them naked and humble like Christ. The Indians would bow and obey, but to the righteousness of the Spaniards' mission, not the frightfulness of their greed and guns. He won another commission and in 1540 led a group of conquistadores to the region of the Río de la Plata in today's Argentina, Uruguay, and Paraguay. Cabeza de Vaca walked barefoot before his mounted men. He offered the Indians an embrace instead of a mailed fist. But in the end his gentle tactics worked no better than Narváez's brutal ones. The soldiers mutinied, and the Indians rejected all efforts to Christianize them. The onetime castaway-turned-miracle-worker was sent home to Spain, where he watched his career sink like a raft in the breakers. Yet Cabeza de Vaca demonstrated how experiences on the margins could change people. Far from home, on the edge of death and at the fringe of native society, he saw openings for peace and mutual benefit among Indians and Europeans, possibilities to which most of his compatriots remained blind.

———

Cabeza de Vaca wasn't the only Spaniard to protest the horrors of conquest and work to obtain justice for the Indians. The most notable critic was Bartolomé de Las Casas, a priest who assisted in the plunder of Cuba in 1511 and was awarded a large encomienda but afterward suffered a crisis of conscience and began to denounce the conquest. The whole point of coming to the New World was to convert the Indians, he declared, "not to rob, to scandalize, to capture or destroy them, or lay waste to their lands." They might be bizarre, ignorant, lewd, and even violent, but the Indians were first and foremost human beings, God's children, and "the entire human race is one." It was one of the first declarations of universal human rights.[9]

Las Casas's argument reached the highest levels of the Spanish state. Appointed "Protector of the Indians," he spent the next twenty-five years thundering against the abuses of the conquest, arguing that colonization and conversion could be carried out by peaceful means. Largely as a result of his brave efforts, in 1537 the Catholic Church officially condemned the enslavement of Indians, and five years later the Spanish monarchy issued new colonial regulations prohibiting Indian slavery and ending the encomiendas. Las Casas was appointed bishop of the Mexican province of Chiapas, where he attempted to enforce the new laws. But the Spanish colonists violently resisted. They threatened the life of the new bishop, and Las Casas was forced to return to Spain, where he continued to argue for a more humane approach to colonization.

Bartolomé de Las Casas.
From Oeuvres de . . . las
Casas *(Paris, 1822).*

Finally, in 1550, King Charles I of Spain invited Las Casas to participate in an official debate over the treatment of the Indians. His opponents, seeking to justify the conquest, argued that the Indians practiced horrible vices that underscored their savagery. They snorted drugs until senseless and had sex with people outside their marriages and inside their genders. To let these sinners go unpunished would be to go against God. Las Casas dismissed these accusations as slander intended to denigrate all the native peoples of America based on the actions of few reprobates. "The Spaniards have defamed the Indians with the greatest crimes," he wrote, making all Indians seem "ugly and evil." The charge of sodomy he dismissed as a "falsehood," and he compared the native use of drugs to the Christian ritual of communion. He even tried to explain Aztec human sacrifice in its own terms. "It is not surprising that when unbelievers who have neither grace nor instruction consider how much men owe to God," he explained to the court, "they devise the most difficult type of repayment, that is, human sacrifice in God's honor." The Aztecs were wrong in their belief, he said, but they believed with enthusiasm, and their passion signaled their readiness for conversion.[10]

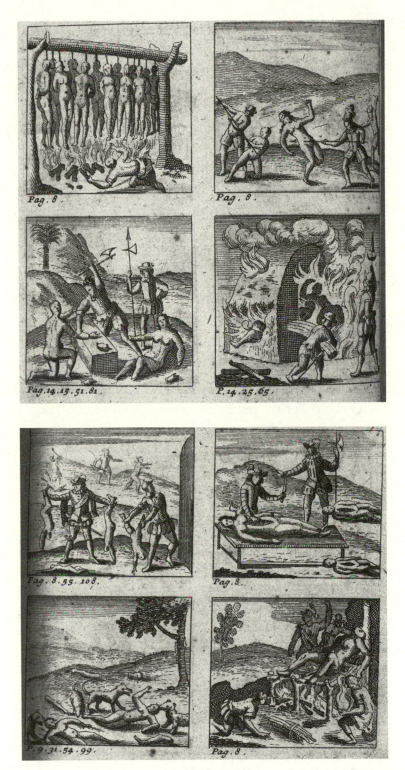

"*The Cruelties used by the Spaniards on the Indians.*" From An Account of the First Voyages and Discoveries Made by the Spaniards in America *(London, 1699). Beinecke Rare Book and Manuscript Library, Yale University.*

The outcome of the debate was inconclusive. Las Casas won the moral argument, but there was little change in policy. He responded in 1552 by publishing a brilliant, muckraking history of the conquest, *The Destruction of the Indies*. In this powerful text, one of the most influential books published in the early modern period, Las Casas blamed Spaniards for the deaths of millions of Indians and indicted them for what today we would call genocide. His arguments were later used by other European powers to condemn Spain while covering up their own dismal records of colonial aggression. Subsequent scholars, doubting the high death rates and huge declines in population that Las Casas threw about, accused him of exaggerating and contributing to the "Black Legend," which mistakenly blamed Spain for being more criminal than any other colonial power. Today his big estimates look spot on, although not for the reasons he proposed. Las Casas was a perceptive man, yet even he couldn't see the primary cause of native mortality: lethal microbes.

Because we lack solid numbers, population figures for this period are educated guesses. Estimates of the size of the native Mexican population on the eve of conquest, for example, vary between 8 and 25 million. A century later it stood at little more than a million. For the rest of the continent, north of Mexico, historical demographers argue over estimates varying from 4 million to 18 million native inhabitants before colonization. But no one disputes that over the subsequent four hundred years the native population dropped to a mere 250,000.

Disease or its ripple effects seeped into every North American frontier. Microbes altered the course of history more than any other factor. Next to a smallpox or influenza virus, the leading characters usually cast as the prime movers of history—Columbus, Moctezuma, Cortés, Malinche, and all the rest to come—look like bit players. Without killer germs, the West as we know it wouldn't have happened. The American region would have developed into something else, an Aztec hinterland, perhaps, or the territory of a confederation of native bison hunters and salmon fishers. But the microorganisms invaded, and the unequal responses of human immune systems guided the course of history.

Indians had little experience with the aggressive crowd diseases that had plagued the residents of the Eurasian continent for centuries. That's not to say that native peoples lived in a world without maladies. They suffered from rheumatoid arthritis, pinta, yaws, hepatitis, encephalitis, polio, tuberculosis, intestinal parasites, and venereal syphilis. But these were hangnails compared to the depopulation bombs that the Europeans carried unseen in their bodies. Smallpox, measles, influenza, malaria, bubonic plague, typhoid, and cholera decimated the humans whose ancestors had crossed the Bering land bridge, distancing their immune systems from these killers As a general rule, European diseases cut native populations in half within a decade of exposure.

Different groups encountered different diseases at different times. Epidemics came and went, and their timing influenced the outcomes of history as much as their virulence. European germs rocked the Western Hemisphere, yet the reactions of survivors mattered just as much. The dead and the living wrote history together. Crowd diseases radically altered the balance of power among humans. Native groups gained and lost power in relation to one another and in relation to colonizers. Overall, disease empowered Europeans, and it helps explain the almost unbelievable success of some of their conquests.

The invasion of America had another profound demographic consequence. Columbus and his crew unknowingly passed germs to the Taínos of Hispaniola. Estimates of the preconquest population of the island range from several hundred thousand to several million, but within a quarter century, the Indians had diminished to "as few as grapes after harvest," in the words of one colonial official. To replace their workers, the Spaniards began importing slaves from Africa, and by 1560 Africans had become the majority population on Hispaniola. By the end of the sixteenth century African slaves vastly outnumbered both native and European populations throughout the Caribbean. The European colonization of the Americas thus commenced with twin demographic catastrophes: the decimation of hundreds of thousands of native Americans through violence and disease, and the enslavement and forced relocation across the Atlantic of hundreds of thousands of native Africans.[11]

Germs eased invasions yet hampered colonization. The destruction of native populations capsized schemes for turning profits. The Spanish wanted the Indians to work, not to die. Immigration from Spain remained low. Even with crowd diseases thinning their numbers, Indians continued in the majority on the Mexican mainland, and by the end of the sixteenth century native populations there had begun to rebound from their disastrous collapse. The Spaniards inhabited the cities, whereas the countryside stayed predominantly Indian. "This state of New Spain," observed a convention of missionaries meeting in Mexico City in 1594, "is made up of two nations, Spaniards and Indians."[12]

A third "nation," however, rose quickly. New Spain attracted young, single men eager for opportunities denied them in their home country. These men desired families, and they created them with native women. Their unions created a large population of mixed ancestry known as mestizos. By the eighteenth century mestizos constituted nearly a quarter of the population of New Spain, and by the nineteenth century they had become the majority. While high-level clerics and

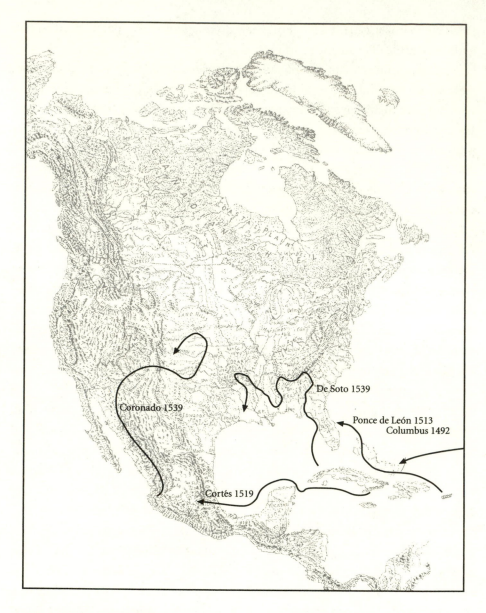

THE SPANISH INVASIONS

philosophers questioned the humanity of Indian people, Spanish men and Indian women ignored the debate and closed the argument with the smiling faces of their children.

The Spanish organized their empire into two parts: New Castile in South America, and New Spain, stretching from the Isthmus of Panama to Mexico, from the Caribbean islands west across the Pacific to the Philippines. At the heart of New Spain was Mexico City, an imperial seat with shady parks, high-fashion colonists parading in coaches, splendid churches towering over the sites of Moctezuma's temples, a university (founded in 1553), a government mint, hospitals, monasteries, and sumptuous homes for the wealthy. Commanding this colonial empire was the viceroy—the new Moctezuma—regent of the Spanish king and, in the New World, a man as powerful as the king himself. There were sixty-one viceroys during the three hundred years before Mexico gained its independence from Spain in 1821. Beneath them, bureaucratic control reached down through provinces and finally to the local magistrate—the alcalde—who administered justice, executed imperial policies, and collected taxes in more than two hundred cities and towns. The empire ran on the suffering labor of millions of peons and slaves, Indians and Africans.

Aztec civilization provided the base for Spanish colonization. Cortés dislodged the top tier of the society and ruled through class structures, communication networks, and alliance systems already in place. The vectors of colonization—among them disease, violence, intermarriage, proselytizing, theft, and slavery—radically altered native societies, but the transformations took hold in a human environment filled with cities, divisions of labor, and religious hierarchies laid down by the Aztecs.

———

Rumors of Indian empires elsewhere inspired more Spanish expeditions. In 1526 the conquistador Francisco Pizarro invaded the homeland of the Incas and commenced the conquest of their Andean kingdom. Other conquistadors turned north. In 1539 Hernando de Soto, who had been one of Pizarro's officers, landed at Tampa Bay with a Cuban army of seven hundred men and thousands of hogs and cattle, and pushed hundreds of miles through the heavily populated Southeast. He found plenty of towns ruled by chiefs, but nothing like Tenochtitlán and no one like Moctezuma. A brutal man, "much given to the sport of hunting Indians on horseback," de Soto tormented new acquaintances, and native leaders developed a strategy to keep him and his men on the move. De Soto badgered chiefs to reveal the location of the "cities of gold," and they played along, pointing their fingers toward the horizon. Paradise was always just a town away. Lured on by his fantasies, de Soto reached today's Alabama, where armies of Tuscaloosa and Chickasaw warriors chewed the Spaniards up. De Soto died on the banks of the Mississippi. Some three hundred survivors of the expedition reached Mexico on rafts in 1543. The invasion repelled, the native peoples of the South retained control of the region for another 250 years.[13]

Another sort of vision, this one a specter of ungodly competition, brought the Spanish back to Florida to stay. In the 1560s a group of French Protestants from Normandy, led by Jean Ribault, established a colony on Florida's Atlantic coast.

Timucua chief and French Huguenots in Florida. From Theodore de Bry, Brevis narratio
eorum quae in Florida Americae . . . [America, Part 2] *(Frankfurt, 1591). Beinecke Rare Book
and Manuscript Library, Yale University.*

At their first location, on Parris Island along the South Carolina coast, the colonists nearly starved. They saved themselves by relocating to a location south of
present-day Jacksonville, near a cluster of villages inhabited by a people known
as the Timucuas. The Timucuas were hospitable, welcoming the French into their
homes with food and drink, likely seeing them as potential allies against the slave-
raiding Spaniards.

A French colony just off the sea lanes that Spanish galleons traveled to bring
Mexican treasure home was unacceptable. A French colony populated by infidel
Protestants was unthinkable. In 1565 the Spanish crown sent Don Pedro Menéndez
de Avilés, captain-general of the Indies, to crush the Huguenots. He established
a base south of the French, then marched overland through swamps to surprise
them with an attack from the land. "I put Jean Ribault and the rest of them to the
knife," Menéndez wrote the king, "judging it necessary to the service of the Lord
Our God and Your Majesty." The dead bodies of five hundred French colonists
bobbed in the surf of the white, sandy beach, ending the French attempt to colonize the temperate latitudes of North America. The Spanish built a fort at their
base camp and set about enslaving and infecting the Timucuas. Thus, Europeans
claimed their first permanent address in North America: Saint Augustine, no city
of gold but a monument to religious intolerance, ocean traffic, and for the Timu-

cuas the end of the world. Over the next two centuries slavery and disease erased them as a distinct people.[14]

———

Saint Augustine watched the sea. A built expression of the Atlantic world, the fort protected shipping lanes that linked Europe, Africa, and North and South America. The second Spanish *entrada de conquista* into North America was a more continental affair. Far more mysterious than the ocean by 1539, the interior beckoned with visions of golden cities and undiscovered civilizations. Francisco Vásquez de Coronado led three hundred Spaniards, both mounted troops and infantry, as well as eight hundred Tlaxcalan warriors north along a well-marked Indian trading path that connected central Mexico to the northern region known as Aztlán—the legendary homeland of the Aztecs.

The expedition passed through the settlements of the Pimas, near the present border of the United States and Mexico, and finally reached the village of the Zunis, the southernmost town of the Pueblo peoples. The Zunis resisted, but the invaders smashed them. Coronado continued north, where after some persuasive violence the Indians allowed him to establish a base camp among the villages in the valley of the Rio Grande. The Indian towns disappointed the Spaniards. Constructed "of stone and mud, rudely fashioned," as one of the Spaniards described them, the homes exuded a depressing plainness. "I have not seen any principal houses," wrote this chronicler, "by which any superiority over others could be shown." Coronado moved on in search of a social hierarchy to molest. But moving north made the situation worse. The grasslands yielded no cities, no ruling classes, no treasure vaults, only vast herds of "shaggy-cows" (bison) and mobile human communities camping in huts. The void repelled the entrada. Coronado and his army limped home to lower everyone's expectations. For the next half-century Spain lost interest in the Southwest.[15]

Souls, not spoils, drew them back. Catholic missionaries targeted the dense, settled communities of the Pueblos. Franciscan missionaries hiked up the trading road and began proselytizing among the Pueblos during the 1580s. Rumors of underground mineral wealth drifted from the friars. After emptying other people's treasuries, the residents of New Spain had developed a booming silver- and gold-mining industry. Always on the lookout for new strikes, especially in the silver-rich north, the reports from the Rio Grande valley sparked a sustained colonization effort.

In 1598 an expedition left New Spain led and financed by Juan de Oñate, a member of a wealthy mining family from northern New Spain and married to a woman descended from both the emperor Moctezuma and the conquistador Cortés. Oñate's party reflected the mingling of peoples and priorities on the northern

The arrival of the Spaniards. Petroglyph, Canyon del Muerto, Arizona, c. 1700. Photograph by Richard Erdos, c. 1965. Beinecke Rare Book and Manuscript Library, Yale University.

Spanish frontier. One hundred and thirty predominantly mestizo and Tlaxcalan soldiers and their families would safeguard and populate the colony while some twenty Franciscans would reap a harvest of converts. The name Spanish officials bestowed on the region—Nuevo Mexico—registered their high hopes. Oñate and his sponsors anticipated a payoff that rivaled the toppling of the Aztec empire.

Oñate soon displayed a cruel streak that matched his forebears. Reaching the valley of the Rio Grande, Oñate advanced from town to town, announcing the establishment of Spanish authority. The reaction of the Pueblos ranged from skepticism to hostility. Acoma, "the sky city," built atop a commanding mesa, offered the most resistance. After tensions irrupted into violence, with Acoma warriors killing soldiers stationed in the town, Oñate laid siege to the city, intent on making an example of the rebels. Indian fighters (both men and women) killed dozens of invaders with arrows and stones. The Spaniards clawed their way up the rock walls and eventually took the city, killing eight hundred men, women, and children in the battle. They torched the Acoma homes, and Oñate ordered his men to sever one foot from each surviving warrior. He sold five hundred Acoma residents into slavery.

Oñate's throwback conquistador behavior displeased some of the Franciscan missionaries while his inability to locate sumptuous gold and silver mines upset his superiors in Mexico City. There would be no grand conquest, no epic con-

Zuni Pueblo in the valley of the Rio Grande. Photograph by Timothy O'Sullivan, c. 1872. Beinecke Rare Book and Manuscript Library, Yale University.

quistador in Nuevo Mexico. Oñate lost his command and was recalled. Officials debated abandoning the colony, but the Franciscans lobbied for more time and funds. The king agreed. He would bankroll the New Mexico colony as a religious experiment. In 1609 a new governor founded the capital of La Villa Real de la Santa Fé de San Francisco de Asis—"the royal town of the holy faith of Saint Francis of Assisi"—and from their base at Santa Fe the missionaries infiltrated the surrounding Indian villages.

———

The Franciscans used the marginality of New Mexico to wage a culture war. The Pueblos and the friars struggled over definitions of morality, truth, and eternity. Their fights spilled into everything—food, sex, marriage, work, clothing, posture, child-rearing, worship, habits, and hygiene. They argued about the meaning of the universe and the appropriate styles for hair. The comprehensiveness of their quarrels hinted at the costs of winning or losing them. Both sides sweated the small stuff because they foresaw enormous risks and rewards. The Franciscans labored to destroy what they considered a heathen culture in order to save the Pueblos from eternal damnation while Pueblo religious leaders worked to save their culture to prevent the world from tumbling into chaos. Only with the stakes so high would both sides stoop so low.

The missionaries entered an Indian world they found difficult to understand. Pueblo society turned Spanish assumptions about gender and property on their heads. The Pueblos, for example, reckoned descent through the mother's line, with women exercising control over their households. "The woman always commands and is the mistress of the house," wrote one Franciscan, "not the husband." Men and women, wrote another, "make agreements among themselves and live together as long as they want to, and when the woman takes a notion, she looks for another husband and the man for another wife." Pueblo men's power resided outside the home, an alien concept for the Spaniards, who thought that authority radiated out from a man's status as father and patriarch. Pueblo men formed religious societies, and they oversaw external affairs—hunting, trading, warfare, and ceremonial religion.[16]

Though they swore off fatherhood and family-making themselves, the Franciscans assumed that patriarchal households defined a good, godly society. The contentiousness that invigorated gender relations among the Pueblos confused and upset the friars. One missionary reported that when Pueblo women bore a girl-baby they placed a seed-filled gourd over her vulva and prayed that she would grow up to be fertile, but they sprinkled a boy-baby's penis with water and prayed that it would remain small. This angered Pueblo men. They responded by strapping on giant phalluses during public ceremonies and sang the praises of their genitalia, "the thing that made the women happy." Suffice it to say, the Pueblos and the Franciscans had very different understandings of sexuality. The priests were celibate, whereas the Indians perceived sexual intercourse as a mighty force bringing together the worlds of men and women. The absence of sex defined the Franciscan order just as the open practice of sex defined the Pueblo community.[17]

An incident during an outdoor ceremony arranged by the missionaries illustrated the difference in the Pueblo and Franciscan points of view. A friar preaching the benefits of monogamy drew a fierce rebuttal from a Pueblo woman. Suddenly, according to the missionary sources, "a bolt of lightning flashed from a clear untroubled sky, killing that infernal agent of the demon." To the priest, God had struck her dead. But the Pueblos reached an opposite conclusion. For them, lightning-struck persons became cloud spirits, they got a metaphysical raise, and the woman's flash-bang ascendancy confirmed the rightness of her ideas.[18]

The missionaries found full-grown minds with engrained beliefs hard to change, so they targeted Pueblo youth, many of whom the priests took from their families. The religious leaders of the Pueblos labeled these baptized converts "wet-heads." Along with age, geography influenced the spread of Christianity. Pueblos in outlying villages—the Acomas, the Zunis, and the isolated Hopis—resisted the

Franciscans and retained their old customs including the system of matrilineal kinship. In the heart of the Rio Grande valley, however, Catholicism took root. Over time the power of women and mothers' lineages faded. European and Indian ideas intertwined in the frontier process known as acculturation. As with most developments on the margins, acculturation calls forth mixed emotions. Did the Franciscans and Pueblos create a new society that fulfilled Cabeza de Vaca's vision of peaceful coexistence? Or did the priests destroy a culture in a fit of self-righteous genocide? One Pueblo tale focused on what was lost when the Franciscans arrived. "When Padre Jesus came," the story goes, "the Corn Mothers went away." But if Jesus and his robed friends left, would the old ones return?

———

Acculturation extended beyond churches and kivas, crosses and kachinas. It even went beyond humans and their views on sex, heaven, and the proper gender requirements for homeownership. Sheep and cattle played an equally impressive role in bringing—and keeping—these people together. Colonial New Mexico accrued a small-scale agricultural economy centered on imported European domestic animals. Herds of gnarly cows and rangy sheep brought a measure of wealth to some families. Colonists of means exploited the labor of the Indians, recasting themselves as lords with leisure. As one Spanish official put it, "No one comes to the Indies to plow and sow, but only to eat and loaf." Indians—Pueblos and their raiding neighbors, especially a group known as the Navajos—also gathered herds. As the decades passed and generations of lambs and calves wobbled into the brush in search of feed, the alien livestock and their human enablers made the Southwest a permanent home. In time, it became impossible for all sides to conceive of living without hooved property.[19]

It became equally hard to imagine a New Mexico without finely drawn racial distinctions. Most of the soldiers who came with Oñate were themselves Mexican Indians, mestizos or mulattoes, but their service to the crown whitewashed their ancestry. Frontier aristocrats, they bore the title of hidalgo, and their descendants inherited all the rights and privileges of that caste. Rising in rank, the former soldiers of mixed parentage proudly claimed the status of *españoles,* received encomiendas, and exploited Indian labor with a haughtiness that suggested they had come straight from Castile. On the northern fringes of the Spanish Empire, writes historian Quintard Taylor, "color presented no insurmountable barrier to fame, wealth, or new ethnoracial status." Moreover, after the initial conquest, few new colonists ventured up the dusty road from Mexico, and the growth of population came almost entirely from the mixing of Indian women and settler men.[20]

By the late seventeenth century, three thousand mostly mestizo New Mexicans clustered in a few settlements along the Rio Grande, surrounded by fifty thousand

The Palace of the Governors, Santa Fe. Postcard, c. 1870. Author's collection.

Pueblos in some fifty villages. Despite their numerical superiority, the Pueblos were the besieged. European diseases surged through their towns, striking communities nearest the Spanish settlements hardest. Illness and death shrunk the available labor pool, and the encomenderos watched their profits dwindle. Colonists pressed for more land, more pasture for their sheep, goats, and cattle. Conflicts with the Pueblos increased until a severe drought in the 1670s carried them to the edge of endurance. Twenty thousand Pueblos had converted to Catholicism over the previous few decades, but the crises stalled the acculturation process. Traditional Pueblo religion staged a comeback.

The Spanish panicked. They outlawed native rituals and confiscated ceremonial items. Priests sent soldiers to raid underground kivas and destroy such sacred artifacts as prayer sticks and kachina dolls. They publicly humiliated holy men and compelled whole villages to perform penance by digging irrigation ditches and weeding fields. The governor of New Mexico had three Pueblo holy men executed and dozens more whipped for practicing their religion.

One of those humiliated, a native priest from San Juan Pueblo named Popé, started a movement dedicated to overthrowing the colonial regime. In 1680 the Pueblos revolted, killing four hundred colonists and several dozen priests, whose mutilated bodies they left strewn upon altars. They ransacked churches and desecrated sacred objects in retaliation. Two thousand Spanish survivors fled to the Palace of the Governors in Santa Fe. Three thousand Pueblo warriors surrounded the building. After a siege lasting five days, the Spanish counterattacked and fled south, in the words of one account, with "the poor women and children on foot and unshod, of such a hue that they looked like dead people."[21]

In victory, the Pueblos transformed the governor's chapel into a kiva, his palace into a communal home. Pueblo women ground corn on the inlaid floors that decorated the one-time abode of power. The corn mothers had returned. Santa Fe became the capital of a Pueblo confederacy with Popé as a religious headman. He forced Christian Indians to the river to scrub away the taint of baptism. He ordered the destruction of everything Spanish, a command that struck many as wrongheaded. Horses, sheep, fruit trees, and wheat benefited the people. Some Spanish introductions had made life better. The people had jettisoned the bullies; why not keep their stuff? The nomads to the north—the Navajos and the Apaches—were not giving up their herds. Indeed, with the Spaniards gone, the Pueblos faced these traditional enemies alone without Spanish assistance. Their raids proliferated while the drought intensified. Popé lost his sway, and with the chaos mounting, the Pueblos deposed him in 1690.

The Spaniards returned in 1692, launching a violent six-year reconquest that re-established their power. But both sides had learned a lesson, and over the next generation the colonists and the Pueblos reached an implicit understanding. Pueblos observed Catholicism in the missionary chapels, while missionaries tolerated the practice of traditional religion in the Pueblos' underground kivas. Royal officials guaranteed the inviolability of Indian lands, and the Pueblos pledged loyalty to the Spanish crown. Together they fought off the nomads for the next 150 years.

On the Spanish fringes, Europeans and Indians coalesced into frontiers of inclusion. With a great deal of intermarriage between male settlers and native women, their communities were characterized by a process of mixing, or *mestizaje*. Thousands of Indians died of warfare and disease, but thousands more passed their genes on to successive generations of mestizo peoples. The children of the Old World fathers and New World mothers became the majority population of New Spain. Thus Spanish colonization brought forth groups of people even as it destroyed them.

FURTHER READING

Juliana Barr, *Peace Came in the Form of a Woman: Indians and Spaniards in the Texas Borderlands* (2007)

James F. Brooks, *Captives and Cousins: Slavery, Kinship, and Community in the Southwest Borderlands* (2002)

Alfred W. Crosby Jr., *The Columbian Exchange: Biological and Cultural Consequences of 1492* (1972)

Ramón A. Gutiérrez, *When Jesus Came, the Corn Mothers Went Away: Marriage, Sexuality, and Power in New Mexico* (1991)

Miguel León-Portilla, ed., *The Broken Spears: The Aztec Account of the Conquest of Mexico* (1962; rev. ed., 1992)

Andrés Reséndez, *A Land So Strange: The Epic Journey of Cabeza de Vaca* (2009)

Daniel K. Richter, *Before the Revolution: America's Ancient Pasts* (2013)

Kirkpatrick Sale, *The Conquest of Paradise: Christopher Columbus and the Columbian Legacy* (1990)

Edward H. Spicer, *Cycles of Conquest: The Impact of Spain, Mexico, and the United States on the Indians of the Southwest, 1533–1960* (1962)

Quintard Taylor, *In Search of the Racial Frontier: African Americans in the American West, 1528–1990* (1998)

David J. Weber, *The Spanish Frontier in North America* (1992)

2

Contest of Cultures

The first visit went smoothly, at least in the opinion of those whose recollections survived. In 1524 Giovanni da Verrazzano, a gentleman of Florence sailing for the French, reconnoitered the Atlantic coast from Florida in the south to Cape Breton Island in the north. Curious locals paddled out to his ship anchored in a fine harbor at 30 degrees latitude. The greeters looked as fetching as their bay, an inlet that over time would acquire their name—Narragansett. "These are the most handsome people," wrote Verrazzano, "of bronze color, some inclining to white, others to tawny color; the profile sharp, the hair long and black and they give great attention to its care; the eyes are black and alert, and their bearing is sweet and gentle, much in the manner of the olden days." The Narragansetts conjured visions of Eden. With their gorgeous grins and winning shipside manners, they seemed refugees from a lost paradise.[1]

Verrazzano's mood shifted the farther north he drifted. Along the coast of Maine, the crew of the *Dauphine* encountered natives of a different sort. Instead of canoeing out to welcome the ship, the Micmacs kept their distance. They fired arrows at a shore landing party and then signaled their desire to trade for knives, fishhooks, and edged metal. Their wary acquisitiveness marked them as troublesome "mala gente" to Verrazzano, who preferred his Indians smiling and pristine.

Transatlantic commerce and violence had already reached these Indian people. Even before Columbus's voyage to the Caribbean, cod-fishing ships from ports in England, France, Spain, and Portugal were plying the abundant waters of the Grand Banks. The crews met and traded with natives along the coast. They opened a market for European goods; they exchanged bodily fluids and the diseases contained therein; and they laughed, dickered, and squabbled. By the time Verrazzano

Native people of the Northeast. From Samuel de Champlain, Les Voyages du sieur de Champlain . . . *(Paris, 1613). Beinecke Rare Book and Manuscript Library, Yale University.*

arrived, the Micmacs had devised strategies to receive foreign technologies while rejecting the proximity of actual foreigners. Far from timeless savages, noble or otherwise, the Micmacs were experienced traders and diplomats. They set the terms for contact. They were more accustomed to the New World than Verrazzano.

Verrazzano's two encounters underscore key features of sixteenth- and seventeenth-century colonization in North America. First, the meetings illustrated the diversity of native and European peoples and how this diversity shaped their experiences with one another. North America subverted monolithic identities, eroded grand theories, and disrupted entrenched patterns. The fact of multiplicity places a burden on students of this period to absorb a crazy quilt of names, relationships, and storylines. Details ruled early modern North America.

A second key point involves timing. Different groups met each other at different times and under different circumstances. This may seem obvious, but timing tipped power relations and shaped colonial attitudes. For example, Indians living farther from the coast had more time to figure out how to best take advantage of European trade goods and political alliances. Contagious diseases swamped some coastal groups, decimating populations before they could react. But even this pattern had exceptions. The Narragansetts, for instance, avoided the epidemics that would level some of their New England neighbors. They emerged as a political force in the region despite their early encounters with explorers and their seaside living quarters.

Timing also affected the colonial projects of European nations. Latecomers to the scramble for wealth and territories, the English came to North America uncertain of their prowess as colonizers. They stole maps from the French and modeled their early efforts on the conquistadores, all the while dismissing their Christian rivals as unscrupulous barbarians. Yet, even though they borrowed and copied, because they arrived late, the English hit the ground with a novel and idiosyncratic set of troopers. Religious and economic upheaval prompted middling families and unemployed workers to journey to New England and Virginia, where they became farmers and indentured servants. Land, not trade, motivated many of these colonists, and unlike the Spanish and French, most English refused to intermarry (or even interact) with Native Americans.

Timing and diversity carved the frontiers of North America in the sixteenth and seventeenth centuries. Groups disembarked and disappeared; they grew powerful and lost everything; they mingled genes and built fences. Seen from the fringes, the era was a model of inconsistency.

———

Ten years after the Micmacs and Verrazzano met—while Cabeza de Vaca wandered among the tribes of the Gulf coast—the Indians of the Saint Lawrence valley marveled at two amazing ships sailing up their river. Jacques Cartier commanded the vessels. He represented a king, Francis I of France, itching to compete with imperial Spain. Cartier entered the river (today's Saint Lawrence) hoping to find a spectacular exit. He sought a Northwest Passage to India, a continental throughway that would finally complete Columbus's vision and give France claims to lands "where it is said that he should find great quantities of gold." When he asked the natives the name of the country through which he passed, they answered with a word that sounded like "Canada" to him. Who knows what they actually meant.[2]

When Cartier landed upriver, at least a thousand Indians escorted him down a well-worn road to the village of Hochelaga, through what Cartier described as "land cultivated and beautiful, large fields full of the corn of the country." The town was "circular and enclosed by timbers," he wrote, with "galleries with ladders to mount to them, where stones are kept for protection and defense." The fortifications, a costly investment in labor and material resources, symbolized the prominence of warfare in the villagers' lives. These people, who spoke a language known as Iroquoian, fought wars of retribution with rival groups in the Northeast, most of whom spoke in a different tongue—Algonquian. These long-held animosities would expand and intensify in the colonial period. Extreme violence, including scalping and torture, happened on American frontiers, but these acts and the wars that inspired them were older than the frontiers.[3]

"Some fifty houses" composed Hochelaga, Cartier observed, each "fifty or more paces long and twelve to fifteen wide, made of timbers and covered, roof and sides, by large pieces of bark and rind of trees." These were the famous longhouses. "Inside," Cartier continued, "are a number of rooms and chambers and in the center of

A fortified native town under attack by Europeans. From Samuel de Champlain, Les Voyages de la Novvelle France occidentale . . . *(Paris, 1632). Beinecke Rare Book and Manuscript Library, Yale University.*

the house is a large room or space upon the ground, where they make their fire and live together, the men thereafter retiring with their wives to private rooms." Like the Pueblos, these people traced their ancestry through their mothers. A communal clan, headed by a clan mother, inhabited a longhouse. When they married, men left the longhouses of their mothers to reside in the longhouses of their wives.[4]

Women controlled domestic and village space. The women "are much respected," a French priest wrote some years later. "The Elders decided no important affair without their advice." Men took charge of the realm outside the village and the longhouse. They hunted, fought wars, traded, and engaged in diplomacy. Men brought meat back for their sisters and mothers, not their wives, and the most important male figures in the lives of children were maternal uncles, not fathers. Most chiefs were men, but their succession, wrote another missionary, "is continued though the women, so that at the death of a chief, it is not his own, but his sister's son who succeeds him, or, in default of which, his nearest relation in the female line."[5]

Gender differences fascinated Cartier and the European chroniclers who followed him. Like the Europeans, native groups transformed biological sexual dif-

The residents of Hochelaga greet Jacques Cartier and his men. From Giovanni Battista Ramusio, Terzo volume delle nauigationi et viaggi . . . *(Venice, 1556). Beinecke Rare Book and Manuscript Library, Yale University.*

ferences into social and cultural gender identities and roles. The designations male and female leaked into the realms of politics and property. They even marked the land as forest (male) and clearing (female). Europeans elaborated on sex differences as well, but they spun biology into culture differently. Men, for example, worked and owned agricultural plots back home. Gender, therefore, provided a common ground and a point of departure for Indians and colonists, which explains why authors wrote so much about marriage, sex, childbirth, and the gender division of labor, as well as a small number of transgender natives who combined gender roles.

Profit tantalized explorers even more. Like sex, trade brought humans together on the frontiers even as material exchanges revealed cultural gaps and misunderstandings. Cartier provided a detailed description of the Indians' enthusiasm for trading. "The savages showed marvelous great pleasure in possessing and obtaining iron wares and other commodities," he noted. Indians quickly perceived the many jobs—from mundane tasks like butchering and hide scraping to ceremonial uses like diplomatic gifts and burial tokens—that European manufactures might perform. Equally observant, Cartier spotted the pieces of Indian wardrobe he desired. "They make their clothes," he wrote, "of the pelts of otter, marten, lynx, deer, stag, and others." In Europe only nobles and priests had the right to wear ermine, sable, and other luxurious furs, but the demand for other pelts for winter wear was strong. The growing population had stripped Europe of fur-bearing animals; even the immense supply of mammals in Russia and Scandinavia was growing thin.[6]

In the absence of silver and gold, furs paid for the French conquest of a huge swath of North America. "They do not value worldly goods," wrote Cartier, "being unacquainted with such." In exchange for items he considered mere gewgaws and trinkets, the Indians handed over valuable furs, including beaver pelts, which the Europeans prized most. Beaver could be processed into a waterproof material for coats and hats. To seal out the weather and reach the acme of fashion, however, the long outer layer of guard hairs had to be removed. The best pelts for trade, it turned out, were the ones Indians had worn for a season or two. The guard hairs fell off with use, leaving a smooth pelt. The humans exchanged soiled garments for trivial commodities, each side puzzling over the other's foolishness.[7]

Was this fair trade? It depends. Most exchanges satisfied both parties, otherwise the trade in furs and skins would never have become the primary interaction between natives and colonists throughout North America. Indians proved shrewd bargainers and tough consumers. They demanded quality and acquired items that fit their definitions of need. They traded for labor-saving technology and weapons but also for ceremonial possessions that helped them broker diplomatic alliances. They interpreted the trade as a form of gift-giving that established mutual responsibilities. Trade signified peace; its cessation meant war. Europeans understood these transactions differently, and they tried to get the Indians to see the trade as a form of buying and selling with limited interpersonal ramifications. In their ideal economy, after paying and receiving a fair price, both sides walked away happy and unencumbered. The fur trade inspired constant negotiations over prices and meanings. As Europeans grew in numbers and power, they forced natives to adopt their assumptions, and many Indian customers lost their independence as debt and overhunting crushed their options. But economic ruin took a long time and was by no means a universal experience. Trade was a blessing and a curse depending on when and where you looked.

———

The fur trade sent ripples of change through the northeast woodlands and beyond. Exchanges on seashores and riverbanks altered far away bodies and economies as goods and germs flowed along native travel and trade routes. After a winter stopover in the bitterly cold Iroquois village of Stadacona, Cartier sailed back to France in 1536. Cartier had found impressive natives with attractive houses and slick, vintage furs, but he couldn't locate a passage through the continent, and the lustrous rocks he packed into his ships' holds turned out to be iron pyrite—gold for fools, not kings. The French wouldn't return to the Saint Lawrence River to stay until Samuel de Champlain founded Quebec in 1608.

But in the meantime trade continued and grew, especially at the annual summer trade fair at the village of Tadoussac, near the mouth of the Saint Lawrence. In the Northeast, Indians and Europeans sailing under many banners fashioned a colonial history that minimized the significance of actual colonies. The fur trade cemented political alliances, interpersonal relationships, and cultural practices distinctive from those that characterized the Spanish Indian frontiers of northern New Spain, for they were based on commerce rather than conquest. These, too, were colonial relationships, of course, and ultimately there would be negative consequences for Indian peoples. Epidemic European diseases radiated out from places like Tadoussac and ravaged the villages of families who never spied the hairy strangers from across the ocean. As the value of furs increased, intense and deadly rivalries broke out among tribes over access to hunting territories. In the tumult of disease and warfare, the communities of Stadacona, Hochelaga, and numerous smaller villages disappeared, and the Saint Lawrence became a no human's land for Indians, creating the space for European settlements.

The French sent more traders to the Northeast than any other European nation, and at the turn of the seventeenth century they hatched a plan to stymie their competition. Samuel de Champlain, who had traveled to the Caribbean and visited Mexico, commanded a colonizing expedition funded by the crown and private investors. He established the outpost of Port Royal on the Bay of Fundy in 1605, and over the next three years he organized men and materials for a push up the Saint Lawrence. Located at the site of the defunct village of Stadacona, Quebec announced Champlain's and France's intention to make North America yield power and profit on a Spanish scale. Quebec would be their Mexico City, though the ruined village site seemed more ghost town than imperial launching pad.

The colony Champlain governed for twenty-five years until his death in 1635 did indeed turn out differently than New Spain. From the start, Champlain depended on good relations with Indian tribes, and he relied on the tradition of commercial relations that had developed between natives and Europeans during the sixteenth century. Instead of attacking a Moctezuma-like headman, which didn't exist in the Northeast anyway, he quickly forged an alliance with the Huron Confederacy, a nation of several affiliated Iroquoian-speaking tribes that lived north of Lake Ontario. The Hurons enjoyed a material abundance of fish and maize, and they controlled the access to the rich hunting grounds of the northern lakes. They were prime allies, but by siding with them, the French made enemies as well as friends. The Hurons were traditional adversaries of the Haudenosaunee (hoe-dee-no-SHOW-nee), a league of five nations (the Mohawks, Oneidas, Onondagas, Cayugas, and Senecas), more familiarly known as the Iroquois Confederacy. According to their oral history, the league was created in the fifteenth century, before the arrival of the first Europeans, to end violent conflict among the five tribes. Peace at home, however, encouraged war abroad. The Haudenosaunee cemented their cohesion by attacking outsiders, especially their northern neighbors, the Hurons. Now Champlain sealed his alliance with the Hurons by joining them in a raid on the Five Nations. Like the Spanish with the Tlaxcalans, the French found native partners to help install their empire. But Champlain was no Cortés. To stay on good terms with their allies and keep the furs coming, the French bowed to native customs and priorities far more than the Spanish ever did.

The French needed Indians to acquire the beaver and otter pelts that financed their colonial venture. Champlain understood the necessity of native hunters and

Samuel de Champlain joins the Hurons in an attack on the Mohawks. From Samuel de Champlain, Les Voyages de la Novvelle France occidentale . . . *(Paris, 1632). Beinecke Rare Book and Manuscript Library, Yale University.*

trappers and therefore sent his agents and traders in canoes to negotiate with Indians and live in their villages. These emissaries learned Indian languages and customs. They often dressed like natives, and some of them married Indian women. These personal connections kept the furs flowing to Quebec and to Montreal, built upriver in 1642 at the site of Hochelaga.

Along the Saint Lawrence, the French installed a version of a European feudal society. Cardinal Richelieu, prime minister of King Louis XIII, devised a scheme, given royal sanction in 1628, granting a "Company of One Hundred Associates"— young nobles, army officers, and merchants—immense privileges in exchange for overseeing the plantation of farms and churches. The company agreed to transport at least four thousand settlers and an appropriate number of priests, all of whom the company had to support. In return, the king gave the company a monopoly over the fur trade and all commercial activities, except fishing and mining. The company could distribute land to lords, or seigneurs, which it did in large swaths along the Saint Lawrence. Rivers ran through everything in New France. The liquid highways brought furs from the interior and connected colonists to one another and their home country. Seigneurs paid special attention to rivers when they divided up their manors. Farms stretched back from river frontages like ribbons, for everyone needed access to the flow of water and goods. Usually fewer than eight hundred feet wide, these properties would run back ten times that length. The riverbank farmers, the *habitants,* owed their seigneurs homage and dues.

It was easier to dream about reenacting the medieval past than to live as lords and peasants along the Saint Lawrence, however. Habitants struggled with short growing seasons and low productivity. Feudal dues went unpaid and uncollected. The company had trouble attracting its quota of colonists and eventually surrendered its charter, leaving the care of New France to the crown. The economy picked up in the 1660s under the leadership of the royal governor Jean Talon, doubling the French population with an influx of immigrants. Still, by 1700 New France had only fifteen thousand colonists. Quebec City, the administrative capital, paled next to Spanish colonial cities, and Montreal remained little more than a frontier outpost.

———

The French built their North American empire on furs, rivers, and relationships. Furs drew traders into the continent's interior; rivers carried them there; and relationships with Native Americans determined profits and kept the French afloat as a colonial power. Without native suppliers, customers, and military assistance, New France would have drifted into bankruptcy or been sunk by its European rivals. Instead, the French kept paddling and strung a series of colonies along the waterways connecting the Saint Lawrence River to the Great Lakes and the Mississippi River to the Gulf of Mexico. Like the Spanish Indian frontier, the French established a frontier of inclusion, but it developed a unique character based on the small size of the French colonial population and the power of the interior tribes.

To supplement their incomes, habitants sent their sons into the interior to work as agents for fur companies or as independent traders. Most eventually returned to their farms, but some remained in Indian villages, where they married and raised families. The fur trade mixed material possessions and gene pools. Indians absorbed European technology and material culture while French traders—the *coureurs de bois*, or runners of the woods—adopted many of the Indians' lifeways.

Native cultures accorded young women the freedom to choose their sexual partners. The presence of young, unattached European traders led to an outburst of erotic activity. One Frenchman interpreted the rules of engagement: "A young woman is allowed to do what she pleases, let her conduct be what it will, neither father nor mother, brother nor sister, can pretend to control her. A young woman, say they, is master of her own body, and by her natural right to liberty is free to do as she pleases." French youths embraced this liberty with such enthusiasm that one experienced trader wrote in his journal: "Our young Canadians who come here are often seen everywhere running at full speed like escaped horses into Venus's country." Their amorousness led one western chief to wonder "whether you white people have any women amongst you?"[8]

The outcome of frontier liaisons was far less predictable than the arousal that sparked them. Prostitution, unknown among the Indians before the colonial era, soon became a prominent feature at every fur trade post and fort. Many colonists entered the fur trade, took Indian women as lovers, and then abandoned them, along with their offspring. Indians exploited the situation as well. Women targeted lovers as an investment. Sex brought valuable trade connections to their families, their clans, or themselves. Many native women came from matrilineal societies and expected rather weak marital connections. Divorce was common, as were multiple wives, or polygamy.

Because neither partner could force the other to adopt their mores or traditions, most men and women married for mutual benefit. "When a Frenchman trades with them," wrote one observer, "he takes into his services one of their Daughters, the one, presumably, who is the most his taste; he asks the Father for her, and under certain conditions, it is arranged; he promises to give the Father some blankets, a few shirts, a Musket, Powder and Shot, Tobacco and Tools; they come to an agreement at last, and the exchange is made. The Girl, who is familiar with the country, undertakes, on her part, to serve the Frenchman in every way, to dress his pelts, to sell his Merchandise for a specific length of time; the bargain is faithfully carried out on both sides." Most of the connections between traders and Indian women seem to have been stable, permanent, and constant, lasting for years, with a great deal of commitment on the part of the men to their children. But, as the above passage suggests, marrying across cultures was as much about work as about sex. Indian women labored for their husbands, cooking, scraping pelts, and hauling trade goods and households on their backs. Traders reciprocated with material wealth and familial devotion. On the frontier, romance came with a set of responsibilities and a lot of heavy lifting.[9]

The French and Indians learned from one another, and together they created new languages, customs, and children that borrowed from both cultures. The fur trade spawned a special language—a pidgin, as linguists call it—that combined French and native tongues. "There is a certain jargon between the French and Savages," wrote a priest, "which is neither French nor Savage; and yet, when the French use it they think they are using the Savage tongue, and the Indians using it, think they are using good French." This was another of the fictions that kept the system of cultural relations running smoothly.[10]

In the segment of their riverine empire the French called the Illinois Country (in reference to their Algonquian allies living between the Great Lakes and Louisiana), young native women immersed themselves in European material culture. Nearly two dozen Illinois women married French men, and instead of bringing their husbands back to live in their villages, the women resided in French colonial towns, surrounded by imported clothing, furniture, and housewares. Their possessions marked the women as Frenchified, and they encouraged the French to contemplate the possibility of Indians becoming more like them instead of the other way around. The French went back and forth on Indian acculturation. Some thought that the future of their North American empire depended on Indians becoming French subjects, thereby enlarging the ranks of the colonial population. Others argued against it. The natives proved far more adept at converting the French to their habits and beliefs, and the slow rise of racism in the eighteenth century caused some philosophes and policy makers to reject the very notion of darker-skinned people becoming French.

While the pundits hemmed and hawed, a group of Illinois women acted. In 1693 Marie Rouensa married Michel Accault. She was seventeen, he closer to fifty and "famous in all this Illinois country for all his debaucheries." Rouensa's father, a prominent Illinois chief, forced the marriage. Accault ranked high in the fur trade, and the chief wanted to cement ties with him through his daughter. This typical arrangement, however, was thrown off track by Marie's faith. A devout Catholic convert, she wanted "to consecrate her virginity to God," not surrender it to a middle-aged rogue. She agreed to the match only after a showdown with her parents. She would marry Accault in a church ceremony and live with him. This went against both her father's and Accault's wishes. They had hoped for a marriage *à la façon du pays,* a union that conformed to Illinois practices and expectations. Rouensa would hear none of this. Her new mate would give her a French home filled with French things; he would give her a French wardrobe, from undergarments to overcoats; and he would give her the respect of a French wife, including rights to inheritance. And, finally, her parents would give God their souls. She demanded that they convert publicly to Christianity.[11]

Rouensa pioneered a relationship model that others would emulate. Fifty-seven Indian women legally married French suitors in the Illinois Country in the decades following Rouensa's nuptials. Not many, it may seem, but the French excelled at colonizing with scant numbers. Their body counts never amounted to much, which meant that those fifty-seven accounted for a fifth of all the legal marriages in the Illinois Country between 1693 and 1763. Dressed in their French finery, the Illinois brides symbolized how some Indian women found room to maneuver in the overlap of geographic and social margins. Marie Rouensa lived in a world dominated by men who sometimes used women as bargaining chips. She didn't get everything she wanted—a convent seemed her dream—yet she successfully played one patriarch off another to secure some autonomy and property rights that she could pass along to her children. Marie had two children with Accault and at least seven more with Michel Philippe, a Frenchman she married after Accault's death in 1702.

Rouensa's offspring followed her lead, for the most part. Many of her children became Catholics, wore French clothes, and counted as French in the colony's census. Further north, in the Great Lakes region, other children of French and native

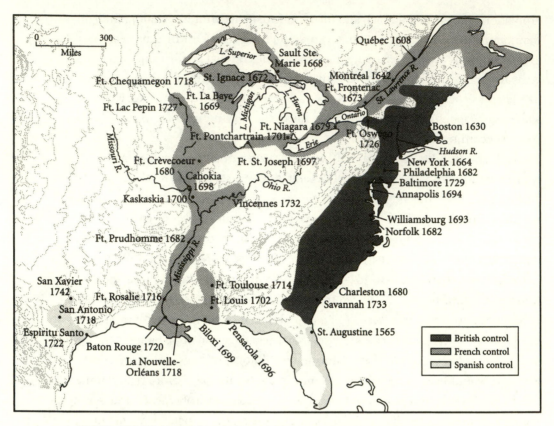

THREE NORTH AMERICAN EMPIRES IN THE EIGHTEENTH CENTURY

unions blended their parents' cultures more thoroughly. The French called this genetic and cultural mélange *métissage* and the new population that emerged the métis. In the Great Lakes region and to the west many of these people of mixed ancestry gradually formed a separate grouping, a people in between. Often bilingual, sometimes trilingual—speaking their mother's, their father's, and sometimes their own métis language as well—with highly developed skills of moving across the cultural boundaries, these people became guides, interpreters, and often traders in their own right.

The French rolled west and south on the river currents and intimate relationships. The coureurs de bois, some of them métis, reached the Great Lakes and found homes in Indian villages as early as the 1620s. Fifty years later they were on the upper Mississippi River. Governor Louis de Bouade, Comte de Frontenac, added official sanction to this French Canadian wanderlust. More than a century after Coronado marched northward into the Mississippi basin, Frontenac authorized expeditions into regions nominally Spanish. In 1673 Jacques Marquette, a Jesuit priest, and Louis Jolliet traveled down the Mississippi to the Arkansas River. Then in 1682 René-Robert Cavelier de La Salle, leading a bickering but audacious expedition, floated all the way to the river's mouth on the Gulf of Mexico. There in the swampy delta, he planted a cross, turned a spade of earth, and claimed all land drained by those waters for King Louis XIV.

By the eighteenth century New France formed a giant crescent, embracing the two immense river systems of the Saint Lawrence and Mississippi joined by the five Great Lakes. Its dimensions were nearly as breathtaking as the sweep of New Spain, whose northeastern borders it touched. The boundaries of the two empires overlapped. The French founded settlements along the Gulf coast—at Biloxi (in 1699, seventeen years after La Salle stood at the mouth of the Mississippi) and New Orleans (in 1718). Except for these ports, however, the French turned inward to the land they named for King Louis XIV, Louisiana.

——————

Commerce motivated French colonialists, just as it motivated their imperial counterparts, the Spanish and the English. Yet global finance drove early modern Europeans only so hard. Money roused them, but religion kicked them into full froth. Both the French and the Spanish wished to see Indians converted to the Catholic faith, and the men put in charge of these missions gave their fingers, toes, noses, and lives to harvest the souls of the New World. In 1611, three years after Champlain founded Quebec, the first Jesuit missionaries arrived in New France, bearing from the king an exclusive jurisdiction to convert the Indians. They replaced the Recollects, the order first given the royal mandate to keep the colony resolutely Catholic (the crown forbade Protestants and Jews from settling there) and the initial job of spreading the gospel to the natives. The Recollects built churches and invited Indians to plant villages next to them. They sought to remake the natives' language and appearance, their work habits, and their incessant roaming, as well as their spiritual beliefs. The Recollects suffered for their high expectations; few Indians took them up on their offers.

The Jesuits planned a different approach. Instead of encouraging Indians to come in close and stay put, they flew to them. The Jesuits studied native languages and cultures in order to know their target population better, and they accepted conversion without any sign of acculturation. The Indians didn't have to adopt the markers of French civilization—monogamy, shirts, and farms—before they accepted Christianity. The Jesuits baptized early and often, hoping that the spirit would carry the savages toward French country living.

At first, the Indians looked upon these Black Robes as culturally inferior. They wore inappropriate apparel that made them look unmanly, they hid their faces behind obnoxious beards, and they displayed little interest in women as sexual partners, a huge surprise given the one-track minds of most European men the Indians had met. And the Jesuits lacked the most basic survival skills. Bumbling, sexually confusing, and adamant, the fathers died by the fistfuls in the seventeenth century, martyrs in the quest to save the aboriginals from eternal damnation.

The Jesuits fumbled taboos, promoted outlandish ideas, and lost philosophical debates. One Micmac chief in present-day Nova Scotia questioned a Jesuit's logic. "Thou sayest of us that we are the most miserable and most unhappy of all men," he told a missionary, "living without religion, without any rules, like the beasts in our woods, and our forests, lacking bread, wine, and a thousand other comforts." Yet, he went on, "we are very content with the little that we have." Then he concluded, "Thou deceivest thyself greatly if thou thinkest to persuade us that thy country is better than ours. For if France, as thou sayest, is a little terrestrial paradise, are thou sensible to leave it?"[12]

The "thous" and "deceivests" in the exchange indicate that the Jesuit, not the Micmac chief, preserved this exchange. He reported it in a letter to his superiors back home to show what he was up against. He may have lost control of his own narrative, revealing his ignorance while trying to display the Indians' naïveté, but his willingness to engage the chief and record his point of view hinted at the Jesuit's patience and flexibility. They studied their adversaries closely and were willing to appear foolish in order to find pressure points in Indian thinking. "One must be very careful before condemning a thousand things among their customs, which greatly offend minds brought up and nourished in another world," a Jesuit wrote in 1647. "It is easy to call irreligion what is merely stupidity, and to take for diabolical working something that is nothing more than human; and then, one thinks he is obliged to forbid as impious certain things that are done in all innocence." Unlike the Spanish Franciscans, who linked conversion to the acceptance of European cultural norms, the Jesuits eventually succeeded because they introduced Christianity as a supplement to the Indian way of life.[13]

Many Indians came to respect the bravery of these priests and their apparent ability, like shamans, to command powers of healing and communion with the spirit world. The enormous social and cultural dislocation that often accompanied the arrival of Europeans and their contagious diseases also prompted natives to accept Christianity. Both the Jesuits and the Indians scrambled to adopt new ideas to meet rapid change. During the 1630s, for instance, the Hurons were struck with a horrible smallpox epidemic. In a few years as many as half the Hurons perished, their population falling from thirty thousand to fewer than fifteen thousand. At first, many Hurons blamed the Jesuits for these plagues. To them, the missionaries were sorcerers who corrupted the spiritual power of communities and introduced disease by practicing their strange rites. Priests rushed to baptize the dying, connecting Christianity and disease in many Indians' opinions. Other Hurons, however, looked to the spiritual power of the Jesuits to save them. Smallpox defeated traditional healing rituals. The treatments proscribed by native ex-

Huron women, Catholic converts. Detail from the map, Novae Franciae accurata delineatio *(Paris, 1657). Beinecke Rare Book and Manuscript Library, Yale University.*

perts backfired—sweat lodges and collective nursing merely spread the disease. As the pox ran rampant and the healers struggled, the Jesuits picked up desperate converts.

The missionaries seemed particularly successful among Huron women. Free to choose their lovers and husbands, the women could also choose to follow the Jesuits if that was their desire. The Jesuits targeted native women through appeals to the cult of the Virgin Mary, the veneration of female saints, and the sisterhood of nuns. They criticized the abuse of women by both natives and Europeans, organized special women's groups, and encouraged adolescent girls to swear lifetime vows of celibacy. The special attention the Jesuits paid to female conversion and the protection of women paid off. By the 1640s they had converted two-fifths of the Huron nation. Native women brought their fathers and brothers with them.

As a rule, the French Jesuits lived and worked with the natives on their own ground, whereas the Spanish Franciscans attempted to concentrate them at their missions. Both empires exploited Indians for commercial profit and to fulfill their evangelical goals, but both also considered them human beings with souls worth saving. By no means would all subsequent inheritors of the North American continent agree.

In the mid-sixteenth century, the English emerged briefly from the political turmoil—spurred by King Henry VIII's decision to take his country and leave the Catholic Church—to sample the riches of the New World. Henry's daughter, Queen Elizabeth I, sanctioned privateers, the so-called sea dogs, to raid Spanish galleons carrying Indian treasure home across the seas. One of the biggest dogs,

Francis Drake, returned from one voyage with booty valued in the millions for him and his investors, which included Elizabeth herself. The English thus began their American adventure by looting the Spaniards, who had looted the Indians. They were parasites on parasites.

Buoyed by their ocean victories, Elizabeth and her councillors shifted their ambitions to the mainland. The time had come to enter the scramble for American territory. In a remarkable state paper, "A Discourse of Western Planting," written in 1584, the queen's adviser Richard Hakluyt laid out the advantages of colonies: they would provide bases for privateers to raid the Spanish Caribbean empire, posts where English traders could tap the Indian market, and plantations for growing tropical products—sugar, for example—that would free the nation from a reliance on the long-distance trade with Asia. These colonies would also help ease England's social ills by giving the "multitudes of loyterers and idle vagabonds" a place to relocate. Hakluyt urged Elizabeth to establish colonies "upon the mouths of great navigable Rivers" from Florida to the Saint Lawrence. The queen backed away from Hakluyt's grandest schemes, but she did authorize and invest in several private exploration and colonization attempts. In the 1570s Martin Frobisher sailed on three voyages of exploration to the North Atlantic. He brought back four kidnapped Inuits, including a woman and her child, as well as hundreds of pounds of what he hoped was gold-bearing ore. The natives soon fell ill and died. The ore proved worthless.[14]

A few years later, in 1585, Sir Walter Raleigh, a favorite of the queen, planted a base for the English to raid Spanish ships on the future Outer Banks of North Carolina. Soldiers and mercenaries landed on an island the local Algonquian-speaking Indians called Roanoke. An advance party treated with chief Wingina, a canny politician who sensed an opportunity. The strangers might help him subdue his Indian rivals. When the English announced their intention to go home and recruit colonizers, Wingina sent two of his men, Manteo and Wanchese, back with them to watch and learn.

They ended up doing some teaching as well. Manteo and Wanchese tutored the Oxford scholar Thomas Harriot and the artist John White. The foursome acquired each other's language and established friendships. Their mutual respect showed in Harriot's published report of the subsequent expedition, a sensitive account of Indian culture providing a detailed description of native culture on the eve of colonization. White's watercolors captured villages, fields, and ceremonies. He recorded native life with an accuracy that would not return to Euro-American depictions on Indians until the nineteenth century.

Respect and understanding, however, couldn't save Raleigh's colony, which he christened Virginia in honor of the Virgin Queen. The men—no women or families accompanied the first round of colonists—proved incapable of support-

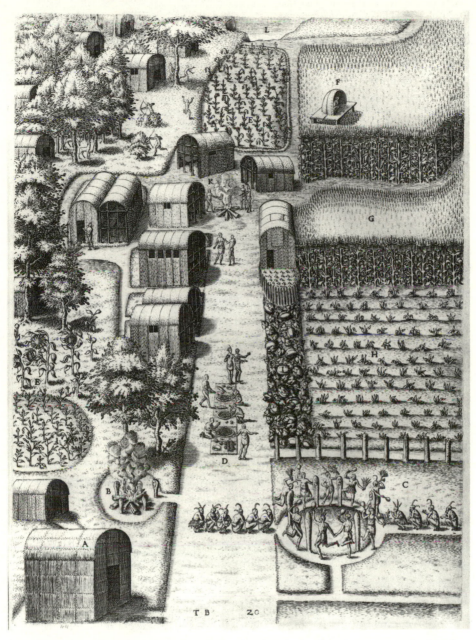

The Algonquian town of Secota. Engraving by Theodore de Bry, based on a watercolor by John White, from Thomas Harriot, A Briefe and True Report of the New Found Land of Virginia *(Frankfurt, 1590). Beinecke Rare Book and Manuscript Library, Yale University.*

ing themselves, preferring to hunt for precious metals or raid nearby villages for treasure, visions of Cortés before their eyes. At first chief Wingina fed them, but when his stores grew short, the colonists took their sustenance by force, beheading Wingina and killing several of his captains. Soon after the sneak attack they returned to England, leaving a legacy of violence and hatred in their wake. In 1587

Raleigh tried again with a mixed cohort of sixty-five bachelors and twenty families. He appointed John White governor, and among the married couples were the artist's daughter, Eleanor, and his son-in-law, Ananias Dare. White envisioned a colony of farmers living in peace alongside (though above) native people. "There is good hope," wrote Thomas Harriot, that "through discreet dealing" the Indians may "honor, obey, fear, and love us." Ever confident in the superiority of their nation and their religion, White and Harriot still held out for love, a sentiment the plunderers never esteemed.[15]

Yet the Virginia slate couldn't be wiped clean. Wingina's people had seen too much. Wanchese told his fellow villagers about England, where the poor begged, the hungry starved, and the wealthy refused to share, and he warned them not to let these people sink roots in the country. Within the first month of White's regime, the natives killed an Englishman while he fished for crabs. Shaken and feeling vulnerable, White sailed for home in the only seaworthy vessel to press Raleigh for reinforcements. War with Spain delayed his return for three years. When he finally made it back, no one was there to greet him. The colonists had vanished without a trace, leaving nothing except the word "Croatan" carved in a fence post. Though Roanoke fit the pattern of early English colonies by ending in miserable failure, the Lost Colony's creepy abandonment endures as a unique and mysterious disaster.

What happened? Did Wanchese rally his people to exterminate them? Or did another group take them in? Unlike Wanchese, Manteo had remained friendly with the English and argued that their goods and technology would be powerful additions to Algonquian life. His home village was called Croatan. Perhaps the colonists followed a far different route than the ones laid out by Raleigh, White, and Harriot. Instead of wealth or love among unequals, they may have found mercy and acceptance on the Algonquian mainland. Perhaps the children of the Roanoke colonists married into Indian families when they reached adulthood. The marriage of John White's granddaughter, Virginia Dare, to an Algonquian warrior would have completed White's picture of Indians and colonists living peaceably side by side, even if the artist would have loathed the idea of happenstance turning his village scenes into family portraits.

Roanoke cost White his family, Raleigh forty thousand pounds, and Wingina his head. Despite the loss of lives and fortunes, the English still desired the mid-Atlantic region, even if no single person wanted to pay for it. In 1604 King James I issued charters to a string of joint-stock companies, which spread the costs and risks of colonization across an array of investors. They sold shares of stock in various quantities, and the money paid for ships, sundries, and equipment. The king liked joint-stock companies because the stockholders dipped into private pockets instead of his coffers, and individual investors approved because they could gamble on the New World without going all in. The stockholders were liable only for the amount they invested, and if the venture failed, individuals could not be sued for their remaining resources. The companies underscored the power of debt on the frontier. Colonial projects might empower, enlighten, and evangelize. But they also had to pay. Investors lurked in the background of most early American dramas.

In 1607 the Virginia Company employed one hundred colonists to build a fort on the Chesapeake Bay they named Jamestown, in honor of the king. The fort came to represent the first permanent settlement in North America, but it looked paltry at the time. The Chesapeake was home to twenty thousand Algonquian-speaking natives, and their villages trounced Jamestown in size, style, and functionality. One chief, a man named Wahunsenacawh whom the English called Powhatan, ruled a confederacy of tribes and saw the English as potential allies. He watched the strangers build in the swampy lowlands on a site more suitable for raising mosquitos, fevers, and poor attitudes than crops.

The Jamestown adventurers, like the early colonists of Roanoke, saw themselves as latter-day conquistadors. Abhorring the idea of physical labor, they survived the first year only with Powhatan's assistance. "It pleased God (in our extremity) to move the Indians to bring us Corne," wrote the colony's military leader, Captain John Smith, "when we rather expected they would destroy us." When the English demanded more than Powhatan thought prudent to supply, events took a familiar turn. Smith inaugurated an armed campaign to grab food from surrounding villages, and Powhatan retaliated by attempting to starve the colonists out. Powhatan thought that the English might help him consolidate his power among local tribes with their trade goods and keep the Spanish—who had irked him with a series of sail-by kidnappings of his people—at bay. But now he realized, he declared to Smith, that "your coming is not for trade, but to invade my people and possess my country." In other words, the English came in the mode not of the French but of the Spanish. Abandoned by their Indian benefactor, scores of English colonists starved in the brutal winter of 1609–10. In their desperation, the wastrels resorted to cannibalism. By the spring, only sixty persons remained of the more than five hundred sent across the Atlantic by the Virginia Company.[16]

Determined to stick it out, the company sent additional men, women, and livestock, committing themselves to a protracted struggle with the Indians. By 1613 the colonists had won firm control of the territory between the James and York Rivers. Worn down by violence and disease, Powhatan accepted a treaty of peace in 1614. "I am old and ere long must die," he declared. "I knowe it is better to eat good meat, lie well, and sleep with my women and children laugh and be merrie than to be

Pocahontas in England. Engraving by Simon van de Pass, from The General Historie of Virginia . . . *(London, 1632). Beinecke Rare Book and Manuscript Library, Yale University.*

forced to flie and be hunted." Powhatan abdicated in favor of his considerably less merry brother, Opechancanough, an implacable foe of the Europeans.[17]

One of Powhatan's daughters lived with the English in Jamestown. The settlers knew Pocahontas as a teenager who hung around the fort and joshed with Captain Smith. (Smith later turned his friendship—perhaps flirtation—with the pubescent girl into a full-blown romance when he concocted his Virginia memoir. The diminutive captain was a magnificent self-promoter at Pocahontas's expense.) With the peace of 1614, Pocahontas returned to Jamestown as a grown woman. She served as a guarantor of the peace as well as an ambassador, interpreter, and lookout for her people. She learned English and received religious instruction. She eventually converted to Christianity, took the name Rebecca, and married a leading Jamestown colonist, John Rolfe. Theirs was the best known of many intimate connections between Indians and English during those early years. Similar to the Spanish and French, early English colonization included a good deal of mixing of Europeans and Indians. There was even hope that the couple would beget a Christian line of succession for the Chesapeake chiefdom of Powhatan. But as it did with many hopes for the future among the English and the Indians in the Chesapeake, disease ruined the chance. Pocahontas fell ill during a visit to England and died in 1617 an ocean away from home. Her only child remained there.

History took a different turn. John Rolfe ensured Virginia's future by developing a hybrid of hearty North American and mild West Indian tobacco, and by 1615 Jamestown was shipping cured tobacco to England. Francis Drake first introduced tobacco to English consumers in the 1580s, and though King James despised the noxious weed as "loathsome to the eye, hateful to the nose, harmful to the brain, dangerous to the lungs," smoking had become a fad by the 1610s. Nicotine addiction made the Virginia colony a success. Soon the company began to send over large numbers of indentured servants—Hakluyt's "loyterers and idle vagabonds"—to work the tobacco fields. The servants came from the young crowd kicked up by the first stirrings of the market and industrial revolutions in England. Most had moved from their homes in the English countryside to cities like London before they signed contracts that financed their journeys to North America. This working population pushed Indians to the edges of the English colonial world. In contrast to the Spanish and French, who built societies based on the inclusion of Indian people, the English established a frontier of exclusion, consigning Indians to the periphery rather than incorporating them within colonial society.[18]

───────

Despite their lack of multicultural desire and imagination, the English could not stay away from the Chesapeake Algonquian tribes. Tobacco drove them together. The boom in tobacco prices encouraged expansion into Indian territories, as did the plant itself. Tobacco leached soils of their nutrients, prompting growers to search for new fields. The colonists pressed the Indians for more land, and Opechancanough prepared for an assault that would drive the tobacco cultivators into the ocean from whence they came. The uprising began on Good Friday, March 22, 1622. Caught off-guard, the colonists lost 350 people, a quarter of their number. Yet they hung on, and instead of delivering a killer blow, the sides settled into a ten-year war of attrition.

The war bankrupted the Virginia Company, and in 1624 the king converted Virginia into a royal colony. The tobacco economy continued to skyrocket, doubling the English colonial population every five years from 1625 to 1640, by which time it numbered approximately ten thousand. The native population headed in the other direction. Disease and warfare decimated them. In 1644, Opechancanough, now almost a hundred years old, organized a final desperate assault. More than five hundred colonists died, but the demographic weight and military aggression of the Virginians crushed the Algonquians within two years. Taken prisoner, Opechancanough died when a Jamestown colonist shot him in the back.

Animosities simmered along the Virginia frontier for decades. Colonists pressed for tobacco lands while their livestock, especially their untended pigs, infested the countryside. By the 1670s the Susquehannocks of the upper Potomac River were under pressure from both human and animal interlopers. Small squabbles turned deadly as tensions reached a boiling point. In 1675 a wealthy frontier planter and his neighbors took the law into their own hands and launched a series of violent raids against belligerent and peaceful Indian communities. The ringleader, Nathaniel Bacon, called his attacks "a mighty conquest." The governor of Virginia disagreed. Sir William Berkeley wanted calm along the leading edges of agricultural expansion. Wars cost lives and money, neither of which he wanted to spend. Who did these frontier malcontents think they were, anyway? They should follow the lead of their royally appointed headmen, not run amok with that rogue gentleman Bacon. Incensed by their governor's passivity, Bacon and his rebels—six hundred in all— turned their fury on Jamestown in the spring of 1676. Berkeley fled by boat into the Chesapeake Bay while Bacon pillaged and burned the place. Soon thereafter, however, Bacon sickened and died in the swamps of the lower James River, cut down like thousands before by an intestinal infection. His revolt died with him.

Bacon's Rebellion of 1676 fed on overlapping discontents. The settlers on the leading edge of English tobacco expansion felt betrayed by their leaders in Jamestown when Berkeley refused to sanction their violence against their Indian neighbors. From the settlers' perspective, they suffered on the margins for the comfort of their downriver countrymen. Their blood paid for the stately homes and the wine cellars enjoyed by the gentlemen along the James River. Class resentment

mixed with geographic marginality, a sense of cultural superiority, and racial en-
titlement to produce the first outburst of agrarian dissent in American history.
During his reign as "General of Virginia," Bacon issued a manifesto demanding
the death and removal of all Indians from the colony as well as an end to the rule
of the aristocratic "grandees" and "parasites." Western settlers tested Indian patience and Eastern Seaboard controls. In 1677, in a replay of Virginia events known
as Culpeper's Rebellion, North Carolina settlers overthrew their local government
and established their own before English authorities ended their rule. But as a
result both Virginia and North Carolina shifted their policy in favor of the armed
agrarians on the margins. Colonial governments put up with incidents of mayhem
and foul play to placate their own subjects and grab huge chunks of Indian territories for themselves. The inability of imperial authorities to manage frontier
anger, greed, and terrorism would become a recurrent theme across time, space,
and nations.

Many Indians withdrew to the west away from the conflict zones created by
the English. Those left behind signed compulsory treaties granting them small reserved territories within colonial bounds. By the 1680s, when the English population of greater Virginia numbered more than fifty thousand, only a dozen tribes
with about two thousand residents remained. Over the next three centuries,
however, these Indian communities hung on to their land through tremendous
struggle. Today some fifteen hundred people claiming descent from the original tribes continue to live in the Chesapeake area. With their own churches and
schools, they fish and farm and commute to jobs in metropolitan Richmond or
Washington, D.C.

In their northern colonies the English carried out a similar policy of exclusion.
Coastal New England seemed an unlikely spot for permanent English habitation.
Traders from Holland vied with traders from New France to control the region's
Indian trade. The Dutch reached north along the Delaware, Hudson, and Connecticut Rivers and found powerful allies and trading partners among the Mohawks, one of the five nations of the Haudenosaunee. The French extended their
trade among Algonquian peoples along the coast as far south as Cape Cod.

The contest for furs and allegiance left scant room for the English until an infec-
tious epidemic that attacked native populations on the northern coast from 1616 to
1618. Whole villages disappeared, and the trade system of the French and the Dutch
collapsed. Indians perished so quickly and in such numbers that few remained to
bury the dead. A surviving Indian reported that "the population had been melted
down by this disease, whereof nine-tenths of them have died." The native population of New England as a whole dropped from an estimated 120,000 to fewer

than 70,000. The scattered "bones and skulls made such a spectacle," wrote one observer, "it seemed to me a new found Golgotha."[19]

In 1620 a group of English religious dissenters and colonial adventurers stepped into one of these graveyards and thought it a promised land. They entered the abandoned Algonquian village of Patuxet, observed the heaps of unburied bones, and fell to their knees to thank God for "sweeping away the great multitudes of natives" to "make room for us." But the Pilgrims and Strangers, as generations of American schoolchildren would come to know them, were not paragons of health themselves. Skinny and debilitated by scurvy, many looked as skeletal as the dead. Nearly half perished the first winter. Like the Virginians, they depended on Indians to feed them. Massasoit, the sachem, or leader, of the Wampanoags, who lived along the coast, offered food and advice in the early months of 1621, anxious to establish an alliance with the newcomers as protection against the Narragansetts, the mighty neighboring tribe who miraculously had been spared the ravages of the plague.[20]

The renegades from the Church of England were looking for a fresh start, but the newness of their New England was an illusion. No one epitomized the wear and tear that colonization had already wrought on the region and its people better than the Pilgrims' liaison and interpreter, a man known as Squanto. Kidnapped from his Cape Cod home in 1614 by an English captain, Squanto returned five years later after completing a tour of the Atlantic world that took him from London to Spain to the Caribbean. Prized for his linguistic skills, he jumped ship when an English vessel that had hired him as a translator entered Massachusetts Bay. Squanto returned to his village of Patuxet to find it abandoned. The plague had killed his friends and family. He found a home with the Wampanoags and became an adviser to Massasoit. He used his knowledge of European ways to broker an alliance with Pilgrims through gifts of seed corn and planting instructions.

The Algonquians of southern New England found these settlers considerably different from the French and Dutch traders. Land fired their imaginations, not trade. Through Squanto, Massasoit tried to use the colonists to his advantage. Yet the Pilgrims proved a blunt political instrument. For example, in 1623, Massasoit urged the Pilgrim military commander Miles Standish to attack a group from the Massachusetts tribe, who resided north of Plymouth. Standish obliged and brought back the severed head of the Massachusetts chief, which he jammed on a pike outside the Plymouth gates as a "warning and terror" to all Indians—Wampanoags included. Though voiceless, the head spoke loudly to the natives. "How cometh it to pass," one asked, "that when we come to Patuxet [using the Wampanoag rather than the English name for the village] you stand upon your guard, with the mouths of your pieces [guns] presented to us?" Soon, their aggressive behavior earned the English a new name, *wotowequenage,* cutthroats.[21]

*Seal of the Massachusetts Bay Company.
Author's collection.*

Radical English-speaking Protestants came in several varieties. The Pilgrims sought a complete separation from the Church of England. North America put an ocean between them and a state-sponsored religion they considered too Catholic. Soon, other groups of reformers joined the Plymouth colonists. These "Puritans" moderated their spiritual aims. Instead of rejecting the Anglican Church, they hoped to restore and purify it. Large numbers immigrated to shores north of Cape Cod. The Massachusetts Bay colonists occupied abandoned Indian fields and village sites, thanking their God for clearing the premises for them. Although the official seal of the Bay Colony featured the figure of a native asking the English to "Come Over and Help Us," the Puritans were actually more interested in helping themselves to "unused" land. "The country lay open," wrote their leader John Winthrop, "to any that could and would improve it." To bolster their own legal claims, settlers bargained with Indians and drew up bills of sale and contracts. These documents often masked the bullying, fraud, and shadiness that prompted land transfers. The Puritans allowed their livestock to graze Indian fields, rendering them useless; they fined Indians for violations to English law, such as working on the Sabbath, then demanded land as payment; they made deals with an assortment of fraudulent "chiefs." As disease and social dislocation crippled the coastal tribes along the bay, many native leaders signed away their fields and hunting grounds and took up residence on the margins of colonial society, trading protection for independence.[22]

Inland and along the shores of Long Island Sound, however, Indian peoples flexed considerable muscle. They blocked Puritan expansion until another

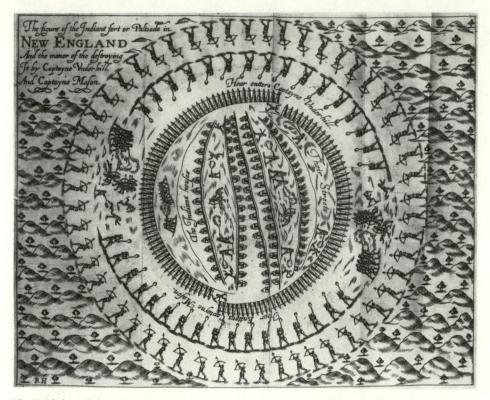

The English and the Narragansetts attack and destroy the Pequot village at Mystic, Connecticut. From John Underhill, Newes from America *(London, 1638). Author's collection*

smallpox epidemic, raging in 1633 and 1634, devastated populations from the Saint Lawrence River south to Long Island Sound. The epidemic opened the way for the thousands of new English immigrants packed in coastal towns to venture into the interior. "Without this remarkable and terrible stroke of God upon the natives," recorded the minutes of one Puritan town meeting, "we would with much more difficulty have found room, and at far greater charge have obtained and purchased land." As the pox spread across Indian bodies, the English planted towns along the lower Connecticut River.[23]

Life in these territories, however, was not free and easy. The Pequots, a powerful tribe that had partnered with the Dutch, served as the teeth in the mouth of the Connecticut River. The Puritans offered an alliance, but the Pequots refused the demand for an acknowledgment of English sovereignty. So in 1637 the Puritans joined the Pequots' traditional enemies, the Narragansetts, and went after the recalcitrant tribe. English soldiers and Narragansett warriors laid siege to the Pequots' fortified main village on the Mystic River, torching homes and shooting men, women, and children as they ran from the flames. The slaughter alarmed the Narragansetts: "It is too furious, it slays too many men." Though savage, the Puritans' butchery was mindful. They intended to send a message to the other tribes in the region. They intended to assert their dominance through terror. The Pequots' territory became English farmland, a pastoral landscape sprung from the flames of Mystic.[24]

The English and the Algonquians settled into an uneasy peace that lasted for forty years. Slowly they built relationships, some happy, most not. Roger Williams, who established his own colony for dissidents in Rhode Island, developed a rapport with his new neighbors, the Narragansetts. Overflowing with zeal to bring Christ to the Indians, Williams occasionally went to live with them in their "filthy, smoky holes," struggling to learn their language and get beyond his sense of superiority. Williams would never appreciate his hosts' decor or sanction their worldview. Still, he defended with ardor their right to the land. Williams rejected the notion that the Indians vacated their land claims by failing to work their fields like Europeans. The English, he argued, had to respect Indian title and bargain for territory rather than simply take it. Williams, writes historian Edward Morgan, "despised their religion and found many of their customs barbarous, but he was ready to live with them and deal with them on equal terms." In Massachusetts, clergyman John Eliot learned Indian languages, translated the Bible into Algonquian, evangelized among the tribes on the outskirts of English settlements, and brought together fourteen villages of "praying Indians." These self-governing communities were the closest the English came to the Spanish missions.[25]

The slow work of getting to know and trust one another could not match the quickening pace of conflicts brought on by English agricultural expansion. Puritan immigration to the region bottomed out in the 1640s, yet the settler population continued to grow through natural reproduction. Compared to England or Virginia, New England harbored fewer diseases lethal to Europeans. Healthier mothers and safer early childhoods bumped up fertility rates, and the recipients of this baby bounty crowed about their capacity "to beget and bring forth more children than any other nation in the world." Population growth produced a hunger for new land, Indian land.[26]

Although still formally allied with the English at Plymouth, the Wampanoags—among the remaining independent and formidable New England Algonquian tribes that also included the Narragansetts and the Abenakis—were ready to alter their foreign policy. English land grabbing and political bullying convinced Metacomet, the English-educated son of Massasoit, that his people had no alternative but armed resistance.

The conflict boiled over in early 1675 when a Christian Indian working as a spy for Plymouth was found murdered. English authorities arrested three of Metacomet's men, tried, and executed them. Within days, Wampanoag warriors attacked a colonial town and killed several residents. Metacomet appealed to their southern neighbors for a defensive alliance, but before the Narragansetts had a chance to reply, the English pounced on the overture to declare war on the Narragansetts and Wampanoags and any other Indians deemed hostile. They invaded Narragansett country and ransacked villages, burning them to the ground. Metacomet, known to the English as King Philip, recruited a guerrilla army and slipped into the interior. The English singled him out for blame, calling what was to become a general Indian uprising "King Philip's War." Fighters from many tribes raided and torched dozens of towns throughout New England. They bashed skulls, disemboweled livestock, and kidnapped women and children. As one strike force left the smoking ruin of what was Medfield, a native scribe tacked a message to a tree. "Thou English man hath provoked us to anger and wrath," it read. "We have nothing but our lives to loose but thou hast many fair houses, cattell and much good things."[27]

Anger and wrath held sway until the beginning of 1676, when the rebels spent a miserable winter in western Massachusetts and the promise of a pan-Indian alliance faded. Metacomet pleaded with the Iroquois for supplies and support. The Mohawks instead attacked and dispersed his army. Metacomet retreated to his Rhode Island homeland, where the English colonial army, aided by Christian Indians and other natives with grudges against the Wampanoags, besieged villages, destroyed crops, and killed hundreds of men, women, and children. Finally, in a battle known as the Great Swamp Fight, the English and their allies defeated the rebels and slew Metacomet. They mutilated his body and marched his head on a pike through their towns. They sold his wife and son, among hundreds of other captives, to slavers in the Caribbean.

The numbers of dead, four thousand Algonquians and two thousand English settlers, appraised the war's brutality. Measured in relation to the size of the population, King Philip's War ranked among the most destructive conflicts in American history. Dozens of English and Indian towns lay in ruins. In the closing months of the fight, terrorized Puritan colonists rounded up hundreds of praying Indians and concentrated them on desolate islands in Boston Harbor. Eliot worked hard to protect his converts, but to little avail. Although a few Christian communities remained after the war—in isolated locations on Cape Cod or Martha's Vineyard—most of the surviving Christian Algonquians fled west. Even Roger Williams, lame and in his seventies, after finding his own house burned along with most of the others in Providence, led Rhode Island troops against his former friends, the Narragansetts. With few exceptions, English sympathies and imaginations extended two alternatives for Indians—removal or extermination.

The war marked the end of large-scale, organized Indian resistance in southern New England. The population of Indians in the region had slipped far below that of the English, from ten to twenty thousand natives compared with fifty to seventy-five thousand settlers. Yet small communities of Narragansetts, Pequots, and other tribal groups survived for centuries, as anyone who has pulled the lever of a slot machine at the Pequots' Foxwoods or the Mohegans' Mohegan Sun casinos in Connecticut can attest. These several thousand native residents tell an alternative history of New England. In the homeland of Metacomet, descendants claim that the ghost of King Philip rises and walks among Indian spirits at night.

———

King Philip's War haunted the larger American culture as well. In its aftermath, commenters spun visions of the frontier as a moral and religious testing ground. Puritans interpreted their defeats and victories as part of God's plan. One of the most popular and enduring statements on this theme appeared in 1682, when Mary Rowlandson published an account of her captivity among the Indians during Metacomet's revolt. Torn from her home and family, several of whom she watched die, Rowlandson described a physical and emotional journey into a dark wilderness. At night, her captors celebrated their victory: "Oh the roaring, and singing, and dancing, and yelling of those black creatures in the night, which made the place a lively resemblance of hell." Exhausted and grieving, Rowlandson accepted her torment as a reminder of *The Sovereignty and Goodness of God*, the title she and her male sponsor, the influential minister Increase Mather, gave to her narrative. The further Rowlandson moved away from her comfortable life, the closer she came to God. Do not let the trappings of earthly happiness distract you from higher callings: this was the lesson God delivered to New England through King Philip—and Rowlandson and Mather. The book found an eager audience. An immediate best seller, the narrative was reissued in at least fifteen editions before the American Revolution. Success brought imitation. Hundreds of captivity stories appeared in print, but most wallowed in gore instead of reaching for glory.[28]

American readers clearly found an enthralling version of the frontier in the captivity narratives. Colonial North America was a hotbed of hostage-taking. Human beings stole, traded, and adopted one another across tribes, nations, and religions. Indians kidnapped other Indians as well as Europeans and some Africans. Europeans purchased African and Indian slaves, and they imprisoned and converted one another. The involuntary traffic of people defined the edges of populations and cultures. Captivity was how early modern people understood their differences and sometimes overcame them. Mary Rowlandson, with Increase Mather's help, drew a sharp line between herself and her captors in her narrative. They were animals— "wolves and bears." She was a reborn Christian. Still, for all her edge-setting, Rowlandson also revealed some feathered joints between herself and the Indians. To earn extra rations, for example, she mended the Algonquians' garments. They provided her with needle, thread, and cloth, and they described the outfits they

*Title page of the 1773 edition of Mary
Rowlandson's captivity narrative. Author's
collection.*

wanted. It turns out that these "dark creatures" preferred English-style shirts. For all their differences, Rowlandson and the Indians shared a sense of fashion.

Mather and Rowlandson half-buried the collusion of frontier cultures under the rhetoric of Indian savagery and religious fatalism, and other New England authors attempted a similar move, publishing divisive accounts that mainly obscured but occasionally offered glimpses of an entwined past. The memoir of Captain Benjamin Church, a second literary classic spawned by the Puritan-Indian wars, combined admiration and belligerence. American-born, Church was a self-declared wilderness expert and innovative Indian fighter. He ridiculed other officers for their "regular" tactics and argued that to wage an Indian war successfully, one had to do battle like Indians. In the course of his narrative, Church becomes more and more like an Indian himself, actively seeking the amalgamation of European and Indian characteristics. After the final battle he sits up all night with Annawon, one of King Philip's lieutenants, swapping tales of their adventures, and Church's narrative implies that a bond of mutual respect and even affection developed between them. Later Church is horrified to find Annawon's head on a pike at Plymouth. His anger at the dishonorable treatment of a fellow wilderness warrior, reported Church's son, led to "the loss of the good will and respects of some that before were his good friends." Church and Rowlandson forged connections to their savage neighbors at gun- and needlepoint. They gave readers a passing glance at the ambivalence and ambiguity that flourished even as relations between Indians and colonists festered.[29]

The English exited King Philip's War ready to mend their ways and placate their deity. After years of bloodshed and woe, they longed to feel the glow of God on their side. But there were too many players with too many motivations to limit colonial conflicts to two sides. They behaved like oil slicks instead of clashes. Groups collided, combined, and dispersed, only to glob into new forms under different conditions. When the Mohawks, for instance, attacked Metacomet instead of supporting him, they did not side with the English. They sought an intermediate space between neighboring Indians and the English colonies. The Mohawks and the other four Haudenosaunee nations sought a dominant position in the middle.

Indian traders from the coast first carried European goods to the peoples of the Five Nations. Archaeologists have found brass, iron, and glass items in Iroquois graves dating from the mid-fifteenth century. The Five Nations first secured direct access to colonial merchandise when Dutch traders established posts along the Hudson River in the 1610s. But the Haudenosaunee had a fur problem. The best source of beaver pelts came from the colder climes to the north. To supply themselves with these valuable items, the Mohawks, Cayugas, Onondagas, Oneidas, and Senecas raided their northern neighbors, plundering their stores of furs and bringing the pelts south to trade with the Dutch. These raids began a long series of seventeenth-century conflicts known as the Beaver Wars. Five Nation warriors attacked Indian peoples as far west as the Illinois Country, building the most powerful Indian confederacy on the North American continent in the seventeenth century.

Trade sparked the Beaver Wars, but population losses to epidemics fed the conflagration of raids and counter-raids. European diseases hit the Iroquois hard. By the 1640s epidemics had cut the population of the Five Nations in half. Warfare against their neighbors not only gave the Haudenosaunee access to the thick-pelted beavers of the northern Great Lakes, but the violence brought them captives to replenish their numbers.

The Haudenosaunee directed their most furious attacks against their northern enemy, the French-allied Hurons. "So far as I can divine," wrote a Jesuit missionary, "it is the design of the Iroquois to capture all the Hurons, if it is possible; to put the chiefs and great part of the nation to death, and with the rest to form one nation and one country." In 1647 and 1648, the Mohawks and Senecas launched a brutal offensive against the Hurons, destroying both Indian towns and Jesuit

Iroquois warriors return from war with scalps and a captive. French drawing, c. 1666. From Edmund B. O'Callaghan, ed., Documents Relative to the Colonial History of the State of New York *(Albany, 1853–87).*

missions. The Iroquois lost many warriors, yet the Huron lost even more. Many Hurons abandoned their homeland near Georgia Bay, Lake Ontario, and fled westward to the Illinois Country. Hundreds more were taken captive and marched south into Haudenosaunee territory, where they were either butchered or adopted into Iroquois families. Left behind, the bones of the dead marked the end of the Hurons.[30]

Many Huron captives were baptized, and they introduced Christianity into the Five Nations. Though ferocious raiders, the Iroquois could not absorb captives through force. To keep their adoptees happy, they eventually invited the Jesuits into their homeland to minister to the Christian Hurons, thus giving the missionaries access to them. Just as the chaos brought on by trade, violence, and illness opened the ears of the Hurons to the preaching of the Jesuits, so the Iroquois listened for personal solace or spiritual advantage, and many converted to Catholicism. The Mohawks, living on the Hudson River, closest to European traders, embraced the new faith the most. By the 1660s strong factions of pro-French Christians had formed in all the towns of the Five Nations.

Christianity disrupted Iroquois life. Many converts rejected traditional ceremonies, saying that they no longer believed in them. "The black gowns had turned his head," the traditionalists said about the converted Onondaga leader Daniel Garokontié. "He had abandoned the customs of the country, [and] had also ceased to have any affection for it." As the level of domestic strife rose, many Christian Iroquois moved north, settling near the French, where the Jesuits created special villages for them. Kateri Tekakwitha, a young Mohawk convert, fled her village in

Iroquois saint Kateri Tekakwitha. Painting by Father Claude Chauchetière, c. 1696. Wikimedia Commons.

1677 and settled in Kahnawake, a Christian Iroquois town near Montreal. An intense believer, Tekakwitha beat and starved her body so aggressively that the Jesuits declared her a wonder. She died young, at the age of twenty-four, and the priests adopted her as a martyr to the cause of New World gospel-spreading. In 2012 the Catholic Church officially elevated Tekakwitha to sainthood.[31]

The Haudenosaunee responded to the cultural crisis of colonization by strengthening their alliance with the Europeans. In the 1660s the English captured Manhattan from the Dutch without firing a shot, and New Netherlands became New York. But the English hoped to preserve the colony's old trading and diplomatic ties with the Five Nations. Traditionalists among the Iroquois warmed to the English, seeing them as a counter to the growing power of the Francophiles and Catholics within their own communities. The lackluster missionary zeal of the English they thought an advantage. When the Mohawks smashed Metacomet's army, the Iroquois cemented their new partnership.

In negotiations conducted at Albany in 1677, the Five Nations and the colony of New York created an alliance known as the Covenant Chain. The Haudenosaunee carefully walked a path between the competing French and English, asserting their autonomy when the European authorities overstepped their bounds. The

Onondaga leader Otreouti ("Big Mouth") put it well in a speech to the English in 1683: "You say we are subjects to the King of England and Duke of York, but we say, we are Brethren. We must take care of ourselves." Haudenosaunee self-determination, military prowess, and diplomatic gymnastics defined the nature of colonization in the Northeast as much as any move by European nations. They were a great power jostling among great powers.[32]

Europeans communicated their high self-regard in published tracts and pamphlets, declaring themselves the rightful heirs to North America due to their correct beliefs and civilized magnificence. But the Iroquois could talk trash, too. They had their own perspective on the history of colonialism. "You think that the Axe-Makers are the eldest in the country and the greatest in possession," declared the Onondaga orator Sadekanaktie in the 1690s. "Yes, all the Axe-Makers think the same. But no! Oh no! We Iroquois are the first, and we are the eldest and greatest. These parts and countries were inhabited and trod upon by the Iroquois before there were any Axe-Makers."[33]

FURTHER READING

James Axtell, *The Invasion Within: The Contest of Cultures in Colonial North America* (1985)
Joyce E. Chaplin, *Subject Matter: Technology, the Body, and Science on the Anglo-American Frontier, 1500–1676* (2003)
William Cronon, *Changes in the Land: Indians, Colonists, and the Ecology of New England* (1983)
W. J. Eccles, *The Canadian Frontier, 1534–1760*, rev. ed. (1986)
Jill Lepore, *The Name of War: King Philip's War and the Origins of American Identity* (1998)
Andrew Lipman, *The Saltwater Frontier: Indians and the Contest for the American Coast* (2015)
Daniel K. Richter, *The Ordeal of the Longhouse: The Peoples of the Iroquois League in the Era of European Colonization* (1992)
Brett Rushforth, *Bonds of Alliance: Indigenous and Atlantic Slaveries in New France* (2014)
Neal Salisbury, *Manitou and Providence: Indians, Europeans, and the Making of New England, 1500–1643* (1982)
Camilla Townsend, *Pocahontas and the Powhatan Dilemma* (2004)

3

The Struggle of Empires

Hacked and hewn by America's original do-it-yourself crowd, log cabins oozed gumption along with buckets of sap. The ultimate starter homes, they stood for hopeful beginnings. Log cabins sheltered working people, regular folks who dreamed of an opening in the forest canopy to grow crops and kids. Yet, even as they came to epitomize homespun Americana, log cabins didn't sprout naturally like mushrooms wherever frontier types roamed. They were actually an invasive architectural species imported from Scandinavia. Finns and Swedes brought the housing style with them from the boreal forests of northern Europe. The dirt-floored, overlapping log constructions with mud-stuffed cracks warmed them after days spent hunting fur-bearing mammals and slashing and burning wood-lands. In 1638 a few of them carried the mental plans for these units to the shores of North America where they staffed the short-lived colony on the mid-Atlantic coast known as New Sweden.

The log cabins took off while New Sweden stumbled. First, in 1655, the Dutch attacked and took the colony. Then, in 1664, the English captured it. In the grand schemes of seventeenth-century colonization, the settlements in the Delaware valley were a sideshow. But in the shadows of the region's great forests, a new culture took root. Just as ranch homes would embody the style and sensibility of post–World War II suburban America, so log cabins announced a way of life. New Sweden's loose organization and confused authority gave people room to experiment. Local autonomy promoted a fusion between settlers and natives, an Algonquian-speaking people who called themselves Lenni-Lenapes but were known by settlers as the Delawares, named for the river that coursed through their homeland. Delaware women raised gardens of corn, beans, and squash,

An early depiction of a log cabin. From Georges-Henri-Victor Collot, A Journey in North America *(Paris, 1826). Beinecke Rare Book and Manuscript Library, Yale University.*

while men hunted for furs, hides, and meat. This gender division of labor mirrored the one practiced by Swedish and Finnish settlers. In the hardscrabble environment of northern Europe, Scandinavian women had been accustomed to practicing forms of shifting cultivation, and they immediately understood Indian horticulture. Colonial women of the Delaware valley quickly adopted the crops of Indian women, while Indian women welcomed European metal hoes, as well as pigs and chickens.

Scandinavian men took to hunting in America just as quickly. Unlike French and English settlers, the Finns and Swedes had backgrounds in killing large mammals for subsistence. Class distinctions regulated hunting in France and England. Royalty and the aristocracy reserved the right to chase and slaughter prize game animals—foxes, stags, and bears—for their sporting pleasure. Lower-class hunters poached rabbits and deer on the sly for fun and protein. Few lords and fewer of the impoverished immigrated to North America; the French and English colonists therefore learned to hunt slowly as they became acquainted with firearms and New World animals. But Scandinavian men hit the ground running after American fauna. They mimicked their Algonquian neighbors' calls, camouflage, and decoys, and they embraced the Indians' surrounds and fire-hunting methods. The Algon-

Dutch colonists and Algonquian Indians in New Sweden. From Thomas Campanius Holm,
Kort beskrifning om provincien Nya Swerige [uit] America . . . *(Stockholm, 1702). Beinecke*
Rare Book and Manuscript Library, Yale University.

quians in turn adopted steel knives, guns, and linen hunting shirts, much more
comfortable in wet weather than buckskin.

The Scandinavians cooked their venison steaks over fires built in log cabin
stone hearths. The homes anchored the composite culture of mobile hunting and
swidden—or slash-and-burn—agriculture that spread with both settlers and natives as they moved up the coastal river valleys and across the Appalachians. With
a few tools and a little training, several men could raise a rough log structure in a
day, a solid house in a week. Indians immediately saw the potential. They traded

for metal tools, then chopped, notched, and chinked their own cabins, probably doing as much as the colonists to spread the practice of building in wood across the frontiers of North America. Descriptions of the Indian towns of Pennsylvania and later Ohio frequently remarked on their resemblance to the settlements of settlers—with the difference being that Indians tended to cluster their cabins rather than scatter them across the countryside, and they often built a large, impressive, log council house in the center of their towns.

The Delaware valley was what geographers call a "cultural hearth," a launching pad for a unique woodland material way of life combining traits from both Indian and European worlds. Indians and colonists even created a lingua franca—a frontier pidgin based in Algonquian but combined with elements of Swedish and eventually English—that allowed them to communicate. In many details, the lifeways of the Indians and colonists came to resemble one another. Mirrors were scarce on the margins, but Indian and European hunters and farmers could look at each other and see a spitting image. Their likeness bespoke a promise of frontier amalgamation rare in the annals of European colonization.[1]

———

William Penn, founder of the colony of Pennsylvania, is remembered for his fair dealings with native people. He came from a prominent English family, his father an admiral and counselor to the king. The religious fervor of the Protestant reformation, however, carried Penn from the centers of power to the fringes of his society. As a young man he converted to the radical sect known as the Society of Friends (ridiculed by outsiders as the Quakers for their religious enthusiasm), and he convinced his father to help him secure a grant of land in North America that could serve as a religious haven for the members. A religious nonconformist, Penn traveled to the geographic outskirts to establish a colony known for peace and toleration. Taking advantage of the tradition of peaceful relations between native Delaware people and Scandinavian settlers, Penn announced that he would not permit colonization to begin until he had negotiated the right to settle and purchased the land.

In 1682, during his first few months in America, Penn met with a council of Delawares he described as made up of "all the old and wise men of the nation" at the village of Shackamaxon near Philadelphia. Warriors from the assembled villages watched from the sidelines, their leaders consulting with them regularly in order to reach consensus. The treaty that Penn and the chiefs signed was commemorated in a Great Treaty Wampum Belt, which the Delawares presented to Penn, an artifact that symbolizes the best hopes of the American frontier experience. In it, a figure wearing a Quaker hat—Penn himself, perhaps—clasps the hand of an Indian said to be Chief Tammany, a Delaware leader who, like Penn, was renowned for

"Penn's Treaty with the Indians." Engraving of a painting by Benjamin West, 1775. Library of Congress.

his benevolence and independent thinking. Over time, North Americans turned Tammany into a cross-cultural hero. He appeared in popular stories and legends among Indians and colonists, and by the time of the Revolution his name was emblematic of the American spirit of independence. Tammany Hall, the Democratic political society of New York City, was named in his honor.[2]

The painter Benjamin West's famous depiction of the negotiations focuses on Penn beneath a spreading elm, presenting a very English version of the treaty to the Indians. Firmly planted in the colonial perspective, the painting veers toward smug fantasy rather than lived ambiguity. But Penn did approach the treaty with goodly intentions. He considered his negotiating partners human beings with rights and feelings. He did his best to protect them from unscrupulous traders and the destructive alcohol trade. As long as Penn lived, there was no frontier warfare in Pennsylvania. Indeed, during his lifetime a number of Indian groups resettled in the Quaker colony.

————

The peace and accommodation of early Pennsylvania fostered the development of the distinctive backcountry culture that changed both colonists and Indians.

But after Penn's death, as his descendants began to pursue an aggressive policy of landed expansion at the expense of native homelands, relations between natives and settlers soured. Instead of marveling at the similarities that united them, natives and settlers in Pennsylvania and elsewhere in the British colonies spent much of the eighteenth century shedding each other's blood. Each group began to see the other as fundamentally different, members of separate and unequal races. And they committed outrageous acts of brutality to prove it. Log cabins thus carry a serious historical burden. They represent both hope and despair, upward mobility and base degradation. They represent both cultural fusion and racial division. They stand for the uneasiness of America's frontiers as diverse people came to know, love, and hate one another through colonization.

The principal cause of the violence was the explosive growth of English settler colonialism. In their outward thrust, Europeans created colonial outposts of varying sorts. The French paddled down the Mississippi, building a watery, canoe-based trading empire stretching from Quebec to New Orleans. The Russians extended their fur-hunting colonial ventures across the Bering Sea down the northern Pacific coast. The Spanish pushed their mission system north from Mexico into Texas and California. All these colonial ventures employed violent means and provoked violent responses. But the greatest conflict took place on the frontiers of the English colonies, where settler families by the thousands came to stay, seizing the land from indigenous people by treaty or warfare, forcing their communities to the periphery or encapsulating them in small reserved homelands.

Demography—the science of counting people—resembles molecular biology in that many of the processes and changes under study occur beyond everyday perception. Few may take notice as populations accumulate, decline, age, and turn over. Such was not the case in British North America during the eighteenth century. So many people moved in and so many people reproduced that demographic change drew eyes and comments like a fireball in the night. "Our People must at least be doubled every 20 years," Benjamin Franklin guessed. (With no census at that time, observers were forced to guess.) He was only slightly off his calculation, the doubling occurring every quarter-century. The 250,000 settlers of the English colonies in 1700 had exploded to more than 1.3 million fifty years later. The British colonial population amazed the grand master of modern head counters, the English economist Thomas Malthus. The settler society of North America, he wrote, was experiencing "a rapidity of increase probably without parallel in history."[3]

What caused the boom? Fertility rates in the colonies considerably outpaced those in the home country. English colonial women commonly bore seven or more children, and birth rates in what English speakers called "the backcountry" made coastal families look modest. Rebecca Bryan Boone, wife of the frontier hero Daniel

Boone, for example, bore ten children, and in the couple's old age they were sur-rounded by sixty-eight grandchildren. Relatively low mortality boosted the effects of high fertility. Blessed with good soil and the productivity of Indian agricultural techniques, settlers did not experience famines in North America. True, colonial cit-ies were notoriously unhealthy places, and some rural areas—notably the lowland South—were plagued by malaria and other tropical diseases. But for most colonists, North American disease environments proved remarkably benign. Death rates were 15 or 20 percent lower than in Europe, and relatively low levels of infant mortality meant that an extraordinarily large number of people survived to reproductive age.

Immigration added even more reproducing bodies. In New York, Pennsylvania, and backcountry Virginia, settlers from Germany, Ireland, and elsewhere pressed into river valleys and mountain hollows, chopping and burning the forest and planting hills of Indian corn in the clearings. William Penn began recruiting Euro-pean settlers for his colony as early as the 1680s, and by the second decade of the eighteenth century, thousands of Germans were streaming from the Rhineland due to depressed farm conditions, religious wars, and New World advertisements. Many were Pietists, pacifists, and excellent farmers. They sought fertile land in the interior, first along the Mohawk valley in New York, where they knocked heads with speculators, then in Pennsylvania, where they flourished. To the immemorial confusion of schoolchildren and tourists who expect to find an enormous popu-lation of clog-wearing, tulip-growing dike-builders in rural Pennsylvania, some of these Germans, such as the Mennonites and Amish, came to be known as the Pennsylvania Dutch because of the language they spoke—Deutsch.

Bewildering in their own fashion, the Scots-Irish poured into the western ar-eas about the same time. They had been transplanted from Scotland to northern Ireland around Ulster, and their struggles with the local Catholics rewarded their aggressive tendencies. They applied these to their English landlords as well, so it is not surprising that they got as far away as they could from the seaboard colonists when they arrived in America. On the geographic margins, the Scots-Irish culti-vated a reputation as fighters, hunters, and marksmen.

By the 1720s these immigrants took the composite Indian-European frontier culture from its hearth in the Delaware valley and pushed it into the backcoun-try, down the immense Shenandoah valley, running southwest along the eastern front of the Appalachians. The Shenandoah became British America's first "west." Within a generation settlers could be found all along the front range of the Ap-palachians, from Pennsylvania south to the Carolinas. Many, perhaps most, of these farmers and hunters held no legal title to the lands they occupied but simply hacked out and defended their squatters' rights.

The squatters built their rights on a fiction. They based their claim to property on the labor they invested in "improving" the land. This assumed that the ground

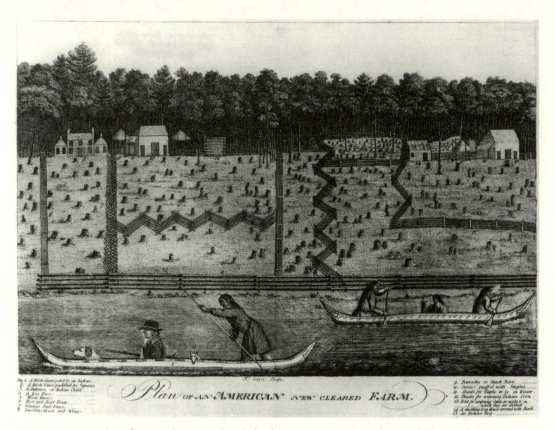

American farm in the Pennsylvania backcountry. From Patrick Campbell, Travels in the
Interior Inhabited Parts of North America . . . *(Edinburgh, 1793). Beinecke Rare Book and
Manuscript Library, Yale University.*

lay fallow, unused, and ripe for manipulation. But the invaders laid claim to the
lands of Indian peoples who found themselves literally pressed to the mountain
wall. While English colonial society underwent rapid expansion, these coastal
Indian societies continued to undergo traumatic population decline, mostly as a
result of the terrific beating inflicted by European epidemic diseases. During the
eighteenth century, the European colonial population overtook the native population of the continent. Accurate counts of people were hard to come by in the eighteenth century; no headlines alerted natives and newcomers to the demographic
shift. They crossed the historical threshold blind to what the future would hold.

In the tidewater region of Virginia, coastal North and South Carolina, and Georgia, where the climate proved suitable for growing tobacco, rice, or indigo, settlers
at first used enslaved Indians or European indentured servants to work the fields,
but they gradually shifted to enslaved Africans, following the pattern that had been
laid down in the Caribbean. Nearly four hundred thousand captive Africans were
landed in the British colonies before the American Revolution, a small portion

of the more than twelve million people who suffered the largest forced migration in world history. Settlers and slaves moved westward from the coast, clearing the piney woods and constructing hardscrabble compounds that in no way resembled the elegant plantations of southern nostalgia. By 1770 Africans made up nearly half the population of the southern colonies.

Population loss did not affect all Indians equally. Although the number of coastal natives declined precipitously, the population of interior peoples such as the Creeks and Cherokees actually stabilized and grew in the mid-eighteenth century. Imperial competition, immigration, natural increase, and territorial expansion would radically alter relationships between human—and nonhuman—populations throughout North America in the eighteenth century. Yet the immense scale of these changes was matched by their haphazard application. Colonization opened new routes to power and wealth even as it foreclosed others. On the grassy plains of the continent's interior, some humans discovered an express to fortune on the backs of Spanish horses. One group, the Comanches, rode this path all the way to their own empire. In the eighteenth century, Europeans monopolized neither the grand designs nor the strong-arm tactics of imperial regimes. Indians could be masters, too.

The Comanches moved from the Rocky Mountains to the Great Plains in the early 1700s in response to the Spanish presence in New Mexico. The Uto-Aztecan–speaking people cared nothing for the Spaniard's God or their claims to New World sovereignty; they were after their animals. During the tumult of the Pueblo Revolt, Spanish horses—a tough breed known as barbs—escaped their owners and galloped onto the southern plains grasslands to find an ungulate paradise. They ate grass, reproduced, and partnered with new sets of caballeros. The Jumanos and Apaches acquired mounts first. They demonstrated the animals' extraordinary potential, and their military and material success attracted imitators, including the mountain-dwelling Utes and Comanches. The Utes and Comanches were allies and indistinguishable in the eyes of the Spanish. The Comanches first appeared in the historical record in 1709. A Spanish official in New Mexico mentioned their presence as an afterthought.

Once they figured out how to fully exploit the power of horses, the Comanches' influence and reputation grew. Unlike the Apache and Jumanos, the Comanches went all in with horses, altering their mixed hunting and farming economy to take advantage of the new technology. They stopped growing food, and they stayed on the plains year-round to hunt bison full time. They raided the villages of vegetable growers to sprinkle their diets with carbohydrates, and they began trading bison robes, horses, and captive slaves with the Spanish in Taos and the French in the Mississippi valley. Trade brought guns, and they used the increased firepower to

The Comanche method of training horses. From George Catlin, Die Indianer Nord-Amerikas . . . *(Leipzig, 1845). Beinecke Rare Book and Manuscript Library, Yale University.*

further escalate their raiding and trading. By the end of the eighteenth century, the Comanches dominated the Southwest. The Jumanos disappeared, the Apache suffered continuous pilfering, and the grand designs of the Spanish in New Mexico and Texas became afterthoughts.

The French colonies also grew in the eighteenth century, but at a much slower pace. Dedicated to keeping its colony exclusively Catholic, officials regulating immigration to Canada refused to admit thousands of Huguenot French Protestants, preventing the colony from achieving the impressive growth of the English. Although Canadian population climbed from fifteen thousand in 1700 to more than seventy thousand by midcentury, it was relatively puny beside the English colonial behemoth of more than a million.

Their low population numbers turned the French into social entrepreneurs. They reached out to Indian peoples through trade and alliances to thwart British and Spanish expansion. They worked to strengthen their great crescent of military posts and isolated settlements extending from the mouth of the Saint Lawrence to the Great Lakes, then down the length of the Mississippi River to the Gulf of Mexico. The scattered French settlements in the western country anchored this meandering hybrid creation of natives and colonists. At each site—from the sugar plantations of the lower Mississippi to the farms of the Illinois Country to the fur posts at Prairie du Chien—the French re-created the "long plot" pattern of the Saint Lawrence; it was the distinctive Franco-American stamp on the landscape,

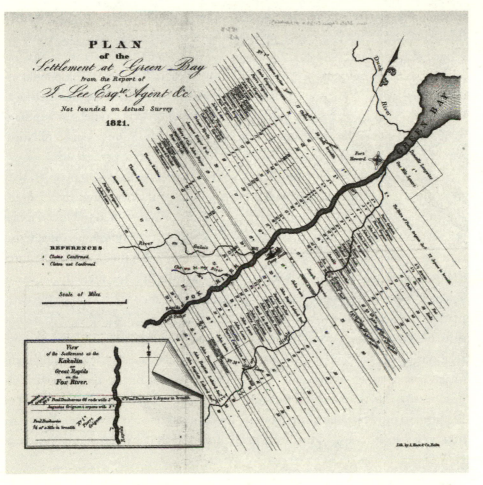

French long lots at Green Bay, Wisconsin. From American State Papers: Documents, Legislative and Executive *(Washington, D.C., 1832–61).*

visible to this day from the air. There were also French settlements at each of the strategic passages of the Great Lakes: Mackinaw, Sault Sainte Marie, and Detroit, this last by midcentury a community of a hundred métis farm families who worked their land near the villages of Ottawas, Potawatomies, and Hurons.

French frontier communities combined European and Indian elements. At first glance, one observer testified, Detroit looked like "an old French village" until he looked closer and noticed that the houses were "mostly covered with bark," Indian style. "It is not uncommon to see a Frenchman with Indian shoes and stockings, without breeches, wearing a strip of woolen cloth to cover what decency requires him to conceal," wrote another visitor; "yet at the same time he wears a fine ruffled shirt and a laced waistcoat, with a fine handkerchief on his head." Family and kinship also took on local Indian patterns. Colonial men and native women intermarried, and soon there were groups of métis in every French settlement. Households often consisted of several related families, and in the Indian fashion, most women limited their fertility, bearing an average of two or three children. There was arranged marriage and occasional polygamy, but wives had easy access to divorce and enjoyed full rights to property. Yet unlike their Indian kin, these people focused their activities on commerce and overwhelmingly identified themselves as Catholics. Choosing a path of mutual accommodation, the French and Indians established some of the most interesting and distinct communities in all of North America.[4]

Although in general the French had better relations with native peoples, they sometimes came into conflict with Indian groups as they pursued their expansionist plans. When the Foxes of the upper Mississippi attempted to block French access to the interior, positioning themselves as lucrative middlemen in the fur trade, the French did not hesitate to wage bloody war upon them, eventually forcing them to sign a treaty in 1738. On the lower Mississippi, the French fought the Natchez Indians, who opposed their arrival, a war that concluded with the decimation and scattering of the entire Natchez tribe in 1731. By force or by friendship, the French strung together a vast territory linked by water and cross-cultural relationships. Like their fellow North American expansionists, they had big plans for an epic continental realm. Although it was true that British colonists far outnumbered them, observed a military officer of New France, numbers were not of first importance, for "the Canadians are brave, much inured to war, and untiring in travel. Two thousand of them will at all times and all places thrash the people of New England."[5]

———

Population increase, territorial expansion, and imperial consolidation: the European colonies in North America bulked up and butted heads throughout the long eighteenth century. Indians cheered and jeered from the sidelines, trading blows when battle met strategic needs from military advantage to cultural survival. The string of colonial wars strengthened some native groups and destroyed others. By the late seventeenth century, for example, the Five Nations had demonstrated their power far to the south and west of their homeland, matching the influence of any European colony. The Osages controlled a vast territory stretching from the Mississippi into the Arkansas River valley, and the Comanches ruled the southern plains. In the Southeast, Indians—including the Cherokees, Creeks, Chickasaws, and Choctaws—joined forces to build new confederacies. The Choctaws allied with the French, the others with the English. Neither Indians nor Europeans understood the colonial wars as racial conflicts of red against white; rather, every group fought for itself, allied as circumstances and interest demanded, in a kind of free-for-all. Indians shot Indians and colonists blew up colonists at least as much as Indians fought colonists and vice versa.

Many of these wars started in Europe, but the North Americans quickly made the hostilities their own. What the English colonists called King William's War in 1689 began when King Louis XIV of France rejected William of Orange as the new ruler of England. In America, this dynastic squabble translated into a battle fought over access to the rich fur ground of the north and west. In 1670 the English had chartered the Hudson's Bay Company to counter French trade dominance in the north, while on the southern flank of New France the English sought to extend their control of the Indian trade through their Covenant Chain allies, the Five Nations. The hostilities opened with an English-supported Mohawk massacre of French settlers at the village of Lachine, near Montreal. The next year the French and their Indian allies counterattacked, burning frontier settlements in New York, New Hampshire, and Maine and pressing the attack on Iroquois towns. The same year, a Massachusetts fleet briefly captured the strategic French harbor and fort at Port Royal in Acadia, but a combined English colonial force failed in an attempt to conquer the French settlements along the Saint Lawrence. The inconclusive war ended with a European treaty of 1697 that established an equally inconclusive peace.

In five short years, the combatants were at each other again, this time over the English refusal to let Louis XIV's grandson ascend to the throne of Spain, bringing those Catholic nations too close for comfort. But in North America what was called Queen Anne's War stoked frontier resentments, and most of the bloodshed occurred on the edges of the empires. The English attacked the French communities in the maritime region, while the French and their Indian allies raided English settlements, such as the outlying village of Deerfield, Massachusetts, dragging more than a hundred prisoners into captivity in 1704. In the South, South Carolina troops invaded Spanish Florida in 1702, burning and plundering Saint Augustine, and four years later, a combined French and Spanish fleet took revenge by bombarding Charleston. Indians fought on all sides of the conflict. The monarchs and their ministers signed a treaty in 1713, but the North Americans kept animosities hot. English slave traders encouraged their Indian allies to continue the attack against natives allied with the Spanish Floridians and French Louisianans. Over the next quarter-century, these raids destroyed the last of the Spanish mission stations in Florida. The raiders captured thousands of mission Indians, and the English sold them into slavery in the Caribbean. Thousands more died in the fighting or bolted for safety. The Creeks resettled in Florida, where they joined fugitive African American slaves from South Carolina and formed a new mixed group known as the Seminoles.

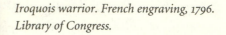

Iroquois warrior. French engraving, 1796. Library of Congress.

Guerrier Iroquois.

The colonial wars went particularly badly for groups like the Iroquoian-speaking Tuscaroras of North Carolina. Defeated in battle in 1713, the surviving families moved north to join their colinguists in New York. In 1722 the Haudenosaunee admitted the Tuscaroras. The Six Nations exploited the violent conflicts, expanding their ranks and their influence over reeling tribes, such as William Penn's old friends the Delawares. Haudenosaunee diplomats became adept at playing the French against the British. Shaken by Canadian attacks on their towns during King William's War, in 1701 they negotiated a treaty of neutrality with New France while maintaining an alliance with the English. "To preserve the Ballance between us and the French," wrote one New York official, "is the great ruling Principle of the Modern Indian Politics." The Haudenosaunee—as well as other powerful nations like the Comanche—benefited from the flexibility of their internal politics. Unlike European monarchical states, Indian confederacies operated through persuasion rather than command. Factions created their own foreign policies to suit their immediate needs. This opened possibilities for the Six Nations: the factions within the Confederacy were free to ally themselves with either the British or the French. They could also withdraw their support without completely wrecking larger agreements. In a similar way the southern confederacies attempted to carve out space for themselves between the British colonies and those of the French in Louisiana and the Spanish in Florida. Onondaga chief Otreouti expressed the Indian position. "We are born freemen," he declared, "we have a power to go where we please, conduct who we will to the places we resort to, and to buy and sell where we think fit."[6]

Yet another succession dispute tested the free-range politics of the Indian confederacies. In the 1740s King George's War broke the peace between the English and French, and both powers sought the help of the Six Nations. The English presented their case at a 1744 conference held at Lancaster, Pennsylvania. The Haudenosaunee were unhappy. Like other native peoples, they felt under siege. A chief named Canasatego gave a long speech that recounted a time before the European invasion: "We then had room enough, and plenty of deer, which was easily caught, and though we had not knives, hatchets, or guns, such as we have now, yet we had knives of stone, and hatchets of stone, and bows and arrows, and those served our uses as well then as the English ones do now." But times had changed: "We are now straitened, and sometimes in want of deer, and liable to many other inconveniences since the English came among us, and particularly from that *pen-and-ink work* that is going on at the table." Here Canasatego pointed at the scribe recording his speech. Through their wars, treaties, and land-grabbing, the English had worn some of the shine off their friendship.[7]

At Lancaster, the Six Nations agreed to support the British—in exchange for payments of gold and promises of fair dealing in the future—and with the Iroquois protecting their northern borders, the English felt safe enough on that frontier to focus on the capture of the strategic French fortress of Louisbourg, at the entrance to the Gulf of Saint Lawrence. But the "pen-and-ink work" remained much on Indians' minds. A series of land deals signed by the Delawares with the colony of Pennsylvania alarmed Indian Country, especially the Walking Purchase of 1737, an event that unfolded on the hazy ground between history and myth. The story was that William Penn had negotiated a treaty in good faith with the Delawares, stipulating the Indians' willingness to cede lands vaguely bounded by the distance a man could travel in a day and a half. Forty years passed, Penn died, and his heirs moved to enforce the treaty. They hired fleet-footed ringers who covered more than sixty miles in the specified time. Historians argue over the accuracy of this tale, but its absolute truth is beside the point. The Walking Purchase symbolized the escalating conflict between Indians and settlers over western land. To install a farmer's paradise in Pennsylvania for Germans and Scots-Irish, Penn's descendants pressured, swindled, and abused the farming peoples already there. The Walking Purchase opened a huge tract in the upper Delaware and Lehigh valleys by dispossessing Indian communities. A stain on Penn's legacy, the story announced an end to fair deals and signaled disturbing things to come.

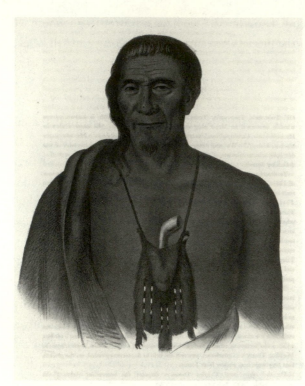

Delaware chief Tishcohan, who was defrauded by the Walking Purchase. From Thomas L. McKenney and James Hall, History of the Indian Tribes of North America . . . , 3 vols. (Philadelphia, 1836–44). Beinecke Rare Book and Manuscript Library, Yale University.

Along with land, trade goods became flash points of resentment. Their growing dependence on European manufactures had, to use Chief Canasatego's phrase, "straitened" some Indian groups. Being able to purchase knives, hatchets, and guns at the trading post gave "a vast advantage to the Six Nations," another Haudenosaunee spokesman declared. "But we think, Brother, that your people who trade there have the most advantage by it, and that it is as good for them as a Silver mine." Trade items bolstered political alliances. The goods cemented friendships and promoted peace. When the Six Nations pointed out an unfair advantage, they were communicating more than their economic displeasure. Unhappy customers meant war.[8]

By the eighteenth century, the easy availability of European goods prompted most native manufactures to cease in the Northeast. A list of items sent to the Iroquois about this time suggests how essential trade had become. It included weapons and ammunition, knives, hatchets, needles, scissors, and flint strikers for starting fires, steel and brass wire, glass bottles, heavy blankets and other textiles, ready-made shirts and dresses, paint for body decoration, glass beads and wampum, tobacco and pipes, and liquor, many barrels of liquor.

Alcohol abuse increased the dizzying effects of colonization. New Englanders manufactured bootleg rum from contraband sugar smuggled from the Spanish or French West Indies. The colonial authorities knew that the addictive substance sometimes turned voluntary economic arrangements into Devil's bargains, and they outlawed the liquor trade to maintain their moral integrity and preserve the peace. Drunks brawled. People died, and survivors sought revenge. The alcohol trade to the Indians resembled the modern cocaine or heroin business, with traders acting like drug lords. They profited from intoxication while Indian communities grappled with addiction. "Strong liquor is the root of all evil," a chief of the Senecas declared, but the chiefs found themselves unable to stop the flow of the drug. One missionary observed a drunken fight among the Senecas in 1750. "The yelling and shrieking continued frightfully in the whole village. It is impossible to describe the confusion to anyone who has not witnessed it."[9]

By the mid-eighteenth century, such violent scenes had become commonplace in eastern North America. To find refuge, many Indian families moved westward, settling in ethnically mixed Indian towns; others remained in their traditional homelands but dispersed to put distance between themselves and their addled neighbors. Gradually, the traditional communal longhouse gave way to single-family log cabins. And the frontier structures took on yet another meaning: they became safe houses from alcohol-induced disruption.

The Ohio country, the great trans-Appalachian watershed of the Ohio River, inspired visions of peace, abundance, and profit. Warfare had kept the human population sparse in the seventeenth century. The Ohio country bloomed as a buffer zone between the warring French-allied Great Lakes Algonquians and the northeastern Haudenosaunee, allied first with the Dutch, then with the English. Animals multiplied in the absence of human predators. In the early 1700s, the fat and numerous bears, deer, and bison proved irresistible, and hunters drifted back into the area. Soon whole communities joined them. The Ohio country became a refuge for Indian peoples sick of the Northeast—Iroquois, Hurons, Delawares, and Shawnees among them. They built multiethnic towns and over time acquired their own leaders and foreign policy. The product of buffer zones, social fractures, and land grabs, these Ohio Indians salvaged a home region from the wreckage of colonization.

The new towns attracted French traders always on the prowl for customers and military allies. The French saw the Ohio country as a crucial hedge against British expansion. The millions of people in the British colonies alarmed them, but also the superior quality and low prices of British trade goods. The rich land of the interior was also a prime target of frontier land speculators and backcountry settlers. Worried that their traders would be crushed and that British settlements would lock up the headwaters of Ohio and thereby break their waterlogged empire, the

French moved to reinforce their claims in 1749. They sent a heavily armed force of Canadians and Indians down the Ohio to warn off the British. In 1753 they began constructing a series of forts that extended south from Lake Erie to the forks of the Ohio River, the junction of the Allegheny and Monongahela Rivers. The forts irritated the British. They threw up their own blockhouses and strengthened their old frontier outposts, and the king gave huge chunks of the region away to a group known as the Ohio Company, a land-speculating venture organized by Virginia and London capitalists. The company made plans to build a fort of its own at the forks of the Ohio.

All this construction upset the residents. The Ohio Indians were suspicious of Europeans with imperial ambitions and blueprints. Many, like the Delawares, had crossed the mountains to rid themselves of scheming speculators and squatters. Most of the Ohio Indians opposed the British and wanted to stop their westward expansion at the Appalachians. They were also disturbed by the French moves into their country, but unlike the British, French outposts did not become centers of swelling agricultural settlements. Indian diplomats understood that it was in their interest to perpetuate the colonial stalemate. They waffled, hoping to forestall a decisive victory by either side.

In 1754 the governor of Virginia sent a young militia officer, Colonel George Washington, to expel the French from the Ohio Company lands. Washington confronted a superior force of French and Indians based in Fort Duquesne, a log bastion erected at the forks of the Ohio and named for the governor of Canada. The Canadians and Indians surrounded Washington and forced him to surrender his troops. From Duquesne, the French commanded the Ohio country (at least in the opinions of the squabbling Europeans). The next year, the British escalated the conflict when they brought in the professionals. General Edward Braddock of the Scottish Coldstream Guards led more than two thousand British troops and fifty Indian scouts from Virginia toward the forks. The French and their Indian allies ambushed the army, and in Britain's worst defeat of the eighteenth century, Braddock lost his life. The survivors buried the general's body on the trail, and the entire English detachment marched over the grave to destroy the traces. Braddock's trouncing launched a global conflagration. The French and British and the many allies on both sides fought on land and sea, embattling North America, India, the Caribbean islands, and Europe proper. The Ohio country became one of the most hotly contested real estate developments in world history.

Braddock's defeat headlined a long series of setbacks for the British. Canadians captured British posts in northern New York, and Indians pounded backcountry settlements, killing thousands of settlers, then raided deep into the coastal colonies, throwing colonists into panic. Prime Minister William Pitt, a passionate advocate of colonial expansion, poured military resources into the North American contest, determined to defeat New France once and for all. To win the support of the colonists, he promised that the war would be fought "at His Majesty's expense." To win the support of the natives, British officials promised the Six Nations and the Ohio Indians that the crown would "agree upon clear and fixed Boundaries between our Settlements and their Hunting Grounds, so that each Party may know their own and be a mutual Protection to each other of their respective Possessions." Pitt dispatched more than twenty thousand regular British troops across the Atlantic, and in combination with colonial forces, he massed over fifty thousand men against French Canada.[10]

The investment in money and manpower reversed the course of the war. A string of British victories culminated in the taking of Fort Duquesne in 1758—renamed Fort Pitt, later Pittsburgh. The last of the western French forts fell the next year. The imperial stalemate in the trans-Appalachian frontier toppled in the South as well. Here, the Cherokees were the key players. Like other Indian confederacies, they tried to balance their alliances to prevent a winner-take-all scenario. During the world war that came to be known in future generations as the French and Indian War in North America, the Cherokees sided with the French to slow British expansion into the interior from the Carolinas. They paid dearly for this choice. Regular and provincial British troops invaded their homeland—no backcountry to the Indians—and crushed them.

The decisive British victory came in 1759. British forces converged on Quebec in the heart of French Canada. Their commander, General James Wolfe, sought a final showdown with the French army led by the Marquis de Montcalm. Wolfe and his men twice made frontal assaults on Quebec from the river, failing both times. He then devised a scheme worthy of a wilderness scout—a night maneuver up a cleft in the bluffs two miles behind the city. At dawn on September 13, 1757, the British met the French on the Plains of Abraham behind Quebec. In a day's hard fight, Montcalm was killed and Wolfe shot three times. Before he died, Wolfe knew he had won, and with the victory England supplanted France in North America.

Benjamin West's painting of General Wolfe's death is filled with last gasps, but the global struggle did not end with the fall of Quebec. For two more years, the British hammered French ships, and since Spain was allied with France, they lost possessions as well. The British invaded and captured several Spanish colonies in the Caribbean and the Philippines in the Pacific. At approximately the same time, England also conquered India, thus becoming the greatest imperial power the world had yet known.

Londoners rang bells while Parisians moped in silence. In the Treaty of Paris, signed in 1763, France gave up all its North American possessions, ceding its claims east of the Mississippi to Great Britain, with the exception of New Orleans, which along with its other trans-Mississippi West claims passed to Spain. In exchange

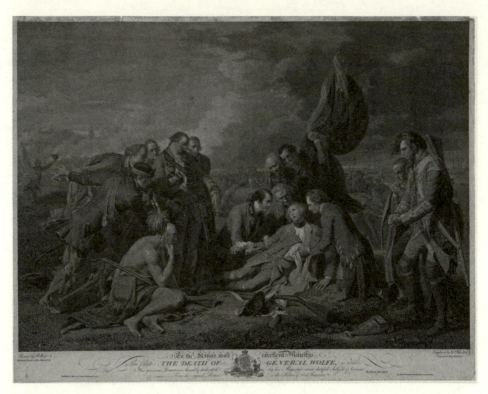

"The Death of General Wolfe." Engraving by William Woollett, based on a painting by Benjamin West, 1776. Library of Congress.

for the return of its Caribbean and Pacific colonies, Spain ceded Florida. In one gulp, the English swallowed France's riverine concoction. As British officials pondered the green valleys, fair forests, and packages of animal pelts that were now theirs, they may have mistaken the pleasant burn in their guts for satisfaction. Wars, however, create as many problems as they solve. The ink had barely dried on the Treaty of Paris when the British began to suffer from indigestion.

When the Ohio Indians heard that the French had ceded their homeland to the British, they were shocked. "Having never been conquered, either by the English or French," British Indian agent William Johnson wrote, the Indians "consider themselves as a free people." A new set of British policies soon turned shock into rage. Both the French and British in America had long given gifts to initiate and renew alliances. This was Indian diplomatic protocol. Friends offered presents; enemies withheld them. The Spanish officials who replaced the French in Louisiana adhered to the old policy to keep the peace, but the British military governor in the western region, General Jeffrey Amherst, in one of his first official actions, banned presents to Indian chiefs and tribes, demanding that they learn to live without

The Indians giving a Talk to Colonel Bouquet in a Conference at a Council Fire, near his Camp on the Banks of Muskingum in North America, in Oct.ʳ 1764.

B. West inv.ᵗ

Grignion sculp.

203

Ohio Indians meet with the British in 1764. Engraving by Benjamin West, from William Smith, An Historical Account of the Expedition Against the Ohio Indians . . . *(London, 1766).*

"charity." As British subjects, Amherst reasoned, the Indians should offer their allegiance to the crown without recompense. The Indians, as "free people," considered this assertion of sovereignty ridiculous and insulting. Amherst's stinginess not only wounded friendships, it hit Indians in the stomach. He refused to supply them with ammunition that they required for hunting. Many Ohio Indians went hungry.[11]

Religion fanned the discontent. An Indian visionary, Neolin, known to the English as the Delaware Prophet, amassed hundreds of followers in the Ohio country. "The Enlightened One" taught that European ways had corrupted native people. To recover, they needed to purify themselves, return to their traditions, and prepare for a holy war against the colonists. "If you suffer the English among you, you are dead men. Sickness, smallpox, and their poison will destroy you entirely," he declared, and urged his followers to "drive them out!" Neolin's message inspired and empowered a collection of native military leaders who laid plans for a coordinated attack against the British in the spring of 1763. The principal figure among them was an Ottawa named Pontiac, a renowned orator and political organizer who admired Neolin's prophecies as much as he despised Amherst's policies. The combination of inspirational religious and political leadership had fired the Algonquian resistance on the Chesapeake early in the seventeenth century, and it would recur numerous times over the long history of Indian resistance to colonial expansion in North America. Religion consolidated military campaigns, welding the fractures of intertribal differences.[12]

In May 1763, the Indians attacked all the British forts in the West. At Mackinaw, located at the narrows between Lakes Michigan and Huron, Indians overran the fort by scrambling through the gates in pursuit of a ball during a lacrosse game, cheered on by the unsuspecting soldiers. Indian raids cost the lives of more than two thousand settlers. At Fort Pitt, General Amherst proposed that his officers "Send the *Small Pox* among those Disaffected Tribes of Indians" by distributing the infected blankets from the fort's hospital. Contagion, whether from Amherst's despicable blankets or the general health disaster that was warfare, struck the Delawares and Shawnees and traveled south to the Creeks, Choctaws, and Chickasaws, killing hundreds. The Indians sacked and burned eight British posts, but the confederacy failed to dislodge the British from key forts at Niagara, Detroit, and the forks of the Ohio. Pontiac fought for another year, but his ranks thinned as rebels peeled off to defend their villages or salvage what was left. Many native groups sued for peace; the British started negotiations by handing out presents. Gifts, it turns out, were cheaper than uprisings.[13]

Even before the revolt began, British authorities were at work on a policy that they hoped would resolve frontier tensions. The king assumed jurisdiction over Indian lands and issued the famous Royal Proclamation of 1763. Some areas at the geographical extremes of British North America—Quebec and Florida—would open for settlement, but the crown forbade its citizens from taking possession of trans-Appalachia. That region was to become Indian Country, and the king's agents controlled access to it. Farmers and speculators would need specific authorization before the purchase of these protected Indian lands. British authorities promised to maintain commercial posts in the interior for Indian commerce and fortify the border to keep out land-hungry settlers. The proclamation gratified Indian leaders, especially the tribes who had sided with the English against the French, but land speculators and their would-be customers grumbled.

Backcountry colonists expected that with the removal of the French threat, they could move unencumbered into the West, regardless of the wishes of the Indian inhabitants. Why would the crown reward territory to Indian enemies who slaughtered more than four thousand settlers during the previous wars? The Royal Proclamation of 1763 seemed absurd, and colonists pushed against the line. They discovered the limits of British power. The king's agents could draw boundaries on maps and declare huge territories off-limits, but they had neither the will nor the manpower to stop the flow of illegal border crossers. Within a few years, New Englanders by the thousands seeped into the northern Green Mountain district, known by the corrupted French name "Vermont." In the middle colonies, New York settlers moved ever closer to the homeland of the Haudenosaunee, while other illegals located within the protective radius of Fort Pitt in western Pennsylvania. Hunters, stock herders, and farmers crossed over the first range of the Appalachians in Virginia and North Carolina, planting illicit pioneer communities in what are now West Virginia and eastern Tennessee.

The western human tide came with sharks. Land speculators and investors saw profit in the king's Indian Country. George Washington considered the proclamation line nothing but "a temporary expedient," and he touted the advantages of investing in western land. "There is a large field before you, an opening prospect in the back Country for Adventurers," he wrote to a contemporary, "where an enterprising Man with very little Money may lay the foundation of a Noble Estate in the New Settlements." The future president himself speculated heavily in trans-Appalachian lands. In 1768 the Ohio Company sent surveyors to mark out its grant in the upper Ohio. In response to settlers and speculators, British authorities pressed the Haudenosaunee and the Cherokees for land cessions. With France gone, native negotiators could no longer play the balancing game between rival colonial powers. They found themselves reduced to a choice between compliance and resistance, and weakened by the recent war, they chose to sign away their rights to land. In 1768 the Cherokees ceded a vast tract on the waters of the upper Tennessee River—where British settlers had already planted communities—and the Six Nations gave up their claim of possession to the Ohio valley, a claim many of the Ohio Indians rejected. The Haudenosaunee sold out the buffer-zone refugees to deflect the British squatters and speculators from their homeland.[14]

Thanks to the French and Indian War, the Ohio country went from a marginal, wartorn no man's land to some of the most hotly contested real estate on the planet. The watershed stoked desire; one group's want begot other groups' wants, and soon colonial rivals had launched a world war to possess the region. The Ohio country epitomized the competition and possessiveness that remade the map of North America in the eighteenth century. Colonial powers scrambled to seize lands and resources, not because they could populate, protect, or use them necessarily, but rather because they did not want their opponents to get hold of them. Empires gobbled territory, at least on paper, in a giant exercise of keep-away.

Thousands of miles from the forks of the Ohio, on the fogbound coasts of the northern Pacific, natives and Europeans battled over a natural resource. Different setting, familiar scene. Driven by the search for valuable furs, the Russians had conquered Siberia and eventually moved across the icy sea to the Aleutian archipelago, homeland of the amphibious Aleuts, master canoeists and hunters of sea mammals. We know this region by the name applied to it much later—Alaska. With the hallmark arrogance of an invading European nation, the invaders called it Russian America.

Tsar Peter the Great commissioned the Danish-born naval officer Vitus Bering to lead a scouting expedition across the Pacific, and in 1741, after several shorter voyages, Bering sailed east across the sea that now bears his name and "discovered" the Aleutian Islands. Although he died on the return passage, his associates brought back a cargo of sea otter furs valued at ninety thousand rubles. This fabulous sum triggered a rush of independent Russian fur trappers and traders called *promyshlenniki*. By 1763 hundreds of Russian traders had followed the Aleutian chain to the mainland and were sending home a steady supply of furs, valued in the millions of rubles, that were traded into China in exchange for the tea to which the Russians were addicted.

The Russians were brutal colonizers, nasty as any expansionist power involved in North America in the eighteenth century. As they had done with native communities in Siberia, the promyshlenniki held Aleut villages hostage, forcing the men to trap and the women to perform sexual services. In 1748 the Russian state declared the Aleuts a conquered people and saddled them with the duty of paying *yasak*, or tribute, to the tsar, effectively legalizing their exploitation. Native resistance was sporadic and local at first, but it soon broadened into a large-scale revolt. The Aleuts had no military tradition, yet in 1762 natives from a number of villages

Russians trade with the Aleuts. From Greigorii Ivanovich Shelikhov, Puteshestvie G. Shelekhova . . . *(St. Petersburg, 1812). Beinecke Rare Book and Manuscript Library, Yale University.*

Колумбы Росскіе презрѣвъ угрюмый рокъ
Межъ льдами новый путь отворятъ на Востокъ.
И наша досягнетъ въ Америку Держава
И во всѣ концы досягнетъ Россово слава.

coordinated an uprising that destroyed a fleet of Russian ships. They prevented the Russians from returning for three years, but in 1766 a force crushed the rebel Aleuts, destroying dozens of native villages and carrying out deliberate "reductions" of the population. When word of the revolt reached Moscow, a shocked Tsarina Catherine ordered her subjects to treat the Aleuts more like Russians, if not human beings: "Impress upon the hunters the necessity of treating their new brethren and countrymen, the inhabitants of our newly acquired islands with the greatest kindness." But the promyshlenniki offered their own moral philosophy of the geographic margins: "God is in heaven, and the tsar is far away." Tsarina Catherine abolished the yasak, but otherwise little changed.[15]

The state-sponsored Russian-American Company, which took charge of operations in 1799, ameliorated the harshest practices, but by then the Aleuts' population had been reduced to six thousand, only a quarter of their previous size. The causes were familiar: disease, warfare, and alcoholism. With so many deaths, hopeful signs of rebirth were hard to find in Russian America. Life did go on, however, and sexual relations and intermarriage between traders and Aleut women created a substantial group of mixed-ancestry people the Russians called Creoles—comparable to the French métis and the Spanish mestizos—who assumed an increasingly prominent position in the northern Pacific fur trade as navigators, explorers, clerks, and traders.

—————

The Russian presence on the Pacific coast upped the anxiety of officials in New Spain. When they looked at their North American domain, they must have felt like a dog with a bone surrounded by a pack of hungry competitors. In the early eighteenth century, the Spanish countered French designs in the lower Mississippi River valley by constructing a string of Franciscan missions among the Indian peoples of Texas. By the time the French ceded their trans-Mississippi claims to the Spanish in 1763, the main Texas settlement at San Antonio de Bexar, including the mission that would later become known as the Alamo, had become the center of a beleaguered frontier province.

Once in Texas, fending off European rivals became a secondary concern to maintaining peaceful relations with the Comanches, who were extending their horse and bison empire into Mexico. They traded horses and mules with the French and English for guns and raided the provinces of Texas and New Mexico for food and captives. Some New Mexicans copied the Comanches and took to hunting bison on the southern plains. They were later joined by mixed-heritage traders known as comancheros, forming an intermediate group between colonials and Indians. Eventually the Spanish negotiated treaties with the Comanches. The peace held in New Mexico and the province thrived, but in Texas the violence continued. The different outcomes suggest the flexibility of the Comanches' empire, playing each province to their advantage.

The Spanish had more success in Alta California, where in 1769 they began planting missions along the coast. Gaspar de Portolá, governor of Baja California, established military headquarters at the fine bay of Monterey. From there he planned to defend the empire against Russian attack. The Russians had yet to establish a single permanent base on the American mainland, so Portolá's fears were overblown. But such emotions stretched the boundaries of empire.

As in Texas, the mission spearheaded colonization in California. Like backcountry log cabins, the old missions with their quaint adobe walls and cracked tiles, have become architectural attractions. But vacationers seldom perceive the flinty core of the mission institution: a tough, pioneering agency that served as church, home, fortress, town, farm, and imperial consulate. Through this corporate entity, two missionaries and three or four soldiers sought to create an orderly

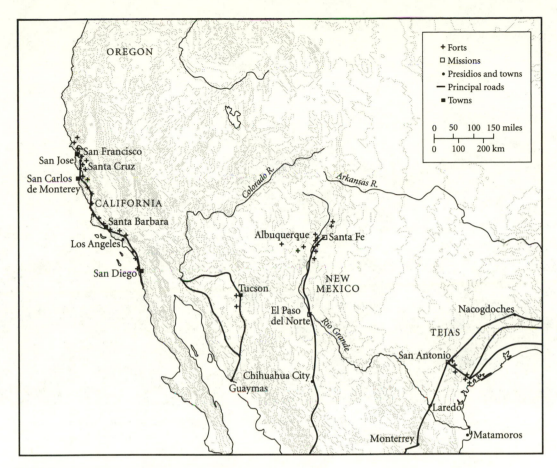

THE SPANISH NORTH IN THE EIGHTEENTH CENTURY

Spanish-style town out of a motley group of several thousand Indians, often from diverse and mutually hostile clans.

Missions were to Christianize nonbelievers. But they did much more. They blended prayer with labor. Friars expected Indians to stop wandering the countryside hunting deer and acorns and settle down at the mission to grow wheat, fruit, and cattle. Native labor supported the colony. In theory it was a winning strategy, advancing Spanish dominion, spreading the faith, and turning a profit. There was no large population in New Spain hankering to move north and populate the frontier. Instead, the Spanish would create new subjects through coercion and instruction. The padres wrote letters extolling not only the conversion of the pagans but their production of wheat, grapes, wine, and cattle. The glowing reports kept support from the royal treasuries coming, though in fulfilling their chief purpose, the conversion and reeducation of Indians, the missions never met expectations. In Alta California, the harvest of souls never matched the harvest of produce.

Spanish lancers bring captured California Indians to the San Francisco mission. From Louis Choris, Voyage pittoresque autour du monde . . . *(Paris, 1822). Beinecke Rare Book and Manuscript Library, Yale University.*

The Franciscans planted twenty missions from San Diego to Sonoma. Father Junípero Serra directed his brothers, while secular officials established a half-dozen garrisoned presidios and pueblos, including San Francisco, founded in 1776, and Los Angeles, started by a group of mestizo and mulatto settlers from Sinaloa in 1781. The colonial population of California never exceeded thirty-five hundred. Indians were the working class. They herded the cattle, sheep, and horses, and they irrigated the fields. The California economy flourished on their backs.

At the end of the eighteenth century, twenty thousand "neophytes" (as the padres called the converts) resided in Alta California's missions. Their rate of mortality was high. Their numbers had already fallen by about a third. They suffered from changes in diet and confinement in close quarters, and they died from dysentery, fever, and venereal disease. Father Felipe Arroyo de la Cuesta, of Mission San Juan Bautista, wrote that "the number of deaths here exceeds that of births," and the mission's funeral records during a terrible smallpox epidemic in 1838 noted that "the old graveyard close to the church is filled up with bodies to such an extent as to saturate the Mission with their smell." The fathers added to the misery

California mission Indians gambling. From Louis Choris, Voyage pittoresque autour du monde . . . *(Paris, 1822). Beinecke Rare Book and Manuscript Library, Yale University.*

by inflicting on their charges harsh discipline. They remedied misbehavior with shackles, solitary confinement, and the lash, always the lash. "The Indians at the mission were very severely treated by the padres," remembered Lorenzo Asisara, who was raised at Mission Santa Cruz. Disobedience brought "the lash without mercy, the women the same as the men."[16]

On occasion, the neophytes met violence with violence. A priest at Santa Cruz, for instance, lost his life when he thrashed his flock once too often. There was native rebellion from the beginning. In 1775 the villagers around San Diego rose up and killed several priests, and the history of many missions is punctuated by revolts, although the arms and organization of Spanish soldiers were enough to quell most uprisings. Flight became the dominant protest, and sometimes whole villages decamped for the mountains.

Observers noted the neophytes' despondence. "I have never seen any of them laugh," wrote one European. "I have never seen a single one look anyone in the face. They have the air of taking no interest in anything." Visiting Frenchman Jean-François de Galaup, Comte de Lapérouse, charged the Franciscans with enslaving rather than enlightening, and compared the missions to slave plantations in the Caribbean. The missionaries, he wrote, were convinced "either by prejudice or by their own experience that reason is almost never developed in these people, which to them is sufficient motive for treating them as children."[17]

For all their moral failings, including acts of spectacular brutality, the Spanish padres were able to imagine a universe where Indians and colonists lived together as Christians, albeit unequal ones. This meager concession to shared humanity was becoming a radical position in eighteenth-century North America. Across the continent, in a colony once considered cutting-edge for its dedication to amity and uplift, people were dividing themselves into races and slaughtering each other. The Pennsylvania frontier made the California missions, which some historians have compared to Nazi concentration camps, look like peaceable kingdoms.

───────

Far on the western fringes of Pennsylvania, in a cluster of log cabins along the Susquehanna River called Paxton, the frontier settlers viewed the government in Philadelphia as negligent if not downright hostile to their well-being. Largely Presbyterian, the Paxton community looked askance at the Quakers who controlled the government. How could those sons of William Penn, elite pacifists snug in their mansions, sympathize with farmers trying to wrest a living from the margins? Thirty miles from Paxton lay a village of Conestoga Indians—poor, peaceful descendants of a tribe that had long lived in submission. There were rumors, though, that the Conestogas were spies and abettors of hostile warriors who raided frontier homesteads. The whispers were enough to raise a lynch mob.

In December 1763, a small band of men calling themselves the Paxton Boys massacred twenty Conestoga men, women, and children. Frightened survivors fled to Philadelphia for protection. Incensed that the government would harbor the Indians, the Paxton Boys marched on the capital. Philadelphia officials sent out the militia, including a troop of artillerymen, and dispatched negotiators led by Benjamin Franklin. Franklin had already written an essay expressing his sympathy with the Indians and calling the Paxton Boys "Christian white savages." But he satisfied the mob that their cause would be heard by the colonial assembly and the governor. After composing a long protest letter, the farmers marched home to Paxton.[18]

The Paxton Boys admitted that their conduct bore "an appearance of flying in the face of Authority." But, they argued, the extremity of their peril demanded radical countermeasures, especially since their own government showed a "manifest Partiality for Indians." The Conestogas had been "cherished and caressed as dearest friends" by the politicians. The public had thereby been made "tributaries to savages," and the poor frontier farmers had been cut loose to fend for themselves. The westerners wanted more effective political representation and the abolition of property qualifications for voting. Underneath the complaints lurked the stark inequality of western farmers in the midst of their fellow white Pennsylvanians. Many owed money to eastern financiers. The Paxton Boys had butchered innocent

The Paxton Boys murder Conestoga Indians, 1764. From John Wilmer, Events of Indian History . . . *(Lancaster, Pa., 1841).*

human beings in the spirit of democratic reform. The inspiring frontier tableau of regular folks seeking social justice through agrarian protest was often marred by the nauseating tendency of these same folks to terrorize their weaker neighbors.[19]

In 1767 in the backwoods of South Carolina, murders, thefts, and anarchy reached a crescendo. Even members of a new religious sect, the Weberites, turned homicidal and murdered their "holy ghost" (a black man) and their "holy son" (a white man). Arrested backcountry criminals were often pardoned in Charleston. Justice seemed literally misplaced, and westerners complained about the failures of their eastern government. So they became law unto themselves. Neighbors profiled their neighbors, declared some outlaws, and drove them out through shows of mob force. The governor of South Carolina disapproved of the farmers' actions, which prompted the farmers to ramp up their extralegal policing. They labeled themselves Regulators, and one thousand signed an agreement to protect one another until the crime wave subsided. Occasionally designated Rangers, they roamed the countryside on horseback, pursuing suspected criminals as far as necessary, whipping some, hanging others, but bringing most in for proper trials. For the most part, the Regulators were law-and-order rebels.

Like the Paxton Boys, the backcountry Regulators dressed up their criminal activities in the cloak of political legitimacy. They wanted better representation in the colonial legislature, better courts in frontier areas, more schools and jails, increased regulation of taverns and public houses, more restrictions on hunters and law-yers (both offensive characters associated with carrion), and even the distribution of Bibles at public expense. A petition signed by four thousand men highlighted these demands. The popularity of populism, however, waxed and waned, and by March 1768 sentiment was rising against the Regulators' illegal actions. Sensing a backlash, the Regulators declared victory—crime had declined and they had made their protest—and went back to shooting deer and squirrels instead of scofflaws.

Paired in time and similarly spewing vitriol and inciting violence, the Carolina Regulators and the Paxton Boys often ride into history books together. They exem-plify frontier rebellion and agrarian protest. Yet in some ways they were radically different. The Pennsylvanians challenged the authority of government. The Regu-lators were more concerned with ridding local areas of crime, and although they acted unlawfully, like the Paxton Boys, they endeavored to reestablish authority, not buck it. Both groups were agrarian dissenters. The men from Paxton, however, functioned like a lynch mob, attacking a minority and then using the occasion to carry their grievances further. The Regulators were vigilantes, allegedly responsible members of society trying to clean up local corruption. Examples of do-it-yourself justice, lynch mobs and vigilantes would appear and reappear in only slightly var-ied guises on every American frontier. Backcountry South Carolina pioneered the terms *regulator* and *regulation,* but the words and ideas spread and became stan-dard until events in San Francisco in 1851 shifted popular usage to *vigilante* and *vigilance committee.*

Frontier mobs and posses have infiltrated American culture as relics of a by-gone era when good men had to take matters into their own hands to beat back chaos. The glow of these gatherings dims on closer inspection. A stew of racist bile and democratic outrage, the groups remind us that on the margins people some-times called for violence and fairness in the same breath. Barbarity and democracy clasped hands in colonial British America. Their grip would grow stronger as new republics took over older frontiers.

FURTHER READING

Richard Maxwell Brown, *The South Carolina Regulators* (1963)
Hector Chevigny, *Russian America: The Great Alaskan Venture, 1741–1867* (1965)
Gregory Dowd, *A Spirited Resistance: The North American Struggle for Unity, 1745–1815* (1992)
Kathleen Duval, *Independence Lost: Lives on the Edge of the American Revolution* (2016)
Steven W. Hackel, *Junípero Serra: California's Founding Father* (2014)
Pekka Hämäläinen, *The Comanche Empire* (2009)
Terry G. Jordan and Matti Kaups, *The American Backwoods Frontier: An Ethnic and Ecologi-cal Interpretation* (1989)

Ian K. Steele, *Warpaths: Invasions of North America* (1994)

Alan Taylor, *The Divided Ground: Indians, Settlers, and the Northern Borderland of the American Revolution* (2007)

Richard White, *The Middle Ground: Indians, Empires, and Republics in the Great Lakes Region, 1650–1815* (1991)

Michael Witgen, *An Infinity of Nations: How the Native New World Shaped Early America* (2013)

4

The Land and Its Markers

The American Revolution unleashed a terraforming spree that turned the maps of colonial North America into antiques. By the nation's centennial in 1876, the geographic footprint of the United States had stamped out empires built over many generations. The Spanish, French, British, and Russian, Haudenosaunee, Cherokee, and Comanche frontiers had given way to new territories and states. Many Americans of the late nineteenth century professed a belief that destiny had propelled them across the continent, that Providence had ordained the nation's birthright to continental dominance, that the new maps were inevitable. In fact, the process was far more contingent and gritty, far less destined or divine.

The United States acquired vast territories, but the incorporation of the West into the economy, the polity, and the culture of the nation took time. This chapter and those that follow tell the story of how the nation gathered, organized, and reimagined the land. It's a story of expedient real estate deals and negotiations conducted at the point of a gun, of democratic yearning and appalling greed, of seemingly boundless opportunity and the destruction of entire ways of life. It's an American story to the core. Several engines of change and development propelled the creation of the American empire, among them nationalism, familialism, capitalism, racism, and religion. Running the gamut from the admirable to the loathsome, they carved out the nation's future.

The American Revolution further fragmented the native and settler peoples of the backcountry. The Carolina Regulators, for instance, balked when coastal planters organized to take up arms against the crown. The politics of independence and loyalty mixed with fiercer animosities on the frontier. The farmers and hunters in the West—native Indian peoples, settlers born and raised in-country, as well as recent migrants from Germany, Ireland, and Scotland—ripped into one another from multiple angles. Relative to population, the backcountry suffered losses greater than any other region during the Revolution. There were some ten war-related deaths for every thousand persons in the thirteen coastal colonies, but more than seventy per thousand over the mountains in Kentucky. Moreover, the violence in the West continued long after the treaty of peace was signed in 1783. The fighting that began with the French and Indian War in 1754 did not cease until the Battle of Fallen Timbers forty years later in 1794. It was the bloodiest phase of the three-century campaign for the conquest of North America.

The British held an essential advantage in the West because they managed to keep their tribal allies from the long fight against the French. But in 1775, when British agents pressed their advantage, urging the Haudenosaunee to attack the Patriots, they received a tepid response. "We are unwilling to join on either side of such a contest, for we bear an equal affection to both Old and New England," declared one Oneida chief. "Let us Indians be all of one mind, and live with one another; and you white people settle your own disputes between yourselves." Disease, alcohol abuse, and economic dependency had weakened the once powerful Six Nations, and the French departure from North America made it difficult for them to play the traditional balancing game. Many Iroquois chiefs saw neutrality as their only course.[1]

Other war leaders, especially the Mohawk leader Thayendanega, known also by his English name, Joseph Brant, saw the situation differently. Descended from a prominent native family, Brant was the brother-in-law of British Indian agent Sir William Johnson, who sent him to Anglican mission school and then to an Indian academy (later known as Dartmouth College), where Brant developed into a brilliant scholar. When the fighting broke out in Massachusetts at Lexington and Concord, Brant went to London at the request of British authorities to negotiate an anti-Patriot alliance between the Six Nations and the British. He toured the capital, dined with luminaries, and sat for a portrait by a fashionable artist. The questions of land and sovereignty, Brant told the British, would determine Mohawk support. The Iroquois would fight for their own independence. Receiving British assurances that the Six Nations would be able to write their own terms at the end of the conflict, Brant returned home to lobby for the British among the leaders of the Six Nations.

Dominated by chiefs seeking neutrality, the Haudenosaunee council refused to let Brant speak, so he called his own meeting of sympathetic chiefs at the British trading town of Oswego. Representatives of the Mohawks, Cayugas, Onondagas, and Senecas agreed to fight for the English king with Brant in command, but chiefs of the Oneidas and Tuscaroras sided with the Patriots. Fratricidal civil war would tear at the bonds of peace and power that had held the Iroquois together since

Mohawk leader Joseph Brant. Painting by Gilbert Stuart, 1786. Wikimedia Commons.

the fifteenth century. For many Iroquois patriots, Joseph Brant was a hero of the resistance against the Americans. But others condemned him for destroying their unity.

Brant's army trounced the Patriots at Oriskany in 1777 and Cherry Valley in 1778, and his name summoned more fear in the hearts of settlers than any Indian leader since Pontiac. The Iroquois absorbed devastating Patriot invasions, then pushed back, ejecting the Americans from their territory and pushing the out-

George Rogers Clark. Engraving by T. B. Welch, c. 1865. Author's collection.

skirts of Albany. "We are now deprived of a great portion of our most valuable and well inhabited territory," announced Governor George Clinton of New York. Meanwhile the Shawnee, Delaware, Miami, and Mingo peoples of the Ohio valley formed their own pro-British military confederacy centered at Detroit, a fur-trade hotspot and supply depot at the strategic junction of Lakes Erie and Huron. In 1777 and 1778, the Ohio confederacy sent warriors south against American communities planted in defiance of the Royal Proclamation in Kentucky and western Virginia. The Americans barely held on.[2]

The only American military leader in the West who could match Brant's leadership was George Rogers Clark. A Virginian and a gentleman planter, warrior, and speculator, Clark had taken part in several western land surveying expeditions. He had a stake in lands along the Ohio and refused to allow them to be abandoned to the British or their Indian allies. His western army conquered the former French settlements in the Illinois Country and captured the British commander. The Spanish, though careful to distance themselves formally from the Patriot cause, supplemented Clark's gains by retaking Florida and the Gulf coast and tossing the British out of the Mississippi River towns of Natchez and Baton Rouge. While the Spanish hoisted their flags over key transportation and trade junctions, the Americans' advance stalled at Detroit. Clark lacked the manpower to attack the garrison. The Americans raided Indian towns across the Ohio River, but they could do little more than defend their forts in Kentucky and hang on to Illinois.

As the British had learned after their victory over the French, starting fights in the West proved easier than ending them. When General Charles Cornwallis surrendered the British army at Yorktown in 1781, concluding the war in the East, the battle in the West intensified. Brant launched new offensives, casting a shadow over Clark's successes. American militiamen from western Pennsylvania marched into the Ohio valley to put a stop to Indian raiding. Finding no enemies, in early 1782 they attacked peaceful Christian Delawares at the mission village of Gnadenhutten. The mutilated bodies of 96 peaceful men, women, and children testified to the levels of violence in the West after the Revolution. The Pennsylvanians nailed Indian scalps over the doors of their log cabins to advertise their victory. Outraged, Ohio Indian warriors invaded Kentucky, and in August, at the Battle of the Blue Licks, they ambushed an army of militiamen, leaving the mutilated bodies of 147 Kentuckians on the battleground.

By 1783 the confederated army of Indian fighters was winning the war for the West. It came as a shock, therefore, when they received news of the British surrender. The Americans had acquired the imperial *right of conquest* to the entire trans-Appalachian country, from the Great Lakes to the Mississippi River to the boundary of Spanish Florida, the region the British had defined as Indian Country in the Royal Proclamation of twenty years before. Given the advantage they held through their Indian allies, why did the British cede the West? Strategists in London believed that they still held an advantage. They understood that gaining the right to the West was not the same as controlling it. By returning Florida to the Spanish and strengthening their fortifications in Canada, the British succeeded in surrounding the infant republic with jealous European powers. The treaty stipulated that the British would evacuate their forts in the ceded territory "with convenient speed," but London issued instructions to "allow the posts in the upper country to remain as they had for some time." These forts supplied guns and ammunition to Indian insurgents. The Americans could have the West—and slowly bleed to death there. At a date in the near future, the British could sweep in and reclaim their empire.[3]

———

The American Revolution was fought over the question, who will rule? In the West, the fighting continued over another, who will own? The answer to both questions seemed the same. The people ruled and the people would own the nearly 230 million acres beyond the accepted boundaries of the Atlantic states. The answer was elegant in simplicity and noble in spirit. But who were "the people"?

Indians at Independence Hall, Philadelphia. From William Birch, The City of Philadelphia . . . *(Philadelphia, 1800). The Winterthur Library: Printed Book and Periodical Collection.*

The Indian residents of the West assumed that they held the equivalent of title to their traditional lands. They had not been defeated, yet the United States assumed that the victory over Great Britain also included victory over their Indian allies. The national government claimed the right to seize the lands and property of all who had opposed the Revolution. When the Indians were informed that they would suffer the same fate as the Tories, they were thunderstruck. "When you Americans and the King made peace," declared the Seneca leader Red Jacket, "he did not mention us, and showed us no compassion, notwithstanding all he said to us, and all we had suffered." The Americans paid no attention to such complaints. Seizing hostages, commissioners of the Confederation Congress forced the Six Nations to sign a treaty in 1784 ceding a large portion of their homeland. Joseph Brant and his followers fled north to British territory, creating a second Iroquois confederacy on the other side of the new international boundary. The next year the commissioners bullied the tribes of the Ohio confederacy into ceding the southeastern portion of what would became the state of Ohio. Even Indian nations that had fought with the Patriots—the Oneidas and Tuscaroras of the Six Nations and the Penobscots and Passamaquoddys of northern New England—were compelled to make large cessions. The Americans translated victory into

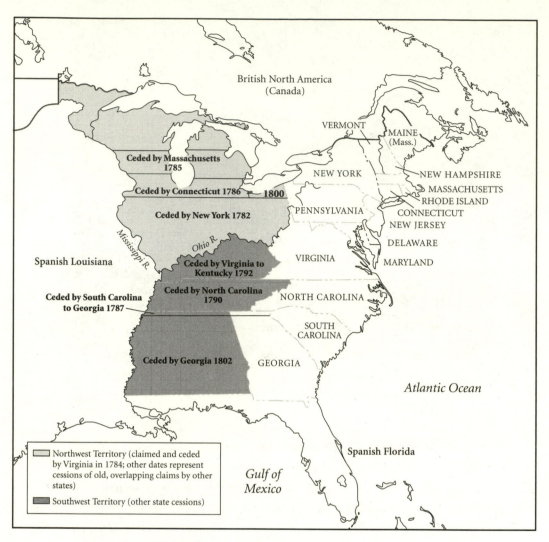

British North America
(Canada)

Ceded by Massachusetts
1785

Ceded by Connecticut 1786 ── 1800

Ceded by New York 1782

Mississippi R.

Ohio R.

Spanish Louisiana

Ceded by Virginia to
Kentucky 1792

Ceded by North Carolina
1790

Ceded by South Carolina
to Georgia 1787 ──

Ceded by Georgia 1802

VERMONT

MAINE
(Mass.)

NEW YORK

NEW HAMPSHIRE

MASSACHUSETTS
RHODE ISLAND
CONNECTICUT
NEW JERSEY

PENNSYLVANIA

DELAWARE

VIRGINIA

MARYLAND

NORTH CAROLINA

SOUTH
CAROLINA

GEORGIA

Atlantic Ocean

Northwest Territory (claimed and ceded
by Virginia in 1784; other dates represent
cessions of old, overlapping claims by other
states)

Southwest Territory (other state cessions)

Spanish Florida

*Gulf of
Mexico*

WESTERN LAND CLAIMS OF THE STATES

arrogance, guaranteeing a bloody aftermath following the Revolution, especially in the West.[4]

There was also a dispute over whether the West fell under the jurisdiction of the states or the national government. The English king had granted several of his American colonies charters that extended westward, in some cases stretching all the way across the continent to the "South Sea." When these colonies became states, they were reluctant to surrender their claims. But the six states without claims demanded that Congress assume authority over the western lands "for the good of the whole." The dispute delayed the ratification of the Articles of Confederation until 1780, when Congress resolved that all ceded western land would "be disposed of for the common benefit of the United States, and be settled and formed into distinct republican States, which shall become members of the Federal Union."

New York immediately agreed to give up its western claims, followed by Virginia in 1781 and soon thereafter most of the others, with the exception of Georgia, which held out for years.[5]

The Congress looked to colonial traditions of land dispersal to guide their decisions about what to do with this vast public domain in the West. The colonies employed systems of land distribution that blended social aims with geographic realities. In New England, a communal ethos prevailed. Colonial governments granted lands not to individuals but to congregations and community groups, and they discouraged migrants from moving too far from existing towns. Before relocating, an advance party surveyed their grant, designating the appropriate place for the town center, with its church, roads, pasturage, and most promising farming fields. Each family in the group received a lot in the center, as well as farm, pasture, and timber lots on the fringes. The enthusiasm for this pattern of settlement outlasted the enthusiasm for the Puritan church's cultural dominance, and Yankees continued to practice prior survey and compact settlement. In the South, where land and climate encouraged staple agriculture (tobacco, rice, and later cotton), a different system, featuring large tracts relatively far apart, took root. Individual

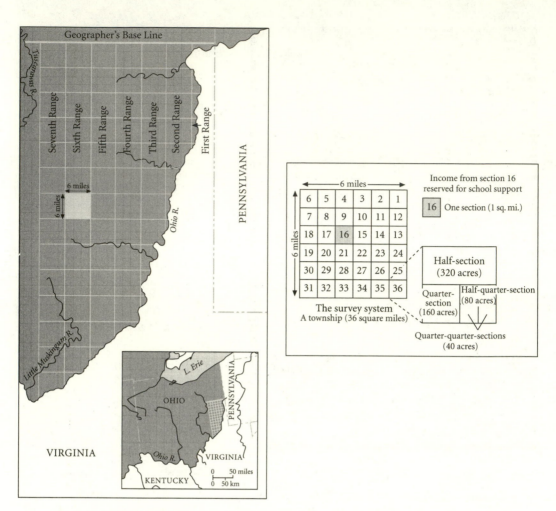

THE SURVEY SYSTEM

planters spread out across the countryside looking for appealing chunks of property, then requested a grant from the colonial government. Unlike New England, southern farmers bore the cost and assumed the obligation of independent development. The law Congress wrote, the Land Ordinance of 1785, drew from both traditions, borrowing from New England the idea of prior survey and orderly contiguous development and from the South the practice of allocating land directly to individuals.

The land law, however, also broke with tradition. The authors tossed out the "metes and bounds" system of surveying, in which each parcel was described by the distinctive lay of the land and the property lines of adjacent plots, and replaced it with an elegant grid mechanism that screamed eighteenth-century enlightened planning. All the western territory would be divided "into townships of six miles square, by lines running due north and south, and others crossing these at right angles." A great grid of "Principal Meridians" and "Base Lines" would divide the whole of the West into numbered ranges of townships, with each township divided into thirty-six square-mile sections, each section further divisible into half-sections, quarter-sections, and quarter-quarters of forty acres. Coordinates framed every farmer's field; you could locate each patch of the public domain by range, township, and section numbers. This system, a product of the Age of Enlightenment, worked well in some landscapes, weirdly in others. The national survey would assure clear boundaries and firm titles, but it would press on the land a uniformity that took no account of the landscape, the climate, or previous human occupation.[6]

The Land Ordinance set the table, but Congress still had to decide who would have access to the public domain as well as who would foot the bill. Thomas Jefferson argued for giving western land away "in small quantities" to settlers. "I am against selling the lands at all," he declared. The people on the margins were poor, and "by selling the lands to them, you will disgust them, and cause an avulsion of them from the common union." Jefferson understood that expansion was the operational dynamic of a settler society. His ideas anticipated the 1862 Homestead Act, but in 1785 his views were out of step with most American leaders. Instead of giving the land away, Congress decided to auction it off in chunks no smaller than 640 acres, at prices no less than one dollar per acre, well beyond the means of most settlers. Revenue concerned Congress more than plowboys. The national government had borrowed heavily to finance its independence, and the nation needed to sell its western lands to people with cash.[7]

But the dream of personal, communal, and national improvement in the West continued. J. Hector St. John de Crèvecoeur echoed the hope in his 1782 book, *Letters from an American Farmer:* "Scattered over an immense territory" and "animated with the spirit of an industry which is unfettered and unrestrained," Americans were building "the most perfect society now existing in the world." A boundless—yet rationally parceled—West would guarantee that the American people would maintain their economic independence, the foundation of republican government. Jefferson seconded these sentiments, writing in 1787 that Americans would remain virtuous as long as they kept their roots in the agrarian soil.[8]

———

The ink was barely dry on the Iroquois and Ohio Indian land cessions when the surveyors headed west in late 1785. Here right angles and Euclidian grids ran headlong into bogs, thickets, and hummocks. Actual terrain slowed the running of lines and the marking of township boundaries. Impatient for the anticipated western payoff, Congress ordered a public auction of the first surveyed ranges. The results disappointed. Land speculators stayed away, no bidding war erupted, and Congress failed to get its windfall. While eastern capitalists waited, western

Daniel Shays (left) and his fellow insurgent Job Shattuck. From Bickerstaff's Boston Almanack *for 1787 (Boston, 1786). Author's collection.*

settlers moved. They sauntered north of the Ohio, picked good-looking spots, and squatted, claiming ownership by right of occupancy. Congress called out the army to evict them. "There is scarcely one bottom on the river but has one or more families living thereon," Ensign John Armstrong reported to his superiors. If Congress did not "fall on some speedy method to prevent people from settling," the West would soon be populated by "a banditti whose actions are a disgrace to human nature." Class resentments flared as land controversies grew. The eastern upper crust feared a settlers' rebellion. Fresh in their memories was the protest of Daniel Shays, a poor farmer and Revolutionary War hero in western Massachusetts, who in the tradition of the Regulators led a protest against monetary policies and farm foreclosures in 1786. Shays and hundreds of his neighbors prevented the local county courts from sitting, and state authorities called out troops to quell the uprising.[9]

Farmers were not the only ones in debt. The federal government also had obligations to pay. In 1787 Congress modified its plans. A Massachusetts lobbyist named Manasseh Cutler approached a number of congressmen with a proposal for a huge western land grant to a group of wealthy New England capitalists known as the Ohio Company of Associates (not to be confused with the earlier Ohio Company of the 1750s). The Ohio Associates wanted one and a half million acres of lush green Ohio hills and valleys but balked at paying the one-dollar-an-acre price mandated by the Land Ordinance. Cutler, a Yale divine and a free-range amateur scientist, was also a dealmaker, and he suggested a scheme: let his associates purchase the block in depreciated revolutionary currency. Desperate for revenue, Congress agreed, and the Ohio Associates bought a principality for a pittance.

If Cutler and his congressional enablers massaged the Land Ordinance, state officials and land speculators in Georgia beat the law to a pulp. The only state that continued to claim trans-Appalachian lands, Georgia in 1795 granted an enormous tract in what would later be the states of Alabama and Mississippi to a group of shady investors ("bribes," as they say, "were paid"). Georgia's ownership of this territory was dubious at best. In fact, the Spanish still claimed most of it. The lack of secure title, however, did not deter the speculators, who sold their "rights" to land jobbers, who resold them to thousands of gullible investors. After President Washington declared the sales a fraud, the Georgia legislature repealed the Yazoo Act, so named for a meandering river in the region. The repeal caused even more controversy, as droves of speculators across the country faced the loss of their investments. A congressional committee investigated complaints and claims for years, and in 1802 Georgia finally coughed up its western lands to the federal government in an attempt to limit its liability in the wake of the scandal. The Supreme Court waded into the Yazoo affair in 1810, ruling in the case of *Fletcher v. Peck* that the constitutional guarantee of the sanctity of contracts prevented Georgia from revoking its actions, however corrupt. Congress voted to award the speculators more than four million dollars. The Ohio Associates and the Yazoo affair tarnished the reasoned planning and democratic impulse behind the Land Ordinance. Debt, speculation, and fraud often drove land policy in the early Republic. The interests of actual settlers trailed in the line of considerations.

―――――

Many politicians, Thomas Jefferson foremost among them, assumed that western lands would move quickly toward full, independent statehood within the Union. After fighting a war to end colonialism, the revolutionaries were hesitant about creating a colonial system of their own. But continuing Indian resistance, squatter infestation, and general western unruliness convinced Congress to reject Jefferson's plan to grant territories immediate self-rule. The "uniformed and perhaps licentious people" of the West, argued the influential Virginia planter Richard Henry Lee, required "a strong toned government."[10]

With the Northwest Ordinance of 1787, Congress provided a structure of government for the territory "northwest of the river Ohio." They devised a regime more strict and authoritarian than the colonial governments overthrown by the

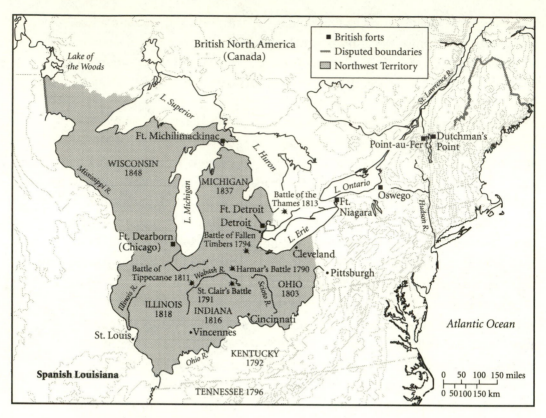

THE NORTHWEST TERRITORY

Revolution. An appointed governor, a secretary, and three judges would rule until the male population reached five thousand, at which time the voters (male property owners) would be allowed to elect representatives to an assembly. But the governor enjoyed absolute veto power. Once the population reached sixty thousand, the territory (or a portion of it) might be admitted into the Union on equal terms with the existing states—the most praiseworthy feature of the ordinance. In the meantime, Congress appointed Arthur St. Clair, a prominent leader of the Ohio Associates, as governor of the Northwest Territory, an early instance of government in the hands of capitalists and developers. With the installation of major players, eastern power brokers announced their intention of keeping violent mobs and frontier roughnecks under supervision. A strong hand, it was hoped, would keep the rubes from reverting to Regulators, Paxton Boys, and Shaysites.

The Northwest Ordinance also outlawed involuntary servitude—slavery—north of the Ohio River. Jefferson's first territorial plan had called for keeping slavery out of the entire West, but Congress rejected that radical idea. Many northern states had already moved to abolish slavery, and the ban north of the Ohio reflected that trend. But southern politicians envisioned an expanding system of slavery. They acquiesced in the antislavery provision for the Northwest, but insisted that the nation do nothing to impede the spread of slavery elsewhere. In 1790, when Congress created the Southwest Territory from the western claims ceded by the Carolinas, southern representatives beat back an attempt by northerners to include the same antislavery clause. "The result, pregnant with meaning for the future" writes historian Don Fehrenbacher, "was a national policy of having two policies." The Ohio River became the dividing line between the slave and the free West.[11]

Americans' unease with the West and westerners colored their legends as well as their laws. To some, the West offered up homegrown American icons, burly nature-men who epitomized self-reliance and wilderness savvy. Others saw these backwoodsmen as lowdown, shiftless, lazy riffraff. The life and legend of Daniel Boone harnessed these ambiguities.

Born on the Pennsylvania frontier in 1734, Boone migrated with his parents to the North Carolina backcountry when he was fifteen. There he married the impressive Rebecca Bryan, a strong and commanding woman who rivaled her husband in height, weight, and household authority. In the typical division of frontier labor, she ran the farm and raised their ten children while Boone hunted professionally and worked as a guide. As a teamster with General Braddock's army during the French and Indian War, Boone heard tales of animal-rich Kentucky, and afterward he found his way there. In 1773 he tried to move his family across the mountains, but Indians perturbed by the flood of Americans into the West attacked the caravan at Cumberland Gap, killing Boone's eldest son and turning the party back. Two years later Boone led another attempt, this one part of a grand colonization scheme organized by North Carolina speculator Richard Henderson. Boone helped found the settlement of Boonesborough and settled the bluegrass with his family and others. But Henderson's company failed and Boone lost the lands promised him. During the Revolution, the Shawnees, allied with the British, captured him. He escaped and led the defense of besieged Boonesborough, an episode that cemented Boone's national reputation.

His stardom would reach international proportions soon after. Following the war Kentucky became the new "land of promise, flowing with milk and honey," where "you shall eat bread without scarceness and not lack any thing," in the words of John Filson, a schoolmaster turned promotional-tract author who in 1784 convinced thousands of settlers to head west through the Cumberland Gap. "What a Buzzel is amongst People about Kentuck," wrote a Virginia minister. "To hear people speak of it one Would think it was a new found Paradise." Like hundreds of others, Daniel Boone staked claims to thousands of acres. But most of his claims

Daniel Boone kills a bear and escapes from the Indians. From Timothy Flint, The First White Man of the West; or, The Life and Exploits of Col. Dan'l Boone . . . *(Cincinnati, 1854).* Author's collection.

proved defective. No single authority directed or sanctioned land titles. Kentucky's true bounty after the war was lawsuits. Boone grew disenchanted with the American West, and in 1799 he and his large extended family crossed the Mississippi and settled in Spanish Missouri. He lived near Saint Charles on the Missouri River for the rest of his life, working as a hunter until his death in 1820.[12]

The world would have remembered none of this had John Filson not included a stirring account of Boone's adventures in his book on Kentucky, presenting him as a pathfinder, a child of nature, and a consummate American. Boone's legend reached astonishingly far. French intellectuals grabbed onto his wilderness image to discuss "natural man" in their toney salons. Closer to home, others saw Boone in the same romantic light. Henry Marie Brackenridge cast Boone and his fellow backwoodsmen as refugees, "placing themselves at a distance from the deceit and turbulence of the world." Yet Boone's woodsy panache was not admired by all. A missionary in North Carolina complained that Boone did "little of the work" around his farm, leaving the drudge agricultural labor to his wife and children. "There are many hunters here who work little," he wrote, and "live like the Indians." Others argued that Boone was a misanthrope, a man who, as one critic put it, wanted "to live as remote as possible from every white inhabitant." Was Boone a lazy, free, white American? Was he a hero or a heel? Depending on who you asked, he was all these things, and this haziness made him the ideal pioneer for an equally unsettled American West.[13]

―――――

From just a few hundred American settlers at the beginning of the Revolution, by 1785 the population of Kentucky stood at thirty thousand; it had grown to nearly ninety thousand by the time Congress made the territory a state. Without waiting for the official opening of the Northwest Territory lands, overrunning the public domain and Indian homelands, American farmers pressed north of the Ohio, squatting illegally. This incursion, combined with the arrogance of the new nation's "conquest" theory—that the Republic's military victory against Great Britain negated the native rights to land—delivered a clear message to the Indians of the Ohio valley: the Americans were about to dispossess them of their lands.

Neither a tribe nor a nation, the Ohio Indians were a patchwork confederacy, as much of a product of the frontier as their white opponents. The confederacy included peoples like the Miamis and Potawatomies, who had lived in the valley for centuries, as well as Delawares, Shawnees, and Mingos, newcomers from Pennsylvania and New York who moved west to escape violent conflicts with Americans. They built communities of log cabins, cleared forests for their fields of corn and beans, grazed their herds of horses and cattle in meadows, and hunted in the woods, very much like the American settlers in Kentucky. In the late 1780s, native and newcomer Indians formed a defensive confederacy with a council fire at Detroit, a choice of headquarters encouraged by the British, who offered supplies. Joseph Brant and the Canadian Iroquois, embittered by the Revolution, preached pan-Indian resistance at Detroit. The Indians east of the Appalachians had lost their lands, one Iroquois chief declared, because they fought one another instead of uniting against the Europeans. The Americans, by contrast, had succeeded because of "the unanimity they were prudent enough to preserve, and consequently none of the divided efforts of our ancestors to oppose them had an effect."[14]

Pan-Indian movements existed before Brant's call, even before the arrival of Europeans. The Iroquois Confederacy proved this. The league strengthened its members by ending internal strife in the name of defeating external foes. In the eighteenth century, both Indians and Euro-Americans developed a new bonding agent that helped unite their diverse peoples. They began to see politics in color. They racialized themselves and their opponents. In Pennsylvania, for example, colonists from Scotland, Ireland, Germany, and England, often at odds with one another, latched onto their "whiteness" to express their common opposition to "dark" savages. Native Americans experimented with the term *red* to declare their difference from Europeans in the seventeenth century. The brutality of the eighteenth-century frontier solidified these racial concepts. By the time Brant rallied the Ohio Confederacy, the notions of "red" and "white" moved large groups of frontier dwellers across cultures to cast their lots together and aim their muskets at a common enemy from another race. Prejudice tricked both sides into seeing the other as fundamentally different. Objectively, whites and reds on the frontier looked remarkably similar. Warriors wore hunting shirts and leggings. Their female partners grew corn and beans. Everybody drank too much whiskey. Hatred masked all that they shared.

When George Washington assumed office as the first president of the new federal government, the problems of the West troubled him most. The western Indian confederacy seemed unified and determined to stop the United States at the Ohio River. Great Britain continued to maintain a force of at least a thousand troops at northwestern posts like Detroit. They traded furs and supplied the Indians with guns and ammunition. Spain also encouraged and supplied native resistance to the expansion of American settlement in the South, refusing to accept the territorial settlement of the Treaty of Paris and claiming that the northern boundary of Florida extended to the Ohio River. The Spanish secretly employed a number of prominent westerners, including George Rogers Clark, as informants and spies.

The West threatened to slip from the Americans. Washington and his secretary of war Henry Knox shifted tactics and reformed the nation's Indian policy. Instead of using the "right of conquest" to squeeze land from the Indians, they suggested a more even hand. Knox had been active in crafting the language of the Northwest Ordinance of 1787, which promised that "the utmost good faith shall always be observed towards the Indians," that "their lands and property shall never be taken from them without their consent," and that "they shall never be invaded or disturbed unless in just and lawful wars authorized by Congress. This amounted to a rejection of conquest theory and a recognition of the independent character of Indian nations.[15]

In 1790, following Knox's lead, Congress passed the Indian Intercourse Act, the basic law regulating "trade and intercourse with the Indian tribes." The act created a legal distinction between the territorial jurisdiction of the states and that region known as Indian Country, a concept taken directly from the Royal Proclamation of 1763. Indians residing within the territory of the United States were not American citizens but rather subjects of their own nations, enjoying jurisdiction over their own homelands, with their own governments and laws. Indian nations retained a form of limited sovereignty. They ruled within their territory, but the United States forbid them from engaging in state-to-state relations, neither with individual states nor with foreign governments—the British in Canada or the Spanish in

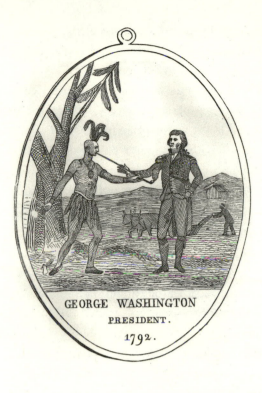

Facsimile of federal peace medallion presented to Seneca chief Red Jacket in 1792. From Red Jacket *(Buffalo, 1885). Beinecke Rare Book and Manuscript Library, Yale University.*

GEORGE WASHINGTON
PRESIDENT.
1792.

Florida and Louisiana. The federal government assumed the sole right to negotiate treaties with Indian groups. Treaty-making became one of the nation's principal tools of conquest, and the desire for legal, peaceful, and clear treaties explains why Washington and Knox wanted Indian sovereignty included in the 1790 act. The United States needed legitimate partners with whom to negotiate. The Constitution, drafted in 1787 and ratified the following year, detailed the government's treaty-making powers—the president negotiated them, while the Senate retained the power to approve or reject them.[16]

Typical was the first Indian treaty negotiated by the Washington administration, with the "Creek Nation of Indians" in 1790. In exchange for Creek cessions of land and an acknowledgment that they were "to be under the protection of the United States of America, and no other sovereign whosoever," the government pledged to protect the boundaries of their nation and acknowledged their right to punish "as they please" Americans who invaded their boundaries or violated their laws.[17]

The 1790 act declared that it was official federal policy "to promote civilization among the friendly Indian tribes." The president was authorized to furnish them "with useful domestic animals, and implements of husbandry." Indians might become eligible for citizenship in the Republic, wrote Knox, once they acquired "love for exclusive property." Moreover, to eliminate unscrupulous abuses, the government created a licensing system for traders and authorized the creation of subsidized federal trading posts (called "factories") in Indian Country, where native traders could obtain goods at fair and reasonable prices. Congress pledged to curtail the destructive flow of alcohol to the Indians. These programs, however, were never adequately funded, and the "civilization program" languished.[18]

Loose ends infested American Indian policy. On the one hand was the pledge to protect native homelands. On the other was the program to survey, sell, and create new political institutions in those very same lands. As historian Elliott West writes, "A policy that could make such promises, all within the same pair of documents, had moved beyond contradiction to schizophrenia." Yet, once established, the legal principles endured. In the twentieth century, many Indian tribes successfully appealed for the return of lands taken by the states or private individuals in violation of the provisions of the Indian Intercourse Act.[19]

———

Legal niceties and good intentions wrecked against the ruthless pressure of settlers seeking rich farm lands in the Ohio country. Squatters ignored the government's ordinances and acts along with Indians' rights. "Though we hear much of the Injuries and depredations that are committed by the Indians upon the Whites," wrote Governor St. Clair of the Northwest Territory, "there is too much reason to believe that at least equal if not greater Injuries are done to the Indians by the frontier settlers of which we hear very little." Juries refused to convict whites for crimes against Indians. Injured parties sought their own justice. The leaders of the Ohio confederacy proved unable to restrain and coordinate the passions of its many members. Chiefs could not control their warriors. Indians struck back at Americans with equally indiscriminate violence.[20]

In the fall of 1790, General Josiah Harmar of the regular army led an expeditionary force made up largely of militia in an invasion of the Ohio country with the mission of pacifying the Indians and establishing order among the Americans. He met a formidable Indian force under the leadership of Little Turtle, a brilliant war chief of the Miamis. Little Turtle trapped Harmar's army and badly defeated them. Encouraged by this victory, the British began the construction of Fort Miami in the Maumee valley west of Lake Erie, well within the region ceded to the United States at the end of the Revolution. To make matters worse, the Spanish had closed the port of New Orleans at the mouth of the Mississippi River to American commerce, threatening to choke off economic development. The West rattled the young nation. Rivals tested the Americans' grip on the territories that symbolized their country's future.

In November 1791, the Americans once again invaded the Ohio country, this time with a large but poorly trained army under the command of Governor St. Clair himself. Little Turtle's army demolished them. With a loss of more than

Little Turtle, Miami chief and war leader of the Ohio Confederacy. Copy of a lost painting by Gilbert Stuart, c. 1796. Author's collection.

nine hundred American dead and wounded, St. Clair's misadventure would go down as the single worst defeat of an American army by Indian warriors, a far more serious loss than the famous toppling of General George Armstrong Custer at the Little Bighorn in 1876. Seen from a native perspective, it was the most breathtaking victory of Indian arms in the annals of American history.

Bloodied and vulnerable, the United States wobbled in the West. President Washington gambled 80 percent of the federal government's operating budget on a massive campaign against the Ohio confederacy that would show not only the Indians but the British and Spanish as well that his nation was in control of its western territory. He picked General Anthony Wayne to lead the surge. On August 20, 1794, at the Maumee villages, three thousand troops under Mad Anthony (a nickname Wayne earned from his own men, who suffered under his fierce discipline) engaged Little Turtle's confederated warriors. The Indians drove back the first wave of Americans, inflicting heavy casualties. Wayne brought up his reserves and overwhelmed the warriors as they tried to press their advantage. The Americans outflanked the warriors, and they broke for the safety of Fort Miami. The British officers at the fort watched the retreat and decided to forgo an international incident. They barred the gates, and Wayne's troops picked off the fleeing fighters. The Battle of Fallen Timbers badly damaged the Ohio confederacy and displayed the determination of the United States to protect its West. The British flinched, demonstrating the emptiness of the promises to their

Indian allies. Their supplies dwindled with their bravado, and they abandoned Fort Miami.

In the negotiations that followed, the representatives of twelve Indian nations, led by Little Turtle, ceded a huge territory encompassing most of present-day Ohio, much of Indiana, and other enclaves in the Northwest, including the town of Detroit and the tiny village of Chicago. The rising threat of the French Revolution further dissuaded the British from investing funds and soldiers to influence the West. They withdrew from American soil. The next year the United States settled its boundary dispute with Spain, which agreed to grant Americans free navigation of the Mississippi River with the right to deposit goods at the port of New Orleans.

Many Indian groups suffered under American rule. Military defeats, lost land and sovereignty, poor hunting and weak trade, alcoholism, and disease pushed societies into desperate corners. At rock bottom, some found salvation in spiritual revitalization. It happened first among the Iroquois. Before the Revolution, the British had estimated Iroquois strength at about ten thousand, but by 1800, as a result of the bloody warfare of the intervening years, their numbers had fallen to four thousand. Their homeland invaded, their hunting territories gone, and their economy in shambles, many Iroquois numbed themselves with rum and brandy. "It appears to me," one Iroquois testified, "that the great Spirit is determined on our destruction."[21]

The Iroquois predicament earned them a plague of enthusiastic Quakers. Preaching a message of Christian love, the Society of Friends set up schools and offered employment, and many Indians came under their influence. Opinions differed about the Friends. The Seneca chief Cornplanter came to appreciate their compassion and their message. "We are determined to try to learn your ways," he declared to one Quaker missionary. But Red Jacket, leader of the traditionalists among the Seneca, opposed them. "You say that you are sent to instruct us how to worship the Great Spirit," he told a missionary, but "we also have a religion, which was given to our forefathers, and has been handed to us, their children. We worship in that way." The Iroquois did not need the Quakers to tell them to love a higher power and one another.[22]

The split connoted by Red Jacket's traditionalism and Cornplanter's progressivism reverberates in many Indian communities to this day. But human beings, historic or otherwise, rarely fit neatly into philosophical camps. Take Handsome Lake, a distinguished war leader of the Six Nations during the Revolution. Postrevolutionary America dealt harshly with Handsome Lake. In defeat, he despaired and he drank. During an epic binge in 1799, he fell into a coma. His family thought

Seneca chief Red Jacket, wearing the peace medallion presented by President George Washington. From Thomas L. McKenney and James Hall, History of the Indian Tribes of North America . . . , *3 vols. (Philadelphia, 1836–44).*

that he would die for sure, but he recovered and began preaching a glorious message of renewal. He inspired hundreds of followers, and within a generation the teachings of Handsome Lake became a rallying point for people throughout the Six Nations. Urging a return to the ancient rites and rituals, Handsome Lake preached traditionalism. But he also advocated progressive reforms like asking men to forsake hunting for farming.

Handsome Lake's followers emulated their American neighbors in many things, but they gathered in traditional longhouses for their services. The Longhouse Religion, as it came to be called, combined Iroquois spirituality with the values of Quaker Christianity: temperance, nonviolence, frugality, and an emphasis on personal good and evil. The Bible resided alongside traditional Iroquois oral stories and teachings within the longhouses. The Longhouse Religion did not lessen the material and political poverty of living as a colonized people in the United States of America, but it did give some Iroquois a sense of cultural self-determination and respect.

—————

Following the Battle of Fallen Timbers, many Ohio Indians exercised their self-determination by leaving for American-free spaces across the Mississippi River. Those who remained accommodated themselves to the onslaught of land-grabbers as best they could. Still, they found living with the Americans difficult. Like the Iroquois, they confronted poverty and alcoholism. Here, too, an Indian prophet arose to point the way to a revitalized future. He was a Shawnee and, like Handsome Lake, a drunk. In 1805 he collapsed and fell into a trance his family mistook for death. But he awoke and told them that the Master of Life had sent him back from the dead to lead the Indians to redemption. He took the name Tenskwatawa, meaning "the Open Door." The Americans called him the Shawnee Prophet.

Tenskwatawa reproached Indians for abandoning traditional values and mores. He condemned alcohol—"the white man's poison." He told his followers, in stark, racialized language, to reject "white" clothing, tools, and weapons and return to old-school styles and technologies. He demonstrated a keen understanding of the dangers of economic dependency. The emphasis on the rejection of colonial ways marked the divergence between Tenskwatawa's teachings and the Longhouse Religion, yet even the Shawnee Prophet's traditionalist message contained Christian flourishes. Sounding very much like a frontier preacher, he promised a glorious afterlife to all his loyal followers and a hell of fire and brimstone to those "bad Indians" who rejected his call. In 1806 he used his knowledge of a forthcoming full eclipse to answer Governor William Henry Harrison's challenge to display his spiritual power by causing "the sun to stand still." Turning day to night, he converted hundreds with his trick that tweaked the governor. Tenskwatawa's faction lived in

Tenskwatawa, the Shawnee Prophet. From James Otto Lewis, The Aboriginal Port-Folio . . . *(Philadelphia, 1835–36). Beinecke Rare Book and Manuscript Library, Yale University.*

TENS QUA-TA-WA
or THE ONE THAT OPENS THE DOOR
Shawnese Prophet
Brother Tecumseh

a new, multitribal Indian community called Prophetstown, near Tippecanoe on the Wabash River.[23]

Little Turtle, of all people, opposed Tenskwatawa. The onetime bane of the American military had come to believe in accommodation. American officials supported Indians seeking peaceful coexistence, but the escalating demands of white farmers and speculators for more land undercut whatever goodwill Indians and whites harbored. William Henry Harrison, new governor of the Northwest Territory, pressed accommodationist chiefs like Little Turtle to sign away another three million acres, tainting progressives in many Indian eyes and increasing Tenskwatawa's appeal.

Joining the prophet at Tippecanoe was his brother Tecumseh, a traditionalist Shawnee chief who adopted his sibling's religious vision and used it to fight progressives and expand the reach of Indian resistance outside the Ohio country. A brilliant orator and racial tragedian, Tecumseh melded Indian grievances into a piercing indictment of white colonization. "Where are the Pequot?" he asked. "Where are the Narragansett, the Mohican, the Pokanoket, and many other once powerful tribes of our people? They have vanished before the avarice and oppression of the white man, as snow before a summer sun." Tecumseh worked to rebuild the Ohio confederation, and he traveled among the tribes of the South with

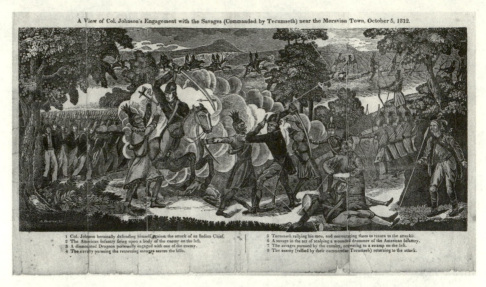

Death of Tecumseh. From Henry Trumbull, History of the Indian Wars *(Boston, 1846).*

his message of racial unity in the coming Armageddon. "Let the white race perish!" he thundered before an assembly of Creeks. "They seize your land; they corrupt your women; they must be driven!—aye, back to the great water whose accursed waves brought them to our shores! Burn their dwellings—destroy their stock— slay their wives and children, that the very breed may perish. War now! War always! War on the living! War on the dead!"[24]

Strong words. But what truly frightened the Americans was the prospect of Great Britain using a pan-Indian uprising in the West to destabilize the young Republic. When Tecumseh and the Prophetstown delegation came to Harrison's headquarters at Vincennes in 1810 and proclaimed their intention to keep federal surveyors off the lands recently ceded by treaty, the governor moved to stamp out a conspiracy that reached far beyond the Wabash. In the fall of 1811, Harrison attacked Prophetstown while Tecumseh was organizing in the South. The Battle of Tippecanoe did not defeat traditionalists, but it began war in earnest. Echoing Tecumseh, Harrison asked, "What other course is left for us to pursue but to make a war of extirpation on them?"[25]

The Indiana racial apocalypse quickly got subsumed by a larger struggle between the United States and Great Britain. The War of 1812 was ostensibly fought over maritime rights. But the congressional War Hawks rode the conflict inland in the hopes of carrying away British real estate. Their Canadian campaign, however, was a fiasco. Instead of grabbing Quebec, the Americans lost Detroit and watched the Canadians burn and sack Buffalo, New York. By 1814 the Royal Navy controlled the Atlantic coast, and British troops invaded Washington, D.C. Satisfied with a public trouncing, the British agreed to settle the conflict without consolidating their gains. Conquering American territory was easier than governing it, and Napoleon Bonaparte's militaristic France loomed as the larger threat.

Great Britain and the United States may have ended the War of 1812 with a collective sigh of "meh," but for the Indians of the Northwest, the conflict was decisive. Supplied by the British, Tecumseh and his traditionalist allies fought the Americans northeast of Detroit in 1813. The Battle of the Thames broke the Indian army and killed Tecumseh. Bullets poked holes in Tenskwatawa's predictions of Indian invincibility. He survived the war and lived into the 1820s, but few people— Indian or otherwise—considered him a prophet after Tecumseh fell.

———

The Cherokees provide a final example of the revitalization movements that swept through the Indian nations of the trans-Appalachian West during the first decades of the nineteenth century. The Revolution devastated the Cherokees. As with the Iroquois, the conflict took on the aspect of a civil war, with the people divided and fighting one another. The Americans invaded and burned Cherokee towns. Hundreds died.

In the aftermath, men of mixed ancestry such as Major Ridge and John Ross, the sons of native mothers and American traders, claimed the leadership of the nation. They supported the Washington administration's Indian "civilization" program. They sought to transform their tribe into a modern nation along the lines of the American states. Their region was undergoing a profound transformation. The invention of the cotton gin in 1793, enabling the easy separation of the seeds from the plant fiber, resulted in a tremendous boom in cotton production. Planters were driving their slaves west, clearing forests and opening new fields. Many Cherokees had taken up farming and slavery, and the new leadership promoted cotton production.

These progressive ideas, however, ran afoul of traditional Cherokee values. Enthusiastic capitalists, the Cherokees with plantations and stores violated the traditional ethics of sharing. Old-school leaders had gathered political influence through the distribution of wealth. The new chiefs practiced real capitalism, accumulating wealth and power for themselves. During the War of 1812, when Tecumseh riled up Cherokee traditionalists with his message of racial unity and revitalization, prophets arose echoing the language of Tenskwatawa. Among the Cherokees, a visionary named Tsali preached to the people to "get the white men out of the country and go back to your former ways." The acquisitive accommodations of the mixed-blood leadership disturbed him: "Destroy the cattle, destroy the spinning wheels and looms, throw away your plows, and everything used by the Americans."[26]

A large faction of Tecumseh's supporters among the Creek Nation, known as the Red Sticks, went to war against the Americans during the War of 1812. In one bloody incident they attacked and killed most of the five hundred men, women, and children held up in Fort Mims on the Tombigbee River. In retaliation, Andrew Jackson, commander of the Tennessee militia, led an army of two thousand against the Creek militants. Hundreds of progressive Cherokees marched with Jackson, upending the racial unity preached by Tecumseh. In March 1814, at the Battle of Horseshoe Bend in what is today central Alabama, Jackson's combined force defeated the Red Sticks, killing more than eight hundred, marking this as the worst defeat of an Indian people in the nation's history. In the aftermath, Jackson forced the Creeks to cede twenty-three million acres, which over the next twenty years would become prime cotton land for slave masters, men such as Jackson himself.

The slaughter at Horseshoe Bend disgusted traditionalist Cherokees. Many left the southern Appalachians and moved west across the Mississippi to the Arkansas River valley. The progressive leadership exploited the exodus to bolster its nationalist credentials. True Cherokees, they pronounced, stayed and adapted to keep their homes. "I scorn this movement of a few men to unsettle the nation, and trifle with our attachment to the land of our forefathers," declared head chief Major Ridge to a large assembly of his people. Ridge and his progressives won the battle for Cherokee hearts and minds.[27]

The Cherokees took the early Indian policy of the United States at its word and transformed themselves into prime examples of so-called civilized Indians. With assurances of federal protection of their homeland and sovereignty, the Cherokees listened to their agents and missionaries. They adopted the American economic system and modeled their government on the institutions of the United States. The nation built a new capital at Echota, in the foothills of the Appalachian Mountains, elected a representative assembly, and codified their laws. Missionaries opened schools; the leading men of the nation learned to read and write English.

The flower of the Cherokee renaissance was the invention by a man named Sequoyah (his English name was George Guess) of a written phonetic system for spoken Cherokee—the first writing system invented by a North American Indian. Sequoyah was a traditionalist who had removed to the Arkansas River and was seeking a way to communicate with family and friends back home in the Cherokee Nation. His syllabary proved easy to learn, and it immediately caught on. Within a few years, a majority of Cherokees both in the West and in the nation had learned to read and write using Sequoyah's system. Literacy among the Cherokee outpaced their American neighbors. The nation set up its own newspaper, the *Cherokee Phoenix*, published in both English and Sequoyan. All these words and activities

Sequoyah with his Cherokee syllabary. From Thomas L. McKenney and James Hall, History of the Indian Tribes of North America . . . , *3 vols. (Philadelphia, 1836–44).*

were sparked by one man's attempt to send a few words back home to friends and family.

Some optimists, like the editor of the *Cherokee Phoenix*, Elias Boudinot, saw the Cherokees moving from the degraded margins to the dignified center of human existence. "There is," he reported in a speech to a white audience, "in Indian history, something very melancholy. We have seen everywhere the poor aborigines melt away before the approach of the white population." But the Cherokees, he intoned, would write a new chapter: "I can view my native country, rising from the ashes of her degradation, wearing her purified and beautiful garments, and taking her seat with the nations of the earth." Arrayed in the trappings of civilization—

capitalism, print, democracy—the Cherokees' passage looked assured to Boudinot. He ended his speech with a rhetorical question: "I ask you shall red men live,
or shall they be swept from the earth? Must they perish? Let humanity answer."
Boudinot thought that he knew what the answer would be.[28]

FURTHER READING

Stephen Aron, *How the West Was Lost: The Transformation of Kentucky from Daniel Boone
    to Henry Clay* (1996)
Colin G. Calloway, *The American Revolution in Indian Country: Crisis and Diversity in
    Native American Communities* (1995)
Andrew R. L. Cayton, *The Frontier Republic: Ideology and Politics in the Ohio Country,
    1780–1825* (1986)
David A. Chang, *The Color of the Land: Race, Nation, and the Politics of Land in Oklahoma,
    1832–1929* (2010)
R. David Edmunds, *The Shawnee Prophet* (1983)
Patrick Griffin, *Leviathan: Empire, Nation, and Revolutionary Frontier* (2008)
William G. McLoughlin, *Cherokee Renascence in the New Republic* (1986)
James H. Merrell, *Into the American Woods: Negotiations on the Pennsylvania Frontier*
    (2000)
Peter S. Onuf, *Statehood and Union: A History of the Northwest Ordinance* (1987)
Daniel K. Richter, *Facing East from Indian Country: A Native History of Early America*
    (2003)
Peter Silver, *Our Savage Neighbors: How Indian War Transformed Early America* (2009)
John Sugden, *Tecumseh: A Life* (1997)

5

Finding Purchase

Daniel Boone exited life two months shy of his eighty-sixth birthday in 1820. In the years before his death, many admirers beat a path to his door—if they could find it. John Filson's romanticized 1783 biography tied Boone's name forever to Kentucky, but in 1799 the legendary hunter had left the state in frustration, and fans had to trek farther west to his new home in Missouri. When the old man saw visitors approaching, he would "take his cane and walk off to avoid them," one of his sons recalled, "but if cornered he would sit and talk with them." Boone was ambivalent about his fame. He appreciated the respect Filson's heroic portrayal brought him, and he offered the author nothing but praise. "All true! Every word true!" he exclaimed after a visitor read a portion aloud. "Not a lie in it." But that didn't mean that Boone was happy with everything near the end of his days.[1]

Filson christened Boone an American original, a "natural man" of the wilderness. But he was no naïf. He had blundered into too many legal tangles, suffered too many business setbacks, and witnessed too many bloodlettings. Following the Revolution, he took up surveying, opened a general store, and planned to settle his children and grandchildren nearby. "But alas!" he lamented, "it was then that my misery began." As recompense for patriotic service to the country, "I thought I was entitled to a home for my family," but "another man bought the land over my head." Forced into court, he lost both his land and his business. Disappointed and downhearted, "I determined to quit my native land," Boone said. He relocated his family to Spanish Missouri, where authorities granted them a generous estate. But "my misfortune did not end," he continued, for when the United States acquired Missouri as part of the Louisiana Purchase, in came the speculators and the lawyers, and eventually his Spanish grant was also declared null and void. "I have lived

Daniel Boone in Missouri, eighty-five years old. Engraving by James Otto Lewis, 1820. Author's collection.

to learn," Boone concluded with a weary sigh, that progress "is nothing more than improved ways to overreach your neighbor."[2]

In legend, Boone moved whenever his elbow room was threatened by new settlers. In real life, he fled from debt collectors and lawyers. Boone found respite from his woes in the company of Indian neighbors, many of whom had removed from places farther east, men who shared his love of hunting and his feeling of persecution. His choice of companions surprised admirers, who expected the celebrated Indian fighter to hate his foes. But Boone disliked telling war stories and refused to count scalps. Legend portrayed him as "a wonderful man who had killed a host of Indians," he said, and he allowed that "many was the fair fire I have had at them." But, he avowed, "I am very sorry that I ever killed any, for they have always been kinder to me than the whites." Some Americans, expecting a fiercer defense of their nation's right to western lands as well as their treatment of the region's perceived savages, found Boone's sentiments embarrassing. He backed away from the greed and rancor he spied in his fellow citizens. If this be civilization, Boone concluded, he would "certainly prefer a state of nature."[3]

Boone's perspective offers a jumping-off point for a consideration of the western expansion of the United States. How did the young nation on the Atlantic coast wind up with a growing western empire that included former Spanish and French territories in Louisiana and Texas, as well as a joint occupation of the Oregon Country with Great Britain? What ideas and emotions did Americans attach to the ground they gained on maps? Where did these new margins fit in their mental cartography of race and nationhood? More importantly, how did the people living in these spaces perceive these changes in ownership?

⸻

The founders believed that expansion was critical to the nation's future. James Madison, often called the father of the Constitution, placed it at the heart of the American political system. "Extend the sphere," he declared in the *Federalist Papers,* "and you make it less probable that a majority of the whole will have a common motive to invade the rights of other citizens." Expansion would ameliorate social conflict. American republican government would thrive with an ever-expanding geography, leading to what he called "one great, respectable, and flourishing empire." George Washington envisioned the United States as a "rising empire," a growing and expanding state, and many Americans entertained continental ambitions. "The Mississippi was never designed as the western boundary of the American empire," declared Jedidiah Morse in *American Geography,* a popular textbook published in 1789, the year the Constitution was ratified. "It is well known that empire has been traveling from east to west. Probably her last and broadest seat will be America. . . . We cannot but anticipate the period, as not far distant, when the AMERICAN EMPIRE will comprehend millions of souls west of the Mississippi."[4]

The patriotic rhetoric camouflaged the vulnerability of a nation still under construction. The United States was by no means a foregone conclusion in the opening decades of the nineteenth century. Napoleon menaced from his sugar islands in the Caribbean, and in 1800, when Spain returned Louisiana to France, the resurgence of the French in North America appeared imminent. Great Britain humiliated the United States during the War of 1812, and Canadian fur trade corporations stretched British influence across North America, allying many interior tribes with the crown. Powerful Indian nations stretched across the Great Plains, controlling trade through their alliances, their military prowess, and their vast herds of horses and mules. The United States struggled to maintain control over its own frontier citizens, and domestic unrest added to the treacherousness of nation-building in the West. In 1794 President Washington led troops into western Pennsylvania to subdue the Whiskey Rebellion. Plots and subterfuge infested the highest ranks of western officials. Men sold their loyalty and hatched schemes that involved founding new nations out west or breaking chunks of American peripheries off and feeding them to Spain or Canada.

Yet many Americans believed that they enjoyed a natural right to the continent. They told a story of their nation's founding that sprung from the geographic fringes. There, they imagined, far removed from Europe's cultural reach, a new breed emerged. Nature remade western Americans into gnarly woodsmen, fiercely independent bark-eaters who bowed to no one. The Boone of legend, the prototype of this distinctive American folk hero, was followed by many more of the same mold. But this national origin myth ignored how things actually worked. The real Boone knew the truth. To acquire wealth, to gain power, and to stay alive, humans needed other humans. Success hinged on reaching across cultural, ethnic, and racial divisions to create friends and family. Friends and families, not solitary masculine heroes, built companies, partnerships, alliances, nations, and empires. In the West, a person or a country was only as strong as the bonds that were made and kept.

In American eyes, the friendship that defined this period of western history was the one formed between Thomas Jefferson's secretary, Meriwether Lewis, and the military captain William Clark. In 1801 Jefferson asked Lewis to prepare a western exploratory mission. The expedition would travel through territory claimed by European empires. In 1762, before Britain and France signed the treaty ending the French and Indian War, the French had transferred their claim to western North America to Spain. The boundaries of Louisiana were huge but vague, beginning at the linchpin port of New Orleans, taking in the entire western watershed of the Mississippi River, and falling off somewhere in the Rocky Mountains. The Spanish closed the Mississippi to American traffic, choking off economic development in the trans-Appalachian West. Finally in 1795, after long negotiations, Spain agreed to open the river to American commerce.

But soon American concerns shifted to France. Napoleon Bonaparte, who seized control of revolutionary France in a coup d'état in 1799, had New World imperial dreams of his own. He envisioned a revived empire that would unify France's Caribbean colonies with the mainland colony of Louisiana. In 1800 he invaded and defeated Spain, then dictated a peace treaty returning Louisiana to French control. President Jefferson, concerned about continued American access to New Orleans, sent an American delegation to France to negotiate the purchase of the city and the surrounding country on the east bank of the Mississippi. In letters he fully expected French censors to read, Jefferson let slip that the Americans would resist French imperialism on the continent by romancing another country. "The day France takes possession of New Orleans," he wrote, "we must marry ourselves to the British fleet and nation."[5]

But it was a slave revolt, rather than Jefferson's threat, that altered Napoleon's plans. François-Dominique Toussaint, one of the era's great generals, broke France's hold on its most profitable Caribbean colony. Born a plantation slave, Toussaint acquired enough education to read the writings of French revolutionaries as well as Julius Caesar's account of his conquests. When Haiti's slaves rebelled against their French masters in 1790, he became their leader, taking the name L'Ouverture, "the Opener." By 1798 the Haitians had thrown out their former French masters and installed L'Ouverture as governor for life, sending panic throughout the slave-holding world. Napoleon sent twenty thousand troops to oppose L'Ouverture's eight-thousand-man army. The Americans encouraged clandestine shipments of supplies to the rebels but refused to support L'Ouverture publicly for fear of inspiring their own slaves to cut their throats. The Haitians' fierce guerrilla tactics as well as an outbreak of yellow fever decimated the French. Captured by his enemies, L'Ouverture died in a miserable dungeon, but his followers fought on. By early 1803, Napoleon had to acknowledge the Haitians' independence, and he decided to cut his losses.

In April 1803, the American negotiators in Paris were shocked when French foreign minister Talleyrand asked, "What will you give for the whole?" The "whole" of what? The Americans responded cautiously. "Whatever it was we took from Spain," the minister answered with a shrug. The Americans offered fifteen million dollars for the French claim, only slightly more than they had been prepared to offer for New Orleans alone. The land, of course, remained in the possession of its Indian proprietors. Every acre would have to be won by treaty or conquest

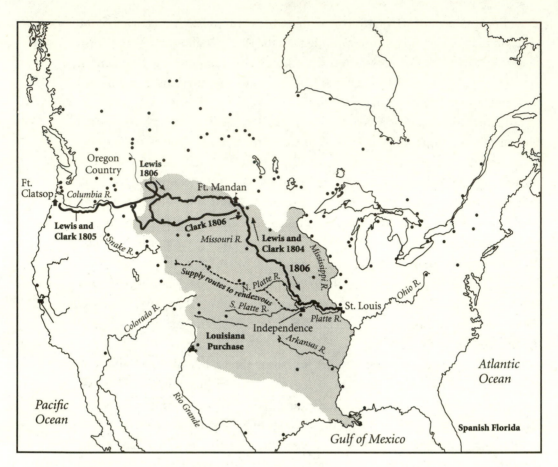

THE LOUISIANA PURCHASE

at a cost that ultimately would be nearly thirty times greater than the sum paid to France. But even that was an incredible deal. "You have made a noble bargain for yourselves," Talleyrand declared at the conclusion of the negotiations. "And I suppose you will make the most of it."[6]

———

Jefferson intended to do just that. The Louisiana Purchase gave his western exploration plans new urgency. Commanded jointly by Meriwether Lewis and William Clark, the expedition combined Jefferson's scientific and nationalistic ambitions. He wanted the captains to find and catalog the interior's botany, zoology, and geology, hoping their investigation would prove North American flora and fauna as diverse and vigorous as any found in Europe. Science would back the naturalness of American power while the captains' survey of the territory would reveal new avenues for this power's expression. It was well and good to admire frontier nature, but to hang onto the West, the Americans must bend that nature

Captain Lewis & Clark holding a Council with the Indians.

Meriwether Lewis and William Clark in council with Indians. From Patrick Gass, A Journal of the Voyages and Travels of a Corps of Discovery under the Command of Capt. Lewis and Capt. Clarke . . . *(Philadelphia, 1810). Beinecke Rare Book and Manuscript Library, Yale University.*

to their advantage. Lewis and Clark explored for the exploitable: a quick passage across the continent to reach the China market; fur resources like beavers and otters; and trading partnerships and military alliances with native nations.

In the spring of 1804, the company shoved off, crossing the Mississippi from Illinois and entering the Missouri River country. The forty men made up a motley crew: backwoodsmen of British and Irish decent, métis of mixed ancestry, and Lewis's black slave, York. As they rowed up the Missouri, they passed communities more motley still: towns of French-speaking Creoles and métis who had lived there since the mid-eighteenth century, villages of emigrant Indians more recently displaced from the Ohio valley, and clusters of recent arrivals from the American backwoods, like Daniel Boone, who lived with his family on the north side of the Missouri.

Pulling against the current, the company spent a summer reaching the earth lodge villages of the Mandan and Minnetaree Indians near "the falls" of the Missouri, in what is now central North Dakota. Farmers, these groups lived in durable towns, which made their lodges trading centers for the northern Great Plains. The Americans found French traders living among them with Indian wives and métis children. Frenchmen had been visiting the Mandans since 1738, when the party of fur trader Pierre de Varennes et de La Vérendrye arrived, part of a wave of French

Mandan village on the Missouri River. From George Catlin, Catalogue of Catlin's Indian Gallery of Portraits . . . *(New York, 1837). Beinecke Rare Book and Manuscript Library, Yale University.*

traders pushing westward from the Great Lakes. After warning the traders that the region was now part of the American West, Lewis hired a number of them, including Toussaint Charbonneau, who offered the interpretive skills of one of his wives, a fifteen-year-old Shoshone captive named Sacagawea. The only woman to accompany the expedition from the mountains to the Pacific, Sacagawea eased the Americans' passage through the social and political crosscurrents of the region with her words as well as her visage. "The sight of this Indian woman," wrote Clark, convinced the Indians "of our friendly intentions, as no woman ever accompanies a war party of Indians in this quarter."[7]

Like Boone's legend, Sacagawea's story—the U.S. Postal Service honored her with a stamp in 1994—distorted the historical circumstances that inspired it. A very young woman who had probably been sold as a slave to her husband, Charbonneau, she bore little resemblance to the plucky feminist heroine others fabricated. (Late nineteenth-century and early twentieth-century women's rights advocates and suffragists latched onto Sacagawea as a role model and female counterpart to Lewis and Clark.) But there was nothing especially unusual about Sacagawea. She belonged to a small but influential group of captive women and children who knit the peoples of the West together. Her legacy to the explorers and to American history was her normalcy. Rather than helping Lewis and Clark to win the West, she helped them figure it out.

To navigate the West in the early nineteenth century, the Corps of Discovery had to establish relationships with the people living there. Women like Sacagawea acted as intermediaries among traders, tribes, nations, and empires. Through marriage, captivity, and slavery, women traversed linguistic, political, ethnic, and racial boundaries. Their travels and travails created kinship networks that made trade and alliances possible. It also made some of them dealmakers and peacekeepers. Some women used their proficiency in multiple languages and their ties to multiple families to secure wealth and independence. Many others, like Sacagawea, however, were not so lucky. They remained on the peripheries of their captors' societies. Essential as go-betweens, their split identities and loyalties roused suspicions and provoked abuse.

The range of captivity and slave experiences signaled a key difference between the West and other sections of the United States. Western enslaved people ran the gamut from oppressed laborers to cherished family members. Some left bondage when they married their captors; others died scraping bison hides for wealthy masters who had no intention of ever freeing them. No racial codes or state constitutions controlled or dictated western slavery. A fluid arrangement, western slavery epitomized the ambivalence of the frontier. Bought and sold, ripped from kith and kin, slaves and captives forged new bonds with their masters and captors. The product of shattered lives, these relationships undergirded the politics and economies of the early West.

Lewis and Clark depended on Sacagawea, on French fur traders, and on informants among the Mandans and Minnetarees to begin to understand the complicated world of the Great Plains, a region that had been transformed over the preceding century. Soon after the Pueblo Revolt in 1680, horses from the Spanish settlements drifted onto the plains, triggering a cultural revolution based on grass. Groups of natives exploited the power generated by the horse's ability to consume sunshine encased in the blades that grew in oceanlike swaths along the continent's midsection. Indians bred, stole, and traded the animals. They used them to move, fight, and hunt. Horses increased wealth by giving hunters greater access to the Great Plains' bison herds. Bison meat filled bellies while their robes bought European trade goods, especially guns. The Indian nations that bet heavily on horses in the eighteenth century grew into formidable nations—some historians call them empires. Equestrian nomads dominated the West that Lewis and Clark encountered in the winter of 1804.

The horse remade life on the plains for better and worse. The social and cultural revolution hobbled native women. Nomadism upped their workload. Men hunted and fought; women did everything else. They struck and moved camp, transporting

Facsimile of a buffalo hide pictogram. Painted by Samuel Seymour, 1820. Beinecke Rare Book and Manuscript Library, Yale University.

tepees, food, and the increasing bulk of hides and trade items to new pastures. They cooked, foraged for wild plants, and cared for children. And they processed hide after hide. Increasingly lethal, male hunters overburdened their female kin with bison hides and robes for trade. It took about three days of constant labor to cure a single hide; and a proficient hunter might bring in a dozen hides from a good hunt. Successful hunters not only acquired many horses but began to take many wives. Female laborers were the bottleneck in the hide business. A hunter could trade only as many as women could manufacture. The hide trade fueled captive-taking and the slave trade. Men stole and bought women to increase hide production.

The nomads of the plains lived most of the year in hunting bands consisting of a handful of families. As the bands moved, their allegiance and loyalty often shifted, and tribal identities emerged only gradually. The nations that confronted the Americans in the West were recent consolidations. The grass revolution inspired massive moves and reorganizations. A rambunctious country with a land-hungry and impressively fertile population, the United States was not the most expansive nation on the frontier. Mounted peoples converged on the interior of the continent from all directions. The Comanches originated as a Shoshone people of the Great Basin. After adopting the horse, they migrated onto the plains, and over several generations they moved southeastward toward present-day Oklahoma and Texas. There, they found some of the best pasture in the world. Their horse herds thrived, and their wealth and power increased. By the early nineteenth century, the Comanches dominated the southern plains.

In the northern plains a number of nomadic groups contested one another for hunting space. The Crows broke away from kindred farming communities along the Missouri River around 1700. A little later the Cheyennes left their farming homeland in present-day Minnesota and moved west. Long before Europeans or Americans reached the area, these two groups met in violent clashes in the vicinity of the Black Hills. The Cheyennes migrated in response to competition from an even stronger and more populous people, the Lakotas. Before the horse, the Lakotas, like all their neighbors, combined hunting, gathering, and a little farming to make a living on the northern fringe of the plains, but as the French traders pushed beyond the Great Lakes, their Algonquian allies, the Ojibwas and Crees, went to war with the Lakotas, driving them west. Indeed, the name by which we generally know the Lakotas—the Sioux—is a French transliteration of an Algonquian word meaning "enemy." The Lakotas' migration brought them into conflict with the Cheyennes and Crows. The groups fought over the Black Hills for decades. The Sioux won, pushing their rivals farther west. By the late eighteenth century, the Sioux rivaled the Comanches in the northern plains.

Nomads such as the Sioux traded with and raided the village dwellers who continued to farm in the West's river valleys. These groups owned horses and ventured onto the plains seasonally to hunt bison. But cultivated food seemed more dependable than roaming with the herds, and they stuck with their older traditions. The nomads depended on the farmers for carbohydrates. They traded robes and horses for corn and took what they needed when the villagers refused to bargain. Tales of Sioux ferocity had reached the Lewis and Clark expedition. The corps had a tense encounter with a Sioux band before their arrival at the Mandan towns. The mounted warriors didn't fail to impress. The Mandans asked the Americans to protect them, and Clark promised to "kill those who would not listen to our good talk." Thus, from the first moment the Americans entered the world of the plains, they joined long-running disputes and conflicts. Clark felt in charge, but it was the Indians who played him to their advantage.[8]

Following charts and maps drawn with the help of their Mandan friends, the expedition followed the Missouri and Jefferson Rivers to the continental watershed. Obtaining horses from Sacagawea's Shoshone relatives, they reached

Page from William Clark's field notes of the Lewis and Clark expedition, January 18, 1804.
Beinecke Rare Book and Manuscript Library, Yale University.

the westward-flowing Snake River and followed it to its junction with the Columbia. Finally, in the rainy November of 1805 they stood on the shores of the Pacific. After a depressing winter, they largely retraced their route, and in September 1806 the hardened band returned, twenty-eight months after it had left.

Was the trip worthwhile? The captains made contact with dozens of Indian tribes and distributed more than a hundred silver peace medals and dozens of American flags. Despite the troubles with the Sioux, they found most Indians eager for allies against their expansionist neighbors as well as for better trading connections. But the commercial objectives of the expedition were at best only partly realized. The Corps of Discovery failed to find Jefferson's primary objective, a commercial route linking the waters of the Atlantic and the Pacific. Lewis and Clark charted an impossibly difficult route over the Rockies. Americans followed the duo's example and traveled west looking for adventure and profit, but they found better paths that eluded the pathfinders.

In the long view, Lewis and Clark succeeded best at fixing the Louisiana territory in the minds and plans of the nation. The Americans especially liked what they read about the Oregon Country and used the corps' trip to claim it as their own, much to the chagrin of the Canadian fur traders already there. Although another generation would pass before actual farmers trekked west to take up land, the expedition aroused popular interest in the Far West that encouraged additional exploratory, artistic, and commercial forays. Government fact finders, painters, and fur traders entered a complex place with a long history and began making sense of the frontier for American consumption.

In 1806, even before the return of Lewis and Clark, President Jefferson dispatched a second military expedition under the command of Lieutenant Zebulon Pike to reconnoiter the southern reaches of the Louisiana Purchase. Pike specialized in seeking and not finding the origins of major North American watersheds. On a previous mission, he missed the headwaters of the Mississippi. On his new one, he would fail to locate the source of the Arkansas River in the southern Rockies. He marveled at the grand summit later named Pike's Peak in his honor—although he did not manage to scale it. He turned south in search of the Red River, by which he was instructed to return, but instead blundered across the Sangre de Cristo range into New Mexico, where Spanish dragoons arrested him as a trespasser and spy.

The Spanish forced Pike and his men to return with them to the New Mexican capital of Santa Fe, then escorted them south to the provincial capital of Chihuahua, where officials questioned the American commander closely before finally conducting him back home through the provinces of Coahuila and Texas to the

American post at the old French town of Natchitoches in Louisiana. Pike's expedition did little to clarify the boundary line between Louisiana and New Spain, but he was the first American to provide detailed intelligence on New Mexico and Texas. The region left him unimpressed. "These vast plains," he wrote, "may become in time equally celebrated as the sandy deserts of Africa; for I saw in my route, in various places, tracts of many leagues, where the wind had thrown up the sand, in the fanciful forms of the ocean's rolling wave, and on which not a speck of vegetable matter existed." The "uncivilized aborigines," he hypothesized, might keep this place while American farmers plowed elsewhere.[9]

Major Stephen H. Long, who led a military expedition along the Platte River in 1820, seconded Pike's grim assessment. After crossing the plains to the Rocky Mountains, he reported the region "almost wholly unfit for cultivation, and of course uninhabitable by a people depending on agriculture for subsistence," and included a map on which the present states of Oklahoma, Kansas, and Nebraska wore the label "Great American Desert." Pike and Long asserted the United States' ownership rights over a wasteland. It would take more active imaginations to envision Americans easing into landscapes that seemed hostile to their agrarian ambitions.[10]

These exploratory missions often included painters, scientists, and traders, which did not make them any less nationalistic. Images, specimens, and trade items carried as much information as official military reports. Samuel Seymour and Titian Ramsey Peale became the first westering artists when they signed on as members of Major Long's expedition. Seymour's instructions were to paint portraits of Indians, to reproduce landscapes noted for their "beauty and grandeur," and to ferret out any and all subjects "appropriate to his art." His superiors invited Seymour to apply his imagination to the region to bring it to life. They wanted to be impressed, even thrilled by their purchase. Although Seymour was not talented enough to take fullest advantage of the opportunity, he became sufficiently excited about some subjects—the first view of the Rocky Mountains or a council between the Americans and the Pawnees—to endow his drawings with a vitality beyond mere record.[11]

Not until the 1830s did artists begin to capture the complex cultural world of the trans-Mississippi West. Karl Bodmer, a Swiss painter who toured the upper Missouri country in 1833 and 1834 with his German patron, Prince Maximilian of Wied, recorded a wealth of ethnographic detail in his images. His celebrated study of a Mandan family relaxing around the central hearth of their earth lodge includes the shields, lances, and medicine symbols of the warriors, the cooking pots and basketry of the women, and the framing timbers and spaciousness of the

Pawnees in council with the Stephen Long expedition. Painting by Samuel Seymour, 1819. Beinecke Rare Book and Manuscript Library, Yale University.

lodge itself. A century and a half later, Indians would mine Bodmer's images to recover traditional clothing styles, haircuts, and clan rituals. But Bodmer excised the evidence of the long history of interaction between Indians and Europeans or Americans. Instead he depicted pristine Indians, erasing the mingling of people, stuff, and styles that defined the frontier.

The cultural mix was better captured by Alfred Jacob Miller, an American artist with European training. In 1837 Captain William Drummond Stewart, a Scottish nobleman on leave from the British army, hired Miller to accompany him on the last of his several trips to the Rockies. Miller's watercolors and drawings feature Indians and mountain men setting traps, spinning tales around campfires, and resting peacefully together in the midday shade. His remarkable images of the fur trade post of Fort Laramie depict a place of intercultural exchange. And more than any other nineteenth-century artist of the West, Miller noticed Indian women— preparing skins and meat, tending children, racing horses, even hunting buffalo. His work places women at the center of fur trade society, reflecting their key roles as workers and instigators of cross-cultural alliances and partnerships. Yet Miller was no sober ethnographer. He enveloped his historical data in a romantic soft

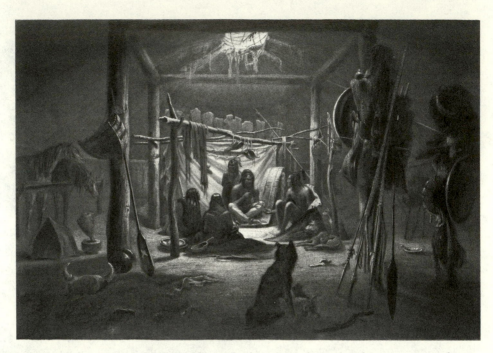

Interior of a Mandan earth lodge. Lithograph of a painting by Karl Bodmer, 1841. Beinecke Rare Book and Manuscript Library, Yale University.

focus. Miller's Indian women are nearly always beauties, and frequently unclothed, bringing to mind the primitive ogling of Paul Gauguin in Tahiti. After all, these paintings were intended for Stewart, a man with wide-ranging and flamboyant sexual tastes. The eroticism of an image like the beautiful *Snake Girl Swinging* (1837) suggests that Miller was after more than facts.

The best-known artist of the early West was George Catlin. By his own account, Catlin experienced a moment of epiphany when, as a young man in Philadelphia, he saw an Indian delegation walk through the city on the way to Washington. The "lords of the forest" so impressed him that he resolved that "nothing short of the loss of my life shall prevent me from visiting the country, and of becoming their historian." In 1832 he worked his way up the Missouri River to the mouth of the Yellowstone, sketching nearly every Indian he met. Over the next several years, Catlin alternated between western jaunts and studio interludes spent transcribing his sketches into finished oils. He asked the public to see his works "as they have been intended, as *true* and *facsimile* traces of individual life and historical facts." Catlin attached certificates, signed by Indian agents, army officers, or other government officials, to back up his claims that they had been "painted from the life."[12]

Despite his factual proclivities, Catlin refracted everything he saw, drew, and painted through a mind preoccupied with the idea that he was salvaging a race on the brink of extinction. He was a man on a mission: "I have flown to their

Snake Girl Swinging. Painting by Alfred Jacob Miller, c. 1837. Beinecke Rare Book and Manuscript Library, Yale University.

The Bear Dance. Lithograph of a painting by George Catlin, c. 1844. Beinecke Rare Book and Manuscript Library, Yale University.

rescue—not of their lives or of their race (for they are 'doomed' and must perish), but to the rescue of their looks and their modes." The Indians themselves would eventually vanish, "yet, phoenix-like, they may rise from 'the stain of a painter's palette,' and live again upon canvass, and stand forth for centuries yet to come, the living monuments of a noble race." Catlin felt deep sympathy for Native Americans and mourned their losses, quite a contrast to the bile spewed by some of his Indian-hating compatriots. But, for all his emoting, Catlin could not see Indians as anything but victims, helpless against the tide of civilization. He was oblivious to the cultural transformations that in fact would insure the survival of these peoples. Aside from the necklaces, the feathers, and the paint that adorn his subjects, Catlin's paintings are peculiarly bereft of cultural dynamism.[13]

Nevertheless, what Catlin called "the mystic web of sympathy" binding him to his subjects comes across clearly in his work. No other artist or writer came as close to depicting the religious communion of Indian dance, for example, a subject Catlin returned to time and again. Bodmer was much better with the human figure, but his dancers are almost mannequins. Though not as perfect, Catlin's images capture the spontaneity of the moment. He presents us with a world he himself barely understood, but had the genius to depict.[14]

The works of these artists were widely distributed in various printed media. Historian Martha Sandwiess estimates that between 1843 and 1863 more than seven hundred engravings and lithographs of western scenes appeared in government reports and documents, many with print runs of thousands of copies. The works of Bodmer, Miller, and Catlin were issued in authorized prints from private publishers, as well as in unauthorized copies without credit, and often became the basis for drawings in popular books, magazines, and dime novels. Engravers and hack artists changed details, altering costumes and sometimes making Indians appear more ferocious and threatening than they appeared in the original sketches or watercolors. Print culture spread and altered the pictorial evidence to suit the emerging nineteenth-century ideology of expansion: that the West was the playground of American destiny, the place where the United States would find its greatness. It was an illusion of foregone conclusions—Indians and bison retreating as farmers and railroads advanced. But the history of the West would take many turns before the United States was able to consolidate its power and possession. The actual course of events was contingent and open-ended.

When Meriwether Lewis, on his return in 1806, described the upper Missouri River as "richer in beaver and otter than any country on earth," he spoke a language of economics and empire that he knew his audience wanted to hear. The fur trade had been the linchpin of frontier commerce for more than three centuries. Beaver and otter were catnip for adventurous capitalists.[15]

The fur trade depended on Indian labor—the work of male hunters and trappers and of Indian women who made jerky and pemmican (buffalo fat mixed with dried berries) and prepared hides and pelts. Indian hands plucked beavers from streams, and their labor initiated a chain of relationships that stretched from the Rockies to company headquarters in London and Montreal. The Hudson's Bay Company, chartered by the British crown in 1670, held the exclusive right to the Indian trade over the entire watershed of Hudson's Bay. It coordinated a far-flung network of field directors and workers (*engagés*), supplying them with traps, horses, boats, food, whiskey, and trade goods for Indians, indicating the best routes for the largest returns, and preparing, collecting, warehousing, and distributing pelts. The company centrally directed the enterprise even in the field, where the business operated out of forts of "factories," with Indians assigned to trapping and bringing furs into the forts, where the engagés readied them for shipment. So great was the power and prestige of the company, it was said, that the initials "HBC" stamped on shipping boxes, invoices, and packs of fur stood for "Here Before Christ."

Immense, but never almighty, the HBC battled with a startup firm from Montreal, the North West Company, a partnership of French Canadian and Highland Scots traders, chartered by the British government in 1784. Unlike the HBC, the

North West Company relied less on factories and traveled to their native suppliers. They fortified their business with family ties and friendships, marrying into Indian families and negotiating alliances. The "Nor'Westers" were dashing opportunists, whereas the HBC men tended to adhere to policy. In 1793 more than ten years before Lewis and Clark, Nor'Wester Alexander Mackenzie became the first European to reach the Pacific Ocean by way of the continental interior. Mackenzie's published account of his Indian-led journey through the maze of western Canadian rivers to the coast was what prompted Jefferson to counter the British with his own expedition.

The North West Company's rambunctious spirit drew young men like John McLoughlin. As a boy in Quebec, he watched Nor'Westers parade through the street. His uncles, Alexander and Simon Fraser, were partners in the company. Sent to Scotland to become a medical doctor, McLoughlin dutifully finished his training, but then he returned to Canada in 1804 and, barely out of his teens, signed on as an apprentice Nor'Wester. He entered a commercial free-for-all in which both companies competed for furs with empty promises and cheap whiskey, undermining their bonds with native suppliers. To curb the excesses of cutthroat competition, the British government ordered the two companies to combine, and in 1821 the Nor'Westers were absorbed into the HBC. McLoughlin weathered the transition and became a partner. In 1824 the company named him general superintendent of the far western Columbia River District.

Like most of his fur trade contemporaries, McLoughlin fell in love with an Indian woman. In 1811 he married Marguerite Wadin, the métis widow of another trader. It was a lifelong relationship, and together they had four children. McLoughlin was representative of those traders who never wavered in their commitment to their native wives, and his children were proud of their métis heritage. McLoughlin's long, prematurely white hair supposedly inspired an Indian nickname: White-Headed Eagle. He ruled the roost at Fort Vancouver for more than twenty years. He epitomized the fur trade's distinctive frontier. Here was a global capitalist enterprise based on local family relationships spanning cultures.

———

John Jacob Astor entered the far western fur trade late and left early. In 1784 he arrived in New York City from his German homeland and within a few years had made a fortune as a wholesaler of furs from the Northwest Territory. Reading reports of the Lewis and Clark expedition, he dreamed of a western trade empire controlled from a post on the Columbia River, where pelts from the interior West could be shipped to China, exploiting the commercial link forged by Russian traders along the northern Pacific coast. In 1811 Astor financed two expeditions to the Pacific, one by sea and one by land. The land travelers had a rough time, and only a handful of survivors arrived at the mouth of the Columbia. They discovered that the seafarers on the *Tonquin*, however, had already arrived and founded a post they called Astoria.

The name sounded grand, but Astor's claim was weak compared to that of the British and the Russians. Captain James Cook of the Royal Navy had explored this coast in 1778, and accounts by his men of the rich trade of the region set off an international rush to those shores. There were sea otter along the coast and beaver in the streams, whales and limitless supplies of salmon, and great stands of spruce and pine, as well as thousands of Indian consumers who promised a brisk trade in goods. As early as 1793, Alexander Mackenzie was reconnoitering the area for the HBC. The Russian-American Company, meanwhile, pushed south to establish its own claim. In 1802 the company established new headquarters on Sitka Sound, in what is now southeast Alaska, and dispatched their Aleut hunters to scour the coastline to the south. The Russians and the British formed alliances with some native groups through trade and battled others for ascendancy. They worked for regional profits while the Americans dreamed of them.

Astoria, 1813. From Gabriel Franchère, Narrative of a Voyage to the Northwest Coast of America . . . *(New York, 1854).*

The War of 1812 capsized Astoria like a rowboat in a tsunami. In October 1813, a British warship threatened to blast the fort to smithereens, and that convinced the men in Astor's employ to surrender it. The British raised their flag, broke open a bottle of wine, and renamed the place Fort George. Soon, however, they abandoned the windswept site in favor of a better location upriver known as Fort Vancouver. Astor remained in the fur business, but he increasingly invested his capital in New York real estate—which made him into America's first million-aire. The Americans would not return in force to the Oregon Country for thirty years. The memory of Astoria served as the legal toehold for the Americans' right to the Pacific Northwest. Yet it was New England captains and sailors that kept the Pacific alive in American commerce and foreign policy. Their ships returned to Boston—so prevalent was this harbor that all Americans were known as "Bostons" in the Columbia region—smelling of tea and spice, their holds spilling out rich profit from a trade that began with barter among coastal Indians for sea otter furs, which were carried to China, where they were traded for East Asian goods.

The Oregon Country prompted some of the dreamiest dreamers in American history. John Quincy Adams, in his various roles as delegate to the negotiations that ended the War of 1812, secretary of state under President James Monroe, ambassador to Russia, and president himself, considered the acquisition of a chunk of the Pacific Northwest for the United States his special mission. "Our proper dominion," he confided in his diary, is "the continent of North America. . . . The United States and North America are identical." He threatened the British with a Russian-American alliance and managed to get them to accept the forty-ninth parallel from the Great Lakes to the Rocky Mountains as the Canadian-American border. The British refused to concede the Columbia River—most of which runs south of 49 degrees latitude—but they agreed to leave the Oregon Country "free and open" to subjects of both countries for ten years.[16]

The British underestimated the loopy enthusiasm that this open competition would inspire. One of the more deeply cracked pots was Hall Jackson Kelley, an eccentric from New England. Roused by the reports of Lewis and Clark, Kelley spewed letters, speeches, and pamphlets in the 1820s proclaiming Oregon "the most valuable of all the unoccupied parts of the earth." In 1832 he organized the "Oregon Colonization Society," a group that talked more than it colonized. Kelley's efforts, however, inspired another dreamer, Nathaniel Wyeth, a Cambridge entrepreneur in the ice business. Wyeth possessed the capacity to act as well as pontificate. From 1832 to 1836, Wyeth sought to lock up the trade in furs and fish along the Columbia River, twice journeying overland to the Oregon Country. But the supply ships he sent around Cape Horn failed to reach him in time, and Wyeth's company collapsed. Still, despite their failure to establish a presence in the Pacific Northwest, through Kelley and Wyeth the Americans accumulated a reserve of bombast. What they lacked in accomplishments, they made up for with their output of propaganda.[17]

Kelley fancied planting a New England–style "city upon a hill" along the Columbia while Wyeth imagined a capitalist empire built on fur and fish. The Reverend Jason Lee contributed another type of hallucination to the American backlog of Oregon dreams. In 1834, in response to a perceived call for missionaries by native people in the region, the Methodists sent a small company led by Lee overland to Oregon with Wyeth's expedition. Unlike Wyeth, Lee built a permanent outpost. Once it was established, however, he quickly forgot about the Indians, ministering instead to a community of retired trappers and their native wives. Lee pioneered the mode of operating for many Protestant missionaries in Oregon who came for the Indians but stayed to service white settlers.

Not to be outdone, the Congregationalists and Presbyterians made plans to send their own missionaries. They selected Marcus Whitman, a young, single medical doctor from western New York. The board frowned on bachelor missionaries—worried, perhaps, that they would succumb to the multicultural world of the fur trade and take up with native women—and so when an associate told Whitman

MASSACRE OF REV. DR. WHITMAN OF THE PRESBYTERIAN MISSION.

Cayuse Indians attack the Whitman mission, 1847. From Francis Fuller Victor, River of the West *(Hartford, Conn., 1870).*

of a young woman in a nearby town whose application for missionary work had been denied because she was unmarried, Whitman hurried there. In a quick weekend courtship, Whitman and Narcissa Prentiss agreed to enter missionary work together. "There was no pretense about romantic love," writes Narcissa's biographer, Julie Roy Jeffrey. "Both saw the marriage as a means of fulfilling their cherished dreams." In 1836 the newlyweds joined Henry and Eliza Spalding, another missionary couple, in the first overland migration of American families to Oregon.[18]

Their marital ties as well as their religious zeal severely challenged the couples. They had formed their family relationships before entering the West, and they expected the Indians to follow their orders. Neither the Spaldings nor the Whitmans succeeded in bridging the many divides that separated them from their targets of conversion. A lack of sympathy separated the Protestants from their potential flock. The local Cayuse people staunchly defended their customs, and the Whitmans saw them as "insolent, proud, domineering, arrogant, and ferocious," in Narcissa's words. "The Dr. and his wife were very severe and hard," the Indians told an interpreter, "which occasioned frequent quarrels." Meanwhile Catholic missionaries in the region, led by the Jesuit Pierre-Jean De Smet, were enjoying more success, precisely because of their skill at crossing cultural boundaries.[19]

Having baptized no more than twenty Indians during their sojourn in the Oregon Country, the Whitmans turned their attention to groups of American settlers who began to appear in the area. "It does not concern me so much what is to become of any particular set of Indians," Marcus wrote to Narcissa's parents. "I have no doubt our greatest work is to be to aid the white settlement of this country." He went east and promoted Oregon as the land of milk and honey for invaders. In 1843 he returned with more than a thousand immigrants bound for Oregon.[20]

The Americans brought hopes and dreams and pathogens. An epidemic decimated the Cayuse in 1847, and the survivors turned on the missionaries who had vexed them for years. On a cold November morning in 1847, with the ghosts of their dead children behind them, Cayuse men broke into the Whitman cabin and murdered Marcus, Narcissa, and ten others.

The Whitman massacre capped a series of missteps and delusions that accompanied the Louisiana Purchase. From Pike and Long to Astor and Kelley to Wyeth and the Whitmans, the Americans stumbled in the West. The place offered geographic, political, and social puzzles few could solve. Their ineptness contrasted sharply with the nimble dealings of virtuosos like John McLoughlin. Put in charge of the HBC's Columbia River Department in 1824, McLoughlin cultivated ties with the Chinooks and the Salishes, salmon fishing tribes who controlled trade along the river. Two daughters of the Chinook chief Concomely married traders under McLoughlin, and he maintained good relations with key native groups near the Columbia and his forts by offering gifts and hospitality and by mediating disputes between Indians and whites. As historian Anne F. Hyde explains, the Columbia region was never a "frontier" for either the British or the Indians but rather "a fully formed system of Canadian trade and culture dropped into another fully formed system of Chinook or Salish trade and culture."[21]

Ignorance defined the Americans' frontier. Still, they flailed with great fanfare. The United States underwent what some historians call a "communications revolution" in the early years of its western expansion. The authors of this outpouring of print tried to distinguish their novels from European competitors, and they looked west for distinctly American characters and storylines. The novelist James Fenimore Cooper led the way with his Boone-like hunter who went by Hawkeye or Deerslayer or Leatherstocking. Despite being the most memorable character in the series of five novels known as the Leatherstocking Tales, Hawkeye was never Cooper's intended hero. The novels' cultivated people, the ladies and gents swooning about and military officers stiffening their upper lips, were supposed to be the stars. But Hawkeye and his Indian mates stole the show.

The two groups of characters, however, enabled Cooper to stage a conflict between civilized restraint and natural freedom. The case for civilization was voiced by esteemed characters like Judge Marmaduke Temple in *The Pioneers* (1823), a visionary town builder modeled on Cooper's own father, the founder of Cooperstown, New York. Temple advocates progress and development: "Where others saw nothing but a wilderness," he now sees "towns, manufactures, bridges, canals, mines, and all the other resources of an old country." Cooper cheered the vision of his nation marching across the continent, yet he also acknowledged the costs of civilization. "The garden of the Lord was the forest," declares Leatherstocking, and was not patterned "after the miserable fashions of our times, thereby giving the lie to what the world calls its civilizing." Francis Parkman, the nineteenth-century historian of the frontier, summarized Cooper's message: "Civilization has a destroying as well as a creating power" and "must eventually sweep before it a class of men, its own precursors and pioneers, so remarkable both in their virtues and their faults that few will see their extinction without regret. Of all these men Leatherstocking is the representative." The printing presses that stoked the communications revolution churned out plays, romances, almanacs, autobiographies, and dime novels that reproduced the frontier hero, the natural nobleman, who led the country west only to be steamrolled by it.[22]

Over the nineteenth century, Leatherstocking was joined by hunters, gunslingers, outlaws, and good badmen and women, characters like Davy Crockett, Seth Jones, Nimrod Wildfire, Kit Carson, Jim Bowie, Jesse James, Deadwood Dick, and Calamity Jane. All appeared in dime novels, cheap paperbacks with sensational themes that began appearing in the 1830s and 1840s. The publishing house of Beadle and Adams issued more than three thousand titles, more than two-thirds of them set in the West. Dime novel characters, some more real than others, shared a common predicament. They thrived on the wild frontier, but they could not abide civilization. The qualities that made them exciting—their freedom, their nonconformity, their penchant for theft and violence—doomed them to extinction. Reading audiences loved these characters because they performed the heavy and sometimes distasteful labor of frontier demolition and then exited the stage at the appropriate moment. In stories, they did not linger to become troublesome neighbors, disreputable colleagues, or embarrassing family members.

The vein of goofiness that ran through western fiction makes all this myth-spinning seem a sideshow to the main drama of western history, which involved real people engaged in substantive activities like overland migration, military operations, and real estate development. How seriously can you take a genre that included a leading man named Deadwood Dick? These stories mattered, though, because they connected a booming and mobile nation with racist inclinations, capitalist ambitions, and a democratic government that could not and would not control its rambling citizens to a region few of these migrants understood and none of them commanded. In the first three decades of the nineteenth century, the Americans gathered territory through purchase, diplomatic negotiation, and political rebellion. But they often misjudged or willfully ignored the political arrangements, family ties, and economic partnerships based in horse trading,

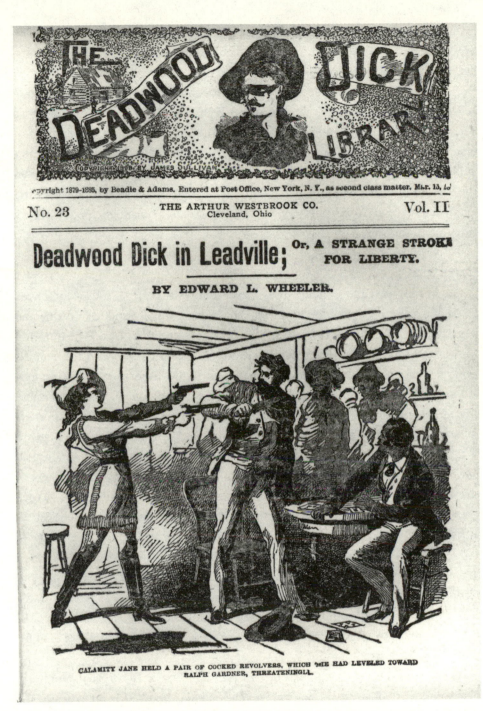

CALAMITY JANE HELD A PAIR OF COCKED REVOLVERS, WHICH SHE HAD LEVELED TOWARD RALPH GARDNER, THREATENINGLY.

Calamity Jane, the first dime novel heroine. From Edward L. Wheeler, Deadwood Dick in Leadville *(Cleveland, 1908). Beinecke Rare Book and Manuscript Library, Yale University.*

bison hunting, captive exchange, and fur profits that governed these places. The West was not new, not wild, not free, and not real to many Americans. Popular culture—paintings, novels, newspaper articles, and memoirs—filled the gaps in their knowledge; it turned the West into a comprehendible and conquerable space. Americans imagined a region filled with aborigines and Daniel Boones. The two groups of romantic wildings would succumb to the inevitable flood of civilization, opening the way for American possession. The consumers of popular culture imbibed in westerns that guaranteed a success certain only to them. To win the West, the United States would have to take it, and this colonial endeavor dirtied the hands of all Americans, not just the semifictional ones clenching Kentucky rifles or six-shooters.

Saint Louis served as an international pivot point between the Indian-dominated Great Plains and Rocky Mountains and the Americans' frontier of dreams and blank spaces. A small French hamlet near the convergence of the Missouri and Mississippi Rivers, Saint Louis became United States territory with the acquisition of Louisiana. The Chouteaus, a prominent family among the town's founders in 1764, handled much of the city's commerce. Led by the widowed matriarch Marie Thèrese, the Chouteaus made a fortune in the Missouri valley Indian trade during the period of Spanish sovereignty. With the coming of the Americans in 1804, Marie's sons, René Auguste and Jean Pierre Chouteau, quickly established connections with the new regime, securing positions as agents and officers of the territory. Jefferson even appointed Auguste Pierre Chouteau, one of Marie's grandsons, to West Point. The Chouteaus' network of personal and political relationships stretched from halls of power in Washington, D.C., to the cabins of influence in Indian Country. The main source of Chouteau influence—the reason why Jefferson paid the family any mind—was their alliance through marriage and trade with the powerful Osage nation. The Osages commanded the gateway to the plains through their dominion over the lower Arkansas River valley. They dictated the terms of trade, and the Chouteaus' wealth derived from the family's talent for meeting these terms.

The Arkansas River led to the southern plains and the massive bison and horse herds that thrived on the region's grass. The valley connected Saint Louis to the Comanches and their allies as well as markets in New Mexico, some sanctioned by the Spanish, most not. The United States government granted the Chouteaus an exclusive trading license with the Osage and made Jean Pierre its Indian agent west of the Mississippi. This gave the Chouteaus a stranglehold on the Arkansas, forcing their competitors to look elsewhere for furs. The Missouri River offered one such opportunity. That river connected to the northern Rocky Mountains and a beaver population that grew thick, musky pelts at the high, cold altitudes.

The first Saint Louisan to exploit the rich beaver grounds of the upper Missouri was one of the Chouteaus' local rivals, Manuel Lisa. Half French, half Spanish, and half grinning alligator, Lisa had moved up the river from New Orleans as a boy of eighteen looking for his main chance. Lewis and Clark's return gave him that opening. He hired John Colter, a hunter and scout from the Corps of Discovery, to lead his trappers into the mountains. On this expedition Colter became the first American to explore the Yellowstone River country. In 1808, in partnership with other Saint Louis traders, including the Chouteaus, Lisa organized the Missouri Fur Company. It proved a very profitable operation. One happy season Lisa made thirty-five thousand dollars, this in an age when a successful merchant might clear a thousand dollars a year.

The fur trade, however, was as mercurial as Lisa's personality. During the War of 1812, the Indians of the northern plains, allied with the Canadian traders, drove the Americans back down the Missouri, ending their dream as effectively as the British had Astor's. A decade of serious depression in fur prices followed. (The beaver trade was a fashion venture. Prices rose and fell according to the whims of hat-wearers in the eastern United States and Europe.) Demand for beaver did not rebound until the early 1820s. The price bump coincided with a loosening of the federal government's trade policy with Indians. The Missouri looked open for business, and Saint Louis entrepreneurs hustled to form companies and send employees into the brink.

William Ashley partnered with Andrew Henry to found the Rocky Mountain Fur Company. Henry had trapped the upper Missouri before, while Ashley brought capital and connections to the operation. A respected Saint Louis gentleman, he was a brigadier general in the militia and the lieutenant governor of the new state. In 1822 Ashley placed an advertisement in a Saint Louis newspaper recruiting one hundred "enterprising young men" for the mountains. The fur trade would make Ashley rich, but not without an alarming physical toll taken on the enterprising young men. The Missouri fulfilled some investors' wildest dreams, but it exposed their employees to a workplace nightmare.

Unlike the Chouteaus, who married into prominent Osage families, and Manual Lisa, who took care to bring gifts to his Indian trading partners, Ashley attempted to circumvent the interpersonal relationships that drove the exchange of furs. He hired his own hunters, supplied them with food and traps, and escorted them up the Missouri River in the style of a military expedition. Whether he realized it or not, he cut out the Indian middlemen and alienated many would-be allies who considered gifts signs of friendship. Ashley's men paid for their boss's business

Fur traders in camp. Painting by Alfred Jacob Miller. Beinecke Rare Book and Manuscript Library, Yale University.

strategy. In 1823 Ashley's second expedition was attacked by the Arikara Indians, a group living in a village along the Missouri who resented the Americans' attempt to sail around them to reach the beavers. The Arikaras killed fifteen men and, despite a punitive military campaign later that year, succeeded in keeping the river route closed for years.

The violence prompted innovation. Ashley strayed from the long tradition of waterborne transportation in the fur trade. He ditched the canoes and keelboats and sent his men directly overland to the mountains. His mounted brigades wintered in their own mountain camps, doing their own trapping. Rather than investing in fixed posts like the Hudson's Bay Company, Ashley gathered furs and resupplied the hunters at an annual summer rendezvous. General Ashley slowly weaned himself from the West. He traveled with the supply caravans several times and explored the headwaters of the Colorado River. Experience taught him, however, that severing relationships brought more money than sustaining them. First he let trusted lieutenants like Jedediah Smith oversee the transportation of trade items and beaver pelts, and then he sold the Rocky Mountain Fur Company outright to his former employees. Ashley continued to negotiate supplies for fur traders, but he let them shoulder the labor and the risks.

The rendezvous system functioned for fifteen years, until falling prices and overhunted beaver populations crippled the Rocky Mountain fur trade. By 1840 the vibrant era of the mountain man was over. The attention of traders and hunters shifted to bison robes and establishing commercial ties with the powerful Plains Indian nations or the newly independent Mexican territories. Though brief, the American beaver harvest was notable for the wealth it generated—Ashley brought home furs worth nearly fifty thousand dollars in 1825—and the rules it broke. In the northern Rockies for a short time, the Americans bypassed many of the customs of the fur trade. Their leaders cut ties and ran from obligations instead of fostering alliances and entering families. Unlike the Chouteaus or John McLoughlin, William Ashley never married an Indian woman, and he retired to Saint Louis as soon as he could. He preferred the cash nexus to interpersonal bonds. He financed and organized the delivery of commodities and let others deal with the human element of the trade.

The successes and strategies of another Saint Louis trading family demonstrate the peculiarity of Ashley and his rendezvous. In 1832 brothers Charles and William Bent brought back 131 packs of beaver pelts from the southern Rocky Mountains, furs that typically went to New Mexico. The Bents established a foothold—and an actual fort—along the upper Arkansas River through careful diplomacy and marriage choices. In 1838 William wed Owl Woman, daughter of a prominent Cheyenne leader. They had four children. The kids had American and Indian names and received formal educations in Saint Louis as well as equally rigorous courses of instruction from their Cheyenne relatives. Schooled in European manners, Indian customs, and trading-post culture, the Bent family secured the fort and sizable profits by blending in with their social surroundings. They inhabited a border world between nations. Their alliance with the Cheyennes—new arrivals to the plains themselves—gave the Bents an opening to the bison-hunting economy, but their marriage and acculturation choices, even more than the adobe walls they built, cemented their place at the crossroads among Saint Louis, New Mexico, and the northern grasslands. Goods moved through this region because multicultural families like the Bents possessed the social relationships to carry them.

The fur trade brought people together on the frontier, creating new living and loving arrangements that proved beyond a doubt that human interactions came in subtler hues than black and white in the West. What capitalism creates, however, it can also destroy, and the fur trade came with ecological cliffs and political tipping-points that unraveled the ties built across cultures. The Rocky Mountain fur trade collapsed for want of beaver pelts. The dam-building mammals entered the 1840s toeing the edge of extinction, and European hatmakers switched to Asian silk to cover their stovepipes and bowlers. The bison herds came under increased hunting pressure as well. As more groups—like the Cheyennes and Arapahos—moved onto the grasslands to participate in equestrian nomadism, competition for bison increased. Indian nations fought each other to preserve their hunting grounds, to protect their horses, and to safeguard their families.

The Comanches tangled with upstarts constantly. Their burgeoning horse herds and bevy of hide-scraping wives and daughters drew raiders across the grasslands. As the nineteenth century wore on, the Comanches learned that wealth brought power and headaches. Eventually, the Comanches' vast horse herds transformed their economy. Instead of mounted bison hunters, they became pastoralists—horse growers who hunted bison on the side. By the time the Americans showed up along the Arkansas River valley and in Texas, the Comanches had ventured into an environmental vice. Their herds overshot the food supply. Feeding the animals through rough winters and lengthy droughts became especially difficult. Historically, the Comanches displayed a spectacular knack for innovation. In the seventeenth century, they moved from the mountains to the plains to take advantage of the escaped Spanish horses known as barbs. Adapting to the perils of abundance proved harder than alterations undertaken to escape poverty. The Comanches declined to a soundtrack of horse teeth ripping their environment to shreds, and their predicament helps explain the subsequent success of the United States' territorial expansion. The great power on the southern plains was reeling before the Yankees got there.

———

The Comanches' struggles created a void that the Americans filled with a surging population. Through the Republic's first seventy-five years, the population of the United States doubled every twenty years, just as Benjamin Franklin had predicted in the mid-eighteenth century. Neither Mexico nor Canada experienced such spikes, and epidemic diseases followed the fur trade, severely damaging western Indian populations. Mexican authorities prodded their people to move to the northern borderlands. The settlement strategy worked pretty well in New Mexico, which benefited from cordial relations with the Comanche, but failed in Texas, where colonists and Comanches fought. The Hudson's Bay Company succeeded in establishing fur posts flung like distant stars across the map of the Far West, but there was no great movement into western Canada before the late nineteenth century. All the while American settlers were pushing their wagons and cattle westward. By 1840 eight new states had formed in trans-Appalachia (Kentucky, 1792; Tennessee, 1796; Ohio, 1803; Indiana, 1816; Mississippi, 1817; Illinois, 1818; Alabama, 1819; Michigan, 1837), with three more carved from the Louisiana Purchase (Louisiana, 1812; Missouri, 1821; Arkansas, 1836). The first federal census in 1790 counted fewer than a hundred thousand Americans west of the Appalachians. Fifty years later, there were more than seven million, better than 40 percent of the nation's population.

Stephen F. Austin. Engraving by an unknown artist, 1836. Author's collection.

The Americans put more boots, bonnets, and hooves on the ground than their rivals. But the hardy pioneers needed government assistance. The federal government of the United States provided exploration intelligence—maps, written reports, and watercolors—but not much else, at least early on. The Spanish government in Mexico City offered more. A political struggle between royalists and rebels seeking Mexican independence had left Texas vulnerable to unsanctioned American expansionists known as filibusters—a word derived from "freebooter," land pirates, basically. In 1813 a filibuster army took San Antonio by storm before being routed by a royalist army whose commander executed three hundred Tejanos (Spanish-speaking Texans) for collaboration, leaving San Antonio in ruins. In 1819 an expedition of American mercenaries took over the east Texas town of Nacogdoches and held it for several months before Spanish forces chased them out. All the fighting and upheaval cut the population of Texas in half by 1820.

Spanish authorities knew that it was only a matter of time before the province would fall victim to American aggression. Unable to attract migration from central Mexico, they opened negotiations with a Connecticut Yankee turned Missouri lead mine owner named Moses Austin. After a visit to Texas in 1820, Austin applied for a large land grant on which he hoped to settle three hundred American families. Turning to Americans to protect from Americans might sound daft, but Austin convinced the authorities that he would bring Americans of a different sort, ones willing to acknowledge Spanish authority and possibly convert to Catholicism. The Spanish placed their bet. In 1821 they approved Austin's plan, granting him two hundred thousand acres of rich Texas soil.

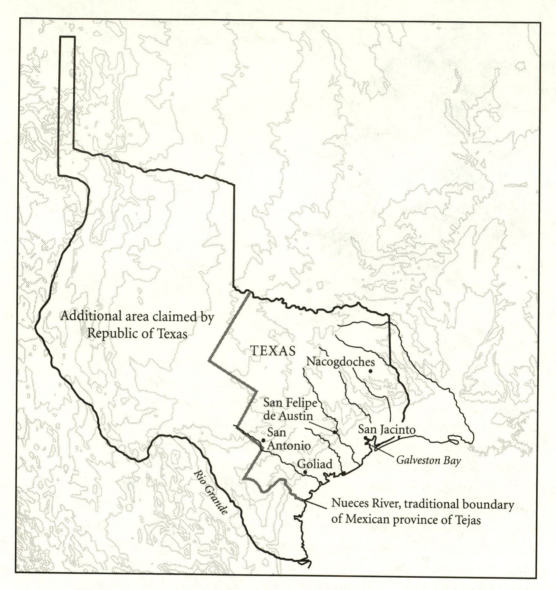

Additional area claimed by
Republic of Texas

TEXAS

Nacogdoches

San Felipe
de Austin

San
Antonio

San Jacinto

Goliad

Galveston Bay

Rio Grande

Nueces River, traditional boundary
of Mexican province of Tejas

TEXAS

On his trip home, Austin fell ill with pneumonia and died, leaving instructions for his son to carry on the Texas enterprise. Stephen F. Austin was a hell-raiser in his youth, if you—like his father—consider a love of dancing and music devilish. Educated in Connecticut, Austin matured into a respected Missouri legislator and circuit judge. He never wed, marking him as an oddity in a region built on extended family. Later, he claimed that Texas was his bride.

By the time the younger Austin arrived to settle his claim, his bride had a new parent. The newly independent government of Mexico confirmed the generous Spanish grant. Austin's lands, some of the richest alluvial soils in the West, stretched along the bottoms of the Colorado and Brazos Rivers down to the Gulf coast. He recruited cotton planters, who came with their slaves. But given the opportunity to receive not only 177 acres of farmland but an additional 4,428 acres for grazing, it is not surprising that most of the colonists declared themselves both farmers and stock raisers. The cotton that flourished in the soil and the cattle that fattened on the range soon became major exports, almost all going to the port of New Orleans.

The Mexican government made three more grants to Austin, allowing him to colonize an additional nine hundred American families. He was one of many empresarios, land speculators given authority to settle families in exchange for awards of thousands of acres for themselves. Austin carefully monitored his land and his families; other empresarios let in American drifters to squat on the best land they could find. Unpredictable as the flooded delta channels of the Mississippi and as irksome as its bars and snags, these squatters were the frontier types—the bad Americans—that Austin excluded from his own "family." By 1823 at least three thousand squatters had joined Austin's fifteen hundred in east Texas. The Texians, as the Americans called themselves, were rapidly outnumbering the Tejanos, concentrated in the southern half of the province.

————

No government promised fiefdoms to the Americans who ventured to Oregon. Propagandists like Hall Jackson Kelley had been working since the 1820s to spur migration to the Pacific Northwest. The Whitmans sought converts and found death in the region. It took a financial panic and an investment by the federal government to start an overland migration. During the mid-1830s, a mania for land speculation caused the disappearance of the last of the public domain lands in the trans-Appalachian West. Soon thereafter the Panic of 1837 inaugurated a prolonged depression. The wholesale price index of farm products fell to the lowest level in American history, prompting many midwestern farmers to wonder whether they would be better off elsewhere. A hatred of slavery kept many from considering Texas, while others believed that the West beyond the Missouri was a desert, fit only for nomads, buffalo hunters, and displaced Indians from the East.

Farmers had plenty of good reasons not to move west. Most of them grew corn and pigs, neither of which thrived in the poorly watered, shadeless expanses that took up huge swaths of the West. But what did they know? They based their decisions on words, maps, and etchings. People heard speeches by Jason Lee and Marcus Whitman or read about them in local newspapers. Others consumed Kelley's pamphlets or perused the accounts of wildcat emigrants who headed west via the Platte River trail blazed by the fur companies in 1841 and 1842. Suddenly hundreds of people throughout the West came down with a new kind of ailment

VIEW DECENDING THE GRAND ROUND   FOOT OF THE BLUE MOUNTAIN.

Emigrant wagons in the Blue Mountains of Oregon. From Major Osborne Cross, A Report
. . . of the March of the Regiment of Mounted Riflemen to Oregon . . . *(Washington, D.C.,
1850). Beinecke Rare Book and Manuscript Library, Yale University.*

communicable through print culture. "The Oregon fever has broke out," wrote
an observer in early 1843, "and is now raging like any other contagion." Oregon
fever was an expression of hope given a boost by the communications revolution
that began connecting the geographically diverse United States in fits and starts
beginning in the 1820s. Print culture infiltrated American society and Americans
moved west at the same time. A booming population met an excess of bombast,
and the volatile combination scattered Americans across the continent from Oregon to Texas. One emigrant from Missouri later recalled hearing the recruiting
speech of Peter H. Burnett, an organizer of the Great Migration of 1843. He stood
on a box and pumped up the crowd. Oregon was a land with soil so rich that a
farmer could raise huge crops of wheat with little effort and with a climate so mild
that livestock fed themselves all winter. "And they do say, gentleman, they do
say," Burnett concluded with a wink, "that out in Oregon pigs are running about
under the great acorn trees, round and fat, and already cooked, with knives and
forks sticking in them so that you can cut off a slice whenever you are hungry."
This indeed was an American paradise, a sylvan wonderland filled with a variety
of hams.[23]

Boosters had told similar tales about Kentucky, Missouri, and Texas. But Oregon was farther—much farther. Emigrants counted off the two thousand miles

of the Overland Trail to Oregon at the rate of just twelve to fifteen miles per day, the speed of oxen and wagons. They departed in spring, as soon as the grass was high enough for stock to graze, and prayed they would make it over the far western mountains before the first winter storms. They spent May and June crossing the Great Plains, following the Platte River to Fort Laramie, a lingering landmark of the fur trade. Heading up the Sweetwater River, they traveled over the broad saddle in the Rockies known as South Pass, then followed timber and water over rough terrain to Fort Hall, which they reached in early August. At that point they had traveled two-thirds of the distance, but their journey was only about half completed. It was here that they began to discover the heart-breaking truth about the Oregon Trail: the closer the destination, the tougher and slower the going. The next two weeks they spent clinging to the torturous cliff ledges of the Snake River leading to the dreaded Blue Mountains, which they could surmount only with the aid of ropes, pulleys, and quickly made winches. Finally, if all went well, they reached the Columbia River in early October and ferried the final hundred miles downriver to the mouth of the Willamette River, their destination.

Getting to Oregon was hard, and the Willamette River valley, which would eventually produce an agricultural bounty, did not spontaneously erupt with loaves and piglets. Early immigrants leaned on the hospitality of John McLoughlin and the Hudson's Bay Company at Fort Vancouver to survive. McLoughlin suffered the interlopers. He had already tried to stop the American onslaught by sending out hunting parties to denude the Columbia watershed of beavers, putting a "fur desert" between his satellite posts and the Saint Louis companies. But conscience wouldn't let him watch the bedraggled immigrants starve, and he spied a business opening he might exploit. The Americans would need the manufactures—cloth, tools, and bullets—that only he could supply. He could fill his forts' larders with their produce and turn a profit for the company. The gambit worked for a few years until the farming population grew numerous and politically bold and their trade and communication linkages to the United States strengthened. The newcomers established a provisional government in 1843, and in 1846 the Oregon Treaty ended the "joint occupation" and settled the boundary between the United States and Canada at the forty-ninth parallel. McLoughlin resigned from the HBC to run a store and oversee his property in the Willamette valley.

The transition from the fur trade society based in family ties to an agricultural democracy dominated by commercial relationships did not proceed smoothly for the man the Oregon state legislature proclaimed "the Father of Oregon" in 1957 for the assistance he offered early settlers. In 1848 his firstborn son and heir died (another son was murdered under suspicious circumstances years before), and then the Oregon territorial government stripped him of a profitable parcel of land near Willamette Falls granted him by the British. McLoughlin watched an American town, Oregon City, overspread the fur post landscape he worked so hard to build. Through his store and other business ventures, he scrambled to find purchase in this new West, but his multicultural family and the trade-through-social-bonds ethos they represented were unraveling by the time of his death in 1857.

That same year, the Oregon Constitution, echoing older territorial laws, forbade free blacks from migrating to the state. The measure was an attempt "to keep" the region "clear" of the race tensions that were plaguing the rest of the nation. But Oregon was and continued to be a multicultural and multiracial place. It was never "white," which gave the provision to keep it so more irony than veracity. The fur trade mingled people in ways that later Oregonians found discomforting. They banished this past in their laws and in their history books, making the dominance of their race seem monolithic and settled.

Wagonloads of misinformation propelled the Americans westward. The federal government supplemented booster pufferies and racial fantasies with maps and statistics. Congress created the Corps of Topographical Engineers in 1838, handing its oversight to the president and the secretary of war. The scientific orientation of the Topographical Engineers was clear; its officers belonged to organizations like the American Philosophical Society, and their ranks grew even more intellectually inclined with the founding of the Smithsonian Institution in Washington, D.C., in 1848. The Topographical Engineers cooperated closely with these and other eastern scientific groups to plan observations and collections in the West. Printed reports of the corps' expeditions typically included expensive illustrations and appendixes detailing the botany, zoology, geology, meteorology, ethnography, and cartography of the new land. But the agenda of the corps was also practical, for its pursuit of knowledge was in service of expansion across the continent.

No one better combined science and colonization, propaganda and practical information than John Charles Frémont. The dashing officer of the Topographical Engineers will end this chapter begun by the reluctant print icon Daniel Boone. If Frémont had a demure bone in his body, he amputated it early and buried it deep. An illegitimate child, he had an eye for opportunity that may have been related to his social insecurity. He took advantage of one friendship to get a naval appointment, which enabled him to master mathematics and engineering. With these scientific tools at his command, he caught his next golden ring in the courtship and marriage of Jessie Benton, daughter of Thomas Hart Benton, senator from Missouri and a powerful western voice in Washington. Benton's contacts were strung along the line of command, and he cried out for attention to the needs of the

John C. Frémont. Engraving by J. C. Buttre, 1856. Beinecke Rare Book and Manuscript Library, Yale University.

West—greater support for explorations and surveys, land developers, and rail-roads. Jessie inherited her father's outlook, energy, and iron will. She defied him and eloped when he opposed her marriage to the young, insubstantial Frémont. In time, daughter and father reconciled, and Benton became Frémont's patron.

Frémont's first assignments for the Topographical Engineers—which Benton secured—made him into one of the great celebrities of his day. From 1843 to 1844, he surveyed the Oregon Trail with a company made up mostly of métis voya-geurs, following a route carefully planned by Benton and President John Tyler. They wanted the expedition to appear strictly scientific, and science did provide an important motivation. The group certainly looked the part, bristling with deli-cate European equipment, including barometers, field telescopes, and chronom-eters. The engineers calculated innumerable latitudes, longitudes, and elevations and observed the emergence of the first satellite of Jupiter. They collected fos-sils from rocks, new plants (such as *Frémontia*), and hundreds of birds, fish, and mammals.

But Frémont's report—skillfully ghostwritten by his wife, Jessie Benton—was more than a scientific treatise. Attention to availability of water and fuel, grass and pasturage, and the ease of the grade all spoke to the needs of overland emigrants. He noted the Americans he saw on the trail and even reported renegade cows,

escapees from the wagon trains, grazing among the bison herds. These passages were calculated to portray a robust Oregon migration fully backed by the federal government. Senator Benton arranged for the printing and distribution, at government expense, of ten thousand copies of the report, including an excellent map of the trail produced by the "Great Pathfinder." In reality Frémont was guided by others. His expeditions included a number of Indian scouts and mountain men, including Kit Carson, who had spent twenty years trapping furs in the southern Rockies. Jessie Benton's narrative neglected the Indians but gave Carson ample time in the spotlight, and he soon became equally famous, the mid-nineteenth-century inheritor of Daniel Boone's mantle (Carson had, in fact, been raised in the home of a Boone descendant). It was a vivid demonstration of the combination of science, practicality, and popular culture that characterized the Topographical Engineers.

Frémont's report became a best seller among easterners as well as emigrants, exciting talk in New York drawing rooms and Missouri barns. Western writer Joaquin Miller later recalled reading the report as a boy. "I fancied I could see Frémont's men, flags in the air, Frémont at the head, waving his sword, his horse neighing wildly in the mountain wind, with unknown and unnamed empires on every hand."[24]

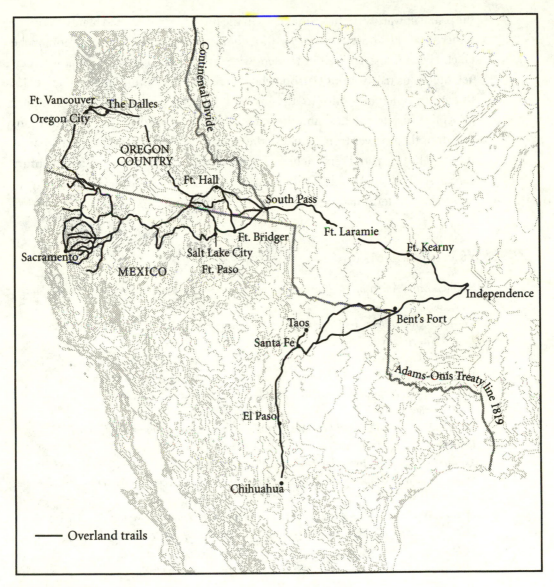

The following labels appear on the map: Ft. Vancouver, The Dalles, Oregon City, Continental Divide, OREGON COUNTRY, Ft. Hall, South Pass, Ft. Laramie, Ft. Bridger, Ft. Kearny, Salt Lake City, Ft. Paso, Sacramento, MEXICO, Independence, Taos, Bent's Fort, Santa Fé, Adams-Onís Treaty line 1819, El Paso, Chihuahua

— Overland trails

THE OVERLAND TRAILS

Thousands of Americans carried Frémont with them. He was the Pied Piper of their empire, and he represented the coming of a new power structure. For most of the eighteenth and nineteenth centuries, families had ruled the West through the ties that bound them. This was due in great part to the influence wielded by the Indian nations tapping into the reservoir of energy sunk in the grass of the Great Plains. Through their horses, the Comanches, the Sioux, the Osages, and the Cheyennes commanded the region and forced their European partners to trade according to their customs, including building alliances through marriage. One of the prime upwardly mobile romancers in the history of the United States, Frémont understood the strategic necessity of a good marriage as well as any Comanche chief. His star rose and fell in tandem with Jessie Benton and her senator father. Yet, unlike his trusty scout Carson, who married across cultures three times, twice to native women and once to a prominent Mexican woman in Taos, Frémont's knots tied him to the East and the federal government, cultures and institutions that drew their power from sources other than grass, horses, and interpersonal alliances. The true path Frémont blazed connected government bureaucrats, venture capitalists, and stockholders to western domains. These outsiders would play an increasingly determinate role in the future of the region.

FURTHER READING

Stephen Aron, *American Confluence: The Missouri Frontier from Borderland to Border State* (2009)

Jon T. Coleman, *Here Lies Hugh Glass: A Mountain Man, a Bear, and the Rise of the American Nation* (2012)

Joseph J. Ellis, *American Sphinx: The Character of Thomas Jefferson* (1996)

John Mack Faragher, *Daniel Boone: The Life and Legend of an American Pioneer* (1992)

Anne F. Hyde, *Empires, Nations, and Families: A New History of the North American West, 1800–1860* (2011)

Richard E. Oglesby, *Manuel Lisa and the Opening of the Missouri Fur Trade* (1963)

Jared Orsi, *Citizen Explorer: The Life of Zebulon Pike* (2014)

Thomas P. Slaughter, *Exploring Lewis and Clark: Reflections on Men and Wilderness* (2004)

Sylvia Van Kirk, *"Many Tender Ties": Women in Fur-Trade Society in Western Canada, 1670–1870* (1980)

David J. Weber, *The Taos Trappers: The Fur Trade in the Far Southwest, 1540–1846* (1971)

David J. Wishart, *The Fur Trade of the American West, 1807–40: A Geographical Synthesis* (1979)

6

War and Destiny

In 1845 a young congressman from Illinois redrew the map of North America on the floor of the House of Representatives. Constrained in stature but bursting with grandiosity, Stephen A. Douglas pronounced the United States too big for its borders. The time had arrived, he announced, "to blot out the lines on the map which now marked our national boundaries . . . and make the area of liberty as broad as the continent itself." His speech merged liberty and the American nation. Both seemed bent on expansion. Liberty was enveloping the globe, and the rebellious spirit of 1776 placed the United States at the leading edge of an antimonarchical wave that had engulfed France, Haiti, Mexico, and huge swaths of South America. Governments everywhere were breaking loose and starting anew. By the time Douglas verbalized this connection, many Americans had subscribed to the theory that their nation had reinvented the ancient human endeavor of territorial aggression. A new-style colonizer, the United States would break shackles as it gobbled up ground. It had become, in a phrase coined by Thomas Jefferson, an "empire of liberty."[1]

The empire of liberty was an unstable celebratory concoction, a homemade cherry bomb that boomed with grand intentions and exploded in its inventors' faces more often than not. The same communications revolution that delivered Frémont's report to households across the country also spread the idea, in the words of newspaper editor John L. O'Sullivan, of the nation's "manifest destiny to overspread the continent allotted by Providence for the free development of our yearly multiplying millions." Congressman Andrew Kennedy of Indiana put it in more prosaic language. "Go to the West," Kennedy declared, "and see a young man with his mate of eighteen, and [after] a lapse of thirty years, visit him again, and instead of two, you will find twenty-two. That is what I call the American multiplication table." What his math elided, of course, was the purposeful federal policy and ruthless military power required to conquer a continent. The American people did not acquire an empire simply by doing what came naturally. The ideology of "manifest destiny" masked the messy business of seizing, occupying, and ruling over foreign peoples and nations. It also attempted to submerge controversies that bitterly divided Americans over expansion.[2]

Manifest destiny was not, as is so often implied, a deeply held American folk belief. It was a self-conscious creation of propagandists like O'Sullivan, who used the megaphone of the penny press in an attempt to uncouple the politics of expansion from the growing sectional conflict over slavery. That dispute first threatened to split the country in 1820, when northern congressmen added the antislavery clause of the Northwest Ordinance to the bill elevating Missouri from a territory to a state. After fierce debate and shrill threats of disunion, Congress crafted a compromise, balancing Missouri's admission with statehood for Maine and agreeing that henceforth slavery would be "forever prohibited" in the territory of the Louisiana Purchase north of the 36 degree, 30 minute latitude line. American political orthodoxy proclaimed that the more ground the United States covered, the less divided the nation would become. But the West would prove more jackhammer than balm. Eventually, all the rattling that came with expansion would tear the country apart.

The West was never free from race, slavery, or a cornucopia of other ethnic, religious, and gender differences. Americans inherited a complex set of racial ideas, captivity arrangements, religious traditions, gender norms, and sexual orientations from the native and European frontiers that came before. The newcomers added their own patterns of difference to this crazy quilt of us-versus-thems. Difference animated conflicts over property, politics, and citizenship. Difference stimulated anger, hate, discrimination, and oppression. Difference ignited violence—riots, lynchings, and massacres. Yet the American West reveals a mixed legacy. Even in opposition—perhaps especially in opposition—humans forged a shared past. Odium and trauma linked entire populations, creating enduring, though at times extremely unhappy, bonds. We confront grim histories not only to recognize victims and expose injustices but to invite the past into the present in the off chance that we might transform tragic opposition into humane reconciliation. That's the hope, at least, that through the honest engagement with history, we can better understand the present.

⸻

The Americans perceived themselves as the harbingers of liberty. Yet slavery was the most expansive force in American life. That was something that no one had expected in the late eighteenth century at the nation's founding. The leaders of

Slaves being driven to the Mississippi frontier. From Wilson S. Armistead, A Tribute for the Negro *(New York, 1848).*

the Revolution—including prominent slave masters such as George Washington and Thomas Jefferson—believed that "the peculiar institution" was on its way to extinction. Instead it became the most important driver of economic growth. The production of upland cotton exploded with the invention of the cotton gin in the early 1790s, and during the first half of the nineteenth century, cotton accounted for more than half the value of the nation's exports. The manufacture of cotton cloth in England, Europe, and the northern United States inaugurated an industrial revolution, stimulated the growth of a proletarian working class, and generated enormous reserves of capital. Slavery was the beating heart of the American economic system, and it grew hand in hand with continental expansion.

Slaves produced cotton on land seized from Indians. Following the War of 1812, planters began colonizing the millions of acres ceded after Andrew Jackson's victory over the Creeks at Horseshoe Bend, Alabama, land that was perfect for cotton production. Soon planters were encroaching on the unceded lands of other southern Indian nations, including the Choctaws, Chickasaws, Cherokees, and Seminoles, whose combined population numbered between fifty and sixty thousand. Southern politicians pressed the federal government to force them all out, but both President James Monroe and his successor, President John Quincy Adams, refused. In 1828 Jackson, who grew cotton and drove slaves on his plantation estate near Nashville, defeated Adams and won the presidency on a platform of forcing all

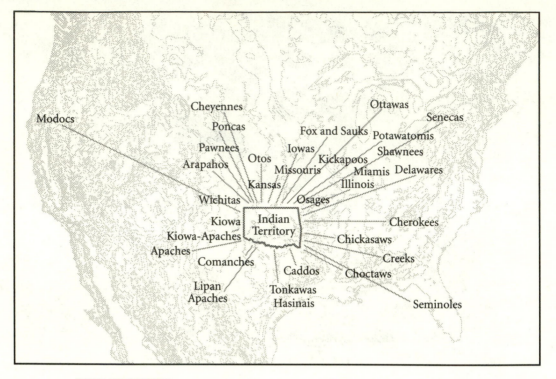

INDIAN REMOVAL

Indian people from the states and relocating them west of the Mississippi. In 1830 Congress followed Jackson's lead and passed the Indian Removal Act. Removal was to be voluntary, the president insisted, but in the context of the times, everyone understood that the law eliminated federal protection and exposed Indian nations to the aggression of the individual states.

Opponents of the Removal Act pointed out the "civilized" accomplishments of Indians like the Cherokees—their syllabary, their Christianity, and their slave-owning. If they could not be absorbed in the nation, then what Indians could? Jackson countered with a theory of history. "Those tribes can not exist surrounded by our settlements," he declared. "They have neither the intelligence, the industry, the moral habits, nor the desire of improvement which are essential to any favorable change in their condition. Established in the midst of another and a superior race, and without appreciating the causes of their inferiority or seeking to control them, they must necessarily yield to the force of circumstances and ere long disappear." In Jackson's twisted logic, he was doing the Cherokees a favor by shoving them out of the way of a runaway train. Federal commissioners, employing bluster, bullying, and bribery, pressured the Choctaws, Chickasaws, and Creeks into signing treaties of removal.[3]

The Cherokees, however, remained adamant in their opposition. They wrote a constitution, elected John Ross as their president, and brought suit in federal court against the infringement of their sovereignty by the state of Georgia. The case soon came before the Supreme Court. Chief Justice John Marshall, who wrote the majority opinion in *Cherokee Nation v. Georgia* (1831), tried to have it both ways. There could be no doubt, he declared, that the Cherokee Nation was "a distinct political society, separated from others, [and] capable of managing its own affairs and governing itself." But, Marshall continued, "it may well be doubted whether those tribes which reside within the United States can, with strict accuracy, be denominated foreign nations. They may, more correctly, perhaps be denominated *domestic dependent nations*." Because they were not completely "foreign" and only foreign nations could sue one of the states, Marshall threw out the Cherokees' suit. President Jackson cheered.

But the decision also bound the federal government to the Cherokees, and within months Georgia tested those obligations by passing an act regulating the presence of white people in Cherokee territory. When two missionaries to the Cherokees defied Georgia's authority over their movements, they were imprisoned, and one of them, Samuel Worcester, brought a federal suit against Georgia. Writing for the majority in *Worcester v. Georgia* (1832), Chief Justice Marshall concluded that the Cherokees constituted "a distinct community, occupying its own territory, with boundaries accurately described, in which the laws of Georgia can have no force, and which the citizens of Georgia have no right to enter." The Cherokees had won and their leaders rejoiced. But President Jackson had the last say. "The decision of the Supreme Court has fell still born," he declared, meaning that the government of the United States would do nothing to prevent Georgia from enforcing its rule over the Cherokees. The president was perfectly willing to violate the Constitution to cleanse as many Indians as possible from the East.[4]

Removal split the Cherokees. In 1835 a minority Treaty Party signed the Treaty of New Echota, which relinquished the Cherokee homeland in exchange for five million dollars and permanent lands on the Arkansas River, west of the Mississippi. Led by President John Ross, fifteen thousand Cherokees, nearly the entire population, signed a petition rejecting that treaty. The dispute reached national attention as the Senate debated the treaty's ratification. What opponents termed the "fraud upon the Cherokee people" passed by only one vote. In 1838 seven thousand troops under the command of General Winfield Scott rounded up the Cherokees who refused to leave Georgia and herded them into camps in preparation for their forced relocation. The federal government asserted its almighty power on the cheap. Underfunded and poorly organized, the ethnic cleansing operation proceeded

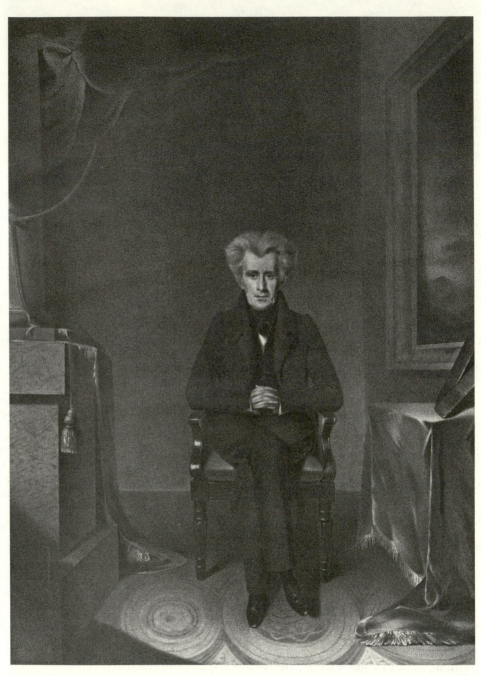

Andrew Jackson. Engraving from a painting by W. J. Hubbard, 1834. Library of Congress.

with little food and poor equipment. Many people suffered from malnutrition and dysentery. Hundreds, perhaps thousands, died of epidemic diseases. On what the Cherokees called the "Trail on Which We Cried," the Americans displayed just how far they would go to expel groups considered racially different and politically uncooperative. The forced removal of Indian peoples, former president John

Quincy Adams wrote in his private diary, was "among the heinous sins of this nation, for which I believe God will one day bring them to judgement—but as His own time and by His own means."[5]

Thousands of eastern Indians, in the North as well as the South, had successfully assimilated into the mainstream of nineteenth-century American society, flourishing in its deepest currents. They were landowners, farmers, stock raisers, and businesspeople as well as citizens of their own nations. Now white Americans pressed them to cede their lands in exchange for territory in the West. Many left and made the best of the situation with little protest; others resisted without resorting to bloodshed. The Winnebagos of Wisconsin, for example, simply drifted back to the former homes after an unpleasant stint in the arid West.

But removal also sparked wars. The Florida Seminoles battled federal troops attempting to remove them for years. Slave owners wanted the Seminoles out of Florida to prevent slaves from running away into their swampy homeland. Several chiefs signed a removal treaty in 1832, but the war leader Osceola represented the will of the majority who wanted to stay. Osceola inflicted a humiliating defeat on the Americans, and the war dragged on for years. By 1842 the majority of Seminoles had been harried west, though hundreds remained in the Everglades, where their descendants still reside. The United States declared an end to the Seminole War after spending twenty million dollars and the lives of more than fifteen hundred soldiers to dislodge some three thousand Indians from their land.

The Sauk and Fox people of Illinois fought a shorter, yet in some aspects nastier, war against the Americans. Again, several chiefs were bribed into signing a treaty ceding their lands east of the Mississippi and settling on reservations across the river. But a dissident leader named Black Hawk protested. "My reason teaches me that land cannot be sold," he declared. "The Great Spirit gave it to his children to live upon, and cultivate, as far as is necessary for their subsistence. Nothing can be sold but such things as can be carried away." In 1832 Black Hawk led two thousand followers back across the Mississippi into Illinois, panicking settlers. The state militia confronted the Indians. Black Hawk sent a delegation to parlay with the skittish volunteers, who promptly fired on the peacemakers. Black Hawk loosed his army and routed the Illinoisans. Then he and his people fled into Wisconsin, where the outraged militia cornered them. Many, including women and children, were slaughtered as they attempted to retreat back across the Mississippi.[6]

The American proponents of removal prettied-up their ethnic cleansing by trumpeting the magical powers of the Far West. Across the Mississippi, Indians

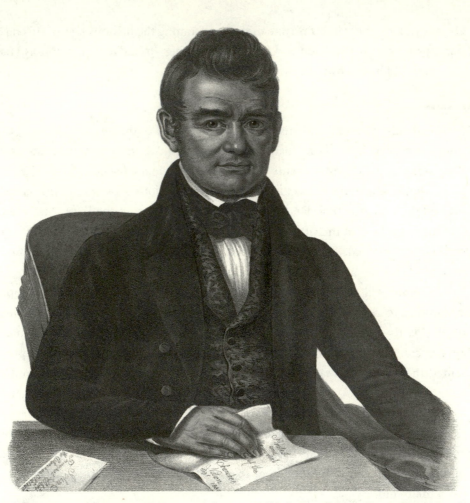

John Ross. From Thomas L. McKenney and James Hall, History of the Indian Tribes of North America . . . , *3 vols. (Philadelphia, 1836–44).*

would discover the ease and space either to disappear gracefully or to learn white ways. Politicians and reformers returned to this logic repeatedly. The West was the American time-out region, where problems were sent to stew and solve themselves. Want to alleviate poverty, banish religious nonconformists, abolish slavery or sustain it, bring the country together under the banner of territorial expansion? The West was the answer. Of course, this line of thinking ignored reality. Many Indians were early adopters of Christianity, market capitalism, and representative democracy, and the same bursting population in need of land and commercial opportunities that propelled Americans west insured that there would be no time out from colonization. Sooner than anyone thought, whites would arrive on the doorsteps of removed Indians, see the evidence of successfully transplanted communities with governments, schools, ranches, and even plantations with slaves, and demand once again that the "savages" hand over the "empty" land.

Planters on the frontier of the Old Southwest—the states of Tennessee, Alabama, Mississippi, and Louisiana, as well as the territory of Arkansas—were infamous for driving their slaves beyond the point of endurance, and slaves in the upper South trembled at the thought of being "sold down the river." Some of them came when their masters relocated, but most were brought in by slave traders. Chained together in long coffles, enslaved men, women, and children were driven hundreds of miles from the upper South to miserable encampments in the wilderness. Black workers cleared the pine forests, drained the swamps, plowed the ground, and then planted, chopped, and picked the cotton. "We require more slaves," settler William Dunbar wrote from the Mississippi frontier; "ordinary men are worth $500 cash, women $400 and upwards."[7]

Slavery lent its full measure to the violent character of frontier life. Samuel Townes was one of many southwestern masters who drove his slaves hard. Impatient that his black women were picking less than half the cotton of the men, he insisted that his overseer "make those bitches go to at least 100 [pounds per day] or whip them like the devil." The lashings, he later noted, improved their productivity. Combining the everyday violence of slavery with the unsettled social conditions of the frontier—large numbers of unattached men, excessive drinking, and endemic Indian-hating—produced a lethal brew. Visitors were horrified by the dueling, fistfighting, and brutal practical joking. These conditions, argues historian Joan E. Cashin, produced a frontier planter class obsessed with independence and inclined toward aggression, both in society and at home. Don't "hang around Mother and drivel away your life," Townes wrote to his younger brother in South Carolina. Come west, where "you can live like a fighting cock with us." Such men emerged as the dominant species in the Old Southwest.[8]

Townes encouraged his brother to relocate, but opportunities for men to rise in the cotton belt quickly grew slim. The Old Southwest was a society of great inequality, a land of "nabobs and nobodies." By the 1820s the nabobs—the elite class of planters—included some of the wealthiest men in America. More millionaires lived in the Natchez district of Mississippi, it was said, than anywhere else in the country, even New York City. But the vast majority of whites were nobodies—small, aspiring planters with a handful of slaves or hardscrabble farmers subsisting on the thin soils of the pine barrens or grazing cattle on the prairie grasses. The

Black Hawk and his lieutenants in chains. From George Catlin, Catalogue of Catlin's Indian Gallery of Portraits . . . *(New York, 1837).*

nabobs grew richer and gobbled up the farms of nobodies. Pushed out of one frontier, they searched for another. An army of nobodies pushed for Texas, including David Crockett of Tennessee, the most renowned ne'er-do-well in American history.[9]

———

In contrast to the United States, newly independent Mexico announced its intention to establish full social equality regardless of caste or color. "All the inhabitants of the country are citizens," declared the Plan of Iguala of 1821, "and the door of advancement is open to virtue and merit." Attracted by these ideals, a small number of free African Americans emigrated from the United States to the northern Mexican province during the 1820s. Samuel H. Hardin and his wife came, he wrote, because Mexico's laws "invited their emigration," and Virginian John Bird moved because he believed that he and his sons "would be received as citizens and entitled as such to land." Several free black heads of household were granted land by the Mexican government.[10]

But the number of free blacks was miniscule compared to the enslaved thousands who were brought by their masters. The arrival in Texas of the Americans— many with slaves—caused enormous concern in Mexico. But in 1824, when Mexican leaders declared their country a republic and adopted a federal constitution, they made no mention of slavery. Texas was joined with Coahuila, its southern neighbor, as one of the states. In 1827, after much debate, the legislature of Coahuila-Tejas adopted a law barring the further importation of slaves and promising the eventual emancipation of the children of existing slaves. There was momentary panic among slave owners, but with the support of leading Tejanos, the legislature passed a new law that allowed planters to import new slaves under the ruse of "contract labor." But in 1829 liberal Mexican president Vicente Guerrero proclaimed an end to slavery throughout Mexico. "It is not conceivable that a free Republic should subject some of its children to slavery," declared one legislator. "Let us leave such contradictions to the United States of North America." Intense lobbying by Austin and leading Tejanos persuaded President Guerrero to issue an exemption for Texas, thereby excluding the abolition order from the only part of Mexico where slavery was important.[11]

But antislavery forces remained powerful in Mexico City. In 1830 Mexican officials canceled all pending empresario contracts, banned further immigration from the United States, and authorized the occupation of Texas by the Mexican army. But Americans with their slaves kept pouring in from the Old Southwest, escalating tensions and adding yet more guns to the Texian cause, whatever that might be. For the crackdown had split the Texians into contending factions. Stephen Austin rallied the moderates in a Peace Party, arguing that Texas should remain part of the Mexican nation but with more autonomy, legalized slavery, and free trade with the United States. Leading Tejanos shared many of these sentiments. Indeed, marriage frequently sealed the alliance of Texians and Tejanos. Erastus "Deaf" Smith, one of the first Anglos to settle in San Antonio, married into the prominent Duran family, and James Bowie, a Louisianan best known for his knife, courted and married the daughter of the vice governor of the province, bringing him into close association with the most prominent Tejano families. Seeking Hispanic allies, Austin asked the *ayuntamiento,* or town council, of San Antonio, where Tejanos were in the majority, to issue a statement in support of his political program. But despite their sympathy for Austin's plan, the San Antonio Tejanos declined, fearful of the Anglo majority in the north of the province, where Texians outnumbered Tejanos seven to one.

That provided an opportunity for Austin's opponents, who organized themselves as the War Party, demanding immediate annexation by the United States. William Barret "Buck" Travis, a volatile and ambitious young lawyer from Mississippi, was ringleader of this group. Travis had come to Texas to escape creditors and a failed marriage, leaving his wife behind to nurse his infant son and fend off bill collectors. As he described in a letter, Texas gave him several comeback options. He might succeed, make a "splendid fortune," and recover his good name and influence. Or he might be killed by the Mexicans and leave a fond memory for his son, who could claim that his father "died for his country." In 1832 Travis and his fellow hotheads attacked the garrison in charge of collecting taxes in Galveston Bay. The moderates tried to distance themselves from the assault, sending Austin to Mexico City to plead their loyalty. But government officials arrested him, and Austin spent the next eighteen months in a windowless cell.[12]

Jail converted Austin to annexation, but leadership of the Texas revolution had already passed to the War Party. The leaders soon included two former Tennessee politicians. David Crockett came to resuscitate his political career after losing a congressional election. And Samuel Houston, whose Tennessee governorship came undone when his wife left him, came on the recommendation of his good friend President Andrew Jackson, who wanted Houston there as his informal agent. Brash, charming, and desperate, Crockett and Houston gambled their future and the lives of their followers on breaking Texas away from Mexico.

In October 1835, in response to the uprising at Galveston and revolts brewing in other provinces, Mexican president Antonio López de Santa Anna issued a decree abolishing all state legislatures and placing the central government directly in charge of local affairs. He then marched north with an army of several thousand, intent on crushing all opponents in his path. Santa Anna's dictatorship unified the moderates and the radicals, the Texians and the Tejanos, and together they took up arms. They besieged the town of San Antonio, forcing the Mexican troops stationed there to withdraw. Houston, placed in command of the rebel forces, withdrew to the east in the face of Santa Anna's advance, leaving behind a detachment under William Travis to hold the town. The defenders—including James Bowie and David Crockett—holed up behind the fortified walls of a ruined mission known as the Alamo.[13]

Travis ought to have retreated, given the Alamo's minimal strategic significance. Santa Anna could have ignored it, sweeping north after Houston's army. But the Alamo fight was not about making smart military choices; it was about defending honor and instilling obedience. Travis sent Tejano captain Juan Seguín to inform Houston that he intended to defend the Alamo to the last, and Santa Anna sent his main force against the fort to deliver his own message: that he would destroy the Alamo and kill every last man to demonstrate his might. The siege ended on March 6, 1836, in a ninety-minute assault that cost the lives of some 250 Texians and several hundred Mexican soldiers. Santa Anna had the bodies of the Alamo defenders burned so that there could be no memorial.

Yet no one forgot the Alamo. News of the defeat arrived at the little village of Washington-on-the-Brazos shortly after a meeting of Texian delegates on March 2 had declared Texas an independent republic. Over the next several weeks, the two sides traded atrocities. At Goliad, Santa Anna captured and executed 371 Texians. At San Jacinto, Texians revenged the Alamo and Goliad by slaughtering more than

"Crockett's Fight with the Mexicans." From Ben Hardin's Crockett Almanac, 1842 *(Boston, 1841). Beinecke Rare Book and Manuscript Library, Yale University.*

600 Mexicans. Captured after the battle, Santa Anna was forced to sign a treaty granting Texas its independence.

In its new constitution Texas legalized slavery and barred the residence of free persons of color. "I love the country, but now look at my situation," free black rancher Greenbury Logan, who owned a spread in the Austin colony, wrote in a petition to Texas authorities requesting permission to remain. "Every privilege dear to a free man is taken away." Texas independence made Tejanos equally leery. Anti-Tejano sentiments flourished among Texians after the war. Juan Seguín, the Alamo veteran and postwar mayor of San Antonio, was forced to flee with his family to Mexico. A group of Texians petitioned to disenfranchise Tejanos, declaring them to be "the friends of our enemies and the enemies of our friends." Texas achieved liberty from a tyrant, but race and ethnic divisions etched the borders of the Lone Star Republic, deciding who would stay, who would go, and who would enjoy the fruits of the wartime sacrifices of both Anglos and Tejanos.[14]

———

The West offered a mirage of an escape: a refuge for the Indians blocking the expanding empire of liberty, a place where nobodies might become nabobs. But bringing western territories into the union threatened to split the country apart rather than heal it. It is not hard to see why some Americans came to reject the theory that territorial expansion would diminish tensions created by territorial expansion.

Juan Seguín. Painting by Jefferson Wright, 1838. Texas State Library and Archives Commission.

The United States recognized the Republic of Texas on March 3, 1837. But the United States did not manifest its destiny by immediately incorporating the breakaway Mexican province into the union. Debate the year before over the admission of Arkansas as a slave state had once again seriously split northern and southern representatives, and politicians feared that the nation might not survive a battle over Texas. Former president John Quincy Adams had returned to Washington as a congressman from his home district in Massachusetts (the only ex-president to serve in elective office), and he led the fight against the admission of any more slave states. How tragic and disgraceful, Adams declared on the floor of the House of Representatives, that the noble Anglo-Saxon race had ceased to carry the burden of freedom and instead had carried slavery into a country where it had been legally abolished. Was there not land enough for slavery already? "Have you not Indians enough to expel from their fathers' sepulchres?" he asked sarcastically.[15]

Presidents Jackson and Martin Van Buren decided to steer clear of Texas annexation, believing that the preservation of their Democratic Party coalition across sectional lines required them to keep mum on slavery. The issue came up again during the term of President John Tyler, a slave owner and a fierce partisan of southern interests, who assumed office after the sudden death of William Henry Harrison in 1841. Tyler negotiated a treaty of annexation with the Texans but failed to win the necessary two-thirds majority in the Senate.

By the presidential campaign year of 1844, expansionists had become desperate to break the logjam. James K. Polk, Democrat from Tennessee, ran on an explicitly expansionist platform calling for the "reoccupation of Oregon and the reannexation of Texas at the earliest practicable period." Linking Texas and Oregon, the Democrats hoped to shift the focus from the expansion of slavery to expansion in general, implying with the curious "re-" prefix that their opponents were stifling Americans' providential right to overspread the continent. Adams and other opponents of new slave states smelled a rat. What Americans needed, they argued, was not more land but more *improvement*—meaning vigorous federal support for economic development—of the land they already had. No, countered the Democrats, more meant better. The federal government should acquire more land and open it to the regular farmers and their multiplying offspring.[16]

The election's outcome demonstrated just how divided Americans were on expansion and many other issues. With just 49.6 percent of the national vote, Polk became the second president to win office without a popular majority, although he carried fifteen of twenty-six states. Had Henry Clay, the Whig candidate, attracted five thousand additional ballots in New York—where a third antislavery party drained support—he would have won the electoral college. But the Democrats took these results and declared a mandate for national expansion. Though he was nominally a Whig, lame-duck President Tyler pressed Congress to admit Texas

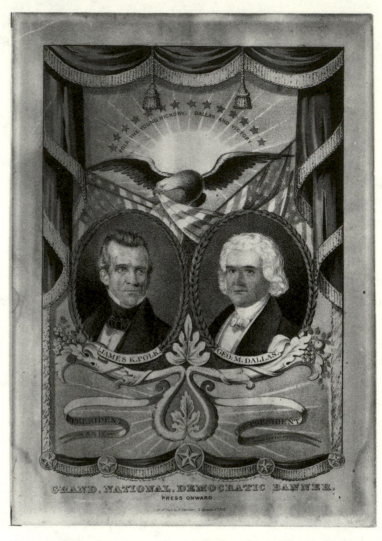

Campaign poster from the presidential election of 1844. Library of Congress.

through the device of a joint resolution, which required only a simple majority. Democrats pushed the measure through, presenting Polk with an accomplished fact when he assumed office in March 1845. The president offered the Texans admission, and by the end of the year the Lone Star had become one of twenty-eight on the flag of union.

Democrats moved next to the Oregon question. In his first annual message to Congress, Polk announced his intention to take all of the Pacific Northwest from the British, prior agreements and claims be damned. "Away, away, with all these cobweb tissues of rights of discovery, exploration, settlement, contiguity, etc.," thundered editor John L. O'Sullivan. But in private, Polk negotiated a treaty with Great Britain, dividing Oregon at the forty-ninth parallel. The Senate ratified the agreement in June 1846. By that time Polk desperately needed a peaceful resolution on the northern border, for he had provoked a full-scale war with Mexico on the southern one.[17]

As soon as Mexican officials heard of the American vote for annexation, they severed diplomatic relations, and both nations moved troops to the contested border region. Polk sent John Slidell of Louisiana on a secret mission to Mexico City with instructions to negotiate a settlement. Although the Mexican press was loud in its denunciation of Texas independence, Slidell found that in private officials were willing to accept annexation if the United States would agree to the old provincial boundary at the Nueces River. But Slidell, adhering to Polk's orders, insisted on a boundary along the more southerly Rio Grande. Mexican public opinion ran hotly against the Americans, which left the diplomats little room to maneuver, so instead of a fixed boundary, the vexed negotiators created a disputed region—the Nueces Strip—a hundred-mile swath along the left bank of the Rio Grande populated by Mexicans that reached from the Gulf to the Rocky Mountains. The talks broke off when Slidell pressed the leaders in Mexico City to sell the provinces of New Mexico and California. If they acceded to his terms, the Mexicans told him, the people would kill them. Slidell returned to Washington empty-handed and offered some advice that suggested why he had failed as a peacemaker: "We can never get along well with them until we have given them a good drubbing."[18]

Though fuming, the Mexicans had no plan to invade the United States to reclaim a province they had lost ten years before and over which the Comanches held the balance of power. Polk, however, was spoiling for a fight. He announced to his cabinet that the acquisition of California—with the fine Pacific ports of San Diego and San Francisco—was the prime goal of his presidency. He ordered General Zachary Taylor—a veteran of campaigns against Tecumseh, Black Hawk, and the Seminoles—to march his Army of Observation into the Nueces Strip. The Mexicans warned Taylor to back off and observe from a respectful distance across the Nueces River, but he remained on the contested ground. On April 24, 1846, Mexican troops crossed the Rio Grande, attacked a party of United States dragoons, and killed eleven of them. Polk leapt at the provocation. "Mexico," he crowed, "has invaded our territory and shed American blood on the American soil." Congress voted for war on May 13.[19]

Not everyone cheered. "That region belonged to Mexico. Certainly it did not belong to the United States," charged Whig senator Charles Sumner of Massachusetts. "Here was an act of aggression." The war was "one of the most unjust waged by a stronger nation against a weaker nation," Ulysses S. Grant, who served as a junior officer under Taylor, wrote years later. "It was an instance of a republic following the bad example of European monarchies, in not considering justice in their desire to acquire additional territory."[20]

Yet for the most part Polk's gambit worked: aggressive expansion brought people together. Most Americans overwhelmingly supported the war. Volunteers from Illinois, Missouri, Texas, and the states of the Old Southwest marched off singing new verses to the tune of "Old Dan Tucker" rhyming lines with "Rio Grandey" and declaring their intention to hike to Matamoros and "conquer all before us."[21]

———

The Mexican War was far easier to start than to finish. The Mexican army performed poorly, but the Mexican people excelled at guerrilla fighting, which exacted a bloody toll from the Americans. In the final tally it cost the United States nearly one hundred million dollars to win California and a new Southwest. By official and conservative government reckoning, it was also the most destructive war to that point in American history, claiming the lives of nearly thirteen thousand Americans and a minimum of twenty thousand Mexicans.

Polk planned a campaign with three principal theaters of operations. In Mexico itself, an American army under General Taylor swept south from Texas and in January 1847 destroyed the numerically superior Mexican army of General Santa Anna at the Battle of Buena Vista, near Saltillo. In the United States, Taylor was celebrated as the hero of the hour. President Polk, viewing Taylor's popularity as a political threat, transferred the bulk of his troops to the command of General Winfield Scott, who in March successfully invaded and seized the Mexican port city of Veracruz and began a slow military march through the mountains to the capital of Mexico City. Battered but unbowed, General Santa Anna refused to negotiate peace as long as an American army remained on Mexican soil.

The conquest of New Mexico, the second theater, was directed by General Stephen Watts Kearny. Like Taylor, Kearny had served on the frontier continuously since the War of 1812. He and his sixteen hundred dragoons took the provincial capital of Santa Fe in August 1846 without firing a shot. Kearney appointed trader Charles Bent as the first American governor of the province. A close associate of former governor Manuel Armijo and married into a prominent Hispanic family, Bent seemed a perfect choice to both keep the peace and represent the Americans. But he had his enemies, and animosities toward the new conquerors simmered beneath the surface. In early 1847, Pueblo Indians and New Mexicans rose in a brief rebellion that claimed the lives of several Americans, including Governor Bent.

California, Polk's dream objective, supplied the third front. After subduing New Mexico, Kearny set out for the Pacific coast. On the way he learned that California

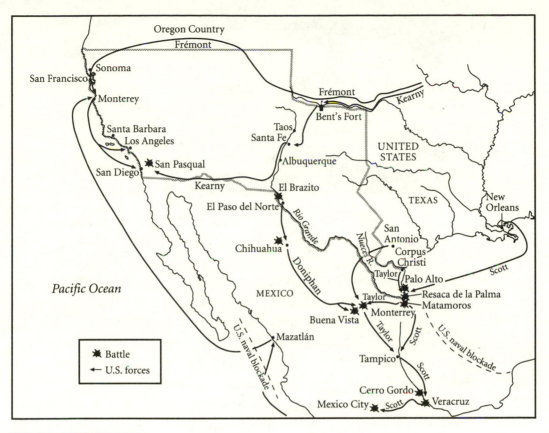

THE U.S.-MEXICAN WAR

had already fallen. In June 1846, a small irregular force of hunters and traders rode into the village of Sonoma, invaded the home of prominent ranchero Mariano Vallejo, and proclaimed the independence of the California Republic. They acted with the backing of Captain John C. Frémont of the Topographical Engineers, in California with a troop of men on what was purported to be a mapping expedition to the Far West. Frémont later acknowledged that he had secret instructions from President Polk to secure California for the United States in the event of war with Mexico. The invasion of Sonoma looked warlike enough for Frémont, and he took command of the uprising.

The American rebels raised a flag with a lone star and a crude drawing of a bear. The star signaled the intention of the Americans to "play the Texas game," while the bear indicated their desire to secure "rough justice." But to the Mexican Californians (known as Californios) cattle-thieving bears, *los osos,* were symbols of piracy, and these "Yankee Osos" were "savage hordes." The Americans barely rose to the Californios' low opinion of them. They insulted and imprisoned Vallejo and other respected Californios, they plundered homes and killed

civilians. "We must be conquerors," declared their leader, William B. Ide, or else "we are robbers."[22]

The Bear Flag Republic lasted only a month. In July, Commodore John D. Sloat of the United States Navy sailed into San Francisco Bay with the news that the United States and Mexico were at war. Promising guarantees of Californio lives and property, Sloat was appalled by Frémont's terror. Many prominent Californios, including Vallejo, favored a break with Mexico and annexation by the United States. But Sloat, who was ailing, was soon relieved by Commodore Robert F. Stockton, an old salt dedicated to bellicose division rather than peaceful congruence. A future presidential nominee of the anti-immigrant, anti-Catholic American Party, better known as the Know Nothings, Stockton escalated the conflict by commissioning Frémont to lead a new fighting unit, the California Battalion of Mounted Volunteers, composed of sharpshooters from the Topographical Engineers, Bear Flaggers, and Indian mercenaries. Frémont and Stockton swept south and took the pueblo of Los Angeles. But they bullied and belittled the locals, stoking an insurgent backlash. Residents of Los Angeles rose up and expelled the invaders.

Unaware of the uprising, General Kearny and his dragoons crossed the desert into California and were badly mauled in an engagement with the Californio insurgents. Not until January 1847 did the combined American force converge on Los Angeles and finally complete the conquest of California. Captain Frémont accepted the surrender, but with egotistical bravado he refused orders from General Kearny, his military superior, and reported instead to Commodore Stockton, who had authorized the formation of the California Battalion. Kearny later charged Frémont with insubordination and treason, a court-martial found him guilty, and he resigned from the service. The jostling among American commanders for power, prestige, and perks forecast conflicts to come.

Meanwhile the American campaign for the conquest of Mexico City slogged on. Mexican losses on the field of battle were followed by rear-guard guerrilla actions harassing supply lines and slowing General Scott's army. The Americans retali-

BATTLE OF CERRO GORDO.
APRIL 18ʸᵗ 1847.

Mexican-American War lithograph, 1847. Beinecke Rare Book and Manuscript Library, Yale University.

ated with outrages against civilians. A Mexican editor described the invaders as a "horde of banditti, of drunkards, of fornicators . . . vandals vomited from hell, monsters who bid defiance to the laws of nature, . . . shameless, daring ignorant, ragged, bad-smelling, long-bearded men with hats turned up at the brim, thirsty with the desire to appropriate our riches and our beautiful damsels." These were understandable feelings from a wartime adversary, but American officers, too, were critical of the operation. Lieutenant Ulysses Grant wrote home that "some of the volunteers and about all the Texans seem to think it perfectly right to impose on the people of a conquered city to any extent, and even to murder them where the act can be covered by dark. And how much they seem to enjoy acts of violence too!" Even General Scott admitted that his troops had "committed atrocities to make Heaven weep and every American of Christian morals to blush for his country," including "murder, robbery and rape of mothers and daughters in the presence of tied-up males of the families." It was six months before the Americans finally reached their objective, storming Chapultepec, the palace of the viceroys in the suburbs, then seizing the center of the city and raising the American flag above the national palace on September 14, 1847.[23]

General John E. Wool and his staff, Saltillo, Mexico, 1847. Beinecke Rare Book and Manuscript Library, Yale University.

President Polk read about the war in the *Baltimore Sun*. Partisan newspapers, fed by Samuel Morse's telegraph system, which began operation in 1844, spread news of the conflict. The Democrats had hoped that expansion would unify the country, but the detailed press coverage only seemed to inflame the opposition. As the war dragged into its second year, public opinion polarized. The majority continued to believe Polk's rhetoric about the duty of the nation to protect the cause of liberty. The president affirmed early in the war that the United States would never fight for conquest and that forced annexation was unthinkable, but he soon began to hedge under the guise of seeking repayment for the escalating costs of the war. There was never any doubt that California, Polk's primary objective from the beginning, would remain in American hands, and geopolitical logic demanded that the territory between Texas and California be included in the package. The region was worthless to Mexico, the argument ran, but the United States might push a transcontinental railroad through it, bypassing the Rocky Mountains and linking New Orleans with Pacific ports.

Polk's conquest struck some as unduly restrained. Extreme expansionists argued that the Mexicans deserved American overlords. Its languishing economy was matched only by its flailing political institutions. The country would be better off and develop more efficiently under new management. While Polk was talking honor and duty, treasury secretary Robert J. Walker commissioned a study of the fiscal implications of total annexation. "Why not take all of Mexico?" asked John L. O'Sullivan in the pages of the *New York Morning News*.[24]

Senator John C. Calhoun of South Carolina had an answer to O'Sullivan's question: because Mexico came with all those undesirable Mexicans. Calhoun's was the loudest voice for white supremacy in the country. "We make a great mistake, sir," he announced, "when we suppose that all people are capable of self-government." More than half of Mexico's residents were Indians, and the rest were "impure races, not as good as the Cherokees and Choctaws." Were Mexico annexed and made a territory of the United States, a mongrel population would be placed on an equal level with racially pure Americans. "I protest utterly against such a project," Calhoun concluded.[25]

A third body of opinion considered the war immoral and unworthy of the nation. Abolitionists charged that a southern president had incited the war as a way of extending slavery farther into Mexican territory. Black abolitionist leader and escaped slave Frederick Douglass condemned the war as an expression of "the spirit of slavery," and so too did the writer Henry David Thoreau, who refused to pay his taxes and spent a night in jail in protest of a war for slavery. Others worried that this war of conquest had done serious damage to the republican ideals of liberty and self-government. Transcendentalist writer Margaret Fuller lamented that the nation's gaze "was fixed not on the stars, but on the possessions of others." Instead of strengthening the United States, the Mexican War threatened to erode its foundations.[26]

Yet even in the writings of these opponents there was little concern for the struggles and bravery of the Mexicans. Antiwar activists tended to adopt the same demeaning and racist rhetoric as the war's supporters. Few Americans paid attention to the Mexican side of the war. Race, religion, and cultural smugness hindered their empathy, shadowing Americans in a common blind spot even as the conduct and aftermath of the war shuttled them into opposite corners.

The increasing force of the political crosswinds encouraged the president to find the nearest exit. He dispatched a peace emissary, Nicholas Trist, to march with Scott and seek negotiations at the first opportunity. Trist's wish list included the Mexican acceptance of Texas annexation as well as a deal on California and New Mexico. Mexican officials, however, were experiencing even fiercer political storms, and they negotiated gingerly. Trist reported their reluctance to Polk. The president responded with a harder line to punish Mexican foot-dragging and

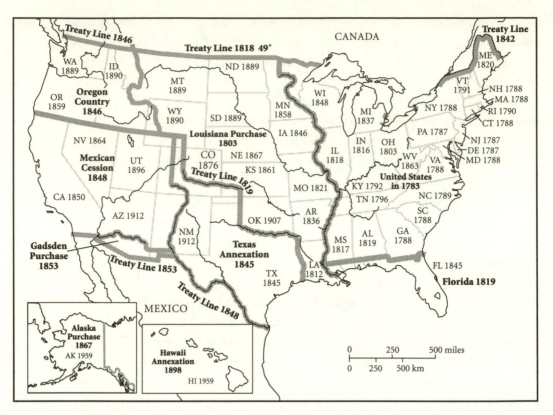

TERRITORIAL ACQUISITIONS AND STATEHOOD

please the "all-of-Mexico" faction of his party. But Trist ignored Polk's bellicosity and kept talking. In January 1848, the two sides agreed on a treaty based on earlier American aims. The Treaty of Guadalupe Hidalgo confirmed the annexation of Texas and set the Rio Grande as the international boundary. As reparations for the cost of the war, Mexico ceded California and New Mexico, a vast territory of 529,000 square miles, that includes not only those present-day states but also Arizona, Utah, Nevada, and southern Colorado. The United States paid Mexico $15 million and reimbursed American citizens for claims they held against Mexico amounting to $3.75 million. That's about five cents an acre.

A joint United States–Mexico commission was established with the power to draw an exact boundary from Texas westward to the Pacific. The American half of the commission split along sectional lines. When the head of the commission, John Russell Bartlett of New England, chose the northernmost of all the boundary options, southerners howled. In 1853, to make up for this "less-of-Mexico" decision and provide a right-of-way for a southern transcontinental railroad, the United States paid Mexico another $10 million for the Gadsden Purchase. Named after its American negotiator, James Gadsden, the purchase bought the land south of the Gila River in present-day New Mexico and Arizona. In all, including Texas, Mexico surrendered a total of 602 million acres, a third of its national domain.

_____

During the negotiations to end the conflict, Mexican officials worried about the status of their citizens residing in territory occupied by the United States. "The condition of the inhabitants," reported Nicholas Trist, "is the topic upon which most time is expended." The Treaty of Guadalupe Hidalgo stipulated that "male citizens of Mexico" in the ceded territory could choose either to retain their Mexican citizenship or to become citizens of the United States and be "maintained and protected in the free enjoyment of their liberty and property, and secured in the free exercise of religion without restriction." In the war's aftermath, however, Mexicans found their civil rights slipping away, their property in jeopardy, and their Catholic religion under assault. The 1850s marked a high tide in intense nativism and anti-Catholicism in the United States, and Anglo newcomers treated the native population as Mexicans, regardless of their formal American citizenship.[27]

Mexican holdings were also treated as fair game by the American settlers pouring into the new territories, and the courts struggled to puzzle through the complicated inconsistencies between Mexican and United States laws. Many Mexican landowners lost their title or were forced to sell to cover legal costs, and the poor people who worked for them were thrown off the land.

Hispanics found solace in stories of outlaws and bandits acting on behalf of the poor and besieged. There were numerous Mexican social bandits in the years following the conquest, but the most famous was Joaquin Murrieta, a semifactual hero who combined the exploits of at least five men. The Murrieta family, according to legend, had been attacked on their land by a group of Yankees. The invaders tied up Joaquin, flogged him, and raped his wife as he watched helplessly. Murrieta vowed revenge, and he and his outlaw band terrorized the Anglos. California's governor offered a thousand-dollar reward for him, dead or alive. Bounty hunters brought back a head pickled in whiskey, claiming that it was Murrieta's. The gruesome trophy went on tour and was viewed by thousands. But Mexican Californians claimed that their hero had escaped, a belief reinforced by a letter, supposedly from Murrieta, printed in the *San Francisco Herald*. "My alleged capture seems to be the topic of the day," the letter read, but "I inform the readers of your worthy newspaper that I retain my head." For the next half-century Murrieta's accomplishments were celebrated in the ballad "El corrido de Joaquin Murrieta," sung throughout communities on both sides of the border. Murrieta turned into an idea that could not die. "To the Mexicans he was a great liberator," his cousin later wrote, "come out of Mexico to take California back from the hands of the gringos."[28]

JOAQUIN, THE MOUNTAIN ROBBER.

Joaquin Murietta. From the Sacramento Steamer, *April 22, 1853. Author's collection.*

Juan Cortina. Drawing by
C. E. H. Bonwill, 1864. Library
of Congress.

In the valley of the Rio Grande in Texas, where Tejanos long remained a majority, discontent moved beyond social banditry into guerrilla warfare. The Texas Rangers, an irregular force originating during the Texas rebellion, administered the law in south Texas, often through assassination and lynching. The Rangers considered Mexicans their natural enemies. "I can maintain a better stomach at the killing of a Mexican than at the crushing of a body louse," a Ranger boasted in the 1850s. Such arrogance and bullying inspired Tejano counterpunchers, including Juan Nepomuceno Cortina, son of a respected ranchero family and veteran of the Mexican War. One day in 1859, while Cortina was conducting business in the predominantly Anglo town of Brownsville, he saw the marshal pistol-whipping an old vaquero who worked for his family. Jumping on his horse and charging forward, Cortina fired a shot and wounded the marshal; then, swinging the old man up behind him, he galloped out of town to the cheers of Tejanos on the street. When the authorities filed charges of attempted murder, Cortina and seventy-five supporters returned to free all the prisoners in the jail, killing four Brownsvillians in the process, two of them Anglos with notorious reputations for abusing Mexicans.[29]

Proclaiming the "sacred right of self preservation," Cortina issued a broadside to Tejanos. "You have been robbed of your property, incarcerated, chased, murdered, and hunted like wild beasts," he declared, and "to me is entrusted the work of breaking the chains of your slavery." During the subsequent Cortina War, several hundred Mexican rebels destroyed the property of dozens of Anglos. Cortina was finally chased into Mexico by federal troops under the command of Colonel Robert E. Lee, but for the next two decades he continued to harass the empire of liberty, and Tejanos celebrated him in *corridos,* the folk ballads of the border region.[30]

The Treaty of Guadalupe Hidalgo ended the war between two nations, drew a line between them, and granted American citizenship to Mexican residents. But violence persisted well into the twentieth century. From Texas to California and beyond, thousands of ethnic Mexicans were lynched by vigilantes and mobs from 1848 to 1928, the date of the last recorded instance of an extralegal execution of a Mexican American. The mob violence, Ranger atrocities, and Mexican American retaliatory strikes suggested the unsettled character of the region. Borders divided people and drew them together. Blood flowed as powerful men tried to etch and enforce lines of difference and inequality in a borderland that fused the destinies of the humans living along its many seams.

─────────

Wars tend to alienate people. To motivate their populations to kill on a massive scale, nations cultivate the otherness of their opponents. They dehumanize their enemies, calling them animals, barbarians, and exemplars of moral rot and insufferable habits. A society marinating in slavery and bigotry, the nineteenth-century United States specialized in deploying race to discredit its foes. But international combat and ideological racism were not the only engines of difference in the American West. Religion fractured nineteenth-century North Americans. Anti-Catholicism fueled the Mexican War and its aftermath, and Protestants contributed their own intramural schisms to the smorgasbord of churches, sects, and belief systems. Religious difference eroded Americans' sense of union. When they surveyed the religious landscape, they saw cracks and tumult, prompting intense worry about the future of the country.

No group kicked up more anxiety than the Church of Jesus Christ of Latter-Day Saints. The Mormons, as they were popularly known, were a uniquely American religious sect. They were also uniquely western. In 1847 thousands of Mormons left the Mississippi valley headed for the isolated desert country of the Great Basin, between the Rockies and Sierra Nevada. They emigrated to escape violence and persecution. The West promised a haven outside the United States where they could be different in peace.

Joseph Smith was the founder of the new sect. A seeker and a visionary, Smith claimed to have discovered, near his home in upstate New York, a set of hammered golden plates covered with strange hieroglyphs. With divine assistance, he said, he had translated those plates into the *Book of Mormon,* published in 1830. The text told the tale of one of the lost tribes of Israel that had wandered to the shores of the New World. Eventually they were blessed by the arrival of Jesus, who after his crucifixion had come to found his true church in America. In the fullness of time, however, decadence overwhelmed the tribe, and it fell into warring factions, which fought a climactic battle reminiscent of Armageddon. The few survivors were the ancestors of the American Indians. The *Book of Mormon,* with its references to America as a "land of promise," offered what historian Jan Shipps calls a "powerful and provocative synthesis of biblical experience and the American dream."[31]

In those days, upstate New York boiled over with religious enthusiasm. In this churning environment, which brought forth prophets and sects in bunches, Smith soon built a following of several hundred. The communitarian emphasis of the Latter-Day Saints appealed to many people vexed by the isolation and competition of market society that pitted neighbors against neighbors and churches against churches. Smith founded an exclusively Mormon community at Kirkland, Ohio, as well as a satellite settlement in western Missouri where he hoped to build a new "Kingdom of God." Pooling labor and resources, and distributing goods according to the needs of the members, the Mormons hammered out doctrines that placed the group above the individual. The Mormons kept their distance from "gentile" Americans, and Smith and his inner circle ruled the group as a theocracy. In Missouri, surrounding farmers grew suspicious of the Mormons' economic collectivism and political authoritarianism, especially when it was practiced by antislavery Yankees, and the Mormons soon found themselves under attack by hostile vigilantes. Smith responded by organizing his men into military companies, which only inflamed the conflict. In 1838 there was an explosion of violence, encouraged by Missouri's governor, that drove Smith and his followers from the state.

The Mormons reassembled on the banks of the Mississippi in Illinois. With renewed vigor they set to building once again, and their new community—which Smith christened Nauvoo—soon became one of the state's largest towns, with more than fifteen thousand residents. Smith oversaw the construction of an enormous temple and organized a large military force known as the Nauvoo Legion. He announced his intention to run for president of the United States and with his closest advisers sketched out a plan for a fabulous Mormon empire in the American West. But trouble followed the Saints, and the Mormons were soon battling with their fellow Americans once again.

In the eyes of many Illinoisans, it was their practice of "plural marriage" that dragged the Mormons outside the perimeter of white Protestant sympathy. For years there had been rumors of sexual improprieties among the Mormon elite, and the evidence suggests that Smith and his inner circle had been practicing polygamy since the early 1840s. Radical change defined the age as expanding commerce and industry reshuffled older ways of living. Utopian reformers began to experiment

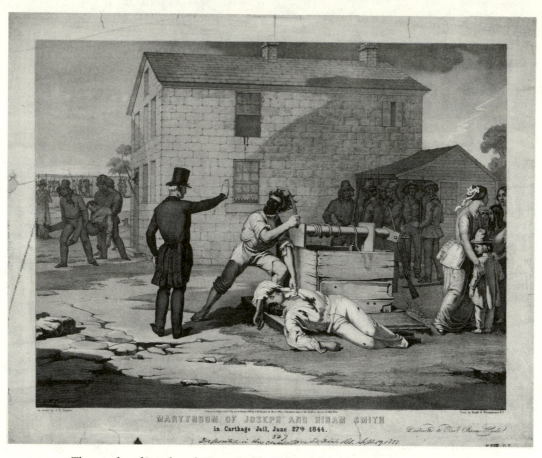

MARTYRDOM OF JOSEPH AND HIRAM SMITH
in Carthage Jail, June 27th 1844.

The murder of Joseph and Hiram Smith. Lithograph by G. W. Fasel, 1851. Library of Congress.

with different ways of organizing social life, and especially the relationships between men and women. The Shakers advocated celibacy, the Oneidans—a utopian community in New York—preached "free love." But plural marriage was a big leap into alternative ways of living, and many Mormons declined to make the jump. When a group of disaffected members published a broadside condemning plural marriage and other secret practices of the Mormon elite, Smith had their press destroyed by the Nauvoo Legion. The dissidents pressed charges, and state authorities arrested Smith and his brother, Hyrum, for destruction of private property. In June 1844, as they awaited trial, an enraged anti-Mormon mob broke into the jail and murdered both men.

For the subsequent two years, the Mormons endured a terrible struggle as factions jostled for control of the sect. Eventually Brigham Young, one of the most talented of Smith's loyal elite, seized leadership. A supporter of the Mormon vision of a western empire, Young laid plans for an exodus that would finally remove the Saints from harm's way. The great migration began in early 1846. As the Mormons evacuated Nauvoo, hostile mobs bombarded the town with cannon, destroying the great temple, the proudest of Smith's achievements. The Saints first moved to temporary winter quarters near Omaha, Nebraska. Then, in the spring of 1847, several thousand set out on the Overland Trail, keeping to the north side of the Platte to avoid conflict with other migrating Americans. Crossing the plains and the mountains, they arrived that fall at the Great Salt Lake, where Young determined to build a permanent refuge. By 1852 more than ten thousand people were residing in the new Mormon utopia of Salt Lake City, irrigating the desert and making it bloom.

———————

Brigham Young used the opportunity of a forced migration to seize the leadership of his church and steer its development. In the end, ethnic cleansing may have empowered the Latter-Day Saints. At the very least, the process of removal kept their movement together and contributed to the migrants' sense of being a chosen people.

American Indians, by contrast, were mostly weakened by their ordeal of removal, largely because they were denied the right to determine their own fate. The principal agent in their western migration was a federal government with fundamentally divided loyalties. In 1849 Congress, in an attempt to govern the territory acquired from Mexico, created the Department of the Interior, consolidating in one agency the Bureau of Indian Affairs and the General Land Office and soon adding the Territorial Office. The federal department charged with protecting Indian rights thus also became responsible for assessing the value of their homelands and distributing it to settlers, creating new territories and states. That this did not strike Americans as an absurd contradiction speaks volumes about the attitude of the government.

Wide open, dry, and blistering, hostile to pigs and corn, the Great Plains were hardly a solace to eastern Indian nations used to growing things in humid environments. Despite the daunting challenges they presented, the western lands would at least be the Indians' in perpetuity, and both native peoples and emigrant Indians signed federal treaties promising to safeguard their homelands "for as long as the grass grows and the waters run." But the geopolitical reality of continentalism invalidated this premise. With new territory on the Pacific coast, the midsection of the continent suddenly became a region binding a nation instead of acting as an outlying dumping ground. Already thousands of Americans were traveling across the Overland Trail to reach Oregon and California. Few Americans claimed land or built homes at this early date, yet their travel exacted a cost. Wagon trains consumed the cottonwoods of the river bottoms for campfires, turning to ashes the strips of bark Indian equestrians used to keep their horses alive through the winter and destroying the windbreaks bison huddled under to survive blizzards. The immigrants

Fort Laramie. Painting by Alfred Jacob Miller, 1838. Beinecke Rare Book and Manuscript Library, Yale University.

grazed their livestock on the crops of native farmers and hunted bison and antelope by the thousands. They blundered into conflicts with Indian hunting parties or sometimes with war parties battling with other native warriors for access to hunting territories. "How are we to develop, cherish, and protect our immense interests and possessions on the Pacific, with a vast wilderness fifteen hundred miles in breadth, filled with hostile savages, and cutting off all direct communication?" asked Senator Stephen Douglas of Illinois. "The Indian barrier must be removed."[32]

In the 1850s the United States negotiated treaties that reconfigured the Indian Country. In 1851 federal officials called on the tribes of the northern plains to send delegates to a conference at Fort Laramie on the North Platte River. More than twelve thousand Indians gathered to watch leaders from the Sioux, Northern Cheyennes, Arapahos, Crows, Assiniboines, Mandans, and Arikaras negotiate with the Americans. In exchange for annuities to compensate for lost game, tribal leaders granted the United States the right to establish posts and roads across the plains. In 1853 the tribes of the southern plains—including the Southern Cheyennes, Comanches, and Kiowas—agreed to similar provisions in the Treaty of Fort Atkinson, which secured the Santa Fe Trail for Americans. These agreements granted American travelers freedom of movement and presaged the end of a meaningful Indian Country by placing limits on native crossings.

Nomadism frustrated the Americans' sense of order and control. They pressed the plains' bison hunters and horse growers to agree to territorial boundaries and to stay within them, hinting at the reservation system that in coming years would become the hallmark of federal Indian policy. Blood would flow on both sides as the colonial impulse to keep people in place battled the nomadic compulsion to move freely.

―――――――

The American West challenged the federal government. With Oregon, Texas, California, and the new Southwest, the unorganized territory of the nation amounted to nearly half of all the country's land. In this vast region, the federal government would assume unprecedented authority over the next forty years. Federal armies would fight native peoples, federal engineers would survey land, and federal bureaucrats would administer territories. By exercising power in the West, argues historian Richard White, the federal government greatly expanded its presence in the everyday lives of all Americans. In the federal system, states counterbalanced the powers of the central government. "The West provided an arena for the expansion of federal powers that was initially available nowhere else in the country," says White. "The West itself served as the kindergarten of the American state."[33]

Still, before the state could be schooled in the West, the nation had to endure a bitter divorce. The Mexican War opened a divisive and violent new conflict on the question of slavery's extension that led directly to the Civil War. The West launched the sectional crises that ended the Union, and the consequences of a war that barely touched the region boomeranged back in full force once the conflict was over. During the Civil War the size and power of the federal government grew exponentially. Following secession, the Republican Party seized control of Congress and enacted key western laws that had been blocked by southern opposition. These laws partnered the federal government with industrial capitalism, a union itself forged in the heat of battle as the North used its manufacturing prowess to break the South. When the United States government granted huge swaths of land and issued low-interest bonds to finance a privately owned transcontinental railroad, it asserted new powers, performed new functions, and used new mechanisms it learned during the war. The West may have been the kindergarten of the American state, but the Civil War bulked the toddler up and supplied it with a gang of arm-twisting friends with names like Jay Cooke, Leland Stanford, and John D. Rockefeller.

The sectional controversy bloomed in the first months of the Mexican War when Congressman David Wilmot of Pennsylvania introduced an amendment to an appropriations bill that applied the antislavery restriction of the Northwest Ordinance to the land acquired from Mexico: "neither slavery nor involuntary servitude shall ever exist in any part of said territory." The debate over what became known as the Wilmot Proviso shattered the expansionist coalition. The amendment passed the House, but southerners in the Senate blocked it. The Compromise of 1850—actually a series of bills passed by shifting coalitions—finally broke the impasse. California, which rejected slavery in its own state constitution in 1849, was admitted as a free state, skipping the territorial interlude altogether. New Mexico and Utah territories were organized without restrictions on slavery, the residents of each territory left to decide the question themselves in good time, a solution the Democrats called "popular sovereignty." As a further sop to southerners, bitterly disappointed over California, the nation's fugitive slave law was significantly strengthened.[34]

But the peace of 1850 was short-lived, broken only four years later when Senator Stephen Douglas of Illinois proposed a bill to organize the old Louisiana Purchase territory beyond the Missouri River into the territories of Kansas and Nebraska. Eager to promote a transcontinental railroad with a terminus in his home state, Douglas proposed abandoning the old Missouri Compromise line to garner votes from southern Democrats. Instead, he argued, the principal of popular sovereignty should decide the issue.

Nebraska was considered too far north for slavery. But slave owners in adjacent Missouri saw Kansas as a prize they might grab, and soon the prairie became a killing field where men took sides and fought for their uncompromising beliefs. Proslavery militias crossed the border to battle heavily armed abolitionist settlers from New England. "Kill every God-damned abolitionist in the Territory," advised Missouri senator and militia leader David Rice Atchison. In the spring of 1856, a "posse" of eight hundred proslavery Missourians invaded antislavery Lawrence, Kansas, demolishing the two newspaper offices, plundering shops and homes, and killing one man. Senator Charles Sumner of Massachusetts condemned this "Crime against Kansas," and in response to this "insult," he received a savage beating from a proslavery colleague on the Senate floor. When abolitionist settler John Brown learned of the assault, he vowed to "fight fire with fire." In an act designed to "strike terror in the hearts of the proslavery people," he and four of his sons seized five peaceful proslavery settlers on Pottawatomie Creek in Kansas and laid open their skulls with broadswords.[35]

The politics of compromise across sectional lines died on the plains of Kansas, and a new arrangement took its place. In order to win a national election, the Republicans, an antislavery party of northeastern interests, needed western support.

Antislavery militia in Kansas, c. 1856. Kansas State Historical Society.

In 1856 they played to western sympathies by running the peripatetic John C. Frémont under the banner "Free Soil, Free Men, Frémont." Frémont lost, but not by much. The Jacksonian coalition had depended on the political alliance of the Old Northwest and Old Southwest, the linking of farmers and planters via the Mississippi. But the construction of the Erie Canal, the development of steam transport on the Great Lakes, and finally the construction of railroad lines redirected the commercial connections from New Orleans to New York City. These prospering economic ties generated increasing support for the Republican program: protective tariffs for northern industry, internal improvements, cheap public land, and railroads for westerners, and an end to slavery's expansion. In 1860 the states of the Old Northwest sealed the new sectional alliance by voting in a block for Abraham Lincoln. When the South refused to accept the election's outcome and seceded, the West and the Northeast not only joined forces to preserve the union, but they also seized the reins of the federal government. Purged of southern representation, Congress moved on two of the West's most cherished political goals: a Homestead Act providing free land for settlers and a Pacific railroad.

When military historians speak of the "western theater" during the Civil War, they refer to battles fought at sites like Shiloh, Chattanooga, and Vicksburg, strategic sites in the trans-Appalachian West. The war in the West meant the war in the

Old Southwest with two exceptions. Confederate president Jefferson Davis took a strong interest in the territory that had been acquired from Mexico. Serving as secretary of war during the 1850s, he had noted with interest the long tradition of irrigated cotton cultivation by Indians and Mexican farmers living there. Some historians argue that slavery was climatically unsuited to the arid West, yet in the twentieth century Arizona and California became two of the nation's largest cotton-producing states using a labor force that was barely free. Historian Donald Frazier argues that the creation of a Confederate slave empire in the West "was a basic goal of Southern independence." It is revealing that one of the first strategic moves of the Confederacy was an attempt to grab the territory of New Mexico. An army of 3,500 Texans pushed up the Rio Grande from El Paso and forced the retreat of Union forces, giving the proslavery minority in the area the opportunity to proclaim the Confederate Territory of Arizona.[36]

During the following winter of 1861–62 the Texans extended their control, capturing the towns of Albuquerque and Santa Fe. Gold had been discovered in the front range of the Rockies in 1859, and with the aim of seizing these valuable Colorado mines, the troops advanced on Fort Union, east of Santa Fe, the largest federal facility in the Southwest. But at Glorieta Pass in the Sangre de Cristo Mountains they were turned back by Colorado volunteers. Leading the charge with "a pistol in each hand and one or two under his arms" was Major John M. Chivington, a Methodist minister known to his men as the "fighting parson." Chivington's maneuver broke the Texan lines and forced a Confederate retreat from New Mexico.[37]

An even more important Confederate goal was control of the state of Missouri, which would put the rebels in command of the entire west bank of the Mississippi River. As part of this strategy, the Confederate government sent agents to court the leaders of the Indian nations in Indian Country, directly south of strongly Unionist Kansas. The Choctaws and Chickasaws quickly signed Confederate treaties without much dissent in 1861, but among the Creeks, Seminoles, and especially the Cherokees, there were strong pro-Union factions. These new divisions reopened old wounds. Chief John Ross of the Cherokees, for example, found his principal support among those who had opposed removal from Georgia, including most of the full bloods and traditionalists. The pro-Confederate faction, by contrast, was led by Stand Watie, the lone survivor of the group of leaders who had signed the removal treaty. Watie's supporters also included most of the Cherokee slave owners. Ross tried to maintain Cherokee neutrality but was seriously undercut when federal troops withdrew from Indian Territory in April 1861. By then Watie was already organizing fighters from the "United Nations of Indians" for the Confederacy.

In Missouri, meanwhile, ad hoc Unionist forces blocked the attempt of the governor to take his state into the Confederacy. When a rebel army composed of troops from Indian Territory and Arkansas invaded the state in March 1862, they were defeated by federal forces at Pea Ridge in the Ozarks, saving Missouri for the Union, at least on paper. But the violence metastasized into a vicious guerrilla struggle. Armed bands of abolitionist Jayhawkers crossed the Kansas border into Missouri, burning and looting. Confederate Bushwhackers like William Quantrill and "Bloody Bill" Anderson answered in kind. Quantrill stormed abolitionist Lawrence in 1863, leaving 182 men and boys slaughtered. "More than any other state, Missouri suffered the horrors of internecine warfare," writes Civil War historian James McPherson, and "produced a form of terrorism that exceeded anything else in the war."[38]

Except maybe in Indian Territory, where factional guerrilla fighting nearly destroyed the Indian nations. "From being the once proud, intelligent, and wealthy tribe of Indians," wrote a federal official, "the Cherokees are now stripped of nearly all." Fleeing the devastation, ten thousand Indian refugees moved north into Kansas, where they mingled with thousands of proslavery refugees who had been evicted from their western Missouri homes. Both western Missouri and Indian Territory would remain wastelands for years. The victorious federal government made the Five Civilized Tribes pay dearly for their Confederate alliance, forcing them to relinquish half their lands. They also had to make room for the emigrant Indians evicted from Kansas to accommodate white settlers.[39]

———

During the war the Republican Congress carved the rest of the trans-Mississippi West into territories in preparation for their settlement. Mapping a domain, however, was not the same as having one. Bringing the West into the nation would require a generation of offensive warfare. For the several hundred thousand Indian people who called the West home, it meant thirty years of desperate resistance.

Suffering and slaughter became commonplace and changed the expectations and behavior of thousands of western Americans. New means of violence facilitated these new habits. In 1836 Samuel Colt patented the first modern revolver, an inexpensive weapon that had no utility as a hunting piece but was designed solely for violent confrontations among men. Colt advertised his guns with heroic scenes—a man protecting his wife and child from Indians armed only with a Colt revolver. Sales were brisk. The weapon soon found its way into the hands of the Texas Rangers, whose example made it the weapon of choice for irregular forces. By the 1850s the Colt factory in Hartford, Connecticut, was turning out a variety of new handguns—the .36-caliber "Navy" model was a favorite among border guerrillas—while the Sharps and Winchester companies perfected the manufacture of new breech-loading and repeating rifles. During the Civil War, the West was flooded with firearms of every type and description, from tiny pocket derringers to .50-caliber buffalo guns.

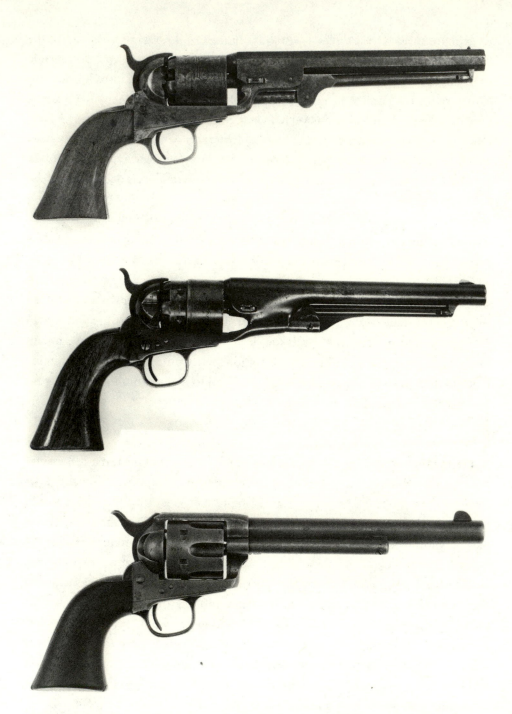

Innovations in handguns (from top to bottom): Colt 1851 Navy Revolver; Colt 1860 Army Revolver; Colt 1873 Peacemaker Single-Action Army Revolver. Buffalo Bill Historical Center, Cody, Wyoming. Gift of Olin Corporation, Winchester Arms Collection.

The arming of western America was accompanied by a hardening and coarsening of attitudes toward the Indians. A new rhetoric of violence appeared in official government discourse. Indian Bureau administrators did not shirk from the draconian design of their new reservation policy. "It is indispensably necessary that [Indians] be placed in positions where they can be controlled and finally compelled by sheer necessity to resort to agricultural labor or starve," one bureaucrat wrote of the Plains Indians. "They cannot pursue their former mode of life," wrote another, "but must entirely change their habits, and, in fixed localities, look to the cultivation of the soil and the raising of stock for future support. There is no alternative to providing for them in this manner but to exterminate them, which the dictates of justice and humanity alike forbid." Coming out of the Civil War, the federal government issued ultimatums in the name of civilization at gunpoint.[40]

The West harvested the first bitter fruits of these trends among the Eastern Sioux of Minnesota in 1862. In treaties of 1851 and 1858, the United States forced these communities to relinquish title to twenty-eight million acres in exchange for annuities and a crowded reservation on the Minnesota River. Their agent described the regimen on the reservation as designed "to break up the community system among the Sioux; weaken and destroy their tribal relations; individualize them by giving each a separate home and having them subsist by industry—the sweat of their brows; till the soil; make labor honorable and idleness dishonorable; or, as it was expressed in short, '*make white men of them*.'" It is hardly surprising that the Sioux resisted. "If the Indians had tried to make the whites live like them," said Big Eagle, one of the Sioux chiefs, "the whites would have resisted, and it was the same with many Indians."[41]

By the summer of 1862, a combination of crop failure and diminished supplies of game reduced the Eastern Sioux to near starvation, yet their authoritarian agent refused to depart from standard procedure and issue emergency stores from the abundant pantry in the agency warehouse. Chief Little Crow, a man inclined to accommodation, approached one of the reservation traders with a group of Sioux men. "We have not food, but here are these stores," he said through a translator. "When men are hungry they help themselves." Furious at what he considered a veiled threat, the trader responded: "So far as I am concerned, if they are hungry let them eat grass or their own dung." Two days later, the reservation exploded. The Sioux attacked surrounding farms, towns, and forts, killing five hundred settlers before the state militia crushed the rebellion. The body of the offending trader was later found, his mouth stuffed with grass. Thirty-eight Sioux were convicted of rape and murder and executed before a cheering crowd of settlers; several hundred more were imprisoned, and the remaining Eastern Sioux were removed to a reservation in Dakota Territory.[42]

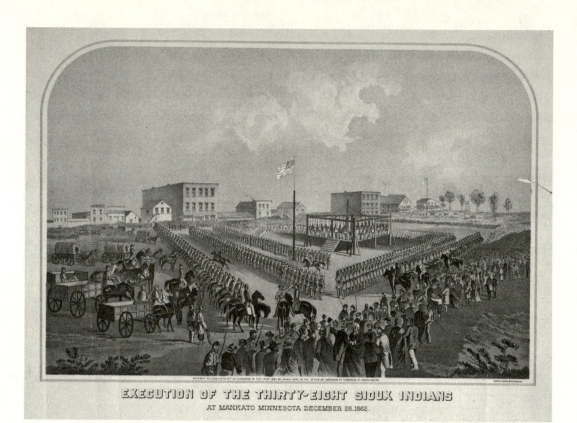

EXECUTION OF THE THIRTY-EIGHT SIOUX INDIANS
AT MANKATO MINNESOTA DECEMBER 26.1862.

Minnesota Sioux executed after the uprising of 1862. Lithograph, 1883. Beinecke Rare Book and Manuscript Library, Yale University.

The Southwest became the focus for the next round of violence between the federal government and the Indians. In the spring of 1862, Colonel James H. Carleton promised the Hispanic and Pueblo residents of the Rio Grande valley to eliminate the raids of the Navajos and Apaches that had been a fact of life for at least three centuries. Yet the raids not only continued, they accelerated, for now American goods and livestock drew them as well.

Carleton commissioned former mountain man Kit Carson—made famous by Frémont's reports—to lead a campaign to eradicate the raiders. "There is to be no council held with the Indians nor any talks," Carleton ordered. "The men are to be slain whenever and wherever they can be found. The women and children may be taken as prisoners." At a desolate spot in arid east-central New Mexico called Bosque Redondo, Carleton established a reservation for the subdued Indians. In a brutal campaign that included the murder of two surrendering Apache chiefs and the torture and beheading of another, several hundred Indians died and several hundred more were forced onto the barren reservation and put to work digging ditches. Most of the Apaches, however, eluded the troops, fleeing into the mountains or south of the border into Mexico. Rather than pacifying the Apaches, the campaign marked the beginning of more than twenty years of their fierce resistance to the Americans.[43]

Carleton next loosed Carson on the Navajos, who lived in the northern border region between New Mexico and Arizona. A group of chiefs attempted to mollify Carleton, but he insisted that their removal to Bosque Redondo was their only option. Like the Apaches, the Navajos had long raided Hispanic and Pueblo communities, but unlike their cousins, they were a farming and pastoral people, with gardens, orchards, and large flocks of sheep and goats. Carson attacked their subsistence, destroying hogans and crops, burning orchards, and slaughtering livestock. By the late winter of 1864, the Navajos were desperate. "Owing to the operations of my command," Carson reported, "they are in a complete state of starvation, and many of their women and children have already died from this cause." By winter's end, some eight thousand Navajos had surrendered and been forced to march four hundred miles through the desert to Bosque Redondo. The Long Walk, as the Navajos call this brutal removal experience, was seared into their collective memory. In 1868 they were finally able to negotiate a return to their homeland—much constricted in size.[44]

From Minnesota to New Mexico, the Americans demonstrated their ruthless pursuit of control through reservations and forced agrarian reform. They were willing to starve people to change them. The Indians could plow furrows or dig their own graves. Yet neither the Long Walk nor the massacre in Minnesota revealed the furthest extent of some Americans' inability to see and to treat different humans as humans in the 1860s. That designation belonged to the hero of Glorieta Pass, John Chivington, a Union man and an abolitionist, who was made a colonel and given command of the First and Third Colorado Regiments.

In 1861, anxious to clear title to land in the newly created Colorado Territory, the Indian Bureau arranged a treaty with some of the region's Arapahos and Southern Cheyennes, assigning them to a barren reservation along the Arkansas River. Hungry and livid as they watched Americans build taverns and ranches near their traditional watering holes, the militant Dog Soldier society of the Cheyennes struck the Platte River road connecting Denver with the East, burning stage stops, driving off livestock, and taking captives. John Evans, the territorial governor, raised a regiment of volunteers and declared war on all Indians.

Some Cheyenne leaders worked hard to prevent this war. They disavowed the Dog Soldiers' belligerence and tried to broker a peace. Black Kettle, a Cheyenne chief, traveled to Denver to request that Evans let his people move closer to their food supply: "We must live near the buffalo or starve." Spoiling for a fight, Evans

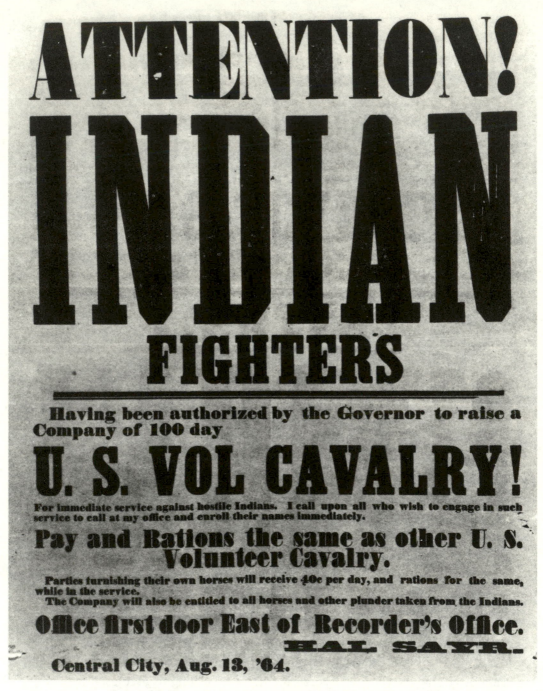

Colorado recruitment poster, 1864. Colorado Historical Society.

George Bent and his Cheyenne wife, Magpie, niece of Chief Black Kettle, c. 1867. Beinecke Rare Book and Manuscript Library, Yale University.

offered nothing but threats. Black Kettle returned to his band and brought them to Fort Lyon in southeastern Colorado, where he sought federal protection from the belligerent Coloradans. Following the instructions of the fort commander, Black Kettle led his people forty miles to the northeast and set up camp on Sand Creek. The encampment was a fair representation of the inclusive world of the upper Arkansas valley frontier; counted among the hundred or more lodges of the Cheyennes and Arapahos were a few white men married to Indian women and a liberal number of métis. Three of the four children of trader William Bent and his two Cheyenne wives were there. "All the Indians had the idea firmly fixed in their minds that they were here under protection and that peace was soon to be concluded," wrote George Bent.[45]

But Colonel Chivington was acting under instructions received from the militia commander of the region: "I want no peace till the Indians suffer more." He led the seven hundred men of the Third Regiment toward Sand Creek. "I have come to kill Indians," he told his men, "and believe it is right and honorable to use any means under God's heaven to kill Indians."[46]

The army surprised the Cheyenne camp at sunrise on November 29, 1864, while most of the young warriors were away hunting. George Bent awoke to the sound of excited people rushing by his lodge. "From down the creek a large body of troops was advancing at a rapid trot," he later wrote. "All was confusion and noise, men, women, and children rushing out of the lodges partly dressed; women and children screaming at the sight of the troops; men running back into the lodges for their arms, other men, already armed, or with lassos and bridles in their hand, running for the herds. . . . Black Kettle had a large American flag tied to the end of a long lodgepole and was standing in front of his lodge, holding the pole, with the flag fluttering in the gray light of the winter dawn. I heard him call to the people not to be afraid, that the soldiers would not hurt them; then the troops opened fire." It was a slaughter. When it was over, the bodies of some two hundred Cheyennes and Arapahos littered the cold ground, three-quarters of them women and children. Chivington boasted that his men killed more, close to five hundred, he guessed.[47]

"Colorado soldiers have again covered themselves in glory," crowed the *Rocky Mountain News*. But there was public outrage in the East. A congressional committee investigated and issued a published report. The summary spared the goriest details, but witnesses testified that troops had carved the genitals from women's bodies, stretching them over their saddle horns or pinning them to their hats. "No attempt was made by the officers to restrain the savage cruelty of the men under their command." Governor Evans was forced to resign, but Chivington escaped court-martial, for he had left the service and was beyond military law. He became the sheriff of Denver and later served as county coroner.[48]

In the aftermath of the Sand Creek Massacre, the entire central plains exploded into war. Previously the Cheyennes had been divided on the issue of peace or war, but the Colorado brutality settled the matter. In early 1865, Sioux, Cheyenne, and Arapaho bands retaliated for Chivington's attack by burning nearly every ranch and stage station along the South Platte, killing scores of American men, women, and children. Efforts to subdue the warriors were ineffective. "At night the whole valley was lighted up with the flames of burning ranches and stage stations," said George Bent. Among the attackers was his métis brother Charles, who became known as the fiercest of the Dog Soldiers. Renounced by his father, Charles swore vengeance on all white people, including his kin.[49]

As the struggle for the Union concluded in the East and war-weary soldiers clamored to be sent home to their families, it became difficult for the U.S. Army to find volunteers to fight Indians in the West. Congress sanctioned the recruitment of soldiers from the ranks of Confederate prisoners of war and authorized the formation of the African American Twenty-Fourth and Twenty-Fifth Infantries and Ninth and Tenth Cavalries, the famous Buffalo Soldiers—as they were christened by the Indians, in reference to the texture of the soldiers' hair. The black troops were segregated and paid significantly less than white soldiers, but they compiled an extraordinary record for discipline, courage, and high morale; over the next

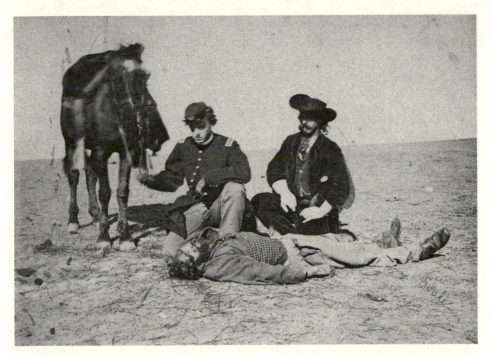

Ralph Morrison, murdered and scalped on the plains of western Kansas, 1868. Photograph by William Soule. Beinecke Rare Book and Manuscript Library, Yale University.

quarter-century fourteen troopers won the Congressional Medal of Honor. Thus, in 1865, regiments of Yankee veterans, "White-washed Rebs," and former slaves joined together to keep Indians on reservations by punishing the "hostiles" who left them. The Americans had managed to create a frontier of inclusion through exclusion.

FURTHER READING

Thomas D. Clark and John D. W. Guice, *The Old Southwest, 1795–1830: Frontiers in Conflict* (1996)

Brian Delay, *War of a Thousand Deserts: Indian Raids and the U.S.-Mexican War* (2009)

William H. Goetzmann, *Exploration and Empire: The Explorer and the Scientist in the Winning of the American West* (1966)

Amy S. Greenberg, *A Wicked War: Polk, Clay, Lincoln, and the 1846 U.S. Invasion of Mexico* (2012)

Robert V. Hine, *Bartlett's West: Drawing the Mexican Boundary* (1968)

Albert L. Hurtado, *John Sutter: A Life on the North American Frontier* (2008)

Benjamin Heber Johnson, *Revolution in Texas: How a Forgotten Rebellion and Its Bloody Suppression Turned Mexicans into Americans* (2003)

Ari Kelman, *A Misplaced Massacre: Struggling over the Memory of Sand Creek* (2013)

David Montejano, *Anglos and Mexicans in the Making of Texas, 1836–1986* (1987)

Raúl A. Ramos, *Beyond the Alamo: Forging Mexican Ethnicity in San Antonio, 1821–1861* (2008)

John D. Unruh, *The Plains Across: The Overland Emigrants and the Trans-Mississippi West, 1840–60* (1979)

Anthony F. C. Wallace, *The Long, Bitter Trail: Andrew Jackson and the Indians* (1993)

7

Machine

Between the end of the Mexican War and the end of World War I, the American West jumped categories. Observers have described this transition variously as proceeding from frontier to region, free to settled, open to closed, mobile to permanent, exuberant to rational, mixed to monochrome, primitive to modern. Western people, places, and animals were incorporated into larger entities, organizations, and relationships. The process began in the mid-nineteenth century as the national economy entered a period of sustained industrial growth. The nation developed—building canals, railroads, and telegraphs, attracting immigrant workers, legalizing corporations, and erecting hierarchies of wealth and class—while it simultaneously settled the West. The twin movements fueled each other. Western colonization supplied raw materials and provided new markets for industrial capitalism. The West helped to build the nation as the nation built the West.

It would be a mistake to attach a single, unidirectional storyline to what transpired. In many ways industrial capitalism introduced yet more chaos and conflict into locales that already had plenty. Colonization prompted booms and busts, and westerners suffered through the vertigo that came with riding the huge swells and valleys of cyclical economics. Industrial capitalism created astonishing monuments to human ingenuity and labor in the West—railroads that crossed deserts and tunneled through mountains, underground mines that honeycombed the earth, cattle drives that turned bison habitats into bovine paradises, and wheat fields that stretched for miles. These accomplishments also produced men of great wealth and power, men like Jay Cooke, Jay Gould, Leland Stanford, Collis P. Huntington, James J. Hill, Henry Villard, John D. Rockefeller, George Hearst, Levi Strauss, and Charles Goodnight. But don't give them too much credit for making

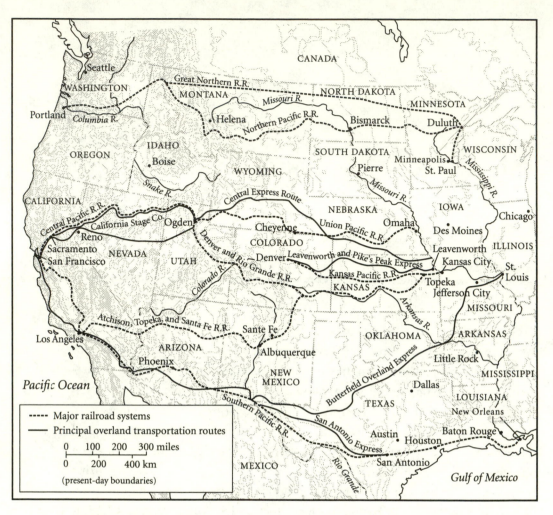

WESTERN RAILROADS

the modern West. In the words of historian Richard White, these captains of industries were "not that smart." They failed as often as they succeeded and often displayed a remarkable lack of insight and mastery over themselves and others, much less the universe. For White, their shortcomings raise an important question about modernity: "How, when powerful people can on close examination seem so ignorant and inept; how, when so much work is done stupidly, shoddily, haphazardly, and selfishly, how, then does the modern world function at all?"[1]

Between 1849 and 1920, the American West was aligned with impersonal large-scale organizations. The federal state exited the Civil War greatly enlarged and empowered, and it grew even more powerful administering the people and resources of the West. Yet the national government paled in comparison to some corporations, especially the railroads, the first truly large-scale economic organizations in American history. The government and the corporations twisted around each other like a double helix. Indeed, the primary skill of many a western tycoon was manipulating the national political process to secure profits and kneecap rivals. The power of these men and organizations was very real and often very dangerous. The wealthy killed people, not necessarily with their own hands, but through their partnership with the army and police forces of the federal state. Yet this power was never total. People resisted, squeezing their own triggers or organizing their own large-scale organizations in labor unions, farmers' alliances, and populist political parties. Squabbles and bumbling defined the industrial West along with technological marvels and titanic undertakings. The region resembled a runaway train more than a well-planned and regulated colony. It pulled into modernity, but only after a hellishly wild ride.

The exuberant origins of the West's major industries—mining, lumbering, railroading, ranching, and farming—suggested none of the sober, top-down management and efficiency of supposedly mature capitalist undertakings. The new era began with the discovery of gold in the foothills of the Sierra Nevada of California on January 24, 1848. People rushed west in an emotional state described in the language of disease. They had caught a fever and made decisions in a state of delirium. The California Gold Rush epitomized the irrationality of western mining booms, but all the other industries also had their wacky moments. The rushes, frenzies, bubbles, and fevers that gripped millions and laid the foundation for the region's economic development were an essential part of modernization. The region was crazed from the start.

John Sutter, a Swiss-born impresario with a huge Spanish land grant along the Sacramento River, attempted to suppress reports of the discovery of gold in a mill race being dug by his employees, but the news reached San Francisco in May. The *California Star* denounced the stories as "a sham, a superb take-in as was ever got up to guzzle the gullible," but within days the town had been emptied of shovel-ready men. The cry of gold quickly spread throughout the territory. One man described the effect of the news: "A frenzy seized my soul. Piles of gold rose up before me at every step; castles of marble, dazzling the eye with their rich appliances; thousands of slaves, bowing to my beck and call; myriads of fair virgins contending with each other for my love, were among the fancies of my fevered imagination. The Rothschilds, Girards, and Astors appeared to me but poor people. In short, I had a very violent attack of Gold Fever." Editors suspended publication of their newspapers, and city councils adjourned for months. Californios, American and Mexican settlers, and indigenous Indians poured into the Sierra foothills.[2]

Fanning outward, they learned that the mother lode of gold ore was contained in a vein of quartz rock that stretched for more than a hundred miles along the

One of the first depictions of the California Gold Rush. Lithograph, 1849. Beinecke Rare Book and Manuscript Library, Yale University.

western slope of the Sierra Nevada range. Icy streams cut and eroded the rock, washing out the gold and depositing it in the alluvial sands of the rivers. A man needed little knowledge and minimal skill to swish the sand in a flat pan with enough water to wash away the lighter ores, leaving behind the heavier gold grains at the bottom. But the work was backbreaking, and the icy waters could quickly bring on a nasty case of rheumatism. This was known as placer mining, and during the summer of 1848 many men struck a bonanza. Those were Spanish terms, *placera* meaning alluvial sand, *bonanza* translated as rich ore, suggesting the critical role the Mexican miners played in educating the first rushers. At first there were plenty of streams for all who came, and the forty-eighters told stories of panning gold worth thousands of dollars in only a few days. A territorial report estimated that ten million dollars was taken out of Sierra streams that first year.

In early December 1848, President Polk kicked off a global rush to California when he confirmed the discovery in his State of the Union address. His announcement hit while the country was still awash with thousands of dislocated and unsettled veterans of the Mexican War, not only in the United States but in Mexico as well. In Europe, residents of the capital cities were recovering from the revolutions of 1848, which had pushed a fearful establishment into severely repressive measures. In Ireland, rural people were in flight from a blight on potatoes, which supplied the food of the masses. In China, people were pushed from their homeland by peasant rebellions and the British-sponsored Opium Wars. By slim clippers around Cape Horn, by square-rigged ships from Hawaii, Australia, and China, over the Isthmus of Panama and across the plains and mountains, tens of thousands of eager men jostled into California.

There their fevered dreams hit rock walls. The easily obtained placer gold soon ran thin, and the miner's take had been drastically reduced before the first of the forty-niners arrived. The big moneymakers of the Gold Rush were the men and women who supplied the miners with food, clothes, equipment, and entertainment. Levi Strauss, a young Jewish dry goods merchant from New York, made his fortune by manufacturing the durable canvas and denim pants ("levis") that became standard-issue work duds. "I find that all shrewd calculating men," Henry Kent noted soon after arriving in California, "get into other business besides mining."[3]

Placer mining gave way to quartz mining, which required the application of industrial processes to extract the gold from the surrounding quartz. In 1852, only four years after the initial discovery, 108 crushing mills were pounding out the ores that time and the river had not yet reached. As early as 1853, men were employing high-pressured jets of water to flush mountains of alluvial deposits into rivers. "The effect of this continuous stream of water coming with such force must be seen to be appreciated," wrote a horrified observer, for "whatever it struck it tore away earth, gravel and boulders. . . . It is impossible to conceive of anything more desolate, more utterly forbidding, than a region which has been subjected to this hydraulic mining treatment." Crushing and hydraulic operations required large capital investments as well as substantial labor forces, so the disillusioned men who had rushed across the continent or sailed across the oceans to get rich quick were forced to go to work for wages. Mining ceased to be an individual pursuit and became a corporate enterprise. "I think all of the old mining ground that is now called worked out will yet pay millions of dollars by working them systematically," wrote miner Seldon Goff in 1850. "Capitalists will take hold of it and make money out of it."[4]

The California experience provided the lodestone for the exploitation of the Far West in the second half of the nineteenth century. Mineral rushes scattered migrants across the West, breaking the pattern of contiguous territorial absorption that had previously defined the nation's expansion. Mining shot-gunned people across the map, sending them into remote deserts and high mountain valleys where no right-minded farmer would go. The census of 1850 revealed the pattern that would characterize the industrial West: clusters of settlement separated by hundreds of miles of undeveloped territory. From California, prospectors spread out, making a series of strikes that spawned a seemingly endless round of rushes: the Fraser River of British Columbia in 1858; the Colorado Rockies west of the

Hydraulic mining in California. Photograph by Lawrence and Houseworth, c. 1860. Beinecke Rare Book and Manuscript Library, Yale University.

settlement of Denver and the Washoe country of Nevada in 1859; Idaho and Montana in 1860 and 1862; the Black Hills of Dakota Territory in 1876; Leadville, Colorado, and Tombstone, Arizona, in 1877; the Coeur d'Alene region of Idaho in 1883; and, closing out the era, the northern Yukon country of Canada in 1896, quickly spreading to Nome and Fairbanks, Alaska. Each rush created new isolated centers of population.

Practically every rush also presented the familiar kaleidoscope of lonely prospectors with their mules and pans, crowds of jostling men of every conceivable nationality, jerry-built saloons and stores clustered along muddy streets, prostitutes and dance-hall girls, outlaws, claim jumpers, and vigilance committees—all soon followed by stamp mills and smelters, slag heaps and underground burrows, company towns and labor unions, leading finally to strikes with the fist instead of the shovel. Mining added a significant dimension to the social, economic, and imaginative development of the West.

———

The California Gold Rush epitomized the splintering effect of industrial colonization. American miners claimed special rights and privileges due to their gender, race, and nationality. California, they argued, belonged to the white citizens of the United States. Yet Gold Rush society was composed of a polyglot collection of nationalities. Louisa Amelia Clappe, who wrote observant letters to eastern newspapers under the pseudonym Dame Shirley, walked through the mining camp called Indian Bar in the Sierras and overheard conversations in English, French, Spanish, German, Italian, and Kanakan (Hawaiian), as well as various American Indian languages. The camp, she wrote, was "a perambulating picture gallery, illustrative of national variety."[5]

But for the lapse of a few years, of course, American citizens would have been the foreigners. In the California mining regions, however, there had been no previously settled Californio population, and with the flood of forty-niners, Americans instantly formed a majority. But some fifteen to twenty thousand Latino miners were not far behind—Californios and Mexicans, as well as Peruvians and Chileans. Many were experienced placer miners and in demand as technical advisers. It was one of the few glimmers of interethnic cooperation.

As it became evident that not everyone was going to get rich in the goldfields, race fused with claims to ownership of the land and its resources. "Mexicans have no business in this country," a reader wrote the *Stockton Times*. "The men were made to be shot at, and the women were made for our purposes. I'm a white man—I am! A Mexican is pretty near black. I hate all Mexicans." The influx of expert Mexican miners from Sonora intensified hostilities. They knew where to look and how to extract the gold. Americans learned from them, wrote English observer William Kelly, but "as soon as [one] got an inkling of the system, with peculiar bad taste and ingenious feeling he organized a crusade against the obliging strangers."[6]

The state backed the crusaders. In January 1849, the military governor of California issued an order warning foreigners that they were mining "in direct violation of the laws." There were, in fact, no such laws. Indeed, until the federal government formally opened the public domain to private mining in 1866, practically every miner in the West was an illegal trespasser. But the order sanctioned the white vigilantes who were enacting their own racial codes in the diggings. The mass expulsions of Mexicans began in the spring of 1850 when the California legislature passed the Foreign Miners' Tax, a prohibitive monthly levy of twenty dollars on all "aliens." Over the next several months, mobs of American miners accompanied tax

Mexican miners. From William Redmond Ryan, Personal Adventures in Upper and Lower California in 1848–9 *(London, 1850). Beinecke Rare Book and Manuscript Library, Yale University.*

THE "DIGGINS"—SONOREANS DRY-WASHING GOLD.

assessors on their rounds, collecting the tax from Mexican miners who could pay and driving the rest away. Ramon Jil Navarro, a Chilean forty-niner who worked a valuable claim near the Mokelumne River with a group of his countrymen, awoke one morning to find notices tacked on the pines and oaks notifying all "foreigners" to abandon the country. A few days later a mob of Americans descended on his camp. They "despoiled every man of everything of value he had on his person," Navarro wrote, "then they demolished each house, not leaving a single wall standing, but taking care to steal the canvas that covered the roofs." Although Navarro's comrades were Chileans, most of the expelled miners probably would have qualified as citizens under the terms of the Treaty of Guadalupe Hidalgo. But American officials and mobs ignored laws and logic to nab the gold. Just as the hydraulic mining hoses eroded hillsides, their racist ideology swept away rights, precedence, tenure, fairness, and decency.[7]

Chinese and American miners in California. Photograph by Joseph B. Stark-weather. California State Library.

The place of thousands of departing Sonorans, Chileans, and Peruvians was soon taken by another group of immigrant miners. Several hundred Chinese arrived in California in 1849, and within a year they were passing through the Golden Gate by the thousands. "Americans are very rich people," read one Chinese circular promoting migration to California. "They want the Chinamen to come and make him very welcome. There you will have great pay, large houses, and food and clothing of the finest description." By 1859 an estimated thirty-five thousand Chinese were working in the California goldfields, and they joined in the rush to each subsequent strike in the West. Dressed in their distinctive blue cotton shirts, baggy pants, and broad-brimmed hats, with a single long braid, or queue, hanging down their backs, the Chinese looked and labored for their main chance, often forming companies to work over the deposits rejected by American miners and making them pay.[8]

Many Chinese came to California as sojourners—as did many Sonorans, Chileans, and Americans. They intended to return as soon as their savings warranted, and every year thousands of them sailed home. Also like their Gold Rush colleagues, the Chinese immigrants were overwhelmingly male. Most were married, but almost none brought their wives along. Respectable Chinese women were expected to remain at home, and families believed that keeping them there would encourage the return of their husbands. The California census of 1852 listed only

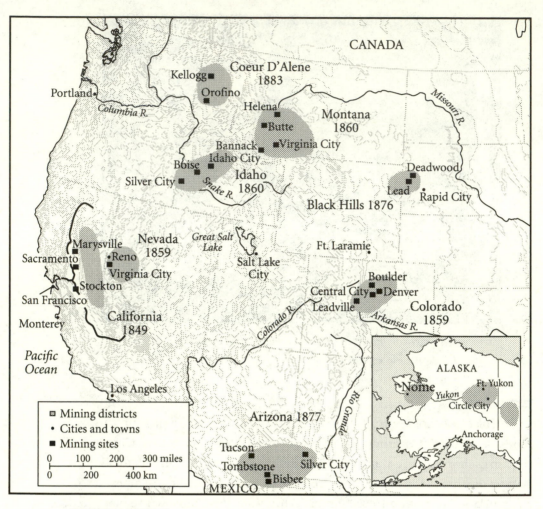

WESTERN MINING

seven Chinese women in the state, and over the next three decades most of the women who immigrated from China were prostitutes, many of them enslaved.

In the cities, towns, and mining camps of the West, Chinese men clustered in "Chinatowns" for protection and camaraderie. In the eyes of many white Americans, this huddling made the Chinese even more suspect than the Mexicans. A California newspaper described groups of twenty or thirty Chinese "inhabiting close cabins, so small that one . . . would not be of sufficient size to allow a couple of Americans to breathe in it." White Americans, however, helped create the clannishness they loathed by targeting the Chinese for abuse and exclusion. In 1852 the California legislature passed a foreign miners' tax aimed specifically at the Chinese. Before the Civil Rights Act of 1870 voided the law, Chinese miners had contributed more than five million dollars to the state's coffers, a quarter of the state's revenue for those years.[9]

Two Chinese toughs, Blackfoot, Idaho, c. 1870. Idaho State Historical Society.

The Chinese helped finance a state that offered them none of the rudimentary protections states are formed to provide. In the case of *People v. Hall* (1854),
the California Supreme Court stripped the Chinese of the most basic legal rights.
George Hall and two white companions had been convicted and sentenced to hang
for the murder of a Chinese man. Hall's attorneys appealed on the grounds that
Chinese testimony was inadmissible, since the statutes excluded the evidence of
African Americans, Indians, and other peoples of color. "This continent," argued
the court, twisting reason into ornate pretzels, "was first peopled by Asiatics, who
crossed Behring's Straits." This made the Chinese virtual Indians, which disquali-
fied them from testifying against white Americans. They were "a race of people
whom nature has marked as inferior and who are incapable of progress or intellectual development beyond a certain point." Hall's conviction was overturned and
the murderer set free.[10]

The Chinese responded to antagonism in a variety of ways. They were among
the first on the scene as mining districts spread across the West. In Idaho, where
they made up nearly 50 percent of the miners in the Boise gold district by 1870, they
used their numbers to enforce their own kind of justice. They also turned to the
Idaho courts to oppose a territorial foreign miners' tax in 1864. They lost the suit,
but the local courts accepted testimony from Chinese witnesses, and most Chinese

miners refused to pay the tax with no punishment inflicted. Idaho proved that numbers mattered, and the Chinese continued to use the courts to settle claims among themselves and with Americans. "Although hardly perfect," argues historian Liping Zhu, Idaho "offered Chinese immigrants opportunities far beyond the proverbial 'Chinaman's chance.'" In spite of prejudice, discrimination, and attempts at removal, the Chinese, the Mexicans, and immigrants from dozens of European countries made the West their new home. Whether the American "natives" liked it or not, the West would be shared by a motley crew of humanity.[11]

The corporatization and industrialization of the West did not mean an end to irrational exuberance. Dreams of quick wealth shifted from alluvial sand to stock portfolios. The western millionaires that capitalized most on the active imaginations of investors, newspaper editors, and congressional representatives were the Big Four—Collis P. Huntington, Mark Hopkins, Leland Stanford, and Charles Crocker—the founders of the Central Pacific Railroad, which built the California-to-Utah section of the first transcontinental line, completed in 1869. The rails carried the hopes for prosperity of many Americans. "The iron key has been found to unlock our golden treasures," gushed the editor of the *Helena Independent*. "With the railroads come population, industry, and capital, and with them come the elements of prosperity and greatness to Montana." Once it was in place, argued the railroad barons, the national railroad system would undergird a fabulously valuable exchange of people and products between East and West. Thousands of settlers would stream onto the plains and over the mountains to the Pacific coast, settling on farms, ranches, and in dozens of rapidly growing cities and towns, scattered like oases across the western countryside. And indeed, the late nineteenth-century West would have been inconceivable without the railroad. "The West is purely a railroad enterprise," declared an executive of one of the transcontinental lines, then with a wink adding, "we started it in our publicity department."[12]

The transcontinentals needed vigorous publicity departments because the notion of a railroad economic bonanza was much like the visions of gold in the streambeds just waiting to be panned—it was a fantasy that existed mainly in people's minds. At the time of their construction, the railroads confronted a West that was conspicuously lacking in customers. That's why few knowledgeable eastern railroad men wanted anything to do with the transcontinentals. The smart money passed, leaving the door open for the Big Four. As principal stockholders of California's first giant corporation, they grew resplendently wealthy, but their nickname came neither from their wealth nor from their power but from their bulk, weighing in collectively at some 860 pounds. Each man hailed from modest roots in the Northeast, and each would later attribute his success to Yankee virtues

Leland Stanford, c. 1870. Wikimedia Commons.

of diligence and thrift. But, as Crocker once admitted, "luck had a hell of a lot to do with it," as did the entrepreneurs' willingness to play hard and fast with the rules when necessary.[13]

The Big Four were all forty-niners. Huntington had come to California via Panama, where, like thousands of others, he was stranded for three months clamoring for passage up the coast to San Francisco. During that time, shrewdly buying and selling whatever he could get his hands on, he increased his initial grubstake by nearly 300 percent. Arriving in California, he immediately grasped the fact that fortune lay not in the gravel at the bottom of a pan but in the sale of the pan itself, and he opened a Sacramento miner's supply. Crocker told a similar story. After trudging cross-country in 1850, his few possessions "tied up in a cotton handkerchief," he worked briefly in the mines before seeing the light and becoming a partner in a general store. Hopkins and Stanford—the first an accountant, the other a glad-handing lobbyist—learned the same lesson before their overland treks, and both went west intending to become prosperous merchants in the gold region.[14]

In 1861, in an upstairs room of the Sacramento store jointly owned by Huntington and Hopkins, this group gathered to hear the pitch of a zealot railroad builder named Theodore Judah. It was not the first time that Judah spread his plans, surveys, and dreams before potential investors. But the Big Four were the first to respond favorably, each pledging to buy fifteen thousand dollars of stock in the company for which Judah had drawn up the articles of incorporation. When Judah died unexpectedly, the operations fell directly to the Big Four. Although they barely knew each other—and would never become friends—they quickly developed an effective division of labor. Hard-headed Crocker supervised construction while inscrutable Hopkins kept the books; Huntington used his talents bidding for supplies in the East while Stanford worked the politicians in Sacramento and Washington, an assignment made easier when in 1861 he won election as California's first Republican governor. The Big Four were about to undertake one of the most spectacular construction projects of the age, yet as Crocker remembered, "none of us knew anything about railroad building."[15]

Not so the leader of the Union Pacific, the Kansas-to-Utah partner corporation to the Central Pacific. Thomas C. Durant, the chief manager of the Union Pacific, learned the railroad business as construction manager for the Chicago and Little Rock Island line built across Iowa during the 1850s. Because every Iowan wanted to be as close to the railroad as possible, Durant threatened to bypass towns or counties that failed to buy sufficient bonds. There are stories of him laying out town sites, auctioning off lots to speculators, then shifting the line to cheaper adjoining land and repeating the whole process. In 1858 Congress awarded the company a large land grant if it completed the Iowa project within ten years. Knowing that this was more than enough time, Durant slowed construction, reasoning that the longer the company took, the more valuable the land would become. It was a preview of what was to come with the construction of the Union Pacific.

Durant invented a way of making fantastic profits on transcontinental lines that looked like boondoggles on paper. Instead of earning their profits through the shipping of people and goods, the transcontinentals would pay off a lucky few through their construction. Durant set up a subsidiary corporation, the Crédit Mobilier, wholly owned by UP stockholders. Through dummy third parties, he channeled all construction contracts to Crédit Mobilier, which in turn exaggerated expenses by double or triple. Though the accounts of the Union Pacific showed little profit, the Crédit Mobilier paid handsome dividends. It was one of the most ingenious swindles in American history. The con was plain enough to see, but Durant used an enormous slush fund to keep official Washington from looking too closely. Republican congressman Oakes Ames, appointed head of the Crédit Mobilier, distributed UP stock certificates, as he put it, "where they will do the most good for us." When the scandal finally broke into the open, the subsequent congressional investigation revealed that the entire Republican leadership, including the vice president and the chairmen of some of the most important House and Senate committees, had accepted Ames's bribes.[16]

The Central Pacific had its own version of the same scam, the Credit and Finance Corporation, which overcharged by millions. But the Big Four avoided public exposure because their records "just happened" to be destroyed in a fire. Huntington distributed more than his fair share of graft, remaining confident in his own righteousness while performing magic with the company's millions. "If you have to pay money to have the right thing done, it is only just and fair to do so," he exclaimed. In his day Huntington corrupted officeholders, lawmen, and regulatory commissioners, just as he pressured and blackmailed newsmen to manipulate public opinion. An acquaintance captured the man's spirit: "Tigerish and irrational in his ravenous pursuit, he was always on the scent, incapable of fatigue, delighted in his strength and the use of it, and full of the love of combat. If the Great Wall of China were put in his path, he would attack it with his nails."[17]

The shenanigans of the railroad tycoons toed the line between farce and tragedy. They captured the spirit of an age filled with slick operators and shifty deals. These fat cats, however, did what they did not because of their cartoonish, mustache-twirling villainy. The federal government encouraged the building of the transcontinental railroads by guaranteeing the right-of-way, supplying low-interest loans, and offering enormous land grants, and the railroad executives corrupted politicians to keep these subsidies coming. The federal government encouraged nefarious behavior by taking on the risk of transcontinental transportation, and the American people were left holding the bag when the operational profits (as opposed to the inflated construction costs) failed to materialize.

Other western industries had their bubbles popped, too. Fly-by-night mining corporations peddled stock in worthless or nonexistent shafts, while investments in cattle businesses reached a fevered pitch in the 1870s and 1880s. In 1881 James Brisbin published *Beef Bonanza, or How to Get Rich on the Plains,* which carried a delirious message of quick wealth that rivaled golden dreams. Capital poured in from New York, London, and Edinburgh. Theodore Roosevelt, the future president, was one of many investors who turned to ranching for fun and profit, investing tens of thousands of dollars in a Badlands ranch in the Dakota Territory. In 1883 Scots investors dumped $2.5 million into the huge Swan Land and Cattle Company, which controlled more than six hundred thousand acres of Nebraska and Wyoming range. Another Scots firm, the Espuela Cattle Company, opened a half-million-acre spread in Texas called the Spur Ranch. British investors financed Charlie Goodnight's huge JA Ranch in the Palo Duro Canyon of Texas. A movement of consolidation swept over the cattle country, inaugurating the brief ascendancy of what historian J. C. Mutchler calls the "super ranch." Sprawling over three million acres in ten counties in the Texas Panhandle was the XIT (which stood for Ten in Texas). Richard King, owner of the enormous King Ranch of south Texas, employed three hundred cowboys to work his sixty-five thousand cattle. On John Chisum's Rancho Grande, a massive spread straddling the Texas–New Mexico border that covered a territory the size of southern New England, wranglers branded eighteen thousand calves in a single season in 1884.[18]

While cattle barons dreamed of spreads that breached horizons—a vision destined to crash when their vast herds ate up all the available grass—western farmers inherited smaller-scale expectations that would prove equally ecstatic. That was not supposed to happen. In the nation's folklore, farmers were thought to be especially virtuous. They were supposed to be the backbone of American independence, their self-sufficiency protecting them from the machinations of tyrants. They owned property and managed the labor of family members and hired workers, so in theory, running a farm prepared them to run the country. Tending crops, herding livestock, and leading households made rural folks into model democrats.

At midcentury Americans continued to believe in the Jeffersonian promise that ordinary citizens could move west, stake modest claims to land, and rise to the ideal level of comfortable sufficiency, neither rich nor poor but simply happy and content. The promise depended on the availability of western land—boundless, fertile, and cheap. In post–Civil War America that availability was underwritten by the Homestead Act, a plan to grant rather than sell public domain land, passed by the Republican Congress in the spring of 1862. The legislation grew out of the political struggles of squatters versus speculators that had animated land policy debates since the passage of the first Land Ordinance of 1785. It was intended to extend and revitalize a nostalgic vision of American success and democracy. The results—as in western railroads, ranches, and mines—combined epic accomplishment with spectacular failure.

The new Republican Party embraced the homestead program as part of its effort to build a political alliance between the North and the West. In exchange for northern votes for homestead legislation, westerners would support higher tariffs to protect infant industries like textiles and iron. Under Republican auspices, the homestead program took on an antislavery cast. "A country cut up into small farms, occupied by many independent proprietors who live by their own toil," George Washington Julian of Indiana told his fellow congressmen, would present a "formidable barrier against the introduction of slavery." Southern legislators, fearing that the agitation for free land inevitably would lead to "free soil"—the political movement to bar slavery from the territories—became implacable opponents of the homestead bill.[19]

The Republican electoral triumph of 1860 and the subsequent secession of the southern states, along with the mass departure of southern politicians from Washington, removed the final obstacle to the passage of the "Act to Secure Homesteads

A homesteading family on the plains. Detail of a photograph by Solomon D. Butcher, 1886. Library of Congress.

to Actual Settlers on the Public Domain." The measure took effect on January 1, 1863, the same day as the Emancipation Proclamation. Persons over the age of twenty-one—without regard to race or ethnicity, women as well as men, immigrants as well as citizens—were eligible to file for up to 160 acres of the public domain. Homesteaders had to cultivate the land, construct a house or barn, and reside on the claim for five years, after which they would receive full title for the payment of a ten-dollar filing fee. By 1935, when President Franklin D. Roosevelt issued an executive order withdrawing the remaining public domain land in the contiguous forty-eight states, the Homestead Act had created farms for more than four hundred thousand families.[20]

It was an achievement of historic proportions, unlike anything tried by any other nation. Still, it should be kept in perspective. Over the same seventy-year period, for every 160 acres of western land given away, another 400 acres was sold. A total of more than 700 million acres passed into private hands through purchase rather than grant. Contrary to American myth, most western settlers were not homesteaders. Most took up public land under the terms of previous laws. Because only surveyed land was open to homesteading, and government surveys of the vast West proceeded at a snail's pace, to get the land they wanted many settlers did what Americans had always done—squatting to establish a preemption claim and purchasing later. Furthermore, homesteading was not available on the land taken from western Indian nations (approximately 100 million acres after 1862) or on the alternating sections the government retained for itself along the rail lines. These plots, with minor exceptions, were available for cash purchase only. The federal government gave away, in the form of subsidies, 183 million acres to the western railroads—an area larger than the state of Texas—and that land was sold at top dollar. Lands along the rail lines, of course, were the most attractive, since by definition they offered access to transportation, without which commercial farming in the trans-Mississippi West was infeasible.

In 1873, the tenth anniversary of the Homestead Act, the federal government circulated a pamphlet boasting that the law had "prevented large capitalists from absorbing great tracts of the public domain." That was a barefaced lie. The Republican Congress had refused to enact limitations on the amount of public land individuals could acquire, and thus the Homestead Act failed to realize reformers' hopes of forestalling land monopoly in the West. Speculators were able to amass large holdings by purchase from railroads or the states, both only too happy to lower prices for big buyers. As a result, speculators grabbed the best farming land in the West before it was available to homesteaders. Almost all the remaining land was far from rail lines.[21]

Then there were the notorious strategies of unscrupulous men devised to defraud the government and frustrate the intentions of the legislation. "Dummy" homestead entries became so common that they were standing jokes in late nineteenth-century America. Working at the bidding of speculators, hired men set up tiny prefabricated shacks on 160-acre quarter-sections to satisfy the minimum legal requirements of "improvement," paid the minimum cash price after the required six months of residence, and then signed the deed over to their employers. Cattlemen and lumbermen were able to acquire tens of thousands of acres by using such methods. In one shocking episode, uncovered by federal investigators at the turn of the century, the California Redwood Company rounded up foreign sailors in San Francisco and marched them, first to the courthouse to file citizenship papers, then to the land office to take out timber claims, then to a notary public to sign blank deeds transferring title to the company, and finally to paymasters who gave them fifty dollars. "Immense tracts of the most valuable timber land," wrote the commissioner of the General Land Office in 1901, "have become the property of a few individuals and corporations." The engrossment of land may have been more prevalent after the Homestead Act than before.[22]

Homesteader fraud: a house "twelve by fourteen." From Albert D. Richardson, Beyond the Mississippi . . . (New York, 1867).

Meanwhile, nearly half of all genuine homesteaders failed to patent or "prove up" their claims. The land may have been free, but the cost of equipment, seed, and supplies for the first year or two was often more than they could manage. Others found themselves unable to stick it out in isolated locations for the required residency period, while still others failed to make their acres pay commercially because of the poor quality of their land or the distance to the railroad. Despite the Homestead Act, the majority of western farmers became tenants on land owned by someone else. The homestead program, supporter George Washington Julian lamented in 1879, had turned out to be "a cruel mockery."[23]

Given all the graft, lies, nostalgia, miscalculations, and delusions that accompanied industrial colonization, it's a wonder that large-scale corporate capitalism survived in the West at all, much less remade the place like a colossus. Perhaps that's the key. The scale of change grew with the scope of malfeasance, inefficiency, and errors. For every successful venture, hundreds of businesses collapsed in the nineteenth-century West. The region filled with gleaming monuments and crumbling ruins simultaneously; both accelerated the pace of change and widened industrial capitalism's footprint. The construction of the transcontinental railroads and the great mines of the West epitomized the epic scale of some industrial undertakings.

Temporary and permanent bridges at Green River, Wyoming. Photograph by A. J. Russell, c. 1869. Beinecke Rare Book and Manuscript Library, Yale University.

The Union Pacific and Central Pacific began their frantic race to see which could build the fastest, get the largest subsidy, and engross most of the future commerce in 1865. Except for winters, when rough weather forced the suspension of construction, there were at least twenty thousand men working constantly to build what Oakes Ames, without exaggeration, called "the greatest public work of this century." Supervising the project for the Union Pacific were the Casement brothers, sons of immigrant parents and experienced railroad contractors, though they were only in their thirties. Jack stood five feet, four inches tall, his brother Dan "five feet nothing," but both were hard bosses who drove their workers demonically. American legend has it that the majority of those workers were Irish, and for the most part they were, although there were also ex-Confederate and Union soldiers, Mexicans, and former African American slaves as well.[24]

At first, the Central Pacific of California had a harder time finding workers. The Gold Rush hordes had rushed elsewhere, and labor in California was scarce and expensive. Charles Crocker considered importing Mexicans but instead decided to give the abundant Chinese population a try. "I will not boss Chinese!" announced

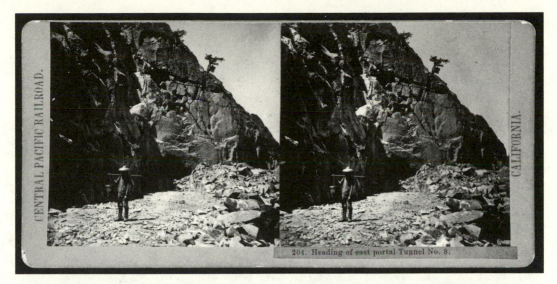

Chinese worker on the Central Pacific Railroad near Donner Pass in the Sierra Nevada. Stereograph by Alfred A. Hart, c. 1868. Library of Congress.

the company's superintendent of construction. "Who said laborers had to be white to build railroads?" Crocker shot back. The Chinese soon quelled all such questions with their persistence, diligence, and courage, and they became the workers of choice. "Wherever we put them we found them good," wrote Crocker, "and they worked themselves into our favor to such an extent that if we found we were in a hurry for a job of work, it was better to put on the Chinese at once." Along some of the nearly impassable gorges of the Sierras, Chinese workers chipped away at solid granite walls with claw hammers, carrying off the rock by the basket load—a job so difficult that in spite of their numbers they were able to average only eight inches per day. They became expert in handling the nitroglycerin used to blast through the mountains, although many died in the inevitable accidents. By 1867 Crocker was paying labor contractors for twelve thousand Chinese laborers, 90 percent of his workforce.[25]

The Casement brothers perfected a highly efficient division of labor with not a single motion wasted. Three strokes to the spike, ten spikes to the rail, four hundred rails to the mile—they pushed the men to quicken the pace, offering time and a half for each mile-and-a-half day, double time for two. At the peak of construction in 1868 and 1869, the workers were whipped into a frenzy of six to seven miles of track daily. The Central Pacific, too, once it had blasted through the Sierras and reached the Nevada deserts, began to calculate its daily distance in multiple miles. Indeed, on one remarkable day in early 1869, the Chinese workers established a world record by laying 26,456 feet of track—more than ten miles—in a single twelve-hour period.

East and West join at the laying of the last rail. Photograph by A. J. Russell, 1869. Beinecke Rare Book and Manuscript Library, Yale University.

The symbolic joining of the rails was enacted on May 10, 1869. Dignitaries from both coasts joined railroad workers and a few reporters for the ceremony. A gang of Chinese workers laid the last few rails and drove all but the last spike, then were hustled off so as not to appear in the official photographs. As the band played and the crowd cheered, Leland Stanford came forward and set in place an eighteen-ounce golden spike, crowned with a large gold nugget. A telegraph wire was attached to the spike and another to the hammer in Stanford's hand, so that on impact the news would flash to a waiting world. Stanford and then Durant took a swing—both missed. The telegraph operator tapped out "DONE."[26]

But the work was not done. The race between the companies had taken precedence over careful construction. "I am very glad to learn that you have made up your mind to go for quantity of road instead of quality," Huntington had written to Crocker in 1868. The result was shoddy work. Ballasts had been improperly laid and roadbeds collapsed; curves had been engineered too sharply and trains derailed. It would cost nearly ten million dollars to correct construction mistakes. As crews tore up railroad sections to make them right, the transcontinental line became both a ruin and a marvel.[27]

By the 1870s the mining industry throughout the Far West had reached economies of scale on par with the railroads. The industry was concentrated in the hands of a wealthy elite. Some of these bonanza kings had clawed their way up from the diggings. George Hearst, father of the newspaper baron William Randolph Hearst, crossed the plains on foot in 1850 and within a few years had made a pile in placer and quartz mining. In 1859 he invested in the Comstock Lode and laid the foundation for an even greater fortune. "If you're ever inclined to think that there's no such thing as luck," Hearst once remarked, "just think of me." In 1877 Hearst and his partner purchased the Homestake Mine in the Black Hills and, by gradually buying up the claims of competing and adjoining miners, turned their property into the most fabulous of all western gold mines. More frequently capital came from investors who had never lifted a shovel. Eastern and British capitalists loaned huge sums to western bankers who in turn invested in western mining. William Ralston of the Bank of California financed the integration of mines, mills, smelters, railroads, and lumber companies on the Comstock Lode. It was classic American capitalism: aggressive, high-risk, and spectacular.[28]

Western miners were laboring for eastern corporations. "The situation is much different from what we in Denmark imagined," a journalist reported home to a newspaper in Copenhagen. "When we speak of a gold miner, we mean a kind of King Midas who simply has to thrust his spade into the ground to find a nugget. But that is not how it is. A gold miner is a common mine worker who labors for a company." Within a few decades, the most fabulous profits were in the mining of base metals rather than precious ones. After a brief moment as a gold and silver mining center, the Montana town of Butte became the mother of all western copper mining—"The Richest Hill on Earth," in the phrase of local promoters. At the turn of the century, there were copper strikes at such places as Globe and Bisbee in southern Arizona and at the Bingham open-pit mine near Salt Lake City—which jokesters lampooned as "The Richest Hole on Earth." These operations were in the hands of large mining corporations with names like Kennecott, Phelps-Dodge, and Anaconda. By the eve of World War I, the West was producing 90 percent of the nation's copper as well as most of its lead and other heavy metals. Work in these hard-rock mines was extremely dangerous. One investigation of Butte's deepest shaft measured the air temperature at 107 degrees Fahrenheit and the

Smelter at Deadwood, Dakota Territory. Photograph by W. R. Cross, 1891. Beinecke Rare Book and Manuscript Library, Yale University.

relative humidity at 100 percent. The heat and humidity magnified the stench of human sweat, excrement, blasting powder, rotting food, and tobacco. Men sometimes dropped dead from such conditions. The accident rate was incredibly high. Western mining was the most hazardous industry in the nation.[29]

Western farmers breathed fresher air than miners, but they too discovered industrial gigantism. Mechanization accelerated following the Civil War. Steel replaced wood and iron in the manufacture of plows; new riding plows allowed farmers to sit and drive their teams; and soon horses were pulling gang plows, which turned over several rows simultaneously. Horsepower was also put to use with new hay mowing, raking, and loading machines. A ton of hay could be loaded from the field in just minutes. The McCormick automatic self-rake reaper of 1867, called "Old Reliable," cut wheat and swept it aside for binding. It was not long before an inventive westerner perfected an automatic binder that gathered the shocks, tied them with a length of twine, and kicked them free. Power threshers appeared, the early ones using horsepower, later models driven by coal-fired steam boilers. In 1880 harvesting and threshing were joined in the "combine" machine, and within a few years, giant steam combines were producing up to eighteen hundred sacks of grain each day. By the end of the century, wheat farming was eighteen times more productive than it had been before the Civil War.

Combined reaper-thresher, pulled by thirty horses, harvesting wheat in eastern Oregon. Photograph by W. A. Raymond, c. 1903. Library of Congress.

Mechanization made possible the giant bonanza farms of the northern plains and the great Central Valley of California. Many of these farms grew from the corporate design of the railroads. After the Panic of 1873, the Northern Pacific attempted to fend off bankruptcy by offering its far-flung acres in exchange for its own depreciated securities. Within two years, the railroad had sold off 483,000 acres in the Red River valley of Dakota Territory at five dollars an acre, with just twenty-three buyers accounting for two-thirds of the acreage. They divided the land according to the most modern principles of efficient production and hired the best foremen and managers they could find. The most famous of the bonanza farms was the thirty-four thousand acres a few miles west of Fargo managed by Oliver Dalrymple, an experienced grain farmer from Minnesota. One of Dalrymple's rippling wheat fields stretched for thirteen thousand unbroken acres. Separate gangs working on distant corners of the farm might not see one another for the entire season. In California, where huge estates were carved from the land grants of the Central Pacific, the largest farms extended over more than sixty-six thousand acres and produced more than a million bushels annually. By 1880 California had become the biggest wheat-producing state in the nation. Whether in the Dakotas or in the San Joaquin valley, these farms embodied the vital components of industrial capitalism—the application of machinery to mass production, absentee ownership, professional management specialization, and proletarian labor.

Combines and megafarms signaled the radical newness that accompanied industrial colonization. The onslaught of machines, international workforces, and global capitalism engulfed western environments and people. The new suffocated the old, breaking time into before and after, glowing past and grim future. Still, industrialization did not bring change to the West: the place had been changing all along. Global capitalism arrived centuries before the railroads, so too technological innovation. The bison-hunting nomads and pastoral horse-herders had demonstrated their adaptive genius, spurring new technologies to military and market dominance. Epidemic diseases disrupted and reshuffled human populations, while earlier colonizers melded with natives creating new groups like the métis and mestizos. Industrial colonization amplified and accelerated change, pushing some western species and communities over the brink. The wreckage of modernization was extreme, quick, and stunning, as were the survival maneuvers of the people that rode the avalanche to worlds undreamed of before the tractors and factories crashed down on them.

The Indians of California had endured Franciscan missionaries, international kingdom-makers, and American interlopers. Though disease had thinned their ranks, they responded to colonization through a mixture of strategies covering the gamut from violent resistance and relocation to Christianization and wage labor. No strangers to abrupt and dramatic change, the Miwoks and Maidus near John Sutter's fort joined the rush to the goldfields as soon as the news reached them. An abusive employer who paid a pittance, Sutter cursed his former workers who fled his dollars that could no longer "bring them to work." The Gold Rush ruined Sutter and his enterprise on the Sacramento. His Indian workers were joined by hundreds of other Native Americans in the rush to the mines. When California's territorial governor toured the diggings in the summer of 1848, he found four thousand miners at work, "of whom more than half were Indians." Many labored for Anglo and Mexican contractors. "A few men who are working 30 to 40 Indians are laying up to $1000 to $2000 a week," American consul Thomas O. Larkin wrote in July. Other Indians mined for themselves or for their communities. A Chilean miner came across a group of Miwoks collectively working a stream in the Sierras. "The men dug and gave the mud to the children, who then carried it in baskets to the women." Panning with "grass baskets of the most perfect construction," the women carefully separated the gold and then tied up small portions in bits of rag. These they used "to trade with, just as if they were money."[30]

Indian mining came to an abrupt end with the arrival of the forty-niners. Suddenly Indian homelands were overrun by tens of thousands of Americans. Violence broke out immediately. In one typical incident in early 1849, a group of Oregon prospectors on the American River shot up a Maidu village, raping women and killing several men. The outraged Indians retaliated by ambushing and killing five of the miners, and in return the Oregonians attacked an unconnected village, murdering twelve people, taking others captive, and then executing them. There were dozens of similar incidents. The Indians "could not understand why they should be murdered, robbed, and hunted down in this way, without any other pretense or provocation other than the color of their skin," traveler J. Ross Browne wrote sympathetically. It "never occurred to them that they were suffering for the great cause of civilization, which, in the natural course of things, must exterminate Indians."[31]

Miners drove the natives into the barren high Sierras, depriving them of their food supplies and forcing them to raid the livestock of valley ranchers to survive. Ranchers retaliated with attacks on Indian retreats in the mountains. Americans, wrote one federal official, "value the life of an Indian just as they do that of a *cayota* or a wolf, and embrace every occasion to shoot [them] down." Federal Indian agents charged with protecting the Indians found themselves powerless to stop the carnage. When one conscientious agent attempted to file charges against a group of murdering miners, the United States attorney in San Francisco refused to act, saying that "he was not aware of the existence of any law that would apply" and suggested turning the matter over to local authorities. But the mob's leader had recently been elected county judge, and the agent questioned whether it would be "worth while to prosecute him in his own county."[32]

As this story suggests, much of the violence was condoned, even sponsored by government officials. In 1851 federal commissioners negotiated a set of treaties with the California tribes, creating a series of reservations scattered across the state, but the governor and legislature opposed the treaties, claiming that they set aside too much land, and instead argued for the removal of all Indians from the state. The treaties were forwarded to the United States Senate, which followed the lead of California's congressional delegation and tabled them in 1853, in effect withdrawing the federal government from its constitutional responsibility to oversee Indian affairs in California. The state assumed unprecedented authority. In a special message to the legislature, Governor Peter Burnett rhetorically shrugged his shoulders at the inevitable, homicidal course of white civilization, declaring that "a war of extermination will continue to be waged between the races until the Indian race becomes extinct." Over the next few years, with the encouragement and sponsorship of the state, thousands of Indians were murdered by miners,

PROTECTING THE SETTLERS.

California settlers attack an Indian village. Illustration by J. Ross Browne, from Harper's Magazine, *August 1861.*

ranchers, and militia. It was the starkest case of genocide in the history of American frontiers.[33]

The "Act for the Government and Protection of Indians" passed by the legislature in 1850 added greatly to the suffering. The pretense was that the law provided a way of disciplining dangerous Indian vagrants and caring for dependent Indian orphans, but in fact, under its cover of legality, thousands of Indian men, women, and children were kidnapped and sold to Anglo and Mexican employers. One federal agent apprehended three kidnappers with a group of nine Indian children ranging in ages from three to ten years of age. The men defended themselves by claiming that taking the children was "an act of charity" because their parents had been killed. How do you know that? asked the agent. Because, one of the kidnappers replied, "I killed some of them myself." A legalized form of slavery, the so-called protection act continued the Californian tradition begun by the Spanish of using forced Indian labor to profit from colonization. The 1850 law was finally invalidated by the ratification of the Thirteenth Amendment to the Constitution, which abolished slavery and involuntary servitude within the United States.[34]

As a result of the genocidal violence, the forced labor, and epidemic diseases, the Indian population of California, estimated at 150,000 in 1848, fell to 30,000 by 1860—120,000 lives lost in just twelve years, a record of human destruction unmatched in American history. A minority of the remaining natives lived in isolated rancherias, but most clustered in dingy shanties on the outskirts of towns like San Jose, San Diego, and Los Angeles, eking out a livelihood as day laborers. It wasn't until the mid-twentieth century that California Indians were able to use the courts to obtain some compensation for the lands stolen from them during the Gold Rush, but the final awards totaled less than a thousand dollars per survivor.

———

In his memoirs, William Tecumseh Sherman, commanding general of the U.S. Army following the Civil War, pointed to the expansion of the open-range cattle industry as a decisive factor in the conquest of the West. "This was another potent agency in producing the result we enjoy to-day," he wrote, "in having in so short a time replaced the wild buffaloes by more numerous herds of tame cattle, and by substituting for the useless Indians the intelligent owners of productive farms and cattle-ranchers." Sherman pegged the animal succession—cattle did replace bison—but he mistook the agency. Cowboys and cattlemen won the grass, but they did not eliminate the ruminant competition. The enormous bison herds were done in by white and Indian overhunting, exotic diseases, shifts in weather patterns, and habitat destruction. No one group deserved sole credit or blame for their destruction.[35]

"Shooting Buffalo on the Line of the Kansas-Pacific Railroad." From Frank Leslie's Illustrated Newspaper, *June 3, 1873. Library of Congress.*

    Plains Indians had long hunted the bison, and the level of their predation increased with the dispersal of horses in the eighteenth century. From a peak of perhaps thirty million, the number of buffalo declined to perhaps ten million by the mid-nineteenth century, partly as a result of commercial overhunting by Indians (for tradable bison robes), but also because of environmental competition from growing herds of wild horses and the spread of bovine diseases introduced by cattle crossing with settlers on the Overland Trail. By overgrazing, cutting timber, and fouling water sources, overland migrants contributed to the degeneration of habitats crucial for the health and survival of the bison. The confluence of factors created a crisis for buffalo-hunting Indians by the 1860s.

    The extension of railroad lines onto the Great Plains and the development in 1870 of a technique for converting buffalo hide into commercial leather (for belts to drive industrial machines) sealed the bison's fate. Lured by hide profits, swarms of hunters invaded the plains. Using a high-powered rifle, a skilled hunter could kill dozens of animals in an afternoon. And unlike the hunter of buffalo robes, who was limited to taking his catch in the winter when the coat was thick, hide hunting was a year-round business. General Philip Sheridan applauded. "They are destroying the Indians' commissary," he declared. "Let them kill, skin, and sell until the buffaloes are exterminated." As the buffalo hunters did their work, Indians also ac-

Mountain of bison skulls, c. 1880. Wikimedia Commons.

celerated their kills, attempting to capture their share of the market. In Dodge City, Kansas, mountainous stacks of buffalo hides awaited shipment to eastern tanneries. Historians estimate that in the five years between 1870 and 1875, five or six million bison were slaughtered on the southern plains, virtually wiping out the southern herds. The hunt then shifted to the north. "It was the summer of my twentieth year [1883]," the Sioux holy man Black Elk later testified, that "the last of the bison herds was slaughtered by the Wasichus [white men]." With the exception of a small wild herd in northern Alberta and a few remnant individuals preserved by sentimental ranchers, the North American bison had been destroyed. Bone collectors piled up the skeletons for rail shipment to factories that ground them up for fertilizer.[36]

Soon the range where the buffalo had roamed was being stocked with Texas longhorns. Battle-ready versions of the domesticated cattle brought north by the Spanish, the longhorns evolved to fend for themselves in arid and predator-rich environments. Their horns could span six feet. Their ornery dispositions were matched by their racy flavor. By the end of the eighteenth century, several million grazed on the thousand hills of the California coastal range and on the grasslands between the Nueces River and the Rio Grande in Texas. Cattle tenders—vaqueros—evolved with their herds. They developed into superb horsemen and ropers, and by the 1760s Tejanos were driving their cattle to market in New Orleans.

It was in Louisiana that Anglo Americans first encountered Hispanic traditions of cattle raising. Herding had long been an occupation in the backcountry of the colonial South. Settlers built cow pens many miles from their farms to corral their stock, leaving them in the care of African or mixed-ancestry slaves and indentured servants. Using dogs rather than horses to tend their short-horned British breeds, these footsore herders, known as "cow-boys," pressed into the Appalachian foothills in pursuit of fresh grazing land. About the time of the Louisiana Purchase, backcountry cowboys and Indian drovers leapfrogged the Mississippi floodplain, and soon both groups were learning and adapting the vaquero traditions of horsemanship and roping. The large number of Spanish loanwords in the lingo of western cattle raising—*lariat, lasso, rodeo, rancho*—testify to this process of cultural fusion.

After the Texas revolution, ranchers violently replaced rancheros across savannas of south Texas. Cattlemen shipped their stock to market by steamer from Brownsville or Galveston, or combined their herds and drove them northeast to Shreveport or New Orleans, following old Tejano trails. Some Texans, however, were lured farther north in an attempt to tap eastern markets in the United States. Texans first trailed longhorns up what was known as the Shawnee Trail to Missouri in 1842, and by 1850 a sizable market for Texas beef had developed in Kansas City. But the Civil War brought to an end these early northern drives, just as the Union naval blockade closed off the Caribbean markets. When Texans went off to fight for the Confederacy, their neglected stock scattered across the countryside, and by 1865 an estimated five to six million emancipated longhorns were grazing on the Texas range.

Cattle outfits sold this free beef to industrial America. Following the war, they gathered herds and drove them north to railheads in Kansas—Topeka, Abilene, Wichita, Ellsworth, and Dodge City. After a bumpy journey, most Texas longhorns ended their lives on the killing-room floors of Kansas City or South Side Chicago, where they were processed along mechanized "disassembly lines." In the 1880s cattlemen drove herds even farther north into Wyoming and Montana, opening new ranches along the watercourses. These invaders took over the niche once reserved for the bison. They became the mammals who turned cellulose into protein and fat, giving their human partners access to the incredible reservoir of sunshine stored in the waving stems of grass.

In 1880 buffalo in Montana far outnumbered the 250,000 cattle; three years later, the buffalo were gone while the range stock had increased to 600,000. Yet, while both gobbled vegetation and supplied leather and T-bones, the beeves and the bison were not interchangeable. The cattle grazed differently, clipping some

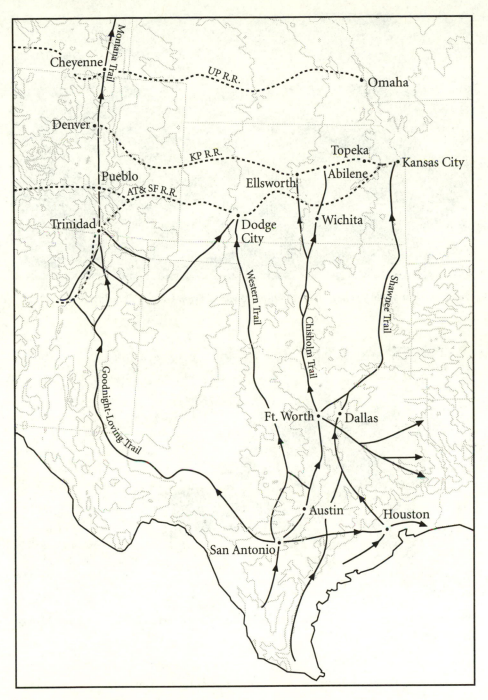

TEXAS CATTLE TRAILS

One of the first published images of American cowboys. From Harper's Weekly, *May 2, 1874.*

Waiting for a Chinook. *Painting by Charles M. Russell, 1886. Beinecke Rare Book and Manuscript Library. Yale University.*

native grass species to death, which created openings for invasive, inedible species like Russian thistle. The cows were also industrialized animals. They sucked energy from the Great Plains and moved it to tables in New York and Boston. The cattle were straws, conducting energy from one ecosystem to others. To capture this bounty, cattle-raisers jammed as many straws into the grasslands as they could. Very quickly, the herds exceeded the carrying capacity of the range. The weather turned, got drier and colder. The grass dwindled. And thousands of cattle died.

The Great Plains phased in and out of extended droughts every twenty years or so. The plants and animals that flourished there evolved to survive, even take advantage of, the cycle. Some grasses, for instance, plunged their roots deep into the soil and weathered the dry spells for the most part underground. American ranchers and farmers moved onto the plains after the Civil War during a particularly wet period. Some thought that the rain would last forever. Cultivated fields, they hypothesized, tamed arid environments. Rain would follow their plows.

But drought returned, the ranching bubble burst, and the wheat farmers retreated from the driest sections of the plains, only to return when precipitation again bumped up during the 1910s. The climate of the Great Plains did not cooperate with industrial colonization. No matter the size and efficiency of the organizations and institutions, no matter how big and plentiful the machines, the jet stream wavered and El Niños happened. Rain fell for years, and then rays baked the place to a crisp.

The United States experienced its first nationwide labor upheaval in 1877. The railroads had connected the continent, organizing Americans into massive networks of production and consumption. Workers, riders, owners, operators, and politicians were joined in a web of rails. When trouble jangled the web, everyone felt the reverberations. During the depression of the 1870s, workers suffered a series of crippling wage cuts; by the middle of the decade, for example, for a grueling twelve-hour day brakemen were being paid only $1.75, down from $2.50 ten years before. When, in the summer of 1877, the nation's four largest railroad companies adopted yet another 10 percent wage cut, eastern workers left their jobs and seized control of switching yards and depots. President Rutherford B. Hayes sent in federal troops, there were armed confrontations, and during the two weeks of the strike more than a hundred people died. The managers of the western railroads at first thought themselves immune to the disorder. "Our people did not think that we would have serious trouble," a prominent San Franciscan later remembered. "The Central [Pacific] Railroad and the system have never had serious trouble with their operatives." In spite of his prediction, the strike spread westward, first to Saint Louis and Kansas City, then to the Union Pacific yards at Omaha, then across the plains to the Central Pacific facilities at Ogden, Utah, and finally to the Pacific coast.[37]

The protest wave hit San Francisco and spilt into the crevices of animosity that radiated through the multicultural, industrial West. Several thousand people gathered before City Hall to hear Dennis Kearney of the Workingmen's Party of California harangue the Big Four. With one breath Kearney argued for popular control of the railroad—"the Central Pacific men are thieves and will soon feel the power of

Dennis Kearney of the Workingmen's Party incites San Franciscans to attack Chinatown. Engraving based on a drawing by H. A. Rodgers, Frank Leslie's Illustrated Newspaper, *March 20, 1880.*

the workingmen"—then with his next appealed to the crowd's worst prejudices— "I will give the Central Pacific just three months to discharge their Chinamen, and if that is not done Stanford and his crowd will have to take the consequences." That set off two days of anti-Chinese rioting. Mobs attacked Chinatown, beating men and women and burning buildings. Four people were killed.

The railroad did not fire the Chinese in response to the demands of the Workingmen's Party, but Congress took note of the anti-Chinese sentiment sweeping the West. The Burlingame Treaty with China, signed in 1868 while Chinese laborers were still hard at work on the transcontinental line, had pledged an open door for Chinese immigration. But in 1882, intoning that "the coming of the Chinese laborers to this country endangers the good order of certain localities," Congress passed the Chinese Exclusion Act, suspending further immigration of "all persons of the Chinese race" for ten years. Thereafter the Chinese exclusion was repeatedly extended until it became permanent as part of the Immigration Restriction Act of 1924.[38]

Exclusion prompted more anti-Chinese violence. Scapegoats for any number of "native" white frustrations, racist populists attacked the Chinese in dozens of western locales. Perhaps the most barbaric incident took place in 1885 in the railroad town of Rock Springs, Wyoming, when the Union Pacific attempted to replace white workers with lower-paid Chinese. In a coordinated attack, workers invaded the Chinese section of town, shooting, burning, and looting, while a group of wives and mothers cheered and fired shots at the fleeing Chinese. Chinatown was burned to the ground, and twenty-eight Chinese died in the flames. In the aftermath of this massacre, there were attacks on Chinatowns all over the West.

Attack on the Chinese, Rock Springs, Wyoming, September 2, 1885. Engraving based on a drawing by T. de Thulstrup, Harper's Weekly, *September 26, 1885.*

Racism eroded class solidarity throughout the West. The West's manifold ethnic and racial divisions aided industrialists. They played workers off one another and erected a labor system that paid "non-natives" less than citizens. Industrialization thus increased racial and ethnic antagonisms and undercut the goal of working-class solidarity, although the West did experience flashes of labor cooperation. Eugene Debs, leader of the American Railway Union (ARU), organized railroad workers across the West in sympathy with the striking workers at the Pullman sleeping car company in Chicago. In 1894 strikers occupied and held rail yards in Omaha, Ogden, Oakland, and Los Angeles; they burned bridges along the transcontinental line in Nevada.

One of the most dramatic and memorable incidents took place on a hot and humid July Fourth in Sacramento. Local militiamen were ordered to the train station to disperse strikers. They arrived to find hundreds of ARU members and sympathizers before the depot, waving American flags. People called out militiamen by name, urging them to put down their guns. "Frank, if you kill me you make your sister a widow," one man was heard calling out. Gradually the soldiers lowered their guns and wandered away to the shade, where ARU women served them lemonade. Community support for the strike also ran high in Los Angeles, where again the militia was called out. "If we had to fight Indians or a common enemy there would be some fun and excitement," one soldier told a reporter. "But this idea of shooting down American citizens simply because they are on strike for what they consider their rights is a horse of another color."[39]

_____

Both strikers and Indians stood in the way of development. But for Indians the situation was much more desperate. For them the spread of mining, for example, was an unmitigated disaster. The California experience was repeated in the Colorado rush of 1859, which led directly to the massacre of the Southern Cheyennes at Sand Creek. Thus when gold was discovered in the Yellowstone country of Montana, luring thousands of miners, the Sioux (longtime allies of the Cheyennes) took it as an ominous sign. As the army worked to construct forts along the road to protect miners, Oglala chief Red Cloud prepared to evict them. "The white men have crowded the Indians back year by year," he declared in a meeting at Fort Laramie. "And now our last hunting ground, the home of the people, is to be taken from us. Our women and children will starve, but for my part I prefer to die fighting rather than by starvation."[40]

In the three years of combat that followed, the Sioux and Cheyennes defeated most of the American forces sent against them. The federal government decided to abandon the forts along the Bozeman Trail, settling for an Indian agreement guaranteeing the security of the main east-west overland routes through the central plains, critical for the construction of the transcontinental railroad. In the 1868 Treaty of Fort Laramie, federal commissioners carved out a "Great Sioux Reservation" stretching from the Missouri River westward through the Black Hills, "for the absolute and undisturbed use and occupation of the Indians." Sioux rights to the adjacent Powder River country of Montana were left deliberately vague.[41]

In spite of his victories, however, Red Cloud sensed that the days of Indian armed resistance were over. A tour of the eastern United States in 1870 opened his eyes to the extent of American power. In the hopes of saving the Sioux from destruction, he and other accommodationist chiefs led the majority of their people onto the reservation. But militants like Crazy Horse of the Oglalas and Sitting Bull of the Hunkpapas opposed the strategy. Drawing followers from across tribes and clans, they refused to participate in what Crazy Horse called the "piecemeal penning" of his people. Crazy Horse asserted his mobility, following the bison, as his fathers had done. Sitting Bull, a holy man as well as a war chief, argued that compromise would get the Sioux nowhere. "The whites may get me at last, as you say," he told a group of reservation Indians, "but I will have good times till then. You are fools to make yourselves slaves to a piece of fat bacon, some hard-tack, and a little sugar and coffee." The factional conflict among Indians sometimes rivaled the hostility and intensity of the fighting with the Americans.[42]

Red Cloud. Photograph by Charles Milton Bell, 1880. Beinecke Rare Book and Manuscript Library, Yale University.

Sitting Bull. Photograph by Zalmon Gilbert, c. 1880. Beinecke Rare Book and Manuscript Library, Yale University.

Then George Armstrong Custer marched into the volatile mix. A dashing Civil War hero who knew the value of publicity, Custer led an armed scientific expedition into the Black Hills on the Sioux Reservation to confirm rumors of gold there. "From the grass roots down," he declared to the press, "it was 'pay dirt.'" Within two years the town of Deadwood was swarming with ten thousand miners and the nearby Homestake Mine was exploiting the richest lode of ore in American history. The Sioux treaty of 1868 required the army to keep miners and settlers off the reservation, but officers looked the other way, hoping that hobnailed boots on the ground would force the Sioux into agreeing to sell the Black Hills. A federal commission attempted to negotiate a purchase, and although Red Cloud and most of the reservation chiefs were willing to sell, they set a price the government was unwilling to pay. Sitting Bull was contemptuous of even a hard-driven bargain.

"I want you to go and tell the Great Father that I do not want to sell any land to the government," he declared. And bending down, he picked up a pinch of dust: "Not even as much as this." With gold beckoning, the federal government was in no mood to wait on stubborn Indians. Smashing the rejectionist Sioux became a bargaining gambit. With Sitting Bull trounced, more cooperative chiefs like Red Cloud might lower their price. American officials began to plan for a campaign of total war.[43]

Knowing what was coming, free bands of Sioux, Cheyennes, and Arapahos congregated in the summer of 1876 to hunt buffalo. In June, along the Powder River and the nearby Rosebud and Little Bighorn tributaries, more than four thousand men, women, and children assembled in what was the largest encampment any of them could remember. At a summer solstice Sun Dance ceremony, Sitting Bull had a vision of many dead American soldiers "falling right into our camp." His dream reflected the Indians' confidence and their determination to bloody the two army regiments of some thousand troops sent against them. In the first major encounter along the Rosebud, Crazy Horse and General George Crook fought with roughly equal numbers, and though Crook claimed victory, he was immobilized for nearly a month.

On June 25, Custer, leading six hundred troops of the Seventh Cavalry, came upon the combined Indian camp. A veteran Indian fighter, Custer had led a charge through a sleeping village of Southern Cheyennes along the Washita River in 1868 that left 103 Indians dead, including Chief Black Kettle, survivor of the Sand Creek Massacre. Instead of trepidation, the massive encampment filled the colonel with glee: "Hurrah, boys, we've got them."[44]

A commotion woke Wooden Leg from his afternoon nap in the Indian camp. The eighteen-year-old Cheyenne warrior roused his sleeping brother. "We heard shooting. We hurried out from the trees so we might see as well as hear. Women were screaming and men were letting out their war cries. Through it all we could hear old men calling: 'Soldiers are here! Young men, go out and fight them.' We ran to our camp and our home lodge. Everybody there was excited. . . . Children were hunting for their mothers. Mothers were anxiously trying to find their children. I got my lariat and my six-shooter." Wooden Leg's memories of that day reflect the power dynamic at play. The U.S. Army charged into the Battle of the Little Bighorn to assert its might. The Americans fought for many things: glory, duty, patriotism, and because, as enlisted men, they had no choice. But they did not fight to protect their families, as Wooden Leg did. The Americans wanted to break Indian resistance by destroying their food, their homes, and their family support. They could do this because trains, steamboats, and wagons supplied them with bacon, bullets, and female camp followers who cleaned their laundry. Industrialization forced the rebel Sioux, Cheyennes, and Arapahos to gamble everything, while Custer and his forces anted up only their lives.[45]

And Custer was no stranger to wagering lives. A reckless man, he refused to wait for reinforcements, divided his forces, and charged. He attacked the camp to the north. Major Marcus Reno hit from the south, where Wooden Leg joined the skirmishing. "Many hundreds of Indians on horseback were dashing to and fro in front of a body of soldiers. The soldiers were on the level valley ground and were shooting with rifles. Not many bullets were being sent back at them, but thousands of arrows were falling among them." Suddenly, the American soldiers panicked, mounted, and raced for the river. "We gained rapidly on them. I fired four shots with my six-shooter. I do not know whether or not any of my bullets did harm. I saw a Sioux put an arrow into the back of a soldier's head. Another arrow went into his shoulder. He tumbled from his horse to the ground. Others fell dead either from arrows or from blows by the stone war clubs of the Sioux. Horses limped or staggered or sprawled out dead or dying. Our war cries and war songs mingled with many jeering calls, such as: 'You are only boys. You ought not to be fighting. You should have brought more Crows or Shoshones with you to do your fighting.'" The warriors killed many of Reno's troops, but they regrouped, dug in, and held their attackers off until they withdrew the next evening.[46]

Custer's men had no such luck. Their days of watching sunsets were done. Custer seems to have directed them in an attack on the northern fringe of the large camp. "I saw flags come up over the hill," recalled the Cheyenne chief Two Moons, "then the soldiers rose all at once." He and hundreds of other warriors raced across the river on horseback and met the charge head-on. Custer's troops were quickly surrounded and overwhelmed. "The shooting was quick, quick," said Two Moons. "Pop-pop-pop, very fast. Some of the soldiers were down on their knees, some standing. Officers all in front. The smoke was like a great cloud, and everywhere Sioux went the dust rose like smoke. We circled all round them—swirling like water round a stone." The battle lasted only a few minutes. Afterward, Sitting Bull's nephew White Bull walked among the dead with a Hunkpapa who had known some of the soldiers. He pointed out a naked corpse and said it was Custer's. "He thought he was the greatest man in the world, and there he is." The flies and worms along the Greasy Grass River (the Sioux's name for the Little Bighorn) devoured the meek and the publicized.[47]

Americans have mourned, celebrated, ridiculed, and scolded Custer ever since his last stand. With his golden locks and chivalrous pretensions, he seems as much a relic of a lost world as the Indians he attacked. But both Custer and Sitting Bull

"Custer's Last Fight." Lithograph for the Anheuser-Busch Brewing Company by F. Otto Becker based on a painting by Cassilly Adams, 1889. Beinecke Rare Book and Manuscript Library, Yale University.

sailed the same current of time. Custer helped create a gold rush to the Black Hills. He was out to prepare the West for industrial absorption, to stifle resistance to railroads, cattle drives, and sod-busting farmers. He represented historical forces of immense magnitude, and his death signaled what was coming rather than what was lost.

The last stand for the Seventh Cavalry turned into the last major stand of the Sioux. The American army pursued the free bands relentlessly, keeping them from hunting or gathering food. No rations were distributed on the reservation. When the war ended that winter, it was not because the Americans had beaten the Indians in battle but because they had starved them into submission. By the end of the year, the reservation chiefs agreed to cede the Black Hills. Not until the following spring, however, did Crazy Horse surrender at the Red Cloud Agency in Nebraska. He would die in custody, bayoneted in the back for "resisting."

Sitting Bull, meanwhile, had escaped with his followers across the border into Canada, where he petitioned the authorities for food and land. But Canadian officials were worried about their own Indian problems and the precedent such an action might set, and they refused. Sitting Bull returned to the United States, where federal authorities imprisoned him. He continued to lead and inspire the Sioux, jibing the Americans and offering his own class analysis of their modern industrial nation. "We have now to deal with another race—small and feeble when our fathers first met them but now great and overbearing. These people have made many rules that the rich may break but the poor may not. . . . They claim this mother of ours, the earth, for their own and fence their neighbors away." Then he concluded. "Possession is a disease with them." Karl Marx couldn't have said it better.[48]

The U.S. Army lost battles but won wars because their meals, clothing, ammunition, and replacement soldiers could be ordered in. Steamboats and railroads carried men and material from a geographic larder and labor pool that stretched to the Atlantic seaboard and beyond. The same immigrant population, for example, attracted by factory jobs in the East signed up for stints in the military. Though vast and constructed over centuries of adaptation, the native traders, farmers, horse mongers, and bison hunters in the Far West drew from a much smaller and vulnerable resource base. In the end, the Americans outprovisioned the Indians, especially in the winters.

Tribes elsewhere worried less about blizzards and subzero temperatures, but the railroads made life miserable for Indians even in more temperate climes. In the Southwest, rail lines encircled the territory of the fearsome Apaches. Most American military officers had trouble finding these elusive guerrilla fighters, much less engaging them. Propelled by sure-footed and durable mules as well as his own mulish personality, General George Crook finally defeated the Western Apaches, the largest of the six Apache tribes, and in 1875 moved them onto a reservation at San Carlos in southeastern Arizona. Crook, following the model of the Sioux wars when officers used Pawnees as scouts, recruited reservation Apaches to assist in tracking down and defeating the "hostiles" from other tribes.

The most feared of the hostiles was Geronimo of the Chiricahuas, famed among his people as a spiritual leader, a healer, and a war leader. As a young man, Geronimo had a vision in which a spirit informed him that "no gun can ever kill you, and I will guide your arrows." From that moment he fought without fear. "Not content to fight according to Apache custom, from behind rocks and greasewood bushes," in the words of one Indian agent, "he rushed into the open many times, running zigzag and dodging so that bullets from the soldiers' rifles did not hit him." Pursued relentlessly by Crook's Apache scouts, Geronimo finally laid down his arms and brought his people into the San Carlos Reservation in the late 1870s. They found it hard to live in this desolate and confining place, surrounded by strangers,

Geronimo. Photograph by A. F. Randall and A. T. Wilcox, c. 1886. Library of Congress.

and in 1885 Geronimo and forty-two of his Chiricahua warriors, along with several dozen women and children, broke out.

For more than a year, these last rogue Apaches eluded the army. Seventeen Arizona settlers died from Chiricahua attacks. "If he were seen by a civilian, it meant that he would be reported to the military and they'd be after us," one of the Apaches later explained, "so there was nothing to do but kill the civilian and his entire family. It was terrible to see little children killed. I do not like to talk about it. I do not like to think about it. But the soldiers killed our women and children, too. Don't forget that." Total war, the modern form of war, provoked savagery on all sides. White Arizonans panicked and alarm spread throughout the nation. Newspapers proclaimed Geronimo the "wickedest Indian that ever lived." Finally, after months of being hounded, he accepted the American promise of a new reservation for his people. But it was a lie. Once they had surrendered, all five hundred Chiricahuas were hustled onto sealed railroad cars and shipped eastward across the continent to an army prison in Florida. Without sanitation facilities or ventilation, their transcontinental journey was hellish. "When I think of that trip, even at this time, I get sick," wrote the officer in command.[49]

Geronimo died of pneumonia in 1909 at age ninety. A prisoner at Fort Sill, Oklahoma, he (and many of the Chiricahua families who followed him) never returned to the Southwest despite a fervent desire to go home. After enshrining Geronimo in their terrorist hall of fame, the American public wouldn't entertain the thought of freeing him. The *New York Times* eulogized the Apache chief as the most sinister, cunning, elusive, and dangerous Indian who ever lived. Missing from the obituary was any sense that Geronimo belonged in the world that buried him. He perished as an unredeemed savage, though the paper did note that he had converted to Christianity. A throwback, he represented a frontier the United States had pacified through military force. The enforcers moved on to inflict progress on others. The paper lauded the white commanders of the Apache scouts, Henry W. Lawton and Leonard Wood, for catching the wily old chief. Lawton became a general and died suppressing insurgents in the Philippines, while Wood hiked up the ranks to an administrative post on Governor's Island in New York harbor. The transpacific imperialist and the paper pusher represented industrial America perfectly, whereas Geronimo embodied a simpler past.[50]

But the chief walked the same earth as Lawton and Wood. He shared their days and had much in common with other industrialized Americans. Like immigrants who journeyed from across the globe to find employment in a growing economy, Geronimo moved back and forth across international boundaries and used his mobility to gain whatever leverage he could on the large-scale organizations that wanted him to stay put and respect their authority. Like the agrarian Populists who would wrestle with corporations, banks, and markets, Geronimo and his followers rejected the raw deal industrial America offered them—poverty on a reservation. Finally, like the labor radicals who tossed bombs and attacked soldiers, the Apaches tried to use violence against a state that sided with corporate interests against them only to suffer the crushing blows of public disapproval and military persecution. Through their violence, anarchists and Apaches were turned into public enemies, leaving them vulnerable to extraordinary punishments not covered in the Constitution. Geronimo never carried a lunch bucket or punched a clock, but he ended up a cog in the machine nonetheless.

Anne M. Butler, *Daughters of Joy, Sisters of Mercy: Prostitutes in the American West, 1865–90* (1985)

Sucheng Chan, *This Bittersweet Soil: The Chinese in California Agriculture, 1860–1910* (1986)

William Deverell, *Railroad Crossings: Californians and the Railroad, 1850–1910* (1994)

Robert R. Dykstra, *The Cattle Towns* (1968)

Albert L. Hurtado, *Indian Survival on the California Frontier* (1988)

Susan Lee Johnson, *Roaring Camp: The Social World of the California Gold Rush* (2000)

Terry G. Jordan, *North American Cattle-Ranching Frontiers: Origins, Diffusion, and Differentiation* (1993)

Rodman Wilson Paul, *Mining Frontiers of the Far West, 1848–1880* (1963; reprint, 1974)

William G. Robbins, *Colony and Empire: The Capitalist Transformation of the American West* (1994)

Henry Nash Smith, *Virgin Land: The American West as Symbol and Myth* (1950)

Elliott West, *The Contested Plains: Indians, Goldseekers, and the Rush to Colorado* (1998)

Richard White, *Railroaded: The Transcontinentals and the Making of Modern America* (2011)

Mark Wyman, *Hard Rock Epic: Western Miners and the Industrial Revolution, 1860–1910* (1979)

8

A Search for Community

Large-scale organizations touched most every westerner. Corporations supplied jobs and set rates. Unions, political parties, and agricultural co-ops offered solidarity and leverage. The federal government bolstered economic development and targeted radicals and hostile Indians. Yet, even though these entities invaded everyday lives and sometimes bullied people, their grip was never as firm as the leaders intended. Large-scale organizations atomized social arrangements. They induced turmoil, and the people churned about by all this change reacted in both new and old ways. Westerners countered upheaval by forming relationships, families, and communities. These bonds held the modern West together, much as they had held people together on earlier frontiers. Communities made the West function well enough for most.

Holding on to families and communities amid constant flux was an old frontier challenge. The movement of people from one place to another is one of the most important factors in American history. By the time of the Revolution, the press for new land and opportunity meant that in typical American communities throughout the nation, at least four of every ten households packed up and relocated every ten years. High rates of geographic mobility have continued to characterize North Americans ever since.

"Many of our neighbors are true backwoodsmen, always fond of moving," John Woods of southern Illinois noted in 1820. Among these "extensive travelers, to have resided in three or four states, and several places in each state, it is not uncommon." His observation is borne out by the migration histories of the residents of Sugar Creek, a pioneer community in central Illinois founded in the second decade of the nineteenth century. Eighty percent of arriving families had made at

"New Country Pioneers." Lithograph by Augustus Kollner, 1858. Beinecke Rare Book and Manuscript Library, Yale University.

least one previous move across state lines, 35 percent two or more. Similarly, eight in ten of the families who traveled the Overland Trail to Oregon and California had already made at least one interstate move, many had made several, and a substantial minority had been almost continuously in motion.[1]

"Everything shifts under your eye," declared frontier minister Timothy Flint. People came and went, blurring the line between neighbor and stranger. Movement led to an "instability of connexions." But Americans connected nonetheless. Considerably more social continuity existed than the raw statistics of mobility suggested. In the Sugar Creek community, for example, a quarter of the early settlers were what western writer Wallace Stegner calls "stickers," laying down roots and living out the rest of their lives in the area. Three-quarters of their children and grandchildren also made permanent homes in the community, most marrying the descendants of other sticker families. Quietly, people wove kinship connections and consolidated their lands. By 1860, four decades after its founding, community life in Sugar Creek was dominated by interlinked lineages of homebodies.[2]

The riddle of community in the American West is solved by recognizing the co-existence of both the movers, a transient majority of settlers who farmed, herded, and mined before pushing on, and the minority of men and women who persisted in the area, intermarried, and passed inheritances of stories, property, and affiliations—to homes, towns, and regions—to their children. Diverse communities formed in the modern American West, and groups counteracted the shattering effects of industrial colonization by making friends, families, and homes.

The big open of the trans-Mississippi West could leave transplants feeling empty, especially rural women. Hamlin Garland, raised on an Iowa homestead, looked upon his graying, wrinkled mother, old long before her time, and thought back over her frontier life. "My heart filled with bitterness and rebellion, bitterness against the pioneering madness which scattered our family, and rebellion toward my father who had kept my mother always on the border, working like a slave."[3]

It was social isolation, however, not movement per se, that took the greatest toll on settler women. On earlier frontiers the distance between farms had been an obstacle to community, but in the trans-Mississippi West it was often an overwhelming problem. "There were few settlers in the valley at that time," one woman recalled of her early years in west Texas, "and it would be two or three months at a time that Mother and I would not see another white woman." The quotation suggests how race also kept women apart. Indian, Hispanic, and black women didn't belong in this daughter's social circle. "I feel quite lonesome and solitary," one woman confided to her diary. "My spirits are depressed. I have very little female society." Journalist Eugene Virgil Smalley was appalled by the isolation of homesteaders on the northern plains in the 1890s: "Each family must live mainly to itself, and life, shut up in the little wooden farmhouses, cannot well be very cheerful." The loneliness affected the children, too. "Mamma, will we always have to live here?" asked a young boy of southwestern Kansas. Yes, replied the mother, sending the boy over the edge of despair. "And will we have to die here, too?"[4]

Communities didn't form spontaneously. Like everything else on a settlement frontier, they required strenuous labor. Communities drew energy from connections forged through work, play, education, and religion. Neighbors exchanged work and participated in barn raisings and harvests, women sewed and quilted together, and men worked on road crews, played on local baseball teams, or joined voluntary organizations. One of the community tasks, strikingly consistent across

Western farm woman. Photograph by Hugh M. Neighbour, c. 1910. Beinecke Rare Book and Manuscript Library, Yale University.

frontier America, was organizing a school. Teachers were most frequently young women, one of the few occupations open to them. Doris Elder Butler of Oregon remembered that "when a girl finished high school, if she had no other definite plans"—getting married, she meant—"it was expected that she would go out into the country to teach school, and it seemed that everyone even remotely concerned took it for granted that I would follow that custom." She did. Schoolmarms not only instructed the children but played a role as community organizers. The one-room schoolhouse often did joint duty as a community center.[5]

Groups of like-minded families might use the schoolhouse as a meeting place for religious services. Little ecumenical congregations formed, bringing together people of various Protestant views, and sometimes they even included Catholics. Eventually the most popular denominations founded churches of their own. Building and running churches brought experience in getting things done, and common beliefs and rituals helped to build sustaining bonds of affections. Religion was the first and most effective tool available to rural community builders.

Getting ministers out to these small and distant congregations was a constant struggle. In 1801 the two largest religious organizations in the country, the Presbyterians and Congregationalists, joined forces in a "Plan of Union" to coordinate

Teacher and students pose in front of their sod schoolhouse, Woods County, Oklahoma, c. 1895. National Archives.

the western expansion of their churches. But their seminaries were never able to supply the demand for ministers in the rapidly growing West, and their missionaries were easily scandalized by the hard-drinking, polyamorous, and cross-cultural fur-trading communities. They damned more than they converted. Other sects were more adaptable, in their tactics if not their moral preferences. Although the Baptists believed in an educated ministry, they hardly considered a college degree a prerequisite to godliness, and the church authorized the use of untrained and unsalaried lay preachers. This army of organizers founded hundreds of Baptist congregations throughout the West. The Methodists were also particularly effective. Francis Asbury, the first Methodist bishop in the United States, invented the institution of the circuit rider, a preacher who sallied forth with his Bible to do battle with frontier irreligion and isolation. As a result, the Methodists became the fastest-growing denomination of the early Republic, expanding from fewer than a thousand members at the time of the Revolution to more than a quarter-million by the Civil War.

The conversion of the West depended on the work of such mobile preachers, itinerants who understood and sympathized with frontier conditions. The archetype of the western circuit rider was Peter Cartwright. Converted to Methodism as a teenager in the opening of the nineteenth century, Cartwright rode the circuits throughout the Old Northwest until his death in 1872. The established eastern

Elders of the Church of God, Broken Bow, Nebraska. Photograph by Solomon D. Butcher, 1892. Library of Congress.

denominations, Cartwright believed, "had no adaptation to the country or people" of the West. "The great mass of our Western people wanted a preacher who could mount a stump, a block, or old log, or stand in the bed of a wagon, and without note or manuscript, quote, expound, and apply the word of God to the hearts and consciences of the people." Western religion melded with the democratic spirit of the times.[6]

The fire of religious enthusiasm in men like Cartwright was first sparked in 1801 at a place called Cane Ridge in central Kentucky. At this "Great Revival" a crowd of some twenty thousand came together to pray, sing, and get saved in the open air. Cane Ridge was the prototype for thousands of camp meetings, ubiquitous in the nineteenth-century West. In late summer—after the crops had been "laid by" and before the intense activity of the harvest—dozens of families converged on some shady grove, many prepared to stay for several days or even weeks. "A camp meeting," wrote one observer, "is the most mammoth picnic possible. As at a barbecue, the very best heart and soul of hospitality and kindness is wide open and poured freely forth." But more was going on in these glades than hearty meals and warm conversations. As one frontier preacher wrote, the occasion offered an opportunity "for the mind to disentangle itself from worldly care, and rise to an undistracted contemplation of spiritual realities." The milling crowds, the campfires casting an eerie light though the trees at evening, the preaching, the singing, the enthusiasm of those being saved—all heightened the sense of the extraordinary that suffused a successful camp meeting. It was an occasion for uniting groups of people, a sacred version of community building.[7]

As churches formed, the founding members often signed covenants that formally bound them together. The covenant of the Buck Run Church in Kentucky, for example, spoke the language of *communitas:* the members solemnly agreed to "watch over each other in brotherly tenderness," to edify one another, to succor the weak, to bear each other's burdens, and to hold in common all "hands and hearts." These were the strongest bonds a community could claim. The ideal of a small, close-knit community was carried deep in the minds of most colonists, and covenanted community was a sacred enterprise, reaching down to the smallest detail of helping one's own neighbor when in trouble or gone astray.

The Church of Jesus Christ of Latter-Day Saints built a covenanted community in the trans-Mississippi West on steroids. The Mormons' epic exodus of the late 1840s took them from Illinois to the Great Salt Lake, where they planted several dozen communities. A theological principle they knew as "the gathering," the imperative to build a Zion, a communal utopia, fortified their group cohesiveness. In order to gather as many believers as possible in the desert, Mormon leader Brigham Young and his advisers dispatched missionaries to the East and across the Atlantic to the industrial towns of England and farms of Scandinavia. Their preaching succeeded spectacularly, pulling thousands of converts looking for salvation, solidarity, and rural simplicity to Salt Lake. The supply was so heavy, and the supply of mules and wagons so short, that Young even organized a series of "handcart brigades." Immigrants pulled inexpensive carts loaded with their possessions across the continent's interior. In 1859 early snows caught two of these brigades and at least two hundred people froze to death in the single worst disaster in the history of the Overland Trail. Young discontinued the handcart experiment, but still the immigrants kept coming. By 1880 some one hundred thousand Latter-Day Saints were living in more than 350 communities scattered across the inland desert. Brigham Young envisioned the creation of a Mormon empire called Deseret, stretching from Idaho to Arizona, from Utah to the California coast.

One of those communities was the little town of Alpine, founded in 1860 in the western foothills of the Wasatch Mountains, south of Salt Lake City. Most of its residents came from England, urban workers sick of the turmoil caused by industrialization. In Alpine, they created a close and supportive rural community, huddling their homes beside a common field where the people labored in concert. The community of Alpine, writes historian Dean May, "drew nearly all adults into some type of voluntary activity that caused them almost daily to talk to, work with, contend with, and in time form enduring ties to others in the settlement." Whereas other western places had difficulty holding on to their residents for more than a few years, Alpine proved stickier than fly paper. At the turn of the century,

Mormon family, Great Salt Lake Valley, Utah Territory. Photograph by A. J. Russell, c. 1869. Beinecke Rare Book and Manuscript Library, Yale University.

forty years after its founding, representatives of every one of its founding families still lived in the village.[8]

The Mormons were practical utopians. Most of Brigham Young's divine revelations, and certainly his leadership, concerned economic matters. Joseph Smith's early doctrines of stewardship and consecration were coupled with a Horatio Alger ideal: every herdboy expected to become a prosperous patriarch. The Mormons' economic system was in fact a bootstrap operation. Foreign and eastern capitalists weren't interested in financing odd fellowships in barren wastes, so the church financed its own ventures, such as sugar beet factories and mining smelters, assigning new recruits to work in those industries. The church became the owner of mercantile outlets, sugar and woolen factories, and a bank and life insurance company, as well as a major stockholder in railroads. The Latter-Day Saints demonstrated a flair for communal capitalism. They prospered materially and took this as a sign of God's favor. However, they struggled with the low opinions of many Americans. The Mormons built communities based on sentiments of fellowship, but these oases of affinity were surrounded by huge swaths of hard feelings.

The federal government created the territory of Utah and appointed Brigham Young governor. But federal officials sent to administer the territory found to their chagrin that the LDS Church retained the real power and that nonbelievers ("gentiles" in Mormon parlance) were excluded. They accused the Mormons of running a "theocracy," and they were partly right. Before his murder, Joseph Smith himself had termed the Mormon system a "theo-democracy," in which voters were asked to confirm God's will as revealed to the church hierarchy.

The conflict between Mormons and gentiles increased greatly in 1852 when the church announced that one of its fundamental tenets was "plural marriage." Rumors of this practice had been one of the causes for the Mormon troubles in Illinois, and this acknowledgment that the church indeed encouraged polygamy set off a firestorm of controversy that blazed for a half-century. Americans focused on the extraordinary cases—like Brigham Young's marriage to twenty-seven women and his paternity of fifty-six children. But Young was hardly a typical Mormon. In its heyday no more than 15 percent of LDS families practiced polygamy, and two-thirds of these plural marriages involved just two wives. Though practiced by a minority, polygamy wove through the fabric of the Mormon community as part of the Saints' conception of their distinctive way of life.

In 1856 the polygamy controversy broke nationally when the newly formed Republican Party included a condemnation of "those twin relics of barbarism—polygamy and slavery" in its political platform. The next year, concluding that the territorial government was a sham cloaking the string-pulling of Young and the LDS Church, President James Buchanan ordered a federal military expedition to Utah to bring the Saints in line. With the memory of persecutions in Missouri and Illinois still fresh, the Mormons prepared to burn Salt Lake City and flee into the desert. At the last minute, negotiators from both sides narrowly avoided armed conflict, but not before an agitated group of Mormon vigilantes attacked a wagon train of Missourians at a spot in Utah called Mountain Meadows, killing 120 men, women, and children. Eventually vigilante leader John D. Lee, a committed Mormon, was executed by federal authorities for directing the massacre.

Saints and gentiles avoided open warfare, but the controversy over polygamy continued. Following the Civil War, feminist advocates of woman suffrage argued that the Mormons presented a case study in the consequences of women's disenfranchisement. If only Mormon women had the vote, surely they would "do away with the horrible institution of polygamy." Sensing a public relations opportunity in addition to a major boost to his voting majority, Young approved and in 1870 the Utah territorial legislature passed the nation's first universal woman suffrage bill. Feminists cheered, and Susan B. Anthony and Elizabeth Cady Stanton traveled to Utah to congratulate LDS women. But the mood shifted when Mormon women, in election after election, voted in concert with Mormon men. Gradually plural wives stopped being seen as victims and began being portrayed as dupes. Proclaiming that "woman suffrage in Utah means only women suffering," the opponents of votes for women seized on the issue as a cautionary tale—married women were incapable of being independent. The Mormons' "theo-democracy" thwarted outsiders' desires for political and propaganda victories.[9]

Although Congress outlawed polygamy in 1862 and 1874, the 1882 Edmunds Act was the first legislation to stipulate harsh penalties for polygamists. Federal authorities began arresting Mormon men for "unlawful cohabitation," imprisoning more than a thousand over the next decade. But the LDS hierarchy refused to relent. In 1887 Congress swung even harder, disincorporating the Mormon church, confiscating its real estate, and abolishing women's suffrage in Utah. The struggle against polygamy widened into a war against the church. Facing institutional collapse, in 1890 the LDS hierarchy agreed to the abolition of polygamy in practice (though not in theory), and in 1896 Congress finally voted to admit Utah to the union as a state. It had been a long and bitter struggle, which the Mormons would always regard as more evidence of the hostility toward their religious beliefs and the communitarian experiment.

In 1879 yet another exodus to the western promised land took place, this one by thousands of African Americans from the Old Southwest. The background of this episode in Americans seeking freedom and plenty through mobility lay in the failure of southern land reform after the Civil War. "Forty acres and a mule"—land and the means to work it—was the cry that echoed throughout the communities of former slaves in the South. In 1866 Congress passed a Southern Homestead Act, extending the terms of the western bill to freedmen and women. But what little remained of the southern public domain was swampy, barren land, far from transportation links, and in the end only a few thousand people benefited from this program. Real land reform required the confiscation of large plantations and the redistribution of land to the African American men and women who had worked the land for years without compensation. But neither Congress nor the southern reconstruction governments wanted to disrupt cotton production or violate private property rights. When, in the 1870s, Republican reconstruction governments gave way to Democrat "redeemer" regimes, soon followed by the withdrawal of federal troops from the South in 1877, many African Americans looked to the West for a better future.

Freedmen and women would have to "repeat the history of the Israelites," declared one assembly of black Alabamians, and "seek new homes beyond the reign and rule of Pharaoh." Benjamin Singleton, a former Tennessee slave, led a group of African Americans to an agrarian colony in western Kansas in 1875, and three years later he circulated broadsides throughout the Old Southwest exhorting other freedmen and women to join him in an even bigger venture. Singleton's plans called for the orderly migration of several hundred families, but the word of mouth soon grew into wild rumors—that there was free land for ex-slaves in Kansas and that the federal government would provide free transportation and supplies. Suddenly,

The Shores family, Custer County, Nebraska. Photograph by Solomon D. Butcher, 1887. Library of Congress.

in the spring of 1879, thousands of African Americans throughout the cotton belt packed up and headed for the fabled land of John Brown. "I am anxious to reach your state," one black Louisianan wrote to John Pierce St. John, the governor of Kansas, "because of the sacredness of her soil washed by the blood of humanitarians for the cause of freedom." Within a few short weeks, more than twenty thousand Exodusters, as they called themselves, flooded into Kansas. The state rose to the occasion. "Kansas has a history devoted to liberty," proclaimed Governor St. John, and its citizens would not deny the freedmen and women in their hour of need, for "when the life of the Nation was in danger, the blood of the negro mingled with our own to sustain the Union." A hurriedly organized state relief association assisted several thousand Exodusters to settle a dozen communities in western Kansas and several more in Indian Territory (later the state of Oklahoma). Eventually some forty black towns were established on the southern plains.[10]

One hundred and fifty black families founded the settlement of Nicodemus on the upper Solomon River in central Kansas. Like most easterners, the transplants found the arid Great Plains an agricultural dustbin, and many moved on during the drought and economic hard times at century's end. A group of stickers, however, found jobs on the railroad or took work with neighboring white farmers as hired hands, and the community survived into the twentieth century. Grant Cushinberry, born and raised in Nicodemus, remembered the heart of the community: the African Methodist Episcopal Church. "Momma didn't allow us to dance or play no music on Sunday," he said, "every living soul had to go to church." After the service his mother "always brought some old preacher home for dinner." At these gatherings the family told stories of their suffering in the South during Reconstruction. Cushinberry remembered a vivid tale of the Ku Klux Klan coming to the Mississippi cabin of an uncle late one night. Dragging the man's pregnant wife into the yard, they strung her up by the heels and "cut the baby out of her stomach." Her husband grabbed his shotgun and slaughtered the night riders, "then he ran all day and all night until he got to Kansas." Cushinberry's relatives cultivated the western dream of finding justice and refuge in community.[11]

Rather than plow the dry prairies, most Exodusters elected to live in established Kansas towns, where they found work as laborers and domestics as well as informal and explicit racial segregation. "We were all pushed back of there (across the railroad tracks)," remembered Dorothy Fulghem, a longtime black resident of Manhattan. "We had our own churches"—three African American congregations that provided a rallying point for the community—and "we were raised in the church," Fulghem remembered. The black congregations led the unsuccessful opposition to a school board plan to segregate the town's public schools. "Compel us to associate with the negro," warned one white resident, "and we become a slave in turn." Soon Frederick Douglass School was opened for the black children across the tracks.[12]

Despite the state's historic "devotion to liberty," white Kansans abandoned their commitment to racial justice at the turn of the century, joining the rest of the nation in establishing separate and unequal institutions for minorities. The writer, photographer, and filmmaker Gordon Parks was born into this broken-promise land in 1912. Nearly all of the public facilities in his hometown of Fort Scott, Kansas, were segregated. "The grade school was segregated but the high school wasn't," Parks writes in his autobiography, "mainly because the town fathers couldn't scrounge up enough money to build a separate one. But even inside those walls of meager learning, black students had to accommodate themselves to the taste of salt. The class advisers warned us against seeking higher education, adding 'You were meant to be maids and porters.'" Even after achieving success in his profession, Parks considered Fort Scott "the place I attack in dreams." He later wrote a poem in which he tried to summarize his ambivalent feelings. He filled the stanzas with June bugs and fireflies, and with warm summer days spent crawdad fishing, but smashed these warm memories in the final lines: "Yes, all this I would miss—along with the fear, hatred and violence / We blacks had suffered upon this beautiful land."[13] In 1985 the Native Sons and Daughters of Kansas selected Parks as "Kansan of the year." During the presentation ceremony in Topeka, sitting with the governor and one of the state's United States senators, Parks listened as the master of ceremonies read his Kansas poem aloud, regaling the audience

Gordon Parks, c. 1943. Library of Congress.

with the cozy details but omitting the crucial last two lines. Parks arose, walked to the podium, and read the deleted lines to the thunderstruck audience. Going back to Kansas was "like returning to a battlefield where a truce has been signed," he mused. "It will always be the identity of my brutal past."[14]

———

Communities offered refuge and comfort—and they could turn cold to those deemed outsiders. The white community in Fort Scott wounded Parks through exclusion and discrimination. Race defined both white and black communities, but whites possessed more resources and stronger allies. In the West the federal government joined groups like the Native Sons and Daughters of Kansas to police the color line. The motivation, though racist, was not always venomous. White Kansas honored Parks even as it insulted him. The reformers and federal officials dismantling Native American communities in the late nineteenth century acted out of kindness more than malice. In the actual West, bad guys didn't wear black hats and twirl long mustaches. They often carried a Bible and a court order and cast themselves as the heroes in the stories they told themselves.

Persecution drove the flight of the Mormons and the Exodusters, though they were at heart migrations of hope. The West, however, witnessed its share of forced removals and relocations—migrations of terror. The Cherokee Trail of Tears was repeated many times, not only for eastern Indians like the Seminoles or the Sauks, but for the native peoples of the plains and mountains, forced to relocate to god-forsaken corners of Indian Territory or squeezed onto small "reserved" portions of

Chief Joseph of the Nez Perce. Photograph by William H. Jackson, c. 1880. Wikimedia Commons.

their former homelands. One memorable migration of terror took place in the Pacific Northwest in the fall of 1877, when the federal government insisted that all the men and women of the Nez Perce tribe of Indians be relocated to a confined reservation. About a quarter of them refused, a group of young warriors led a bloody raid on nearby settlers, and the army attacked. At that point the Nez Perce chiefs decided that their only alternative to destruction was flight. They led fifty fighting men and three hundred women and children over a desperate trail of more than thirteen hundred miles through the rugged mountains of Idaho, Wyoming, and Montana, in the hope of reaching Canada, and successfully beat back three full-scale army attacks. Just fifty miles short of freedom they were surrounded. After five days of watching his people freeze and starve, Chief Joseph, the only surviving leader, surrendered.

The end of three centuries of warfare found western Indians confined to a series of reservations. These reservations were conceived as temporary expedients, not permanent institutions. White Americans premised their Indian policy on the assumption that natives would become farmers, Christians, and citizens. The task, as Sioux agent Thomas J. Galbraith put it, was "to make white men of them." He provided a succinct summary of federal goals for Indians during the era that stretched from the 1870s to the 1930s: "weaken and destroy their tribal relations and individualize them by giving them each a separate home and having them subsist by industry." The goal of federal policy, according to Galbraith, was "to

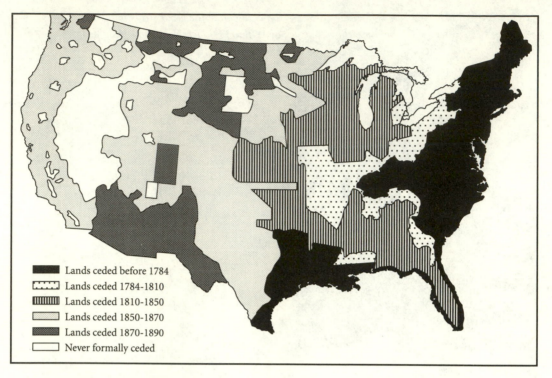

INDIAN LAND CESSIONS

Lands ceded before 1784
Lands ceded 1784-1810
Lands ceded 1810-1850
Lands ceded 1850-1870
Lands ceded 1870-1890
Never formally ceded

break up the community system." At the same time as pioneers spun webs of affinity, creating new communities, the federal government was using its power to smash ancient ones.[15]

The first step: eliminate all vestiges of Indian sovereignty. The limited sovereignty of Indian nations had been a foundation of federal policy since the early days of the Republic, enacted into law in the Indian Intercourse Act (1790) and confirmed by the Supreme Court in 1832 in the famous case *Worcester v. Georgia*. The United States wanted circumscribed political entities to negotiate treaties with and help make sense of a fractious tribal landscape that could be extremely confusing. Now they wanted to sweep away the Indian nations. Ely S. Parker, commissioner of Indian Affairs during the presidency of Ulysses S. Grant, condemned the treaty system for falsely impressing the Indians with notions of their own independence. The time had come, he wrote, when "this idea should be dispelled, and the government cease the cruel farce of thus dealing with its helpless and ignorant wards." Indians had never been citizens of the Republic but constituents of their own tribes or nations, subject to government, law, and custom administered by their own authorities. Without institutions of their own they became subjects of the federal government—"helpless wards," in Parker's words. The sad irony was that Ely Parker himself was an Iroquois, a member of a distinguished family of

Senecas, and he quietly ignored the long struggle of his people to maintain their independence.[16]

In 1870 the Supreme Court ruled that Congress had the power to supersede or even annul treaties made with Indian nations. Given a green light by the court, the next year Congress passed a resolution that once and for all put an end to the system of Indian treaty-making. From that date forward, read the text, "no Indian nation or tribe within the territory of the United States shall be acknowledged or recognized as an independent nation, tribe, or power with whom the United States may contract a treaty." In 1885 Congress passed legislation taking away the right of tribal governments to operate under their own customary laws and extending federal jurisdiction to include felony crimes committed on reservations.[17]

Then the feds rushed in. Federal Indian agents were directed to undertake a sustained campaign of forced cultural modification—outlawing Indian customs they considered "savage and barbarous," such as the Sun Dance of the Plains Indians or the "pagan, horrible, sadistic, and obscene" rituals of the Pueblos. The United States was doing precisely what other imperial powers had done to their colonial subjects. In the Pacific island colonies, for example, the French outlawed singing and dancing at native religious ceremonies, while in southern Africa the British imprisoned "witch doctors." The similarities were noted. The United States was "a great colonial power," wrote Harvard history professor Albert Bushnell Hart, and "our Indian agents have a status very like that of British in the native states of India."[18]

Cultural imperialism invaded the curriculum of reservation schools. "If Indian children are to be civilized they must learn the language of civilization," ruled the secretary of the interior, and the Indian Bureau issued regulations that "no textbooks in the vernacular [the native language] will be allowed in any school." This, too, was a familiar colonial practice. In a similar vein, a British official in South Africa wrote that "primitive customs and taboos must go [and] with them must also go the native mode of life and probably the language which was adapted to that life." Even more severe was the practice of sending children to Indian boarding schools, most famously the Carlisle Indian Industrial School in Pennsylvania, founded in 1879 by Richard Henry Pratt, a former commander of Indian scouts. Carlisle administrators gave the girls Anglo-American names, dressed them as Victorian ladies, and taught them to play the piano. The boys were organized into military companies and drilled in uniform.[19]

"They told us that Indian ways were bad," Sun Elk, a resident of Taos Pueblo, remembered years later of his boarding school experience. "They said we must get civilized. . . . The books told how bad the Indians had been to the white men—burning their towns and killing their women and children. But I had seen white men do that to Indians. We all wore white man's clothes and ate white man's food

A group of Chiricahua Apache students on their arrival at Carlisle Indian School and four months later, c. 1890. Beinecke Rare Book and Manuscript Library, Yale University.

and went to the white man's churches and spoke the white man's talk. So after a while we also began to say Indians were bad. We laughed at our own people and their blankets and cooking pots and sacred societies and dances." After seven years of education, Sun Elk came home. "It was a warm summer evening when I got off the train at Taos station. The first Indian I met, I asked him to run out to the pueblo and tell my family I was home. The Indian couldn't speak English, and I had forgotten my Pueblo language."[20]

On the reservation, federal officials strove to instill work discipline. The Indians were to be placed "in positions where they can be controlled and finally compelled by sheer necessity to resort to agricultural labor *or starve*." By design the government supplied only basic necessities. Indeed, the goods issued to reservation Indians—who had been deprived of their ability to hunt—were the equivalent of only half the daily rations distributed to American troops in the field. Hunger and poverty haunted the reservations. But necessity did not transform Indians into farmers. Tillers of the soil actually need soil, and reservations were often too barren or arid to support crops. And many Indians resisted the agents' occupational advice: "The whites were always trying to make the Indians give up their life and live like the white men," said the Sioux chief Big Eagle, "go to farming, work hard, and do as they did—and the Indians did not know how to do that, and did not want to anyway."[21]

Indian communities reeled from policies administered by government officials and crusading educators, but their so-called allies, the Friends of the Indians, delivered the killer blow, striking at the material foundation of group cohesiveness— the land. Their solution to "the Indian problem" was a program called "allotment in severalty." Collective ownership of the land would give way to individual tenure. Reservations would be divided up and "allotted" in small parcels to each Indian head of household. Once the family had shown a flair for Jeffersonian yeomanry, improving their fields and homesteads, they would become naturalized United States citizens and slip into a highly nostalgic vision of American society. "Selfishness," declared Senator Henry Dawes of Massachusetts, "is at the bottom of civilization. Till this people give up their lands, and divide them among their citizens so that each can own the land he cultivates, they will not make much more progress." After allotment, reformers believed, tribes would wither away.[22]

The majority of Indian tribes opposed allotment. Reformers blamed the lack of enthusiasm on chiefs' reluctance to cede their power. Indian leaders, went the conventional wisdom, didn't know what was good for their own people. Western politicians added to the momentum for allotment. Eastern reformers broke up reservations for philosophical reasons, but westerners joined the movement when it became clear that after reservations had been allotted in parcels of 160 acres to Indian families, there would be tens of thousands of acres of "surplus lands" that would be opened to white settlers. It was a corrupt alliance and a raw deal. Senator Henry M. Teller of Colorado was one of the few who spoke out against the bill. "I want to put upon the record my prophecy in this manner," Teller told his Senate colleagues. "When thirty or forty years have passed, and these Indians shall have parted with their title, they will curse the hand that was raised professedly in their defense." Allotment proceeded precisely as Teller had feared. In 1888 Indian tribes held 138 million acres. By 1934 that number had dropped to 47 million.[23]

With armed resistance impossible and their cultures and communities under attack, the Indian people of the West responded like their fellow modern westerners—they turned to religion to manage the turmoil. The Ghost Dance united seekers across tribal lines, recalling earlier religious movements. This revival also featured a charismatic holy man, like the Delaware Prophet Neolin, the inspiration for Pontiac's Revolt, or Tenskwatawa, the Shawnee Prophet, brother of Tecumseh. The Ghost Dance emerged from the vision of Wovoka, a shaman among the Paiutes of Nevada. Wovoka had a vision in which the Great Spirit instructed him to speak to all Indians. We must act as brothers and never resort to violence, Wovoka preached. If Indians gave up alcohol, lived simple lives, and dedicated themselves to meditation and prayer, the Great Spirit would restore control of their lives and lands. Wovoka foresaw a day when the whites would disappear, along with all their stuff—guns, whiskey, and manufactured goods. Dead Indians would then rejoin their living brothers and sisters and reside together in a world "free from misery, death, and disease." Wovoka's followers developed his message into a ritual that included five days of worship in the form of slow dancing and meditation. Wovoka's was a message of community flowering from the depths of despair. It spread rapidly among tribes throughout the Far West, suggesting yet again the power of religion to bring people together despite the best efforts of large-scale modern organizations—like the Friends of the Indians, the Bureau of Indian Affairs, and the U.S. Army—to pry them apart.[24]

Sitting Bull, still an influential community leader among the Sioux, sent emissaries to meet with Wovoka. They returned to the northern plains in the summer of 1890, stirred by his message. Chiefs like Sitting Bull at the Standing Rock Reservation and Big Foot at Cheyenne River transformed Wovoka's pacifist message into a movement far more militant and confrontational. Sioux Ghost Dancers, including men, women, and children, came together for rituals lasting for several days and nights, singing and dancing themselves into trances. Anthropologist James Mooney translated a Sioux song that he believed "summarized the whole hope of the ghost dance."

Arapaho Ghost Dancers. Photograph by James Mooney, c. 1895. National Archives.

> The whole world is coming,
> A nation is coming, a nation is coming,
> The eagle has brought the message to the tribe.
> The father says so, the father says so.
> Over the whole earth they are coming.
> The buffalo are coming, the buffalo are coming.
> The Crow has brought the message to his tribe,
> The father says so, the father says so.

These sentiments terrified Indian agents who had labored for years to suppress all traces of "pagan" religion among the Sioux. To them, the Ghost Dance crossed the line from revival into rebellion. "Indians are dancing in the snow and are wild and crazy," one agent telegraphed his superiors. "*We need protection and we need it now.*"[25]

The Seventh Cavalry—Custer's old unit, eager for payback for the devastating defeat at the Little Big Horn—responded to the call. But Sioux Ghost Dancers, led by Chief Big Foot, took refuge in the region known as the Badlands, in the northwest corner of the Pine Ridge Reservation. Frustrated, federal officials ordered the arrest of traditional chiefs. "Let the soldiers come and take me away and kill me," Sitting Bull taunted when he heard the news of his impending arrest, but it was Sioux reservation police who came to his door. "We are of the same blood, we are all Sioux, we are relatives," Sitting Bull said, trying to shame them. "If the white men want me to die, they ought not to put up the Indians to kill me." Sitting Bull's friends and family tried to protect him, but in the subsequent skirmish eight men were shot, and afterward Sitting Bull and his seventeen-year-old son lay dead.[26]

Burial of the dead at Wounded Knee. Photograph by George Trager, 1890. Beinecke Rare Book and Manuscript Library, Yale University.

In late December 1890, a few days after Sitting Bull's death, the Seventh Cavalry caught up with Big Foot and his band of ghost dancers and directed them to set up camp on Wounded Knee Creek. Miles away, at the main Sioux on the Pine Ridge Reservation, a young man named Black Elk learned that the troops had surrounded the dancers. "I felt that something terrible was going to happen," he later remembered, and "that night I could hardly sleep at all." Early the following morning, he awoke to the sound of distant gunfire. He and several other young men galloped to Wounded Knee. Topping a ridge, Black Elk and his co-riders looked down: "What we saw was terrible," he remembered. "Dead and wounded women and children and little babies were scattered all along there where they had been trying to run away. The soldiers had followed along the gulch, as they ran, and murdered them in there." Black Elk saw what was left of human beings "torn to pieces" by "the wagon guns." He watched a baby trying to suck milk from its dead mother. The ugly panorama made him wish he "had died too."[27]

What triggered such carnage? The soldiers had been disarming the Sioux when a gun accidently went off. Troops raked the Indian camp with rapid-fire artillery. The Sioux fought back as best they could. The gunfire killed 146 Indians, including

44 women and 18 children. The Seventh Cavalry lost 25 soldiers, most killed by the crossfire of their own weapons. After the battle a blizzard swept the scene, covering the bodies and freezing them in postures of terror and defense.

At Wounded Knee, a community desperate to survive on its own terms met an organization willing to kill to deny those terms. It's easy to view community as a historical force for good, and westerners seemed at their most heroic when they banded together to mitigate the disruptions of modernity. By uniting, people shared their burdens and joys. They cultivated a common purpose, a sense of belonging. Communities brought order to a chaotic universe. Yet, some groups' foundational beliefs appalled others, and groups with power used it to dissolve communities without it. Their acts of destruction sometimes strengthened their communal ties. Hate bonded as well as love, and the Ghost Dancers at Wounded Knee serve as a stark reminder that community was never an easy or unadulterated undertaking.

In the American myth, the frontier was supposed to transform immigrants into generic Americans. But aside from the English and Canadians—who preferred to colonize as individual families, perhaps because they assumed that the English-speaking American or Canadian nation was their community—European immigrants tended to travel west and plant themselves in groups, retaining many of their ethnic traditions through the second generations. These immigrant communities were also "covenant communities," for in nearly all of them the immigrant church became "an institutional rallying point," in the words of historian Kathleen Neils Conzen. "Nobody made us build them, and they weren't put up with tax money," Norwegian immigrant farmer Carl Hanson remarked about the Lutheran churches that appeared on the northern plains. "We scraped the money together for them, not from our surplus, but out of our poverty, because we needed them." The immigrant church was the institution charged with upholding values and preserving continuity with the premigration past. It offered the first and often only defense against the rapid and total assimilation of immigrant children. Here, too, religion was the key to community survival in atomized modernity.[28]

The Irish proved adept at building churches and communities in the West. Often they came west to work as miners, clustering in the mining districts of states such as Montana, Wyoming, and Nevada, where the proportion of Irish-born greatly exceeded the national average. At the end of the nineteenth century the copper center of Butte was the most Irish city in America. Under the management of Marcus Daly, an Irish immigrant, the Anaconda mining corporation favored the employment of Irishmen. Butte miners told the joke of the Irishman who sent a

German immigrants arrive at Lincoln, Nebraska, c. 1895. Nebraska State Historical Society.

letter back home encouraging his brother to come over. "Don't stop in the United States," he wrote, "Come right on out to Butte." The Irish community in Butte was rooted in strong kinship ties, ethnic associations such as the Ancient Order of Hibernians, and, most important, the Catholic parish, staffed almost entirely by Irish priests.[29]

Germans in the West also tended to migrate in chains of kin and cluster in ethnic enclaves. Hessians began arriving in Texas during the 1830s, soon after they obtained a grant of land from Stephen Austin. By 1860 more than thirty thousand populated the Texas hill country, clustered in little farming communities with a Lutheran church planted at the center. Many of these stone churches still stand, and conversations in German can sometimes be heard in the vicinity of New Braunfels, south of Austin. Other common German destinations were Wisconsin, Minnesota, the Dakotas, and Nebraska, where Catholic Rhinelanders began settling in the 1850s. These communities displayed remarkable persistence rates well into the twentieth century. A second-generation German American later recalled how he ended up staying on the family farm in Minnesota. "Dad said, 'I am getting old and cannot work the farm anymore.' That's how I was hooked with it; I couldn't say no and leave them sit alone. I could have gotten a job somewhere, gone away. But I couldn't do that to my parents." Thousands of rural sons did say "no" and left to go farther west, into cities far from their origins. But kinship and community ties proved strong among German Americans. Language, religion, and rural traditions glued many in place.[30]

After the Civil War, each of the states and territories of the upper Midwest and northern plains recruited European immigrants, publishing guides in a variety of

Norwegian American singers in costume at the Minnesota State Fairgrounds, 1925. Minnesota Historical Society.

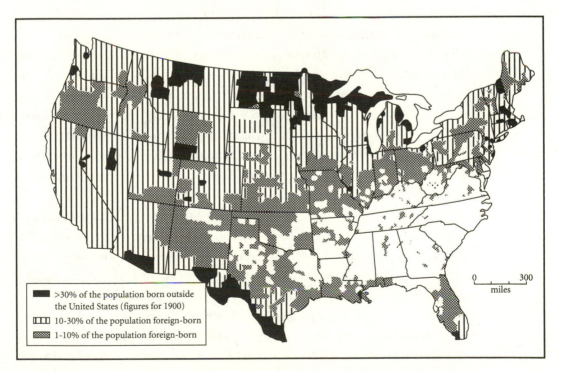

>30% of the population born outside the United States (figures for 1900)

10-30% of the population foreign-born

1-10% of the population foreign-born

0   300
        miles

THE FOREIGN-BORN POPULATION IN 1900

languages and sending agents across the Atlantic to pitch the advantages of their lands. They found plenty of listeners in the tens of thousands of rural Europeans being thrown off their farms through economic and industrial consolidation. During the last quarter of the nineteenth century, from a third to a half of the population of the northern plains was foreign-born, the highest proportion of any region in the nation. The countryside was a patchwork of culturally homogeneous communities of Germans, Czechs, Poles, Russians, Hungarians, and especially Scandinavians.

These immigrants built and attended churches. In Isanti County, fifty miles north of Minneapolis–Saint Paul, more than seven hundred Swedish households made up seven distinct communities, each with its own Lutheran church and pastor. The role of the church as a conservative force cannot be underestimated. Through its ceremonies and its holidays, it helped perpetuate the old customs of the homeland. A pastor, newly arrived from Sweden, wrote of how impressed he was "to see the people coming to Church in festive array, with clothes cut according to the ancient style, the man dressed in the leather apron, the woman with the short waist, red stockings, and large shoes." Church-run "Swede schools" supplemented public education, teaching children to sing Swedish songs and to read the Swedish Bible, Swedish history, and Swedish literature. The church also presided over a pattern of in-marriage. Eight out of ten marriages in these communities were between men and women of the same congregations. Similar patterns were present within other rural immigrant communities.[31]

Cultural homogeneity characterized ethnic communities until the early twentieth century, when to the chagrin of church elders, who equated cultural change with spiritual decline, the third generation began to move toward assimilation. Swedish congregations in rural Minnesota engaged in a prolonged and divisive debate over whether God could hear prayers in English. During the "Americanization" frenzy of World War I—when a number of midwestern governors issued proclamations forbidding the public use of languages other than English (even on the telephone)—Swedish churches finally began to hold their worship services in English.

The drop in the public use of homeland languages paired with increased out-migration and intermarriage fueled assimilation, which alarmed critics like Ole Rølvaag, Norwegian immigrant who became a professor of literature at Saint Olaf College in Minnesota. Famous for his novel *Giants of the Earth* (1927), Rølvaag warned fellow Norwegians that they risked losing the "intimate spiritual association with our own people" by becoming "American." Lecturing to a class on immigration history he urged his students to "show the greatest faithfulness to your race, to the cultural and spiritual heritage which you have received and which you may receive in still larger measure. You must not erase your racial characteristics in order to become better Americans." Rølvaag believed that American culture had little to offer except a preoccupation with material success. "I have met with none but crippled souls," he wrote of his encounters with farmers in the Minnesota countryside. "They are dead, dead, living dead! Their highest interests are hogs, cattle and horses." Strict adherence to community distinctiveness, especially the old religion and culture fused into bones and blood through race, was the only solution to a looming future of a 4-H zombie apocalypse. Rølvaag represented an especially intense denunciation of the "highly praised melting pot," but he was not the only doomsayer preaching the rejection of American sameness. Black Elk, for example, used the carnage of Wounded Knee and the federal government's assimilation policy to argue for a similar return to traditional communal Indian values to counter the ruin of modernity. He, too, sought to repair the damage of acquisitive individualism through spiritual rebirth.[32]

The barren sameness of western community life sometimes even panicked the primary beneficiaries of industrial colonization—native-born, English-speaking white people. Sinclair Lewis skewered humdrum normality in his novel *Main Street* (1920). When Carol Kennicott, Lewis's main character, arrives at Gopher Prairie, it seems scarcely more impressive than a hazel thicket: "There was no dignity in it, nor any hope of greatness. . . . It was a frontier camp. It was not a place to live in, not possibly, not conceivably." Feeling its plainness and flimsiness, Carol walks its length and breadth in just thirty-six minutes. The residents, she concludes, were as "drab as their houses, as flat as their fields." The modern West, like Kennicott, was in danger of being bored to death. Lewis knew the sensation of small-town stultification. He had grown up in a small town and fashioned Gopher Prairie after similar burgs from Peoria to Petaluma. "Main Street," he wrote, "is the culmination of Main Street everywhere." The identical grid pattern, ignoring the terrain, borrowed from Philadelphia because it communicated regularity. The same false fronts dressed up the dry-goods store and the post office, the saloon and the livery stable, the schoolhouse and the church. From the Mississippi River valley to the Pacific coast, these towns were shockingly similar, an idea of place beat to death through repetition.[33]

For decades Americans had held up small towns as the best the nation had to offer. Writer Zona Gale looked back on her Wisconsin hometown of Portage with quiet affection. The main street of "Friendship Village" (1908) held memories of tulip beds and twilight bonfires, with people concerned enough to help one another through illness and hard times. The fellowship of small communities warmed the memories of writers like Gale, but other observers found this nostalgia old-fashioned and misguided after World War I. Lewis's *Main Street*—published

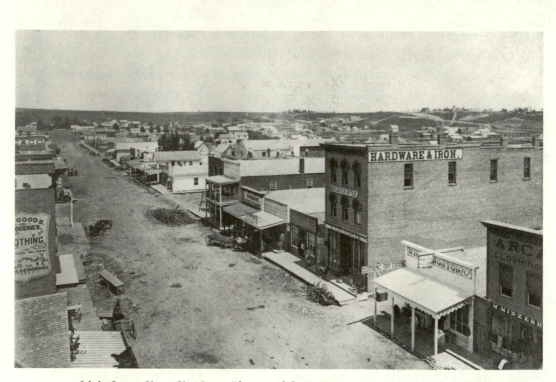

Main Street, Sioux City, Iowa. Photograph by B. H. Gurnsey, 1869. Beinecke Rare Book and Manuscript Library. Yale University.

the same year the Census Bureau announced that the population of urban America outnumbered rural America for the first time—marked an attitudinal sea change. Novelists Hamlin Garland and Edgar Lee Masters had depicted the crimped lives of small-town residents before Lewis, but with *Main Street* the cynical view became the dominant perspective.[34]

The myth of small-town life had pictured a homogeneous, classless society in which anyone with ambition, thrift, and diligence could easily move upward. But in fact class structured small towns. During the early years, economic lines blurred, but by the end of the Civil War, when industrial colonization reached full-steam, rigid class lines appeared nearly everywhere, even in supposedly wide-open cattle towns of the Great Plains, where within a few years of their founding the richest 20 percent of the population controlled more than 80 percent of the real estate. The working classes were divided between craftworkers, transients, and drifters. African Americans, Mexicans, Asians, and Indians were isolated at the bottom of the social ladder.

Toward the end of the nineteenth century, the atmosphere of small western towns seemed increasingly uneasy. The industrial promise of links between farm and market had not been fulfilled; clearly, the railroads served eastern capital almost exclusively. Conflicts within the community burst into public view, especially as the quarter-century of depression from 1873 to 1898 exposed the vulnerability of the poor. The hardening of class lines bred dissatisfaction, and small-town newspaper editors had to admit the existence of discord. Social conflict became the rule rather than the exception, and cohesiveness degenerated into narrow morality. Frederick Russell Burnham, who lived in a small Midwest town in the 1870s, thought that most people spent half their life trying to reform someone else in a quiet fervor of "intolerant religiosity." This oppressive, narrow morality—peeping through keyholes—was the cause of Carol Kennicott's rebellion in *Main Street*. Intellectuals fled to the cities and began to describe their former environment as smug, prejudiced, sterile, and joyless.[35]

Much of the trouble stemmed from the backward glance of many small communities. Dedicated to timeless virtues and the good old days, townspeople saw corruption in industrial values and sighed, in the words of poet Vachel Lindsay, "for the sweet life wrenched and torn by thundering commerce, fierce and bare." True, towns often courted small-scale industry in the hope of creating more jobs and revenue, but monopolies, large-scale corporations, and the interventions of the federal government tossed communities about like corks in a swell. Turning inward, the residents of small western towns developed intense localism as a shield against unwelcome change. Confronting fears that the "end of the frontier" would bring an end to the assimilation of foreigners, the white middle class of the small town lashed out against "un-American" immigrants. Fear and loathing marked the end of one West and the creation of another.[36]

The closing of the frontier prompted fears of scarcity and the loss of identity as industrialization prompted the rearrangement of global populations. In the Pacific and Indian Oceans, people from all points rushed to California, Australia, India, and South Africa. In these places, Europeans and Euro-Americans encountered immigrant workers from China, India, Hawaii, Japan, and Indonesia. Racial animosities flared when white immigrants declared a racial monopoly on resources and opportunity. From South Africa to Australia to California, democratic political movements rallied around immigration restrictions to protect places deemed "white men's countries."

These pronouncements cut against powerful ideologies and political forces that were themselves reshaping the Pacific world. Industrial capitalism thrived on the free movement of people and goods. Great Britain and the United States negotiated treaties with China to gain access to Chinese markets. In the Treaty of Nanking (1842) and the Burlingame Treaty (1868), the nations established and then enhanced the principle of free movement and migration as a universal human right. Empires could also facilitate the movement of people. The color of one's skin did not determine one's membership in the British Empire, for example. Theoretically, once conquered and incorporated into the realm, all people were subjects of the same monarch. In the face of escalating prejudice, oppressed groups turned to the market and the courts to protect their rights. They used concepts of individual freedom, property rights, and citizenship to counter democratic bigotry that equated national belonging with whiteness and manhood.

In the modern West few groups suffered more fear and loathing than Chinese and Japanese immigrants. In 1878 a federal judge in California ruled that Chinese immigrants could not become naturalized citizens because they were not "white persons" within the meaning of the Naturalization Act of 1790, a decision extended to the Japanese by the Supreme Court in 1922 and not repealed until after World War II. Throughout the West, states and localities passed laws denying Asians the right to vote, forbidding their employment by public agencies, and restricting them to residential ghettos. But with the same dream of land ownership and prosperity motivating them as other immigrant groups, many Asians stayed in the West, created families, and built communities. Their children became citizens by birth.

"They form little communities among themselves," wrote a landlord in the Sacramento delta in the 1860s, "do their own cooking, live in little camps together. If you can get them this year you can get them next year and the year after. They become attached to your place and they stay with you." Similarly, in the 1870s growers in the citrus belt of southern California began employing Chinese men in their groves and packinghouses. They perfected what became known as the "China pack"—each piece of fruit individually wrapped in tissue paper before being carefully packed into a crate. It was like a work of art, one grower remembered, "every wrapper smooth, not a wrinkle, and the tissue triangled to a point at the top so that when the box was opened it was something to display in a grocer's window." Citrus growers came to depend on the industry and careful work of these Chinese laborers, and soon every town in the citrus belt had its own Chinatown, usually on the poor side of the tracks.[37]

By the 1870s Chinese workers composed half of California's agricultural workforce. Growers cheered their diligence and reliability, but white workers growled, and violence against Chinese surged during economic depressions. In 1873 white farmworkers in California held rallies demanding the firing of Chinese laborers. In the Sacramento delta, vigilantes invaded Chinese communities, bullied families into leaving, and set fire to their homes. The old pioneer John Bidwell, who employed Chinese on his ranch, had his buildings burned after ignoring a threatening note: "You are given notice to discharge your Mongolian help within ten days or suffer the consequences." Authorities tracked down and convicted the arsonists and Bidwell rebuilt. The night before his reopening, white malcontents torched the new structures. In Chico, a mob shot five Chinese tenant farmers and burned their bodies with their cabins. In the terrible depression year of 1893, armed mobs

Anti-Chinese riot in Denver, 1880. Engraving based on a sketch by N. B. Wilkins, in Frank Leslie's Illustrated Weekly, *November 20, 1880.*

attacked Chinese workers in several San Joaquin valley towns. They drove Chinese men from the fields and loaded them onto railroad cars at gunpoint. In the citrus town of Redlands, east of Los Angeles, vigilantes swept into Chinatown in September. Growers denounced the mayhem—looting, arson, beatings—and argued that they couldn't "afford to pay the wages demanded by the whites." But Senator John Miller argued that because Chinese workers were inferior human beings, they could "dispense with the comforts of shelter and subsist on the refuse of other men, and grow fat on less than half the food necessary to sustain life in the Anglo-Saxon." Chinese Americans remembered this period as "the driving out." By the turn of the century, most had relocated to the Chinatowns of the largest western cities, where they found an uncertain refuge.[38]

"Now that the Chinese have been excluded," Methodist missionary Merriman Harris wrote from California in 1888, "there is a demand for cheap labor and it is probable that Japanese laborers will be brought over to supply the demand." The Japanese government did not allow emigration until the end of the century, so it was not until the 1890s that Japanese men began arriving to seek work on the railroads and especially on the commercial farms of the West. In 1900 Harris reported "an unusually large influx of Japanese to the Pacific coast" and noted that they "go into the country districts and readily find work in the fruit orchards and on the ranches." By 1910 more than thirty thousand Japanese worked on farms in California, the single largest ethnic group toiling in what California journalist Carey McWilliams would later call the "factories in the field."[39]

Japanese workers evoked a familiar response from racist westerners, a group not known for original or consistent thinking. Senator James D. Phelan, former mayor of San Francisco, declared that white men could not compete with the Japanese because "they know no rest and respect no standards," and he warned his constituents that the Japanese were "rapidly acquiring the most productive lands." Some commentators saw the Japanese as an even greater threat than the Chinese. They leased and purchased their own land and soon were supplying most of the vegetables and much of the fruit sold in the urban markets of California. Reacting to pressures from exclusionists, in 1908 President Theodore Roosevelt negotiated the so-called Gentlemen's Agreement with the Japanese government, ending the immigration of Japanese men to the United States. And in 1913 the California legislature prohibited the ownership or long-term lease of land by aliens of Asian descent, legislation imitated by several other western states. But Japanese immigrants (the Issei—the first generation in America) simply shifted the title of their farms to their American-born children (the Nisei), who were legal citizens. By 1920 Japanese farmers, who owned 1 percent of California's agricultural land, were raising and marketing crops equal to 10 percent of the total value of the state's production. Instead of trumpeting their success, the

Campaign poster for Senator James D. Phelan, 1920. National Archives.

California legislature, a body never shy about promoting the agricultural bounty produced by the state's white farmers, strengthened the anti-Asian leasing law in 1921. Try as they might, the politicians could not obliterate the property and citizenship rights in the American Constitution to prohibit landownership among the Nisei.[40]

The Gentlemen's Agreement had permitted the continued immigration of wives of Japanese men already in the Pacific states, and from 1908 to 1924—when the federal Immigration Restriction Act of 1924 ended all Japanese immigration—approximately sixty thousand Japanese women entered the country. Perhaps half were so-called picture brides, women whose families had arranged for their marriage by proxy to immigrant Japanese men in America. "When you think about it, my god," one Issei remembered, "those girls were only eighteen or nineteen and came across to meet somebody they didn't even know. They had guts." Women and men formed families, and those unions irked racist power brokers like Senator Phelan. "The rats are in the granary," Phelan declared when asked about the immigration of Japanese women. "They have gotten in under the door and they are breeding with alarming rapidity." In his campaign for reelection to the Senate in 1920, Phelan adopted the slogan "Keep California White." At the time the Japanese made up less than 3 percent of the state's population.[41]

Most of the Japanese minority lived in isolated rural communities, many in California's fertile San Joaquin valley. The town of Del Rey, "20 miles south of Fresno, 200 miles from San Francisco or Los Angeles, and 100 years from Japan," according to one local Nisei, resembled many of these communities. A center of California's raisin industry, Del Rey began attracting Japanese laborers at the turn of the century, and within a decade Japanese farmers had begun leasing and buying land in the names of their Nisei children. They joined a multiethnic town with Armenians, Mexicans, and Chinese enclaves. "Japtown," as the Japanese section of Del Rey was locally known, was like a little neighborhood in Tokyo, its wooden buildings packed tightly together, opening onto courtyards with koi ponds and ornamental trees.[42]

Historian Valerie Matsumoto studied another Japanese community in the San Joaquin valley, the Cortez Colony of Merced County, established by Japanese Christians in 1920. Like many western communities, the settlers' first priority was founding a church, which, in the words of Matsumoto, "cemented the bonds of friendship and support." At Del Rey, where Japanese farmers were evenly divided between Christians and Buddhists, the center of community was the nonsectarian *kyowakai,* a community club. "Everybody that's Japanese in Del Rey, they had to join kyowakai, an automatic member," one longtime resident recalled. The kyowakai building, known as Del Rey Hall, hosted the meetings of both Christian and Buddhist congregations, children's Japanese-language classes, and other community gatherings. Painfully aware of the prejudice against them in the larger world, the Japanese of Del Rey tried to keep to themselves. "We always stood together, whether we liked it or not. . . . That's why the community remained so important."[43]

With nativist sentiment on the rise after World War I, the Japanese communities in the West found themselves under increased attack. In Oregon's Yakima valley a politically ambitious attorney led a local movement to evict Japanese farmers from their leaseholds on Indian reservation land, which was under federal control and thus exempt from the state's anti-Asian leasing law. "THE JAP MUST GO," he declared in a manifesto that accused Japanese farmers of "slowly but surely" acquiring all the best land in the valley. When the economy went sour in the 1930s, the verbal attacks turned violent. Terrorists bombed homes and farm buildings of two Japanese families. "All our forefathers, yours and ours, came across the oceans," the Japanese American Citizens League appealed to valley residents, and "we should all have the same equal rights." Two more dynamite bombs exploded on Japanese farms. "We're charged with wanting to get rid of the Japs for selfish reasons," a farmer from California's Central Valley told a reporter. "We might as well be honest. We do. It's a question of whether the white man lives on the Pacific Coast or the brown man."[44]

Violence against Japanese farmers erupted in Arizona's Salt River valley. Four thousand families farmed in the district. Only 120 were Japanese, but they received

Japanese farmworkers, Etiwanda, California, c. 1920. Beinecke Rare Book and Manuscript Library, Yale University.

the lion's share of hatred, especially after Japanese families responded to the state's Alien Land Law by shifting title to their Nisei children. "Let it be suggested that the newcomers depart quietly while they are still safe and before a war starts," a local newspaper warned. "Unless something like this is done at once—look out!" In August 1935, fifteen hundred white farmers drove through the streets of Phoenix carrying banners proclaiming, "We Don't Need Asiatics," and "Get Out or Be Put Out." Before the hate campaign sputtered to an end months later, there were sixty-nine violent incidents, including dynamite attacks on Japanese homes and drive-by shootings of Japanese men and boys working in the fields. Fortunately, no one was killed. A group of Japanese farmers suggested negotiations. "We don't care to hear them talk," answered a leader of the expulsion movement. "All we want is to see them walk."[45]

By suggesting that offending immigrants "go home," white supremacists denied the world that global capitalism was creating and the new streams of human movement that tied the American West into a Pacific network of trade and travel. Focused on closing doors to those with the wrong skin color, local racists ignored the larger communities based in such ideas as the freedom of movement and individual rights. Historical creations themselves, these Western ideas of individualism were used by Great Britain, the United States, and others to pry open Chinese and Japanese markets. As Chinese and Japanese laborers traveled to the American West to improve their lives, they deployed these notions in their defense. They sued, and cases wound their way to the highest court. Some cases, like *Chae Chan Ping v. United States* (1889), ended badly, with the Court siding with the exclusionists, but others brought victories. In 1898 the Supreme Court decided in *United States v. Wong Kim Ark* that Chinese Americans born in the United States were naturalized and possessed American citizenship. Going to court, opening businesses, and moving back and forth between countries in search of work, profit, and advancement, these activities defined the West and the Pacific as much as did riots and slurs.

––––––––

Chinese immigration to the American West all but ceased with the Exclusion Act of 1881, and the Gentlemen's Agreement severely restricted Japanese immigration in 1908. Neither of these controls slowed immigration; they simply changed the immigrants. In the early nineteenth century, Mexican immigration to the western United States took off like a rocket. Official statistics recorded the entry of 728,171 Mexicans between the turn of the century and 1930, but historians estimate that many more crossed the border, upping the total immigration to about 10 percent of the entire population of Mexico. This northbound mass migration determined the future of the American West as much as any westward movement.

Many immigrants came as war refugees attempting to escape the revolution in Mexico that followed the overthrow of the dictator Porfirio Díaz in 1911 and engulfed the country for nearly ten years. Some of the bloodiest fighting took place in Mexico's northern states, and thousands of civilians looked toward the United States for their safety. During one week in 1916, U.S. immigration agents counted nearly five thousand Mexicans attempting to cross the Rio Grande at El Paso. Unable to cope with such numbers, officials closed the border, but refugees kept coming over, unofficially, downriver, in the city's eastern section.

Revolutionary sentiment crossed over with the refugees. In the Rio Grande valley of Texas, farmers from the Midwest and South had been buying up large tracts, irrigating them to grow cotton and vegetables—crops dependent on Mexican labor at harvest. Commercial agriculture squeezed the traditional ranchero world of south Texas. Tejanos resisted, but commercial farmers took over county governments and instituted laws segregating public accommodations and schools. Texas enacted a statewide poll tax in 1902, effectively disenfranchising thousands of poor blacks and Tejanos. Frustrations erupted into violence. In 1915 a group of Tejano rancheros and businessmen met in the small town of San Diego on the Nueces River—not far from the spot where the Mexican War had begun seventy years

Texas Rangers pose with the corpses of Mexican raiders near the Rio Grande. Photograph by Robert Runyon, 1915. Library of Congress.

before—and issued a proclamation calling for armed insurrection by a "liberating army" of the oppressed castes of the Southwest—Hispanics, Asians, African Americans, and Indians. Several hundred (perhaps several thousand) Tejanos pledged themselves to *El Plan de San Diego*, as the manifesto was known. Tejano raiders attacked farms and railroads, burned bridges, and sabotaged irrigation systems. They killed several dozen Anglos.[46]

Texas authorities responded with what historian Walter Prescott Webb described as "an orgy of bloodshed." Anglo vigilance committees lynched suspected insurrectionists while the Texas Rangers conducted punitive raids against Tejano communities. The revolutionaries attacked the symbols of the white commercial agricultural regime, the Texas authorities counterattacked with the actual power of that regime. And they spread the pain to non-combatants to shore up the class and racial order that consigned Mexicans and African Americans to the lowest ranks. According to longtime resident Emma Tenayuca, the Rangers invaded "villages in the border country, massacred hundreds of unarmed, peaceful villagers and seized their lands." Historian Webb estimated that as many as five thousand Tejanos and Mexicans were killed. Soon Mexican supporters were retaliating from across the Rio Grande, terrorizing Anglo communities in Brownsville and other

south Texas towns. In 1916 Francisco "Pancho" Villa and his northern Mexican vaquero army threatened an invasion of the city of El Paso, then shifted west to loot
and burn the border town of Columbus, New Mexico. President Woodrow Wilson
sent an American army on a "Punitive Expedition" across the border, and for the
next several months, troops exhausted themselves chasing Villa's forces through
the deserts of Chihuahua. The border war acquired a global menace when American spies intercepted a secret telegram from the German foreign secretary, Arthur
Zimmerman, to his ambassador in Mexico. Zimmerman proposed a deal in which
Mexico would declare war on the United States and in exchange Germany would
support the return of "lost territory in New Mexico, Texas, and Arizona." The
border violence gave the Zimmerman telegram bite and helped prompt the United
States' entry into World War I.[47]

————

Revolutionary violence pushed refugees across the border, but jobs in orchards
and fields across the Southwest pulled them as well. "The cry of the hour is con-
tinually for more dependable labor," reported the *El Paso Daily Times* in 1912. Encouraging Mexican immigration—and thus increasing the supply of labor and
lowering wages—was clearly in the interest of the powerful farmers' associations
of the Southwest, who were engaged in fierce struggle with unions for higher wages
and better working conditions. City officials of El Paso and other border towns
equally overwhelmed with immigrants appealed to the federal government to stem
the tide, but the growers opposed every attempt to restrict the Mexican exodus. By
the 1920s Mexican migrants made up about three-quarters of the more than one
million farm laborers in the American West.[48]

Mexico's proximity distinguished Mexican communities from other immigrant
communities in the American West. When Mexico ceded the territory to the United
States, many Latino families were divided, and there was regular movement back
and forth across the untended border. The border did not stop movement; it invited crossings. A typical Mexican farmworker of the early twentieth century might
follow the harvest cycle through the irrigated fields of the Southwest, then return
to his Mexican village for the winter. A cross-border migration pattern was the
preference of many workers and employers alike. Early in the century, an inspector
interviewing Mexicans at the border found that 69 percent had been to the United
States at least once before. During the mass exodus of the Mexican Revolution,
however, thousands of families decided to settle permanently in the United States.
They founded new colonias in the dozens of farm towns servicing the intensive agricultural districts—usually on the rough side of the tracks, often on the site of former Chinatowns, abandoned during earlier bouts of vigilante violence. Newcomers headed for *tenemos familias,* places where extended family or former neighbors

resided; colonias often had strong links with one or two villages back home. These allegiances influenced the immigrants' worldview. Instead of seeing themselves as members of a region (the American West) or a nation (the United States or Mexico), the migrants perceived a borderland that transcended regions and borders. Anticipating the globalized linkages that would define the postregional, postmodern West, Mexican migrants spied a world *sin fronteras*—without borders.[49]

Growers were fond of assuring themselves that this pattern of continued loyalty to Mexico operated in their favor. As a spokesman for California growers put it, the Mexican was "a 'homer'—like a pigeon, he goes back to roost." Another grower condescended that "the Mexican likes the sunshine against an adobe wall and a few tortillas, and in the off season he drifts across the border where he may have these things." In other words, the border made Mexicans pliable peasants, grateful for the employment that growers provided, unlikely to cause labor trouble. Mexicans did remain loyal to the country of their birth. They had one of the lowest rates of naturalization of any group in American history. But equating this ambivalence about citizenship with docility was foolish thinking. Consider how one immigrant responded when asked whether he planned to become an American citizen: "I would rather cut my throat before changing my Mexican nationality. I am only waiting until conditions get better, until there is absolute peace before I go back." Not the words of a quiescent man. For many Mexican immigrants, memories of the native land included traditions of militancy. Parents taught children to admire grandfathers who had fought with Benito Juárez, fathers who had stood with Emiliano Zapata, mothers who had been soldaderas in the army of Pancho Villa. Far from apolitical simpletons, most migrants came from those areas where the Mexican Revolution had been most intensely argued and fought, and many had participated in peasant rebellions and union struggles.[50]

Working conditions in the fields and orchards of the Southwest provoked and tested these traditions. "The growers considered us slaves," remembered one migrant Mexican worker; they "treated the horses and cows better than the farm workers. At least they had shelter, but we lived under the trees." According to a report of the California Department of Immigration and Housing, most migrant farmworkers were forced to provide their own accommodations; some had their own tents, but others "fix[ed] a rude shelter from the limbs of trees." Grower-owned labor camps were little better. California investigators found "filth, squalor, and entire absence of sanitation." To make matters worse, the wages of farmworkers began to fall in the mid-1920s and kept falling during the Depression years. In 1935 a typical migrant worker earned only $280 per year (the equivalent of about $4,800 today). Mexican farmworkers responded by organizing unions and battling growers for better working conditions and higher wages. "We would have starved working," declared one organizer, "so we decided to starve striking."[51]

Mexican cotton pickers on strike in California's San Joaquin valley, 1933. Bancroft Library, University of California, Berkeley.

Historians have documented 160 major farm-labor strikes in California alone during the 1930s, most of them featuring Mexican workers and organizers. High tide came in 1933, when growers were hit with 37 strikes involving forty-eight thousand workers and affecting two-thirds of the state's agricultural production. In the words of Carey McWilliams, who served as chief investigator for California's Department of Immigration and Housing in the late 1930s, these strikes were "the most extensive in the farm labor history of California and the United States; in scale, number, and value of crops affected, they were quite without precedent." Organized by the Cannery and Agricultural Workers Industrial Union, the actions began in April among pea pickers in the Bay Area, spread in June to the berry fields of southern California and in late summer to the fruit orchards and vineyards of the Central Valley, and concluded with a massive strike of fifteen thousand cotton pickers in the southern San Joaquin valley in October. Forcibly evicted from grower-owned camps, strikers set up their own makeshift communities on unoccupied land, including a huge tent city housing three thousand near the dusty valley town of Corcoran. A traveling troupe of Mexican actors known as Circo Azteca raised a platform near the center of camp and staged reenactments of radical events from Mexican and American history. Many of the strike organizers were veterans of the Mexican Revolution.[52]

These attachments to Mexico could inspire, but revolutionary memories and symbols paled next to the allies the growers could recruit. When the 1933 strikes were broken, as all eventually were, it was not because of the absence of worker resolve, for there was plenty of that, nor because of grower violence, although there was plenty of that, too, including three strikers shot dead and many more wounded during the cotton strike. No, most strikes were ended by the intervention of Mexican consular officials who arranged meager deals with growers under the assumption that the Mexican state represented the interests of Mexican migrants. Union organizers were infuriated by this violation of the principle of solidarity, but the Mexican government had decided that the continuation of these strikes was not in Mexico's national interests. "The Mexican consul played a major role in California's labor struggles in the 1930s," writes historian Gilbert G. González, "providing a prominent bulwark against working class radicalism." Stuck between states, Mexican laborers pondered various futures. Some would remain borderlanders, pioneers of the great muddled ground on the edges of nations, while others considered the implications of becoming Mexican Americans and joining the panoply of communities that made the modern West work.[53]

FURTHER READING

John Mack Faragher, *Sugar Creek: Life on the Illinois Prairie* (1986)

Matt Garcia, *A World of Its Own: Race, Labor, and Citrus in the Making of Greater Los Angeles, 1900–1970* (2002)

Jon Gjerde, *The Minds of the West: Ethnocultural Evolution in the Rural Middle West, 1830–1917* (1997)

Gilbert G. González, *Labor and Community: Mexican Citrus Worker Villages in a Southern California County, 1900–1950* (1994)

Linda Gordon, *The Great Arizona Orphan Abduction* (2001)

Robert V. Hine, *Community on the American Frontier: Separate but Not Alone* (1980)

Karl Jacoby, *Shadows at Dawn: An Apache Massacre and the Violence of History* (2008)

Valerie J. Matsumoto, *Farming the Home Place: A Japanese American Community in California, 1919–1982* (1993); *City Girls: Nisei Social World in Los Angeles, 1920–1950* (2014)

T. Scott Miyakawa, *Protestants and Pioneers: Individualism and Conformity on the American Frontier* (1964)

Sandra L. Myres, *Westering Women and the Frontier Experience, 1800–1915* (1994)

Jeffrey Ostler, *The Plains Sioux and the U.S. Colonialism from Lewis and Clark to Wounded Knee* (2004)

Nell Irvin Painter, *Exodusters: Black Migration to Kansas after Reconstruction* (1976)

Devra Weber, *Dark Sweat, White Gold: California Farm Workers, Cotton, and the New Deal* (1994)

9

The Urban Frontier

For most Americans, spaciousness defines the West. How else would pioneers advance, buffalos and antelopes roam, and tumbleweeds tumble? These are not activities performed in close quarters. In a memorable 1893 essay, historian Frederick Jackson Turner articulated a unique American need for elbow room. The settlement of an "area of free land," he wrote, was "the really American part of our history." Turner's thesis proved as durable and free-ranging as a tumbleweed. But only six years after his star turn, another historian, Adna Weber of Columbia University, published a study that challenged Turner's ruling assumption. "In the Western states a larger percentage of the people dwell in cities," Weber demonstrated, "than in any other part of the nation except the North Atlantic states." The West was more urban than rural. Instead of a free space or a throwback region defined by uninhabited wilderness, the West represented the cutting edge of an industrializing nation.[1]

You would not know this from many of the histories written about the region. Weber's thesis sunk into obscurity as Turner's rose to orthodoxy. It didn't take a statistician to see that the twentieth-century West was increasingly urban and included the fastest-growing cities in the country, but this fact was taken as confirmation of Turner's assertion that the "close of the frontier" at the end of the nineteenth century marked the end of one era and the beginning of another. The modern West might be urban, but westering had been predominantly rural, and nearly all of the history written under the influence of the frontier thesis echoed this belief.

In fact, cities had always been central players in westward expansion. Eyewitnesses said as much. "Without transition you pass from a wilderness into the streets of a city, from the wildest scenes of the most smiling pictures of civilized life," remarked the Frenchman Alexis de Tocqueville after traveling through the trans-Appalachian West in the early 1830s. "Here it is not uncommon to have large cities spring up in a few years," a Scots farmer in Illinois wrote to his family. The urban quality of colonization intensified in the trans-Mississippi West, where the aridity dictated a low density of rural population and the extractive economy encouraged the development of industrial urban centers. In the modern West, bustling cities provided a roadside sobriety checkpoint to writing under the sway of the frontier thesis. It took some serious mind alterations not to see the metropolitan character of living in what would become the most urban region of the United States.[2]

Americans' first interior cities grew like fruits near the river branches that flowed into the main trunk, the Mississippi River. Town builders platted Lexington and Louisville in Kentucky during the American Revolution, years before the great postwar migration that filled the Ohio valley with Americans. Even as American armies continued to battle the confederated Indian tribes for control of the region, eastern developers laid out the town of Cincinnati as the administrative capital of the Old Northwest. In the Old Southwest, the entrepôts of Nashville, Natchez, and Memphis gathered plantation crops for marketing and shipment. They also provided a place for western grandees and granddames to display their wealth in mansions, carriages, slaves, and hoopskirts.

These incipient western cities were ruthless competitors for the trade of the extensive agricultural hinterlands of the Mississippi valley. Urban merchants sought to capture the business of thousands of farmers who were moving beyond subsistence and devoting more and more of their time and energy to the production of a "surplus" for market. What historian Richard Wade calls "urban imperialism"—the constant competition among towns for new rural markets—stimulated the expansion of commercial and industrial enterprises.[3]

Cincinnati won the early rounds for western urban supremacy. Founded in 1789, the Ohio River town had become a market center by 1800. "I could scarcely believe my own eyes," a visitor from New Jersey wrote home, "to see the number of people and wagons and saddle horses and the quantities of meat, flour, corn, fish, fowl, and sauce [preserves and jams] of all kinds that were offered and actually sold." Bread and jam, however, didn't turn Cincinnati into a regional power: steamboats did. Henry M. Shreve, a Pittsburgh keelboat captain, launched the *Washington*, a double-deck, shallow-hull side-wheeler able to carry heavy cargoes in the relatively shallow waters of the upper Ohio. Taking advantage of its location at the center of the nineteenth-century corn belt, Cincinnati's merchants concentrated on the slaughter and packing of pork ("corn on four legs") for shipment downriver to New Orleans, from where it was distributed to butchers along the Atlantic coast.

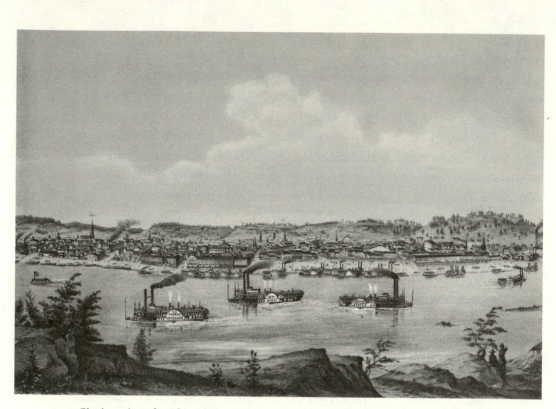

Cincinnati on the Ohio River. Lithograph by Otto Onken, c. 1850. Beinecke Rare Book and Manuscript Library, Yale University.

Lard they exported by the hundredweight for use as cooking fat in the Caribbean and South America. By the late 1820s, Cincinnatians squealed with delight at their status as the nation's unrivaled meat-packing champion. Boosters crowned it the "Queen City" of the West while locals, less regally but more to the point, called it "Porkopolis." Pork packers contracted for hogs not only in Ohio and Indiana but deep into Kentucky and far down the Ohio River, stealing business from Lexington and Louisville, and by the 1840s the butcher sheds were processing an estimated four hundred thousand hogs a year.[4]

From the mountains of slaughterhouse refuse, enterprising capitalists created new industries—producing leather, brushes, glue, soap, and chemicals—and on this economic base Cincinnati rose to become the first industrial city west of the Appalachians. At midcentury some twenty thousand workers manufactured clothing, furniture, building materials, and cooking stoves, as well as such capital goods as steam engines and mills. "The city's smokestacks," writes historian Carl Abbott, "emitted a perpetual blanket of smoke as dense and black as that over the mill towns of England." Cincinnati produced culture alongside smog. Numerous academies and "commercial colleges" sprang up. Scholars and everyday readers could peruse the scores of magazines, dozens of newspapers, and hundreds of books printed by local publishing houses. A Cincinnati firm published the famous McGuffey's Eclectic Readers, the most common texts used in western schools during the nineteenth century. All this development came from the close relation of city and country. "The pride and support of Cincinnati is her rich and extensive backcountry," wrote an editor of one of the city papers.[5]

While steamboats on the Ohio River kept Cincinnati's economy churning, farther downriver another western metropolis drew people and goods. Founded by French traders from New Orleans in 1762, Saint Louis benefited from its strategic location at the junction of the Missouri and Mississippi Rivers. The town long served as the headquarters of the Rocky Mountain fur trade, but it was lead—essential for ammunition—that accounted for the economic boom that produced a city. During the territorial period, Moses Austin and other businessmen opened a number of successful lead mines in eastern Missouri, giving the city its start in the business. When steamboats began operating on the Mississippi after the War of 1812, experienced lead traders from Saint Louis were able to seize control of the commerce of the mining district upriver at Galena, Illinois. Control of the nation's lead trade enabled Saint Louis to free itself from the economic dominance of Cincinnati and establish its own hinterland along the Mississippi corridor north of the city. By 1830, according to Thomas Ford, who served a term as governor of Illinois, "nearly the whole trade of Illinois, Wisconsin, and the Upper Mississippi was concentrated at Saint Louis."[6]

For every Saint Louis and Cincinnati, hundreds of would-be king and queen cities stumbled and fell. Consider Alton, Illinois, upstream and across the river from Saint Louis. Illinois leaders, chagrined to find the commerce of their lead district in the hands of Missourians, arranged for the state bank to finance a plan by Alton businessmen to recapture the trade. But Saint Louis merchants, leveraging their commercial dominance, were able to prevent their Alton competitors from chartering enough steamboats, driving them into bankruptcy. Alton hung on as a second-class river town, but dozens of aspiring cities were ruined by competition. On a trip down the Ohio, landscape architect Frederick Law Olmsted was startled by the number of forlorn and abandoned towns he saw. "Each had its hopes," he wrote, "of becoming the great mart of the valley, and had built in accordant style its one or two tall brick city blocks, standing shabby-sided alone on the mud-slope to the bank, supported by a tavern, an old storehouse, and a few shanties. These mushroom cities mark only a night's camping-place of civilization." Capitalism moved, convincing people and places that they had arrived only to leave them slumped in the dark like fungi.[7]

The busy Mississippi River levee at Saint Louis. Photograph by Boehl and Koenig, c. 1875. Beinecke Rare Book and Manuscript Library, Yale University.

Nineteenth-century Americans tossed around theories that explained why some cities succeeded while others failed. They cited geography, the urban "law of gravitation," and the "immortal fires of civilization." The urban theorists were accomplished back-casters. They looked to nature, history, and "Isothermal Zodiacs" to explain why destiny chose their hometown for greatness. But advantage could quickly turn to disadvantage, as western capitalists learned repeatedly that their future belonged, not to God or the stars, but to Wall Street and State Street bankers.[8]

Eastern control became clear during the mid-1850s, when Saint Louis was thrown into turmoil by the border war that broke out over the future of slavery in Kansas. Proslavery mobs threatened eastern merchants, and in 1856 several incoming shipments of goods were destroyed in a desperate search for rifles being sent to free-soil forces. These attacks were front-page news in the East. In a powerful series of editorials, William Cullen Bryant of the *New York Post* discouraged his readers from further investment in Saint Louis. "Men who have no regard for the rights of others," he warned, "cannot be expected to pay their debts." Frances Hunt, a Bostonian doing business in Saint Louis, admonished his local associates that unless the attacks ceased, the "source of their prosperity shall be cut off and driven to

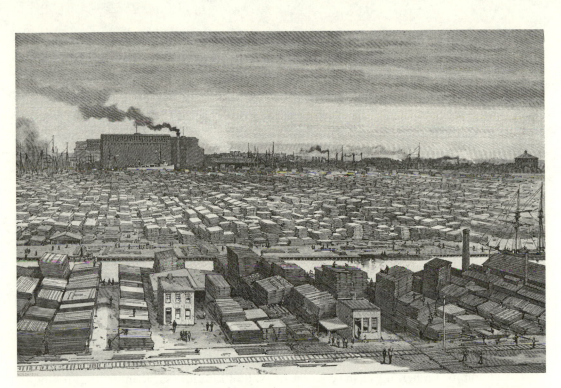

The Chicago lumber district. Harper's Weekly, *October 20, 1883.*

a northern route." With the open hostility toward "Yankees" unabated, Hunt soon closed his doors and joined the flight of eastern businessmen from the city. Almost overnight the city's economy collapsed.[9]

Saint Louis's loss was Chicago's gain. Little more than a swampy outpost on the southwestern shore of Lake Michigan in the 1830s, Chicago was the creation of eastern capitalists in collaboration with the state of Illinois. While speculators invested in unimproved city lots, driving up property values, the state undertook an ambitious program of lakeshore harbor improvements and canal construction. During the 1840s, the city captured the grain trade of northern Illinois and southern Wisconsin. Chicago's fortunes boomed just as eastern investors were pouring capital into railroad construction, and by the early 1850s a number of eastern railroad companies had selected Chicago as their western terminus, while several western companies were constructing lines radiating outward from the city into the adjacent countryside. One of them, the Chicago and Rock Island Railroad, struck at Saint Louis merchants. Ambitious Chicago businessmen hoped that the railroad would give them the wherewithal to capture the lead trade of Galena from Saint Louis control. The Rock Island line reached the Mississippi in 1854 and during its first season of operation succeeded in diverting half the output of the lead mines to Chicago. Two years later, the Rock Island became the first railroad to bridge the Mississippi.

"The faces of the men of business of the valley of the Upper Mississippi, who have heretofore looked Southward and downward, will now look upward and Eastward," crowed Chicago's *Daily Democratic Press*. "How can they resist it?" When in 1856 a Saint Louis steamboat crashed into the Rock Island bridge and exploded in flames, its owners sued the bridge company and the railroad. The case was a showdown between the two cities. "If we are beaten," warned the Saint Louis Chamber of Commerce, "the commercial position of Saint Louis, which is now the pride and boast of her citizens, would be counted among the things that were." And so it was. Abraham Lincoln, then an Illinois attorney in private practice, effectively argued in federal court that the railroad bridge represented the best hopes of a developing West. The jury deadlocked, the judge dismissed the suit, and Saint Louis was forced to concede the loss of the upper Mississippi. A reporter saw the evidence of Chicago's victory on a visit to a mercantile establishment in Omaha. "The ancient store boxes in the cellar have 'Saint Louis' stenciled on them; those on the pavement, 'Chicago,'" he wrote. "Omaha eats Chicago groceries, wears Chicago dry goods, builds with Chicago lumber, and reads Chicago newspapers." Chicago's triumph did not result simply from the "natural advantage" of its geography. Rather, it was the combined result of location, savvy investing, an innovative new mode of transportation, cutthroat competition, and the political crisis that marked the coming of the Civil War.[10]

Chicago emerged as the dominant western metropolis, the city with the strongest links to eastern markets, just as the explosive settlement of the trans-Mississippi West got under way. Chicago became what geographer Andrew Frank Burghardt calls a "gateway city," the link between the settlements and resources of the West and the cities, factories, and commercial networks of the Northeast. Within a few years, the completion of the transcontinental railroad opened a hinterland of unprecedented size, one stretching from the Great Lakes to the Rocky Mountains and beyond. "The range of the trade of Chicago," wrote an economist for the federal government in 1881, "embraces an area constituting more than one-half of the territorial limits of the United States." Historian William Cronon has detailed the city's role as headquarters for the late nineteenth-century colonization of the trans-Mississippi West. Chicago lumber merchants set thousands of men to work cutting the pine forests of the Great Lakes and shipped westward billions of board feet of lumber needed for the construction of the railroad system as well as for countless homes, towns, and cities on the Great Plains. Chicago entrepreneurs built dozens of grain elevators and devised the practice of commodity trading on the city's board of trade, providing a world market for the thousands of farmers who converted the grasslands into produce. Chicago meatpackers financed the western

A deserted railroad town in Kansas. Harper's Weekly, *February 28, 1874.*

cattle industry, and the South Side stockyards became the city's largest employer, drawing tens of thousands of immigrant workers from Ireland, Germany, Bohemia, Poland, and Slovakia. Workers and raw materials rode the rails into town, and commodities exited in the cars. Chicago surpassed the river towns as the gateway to the West because the railroads tied the city to the region's natural bounty.[11]

By the 1880s Chicago stood atop a western urban hierarchy that included some two dozen cities in the trans-Mississippi West, each with its own commercial hinterland. The "railroad capitalism" of the late nineteenth century concentrated decision making in the great urban centers, arranging lesser cities into a pecking order. With Chicago at its center, this interconnected urban system, writes Gilbert Stelter, "reflected the basically colonial nature of western life."[12]

William "Buffalo Bill" Cody told a story that illustrates this point. As a young buffalo hunter supplying meat for construction crews on the Kansas Pacific in the 1860s, Cody and a friend went into a partnership to develop a town they called Rome at a spot on the prairie where the railroad had announced that it would locate its repair shops. The partners staked out lots, and soon merchants, saloonkeepers, and ordinary settlers arrived and built on them. But returning from a hunt one afternoon, Cody discovered that "the town was being torn down and carted away. The balloon-frame buildings were coming apart section by section.

I could see at least a hundred teams and wagons carting lumber, furniture, and everything that made up the town over the prairies to the eastward." Officials in some far-flung corporate office had decided to relocate the repair facilities to Hays City, and Rome was unbuilt in a day.[13]

Denver nearly avoided duplicating Rome's fall when the Union Pacific bypassed the town in 1867. The skittish among Denver's business elite panicked, rushing north to Cheyenne on the rail line. A number of the city's more determined and optimistic citizens, however, organized a railroad company of their own called the Denver Pacific and used their Washington connections to win a land grant and subsidy from Congress. The Denver Pacific ran tracks north and tapped into the transcontinental line. The Denver example proved the importance of aggressive boosters. Cities didn't make themselves; blowhards with political connections were critical to the emerging urban system. Consider the case of the neighboring towns of Leavenworth and Kansas City, both aspiring to the status of regional metropolis. While Leavenworth's citizens quarreled over the financing of a bond issue, the business and political community of Kansas City unified behind a plan to win a rail connection and offered choice lots to influential railroad men. Kansas City secured rail access across the Missouri River first, and Leavenworth fell in line as the tributary of its neighbor. The Texas towns of Houston and Galveston waged a similar struggle. Feeling secure with a fine bay and harbor, Galveston's leaders wasted time squabbling over which railroad they should invite into the city, providing Houston's inland elites with time to construct an ambitious canal to the Gulf, dredge a deep harbor at Buffalo Bayou, and finance a railroad of their own, linking them to the national transportation system. Houston captured a vast Texas hinterland while Galveston whined for years, teaching local schoolchildren that crass, commercial Houston had stolen their natural port.

In the Great Basin, the Mormons at first sought to remain apart from the developing urban network of the West. Brigham Young warned against commerce with outsiders, and the church leadership tried to link together its own hinterland through a series of ninety-six outposts extending southwest from Salt Lake City to the port of San Diego on the Pacific Ocean. The church assisted the settlement of more than seventy thousand emigrants on small farms and ranches along this corridor. But railroad construction and mining rushes subverted the Mormons' careful isolation. Salt Lake City became a critical way station, attracting thousands of travelers and hundreds of gentile businessmen eager to profit from their movement. The Mormon leadership came to the conclusion that their economic isolationism was only enhancing other people's profits, so in 1869, when the Union Pacific line reached north of Salt Lake City, the church financed a line connecting the city with the depot at Ogden, and over the next decade the Mormons undertook a program of industrial development. By the mid-1870s, manufacturing had grown

Temple Square, Salt Lake City. Photograph by Charles Roscoe Savage, 1889. Beinecke Rare Book and Manuscript Library, Yale University.

in the local economy to such an extent that a local magazine could write that Salt Lake City was "eminently a manufacturing community."[14]

By the end of the nineteenth century, a handful of western cities had escaped tributary status to become industrial and financial powers unto themselves. The twin cities of Minneapolis and Saint Paul, for example, took advantage of the cheap waterpower available at the Falls of Saint Anthony on the Mississippi River and built a lumber and flour milling industry. Using their own capital, local millers helped finance the construction of rail lines into the Dakotas and western Canada to capture the wheat and lumber trade. By 1880 the combined output of Minneapolis companies such as Pillsbury outpaced Milwaukee, Saint Louis, and Chicago in flour production. While the twin cities road processed carbohydrates to glory, Denver concentrated on smelting the ores from the Rocky Mountain's numerous mines. In 1870, when the population numbered just 5,000, the city's annual industrial output was only $250,000, but thirty years later Denver's 134,000 residents were producing commodities valued at more than $50 million. Denver was able to circumvent Chicago and establish direct connections with New York financiers, becoming the regional command post for the great mining interests controlled by the Rockefeller and Guggenheim families.

An oil field near Houston. Photograph by Homer T. Harden, c. 1919. Library of Congress.

Houston's rise as one of the great cities of twentieth-century America dates from the huge oil gusher unloosed in 1901 at Spindletop, in nearby Beaumont. Spouting two hundred feet high, it blew off a hundred thousand barrels a day for ten days, creating a huge oil lake that caught fire and burned for weeks. Within months, engineers tapped other vast oil fields along the Gulf coast. Local companies with names like Gulf, Texaco, Shell, and Humble (later Exxon) built refineries and established headquarters in Houston. With federal help, the city dredged Buffalo Bayou deep enough to permit oil tankers to reach the city. Petroleum became the foundation for an industrial economy that included chemicals, machine tools, and warehouses. By 1910 Houston's economy had moved into the state of self-financed growth.[15]

The success of Houston, Denver, Salt Lake, and Minneapolis did not alter the basic flow of power from urban centers to rural hinterlands. Command and control lingered in the hands of a few men ensconced in high places in a few metropolitan areas. But the rise of regional cities did increase the number of high places. By 1900 Chicago had to share the roost with the upstarts as well as a West Coast competitor with gold claws.

San Francisco was the first regional city of the trans-Mississippi West to truly achieve takeoff, but even it began as a creature of the East. The Gold Rush drew people from many quarters, with a majority from the rural Mississippi valley. The residents of San Francisco, however, hailed mainly from the urban Northeast. During the city's first decade nearly all the principal merchants and bankers were agents or associates of Boston and New York firms. A survey of the city's lawyers found that 40 percent had been licensed to practice by the New York State bar. But the fabulous wealth of the mines led to the early creation of a powerful group of local capitalists. The event that signaled the arrival of San Francisco's financial class

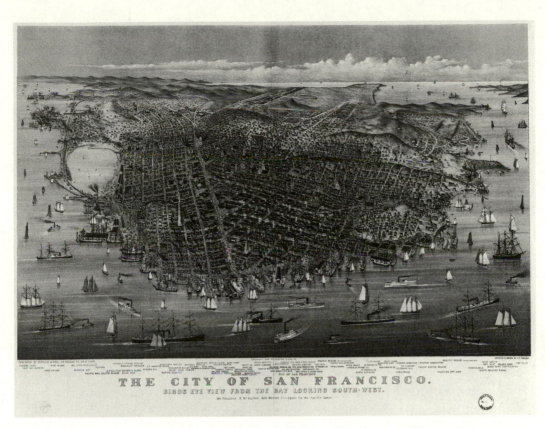

Bird's-eye view of San Francisco. Lithograph by Charles R. Parsons for Currier and Ives, c. 1878. Library of Congress.

was when its bankers and Silver Kings cornered the unprecedented wealth of the Comstock Lode in the late 1860s. From their headquarters on San Francisco's Nob Hill, noted historian Rodman Paul, "Comstock millionaires underwrote many a new venture in the American West and abroad."[16]

Henry George, San Francisco's radical journalist, was one of the first to note the city's bump in status. "Not a settler in all the Pacific States and Territories but must pay San Francisco tribute," he wrote. "Not an ounce of gold dug, a pound of ore smelted, a field gleaned, or a tree felled in all their thousands of square miles, but must . . . add to her wealth." By 1880 San Francisco's commercial hinterland stretched from Panama to Alaska, from the sugar plantations of the Hawaiian Islands to the mining districts of northern Idaho. In 1880 approximately thirty thousand workers produced output valued higher than the combined total of all the other urban centers of the West. "San Francisco dwarfs the other cities," the English scholar and diplomat James Bryce wrote in 1888, "and is a commercial and intellectual centre and source of influence for the surrounding regions, more powerful over them than is any Eastern city over its neighborhood. It is a New York which has got no Boston on one side of it, and no shrewd and orderly rural population on the other, to keep it in order."[17]

In the 1870s San Francisco investors began spreading their capital to other sections of the state. Los Angeles, with a population of only ten thousand, was "still a mere village—mostly Mexican," wrote visitor David Starr Jordan, "and the country round was practically a desert of cactus and sagebrush." But investors from San Francisco took notice when the Southern Pacific and Santa Fe linked L.A. to the nation's railroad network. Although the first transcontinental connection was built in 1876, it was the arrival of the Santa Fe Railroad in 1887 that commenced the city's first boom. A fare war drove ticket prices down so far that a passage from Saint Louis cost as little as five dollars. That brought in an estimated two hundred thousand tourists, curiosity-seekers, and land speculators. Boosters pitched southern California to the crowds much as they had promoted Kentucky and Texas in earlier years. "There are calla lilies by the acre," read one guidebook, "and tall enough to be picked by a man on horseback; hedges of geraniums, fifteen feet high; . . . roses of a thousand varieties, by the million, it being no rare thing to see a hundred thousand, two hundred thousand, or more, buds and blossoms and full blown roses on a single bush at the same moment." One visitor wrote home: "I apparently have found a Paradise on Earth."[18]

The cost of paradise rose with the resulting frenzy of buying and selling. In less than two years, developers laid out more than sixty new towns on nearly eighty thousand acres. The real estate bubble burst in 1889, yet the long money stayed in southern California. "People," wrote the vice president of the Santa Fe, "will continue to come here until the whole country becomes one of the most densely populated sections of the United States."[19]

Dense populations and desert environments do not make good partners unless water is added. With only enough precipitation in most years to avoid being classified as a semiarid climate, Los Angeles impressed many onlookers with its obvious deficiencies. The village lacked a proper harbor, and critics wondered why a city would develop there. "It is difficult to find any really good reason why the city of Los Angeles should have come into existence," the ecologist Raymond Dasmann once wrote, reflecting the opinion of many of his fellow San Franciscans. But in the twenty years following the initial boom, the leaders of Los Angeles took aggressive steps to solve their problems. After intense lobbying, Congress voted in 1897 to "improve" the anchorage at the harbor of San Pedro, a part of greater Los Angeles.[20]

Meanwhile, the city prowled for new sources of water. In 1905 and 1907, the L.A. water commissioners proposed, and the voters approved, more than twenty-five

A crowd celebrates the completion of the Los Angeles Aqueduct, bringing Owens River water to southern California. Photograph by Los Angeles Department of Water and Power. Beinecke Rare Book and Manuscript Library, Yale University.

million dollars in bonds to finance the construction of an aqueduct diverting the flow of the Owens River, some two hundred miles northeast in the Sierra Nevada. The water arrived in 1913, providing Los Angeles with more than enough capacity to satisfy its 350,000 residents, enough indeed to sustain a population numbering in the millions. What L.A.'s citizens had not been told, however, was that a syndicate of wealthy citizens—including government insiders—had previously bought up more than one hundred thousand acres in the adjacent San Fernando valley, where Owens River water would be stored in reservoirs. "Anyone who knew this, and bought up more than one hundred thousand acres in the adjacent San Fernando valley while it was still dirt-cheap," wrote historian Marc Reisner, "stood to become very, very rich." The syndicate made an estimated profit of one hundred million dollars. In an era of aggressive promotion, the elite of Los Angeles set a new standard for urban buccaneering.[21]

Henry E. Huntington stood among L.A.'s elite real estate tycoons. Nephew and heir of Collis P. Huntington of the Southern Pacific Railroad (corporate successor to the Central Pacific), one of the legendary Big Four, Huntington invested his family wealth in Los Angeles trolley companies and real estate. By 1900 he had become southern California's single largest landowner and majordomo of the interurban rail system known as the Pacific Electric. Huntington built dozens of new trolley lines, connecting his undeveloped tracts to the city center. "Railway lines have to keep ahead of the procession," he instructed his lieutenants. Leaving nothing to chance, Huntington had his land subdivided into lots and planted with pepper trees from Peru, jacarandas from Brazil, and palms from Asia and Africa, had the streets surveyed and paved, and even had the utilities laid out in advance of building. He thus created the conditions for what became the southern California—and then suburban America's—preference for detached single-family homes with private landscaped yards. Huntington helped invent a new kind of dispersed urban landscape, what a later generation would call sprawl. "As much as any single person," writes historian Kenneth T. Jackson, Huntington "initiated the southern California sprawl that still baffles visitors."[22]

Siphoned water encouraged far-flung real estate development, priming Los Angeles for an automotive takeover. The country's first filling station appeared there in 1909, the same year that California authorized the first bond issue for a paved state highway system. Cars accelerated the process of decentralization that Huntington began. In the 1920s builders developed some 3,200 new subdivisions with 250,000 new homes in outlying areas. Los Angeles, quipped Carey McWilliams, has from its beginnings been "a collection of suburbs in search of a city."[23]

Early twentieth-century L.A. served as the urban hub of a booming agricultural hinterland. Citrus fruit orchards, for example, covered the foothills and valleys throughout the southland, but the association that organized the picking, packing, and national distribution of Sunkist oranges was located in the city. "The center of power in the industry is not to be found in the elegant residences on Smiley Heights in Redlands," wrote McWilliams, "but in the offices of the California Fruit Growers Exchange in Los Angeles." Real estate and tourism provided other sources of economic vigor. But L.A.'s industrial sector was remarkably anemic in the early twentieth century. James M. Cain, who moved to the area in the 1920s to work as a Hollywood screenwriter, was appalled by "the piddling occupations" of his neighbors, and in *The Postman Always Rings Twice* (1934), his classic noir novel of southern California, one of his characters remarks that the "whole goddam country lives selling hot dogs to each other." Yet the future belonged to the peddlers of services, including food, tubular or otherwise. Southern California would cultivate many of the ideas and economies that would make the West a national trendsetter.[24]

The West led the way as the United States moved from a rural to an urban nation in the second half of the nineteenth century. The movement from farm to city defined industrial America. Farmers sought to increase their productivity through mechanization. Economic development in the countryside inevitably meant depopulation. Compare this to the pattern of the cities, where innovations in manufacturing led to the creation of new jobs through what economists call a "multiplier" effect. Rural townships in the Midwest had begun to lose population by the 1880s, and over the next half-century most of the rural West was overtaken by this trend. For every industrial worker who became a farmer, twenty farm boys rushed to the city to compete for his job.

Less well known is the fact that for every twenty farm boys, as many as twenty-five farm girls moved from the rural West to the cities. This migration reversed the gender blueprint of western movement, which featured young, unattached men rushing about, with single women conspicuous in their absence. Now rural men stayed put while young women took off. One historical study of rural households in late nineteenth-century Illinois, Iowa, and Minnesota details the "defeminization" of the countryside, with six in ten daughters of typical families leaving the area while seven in ten sons remained. Many of these young women married farmers from other communities, but even more headed for cities. There is evidence for this at the urban end of the trail where, by the 1880s in most western cities, American-born young women had begun to outnumber American-born young men. Over the next half-century, the proportion of young women in the urban population continued to rise.[25]

What explains the greater rates of female migration to the city? In the opinion of many contemporaries, young women were pushed out of the countryside by the lingering legacy of patriarchy. "I hate farm life," declared a disillusioned bride in Hamlin Garland's *Main-Travelled Roads* (1891). "It's nothing but fret, fret, and work the whole time, never going any place, never seeing anybody but a lot of neighbors just as big fools as you are. I spend my time fighting flies and washing dishes and churning. I'm sick of it." In 1913 the Department of Agriculture, seeking an answer to perceived rural decline, surveyed several thousand farm wives. The results confirmed the worst. The consensus among women was that they were overworked, that they had limited educational and vocational options, and that "old fashioned" male attitudes kept them at home and prevented their full participation in public and community life. "Isolation, stagnation, ignorance, loss of ambition, the incessant grind of labor, and the lack of time for improvement by reading, by social intercourse, or by recreation of some sort are all working against the farm woman's happiness," wrote one woman. Daughters fled farms for better lives.[26]

A young Colorado emigrant in Los Angeles, c. 1925. Author's collection.

They may also have been fleeing male violence. Historian David Peterson del Mar has found a good deal of provocative evidence in the records of divorce courts in rural Oregon. One man, defending himself against the charge of battering his wife, explained to the judge that he beat her because "a man should rule over his wife in everything except religion." Another man argued that he had used only the violence "necessary and reasonable to enforce rightful obedience" and swore that he would hit his wife again "if she did not do to suit." A father, testifying on behalf of his daughter, told the court that he had seen evidence of her husband's abuse many times: "I saw her with a very black eye." She told him, "Pa, the world will never know what trouble I have seen." Del Mar concluded that "husbands commonly used physical force on their wives." His documentation comes from only a single state, and divorce records typically emphasize the worst, but other kinds of evidence suggest that domestic violence was commonplace in the West. Readers of Mari Sandoz's biography of her homesteader father, *Old Jules* (1935), are shocked at his violent treatment of women. When Sandoz's mother asks Jules to help her with the work around the farmyard, he rages—"You want me, an educated man, to work like a hired tramp!"—and throws her against a wall. Yet Sandoz makes it clear that her father was not different from the other men she knew growing up in Nebraska.[27]

According to historian Joanne Meyerowitz, the records of welfare agencies in early twentieth-century Chicago are filled with stories of rural women who came to the city to escape abusive male relatives. One such girl sought protection from Travelers Aid when she arrived at Union Station late one evening in 1912. "Her stepfather had been making improper advances toward her for some time," reads the case record, "but so far she had been able to resist them. Her life was threatened if she told her mother. But the importunities of the man had become so insistent that the girl was afraid to remain longer and she fled." Another young migrant reported heated arguments with her father about dating. She resolved to leave home when her father threatened to whip her. "I was always willing to stand up for my rights," she told the social worker.[28]

Hope combined with fear to motivate women to leave rural homes for city opportunities. One rural mother wrote that her country daughter left the countryside in pursuit of greater economic freedom. "She isn't going to 'stay put,' but will get out where she can earn some money of her very own, to buy little things so dear to the hearts of girls." The city pulled rural women. Urban employment offered them independence, incomes of their own—which were hard to come by in the country, where just about the only paid work available was teaching school. As early as the 1890s there were reports of working women in western cities spending substantial sums on clothing, makeup, and amusements. After a ten-hour day working in shops, restaurants, or factories, young women sought recreation in dance halls, the theater (or movies a few years later), or simply strolling the streets with the companions of their choice. "Dallying in front of display windows, women announced themselves as independent wage-earners and consumers," writes Mary Murphy, who studied young women in early twentieth-century Butte, Montana. "Their dress, their assertive presence on the sidewalk, and their flirtatious manners proclaimed their right to share the street—and by extension movie theaters, dance halls, restaurants, and nightclubs—with men and do so on their own terms." Urban working women, many fresh from the farm, charted a course for economic independence and the possibility for life apart from family. They deserve a featured spot in American frontier history, for they as much as the forty-niners or the families rolling overland in their Conestoga wagons made the case for associating personal freedom with western locales. And they found their unfettered range in cities.[29]

————

From many vantage points, western cities were hardly unique. They were transportation crossroads, industrial hubs where people could find work. As such they drew immigrants from near and far. Western cities differed from their eastern counterparts only in the intensity of their diversity. A third or more of the populations of Salt Lake City, Portland, Sacramento, and Omaha were foreign-born in 1880. These were immigrant cities on par with Cleveland, Buffalo, or Scranton. In

1880 San Francisco had the highest proportion of foreign-born (45 percent) of any city in the nation, more than either New York (40 percent) or Chicago (42 percent). An early visitor was struck by the astounding ethnic diversity: "French, Germans, Mexicans, English, Americans, Irish, and even Chinese, white, black, yellow, brown, Protestants, Catholics, atheists, thieves, convicts, assassins—behold the population of San Francisco." Immigrant groups carved out neighborhoods along the crowded, hilly streets. Several thousand French residents lived on or near Commercial Street. Up Montgomery, beyond Pine, resided the Germans, and a few blocks farther north was a substantial neighborhood of German Jews. The Irish, the city's largest ethnic group, lived on the slopes of Telegraph Hill along with many Mexican and African Americans, while the Italians clustered along Broadway and in North Beach.[30]

In a city with little manufacturing, the Italians moved into fishing, skilled craftwork, and small business. Italian workers rose to leadership in the city's labor movement as well as the business community. Amadeo Peter Giannini spent his early years in the family wholesale produce business, selling crates of lettuce and peaches in San Francisco's foggy predawn. But in his thirties he switched to banking, opening Banca d'Italia in North Beach. After the devastating 1906 earthquake, he carted eighty thousand dollars out of the burning city hidden in fruit crates from his old produce business. While the city smoldered, he reopened for business. In an era when banks were austere places frequented only by capitalists and businessmen in the dark suits and starched shirts, Giannini pitched his services to consumers, offering small loans to ordinary people at reasonable rates of interest and opening friendly "branch banks" in urban and ethnic neighborhoods. In 1930, the year he renamed his institution Bank of America, he claimed some 280 branches scattered throughout the West.

The most distinctive of San Francisco's ethnic communities—and the one most characteristically western—was Chinatown, a place the English writer Oscar Wilde described as "the most artistic town I have ever come across." Chinatown bustled with tenements, boardinghouses, small factories, restaurants, and shops, "stocked with hams, tea, dried fish, dried ducks, and other Chinese eatables," wrote one visitor. "Suspended over the doors were brilliantly-colored boards covered with Chinese writings, and with several yards of red ribbon streaming from them; while the streets thronged with Celestials, chattering vociferously as they rushed about from store to store." In the 1880s approximately twenty-five thousand Chinese, nearly 2 percent of the city's population, squeezed into Chinatown's eight to twelve city blocks in the shadow of the millionaire enclave on Nob Hill.[31]

By custom, San Francisco's Chinese were not permitted to live outside Chinatown. "If you passed the boundaries," wrote a longtime Chinatown resident, "the white kids would throw stones at you." In 1868, while walking home with a bas-

San Francisco's Chinatown before the earthquake, c. 1898. From Arnold Genthe, Pictures of
Old Chinatown *(New York, 1908).*

ketful of crabs, one Chinese man was attacked by hooligans who beat him with
hickory clubs, branded him with a hot iron, and left him to die. Yet, as bad as it
got in San Francisco, Chinese immigrants preferred cities to rural towns. They
concentrated in Chinatowns where at least they could practice their own customs,
speak their own languages, and find security in numbers. They were protected
(and exploited) by the powerful Six Companies, a merchant-dominated director-
ate of clan associations that governed the Chinese community.[32]

During the first three decades of San Francisco's history, whites excluded Chinatown's children from city schools. "The prejudice of caste and religious idolatry
are so indelibly stamped upon their character," declared the city's school superintendent, that educating them was "almost hopeless." Then in 1884 a Christian
Chinese couple, Mary and Joseph Tape (themselves educated in foreign mission
academies), sued the board of education to admit their daughter to the local elementary school. "Is it a disgrace to be born Chinese?" Mary wrote in a letter to
the board. "I will let the world see, sir, what justice there is when it is governed
by the race of prejudice men!" The Tapes won their suit, the court deciding that

discrimination in education was unconstitutional, but the city circumvented the ruling by establishing a separate school for Chinese children in Chinatown. Educational discrimination would continue to harm them for decades to come. Esther Wong, a Chinatown schoolgirl in the 1920s, remembered a time when her teacher instructed her to read aloud. "Well, I read for her, and there were no mistakes," Wong told an interviewer, and then the teacher said, very slowly, "Well, you read all right, but I don't like you. You belong to a dirty race."[33]

During the late nineteenth century, San Francisco's immigrant working class succeeded in organizing one of the most powerful labor movements in the country. Secure jobs and good wages lifted working-class families up, and they used their rising incomes to move out of old ethnic communities and into new neighborhoods on the west side of the city or into newly developed suburban towns to the south. The workers, however, rejected and vilified the Chinese. One of the fundamental principles of western labor solidarity was the exclusion of the Chinese from unions. And because many of the male workers in Chinatown had been fraudulently admitted to the country as the "paper sons" of wealthy merchants (the only group allowed to bring over family members by the Exclusion Act), they found themselves without legal protection and became prime targets for exploitation and abuse by those same businessmen. Representatives of the Six Companies cut deals with city officials that allowed them to circumvent zoning and labor laws. About half of the city's manufacturing labor force was Chinese, but Chinatown was the center of the city's sweatshop district. Segregated and excluded, the Chinese workers in San Francisco could have used some help from fellow laborers, but the unions defended their turf by tossing rocks at nonwhites.

━━━━━━

In contrast to San Francisco, few European immigrants settled in early twentieth-century Los Angeles. The white population filtered in from the Midwest and plains, from the farms and small towns of Indiana, Illinois, Nebraska, Iowa, and Kansas. This was a gray wave, made up largely of the elderly, "retired farmers, grocers, Ford agents, [and] hardware merchants," wrote Louis Adamic, author of an early debunking history of the City of Angels. "They sold out their farms and businesses in the Middle West or wherever they used to live, and now they are here in California—sunny California—to rest and regain their vigor, enjoy the climate, look at the pretty scenery, live in little bungalows with a palm-tree or banana plant in front, and eat in cafeterias. Toil-broken and bleached out, they flocked to Los Angeles, fugitives from the simple, inexorable justice of life, from hard labor and drudgery, from cold winters and blistering summers of the prairies." Go west, old man.[34]

"As New York is the melting-pot for the peoples of Europe," wrote novelist Sarah Comstock, "so Los Angeles is the melting-pot for the peoples of the United States." Actually, there was little melting. Many transplants, lonely for their old homes, joined the several dozen state societies of southern California. Thousands joined the Pennsylvania Club and the Illinois Association, and crowds estimated at 150,000 people or more attended the annual Iowa Society picnic.[35]

Los Angeles rapidly industrialized after World War I and began attracting a different, more diverse crowd. Stimulated first by the enormous expansion of the federal government during the war, industrial development took off with the discovery of vast local petroleum fields. Oil was discovered in the 1890s, but the really big strikes took place after the war, the first in 1920 at Huntington Beach (one of Henry Huntington's many developments), followed by several more in quick succession. Almost overnight the region was supplying nearly 10 percent of the nation's fuel oil and gasoline. In California, as in Texas, local capital financed petroleum development, supplying one of the most important early examples of western industrial development. California overtook Texas and Oklahoma as the largest oil-producing state during the 1920s, and by 1930 refining was the state's largest industry. Between the wars, Los Angeles rose to become the West's largest industrial center—the nucleus of the nation's oil equipment and service industry, the second largest tire-manufacturing center, and the largest producer of steel, glass, chemicals, aircraft, and automobiles in the West. Perhaps the most visible sign of the region's growth was the motion picture industry, which by the end of the 1920s employed more than fifteen thousand people.

Prosperity brought people. More than a hundred thousand new residents arrived each year during the early 1920s, part of the massive national relocation taking millions from farms to cities. From states like Arkansas, Oklahoma, and Texas came thousands of poor folk in search of work. "Like a swarm of invading locusts," wrote essayist Mildred Adams, "migrants crept in over the roads. They had rattletrap automobiles, their fenders tied with string, and curtains flapping in the breeze; loaded with babies, bedding, bundles, a tin tub tied on behind, a bicycle or a baby carriage balanced precariously on top. Often they came with no funds and no prospects, apparently trusting that heaven would provide for them. They camped on the outskirts of town, and their camps became new suburbs."[36]

The migration to southern California included thousands of African Americans, Mexicans, and Japanese, who collectively by 1930 made up approximately half of the unskilled workforce at the base of the region's industrial economy. The rapid rise in the proportion of these groups in the population—from 6 percent in 1910 to nearly 15 percent in 1930—alarmed many of the region's white residents. "Negroes: We Don't Want You Here," screamed the headline in one local paper

Restricted housing tract, Los Angeles, c. 1940. Southern California Library for Social Studies and Research.

in 1922. "Now and forever, this is to be a white man's town." Local chapters of the Ku Klux Klan staged nighttime rallies in public parks and organized auto caravans through minority neighborhoods, "to put us in our place," one Mexican immigrant told his son. In the area surrounding the downtown campus of the University of Southern California, homeowners formed the Anti-African Housing Association (later renamed the University District Property Owners Association), a coterie of respectable citizens who specialized in burning crosses on the lawns of the black transgressors of the association's "color line." White residents harassed Japanese families moving into white neighborhoods, and in one particularly frightening case, vigilantes burned one Japanese family out of their home. Silent "restricted covenants" were more common and insidious. Written into the deeds of homes in most sections of the city, these covenants excluded "Negroes, Mongolians, Indians, and Mexicans" from occupancy. By the 1920s, 95 percent of the city's housing had been declared off-limits to racial minorities. Minority home buyers brought suit to challenge the legality of these deed restrictions, but local courts continued to uphold them until 1948.[37]

The African American population of Los Angeles—which grew from eight thousand in 1910 to nearly forty thousand in 1930, making it the largest in the

West—was confined to an area along Central Avenue in the southern section of the city and to a rural district farther south initially known as Mudtown. The writer Arna Bontemps, who attended school in L.A. in the 1920s, remembered the black neighborhood as an agrarian place complete with "pigs and slime holes." Most of the black residents had emigrated from Louisiana, Arkansas, and Texas, and Mudtown "was like a tiny section of the deep south literally transplanted." After World War I, the area was renamed Watts, for real estate agent C. H. Watts, who developed a tract of inexpensive bungalows there for black families.[38]

Southern California was a space divided by race. Segregation marked (and marred) public education and transportation, parks, swimming pools, hotels, restaurants, and theaters. Edward Roybal, a social worker who in 1949 became the first Mexican American elected to the Los Angeles City Council, remembered that during the 1930s it was common to see signs in the city's establishments warning, "No Mexicans or Negroes Allowed." Los Angeles, of course, was not uniquely racist. The western states of Texas, Oklahoma, and Arizona wrote segregation into law. "Nowhere in the United States did minorities enjoy complete equality and integration," writes historian Robert Fogelson. "But in Los Angeles, where they were distinguished by race rather than nationality, the majority subjugated and excluded them even more rigorously." Dwight Zook, for many years a member of the county's Fair Employment Practices Commission, put it more boldly in an interview in 1965. Los Angeles, he declared, was "probably the most segregated city" in the United States.[39]

Mexican Americans made up the largest and fastest growing of the minority communities in Los Angeles, climbing from only six thousand in 1910 to nearly one hundred thousand in 1930. Their experience illustrates another dimension of the centuries-long conflict over acculturation and assimilation that lies at the heart of the history of the American West. The Mexican immigrants arriving in the city during the 1910s and 1920s first settled in the old city center, near the nineteenth-century Catholic church. But as that area filled up, they began streaming eastward, over the Los Angeles River and into the area that has become known as East L.A.—the Mexican American capital of the West. By the late 1920s East L.A. had stabilized into a durable community, a place where, as historian George Sánchez discovered, 44 percent of Mexican families owned homes. "Home ownership," Sánchez writes, "symbolized adaptation: permanent settlement in the city."[40]

The prosperity of the 1920s was short-lived. The Great Depression hit Los Angeles hard, with a third or more of the county's workforce unemployed by 1931. Clamor grew for the deportation of Mexicans. In several neighborhoods of the Los Angeles barrio, immigration agents went door to door, demanding that residents

Mexican deportation: "Sometimes I tell my children that I would like to go to Mexico, but they tell me, 'We don't want to go, we belong here.'" Photograph and caption by Dorothea Lange, 1935. Library of Congress.

produce documents proving their legal residency, summarily arresting and jailing those unable to do so, many of them American citizens. "It was for us the day of judgment," one resident wrote in 1931 in the pages of the local Spanish-language newspaper, *La Opinion.* "The *marciales,* deputy sheriffs, arrived in the late afternoon when the men were returning home from working the lemon groves. They started arresting people. . . . The deputies rode around the neighborhood with the sirens wailing and advising people to surrender themselves to the authorities. They barricaded all the exits to the *colonia* so that no one could escape." Raids like this one frightened many Mexicans into joining voluntary programs of repatriation by officials of Los Angeles County, and between 1930 and 1933 tens of thousands of Mexican citizens boarded buses and trains for the border. There are not reliable statistics on the total number of Mexicans deported from Los Angeles, but in the authoritative study, Francisco E. Balderrama and Raymond Rodríguez estimate that at least a million Mexican citizens from the Southwest were repatriated during the 1930s.[41]

Intended to exclude Mexicans from America, the deportations ended up binding the next generation more to the United States. "What had been largely an immigrant community before the Depression," argues George Sánchez, "became one dominated by the children of immigrants. While maintaining their Mexican identity, these children had grown up in the states, absorbing American culture. The conflict between generations often focused on gender. "Here the old women want to run things," grumbled one Mexican immigrant, "and the poor man has to wash the dishes while the wife goes to the show." One young woman, pointing out that her parents had been "born in old Mexico," complained to an interviewer that "as soon as I was sixteen my father began to watch me, and would not let me go anywhere or have my friends come home." Another boasted that the first thing she did when she left home was bob her hair in the fashion of the day. "My father would not permit it and I have wanted to do it for a long time. I will show my husband that he will not boss me the way my father had done all of us."[42]

Impatient with their immigrant parents, yet outraged by racism and segregation, Mexican American youths created a pachuco subculture, a defiant style of talking, dressing, and behaving that included talking in a slang "Span-glish," dressing in the long coats and pegged pants of the zoot-suiter, joining gangs, and rumbling in the streets. During World War II, pachuco gangs roused public controversy, and in 1943 hundreds of sailors from the port of Long Beach invaded East L.A., assaulting young Mexican Americans and African Americans, stripping them of their clothes, and beating them senseless as the police stood by and white bystanders cheered. As sociologist Alfredo Guerra Gonzalez suggests, what have been called the Zoot-Suit Riots should actually be remembered as Serviceman's

Riots. For the Mexican American community, which sent its sons to fight in the war in greater proportion than any other group in the West, these riots would remain a bitter memory. A young Mexican American, arrested in 1943 as a public nuisance, eloquently expressed the feelings of his generation to the judge. "Pretty soon I guess I'll be in the army and I'll be glad to go. But I want to be treated like everybody else. We're tired of being pushed around. We're tired of being told we can't go to this show or that dance hall because we're Mexican, or that we better not be seen on this beach front, or that we can't wear draped pants or have our hair cut the way we want to. . . . I don't want any more trouble and I don't want anyone saying my people are a disgrace. My people work hard, fight hard in the army and navy of the United States. They're good Americans and should have justice."[43]

In Los Angeles, justice could be as scarce as a rain shower in August. Crowded into Little Tokyo in the downtown section of the city, the immigrant Issei and their Nisei children seemed willing to ignore discrimination and dedicate themselves to hard work and prosperity. "Scratch a Japanese American," writes scholar Harry Kitano, "and find a white Anglo-Saxon Protestant." Until the 1920s, the Japanese in America seemed headed for assimilation and a weakening identification with Japan, but the passage of the Immigration Restriction Act of 1924, completely barring Japanese immigration, "was a stinging rejection of their hopes for economic and social assimilation," according to historian Brian Masaru Hayashi. "We are not whole-heartedly accepted by the country we reside in," one Nisei concluded. "True, we are American citizens, but only in a statutory sense. Socially we are just another foreigner, compelled to huddle into a small quarter of our own, unable to take part in American social activities, and above all denied positions in American firms, simply because of our race."[44]

During the 1930s, Japan's aggressive expansion into China sparked considerable controversy within the Japanese American community. Nisei Monica Sone later remembered bitter debates with her Issei parents. "I used to criticize Japan's aggressions in China and Manchuria while Father and Mother condemned Great Britain and America's superior attitude toward Asiatics and the interference with Japan's economic growth," she wrote. "During these arguments, we eyed each other like strangers, parents against children. They left us with a hollow feeling in the pit of the stomach." The Japanese American Citizens League, a Nisei organization formed in 1930 to promote assimilation, was critical of Japan. But allegiances didn't break cleanly along generational lines, for other Nisei publicly supported the empire. "I cry for joy over the Imperial favor that is now extending to the 400 million Chinese people," wrote a Japanese leader in Los Angeles. Another

Troops supervise the evacuation of Japanese families from Los Angeles to Manzanar. Photograph by Russell Lee, 1942. Library of Congress.

Nisei condemned the idea that "American culture was the only possible lifestyle." In the coming "Era of the Pacific," he wrote, the Japanese should seek less "Americanization" because Americans would have to pursue more "Pacific-ization."[45]

The loyalty of some Japanese to their homeland was not unique, and the American proponents of empire should have recognized the Japanese rhetoric, for it echoed their own expansionist propaganda. German Americans belonged to the Nazi Bund party and Italian Americans applauded Mussolini. Members of the American Communist Party backed Stalin, a transnational loyalty made palatable when Hitler broke his nonaggression pact with the Soviets. But Japanese-Americans were the only ones subjected to mass incarceration during World War II. Two months after the attack on Pearl Harbor, President Franklin D. Roosevelt signed Executive Order 9066, suspending the civil rights of both citizens and aliens of Japanese background in the western states and authorizing the confiscation of property and "removal" of families from their homes and communities. Defended on the grounds of "military necessity," the order withstood a review by the Supreme Court in 1944, although in 1982 a federal commission concluded that the United States possessed no evidence linking West Coast Japanese Americans with espionage and that internment resulted from "race prejudice, war hysteria, and a failure of political leadership." The residents of L.A.'s Little Tokyo were rounded up and sent to one of the ten camps set up across the trans-Mississippi West. Many ended up at Manzanar in the Owens valley, left an arid waste by the diversion of water for urban Los Angeles. Manzanar was "the scene of a triple tragedy," says Richard Stewart, a Paiute Indian who leads tours around the abandoned site of the camp. First native Paiutes and Shoshones lost their homes, then farmers and ranchers lost their water, and finally Japanese Americans lost their rights. A total of 120,000 people entered these detention camps. Some stayed for up to three years.[46]

"The evacuation and establishment of relocation centers were actions without precedent in American history," wrote Dillon S. Myer, director of the War Relocation Authority, commander of the operation. The Cherokees and the Creeks, the Shawnees and the Nez Perce, might disagree. Was it mere coincidence that Myer found many of his lieutenants among those historical relocation and reservation specialists in the Bureau of Indian Affairs? Ethnic cleansing and prison camps were not alien concepts dropped into American minds like bombs from Japanese Zeros. They represented a culmination of American fear and racism. "A Jap's a Jap," declared General John L. DeWitt of the Western Defense Command. "It makes no difference whether he is an American."[47]

FURTHER READING

Adam Arenson, *The Great Heart of the Republic: St. Louis and the Cultural Civil War* (2011)
Gunther Barth, *Instant Cities: Urbanization and the Rise of San Francisco and Denver* (1975)
William Cronon, *Nature's Metropolis: Chicago and the Great West* (1991)
Brian Masaru Hayashi, *"For the Sake of Our Japanese Brethren": Assimilation, Nationalism, and Protestantism among the Japanese of Los Angeles, 1895–1942* (1995)
Andrew Needham, *Power Lines: Phoenix and the Making of the Modern Southwest* (2014)
George J. Sánchez, *Becoming Mexican American: Ethnicity, Culture, and Identity in Chicano Los Angeles, 1900–1945* (1993)
Robert O. Self, *American Babylon: Race and the Struggle for Postwar Oakland* (2003)
Richard Wade, *The Urban Frontier: The Rise of Western Cities, 1790–1830* (1959)
Judy Yung, *Unbound Feet: A Social History of Chinese Women in San Francisco* (1995)

10

New Frontiers

Frederick Jackson Turner faced the end of the frontier without tears. The young man, after all, was a professional, part of the vanguard of the first academically trained generation of historians in the United States. His argument came from evidence he found in the published report of the 1890 federal census: "Up to and including 1880 the country had a frontier of settlement," it concluded. "But at present the unsettled area has been so broken into by isolated bodies of settlement that there can hardly be said to be a frontier line." From this, Turner deduced a pattern that, he argued, explained America's unique development and pointed to an uncertain future. He announced his "frontier thesis" at a meeting of historians held in conjunction with the 1893 World's Columbian Exhibition in Chicago, a celebration of the four-hundredth anniversary of Columbus's first voyage to America. "Up to our own day American history has been in large degree the history of the colonization of the Great West," Turner wrote. "The existence of an area of free land, its continuous recession, and the advance of settlement westward, explain American development." But now, he concluded, "four centuries from the discovery of America, at the end of a hundred years of life under the Constitution, the frontier has gone, and with it has closed the first period of American history."[1]

There were problems with the notion of a closed frontier. Farmers and ranchers took up far more land in the trans-Mississippi West after 1890 than before. Western settlements continued to expand in the years after 1890, yet on the census map of 1900 and 1910, the "frontier line" made a mysterious reappearance. Settlement was an uneven process, with advances and retreats. In the twentieth century, many rural counties suffered depopulation, as the children of hard-pressed farmers left for the nation's towns and cities. Using Turner's own definition of "unsettled,"

Homesteading family in east Texas, 1918. Author's collection.

at the beginning of the twenty-first century there were more than 150 "frontier" counties in the West, and the number continues to grow. The geography that so inspired Turner turned out to be less a work of science than that of the imagination. Well into the twenty-first century, the West has yet to fill up.[2]

But the notion of a closed frontier resonated emotionally with Americans. During the long cycle of economic hard times that began with the Panic of 1873 and lasted through the late 1890s, Americans grew anxious about "the close of the frontier"—an end to the availability of "free land" and the exhaustion of the West's natural resources. The worry echoed in government reports, scholarly treatises, and ministers' sermons but was not confined to intellectuals. Western newspaper editor and humorist Bill Nye expressed the fears of ordinary folks: "No, we don't have the fun we used to," he quipped. "There ain't no frontier any more."[3]

Appealing to reason, Turner's words moved hearts. Even if parts of the frontier thesis were factually wrong, it felt right. Every period of history appears rough and conflicted to those experiencing the dips and swells of the moment, but the second half of the nineteenth century was especially tumultuous for an industrializing United States juggling several distinct regions. North and South coalesced into arguing "sections"—ornery regions—and fought a civil war that ended slavery and settled the question of whether the individual states were sovereign. Like

Indian to Filipino: "Be good, or you will be dead!" Cartoon by Victor Gilam, Judge, April 22, 1899.

the South, the West was brought into the nation through federal intervention and violence. Reconstruction, western historian Elliott West observes, was a national program that integrated all the regions into the union—at gunpoint. Warfare and industrialization empowered the federal government and enlarged corporate entities like the railroads. They could reach out to the far corners of the West and into the daily lives of farmers, workers, and Indians. These changes prompted anxiety. Americans looked for answers and solace.[4]

Turner's frontier thesis both stoked and calmed vexations. Some interpreted the "closing of the frontier" to mean that Americans should colonize other places and people. After reading Turner's essay, Woodrow Wilson wrote that with the continent occupied "and reduced to the uses of civilization," the nation must inevitably turn to "new frontiers in the Indies and in the Far Pacific." Future president Theodore Roosevelt agreed, arguing that America's westering tradition should transition to the seizure of colonies. He likened Filipinos to Apaches and condemned anti-imperialists as "Indian lovers." If the United States was "morally bound to abandon the Philippines," he blustered during the debate on annexation after the Spanish-American War, "we were also morally bound to abandon Arizona to the Apaches."[5]

Just as expansionists of the 1840s had marshaled public enthusiasm for westering to justify a war against Mexico, so imperialists of the 1890s exploited fears of the end of frontier opportunity to build support for the creation of an American overseas empire. As historian William Appleman Williams observed, it offers "a classic illustration of the transformation of an idea into an ideology." But even as Roosevelt was acclaimed for the charge up San Juan Hill in Cuba with his cowboy cavalry, Turner was lamenting the "wreckage of the Spanish War." Rather than expansion overseas, Turner placed his hopes for the American future in the expansion of higher education. "The test tube and the microscope are needed rather than ax and rifle," he wrote. "In place of old frontiers of wilderness, there are new frontiers of unwon fields of science." Turner made a case for what amounted to a moral equivalent to westering.[6]

Americans looked for new frontiers, but they also looked back to the passing of the old ones. The individual most identified with frontier nostalgia was William Frederick "Buffalo Bill" Cody. As a teenager he tramped to the Colorado gold rush; he fought with an irregular force of border Unionists (Jayhawkers) during the Civil War, scouted for the frontier army in campaigns against the Comanches, Sioux, and Kiowas, and earned his nickname hunting buffalo to feed railroad construction gangs. In 1869 dime novelist Ned Buntline wrote Cody up in the fanciful *Buffalo Bill, the King of Border Men* as "the greatest scout of the West." Honor motivated all his actions, whether protecting public virtue or rescuing white women from dastardly attacks by Indians. Before Cody's death in 1917, he had been the subject of no fewer than fifteen hundred dime novels.

Cody was such a showman, such a ham actor, that he tried his best to live the role in which Buntline had cast him. He went on the stage playing himself and organized a troop of cowboy and Indian actors who reenacted actual events in western history. In 1882 Cody organized the greatest of his shows, "Buffalo Bill's Wild West," which toured the United States and the world for the next three decades. The performance began with an overture played by thirty-six "cowboy" musicians wearing flannel shirts and slouch hats. Laced throughout were exhibitions of shooting and riding. Annie Oakley, the sweetheart of the show, entered trippingly, throwing kisses. Then her rifle would begin to crack as she dispatched glass balls, clay pigeons, and little three-by-five-inch cards embossed with her picture, thrown high, sliced by her bullets, then tossed to the delighted audience. Buck Taylor, King of the Cowboys, clung to bucking broncs and led a group in square dances and Virginia reels on horseback.

There was always a large contingent of Indians, mostly Sioux, performing their dances and displaying life as it had been lived on the plains. Sitting Bull joined the tour for the 1885 season, but when the great Sioux chief appeared in his ceremonial feathers, the audience hissed him, and he refused to tour for another season.

Sitting Bull and William "Buffalo Bill" Cody. Photograph by W. R. Cross, c. 1885. Beinecke Rare Book and Manuscript Library, Yale University.

Reformers complained that Cody exploited his Indian performers, but most of the historical evidence suggests that Indians enjoyed the work and considered themselves well treated. Black Elk, a young Oglala dancer who later became a famous spiritual leader, came down with a bad case of homesickness while touring with Cody in England in the early 1890s. Cody gave him a ticket home and ninety dollars. "Then he gave me a big dinner," Black Elk remembered. "Pahuska [Long Hair] had a strong heart."[7]

Authenticity through historic reenactment was the highlight of the Wild West. Hunters chased buffalo, Indians attacked the Deadwood stage, and the Pony Express once again delivered the mail to isolated frontier outposts. The climax was a staging of "Custer's Last Fight," with Buffalo Bill arriving just after Custer's demise, the words "Too Late" projected by lantern slide on a background screen. In the grand finale, Cody led a galloping victory lap of all the company's players—"The Congress of Rough Riders of the World"—with the American flag proudly flying in the company van. The whole spectacle, in the words of the souvenir program, was designed to illustrate "the inevitable law of the survival of the fittest."[8]

Simultaneous with Turner's thesis and Cody's Wild West, a group of prominent easterners brought the frontier to literary and artistic attention. The most notable among them was Theodore Roosevelt. No one rode the frontier hobbyhorse harder or into more divergent fields. Roosevelt and a number of friends—including writer Owen Wister and artist Frederic Remington—turned a lament over the passing of an epoch into an ideology that shaped American culture and politics well into the twentieth century. All three were born into prominent families in the era of the Civil War and educated at Harvard or Yale. At a critical point in their early twenties, each man went west seeking personal regeneration. The experience convinced all three that only by coming to grips with the experience of westering could Americans preserve the traditional values being swept away by the rush of industrialization. Most importantly, these men—and they wallowed in their manliness—sought to encourage a rugged version of American manhood. Their heroes were all "men with the bark on."

Roosevelt's encounter with the West followed the devastating death of his young wife (in childbirth) and his mother (from disease) on the same day in 1884. Leaving his baby daughter in the care of the extended family, he left New York and for three years lived on a Dakota cattle ranch, "far off from mankind." This western sojourn became a critical test of his manhood. The cowboys at first ridiculed him for his city ways, but after Roosevelt demonstrated his vigor by flooring a bully with a lucky punch, they came to admire him. Roosevelt learned to hunt and graduated

Theodore Roosevelt, c. 1910. Library of Congress.

from killing deer to stalking panthers. He joined a posse and participated in the
capture of a gang of desperadoes. "We knew toil and hardship and hunger and
thirst," he wrote, "but we felt the beat of hearty life in our being, and ours was the
glory of work and the joy of living." He returned to New York in 1886, a rough-
and-tumble westerner. This experience would inform all his subsequent work—as
author of hunting memoirs, including the best-selling *Ranch Life and the Hunting Trail* (1887), a multivolume history, *The Winning of the West* (1889–96), and
a dozen other popular books with similar themes; as president of the Boone and
Crockett Club, conservationist, sports hunter, and advocate of "the strenuous life";
as commander of the Rough Riders during the Spanish-American War; and finally
as America's first and foremost "cowboy president." An appreciation of the West
and its traditions, Roosevelt believed, would cultivate "that vigorous manliness
for the lack of which in a nation, as in an individual, the possession of no other
qualities can possibly atone." To save their country, Americans must reach to the
frontier and rediscover their testicular fortitude.[9]

Owen Wister also traveled west to recover both his health and his pride. At
twenty-five in 1885 he traded a career as a Harvard-educated Boston businessman

for a manager's position on a large Wyoming cattle ranch, sleeping outdoors with the cowboys, bathing in an icy creek, drinking his steaming coffee from a tin cup, and joining in the roundup. "The slumbering Saxon awoke in him," Wister wrote in a story with autobiographical implications, and he reinvented himself as "kin with the drifting vagabonds who swore and galloped by his side." He soon returned to his eastern home but began writing and publishing short stories, essays, and novels about cattle country. His ultimate triumph came with *The Virginian: A Horseman of the Plains* (1902), a runaway best seller and the model for countless subsequent western novels.[10]

Set in the mythical country of the open range, *The Virginian* is staged as a series of tests of manhood. The hero—the nameless Virginian of the title, who lives by a code of honor—rides at the head of a posse that captures and lynches a group of cattle rustlers, including his best friend. Once they had ridden together as wild and woolly bunkmates, but the Virginian has the foresight to see that the old days are passing. He confronts the threatening outlaw Trampas—"When you call me that, smile!"—and in the prototype of the western gunfight shoots him dead in the dusty main street of Medicine Bow, Wyoming. By dint of intelligence and industry, he rises from cowboy to foreman, eventually becoming "an important man, with a strong grip on many various enterprises." But the central test is the Virginian's courtship of Molly Wood, the eastern schoolmarm. In a series of arguments, the cowboy convinces the lady to abandon sentimental attachments and accept his moral code, the rule of honor. "Can't you see how it is about a man?" he implores as he rejects her pleas to leave town and avoid the final confrontation with Trampas. She cannot see—but in the end she accepts. After all, Molly had come West because she "wanted a man who was a man." Old South is united with Old East in the New West.[11]

Young Frederic Remington also went west for a booster shot of masculinity, leaving behind a domineering mother who ridiculed his ambition to be an artist, insisting that he "take a real man's job." Writing that he wished to "cut women out of his life altogether," Remington used a small inheritance to purchase a Kansas ranch. Although he failed to make the operation pay and eventually lost it to creditors, he considered his three years in the West the happiest of his life. Western men "have all the rude virtues," he wrote. They were "untainted by the enfeebling influences of luxury and modern life." His admiration was mixed with a heavy dose of nostalgia. "I saw the living, breathing end of three centuries of smoke and dust and sweat," he later mused. Following in the footsteps of George Catlin and Missouri artist George Caleb Bingham, Remington thought that he could preserve history through art. Thus, he found an answer to his art problem—he could become an artist with the bark on by capturing the last gasps of an obviously macho epoch in American history.[12]

"A Daring Feat of Horseman-ship." Illustration by Frederic Remington, from Owen Wister, The Virginian *(1902; New York, 1911). Beinecke Rare Book and Manuscript Library, Yale University.*

In 1885 he accompanied troopers through New Mexico during the campaign against Geronimo and placed his sketches in *Harper's Monthly* and in *Outing*, one of the new men's sporting magazines. Returning east in the wake of this success, Remington struck his friends as a man transformed. "He had turned himself into a cowboy," wrote a former Yale classmate. Captivated by Remington's work, Roosevelt asked him to illustrate his ranch and hunting book. And the projects kept coming. Remington became one of America's most successful commercial illustrators. Soon oils and bronzes were also pouring from his studio, commanding top dollar. "It is a fact that admits of no question," wrote an art critic in 1892, "that Eastern people have formed their conceptions of what the Far-Western life is like, more from what they have seen in Mr. Remington's pictures than from any other source."[13]

Remington marinated his western conceptions in manhood, race, and violence. The result could be invigorating and it could be repellant. Remington excised women from his West just as he excised them from his life and art. He claimed to have "never drawn a woman—except once, and then had washed her out." He exaggerated, but not by much. Amid the thousands of men in his many works, women appear only four times. True manliness, he believed, developed in the struggle with raw nature. His works include dozens of images of men against a barren landscape. In *Friends or Foes? (The Scout)* (1902–5), a lone rider strains his eyes to identify a barely visible speck on a bleak horizon. Remington placed Indians among the existential hostilities (drought, wind, hunger, rowdy broncos) that threatened and sharpened true white men. *Downing the Nigh Leader* (1907), one of his most celebrated paintings, features a group of mounted Indians attacking a speeding stagecoach. The lead horse on the left pitches violently to the ground, felled by a spear from a galloping warrior, while the drivers stoically struggle against their impending destruction. In *The Last Stand* (1890), Remington's ode to Custer, a group of cavalry troopers converges in heroic formation against an unseen enemy. The missing Indians typified the mindset of Remington and his ilk. They felt besieged in modern America, and they imagined an array of hostiles out there. In a letter to a friend written at about the same time he painted that image, Remington lumped Indians together with immigrants. "Jews, Injuns, Chinamen, Italians, Huns—the rubbish of the earth I hate—I've got some Winchesters and when the massacring begins, I can get my share of 'em, and what's more, I will." In his art, Remington proclaimed the American male triumphant over nature and the Anglo-Saxon dominant over "the rubbish of the earth."[14]

———

The notion of a closing frontier prompted the searching of souls alongside the beating of chests. Americans mourned the wild things they believed they had lost. Sometimes these feelings coalesced around a mascot, such as a buffalo, a wolf, or perhaps a scrumptious bird. In the nineteenth century billions of passenger pigeons inhabited eastern North America. Their sudden appearance in forests during their migrations triggered celebrations and mass killings. Rural Americans interpreted the flocks that blotted out the sun as symbols of abundance, and they slaughtered railroad cars full of them to fill pigeon pies in urban restaurants. To most, the passing of the pigeons represented the high point of the year, an unexpected reason to rejoice. But others were repelled by the slaughter and waste. James Fenimore Cooper included a scene in his novel *The Pioneers* (1832) critical of the birds' destruction, and Americans noted the population's decline as early as the 1850s. By the end of the century the species had been driven to extinction in the wild. The last known passenger pigeon—an elderly female named Martha—died in the Cincinnati Zoo on September 1, 1914.

The extinction of wild animals elicited lament, but these pronouncements of sorrow often came with statements of inevitability in the fine print. Passenger pigeons, bison, and gray wolves, like cowboys and Indians, *had* to die along with the frontier. There was no place for them in a modern West filled with farms, factories, cities, and (soon) motor cars. History moved forward, never in reverse, and

"Shooting Wild Pigeons in Iowa." From Frank Leslie's Illustrated Newspaper, *June 3, 1871.*

progress came with casualties. Extinction thinking blended facts with feelings. The tragic inevitability of loss motivated artists, historians, and politicians. A prime example of Americans drawing a stark line in time to organize their country into past and present, antique and modern, wild and tame, violent and subdued, the frontier entered the twentieth century a very active corpse that continued to inspire painters, film-makers, historians, biologists, and lawmakers long after Turner had buried it.

Scientists have compiled a list of approximately seventy known American species that went belly-up over the past two centuries, including the Labrador duck, New England heath hen (a relative of the prairie chicken), and Carolina parakeet (valued for its colorful plumage), the eastern sea mink and eastern elk, and the Wisconsin cougar and Great Plains wolf. By the early twentieth century the only California grizzly left in California prowled on the state flag. The beaver disappeared from most of its habitat by the 1840s, although it managed a revival after beaver hats fell out of fashion. The sea otter and the fur seal of the Northwest coast verged on extinction when saved by an international ban on commercial hunting in the early twentieth century. The bison perished by the tens of millions, of course, and by 1890 just eight hundred remained in several isolated herds. Other game animals in the West also declined in numbers, some drastically like grizzlies and wolves. Americans blasted their way across the continent, says environmental historian Donald Worster, leaving in their wake "a landscape littered with skulls and bones, drenched in blood."[15]

They left stumps and sawdust as well. By the early nineteenth century, the massive trans-Appalachian deciduous and evergreen forests were dwindling. Farmers by the hundreds of thousands girdled, chopped, and burned. The pungent smell of wood smoke filled their nostrils with the sweet perfume of "improvement." Eventually, they reduced the woodlands east of the Mississippi to only about 2 percent of their former extent. The timber of the great woods also fed hundreds of small sawmills and pulp mills scattered throughout the West. By midcentury the construction of the rail network and the rise of Chicago as a distribution center led to the industrialization of logging. The greatest volume and value came from the forests of the Great Lakes. Some logging companies purchased huge stands of white pine from state and federal governments, but others perpetrated enormous frauds by paying their employees to enter phony homestead claims. "In all the pine region of Lake Superior and the Upper Mississippi where vast areas have been settled under the pretense of agriculture," the commissioner of the General Land Office reported in 1876, "scarcely a vestige of agriculture appears." In the vicinity of Duluth, Minnesota, for example, more than 4,300 homestead entries had been filed and completed, but an investigation found that only a hundred settlers were actually living and working on farms. The bulk of the land had been logged and abandoned.[16]

Loggers systematically cut over huge areas, floating great rafts of logs downriver to giant steam-powered sawmills and leaving forests of stumps for hundreds of miles. The slash cover of dead wood and brush fueled terrifying fires that consumed millions of acres, destroying the humus layer of the already nutrient-poor soil. In 1871 an inferno raging through the woods of Wisconsin destroyed the town of Peshtigo and killed more than fifteen hundred people, far more than died in the famous great Chicago fire of the same year. By the turn of the century, the logging industry had used up the timber in the Great Lakes region and was moving on to the South and the old-growth forests of the Pacific Northwest.

Logging was unsightly, but mining pushed the boundaries of scenic ugliness. In California, the use of high-pressure water jets to wash down mountains of deposits, so that laborers could cheaply and quickly separate the gold from the rubble, washed tons of silt downriver, burying plant life in avalanches of debris. Farmers with clogged irrigation systems and inundated crops fought bitter legislative battles against mining companies. But by the time the federal judge declared hydraulic mining a public nuisance and issued a permanent injunction in 1884, an estimated twelve billion tons of earth had been eroded away. The resulting silt reduced the depth of San Francisco Bay by three to six feet. Even greater destruction to the bay came from the mercury mines in the foothills surrounding the town of San Jose. Mercury was used to separate gold from quartz rock, and mining operations

The Lakeview gusher, Kern County, California. Photograph by the U.S. Geological Survey, 1910. Library of Congress.

dumped tons of the stuff into streams that fed the bay, leaving a legacy that poisons the fish to this day.

Petroleum drilling also left ecological scars. The oil spills from gushers polluted soil and water and, catching fire, sent heavy clouds of acrid smoke drifting across the countryside. The Lakeview gusher in Kern County, California, spewed out 378 million gallons of crude before it was capped, making it the largest oil spill in U.S. history. Plunder and pollution defined frontier economies. Americans scrambled to grab resources and profits. Rapid exploitation rewarded the fiercest competitors, and a laissez-faire government stood aside—or enthusiastically aided the sharks. There seemed to be plenty of nature to go around. The frontier idea was premised on vastness. Fish, furs, minerals, timber, oil—all were available in unending supply. Or so it seemed, until the fear of the closing frontier woke Americans to the dangers.

———

Nineteenth-century landscape artists promoted the awesome bigness of the West. Albert Bierstadt, an American who trained in Europe painting Rhine castles and snow-capped Alps, specialized in the monumental. Returning to the states, he joined a government survey party headed west and found the Rockies "the

"The Rocky Mountains, Lander's Peak." Engraving by J. Smillie, 1866, based on a painting by Albert Bierstadt, 1863. Beinecke Rare Book and Manuscript Library, Yale University.

best material for the artist in the world." Entranced, he tramped and sketched his way through the Wind River Mountains, then returned to his studio in New York City to paint a number of huge finished works. In *The Rocky Mountains, Lander's Peak* (1863), nature loomed and belittled man. On a canvas measuring six feet by ten, Bierstadt brought viewers into a panoramic and infinitely receding landscape of valley, lake, and mountains, replete with a busy Indian encampment in the foreground. Dramatic interplays of shadow and sunlight embolden the distant peaks and overwhelm the human subjects. The critics were impressed: "No more genuine and grand American work has been produced of that majestic barrier of the West where the heavens and the earth meet in brilliant and barren proximity." Bierstadt took the canvas on a triumphant tour through the United States and Europe, then sold it for the unprecedented sum of twenty-five thousand dollars (half a million today). Bierstadt arranged to have the picture engraved and sold subscriptions during the tour, netting him thousands of dollars more.[17]

The idea that human beings could subdue this place seemed silly. Bierstadt's West exhausted humans, they did not exhaust it. In fact, Bierstadt exaggerated his western landscapes to illicit emotions of awe and sublimity. Along the way, he roused skeptics as well. Mark Twain once described one of his Yosemite landscapes as "beautiful—considerably more beautiful than the original," and joked that the painting had "more atmosphere of Kingdom-Come than California." Verisimilitude, however, was never Bierstadt's shtick. He offered magic and mystery to a wartorn nation that hungered for magnificence and a deep connection to North American nature. Europe had its castles, cathedrals, and centuries of recorded history. Nineteenth-century Americans countered with purple mountains. Not everyone approved of Bierstadt's maximalist style, but his massive canvases represented a vision of western nature as beyond human comprehension, much less domination. The images suggested that dramatic western scenery was a national treasure.[18]

The other great late nineteenth-century painter of monumental western landscapes was Thomas Moran, an artist as well steeped in English romanticism as Bierstadt was in its German form. Studying in London, Moran fell in the thrall of the romantic landscapes of J. M. W. Turner, a colorist who in his last canvases seemed to anticipate impressionism. Longing for dramatic western vistas to feed his style, in 1871 Moran joined the Yellowstone survey party of Ferdinand V. Hayden. Jay Cooke, the financier and railroad tycoon, loaned Moran five hundred dollars for the trip, hoping that his paintings would rouse interest in the region for his Northern Pacific Railroad. After the expedition, Moran produced a series of watercolors for Cooke, engraved for reproduction. Together with the photographic prints of William Henry Jackson, another artistic member of the Hayden party, Moran's images of towers, geysers, and pinnacles helped convince Congress to create Yellowstone National Park. Like Bierstadt, Moran believed in gigantism. He hung canvases over entire walls to bully viewers with his perspective. Congress purchased his *Grand Canyon of the Yellowstone* (1872) for the astounding sum of ten thousand dollars. And Americans could hang smaller versions of Moran's work on their living room walls when chromolithographs of his Yellowstone views became available in 1876.

Moran and Bierstadt encouraged the public to think of western landscapes as a spectacular emblem of America. The artists connected people to iconic places, giving New Yorkers and Philadelphians a stake in corners of Wyoming and California. This art promulgated many mistaken notions. The mountains were never that tall, the valleys never that deep. But the point was the emotions these images conjured, not the facts they transmitted. Moran and Bierstadt made Americans feel for the West, and they induced mixed sensations. Their images played on the environment's grandeur and vastness. Their West seemed to have plenty of room for miners, farmers, and nature lovers. But they also splashed their canvases with worry. The places could be lost. If Americans cut the forests and ground the mountains to dust, what would signal their uniqueness? The anticipation of ruin made this art compelling. Americans bought both the promise of abundance and the sense of loss when they purchased a knockoff.

"The Grand Canyon of the Yellowstone." Lithograph by Thomas Moran, 1875. Beinecke Rare Book and Manuscript Library, Yale University.

In 1892 Thomas Moran produced one of his most striking watercolors. In *Smelting Works at Denver,* huge smokestacks belch toxic wastes into the crisp air, the smoke, mountains, and sky dissolving into a haze of yellows, browns, and blacks. Moran found a terrible beauty in both the towers and pinnacles of Yellowstone and a cityscape of the emerging industrial West. Americans appreciated both landscapes for they communicated a similar idea—abundance and ruination traveled on the same breath of western atmosphere.

The mingling of industrial might and nature appreciation didn't end with Moran's smelter haze. The same people who benefited most from the West's mines, oil patches, and urban sprawl often led and financed the preservation of iconic

"Smelting Works at Denver." Watercolor by Thomas Moran, 1892. © The Cleveland Museum of Art. Bequest of Mrs. Henry A. Averett for the Dorothy Burnham Everett Memorial Collection.

animals and landscapes. Missing from Moran's watercolor was the owner of the smelter, the capitalist who produced the smoke and collected profits, who could also invest in philanthropic causes and such aesthetic pursuits as protecting natural beauty and purchasing nature paintings.

Elites were prominent in the environmental movement from the start. Game animals caught their attention first. Traditionally Americans hunted to eat, to cover their bodies, and to acquire skins for trade, but by the mid-nineteenth century sport hunting had become popular, especially among men of the American upper class. Sport hunting, as opposed to traditional hunting, focused on means rather than ends. There were fair and foul ways of taking game. Sport hunters were outraged, for example, by the continuing war of market hunters on the passenger pigeon. On a number of occasions groups of sportsmen attempted to prevent the attacks on large nesting colonies of pigeons; there were armed confrontations and occasionally even exchanges of gunfire, but they did little good. Eventually the depletion of their favorite trout streams and hunting ranges pushed sportsmen to organize, pressing state legislatures for laws limiting and regulating the take of wildlife. The campaign for hunting laws began after the Civil War, and by century's end a majority of states and localities had established fish and game commissions, defined fishing and hunting seasons, and set licensing requirements and bag limits. Wealthy sportsmen initiated the first organized efforts to regulate the use of the environment.

George Bird Grinnell, a patrician New Yorker with a doctorate in zoology from Yale University, rallied support for protecting iconic western animals. In 1880 Grinnell became editor of *Forest and Stream,* one of a number of sportsmen's magazines founded in the late nineteenth century, and he used its pages to condemn the destruction of the buffalo as "mercenary and wanton butchery" and to decry the "corruption" of hunting by "the mighty dollar." In 1887 Grinnell joined with Theodore Roosevelt in convening a group of wealthy sportsmen to establish a national society for the promotion of sports hunting. The Boone and Crockett Club—named for two of the nation's legendary backwoodsmen— sought to perpetuate the traits of "energy, resolution, manliness, self-reliance, and capacity for self-help." The frontier experience had cultivated a "vigorous manliness" among Americans, Roosevelt wrote, and "unless we keep the barbarian values, gaining the civilized ones will be of little avail." The Boone and Crockett Club quickly became the nation's most influential lobby, working for the protection of threatened species and the creation of a system of wildlife refuges.[19]

Conserving nature involved police work, and the humans most likely to be policed were the same ones Frederic Remington feared. Hunting regulators targeted Italian immigrants in rural Pennsylvania who hunted songbirds for recreation and a gustatory treat. Other reformers went after middle-class city women who purchased hats decorated with the plumes of endangered species. Game wardens patrolled parks and reserves in the Adirondacks to stop locals from using (in their language, "wasting") forest resources. The United States Army oversaw Yellowstone National Park from 1886 to 1918, arresting American Indian trespassers—Eastern Shoshones and Bannocks—as well as white poachers who entered the park for elk and bison trophies. In Glacier National Park, created in 1910, officials excluded the Blackfeet from their traditional hunting grounds and policed the boundary line that separated federally conserved nature from federally reserved Indians. The park's eastern edge abutted the Blackfeet Indian Reservation for hundreds of miles.

Saving beautiful places from unethical despoilers reversed the federal government's long-standing practice of selling or donating the public domain to private owners. Some landscapes and resources, conservationists argued, were too valuable for the market. Federal power must be exerted to keep the scenery intact or the stock well managed so that future generations could enjoy the grandeur, the board-feet, or the irrigation water. The glacier-carved Yosemite Valley in the central Sierra Nevada of California went public first. Gold miners "discovered" the gorgeous valley in 1851 and attacked the villages of the native Yosemite people, driving them from the site the Indians knew as Ahwahnee—place of deep grass. Within a few years, tourists trekked into the area, and their published accounts and drawings brought the spectacular vistas to national attention. The combination of granite cliffs, lofty waterfalls, verdant meadows, clear streams, and huge redwoods made Yosemite the perfect subject for romantic art of the sublime and picturesque, exemplified by Albert Bierstadt's paintings of the valley, widely distributed as engravings and chromolithographs. In 1864 a group of prominent citizens, including Frederick Law Olmsted, designer of New York City's Central Park, persuaded Congress to grant the valley to the state of California for "public use, resort and recreation." Small, only ten square miles, the reserve bubble-wrapped the scenery. Nineteenth-century visitors did not think in terms of environments or ecosystems. Soon tourist facilities cluttered the valley floor. But Yosemite escaped the shearing force of sheep and cow teeth; the destiny of most grassy locales in the West at this time was a vigorous gobbling, not an aggressive ogling. Compared to other sites, Yosemite was lightly exploited, and writers and artists called for more "nature reserves." These voices were given a powerful boost when the Southern Pacific Railroad noted a significant uptick in tourist traffic along the rail lines leading to Yosemite.[20]

Railroad tourism dated from the advent in the late 1860s of Pullman sleeper cars—rolling hotels, paneled in mahogany, lights shaded with Tiffany glass—bringing travelers west in comfort and style. Western railroads needed places to transport the plush crowd, and federal parks became destinations. Long treasured by Indians as a rich hunting and fishing ground, the headwater region of the Yellowstone River, high in the Rocky Mountains, was legendary among fur trappers for its iridescent pools, roaring waterfalls, and mirror lakes. The trappers' reports seemed ludicrous—water exploding from the ground, boiling springs beside icy streams. But in 1870 a party of scientists and local boosters hiked into the area and confirmed the tall tales. The next year, University of Pennsylvania geologist Ferdinand V. Hayden, founder of the United States Geological Survey, led a Yellowstone expedition (the one that included photographer William Henry Jackson and artist Thomas Moran). Hayden's report—and particularly Jackson's photographs and Moran's watercolors—generated considerable interest. Railroad financier Jay Cooke, mindful of the profits that ticket-buying tourists would bring his Northern Pacific Railroad, capitalized on the publicity to strongly suggest that Congress consider declaring Yellowstone "a public park forever—just as it reserved that far inferior wonder, the Yosemite Valley."[21]

Mammoth Hot Springs, Yellowstone National Park. Photograph by William Henry Jackson, 1873. Beinecke Rare Book and Manuscript Library, Yale University.

Unlike Yosemite, the Yellowstone region belonged to the federal government (Wyoming, Montana, and Idaho did not become states until 1890), so Congress would have to create the park. Assured that this remote and cold terrain would defy agriculture and other normal capitalist manipulations, that being set aside would do "no harm to the material interests of people," in March 1872 Congress designated more than two million acres on the Yellowstone River as "a public park or pleasuring ground for the benefit and enjoyment of the people," stipulating that all the timber, minerals, wildlife, and "curiosities" be retained "in their natural conditions." Withdrawing land from the survey and dispersal system for "pleasure" brought vociferous protest. One congressman barked that commercial development was being stymied to placate "a few sportsmen bent only on the protection of a few buffalo," and another snorted that this heralded the government's entry into "the show business." Others thought differently. A Missouri senator declared Yellowstone a "great breathing-space for the national lungs," and the support of the railroad interests helped redirect American land policy from a blanket-

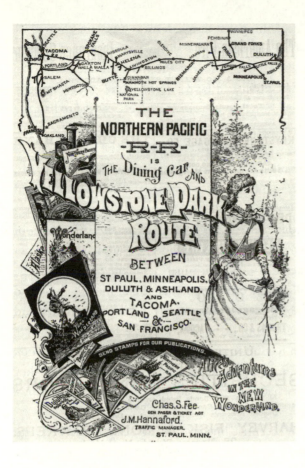

Railroad tourism: an advertisement by the Northern Pacific Railroad promoting Yellowstone National Park, 1889. Author's collection.

order "survey and sell" to a stance that had the state keeping the spectacular stuff. Yellowstone remained the only national park until 1890, when the Southern Pacific successfully lobbied for federal legislation creating a wilderness sanctuary in the area surrounding Yosemite Valley and another to protect the groves of huge sequoias in the southern Sierra Nevada.[22]

From these beginnings, wilderness and commerce were entwined around a staff of tourism in the national park system. Advocates for scenic landscape protection, however, framed the debate as a conflict between capitalism and nature. No nineteenth-century American played this refrain with more verve and eloquence than John Muir. Born in Scotland and raised on a hardscrabble Wisconsin farm, Muir escaped his domineering Presbyterian parents through reading, fiddling with mechanical devices, and exploring nature. He left home, labored in an Indianapolis carriage factory, and, after a workplace accident temporarily blinded him, tramped from Canada to Mexico and sailed from Alaska to the South Seas, writing about his experiences. A fervent disciple of transcendentalism, Muir once invited Ralph Waldo Emerson, who was touring California, to "worship" with him at Yosemite. Emerson accepted, but instead of sleeping with Muir under the stars, he bunked in one of the park's tourist hotels, explaining that the wilderness was "a sublime mistress, but an intolerable wife." For Muir, nature was all—wife, mistress, offspring, even God, though quite unlike the God of his strict Presbyterian ancestors. The forests, he wrote in one of his first published essays, were "God's first temples." Muir's wilderness philosophy drew heavily on the contrast between sacred nature and what he called "the galling harness of civilization."[23]

In truth, no clear line divided wilderness and civilization. The national parks mixed motivations. Tourists demanded the construction and maintenance of roads, trails, and buildings; park visitors required hotels, restaurants, campgrounds, and garbage dumps, water, sewage, and power systems. Moreover, the mandate to retain the parks' "natural conditions" was interpreted to mean the cultivation of landscapes that conformed to the public's notion of wilderness. Officials at Yellowstone worked hard to encourage what one park superintendent called "the type of animal the park was for." To protect browsing herds of elk, moose, deer, and bighorn sheep, park managers went to war against wolves, mountain lions, and coyotes. To save the last bison herd from extinction, they created a ranch where the animals were fed park-grown hay. To improve fishing, they introduced brook and rainbow trout in the streams. And to protect this concocted "wilderness," they suppressed forest fires, those very natural conflagrations that had shaped Yellowstone for eons.[24]

While John Muir cultivated an eccentric image—letting his hair and beard go untrimmed, living in the woods, and dedicating himself totally to "nature"—he understood better than most the practical side of national parks. Without hesitation he assisted the efforts of the railroads to generate more tourist business. He worked with the Northern Pacific, lobbying for the creation of Mount Rainier and Glacier National Parks in 1899, and with the Southern Pacific in 1906 to convince California to cede Yosemite Valley back to federal jurisdiction. To monitor federal administration of the parks and counter new threats to his mountain sanctuaries, in 1892 he organized the Sierra Club—an organization that would "be able to do something for wildness and make the mountains glad"—and served as its president for the next twenty-two years. Muir was an idealist and a romantic. But he was also an environmental politician. His activism crisscrossed the frontiers of art, ideology, religion, and policy.[25]

The advocates of national parks offered them as healthy alternatives to rapacious capitalism. They were supposed to be "time-out" locales, sites where harried moderns could breathe freely and still their demons. Yellowstone and Yosemite stood for nature as Americans increasingly gathered in smog-choked cities. But rural landscapes could inspire modern nightmares as well. Clear-cut forests conjured visions of loss as well as extinct bison or sublime vistas. The indiscriminate felling of trees appeared thoughtless and poorly planned to some Americans. They advocated new policies to insure the perpetual use of natural resources. Management and efficiency were the watchwords of the conservationists. They did not worship the West's trees and rivers, they wanted them put to better use.

As early as the 1870s, government officials expressed concern over deforestation, especially in the cutover Great Lakes Region. But at that time—the heyday of expansion in the trans-Mississippi West—Congress was in no mood to restrict access to western resources. Instead, the American people got the Timber Cutting Act of 1878, a law that made it even easier for private citizens and companies to cut timber on federal land. The legislation amounted to what one disapproving congressman called a "license for timber thieves on the public domain."[26]

After 1878 loggers cut more lumber while scientists reconsidered the damage. Trees, they argued, belonged to a web of connections among living things, rooting an "ecology" of birds, soil, worms, fish, and streams that fell with them. An important contribution to this thinking was the book *Man and Nature* (1864), written by American diplomat and amateur scientist George Perkins Marsh. Deforestation concerned Marsh. He watched the trees go in his boyhood home in the Green Mountains of Vermont and then pondered the denuded Mediterranean hills of Turkey and Italy during his diplomatic assignments. Without forests to hold thin mountain soils, rains produced torrents that swept down hillsides, washed away topsoil, destroyed undergrowth, drove away wildlife, and flooded agricultural valleys. Deforestation and erosion, he implied, had contributed to the fall of Old World civilizations and might produce the same result in America. By the 1880s other Americans were repeating Marsh's warnings. "We are following the course of nations which have gone before us," admonished the author of a federal report of 1882. To stave off a future of deserts fit for biblical wanderings, Americans needed to rein in their frontier exuberance and keep their canopies intact. By the end of the decade, the American Forestry Association (founded in 1875) was calling for a moratorium on the sale of all public forest lands.[27]

The forestry movement registered a mere peep compared to the roar of loggers' saws. The timber industry rapidly moved the center of its operations from the Great Lakes states to the Pacific coast. By 1890 the easily accessible forests of Douglas fir, spruce, and redwood along the California, Oregon, and Washington coasts had already fallen, their ancient logs ripped into boards and shipped to San Francisco or Los Angeles for the booming home construction market. Loggers chugged into the mountainous backcountry on large tractors called "steam donkeys" to open hauling trails, clear-cutting huge patches of forest, and shipping out the harvest of logs on precarious narrow-gauge railroads. In regions too rugged or isolated for rails, they built mountain "splash dams," where they dumped their

Lumberjacks fell a giant spruce in Washington State. Photograph by C. Kinsey, c. 1900. Beinecke Rare Book and Manuscript Library, Yale University.

logs and, when the ponds were full, blasted the dams with explosives, producing floods that washed the logs downstream to the sawmills. These practices blurred the line between industrial tactics and natural disasters.[28]

 Responding to considerable public concern that the Northwest would suffer the same fate that had befallen the Great Lakes states, Congress undertook a complete revision of the nation's land laws in 1891. They botched the job, repealing some programs, extending others, and in the end failing to address adequately the worries about deforestation. At the last minute, however, friends of forest reform slipped in an amendment—later known as the Forest Reserve Act—giving the president the authority to carve "forest reserves" from the public domain. The expectation seemed to be that this power would be used sparingly, but over the next decade Presidents Benjamin Harrison, Grover Cleveland, and William McKinley used it to withdraw more than forty-seven million forested acres. Preservationists hoped— and loggers feared—that these reserves would be closed forever to commercial exploitation. This is precisely what John Muir and the Sierra Club proposed. But following the advice offered by a special Forestry Commission, Congress in 1897 made it clear that the reserves were intended not for the preservation but rather the use of the forests. The Forest Management Act declared that the reserves should "furnish a continuous supply of timber for the use and necessities of citizens of the United States." The executive branch was directed to establish regulations for the management of the reserves, auctioning to the highest bidder the right to harvest timber in them.[29]

The legislation swung history and policy in the direction of the rambunctious leader of the commission, Gifford Pinchot. Born to a wealthy family, Pinchot traipsed through the woods from a young age. His classmates at Yale called him "tree mad." After graduation he went to Germany and France to pursue advanced studies in forestry, then returned to spend several years as the forester at Biltmore, the huge Vanderbilt family estate in the North Carolina hills, where he restored cutover lands. This work got him appointed to the Forestry Commission, bringing him to the attention of President McKinley, who named him chief forester of the United States at the age of thirty-three. When Roosevelt became president in 1901, Pinchot quickly became his closest adviser on environmental policy. Both men were members of the Boone and Crockett Club and lovers of what Roosevelt called "the strenuous life." They boxed and frequently sparred with each other. Both were iconoclasts willing to raise hackles in pursuit of their goals.

"Conservation," the name Roosevelt and Pinchot chose for their approach to the national domain, was an ideology for postfrontier America. "When the American settler felled the forests he felt there was plenty of forest left for the sons who came after him," Roosevelt lectured. "The Kentuckian or the Ohioan felled the forest and expected his son to move west and fell other forests on the banks of the Mississippi." The era of indiscriminate hacking had ended. The future required a dash of forethought and restraint. "The right of the individual," Roosevelt argued, "to injure the future of us all for his own temporary and immediate profit" had to be checked by an activist federal state. Manly experts with the government would manage the West's natural endowment.[30]

The president encouraged Congress to establish several new national parks, and using his presidential power to declare national monuments, he set aside sixteen areas of unique national and historical value, including Devil's Tower in Wyoming, the Olympic peninsula in Washington, and the Petrified Forest and Grand Canyon in Arizona. He founded fifty new wildlife preserves and refuges and sponsored legislation creating the Bureau of Fisheries and the Bureau of Biological Survey. He withdrew oil, coal, and phosphate lands from the public domain in order to forestall, at least temporarily, their engrossment by corporate monopolies. In 1905 Roosevelt engineered the transfer of the forest reserves (renamed "national forests") from the Department of the Interior to Pinchot's National Forest Service in the Agriculture Department. In his first directive, Pinchot laid out the "wise use" environmental perspective he shared with Roosevelt: "All the resources of forest reserves are for use, and this must be brought about in a thoroughly prompt and businesslike manner, under such restrictions only as will insure the permanence of these resources." In postfrontier American forests, Pinchot's "gospel of efficiency" shook the leaves alongside Muir's transcendental exultations.[31]

The concerns of the "utilizers" and the "preservationists" overlapped, but their solutions differed. Both opposed heedless exploitation of natural resources, and both believed that Americans had crossed a threshold into a new epoch of history with the end of the frontier. Pinchot once joined Muir on a tour of the western forests. "I took to him at once," Pinchot remembered, finding his companion "a most fascinating talker." But the two men squabbled over the federal policy of allowing sheep ("hooved locusts," according to Muir) to graze on the public domain. For Muir, "the hope of the world" was "fresh, unblighted, unredeemed wilderness." Preservationists sought to consume an ideal nature free of bleating ewes and rams or the rattle of steam donkeys and chainsaws. They preferred forests that rejuvenated tourists rather than produced two-by-fours. Pinchot disagreed, declaring that "wilderness is waste." To survive in postfrontier America, the "water, wood, and forage of the reserves" needed to work "for the benefit of the home builder first of all." The forests would supply the wherewithal to build the suburbs.[32]

The truth is, neither Roosevelt nor Pinchot spent much time worrying about Muir. They were too busy putting their conservation programs into operation and fending off attacks from critics who wanted to dismantle federal authority over the forests. An alliance with large logging companies helped preserve the National Forest Service. By the early twentieth century these corporations had gained control of nearly 50 percent of the nation's standing timber, and locking up an additional 35 percent in the national forests suited them just fine. It would stifle competition from smaller loggers. In exchange for federal acquiescence to timber corporation gigantism, Pinchot expected companies to manage the forests scientifically. The

President Theodore Roosevelt and John Muir at Glacier Point, Yosemite, 1903. Library of Congress.

Weyerhaeuser Company—the world's largest private owner of standing timber, holding resources equal to half the national forest system—instituted extensive reforestation programs. Corporate lumbermen, argues historian William Robbins, used the Forest Service "as a tool to achieve stability," to avoid overproduction, glutted markets, and low prices in their industry. The cozy relationship between industry and government insured the measured exploitation of forests instead of their being gobbled in manic episodes of "cut and get out."[33]

It was the small loggers—and there were a great many of them—who opposed federal regulation. "Czar Pinchot" constricted their opportunities with the creation of national forests and bureaucratic regulations. Although big logging companies had more land, small loggers possessed political clout, and in 1907 they won congressional repeal of the president's authority to declare national forests by executive order. Before Roosevelt signed the legislation, however, he and Pinchot pored over maps of the West and selected more than 16 million acres of new forest reserves, sending independent loggers into a tizzy of these "midnight reserves" that increased the size of the national forests to more than 150 million acres. Roosevelt and Pinchot were not deterred. In 1908 they convened a White House conference of the nation's governors, congressmen, Supreme Court justices, and leading scientists to consider the future needs of environmental policy, "the weightiest problem before the nation" in Roosevelt's estimation.[34]

Pinchot stayed on at the Forest Service when Roosevelt left office in 1909, but he found the administration of President William Howard Taft far less friendly to him or to conservation. Interior Secretary Richard Ballinger, a former mayor of Seattle, represented westerners irked by federal resource meddling and wanted to transfer national property to the states to facilitate private development, a policy antithetical to Pinchot's plan of rational development under federal management. The two men tangled, and when Pinchot publicly accused Ballinger of a conflict of interest in 1910, Taft dismissed the chief forester. By the time he left office, Pinchot had built the Forest Service into a proud and formidable organization with fifteen hundred committed employees. The national forests and the bureaucracy that oversaw their rational dispersal to giant corporations were not going anywhere.

The forest ranger personified the Forest Service. A mounted authority figure, supervisor of the timber harvest, enforcer of regulations governing loggers and hunters, and battler of forest fires, the twentieth-century conservation woodsy bureaucrat applied a new twist to frontier persona with a long, troubled history. The word *ranger* roamed American English signifying initially seventeenth-century gamekeepers who targeted poachers on the crown's domain. Rangers then acquired a military meaning as light infantry who "ranged" over the country, matching the guerrilla tactics of Indian fighters. Most famous in the history of the West, of course, were the Texas Rangers, the irregular force first organized during the Mexican War, later designated the official constabulary of the Lone Star State. The Forest Service tapped into these traditions by declaring its employees rangers and dressing them in khaki shirts and jodhpurs, knee-high riding boots, and flat brimmed

Stetson "campaign" hats. The rangers epitomized postfrontier authority. They were swashbuckling paragons of the rising power of large organizations—the federal government and Weyerhaeuser—and the service industry. Rangers policed nature and assisted tourists. Over time, their image broadened and softened to include Edward Pulaski, a ranger who saved his crew from a raging forest conflagration by shuttling them into an abandoned mine and blocking the entrance with his water-doused body, as well as Ranger Rick, the raccoon cartoon character invented by the National Wildlife Federation to introduce suburban children to wild creatures and places. Rangers went from vessels of white supremacy—Roosevelt declared Ranger Pulaski as the preserver of "the virtues which beseem a masterful race"—to well-meaning public servants protecting picnic baskets from Yogi Bear.[35]

In 1916 Congress created the National Park Service, and a force of park rangers in khaki replaced federal troops as the managers of the parks. The romance and goodwill the ranger persona generated for the agencies managing the nation's parks and forests proved a valuable asset that some male bureaucrats fiercely guarded. Both agencies pushed their manliness, and until the 1970s the Forest Service had a policy against hiring women as forest rangers. It took a federal suit by female employees in 1981 to convince the agency to institute an affirmative action plan to advance women up the ranks. The ranger identity, however, was surprisingly flexible from the start. The title, as historian Polly Welts Kaufman has shown, did not necessarily imply a man who ate nails and sprouted a luxurious growth of chest hair. In its very early years, the National Park Service employed women as rangers and no heads exploded from contradiction.

Horace Albright, the first civilian superintendent at Yellowstone, hired at least ten women for his force of rangers. The first was Isabel Bassett, a nature aficionado with a degree in biology from Wellesley College who came to the park looking for work about the same time Albright assumed his duties in 1919. "I am to be a government ranger in Yellowstone Park," she wrote excitedly in a letter home. "You never heard of a woman ranger? Well, neither have I." Another of Albright's early recruits was Marguerite Lindsley, the daughter of a former Yellowstone superintendent, born and raised in the park. She came home after earning an M.S. in biology and Albright hired her on the spot. No one knew the park better, or with more scientific understanding, something she amply demonstrated in the more than fifty articles on local flora and fauna she published in *Nature Notes*, the Park Service newsletter. Lindsley was also a character, displaying a Pulaski-level zeal for exercise and adventure. During the winter of 1925 she and a female companion made the complete 143-mile transit of the park on cross-country skis. And one summer she bought a secondhand Harley with a sidecar, and, disguised as men, she and her friend took a cross-country road trip, riding through "hail, sleet, mud, and washouts," camping along the way.[36]

Naturalist Herma Albertson Baggley (second from left) poses in ranger uniform with coworkers at Yellowstone National Park, 1933. National Park Service History Collections.

When the chief inspector of the Interior Department came to Yellowstone in 1926, the number of female rangers Albright had hired shocked him. Nosing around, he found angry male rangers who complained about "posy pickers" and "tree huggers." Albright defended his policy. "Women can do just as well or better than men." He found that women did a much better job interacting with the public. Not a man on his force could give a lecture, "even if his life depended on it." In spite of Albright's defense, the inspector's report caused a stir in Washington, D.C., and resulted in a director's decree that the Park Service would no longer hire women as rangers. At almost the same moment, *Sunset Magazine* published an adoring profile of Marguerite Lindsley and her exploits entitled "She's a Real Ranger." Lindsley received dozens of letters from young women asking her for advice on becoming a ranger, and she was forced to write back with the news that for the foreseeable future "the ranger staff will be made up entirely of men." The next year Lindsley resigned from the agency to marry another ranger.[37]

In 1929 Albright was elevated to the directorship of the National Park Service. He reversed the previous order and did his best from Washington to encourage his superintendents to adopt his open attitude about women. But Albright's retirement in 1933 marked the end of this bold experiment. Within a few years the Park Service was looking back on the days of female rangers with considerable loathing. The employment of women, one official believed, had resulted in rangers being ridiculed as "pansy pickers and butterfly chasers." Rangers, insisted another macho critic, needed to maintain their image as "the embodiment of Kit Carson, Buffalo Bill, Daniel Boone, the Texas Rangers, and General Pershing," all men with the bark on.[38]

History, especially frontier history, can play havoc with entrenched ideologies. Male chauvinists held sway in the National Park and Forest Services until the 1970s, but their grip on the English language proved far weaker. Thanks to heroic pioneer women like Bassett and Lindsley and the development of national parks and forests as tourist destinations, Americans came to expect more from their rangers than Carson- or Boone-types could provide. They wanted accurate information and professional courtesy. The ability to shoot a bear (or a human being) ranked below hospitality and scientific knowledge in the skillsets of modern rangers. The frontier past is littered with enforcers outfitted in military garb, but the future would include rangers of a different sort, ones who assisted instead of assailed. The ranger icon endured because some women and men remodeled it into a kind helper—a public servant—and placed their version alongside men taking the law into their own hands.

By 1920 the forested area of the United States stabilized around 730 million acres, approximately 32 percent of the nation's land, about where it has remained in the years since. Conservation helped prevent the much-feared "timber famine"; so did larger demographic shifts, especially Americans' journey from a rural population to a primarily urban one. The country's forests stabilized when fewer Americans desired cleared farmland. The proportion of land devoted to growing crops had risen 5 percent in 1850 to 20 percent in 1920, and at least half of this increase had come at the expense of forest clearing. By the second decade of the twentieth century, however, American agriculture was well into a mighty transformation characterized by the development of high-yield hybrid crops, the application of chemical fertilizers, and the introduction of labor-saving machinery. Farmers squeezed more crops and profit from less land. The demand for growing space withered. Consider just one aspect of this transformation, the shift from draft animals to internal-combustion engines. Before World War I more than a quarter of the nation's cropland produced feed and fodder for mules and horses. By the end of World War II the replacement of livestock by tractors freed up all this land, 70 million acres, for growing marketable crops.[39]

Americans struggled with a bounty of agricultural products in the twentieth century, a quandary of too much. Postfrontier thinkers like Roosevelt and Pinchot were not wired to confront surplus crops and surplus farmers. Scarcity drove their opinions and politics. Nothing demonstrated this more clearly than another program of Theodore Roosevelt's, the federal support for western irrigation, flood control, and hydraulic power that would fundamentally reshape the twentieth-century West. Interest in irrigating arid lands escalated in the last third of the nineteenth century, and by 1900 public and private projects were watering some eight million acres in the western states. Further development, however, would require massive dams, substantial reservoirs, and long-distance canals, capital investments beyond the means of most corporations, municipalities, or even states. "Great storage works are necessary," Roosevelt declared in his first presidential message to Congress, but "their construction has been conclusively shown to be an undertaking too vast for private effort." If Americans wanted their desert "wastes" to bloom, the feds would have to involve themselves.[40]

In the debate over federal legislation, few congressmen questioned the country's need for more farmland. The winning arguments plowed over reason with antiquated visions of the yeoman republic. Federal support for irrigation would open new lands and "furnish homes for the homeless and farms for the farmless." More farms would pacify urban conflicts and replant the country in the soil. The arguments ignored the world in which Americans were actually living, the one where farmers repeatedly abandoned their fields for cities. The federal government poured funds into dikes and ditches that collected runoff along with mistaken assumptions.[41]

In 1902 Congress passed the Reclamation Act, establishing a new agency in the Interior Department—the Bureau of Reclamation—to administer a massive federal effort in the states of the trans-Mississippi West. A curious term, "reclamation" implied that arid lands—the product of weather patterns and geologic processes—needed to be taken back from a nature that had gone astray. Western precipitation, or the lack thereof, took on a religious meaning. As one minister sermonized, "It is meet that God should be glad on the reclamation of the sinner." God, the rhetoric suggested, intended the West to be suitable for agricultural development, and the Almighty had tasked Americans with the job of redeeming the place. As the preacher helped rescue the backslider, so the irrigator helped reform the land, bringing it into a state of grace.[42]

Irrigation came with ideological aspirations no capital development could meet. Reclamation schemes uplifted some rural westerners at the expense of others.

Water projects often destroyed traditional ways of life that had served residents for generations. Elephant Butte Dam on the Rio Grande in central New Mexico created a system of modern reservoirs and canals that replaced the ancient complex of acequias (ditches) that had watered the land of hundreds of Hispanic subsistence farmers, forcing them to become agricultural laborers. Western water projects also ran roughshod over Indians. In 1908 the Supreme Court ruled that a reclamation project on the Milk River in Montana was illegally diverting a river that ran through the reservation of the Gros Ventre and Assiniboine tribes. Indians, the Court announced, retained an inviolable right to the waters of their homelands. Yet over the next half-century the Interior Department—the very agency entrusted with protecting Indian rights—approved dozens of projects that flooded reservation lands, dammed salmon runs, and drained reservation rivers but provided little or no benefit to reservation people.

Every human manipulation of critical natural resource comes with a cost. Why should reclamation be different? Some people win and others lose when economies develop. Perhaps, but reclamation produced few winners according to its own score sheet. The Reclamation Act included provisions restricting the use of irrigation water to residents (not absentee) farmers with plats of 160 or fewer acres. From the program's beginning, however, bureaucrats found it inconvenient to enforce these limitations and generally ignored, waived, or overrode them. Agribusiness, not the small farmer, was the big beneficiary of federal irrigation. The men and women laboring in reclaimed fields and orchards were not independent proprietors but migrant farmworkers. Moreover, reclamation projects meant to benefit rural residents were sometimes hijacked by urban interests, most famously when the city of Los Angeles commandeered the Owens River project that was supposed to benefit local farmers. Utilitarian ethics demanded that the few denizens of the Owens valley suffer for the many in Los Angeles. But reclamation was launched on ideals loftier than the greatest good for the greatest number. These projects were supposed to grow Edens overrun with happy yeomen and women, not factories in the fields or smoggy metropolises.

Frequently rivers were dammed and valleys flooded with little concern for the loss of ecosystems or natural wonders. The most infamous example was the Hetch Hetchy valley in Yosemite National Park, whose sharp glacial walls and meadow floor sent John Muir into rapture. "A grand landscape garden," he declared it, "one of Nature's rarest and most precious mountain temples." Some two hundred miles to the west, San Francisco engineers in search of a dependable urban water supply fastened on Hetch Hetchy as the best place to impound city water. The case sorely tested the priorities of the Roosevelt administration. When the city first approached the federal government for approval in 1903, the immediate reaction was negative. The reservoir would besmirch the valley's "wonderful

Hetch Hetchy valley, before and after damming. Wikimedia Commons.

natural conditions and marvelous scenic interest." But Roosevelt soon decided that "domestic use, especially for a municipal water supply, is the highest use to which water and available storage basins can be put," a decision that sent Muir into orbit. He attacked Roosevelt, Pinchot, and San Francisco politicians as "devotees of ravaging commercialism." "Dam Hetch Hetchy!" he thundered. "As well dam for water-tanks the people's cathedrals and churches, for no holier temple has ever been consecrated by the heart of man." Roosevelt vacillated, passing the matter on to his successors when he left office. Finally, in 1913, the project won approval by the Wilson administration. It would be Muir's last stand. He died a year later, deeply saddened by his defeat. "We may lose this particular fight," he wrote shortly before his death, "but truth and right must prevail at last." San Francisco got its water. Environmentalists inherited a cautionary tale.[43]

During its first three decades, the Reclamation Bureau completed twenty-two western projects that watered some fourteen million acres of western land, on which were grown major portions of the nation's fruits and vegetables, sugar beets, alfalfa, and cotton. Yet the very real success in increasing output was the program's greatest weakness. Reclamation heaped more on the economy's agricultural surplus. This was not immediately apparent. The industrial expansion of the early century and the extraordinary demand for foodstuffs during World War I kept farm prices high, encouraging large farmers to mechanize their production and irrigators to invest in expensive water distribution systems. But following the war, when demand shrank and farm prices dropped, not only did farmers have a tough time servicing the debts they had assumed to buy equipment but many irrigators found themselves unable to pay for construction costs and water fees. Individual farmers responded to lower prices the only way they knew how, by growing more in the hope of increasing their revenue. Western irrigators planted more sugar beets and alfalfa, wheat farmers plowed up millions of acres of raw prairie, and ranchers overstocked the range with cattle and sheep. Prices fell even further. By 1929 average farm income had declined to 64 percent of its level ten years before. American farmers hit bottom *before* the stock market crash sent the rest of the country into the Great Depression. By 1932 farm income was a fifth of its postwar high. What future was there in a program designed to increase the nation's cropland when the nation could not market the crops it was already producing?

In the late 1920s Congress passed legislation empowering the federal government to purchase surplus crops to push up prices, but President Calvin Coolidge vetoed it and his successor, President Herbert Hoover, indicated that he would do the same. Franklin D. Roosevelt, elected president in 1932, finally confronted farm overproduction. In one of his first acts, Roosevelt signed the Agricultural Adjustment Act, passed by the New Deal Congress, authorizing the government to fix production quotas, purchase surplus crops at a guaranteed price (based on the "parity" between industrial and agricultural purchasing power during the boom years 1909 to 1914), and store those surplus commodities in government granaries for sale during years of crop failure. Western populists had argued for some of these reforms for decades, and the New Deal policies would remain the foundation for federal agricultural policy for the rest of the twentieth century. Indeed, today some American farmers are paid by the government not to plant certain crops. Gradually prices climbed back up. Yet primary beneficiaries of the reforms were large operators. Small producers continued to lose their farms at an alarming rate, and tenants and sharecroppers were tossed off their rented land because their plots became the ones landlords retired from production to receive their subsidies. "I let 'em all go," a Texas farmer told a sociologist who inquired about his tenants. "I bought tractors on the money the government give me and got shet of my renters. . . . I did everything the government said—except keep my renters. The renters have been having it this way ever since the government come in. They've got their choice—California or WPA." A displaced Oklahoma tenant described his family's options more starkly: "move or starve."[44]

The Great Depression enhanced a western migration well under way before the economy crashed. Americans began moving from rural Oklahoma, Kansas, Texas, and Arkansas to California and other western Sun Belt states in the 1920s. During the Depression, the emigrants acquired national publicity to go along with the perambulations. John Steinbeck immortalized the "Okies" in his vivid period novel *The Grapes of Wrath* (1939). His Joad family captured the desperation and hopes of another of the epic migrations of western history, this time with the pioneers traveling by automobile rather than covered wagon. California seemed a new promised land. "By God, they's grapes out there, just a-hangin' over inta the road," says Steinbeck's Grandpa Joad. "I'm gonna pick me a wash tub full a grapes, an' I'm gonna set in 'em, an' scrooge aroun', an' let the juice run down my pants." But instead of an agrarian dream the family finds an industrial nightmare, California's factories in the field. Like the Joads, tens of thousands of "Okies" and "Arkies" found work as fruit and vegetable pickers, but even more joined an ever-increasing human flood into greater Los Angeles and other western urban centers.[45]

The states of the Pacific coast received more than 750,000 migrants during the 1930s. They came not only from Oklahoma and Arkansas but from Texas, Kansas, Nebraska, and the Dakotas, all areas where the agricultural crisis was compounded by the extraordinary environmental crisis known as the Dust Bowl. Drought gripped the entire nation during the 1930s, but had its most dramatic effects on the Great Plains. Huge dust storms began sweeping across the prairies in the early spring of 1932. The next year the dust rose so high that the jet stream sucked it up and deposited it like volcanic ash on Chicago, Washington, D.C., and even ships in the Atlantic. With each passing year the storms grew fiercer. The worst was 1935. The storms began in February and reached a terrible climax on April 14, "Black Sunday," when a huge duster enveloped nearly the entire state of Kansas. It was "the greatest show since Pompeii was buried," wrote newspaper editor William Allen White.[46]

What caused the Dust Bowl? Drought recurs naturally on the plains, and there had been small dust storms during the previous dry cycle in the late nineteenth century, but nothing in recorded history approached the ferocity of the Dust Bowl. The difference was the extent of the grassland lost since the 1890s, especially the excessive plowing and grazing of the 1920s that denuded millions of acres of their drought-tolerant native plants. Plains' grasses evolved to survive recurrent droughts. Some drove roots deep into the soil and withstood dry spells by subsisting on the nutrients in these subterranean tangles. Steel plows driven by tractors removed the root systems, exposing the soil—some of the richest on

"Farmer and Sons Walking in the Face of a Dust Storm, Cimarron County, Oklahoma."
Photograph by Arthur Rothstein, 1936. Library of Congress.

earth—to erosion. Dry prairie winds scoured the unprotected humus, turning some twenty-four million acres into barren desert by 1938. Environmental scientist Georg Borgstrom ranked the Dust Bowl as one of the three worst ecological blunders in world history. But unlike the other two—the deforestation of China's uplands in the third millennium B.C.E. and the erosion of Mediterranean hills by overgrazing sheep two thousand years ago—this disaster took only half a century to accomplish.

The rural West faced an economic and ecological catastrophe. Franklin Roosevelt answered with reinvigorated conservation programs. "Long ago, I pledged myself to a policy of conservation," FDR told a campaign crowd in 1932, and promised that he would "guard against the ravaging of our forests, the waste of our good earth and water supplies, the squandering of irreplaceable oil and mineral deposits, the preservation of our wildlife, and the protection of our streams." He appointed Harold Ickes the secretary of the interior (or secretary of the West, as some called the position). A lifelong Republican, Ickes had entered politics in support of Teddy Roosevelt, FDR's distant cousin. But frustrated with the foot-dragging of his party, he supported FDR in 1932. "We have reached the end of the pioneering period of 'go ahead and take,'" Ickes declared upon assuming his duties at the Interior Department, "we are in the age of planning for the best of everything for all." Ickes and Roosevelt moved on several fronts to repair the Great Plains. Thousands of young men in the Civilian Conservation Corps were set to work planting hundreds of millions of trees in "shelterbelts," designed to provide windbreaks, slow soil erosion, and create habitat for wildlife. The Taylor Grazing Act of 1934 brought the public range lands under the regulation of a new agency, the Grazing Service (renamed the Bureau of Land Management in 1946), with the mandate of ending overgrazing. The Soil Conservation Service, established the following year, targeted seventy-five million acres of plains cropland that should be retired from production, and though Congress failed to provide funding sufficient to meet that goal, the administration returned more than eleven million acres to grass.[47]

Critics look at these efforts and see the work left undone. The conservation reforms, argues environmental historian Donald Worster, were half measures that reflected "no fundamental reform of attitudes." Perhaps, but the old ideas the New Dealers resuscitated signaled another watershed moment for the West. FDR closed the frontier, once again. "Our last frontier has long since been reached and there is practically no more free land," he declared during the 1932 campaign. Americans now faced the "soberer, less dramatic business of administering resources . . . , of distributing wealth and products more equitably." In 1935 FDR signed an executive order withdrawing all remaining public lands from entry and placing them under federal conservation authority. The selling off or giving away of the public domain—a cornerstone of the nation's conquest and redistribution policy since

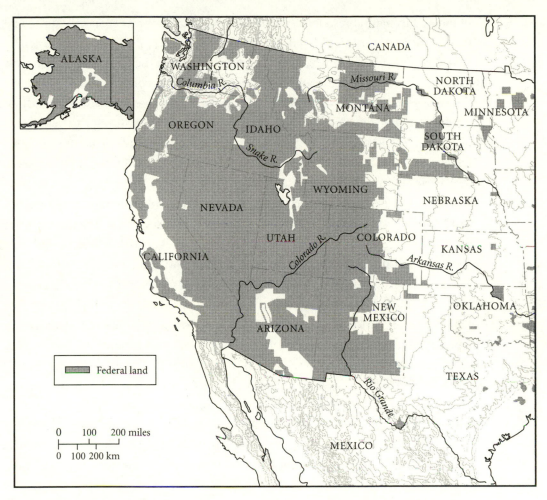

FEDERAL LANDS IN THE WEST

the Land Ordinance in 1874—came to a halt. Truly, this marked the passing of the nation's long frontier era.[48]

President Franklin D. Roosevelt split history into before and after. He drew a line in time and suggested that westerners cross over and embrace different values—sober capitalism (ironic for the man who ended prohibition), scientific management, and federal conservation. The region's economic problems, however, still bedeviled its residents. Roosevelt may have buried the frontier period of "go ahead and take," but the stench of the corpse lingered for years. During the 1930s westerners Bernard DeVoto and Walter Prescott Webb again voiced the old western complaint of colonial exploitation. In an influential jeremiad of 1934, DeVoto argued that the East had created the West as a colonial dependency, had plundered its natural resources, and didn't give a damn for its economic development. A few years later Webb published the angry *Divided We Stand: The Crisis of a Frontierless Democracy* (1937), which argued further that the Great Depression was largely the result of the close of the frontier and uneven economic development of the West and South. New Dealers largely agreed. To survive, the nation's economy needed its lagging sections to catch up. One of the most enduring legacies of the New Deal was Roosevelt's decision to build an industrial infrastructure in these regions. The New Deal's program of public investment was unlike anything seen in American history, and it transformed the West.[49]

The New Deal program focused on multipurpose river development. Reclamation concentrated on irrigation, but chronic surpluses altered the justification for water projects. Dams would produce electricity, regulate floodwaters, and impound runoff for redistribution. Electric utilities and companies manufacturing electrical appliances were two of the fastest-growing sectors of the American economy in the 1920s. Yet only 10 percent of rural households enjoyed electricity for their homes and work. Plugging farmers and ranchers into the electric grid became a philosophical bridge across regions. In 1928 a coalition of southern Democrats and western Republicans ("the alliance of cotton and corn") passed the first multipurpose river bill—a huge dam and hydroelectric complex at Boulder Canyon on the Colorado River, designed to provide irrigation, flood control, public water supplies, and hydroelectric power to Arizona, Nevada, and California. President Hoover took the credit and named the dam for himself but blocked congressional attempts to secure federal funding for similar projects on the Tennessee and Columbia Rivers.

Roosevelt, however, was an enthusiastic supporter of river development. During his campaign for the presidency he came out in favor of the Columbia River project. "Vast water power can be of incalculable value to this whole section of the country," he told a crowd in Portland. "It means cheap manufacturing production, economy, and comfort on the farm and in the household." Massive infusions of federal investment could provide the spark to ignite regional economic growth. Even before he took office, Roosevelt announced the model New Deal river project, the Tennessee Valley Authority (TVA). Congress approved the TVA in the spring of 1933, and over the next several years New Dealers in Congress won approval for similar projects on the Columbia, the Sacramento and San Joaquin in California's Central Valley, and dozens of smaller rivers throughout the West. Congressman Sam Rayburn of Texas sponsored the Rural Electrification Act of 1936, which connected tens of thousands of rural households to the nation's power grid. "I want my people out of the dark," Rayburn told his colleagues. "Can you imagine what it will mean to a farm wife to have a pump in a well and lights in the house?" With clout as both southerners and westerners, Rayburn and other Texas

Hoover Dam with Lake Mead in the background. Photograph by Andy Pernick, 1996. Bureau of Reclamation, Department of the Interior.

Democrats were congressional leaders for Roosevelt's program of development for the provinces.[50]

The projects employed tens of thousands of workers and helped launch some of the West's biggest corporations. "The big winner of the New Deal," wrote historian Jordan Schwarz, "was the West." The river projects enriched regional construction companies and their leaders, such as Henry J. Kaiser, who became known as the New Deal's "favorite businessman." An able and energetic industrialist, Kaiser directed a crew that built the superstructure at the Grand Coulee Dam on the Columbia (three times the size of Hoover Dam) and the gigantic pilings for the San Francisco Bay Bridge. When he failed to win the contract for the construction of Shasta Dam on the Sacramento, Kaiser successfully bid to supply the cement, then in just six months constructed his own cement plant, the largest in the world. Cheap electricity from government-built dams stimulated the industrialization of the Columbia and Tennessee basins and propelled California forward as the nation's leading industrial state during World War II. New western aluminum and steel mills provided the materials needed by western shipyards and aircraft plants. Kaiser turned from erecting dams to assembling aircraft carriers during the war. Power generated by dams on the Tennessee, Columbia, and Colorado Rivers fueled the industrial complexes that invented and manufactured nuclear weapons. Dams and construction projects intended to employ beleaguered Okies and brighten the nights of isolated farm families helped turn the United States into a superpower.[51]

The New Deal belief in the closing of the frontier also stimulated a rethinking of Indian policy. A cornerstone of frontier economics was the "freeing up" of Indian land and resources for private exploitation and development. The Allotment Act of 1888 was proposed as a departure from this pattern, but in fact allotment accelerated the assault on Indian lands. A study conducted in 1928 by Lewis Meriam of the Brookings Institution (a Washington think tank funded by the Rockefeller Foundation) concluded that allotment had "resulted in much loss of land without a compensating advance in the economic ability of the Indians." In Oklahoma tribes such as the Cherokees were stripped of 40 percent of their holdings, with the rest being distributed in small parcels to Indian families. The lands of the Sioux were reduced by a third, the Ojibway estate by fully 80 percent. The total Indian land base stood at forty-seven million acres—only a third of what it had been when allotment was proclaimed as the solution to further Indian dispossession. Moreover, the report declared, the policy of assimilation had been nothing more than an attempt to "crush out all that is Indian" and had demoralized many tribes, making Native Americans the most impoverished group in the United States.[52]

The Meriam Report underscored allotment's marginalization of American Indians. Instead of assimilating them into the mainstream, the program drove many to the desperate fringes. The wonks at the Brookings Institution felt free to criticize the sorry promises of assimilationists because they no longer believed in assimilation. The theory of human development and interaction that motivated them was "cultural pluralism," a term coined in 1915 by the Harvard philosopher Horace Kallen. America, Kallen argued, was best understood as a "federation or commonwealth of national cultures," a "democracy of nationalities, cooperating voluntarily and autonomously through common institutions in the enterprise of self-realization through the perfection of men *according to their kind*." Kallen and the pluralists leaned heavily on this last phrase. Assimilationists assumed the superiority of Anglo-American culture. Pluralists, by contrast, were influenced by new perspectives in anthropology being advanced by Franz Boas of Columbia University and his students Ruth Benedict, Robert Lowie, and Margaret Mead, all of whom had studied the Indians of North America. Impressed by the enormous diversity among cultures, the pluralists argued that each should be considered from within the framework of its own values and assumptions.[53]

John Collier attended some of these Columbia classes. A young southerner from Atlanta, he came to New York City in the early twentieth century and after a few years of course work became a social worker in the city's settlement houses. But the pluralist perspective he had imbibed at Columbia clashed with the paternalism he found rampant in his profession. In 1920 Collier had relocated to Taos, New Mexico, where he became a great admirer of the communal culture of the Pueblo Indians. The Pueblos' determination to preserve their traditions against assimilationists was what impressed him most. When the Pueblos became involved in a fight to defend their land and water rights, Collier jumped to their support and organized a network of reformers around the country. Eventually this network grew into the American Indian Defense Association, and Collier secured a national reputation as a critic of Indian policy. One of the charter members of Collier's association was Harold Ickes, and when Ickes became Roosevelt's interior secretary in 1933, he asked Collier to join the administration as the new commissioner of Indian affairs.

His policies, Collier announced at his swearing in, would focus on "ending paternalism and extending civil rights" to Indian people. "Indians, whose culture, civic tradition, and inherited traditions are still strong and virile, should be encouraged and helped to develop their life in their own patterns." Collier drafted a set of reforms that were included in the Indian Reorganization Act, passed by Congress in 1934. The Indian New Deal represented a radical shift in Indian policy. It put an end to the government campaign of repression and inaugurated an unprecedented era of Indian cultural freedom. Boarding schools were phased out and replaced

John Collier with Blackfoot Indian leaders, 1934. Library of Congress.

by reservation day schools in which Indians themselves had an impact on the curriculum. The bureau sponsored the publication of bilingual textbooks printed in both English and native languages. Indian people began to take a more prominent role in the running of the Bureau of Indian Affairs (BIA), and by the early 1940s the number of Indian employees at the BIA had increased to several thousand.[54]

Collier issued a directive to Indian agents proclaiming religious freedom on all reservations. "There have existed tribal religions which have been forged through thousands of years of endurance," he wrote, "which contain deep beauty and spiritual guidance, consolation, and disciplinary power." Collier's thinking and policies celebrated old—or old-seeming—traditions. While his pluralism and radicalism distanced him from the likes of Gifford Pinchot and Owen Wister, Collier shared their sense that modernity imperiled traditional practices and values. Wister wrote novels to preserve a white manly code of conduct, Pinchot organized the Forest Service to protect natural resources from rapacious capitalists, and Collier dedicated his stewardship of the Bureau of Indian Affairs to saving Indian cultures. Collier wanted to strengthen the tribes, not dismantle them for mainstream absorption. The Indian New Deal ended the policy of allotment. Remaining unallot-

Apache cowboys on a roundup in Gila County, Arizona. Photograph by Gilbert Campbell, 1941. Arizona Collection, Arizona State University Libraries.

ted reservations lands were reconsolidated and placed under the control of tribal corporations. Individual Indians who had been awarded allotments were encouraged to exchange those lands for shares of common stock in Indian corporations. The BIA also established a fund from which tribes might borrow in order to purchase reservation lands from non-Indian owners.[55]

The Meriam Report had suggested that stock raising seemed to offer the most promise for the economic renewal of western Indians. "Not only does the average Indian show considerable aptitude for this work, but enormous areas of Indian land, tribal and individual, are of little value except grazing," the report concluded. Encouraged by Collier's BIA, the number of Indian cattle ranchers doubled and the value of Indian cattle sales increased more than tenfold, reaching three million dollars by 1939. One of the most successful examples was the San Carlos Apache tribe located in the Gila Mountains of southeastern Arizona. By 1940 the tribe's twenty-eight thousand head of registered Herefords had become the largest in the Southwest. "The cattle industry is undoubtedly a fortunate choice for the reservation," wrote an anthropologist studying the tribe. "Indians I have known like the idea of cattle work, for they feel it is worth a man's effort." The Apache cowboys tapped into the same reservoir of virile associations that attracted Wister and Teddy Roosevelt to ranch work, but they achieved a different outcome. As historian Peter

Iverson notes, the mastery of animals while dressed in boots, spurs, and Stetsons "increased rather than decreased their identity as San Carlos Apaches. Being cowboys had allowed them to be Indians."[56]

These successes depended on Indian peoples' ability to exercise sovereignty over their affairs. Under the auspices of the Indian Reorganization Act, 181 tribes voted to organize new forms of representative self-government, and during Collier's tenure about half of those tribes adopted written constitutions and elected leaders. To be sure, the BIA continued to have extraordinary authority in the affairs of reservation Indians, retaining veto power over the decisions of tribal councils and supervising the fiscal and economic arrangements of Indian nations. Indian agents and reservation superintendents continued to dole out jobs and funds, and many tribal councils acted as little more than rubber stamps. Nevertheless, the New Deal declared—for the first time in U.S. history—that tribal government had the right to exercise what the chief legal adviser of the Interior Department called "internal sovereignty." Except in cases where tribal jurisdiction had been limited by the express action of Congress—as it did in 1885 when it extended federal jurisdiction to felony offenses such as murder, rape, and robbery committed on reservations—Indian nations were to enjoy all their "original sovereignty." In the coming years, the federal government would violate its own directives, and many states encroached on tribal sovereignty without federal sanction, yet the legal principles the New Deal established set important precedent. Upheld by a series of federal court decisions after World War II, Indian sovereignty would become the cornerstone of Indian law in the second half of the twentieth century.

Sovereignty as the Indian New Deal defined it led to striking contradictions. The Tohono O'odham tribe of southern Arizona, for example, had no words in its language for "representative" or "budget." In this instance, culture frustrated the reformers' efforts to preserve culture. In other situations, political reorganization ran into long-standing disagreements within Indian communities between progressives and traditionalists, assimilationists and separatists, mixed-bloods and full-bloods. Among the most acculturated Indians—many of whom had accepted allotments and now operated farms or ranches—there were fears that reorganization of Indian policy might threaten their titles. Other acculturated Indians criticized what they thought was Collier's sentimental and romantic attachment to traditional Indian culture. These critics argued that the Indian New Deal was a "back to blanket" program that would retard progress and condemn Indians to perpetual poverty and subjugation. The Iroquois leader Alice Lee Jemison, for example, argued that "reform only meant the strengthening not the diminishing of bureaucratic control in the lives of American Indians."[57]

Traditionalists had their own bones to pick. Among those Indians who continued to believe in the viability of traditional forms of tribal government, there was

Navajo shepherds with their flock. Photograph by Edward S. Curtis, c. 1905. Beinecke Rare Book and Manuscript Library, Yale University.

considerable opposition to the establishment of democratically elected tribal councils and chairs. Many traditionalists feared that these councils would be dominated by assimilated Indians educated in boarding schools. At Pine Ridge Reservation in South Dakota, for example, a representative council replaced the traditional self-selected one in an election in which most traditionalists refused to participate. Disagreements over Indian reorganization fed into the politics of factionalism that existed on nearly every reservation in the country. Although most Indian tribes and communities accepted the Indian New Deal, seventy-seven tribes rejected it, among them the Navajos and Iroquois, two of the most influential Indian nations in the United States. Both already had traditional council governments of their own. The Iroquois feared that acceptance would compromise their hardline position on questions of sovereignty. In 1924, when Congress passed the Indian Citizen Act, declaring for the first time that Indians were U.S. citizens, the Iroquois council rejected it, insisting that the Iroquois people were already citizens of the Iroquois nation.

Collier had nothing to do with the Iroquois situation, but he was implicated in the rejection of the reorganization by the Diné (Navajos), a case that illustrated once again how good intentions and pluralist aspirations failed to mend the federal relationship with Indian people. According to federal studies of the multipurpose development project on the Colorado River, herds of Diné sheep were overgrazing grasslands and causing serious erosion, and the soil carried down to the river threatened to silt up the reservoir behind Hoover Dam. "Down there on the Colorado is the biggest, most expensive dam in the world," Collier told a meeting of the Navajo council in 1934, "which will furnish all southern California with water and electric power." He wanted the Diné to cull their herds, voluntarily he insisted in public at the time, but later he admitted that federal agents had bullied and intimidated Diné stock raisers to accomplish the slaughter of tens of thousands of sheep and goats. The Navajo stock-reduction program hit the smallest and most economically vulnerable Indian herders worst, devastating thousands of native families and reducing them to dependency on federal assistance. Collier and the BIA became anathema to most Diné, and the resentment over stock reduction resulted in a protest vote that killed the new constitution. Collier failed to strike a new deal with the largest tribe in the United States.[58]

In the name of reclamation, bringing water to southern California fruit orchards, and Los Angeles real estate developments, John Collier, pluralist defender of Indian culture, damaged one of the few remaining viable Indian economies in the West. Exemplars of survival against impossible odds, the Diné and their herds were sacrificed to the crosscurrents of the postfrontier West in which bureaucrats managed land, people, animals, and rivers in an atmosphere of eminent extinction and profound loss.

FURTHER READING

Thomas G. Andrews, *Killing for Coal: America's Deadliest Labor War* (2008)

Jon T. Coleman, *Vicious: Wolves and Men in America* (2004)

Robert V. Hine, *In the Shadow of Frémont: Edward Kern and the Art of Exploration, 1845–1860*, 2nd ed. (1982)

Karl Jacoby, *Crimes against Nature: Squatters, Poachers, Thieves, and the Hidden History of American Conservation* (2001)

Jules David Prown et al., *Discovered Lands, Invented Pasts: Transforming Visions of the American West* (1992)

Richard Slotkin, *The Fatal Environment: The Myth of the Frontier in the Age of Industrialization, 1800–1890* (1985)

Mark David Spence, *Dispossessing the Wilderness: Indian Removal and the Making of the National Parks* (1999)

Louis S. Warren, *Buffalo Bill's America: William Cody and the Wild West Show* (2005)

G. Edward White, *The Eastern Establishment and the Western Experience: The West of Frederic Remington, Theodore Roosevelt, and Owen Wister* (1968)

Richard White, *The Organic Machine: The Remaking of the Columbia River* (1996)

Donald Worster, *Dust Bowl: The Southern Plains in the 1930s* (1979)

David M. Wrobel, *The End of American Exceptionalism: Frontier Anxiety from the Old West to the New Deal* (1993)

11

As the West Goes . . .

Though his screeching vocals, tattooed limbs, and teased-out hair would have blown ancestral minds, long-dead Americans would recognize elements of the story Axl Rose wailed in 1987's "Welcome to the Jungle." Rose and his heavy metal bandmates blasted a narrative of corrupted innocence, a tale of a young woman seeking fame in Hollywood. Ever since Americans have had cities they've told of rural innocents led astray by urban corruptors. Guns N' Roses updated that cautionary tale, warning impressionable starlets to watch out for drug dealers and sleazy agents. The song's environment—the jungle—harkened even further back into North America's frontier history, to captivity narratives like Mary Rowlandson's.

Getting lost in the wilderness is one of the oldest plots around. Guns N' Roses simply dressed it up in 1980s "hair metal" glam and cranked up the tempo. That's how stories endure. The living grab onto them, renovate the setting and the delivery, and offer them as new products. Audiences latch onto deep history resurrected as a pop sensation. They get their ancient wisdom and their MTV.

The band could have set their story in any number of American metropolitan jungles. The 1970s and 1980s blighted urban cores across the country. Interstates plowed through downtown neighborhoods, dividing communities and providing an exit ramp to the suburbs for those with means. The federal government pulled back on spending and support at the same moment that local tax bases shrank. In the 1980s, when Americans pictured a wild or dangerous place, they envisioned burned-out sections of New York City's South Bronx or Chicago's crumbling Cabrini-Green housing project. But Guns N' Roses picked Los Angeles, and their choice spoke volumes about the leading role that city played in modern American society and mythology. L.A. was the preferred location for twentieth-century

Americans to lose their way. The relentless California sunshine teamed with Hollywood neon to dazzle transplants into ethical missteps. The contrast between gleaming surfaces and dark underbellies gave L.A. a noir shading. Both the bright light and the deep shadow contained iconic Americans with historical antecedents. If the wide-eyed starlet replayed the role of wilderness captive, her male counterpart was the hardboiled private detective. The gumshoe anchored noir films and novels, kicking the stories into action by exploring the recesses of urban corruption. In the beginning he thinks he understands evil, but he finds that the human heart has no ground floor. A case-hardened student of savagery, he was the reincarnation of Benjamin Church, the man-who-knew-Indians.

Specters from the outer limits of the colonial backwater, Mary Rowlandson and Benjamin Church, had no business haunting 1980s Los Angeles, arguably the dominant city of post–World War II America. The City of Angels sprawled at the center of a region at the center of a nation at the center of the world. Jumpstarted by New Deal projects and the preparation for war, economic development washed over the region, reordering relations among East, West, and South. Certainly the postwar West could no longer be considered a colonial periphery, what Bernard DeVoto termed the nation's "plundered province." Millions of newcomers poured into the region, a westward tilt toward the booming cities and suburbs of the Sun Belt, a shift that altered not only addresses but attitudes. For the first time in American history, the West became the economic, political, and cultural pacesetter for the nation as a whole. "Western" became a brand, a set of cultural associations, an ideological affiliation, disconnected from geographic location. A suburbanite could pull her Chevy Silverado into the garage of a three-bedroom ranch house with "Hotel California" playing on the stereo whether she lived in New Jersey, Peoria, or Flagstaff. Levi's, surfboards, Scientology, pinot noirs, and chimichangas infiltrated the far corners of the nation. This shift was so fundamental that it calls into question the continued relevance of a sectional interpretation of American society. In the twenty-first century the attachments and identities of trans-Mississippi Americans are no longer defined by the huge and amorphous region known as the West but rooted in more discernible cultural provinces.[1]

If *West* lost its salience as a way of understanding contemporary history, the notion of *the frontier* also came under serious interrogation. *Frontier* became a cliché of American political rhetoric, appealing to the optimism and nationalism of voters. John F. Kennedy called for a "New Frontier," and Ronald Reagan celebrated the trek of westering settlers into ever brighter futures. But as presidents mythologized, others wondered. Wasn't *frontier* an ideological concept, an excuse for violent colonization that masked the evidence of conquest with its celebration of American progress?

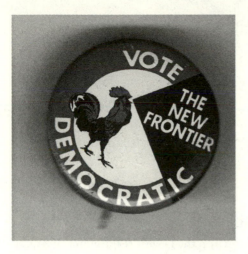

John F. Kennedy presidential campaign button, 1960. Author's collection.

Yet borders and borderlands proliferated in the second half of the twentieth century. The historic pattern of frontier migration and settlement continued. The massive western migration of eastern Americans was matched by equally massive migrations from Mexico, Central America, and Asia. Millions poured across borders to join in making one of the world's most multicultural societies. Moreover, American Indian peoples not only survived but began pushing back, successfully reclaiming important elements of their original sovereignty. The lines among ethnic groups became zones of interaction filled with diverse encounters, conflicts, and exchanges. They fit the enduring pattern of multicultural cross-fertilization that had defined American frontiers from colonial times. As the old notion of *the frontier* came under intellectual assault, a powerful upwelling of new frontiers took place.

In terms of economic development and political clout, the modern West exceeded nineteenth-century boosters' wildest dreams. In the argot of Hollywood, the West became a star, with an increasingly strong gravitational pull that brought money, people, and ideas into its orbit. The New Deal set out to build an industrial infrastructure in the West, and those efforts laid the foundation for what was to come. The influx of federal investment during World War II telescoped decades of development into a few years. The Atlantic coast was deemed vulnerable to German attack, and military planners looked west to disperse vital industries. Then, with the Japanese attack on Pearl Harbor, the West became the staging ground for the Pacific theater. The federal government supplied 90 percent of the capital for western industries and military installations during the war. The aircraft industry expanded spectacularly in Texas, Washington, and California, aluminum plants sopped up the hydroelectric power of the Northwest's great rivers, and steel foundries arose in Texas, Utah, Oklahoma, and southern California.

In April 1942, Henry J. Kaiser broke ground for a huge steel mill in the quiet, rural town of Fontana, fifty miles east of Los Angeles. During the 1930s, Kaiser became the West's most prominent industrialist by building hydroelectric dams on the Colorado and Columbia Rivers. When the priority turned to winning the war, he quickly arranged for federal loans in order to build the world's most modern and efficient facility for producing steel. The Fontana mill fabricated mammoth plates for the hulls of wartime merchant ships built at Kaiser's new shipbuilding plants on the Pacific coast. By the end of the war, a new Liberty Ship was emerging from Kaiser's plant every ten hours, making him the largest shipbuilder in American history. He drew his workforce—including a large percentage of minorities and women—from all over the country, luring them not only with high wages but with child care facilities and subsidized health care. The Kaiser Permanente health plan was one of the first health maintenance organizations in the nation and remains in operation to this day.

Kaiser's biggest financial partner—aside from the feds—was Amadeo Peter Giannini, owner of the Bank of America. Giannini championed the West and invested in many western enterprises. He bankrolled the Hollywood studios of United Artists and Walt Disney, financed the construction of the Golden Gate Bridge, and as a strong supporter of the New Deal reaped his share of investment opportunities during the 1930s. He and his bank were perfectly positioned to supply most of the private financing for the wartime economic boom that started in the West and radiated outward. By 1945 Giannini's Bank of America had become the largest commercial and savings institution in the world. It was the first bank to fully computerize, to introduce direct deposit, and in 1958 to offer the first all-purpose consumer credit card, the BankAmericard (later renamed the Visa card).

Bankrolled by his family's Houston petroleum fortune, Howard Hughes epitomized the capital flows that raised the postwar West to international prominence. He invested in aircraft and built the Hughes Aircraft Company into a giant of western industry. He won lucrative government contracts during the war and in the subsequent Cold War developed weapons-guidance systems, satellites, and clandestine projects for the Central Intelligence Agency. He put capital into Trans World Airlines, selling his share in 1966 for half a billion dollars. He started a regional airline specializing in short hauls not served by major carriers (a critical transportation resource in the spread-out West). Hughes also invested in Hollywood, financing films like *The Outlaw* (1943), featuring voluptuous Jane Russell. After the war Hughes bought RKO Pictures—a major Hollywood studio—and

Howard Hughes, Inglewood, California, c. 1940. Wikimedia commons.

diversified its operations by buying into television stations and broadcasting old movies, demonstrating the profitability of film archives to a media hungry for programming. Hughes was also one of the twentieth century's great eccentrics. His fear of germs and disease caused him to withdraw from public view. Still, though he never left his room, his money moved and grew. In 1967 Hughes began buying properties in the gambling mecca of Las Vegas. By the time he died in 1976, he had become one of the wealthiest men in the world.

While they represented the splashiest (and in Hughes's case the weirdest) of the West's postwar entrepreneurs, Henry Kaiser, Peter Giannini, and Howard Hughes ran with a pack energetic industrialists who parlayed regional economic development into corporations with global stature. The dams and public works of Kaiser had counterparts in the huge construction firms of Stephen Bechtel and John McCone, which moved from building dams in the 1930s to constructing military bases and freeways during and after the war. The Bank of America was only the largest of a number of powerful western banks; in Los Angeles, Security-First National financed much of the home construction boom in postwar southern California. Hughes was but a bit player in Hollywood's growth as the capital of the nation's culture industry, and the gamblers he looked down upon from his hermetically sealed Vegas penthouse were part of a growing tourism industry that stretched from the ringing slot machines of desert casinos to the dude ranches of Phoenix, from the ski slopes of the Rockies to the surfing beaches of southern California. Hughes was also just one of a group of western aerospace capitalists that included John Northrop, Allan Lockheed, Donald Douglas, and William

The Hanford Nuclear Reservation on the Columbia River in Washington State, 1960. Wikimedia Commons.

Boeing. In the late 1950s both Boeing and Douglas created worldwide markets for their new passenger jets.

The West excelled in high-tech. Petrochemical industries in Texas and California laid the foundation for a superstructure completed during the war. "The center of gravity of scientific talent in the United States had definitely gravitated westward," a prominent scientist observed in 1945. An early wartime model was the atomic laboratory at Los Alamos, New Mexico, where the University of California assembled one of the most impressive groups of scientists in the world to build the first atomic bomb. At Hanford, Washington, forty thousand scientists and technicians produced the plutonium for those bombs, an assignment made possible by electricity from the hydroelectric dams on the Columbia River. At Pasadena, in southern California, the Jet Propulsion Laboratory of the California Institute of Technology conducted research in rocketry that would place it at the leading edge of space technology.[2]

Defense spending spurred this growth. In Seattle, where Boeing Aircraft dominated the local economy, military expenditure accounted for 40 percent of job growth in the postwar period. Near Denver, the nuclear production facility at

Rocky Flats and the federal Rocky Mountain Arsenal employed more than twenty thousand people. In the postwar period, 40 percent of all federal aerospace contracts went to firms operating in California, an annual subsidy to that state's economy that hovered near twenty billion dollars. "Defense spending," wrote historian James L. Clayton, was "the primary reason for the extraordinary rapid expansion of industry and population in California since World War II." Federal military demand, he estimated, accounted for two-thirds of the state's manufacturing growth in the twenty years after 1945.[3]

In the 1950s Stanford University encouraged a consortium of science and industry in the nearby Santa Clara valley, and new electronics companies such as Hewlett-Packard accumulated the critical mass for what became known as Silicon Valley, a place where high-tech startups such as Intel, a computer chip maker founded in 1968, could prosper and grow into manufacturing giants. The founding stories of some of these companies is the stuff of modern business legend. In 1976 Steven Jobs and Stephen Wozniak, two college dropouts tinkering in a suburban garage near San Jose, developed an easy-to-use-desktop computer they called the Apple. Five years later, their company, a startup they financed by selling a Volkswagen bus, was marketing thousands of personal computers and threatening IBM, the eastern computing tyrannosaurus. IBM jumped into the personal computer market after purchasing operating software from Microsoft, a company based in Redmond, Washington, led by Paul Allen and Bill Gates. By the end of the century, Gates was the wealthiest individual in the world (with a fortune estimated at more than a hundred billion dollars) and Steve Jobs had become the closest thing to a Silicon Valley rock star, complete with acolytes eager to purchase his company's latest creations.

The economy of the postwar West, wrote historian Gerald Nash, "became a pacesetter for the nation." In 1950 only 10 percent of the nation's two hundred largest firms were headquartered west of the Mississippi. A half-century later that proportion had climbed to 37 percent. The West was home to some of the nation's largest corporations: in electronics, computers, and software (Amazon, Apple, Cisco, Dell, eBay, Facebook, Google, Hewlett-Packard, Intel, Oracle, Texas Instruments, Western Digital), aerospace (Boeing, Northrop Grumman), petroleum refining (Chevron, ConocoPhillips, Exxon-Mobil, Marathon, Murphy Oil, Tesoro), wood products (Kimberly-Clark, Weyerhaeuser), and commercial banking (Wells Fargo). The West's long colonial dependence on the East had ended.[4]

Yet while the powerbrokers looked out at the new West from their high-rise office towers in Los Angeles and Houston or their corporate campuses near Seattle and San Jose, others glared back in resentment. At the end of the twentieth century much of the farming, ranching, and mining West remained tied to a cycle of boom and bust. During the period of national economic stagnation that began in

1973 and extended into the early 1980s, the combined effects of tight money and double-digit inflation created the worst depression in western extractive industries since the Great Depression. As the price of commodities fell, mines and lumber mills closed their doors, throwing tens of thousands out of work. Rural westerners by the thousands lost their land. Over the second half of the twentieth century the number of independent western ranchers and farmers fell by half while the size of the remaining operations increased by 125 percent. Farming and ranching became more concentrated and mechanized, and many small operations were priced out. Unable to buy astronomically expensive tractors and other mechanical devices to keep pace with the corporate "factories in the fields," tens of thousands of farm families left the land. From 1940 to 2010 the percentage of westerners living in rural areas fell from 42 to 10 percent of the total population, a decline of 76 percent. Hundreds of rural counties suffered devastating population losses, and crossroad communities became ghost towns. As the region's economic profile rose, the rural and urban split widened, creating an opening in the middle ground for track homes and strip malls.

The people that streamed into western cities and suburbs pushed economic expansion. The West's population boom began in the early twentieth century, but after World War II the influx was staggering. From 1945 to 1970 more than thirty million people moved beyond the Mississippi, the most significant redistribution of population in the nation's history. In 1964 California surpassed New York to become the nation's most populous state, and in the early 1990s Texas pushed into the second spot. Metropolitan areas experienced the greatest growth. The numbers are stunning. Between 1940 and 2010 the proportion of westerners living in urban areas jumped from 48 to 90 percent, making the West the most urban region in America. Of the nation's twenty-five largest metro areas in 2015, twelve were in the West. Such growth is predicted to continue. According to the Census Bureau's projections, over the next few decades six of the ten fastest-growing states will be in the West.

Cities reordered economic relations. Western cities traditionally acted as funnels for exporting extractive commodities (grain, meat, metals, lumber) and importing manufactured goods. In the nineteenth century, Chicago and San Francisco served as gateways between western resource regions and the industrial and financial centers in the East. But in the second half of the twentieth century, urban growth broke free of the countryside. The extractive economy became less significant than urban manufacturing and service industries. As geographer John Borchert has argued, the rapid growth of western cities in the postwar period cannot be explained simply by connections with the hinterland. Rather, intermetro-

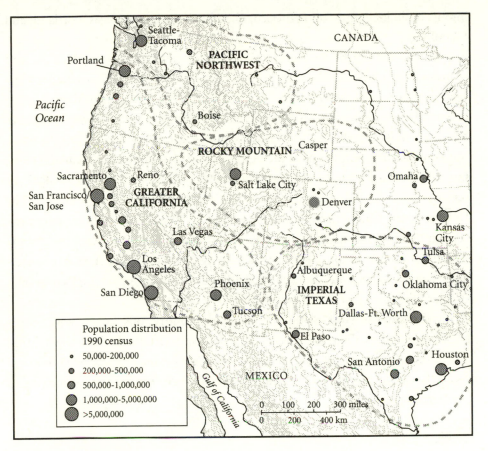

WESTERN CITIES, 1990

politan links account for the development. The cities bolstered one another, and instead of a source of raw materials, the hinterlands became drive-by and flyover zones, wastelands to get through or wonderlands to visit on holiday.[5]

What once captured imaginations as a vast region consisting of half the continent now might be better viewed as a series of metropolitan regions—city-states—with large dependent hinterland districts. Imperial Texas centers on the Houston–Dallas–San Antonio triangle and dominates a huge region that extends from the Gulf coast to the oil fields of Oklahoma, from the cattle range of the southern plains to the industrial transborder zone encompassing the twin cities of Brownsville–Matamoros and El Paso–Ciudad Juárez. The Pacific Northwest, an urban empire with a virtual capital at Seattle, includes Washington, much of Oregon, Idaho, and Montana, pulls in Alaska, and encompasses cross-border ties with Vancouver and trade with Asia. The granddaddy of western urban empires is Greater California, based at Los Angeles, the largest and most diversified urban economy in the nation, with gross revenues totaling $575 billion in 2015. The gravitational pull of the southern California economy swept other urban systems into its orbit, including San Francisco, Phoenix, Tucson, Las Vegas, Portland, and Honolulu.

Busy harbors on the Pacific and Gulf coasts helped launch Seattle, L.A., and Houston. The landlocked metropolis of Denver was for years subordinate to Chicago until the development of air transport in the final decades of the twentieth century. Denver International Airport, opened in 1995, became the focus of hopes for the city's rise as hub of a major metropolitan region, the Interior West. Its traditional economic strength was in the export of basic commodities (grain and meat, minerals and coal). But the airport stimulated the production of high value, time-sensitive products shipped by air cargo to domestic and international markets. The Denver metro region added thousands of highly skilled positions in aerospace, telecommunications, and finance, and job growth stimulated migration into the region. From 1990 to 2010 the population along Colorado's Interstate 25, connecting the Front Range cities and suburbs of Pueblo, Colorado Springs, Denver, and Greeley, grew by an astounding 425 percent.

Residents of the West's large metro regions identify most strongly with their local communities, their urban cores, and their states, for that's where the political action is. Sometimes they identify as natives of multistate regions, like the Rockies or the Pacific Northwest. But there is little salience for them in identifying as "westerners."

How people lived in these new megalopolises mattered just as much as their geographic location. The space that postwar Americans seemed to care about most was the expanse stretching from their front door to the curb and from their sliding-glass patio door to the backyard fence. The suburban plot became cosmic center for the postwar generations. For many, the allegiance to cities, regions, and even the nation grew from their attachment to the "good life" these spaces represented. While suburban development occurred across the nation, the association of detached homes surrounded by swaths of manicured lawn as the foundation of a triumphant "lifestyle" emerged from the West.

The search for open space, for a freer, cleaner, less encumbered life, especially in an appealing climate, drove the West's urban growth. Most of the searchers landed in the Sun Belt, a place-name that originated among wartime planners who sought to locate the majority of the military's training facilities in what they called the "sunshine belt." The enormous swath of arid country stretching from Texas to southern California became the postwar destination of millions of Americans, and almost overnight there appeared thousands of tracts of detached homes, each framed by ample lawns with clusters of palm, avocado, or jacaranda trees and perhaps a backyard swimming pool.

The best known Sun Belt mecca was southern California. "More than any-place else," writes historian Kenneth T. Jackson, it "became the symbol of post-war suburban culture." Southern Californian developers mass produced islands of middle-class satisfaction. Builders moved beyond the innovations of Henry E. Huntington in the early century to consolidate subdivision, home construction, and sales into a seamless operation. In the late 1930s they devised the techniques of tract construction, in which specialized teams of laborers and craftsmen moved sequentially through the project, grading, pouring foundations, framing and sheathing, roofing, and completing the finishing work. With the boom in wartime industry, developers rushed to meet an enormous demand for housing, subsidized by federal loans and income tax reductions for home mortgage interest. Sunshine, tract homes, and easy credit: these were the ingredients of the postwar real es-tate boom. Development intensified beyond all experience. Southern California sprawled. Builders extended their projects in successive rings outward from cen-tral L.A., bulldozing citrus groves and walnut orchards to make way for housing subdivisions, factories and offices, shopping centers, and freeways. Instead of a symptom of economic expansion, homebuilding became a source of growth. Both developers and home buyers basked in the glow. During the 1950s profits in south-ern California homebuilding averaged an impressive 21 percent annually, while the steady inflation of real estate prices turned a generation of homeowners into speculators. Buy a bungalow, sit back, and watch its value grow faster than any savings from hard labor.[6]

Dozens of "instant cities" appeared, places like Lakewood, south of Los Angeles, where housing for seventy-seven thousand sprouted overnight from former bean fields. Critics point at such subdivisions as development gone mad, but places like Lakewood were in fact the result of careful planning. Located near several aero-space plants and including a huge shopping mall (one of the first in the nation), Lakewood was intended to be a complete community. Rather than establish their own police, fire, and other public services, Lakewood residents contracted with Los Angeles County to provide them, enabling them to keep property taxes low. The "Lakewood Plan" served as the model for numerous other developments, essen-tially forcing the general county taxpayer to subsidize these middle-class enclaves. And like nearly all other southern California subdivisions, Lakewood's developers insisted on "restrictive covenants" that excluded all "non-Caucasians" from ever buying a home there. Racial exclusion was part of the plan.

Southern California, wrote journalist Carey McWilliams, became "the first modern, widely decentralized industrial city in America." In just twenty years the citrus groves of Orange County, southeast of Los Angeles, were transformed into one of the world's major metropolitan systems, with an industrial and service econ-omy that by the end of the twentieth century was producing goods and services

The intersection of San Vicente and Fairfax Avenues, Los Angeles, 1922 (top) and 1966 (bottom). The Spence Air Photo Archives, Department of Geography, University of California, Los Angeles.

worth sixty billion dollars annually, equivalent to the economy of Argentina. The vast area from Santa Barbara to the Mexican border, the coast to the mountains, was converted into the nation's largest metropolis. The California dream sprawled across the land.[7]

Families delighted in the opportunity to own their own detached house and yard on a cul-de-sac miles from the central city. But the shadows grew with the subdivisions. Abandoned inner cities, polluted air, and congested freeways alarmed onlookers. Phoenix, Las Vegas, Seattle, Salt Lake City, and Denver were a few of the cities that attempted to avoid L.A.'s sprawl (with local groups vowing "Not L.A."), but they produced more grumpy proclamations than compelling alternatives. Sprawl turned suburbanites into road warriors. A 1999 national study of "road rage" found that Sun Belt metro areas led the country in driving deaths associated with speeding at more than eighty miles per hour, tailgating, failing to yield, or yelling and gesturing lewdly to other drivers. An official of Riverside County in southern California spoke of the frustration of commuters: "Your family is 40 miles away and you're driving one or two hours to get home after putting in 8 to 12 hours on the job, and you're tired and hungry, and you're worried about getting your kids to soccer or keeping the appointment with your child's teacher, or you just want to spend some quality time with your family. But you're stuck in traffic." What good was a private fiefdom if the hours spent rolling slowly behind an eighteen-wheeler rivaled the hours spent enjoying the master suite or the granite countertops?[8]

It didn't necessarily have to end this way. Through some thoughtful planning, for instance, Portland, Oregon, bypassed some of the problems associated with sprawl. In 1973 leaders struck at the heart of the problem and drew a line around their city—within that boundary there would be high-density settlement, outside it, low-density development. Jobs, homes, and stores were forced into a compact area, catering to pedestrians and served by popular light transit, buses, and fewer cars. The downtown freeway was torn up, a park put in its place, and parking restricted to designated areas. Expansionists predicted economic calamity—disappearing jobs, decreased sales, and declining property values. But in fact all soared. "We have been careful stewards of the land and have fought to protect our natural resources against the urban sprawl that has plagued almost every other metropolitan area in this country," said one planner. A number of other western cities are attempting to emulate Portland's success.[9]

Suburban sprawl, congestion, and overdevelopment were not just western problems, of course. In the postwar period subdivisions ate up the countryside on the edges of every major American city. In accounting for this trend, most histories begin with Levittown, the famous Long Island subdivision that opened in 1947,

Advertisement for tract homes in Los Angeles, featuring "The Rancho" model, 1042.
Westchester/Playa Del Ray Historical Society.

but in fact Levittown was built on the model pioneered by southern California builders (including racial exclusion). Not only western construction techniques but western home styles went national after the war.

Although not everyone moved west, millions looked forward to living in a western house. The classic house of the postwar building boom was the ranch, a domestic style that originated in California between the wars, particularly in the work of San Diego architect Cliff May, who was inspired by nineteenth-century haciendas, with their rooms opening onto wide porches and interior courtyards. By the early 1940s the basic design began showing up in architects' plan books. "The style that had captured the attention of the American public is the Ranch-House," wrote the authors of a homebuilder's guide in 1942. The very name evoked myth. "When we think of the West," they mused, "we picture to ourselves ranches and wide open spaces where there is plenty of elbow room." The ranch house sought to capture this feeling with its horizontal orientation: low-slung roof, rooms flowing one into the other, picture windows and sliding glass doors inviting the residents outdoors to the patio (another western loan word) and barbecue grill. The ranch house, writes historian Thomas Hine, "conjured up powerful dreams of informal living, ideal weather, and movie-star glamour." At Levittown ranches commanded a 20 percent premium over Cape Cods, although both were based on the same compact floor plan.[10]

Americans bought the ranch and filled it with many things western. After the war Levi's became the everyday choice of young Americans from coast to coast. By the 1980s not only jeans but western shirts, belts, boots, bandanas, and even Stetson hats were fashionable. Western clothing, writes cultural critic Michael L. Johnson, was "portable Western atmosphere, identity, transWestite statement." Meanwhile country and western music went urban and national, and by the 1990s "hat acts"—performers such as Garth Brooks and Dwight Yoakam—sold more CDs and packed more stadiums than rock stars. A country ditty might play in the background of television commercials for pickup trucks and all-wheel-drive SUVs—heavy-duty contraptions that were basically trucks with lids (and because they were classified as trucks, they were exempt from federal fuel efficiency regulations). Rather than bales of hay and spools of barbed wire, middle-class Americans hauled their kids (the nongoat kind) in farm-grade equipment. Epic names taken from the West gave these poor transportation decisions a cultural free pass. Taking a cue from the movies, commercials for Durangos and Dakotas, Comanches and Cherokees frequently featured the vehicles driving through the splendors of Monument Valley on the Navajo reservation. Consumers bought nature, freedom, and self-sufficiency along with their gas-guzzlers.[11]

American drivers parked three-ton symbols of western power in their garages at the same time as American voters expressed a preference for western power brokers on their presidential ballots. Consider the ten presidents who served from the end of the war to the end of the twentieth century—six were westerners. Harry Truman was born and raised in Independence, Missouri, the jumping-off place for the Santa Fe Trail, and Dwight Eisenhower grew up in the former cattle town of Abilene, Kansas. Some might object that Missouri wasn't especially western by the time Truman reached the White House or that Kansas had little to do with Eisenhower's career. But being perceived as coming from the outskirts of national power helped both men, and the outsider status, real or perceptual, runs through every presidential candidacy since the rise of the United States as a superpower. Jimmy Carter, Bill Clinton, and Al Gore played up their southern roots, while Barack Obama, who grew up in Hawaii, launched his presidential campaign in Springfield, Illinois, to accentuate his Lincoln ties. A frontier rail-splitter as well as a freer of slaves, Abraham Lincoln underscored the multiple peripheries from which Obama emerged.

Texan Lyndon Johnson had been one of the key players in pushing the New Deal programs of economic development, and George H. W. Bush made his reputation as an oil entrepreneur in the postwar boomtown of Houston. Likewise Richard Nixon's political career paralleled the ascent of his native southern California, and Ronald Reagan was California politics incarnate. George W. Bush presided over the Texas Rangers baseball team before his stint as governor of the Lone Star State. Add to this list of the names of western also-rans: Henry Wallace of Iowa, Barry Goldwater and John McCain of Arizona, George McGovern of South Dakota, Ross Perot of Texas, and Robert Dole of Kansas. Of the twenty-six major party candidates who stood for election between 1948 and 2012, thirteen hailed from the West. Even Mitt Romney, the former governor of Massachusetts, rose to national prominence when he took over the management of the 2002 Winter Olympic Games in Salt Lake City after a bribery scandal. His leadership in that crisis as well as his Mormon faith connected him to the West. And for most candidates, a vague connection and the wearing of a cowboy hat at strategic campaign events was enough.

For much of the postwar period, the West and the need for candidates to appear as coming from outside the halls of power converged with conservative politics. Conservatives had been on the outside of national power since FDR's New Deal. But meanwhile, conservative "businessman's governments" held sway over state and local politics in the West. Their agendas were heavily laden with economic restructuring, big capital projects promoting irrigation, freeway construction, airports, urban renewal, convention centers, and sports and office complexes. The full force of taxpayer financing was put behind the continued growth of urban empires. Private property was sacred, and true to old western traditions, no one had the right to tell developers where or how they could build on their own property. In the mid-1960s this conservative tradition ran headlong into a rising clamor of social protest. Women, African Americans, Mexican Americans, and American Indians were demanding their civil rights. Students were marching in the streets and demanding an end to the war in Vietnam. More perplexing was the outcry over the "alienated" life of the suburbs—the gross materialism, the excessive competition, and the loss of community.

No one exploited these tensions better than Ronald Reagan—a former movie actor who starred in a number of Hollywood westerns and loved nothing better than riding horses and chopping wood on his ranch in the southern California foothills. Immigrating to Hollywood from the Midwest in 1937 at the age of twenty-six, he enjoyed modest success as a leading man but discovered his real talent when he became the leader of the Screen Actors Guild in the late 1940s. Reagan turned to the right during the era of communist hunting and blacklisting, and when his movie career began to sour he went to work as a spokesman for the General Electric Company and added a probusiness, anti–big government perspective to his anticommunism. He burst onto the national political scene in 1964 in a televised speech endorsing Republican right-winger Barry Goldwater's presidential campaign. Two years later he ran for governor in a campaign featuring promises to "cut and squeeze and trim" state government, attacks on ungrateful demonstrators, and endorsements of the California "way of life." Reagan's rhetorical skills and personal charm combined to win the election. As governor, however, his attacks on state programs were selective. Although he cut funds for mental health care, higher education, and social welfare ("a cancer eating at our vitals"), he lobbied vigorously for federal defense dollars and supported federally subsidized water for agribusiness.[12]

Rising property taxes precipitated a taxpayer revolt in California in 1978 that quickly swept the nation. Although Reagan had done little to cut taxes during his two terms as governor, he used that movement successfully to ride into the White House in 1981 after defeating the weary and beleaguered incumbent Jimmy Carter. He sponsored massive tax cuts while simultaneously pumping up military spending. The deficit spending produced an economic spurt but also the biggest deficits in the nation's history. During his two terms better than 50 percent of federal military dollars went to defense contractors in the West, many of them in California.

Reagan's popularity was due in large part to the economic good times that prevailed during most of his tenure. But his advisers were masters of the use of western imagery. An excellent horseman, Reagan had been accustomed to dressing in jodhpurs and riding boots but was told that it wouldn't wash, that he had to act the part of the cowboy. Costumed and frequently photographed in Stetson, Levi's, and Justins, Reagan inherited Teddy Roosevelt's mantle of "cowboy president," a distinction he wore with pride. In his most soaring rhetoric, he called on the frontier myth. "I have always believed that this land was placed here between two great oceans by some divine plan," he offered in the first debate of the 1980 presidential campaign. "It was placed here to be found by a special kind of people—people who had a special love of freedom and who had the courage to uproot themselves and leave hearth and homeland and come to what in the beginning was the most undeveloped wilderness possible. We came from 100 different corners of the earth. We spoke a multitude of tongues—landed on this eastern shore and then went out over the mountains and prairies and the deserts and the far Western mountains of the Pacific building cities and towns and farms and schools and churches."

Unlike Teddy Roosevelt, Reagan didn't compose odes to the frontier himself. His speech writers put the words before him on a teleprompter. Yet Reagan knew a good part when he saw it, and he played the son of the frontier with gusto, especially in the closing lines of his second inaugural address in 1984: "History is a

Ronald Reagan, 1976. National Archives.

ribbon, always unfurling; history is a journey. And as we continue on our journey we think of those who have traveled before us. . . . The men of the Alamo call out encouragement to each other; a settler pushes west and sings a song, and the song echoes out forever and fills the unknowing air. It is the American sound; it is hopeful, big-hearted, idealistic—daring, decent and fair. That's our heritage, that's our song. We sing it still. For all our problems, our differences, we are together as of old."[13]

"Together as of old." Reagan's speech writers attempted a final twist by ending with these words. They bent the frontier story of pushing west, taking land, and building communities into an inclusive process. In the past, they suggest, Americans came together through colonization. Missing were the people being colonized, a truth as inconvenient in 1984 as it was when Frederick Jackson Turner launched his frontier hypothesis in 1893. At the beginning of the twentieth century the assumption had been that Indians and their cultures would vanish, but during the post–World War II period they ranked as one of the fastest-growing ethnic groups in the country. The population of American Indians and Native Alaskans rose from about 350,000 in 1950 to nearly 3 million in 2010. What explains such growth? Individuals self-identify their race and ethnicity on the census questionnaire. "There's been a clear trend," says demographer Jeffrey Passel, "for increasing numbers of those people to answer the race question as American Indian." Not only has the number of Indians grown, but several million Americans who otherwise consider themselves "white" or "African American" claim descent from at least one Indian ancestor—as President Bill Clinton did when he remarked in 1997 that one of his grandmothers was a quarter Cherokee. The Cherokee Nation of Oklahoma receives several hundred queries each month concerning enrollment. "We have a lot of people who show up here who may be Indian," the tribal registrar reports, "but they can't prove it." (Neither, it turned out, could President Clinton.)[14]

Applicants must demonstrate lineal descent from persons on the 1907 Cherokee allotment rolls, something few can do. Some may be grifters angling for tribal benefits, but mostly the numbers reflect the long practice of Euro-Americans who adopted Indian costumes and identities to enhance their "American-ness." Wearing a headdress and enlisting in a fictional tribe—like the protesters at the Boston Tea Party—were ways Europeans in North America declared their independence from their homelands. By the 1990s the civil rights movements that emphasized the "power" and "pride" of racial and ethnic minorities further enhanced the cachet of Indian people. "It's the *Dances with Wolves* syndrome," says Rutgers University demographer Ross Baker. "It has sort of become neat to be an Indian." By claiming Indian ancestry, whites drew on an impressive history of survival and improvisation. Like Reagan's speech writers, they dipped into the frontier past to rewrite "our" past. Both the shared pioneer and Indian good old days could be equally fanciful, but in their revisions and mythmaking Americans reached to the margins to conceive of their place in their nation and its history.[15]

Actually living on the American margins was far more brutal than romantic. Native Americans fought daily to improve their lot in a country that repeatedly tried to turn them into mascots or make them disappear. During World War II, 25,000 Indians served in the armed services, including several hundred who acted

Marine "code talkers" Preston (left) and Frank Toledo transmit messages in the Pacific theater, 1943. Marine Corps Archives and Special Collections.

as "code talkers," using their native language as a means of secret communication over the air waves. Another 125,000 native people worked in war industry. Pointing to this patriotic record, at war's end the National Council of American Indians—a group including leaders from many of the nation's 554 tribes—argued that the time had come for the country to make a fair reckoning with Indians for stolen lands and broken treaties. Congress responded positively, creating the Indian Claims Commission and empowering it to investigate tribal claims and award monetary compensation. By the time the commission finished its work more than thirty years later, it had heard and considered nearly four hundred cases and awarded more than eight hundred million dollars in damages (much of which remained in the hands of lawyers). There was, however, an important catch to these proceedings. The settlement claims, declared Commissioner of Indian Affairs Dillon S. Myer (the federal official who had supervised Japanese internment), would be "the means of removing a major Indian objection" for the termination of official relations with the federal government. That would mean the end of all remaining treaty obligations. The limited sovereignty guaranteed to tribes by the Indian New Deal would be revoked. This program, which became known as Termination, was made official by act of Congress in 1953 and became the primary goal of Indian policy during the Eisenhower administration.

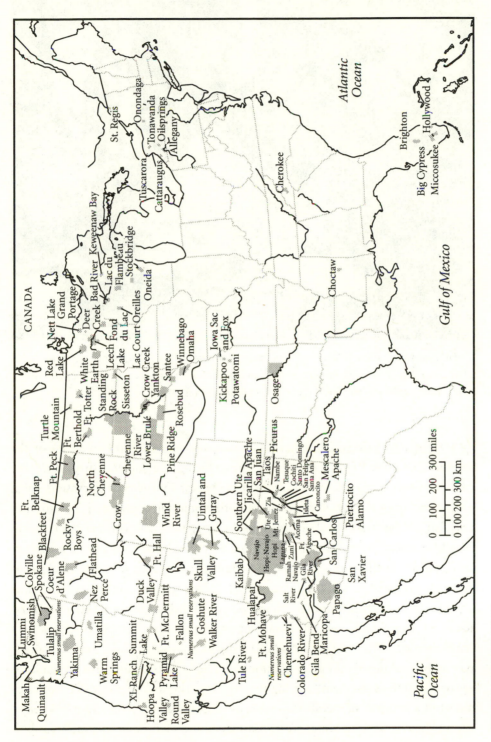

INDIAN RESERVATIONS

Tribal chairman George Gillette weeps as Secretary of Interior J. A. Krug purchases 155,000 acres of the Mandan-Arikara-Hidatsa reservation in North Dakota for use as a Missouri River reservoir. Photograph by William Chaplis, 1948. Associated Press / World Wide Photos.

Termination worked in an insidious manner. Consider the example of the Menominee tribe of northern Wisconsin. During the nineteenth century the Menominees ceded millions of acres in exchange for a protected reservation, tribal exemption from state interference and taxation, and the continuing right to hunt and fish in their traditional territory. In the early twentieth century the tribe resisted allotment, retaining collective ownership of 230,000 acres of prime timberland, on which they ran a lumber operation that provided jobs and modest incomes for reservation residents. After the war the tribe filed a suit with the Claims Commission charging federal mismanagement of their trust fund, and in the early 1950s the Menominees won an award of $7.6 million, to be split evenly among tribal members. Then came the kicker: Congress appropriated the funds but made payment conditional on the Menominees' agreement to termination. Tribal leaders opposed the settlement, arguing that maintaining sovereignty was more valuable, but a majority of members—most of whom lived off reservation—voted to accept the checks. The results were disastrous. The Menominee nation was abolished, replaced by a tribal corporation. Tribal lands became subject to state taxes, forcing the corporation to sell land and raise revenue. Lumber production fell and workers lost their jobs. Reservation schools and clinics closed. Hunting and fishing rights disappeared. Termination struck at the three foundations of reservation people—sovereignty, land, and culture.

Although termination obliterated only a few tribes, its threat hung over them all. "Fear of termination has poisoned every aspect of Indian affairs," a federal study of the early 1960s concluded. Fear and anger led to a broad movement of pan-Indian activism. In 1961 the National Council of American Indians passed a "Declaration of Indian Purpose," calling on the federal government to end termination and begin a new era of "Indian Self-Determination." The declaration was endorsed by President Kennedy, then in turn by Presidents Johnson and Nixon. By that time western state officials had lost their enthusiasm for termination, concluding that the program would result in higher burdens for state-funded welfare programs. Johnson declared an official end to the policy in 1968, and in 1975 Congress passed the Indian Self-Determination and Educational Assistance Act. This measure strengthened tribal governments by giving them the opportunity and the funds to administer their own programs to promote education, welfare, the administration of natural resources, and the improvement of reservation infrastructure.[16]

Termination, meanwhile, accelerated the migration of young Indians to the cities. Indian reservations in the postwar period were some of the most depressed places in America, with a well-established litany of problems from unemployment to alcoholism, a situation that termination did nothing to improve. Like other rural westerners, Indians increasingly looked to western urban enclaves for employment. During the second half of the century the proportion of the American Indian population living in cities rose from 13 to 60 percent. Large Indian communities developed in all major metropolitan areas of the West, the biggest in southern California, which in the 1990s was home to at least a hundred thousand Indians from more than a hundred different tribes. Many Indians maintained their tribal identity by frequent visits to extended family and friends on the reservation, but at least a third claimed no tribal affiliation. A new pan-Indian identity grew. As early as the 1920s Indians in Los Angeles were organizing "Powwow Societies" that sponsored informal get-togethers and ceremonial dancing in an eclectic mix of tribal styles. "I knew I lost a lot when I left the reservation," Joe Whitecloud, a leader of L.A.'s "powwow people," told an interviewer. Powwows, he believed, enabled urban Indians "to pass on our traditions to the kids coming up." Their exchange proved more important than the actual age of traditions, many of which were recent inventions.[17]

The best-known pan-Indian activist organization of the postwar period, the American Indian Movement (AIM), developed in the urban community of Minneapolis. In the words of Dennis Banks, a Chippewa who became the group's most articulate leader, AIM was "a coalition of Indian people willing to fight for Indians."

Russell Means and other occupiers of Wounded Knee. Photograph by Richard Erdoes, 1973. Beinecke Rare Book and Manuscript Library, Yale University.

The group patrolled streets to check police brutality, which captured the imaginations of young urban Indians (as well as considerable attention from the press) much as the Black Panthers inspired young urban blacks. In 1969 AIM organizers joined local Indian activists in occupying San Francisco Bay's Alcatraz Island. "We, the native Americans," the occupiers announced, "reclaim the land known as Alcatraz Island in the name of all American Indians by right of discovery." They employed the language of tribal sovereignty, but this protest was rooted in cities, not reservations. AIM with its "Red Power" slogan was thrilling, and Indian activism spread throughout the urban Indian communities of the West.[18]

An important recruit was Russell Means, an Oglala Sioux born on the Pine Ridge Reservation but raised in the San Francisco Bay area. Means proved himself a genius at confrontational politics. In one of his first AIM actions, Means led a group who for three days in 1972 occupied the offices of the Bureau of Indian Affairs in Washington, D.C. The next year he was instrumental in getting AIM involved in the internal politics of the Oglala reservation at Pine Ridge, South Dakota, the most impoverished place in the United States. Frustrated by a conservative tribal government, AIM activists and a group of reservation supporters armed themselves with rifles and shotguns and occupied a church at the site of the Wounded Knee massacre of 1890, vowing not to leave until the tribal chairman resigned. It was a brilliant bid for national media attention at the site many Americans had recently learned about from historian Dee Brown's best-selling *Bury My Heart at*

Wounded Knee (1970). Besieged by FBI agents and federal marshals armed with automatic weapons, tanks, and helicopters, many Americans saw the incident as a replay of the nineteenth-century Indian wars—although this time opinion polls suggested that the majority sympathized with the Indians, not the cavalry. It was a public relations disaster for the government. After seventy-one days the occupiers finally surrendered with federal promises of negotiations. But afterward the FBI hounded AIM to extinction, and many tribal Indians considered the occupation a political disaster.

More effective change came through the struggles of tribal governments to regain lost lands or treaty rights. One of the most publicized efforts was the struggle of the Taos Indians to regain control of Blue Lake in the Sangre de Cristo Mountains. Seized by the federal government and incorporated within a national forest reserve in 1906, the crystal lake not only fed the stream that flowed through Taos Pueblo and gave it life but was one of the people's most sacred places. After nearly a decade of petitions, protests, and bad publicity for the federal government, President Nixon finally returned forty-eight thousand acres, including Blue Lake, to the control of the Taos tribe in 1970. In the Pacific Northwest, meanwhile, Indians staged "fish-ins" to assert their right to fish despite state game laws. In 1974 they won a major victory when a federal judge vindicated their treaty rights to hunt and fish in "the usual and accustomed" places. Using the law, other tribes won an impressive series of Supreme Court cases that reaffirmed limited tribal sovereignty and exemption from state taxes. "What's happening is that tribal governments are becoming a permanent part of the fabric of American federalism," said John Echohawk, executive director of the Native American Rights Fund. "You have a federal government, state governments, and tribal governments—three sovereigns in one country."[19]

Some tribes used their sovereignty to stimulate economic development on the reservations. At Laguna Pueblo, for example, the tribe created Laguna Industries, a tax-exempt entity that gave it an advantage contracting work with the country's major defense industries. During the 1980s and 1990s tribal and Indian-owned businesses grew by a rate nearly five times the national average. Western Indian tribes control a vast resource base: 30 percent of the coal deposits west of the Mississippi, 50 to 60 percent of the country's uranium, 5 percent of the proven oil and gas reserves, fifteen million acres of timber and watershed, and extensive fish and wildlife habitat. The problem is getting development capital. "We just need to develop more," declared Laguna planner Nathan Tsosie. "People leave the reservation to get jobs. If there were jobs here, they'd stay."[20]

During the 1990s profits from Indian gaming seemed a likely source of development capital. The boom began when the Seminoles opened a high-stakes bingo parlor near Fort Lauderdale in 1978. Florida sued because gaming was illegal in

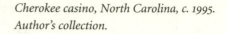
*Cherokee casino, North Carolina, c. 1995.
Author's collection.*

the state, but a federal appeals court ruled in favor of the Seminoles' sovereignty. Other tribes around the country were soon opening gaming operations. In 1988 Congress passed the Indian Gaming Regulatory Act, which required tribes and states to agree on ground rules. By the first decade of the twenty-first century about 40 percent of the nation's 566 tribes were doing a gross annual business of twenty billion dollars, about a quarter of which went to tribal governments. But prosperity depended on location. Ten reservation casinos accounted for more than 50 percent of the take—the Mashantucket Pequots and Mohegans of Connecticut, for example, operated two huge casinos and entertainment complexes within easy reach of Boston and New York. But the Pine Ridge Reservation of the Oglalas, hundreds of miles from a major urban center, remained the most impoverished community in the nation. Pine Ridge was all too typical. At the beginning of the new century, with the national economy booming, unemployment among adult Indians stood at 15 percent, three times the national average, and a majority of reservation households continued to live far below the poverty line. On the ten largest reservations, 15 to 20 percent of residents had no indoor plumbing, no adequate sewage disposal, and no electricity.

Problems and controversies endure, but that should not be allowed to obscure the remarkable resurgence of Indian nations since the end of Termination. Tribes founded forty reservation colleges that annually enroll more than thirty thousand students, and many instituted programs to revive the use of native languages. These developments were part of a cultural renaissance and a resurgence of pride among both reservation and urban Indians. "We alerted the entire world that the American Indians were still alive and resisting," proclaimed activist Russell Means. Declarations of protest joined the clangs of slot machines to answer Reagan's pioneer song. "We're still here, and we're still resisting. John Wayne did not kill us all."[21]

─────────

If frontiers happen when cultures collide and attempt to find ways of living together, the postwar period deserves prominence in the annals of American frontier history. Not only were Indians resurgent, but Mexican Americans and African Americans rattled the ethnic and racial order that had been established during the nineteenth century—the ethnic labor system, the segregation of minorities, and their exclusion from the political process. World War II marked a decisive moment when marginalized groups confronted entrenched powers and forced them to re-negotiate the terms of their frontier settlement—the laws, rights, and economics that determined the shape and rigidity of the seam that joined them.

Booming wartime industry in western cities, particularly on the Pacific coast, encouraged the migration of African Americans from the rural South and Mexican Americans from the rural Southwest. Men and women from both groups found jobs building ships, airplanes, and new housing. They might have lacked experience, but that hardly mattered. At a southern California aircraft plant, a black applicant was asked if he had any experience building B-17 bombers. "Man, I didn't know what a P-38 or a B-17 was, but I wanted to learn, I wanted an opportunity," he remembered. "I was honest and told him I didn't know if he were talking about a gun, a battleship, or a plane." Nevertheless, he got the job. Such opportunities, so rare in segregated industries before the wartime emergency, drew thousands. Historians lack precise numbers for the growth of the urban Mexican American population during the war (the Census Bureau didn't collect data on Hispanics until 1970), but the black population of Seattle, Portland, greater San Francisco, and southern California doubled or tripled.[22]

Opportunity pulled African Americans west as forcefully as the daily humiliation of life in the segregated South pushed them. "You just don't know what it was like," Theresa Waller told an interviewer about life in her native Houston. "They would try to make you feel like you weren't human." She dreamed of leaving for California, where she could "be somebody." In 1943 she and her husband heard of work in the shipyards and canneries of the Bay Area, and he went on ahead to get established. When he called for her to meet him in Oakland, she left Houston "on the Jim Crow car," then changed trains and boarded an integrated car in El Paso. It was filled to overflowing, and a young serviceman rose to offer his seat. "You can relax now," he said when he noticed her shock, "we're at the Mason-Dixon line." Earlier that summer in the Gulf coast town of Beaumont, only a few miles from Houston, there had been a brutal reminder of why it was difficult for African Americans to relax. Inflamed by false rumors that a white woman had been raped by a black man, a mob of several hundred whites invaded the black side of town, looting, burning, and leaving four hundred injured and three dead.[23]

The West may have existed on the freer side of the Mason-Dixon line, yet racial discrimination and segregation were realities there, too. The U.S. government interned Japanese Americans during the war, soldiers and sailors pummeled zoot-suiters in Los Angeles riots, and black and white soldiers and workers fought in numerous western cities. "Things were going to be different out here," remembered Ruth Gracon, a young black woman who migrated to Oakland from Arkansas. "But they weren't like we thought they'd be. They didn't have 'No Colored' signs or anything like that, but they had other ways of telling you they didn't want you." In fact, businesses near western army bases where black units trained posted signs warning, "We Cater to White Trade Only." Restaurants and hotels refused service to African Americans and Mexican Americans. Theater owners reserved balcony spaces for nonwhites, and municipal authorities banned them from parks and pools (except perhaps for a single weekday, usually just before draining and cleaning). The West was famous for its open spaces, not its open minds. A black serviceman stationed in Salina, Kansas, bitterly recalled being turned away with his buddies from a café by the owner—"You boys know we don't serve colored here"—a rejection made all the more painful when he noticed a group of German prisoners of war eating at the counter.[24]

Jobs were abundant, but assurances of equitable treatment were few. African Americans in the wartime shipbuilding industry, for example, were subjected to systematic discrimination—not by the companies but by the International Brotherhood of Boilermakers, the American Federation of Labor union that represented workers. The union segregated blacks (though apparently not Hispanics) in auxiliary locals without representation at the higher levels of the international. "We pay our dues but what do we get?" complained one black worker. "Nothing but discriminated against and segregated." After protests, the union instigated the firing of black activists. With support of the federal Fair Employment Practices Committee, African Americans went to court, and in 1944 the boilermakers were ordered to end their discriminatory practices.[25]

After the war, returning African American and Mexican American combat veterans worked to keep from sinking back to the bad old days. Edward Roybal of Los Angeles told how military service taught him to confront racism. "I was assigned to a barracks full of Texans," he recalled, and "one of them woke up every morning

Edward Roybal of Los Angeles, c. 1950. Roybal Institute for Applied Gerontology, California State University at Los Angeles.

and cursed Mexicans in general. Then one day he cursed me. So, I turned around and socked him." To his surprise Roybal found that his commanding officers approved. They placed unit cohesion above expressions of bigotry—"not because they loved us, but because they wanted things to run smoothly. It dawned on some of us for the first time that the Anglos were divided. And if we united, we could win concessions." Returning to Los Angeles after the war, Roybal ran for a seat on the city council and lost. After the election, he and others founded a group called the Community Service Organization that registered fifteen thousand new Mexican American voters. In a second try two years later, Roybal won the position and became the first Hispanic on the council since 1888. He vividly remembered the council president introducing him at his first meeting as the "Mexican-speaking councilman representing the Mexican people of Los Angeles." Calmly Roybal laid aside "the baloney speech" he had prepared and corrected the man: "I'm not a Mexican, I am a Mexican American. And I don't speak a word of Mexican, I speak Spanish."[26]

The mobilization of minority voters was one of the most crucial postwar struggles. At first electoral activity focused on the municipal and state levels. Then, in

1961, Henry B. González of San Antonio, who like Roybal had begun his political career on the city council, became the first Mexican American elected to Congress. In 1962 he was joined in the House of Representatives by Roybal, who was elected to represent East L.A. That same year Los Angeles voters in South Central also sent Augustus Hawkins, an African American born in Louisiana who had migrated to southern California to escape "the ruthlessness and ugliness of segregation." Most African Americans in Texas could not participate in electoral politics until the Supreme Court declared the poll tax unconstitutional in 1966. That year the voters of Houston elected Barbara Jordan to the state legislature, and six years later she became the first African American to represent Texas in Congress.[27]

The push for voting rights and electoral victories happened in concert with attacks on segregation. The case of Felix Longoria, a young Mexican American serviceman killed in action, provided an early symbol. After the war, Longoria's family arranged to have his body moved from an overseas cemetery to one near their home in Three Rivers, Texas, but they were outraged to discover that the local funeral home would not handle the remains of Mexican Americans. The American G.I. Forum, an activist group of Mexican American veterans, appealed to Senator Lyndon Johnson, who arranged to have the body reburied with full military honors at Arlington National Cemetery in Washington, D.C. Jim Crow in Texas proved unable to defend itself against American heroism, military and otherwise.

The most important arena for desegregation was public education. The League of United Latin American Citizens (LULAC) had gone to court to end school segregation in Texas during the 1930s, and although the league lost, their legal briefs aided later efforts. Immediately following the war LULAC offered legal assistance to a group of frustrated Mexican American parents in the southern California citrus town of Westminster, which confined Hispanic children to a separate and inferior "Mexican school." In a landmark decision in 1947, the California Supreme Court found for the parents, although they tried to limit its national impact by declining to make a broad constitutional ruling. The decision, editorialized *La Opinión*, the leading Spanish-language newspaper in southern California, was a blow to "those who believe in the anti-Semitic theories of Adolph Hitler." Families who had sent men to fight and die in an antiracist war abroad were not going to tolerate it at home. Westminster integrated its schools, and other southern California districts soon followed.[28]

The victory of the Mexican American parents in the Westminster case inspired others to think that the West was perhaps the place to challenge the national system of segregation. "The die is cast in the South, or in an old city like New York or Chicago," Phoenix activist William Mahoney declared in 1951. "But we here are present for the creation. We're making a society where the die isn't cast. It can be for good or ill." Such flights of fancy (institutional discrimination had been going on in the Southwest for seventy-five years) captured the optimism of the immediate postwar period. People began to believe that the United States might live up to its rhetoric of freedom and equality for all. In 1952 a group of black parents in Phoenix won a state court ruling against segregation of the public schools of Arizona. At the same time black parents in Topeka, Kansas—represented by a group of attorneys that included the descendants of Exoduster pioneers—filed a suit in federal court. Although they lost the first round, they quickly appealed. In *Brown v. Board of Education of Topeka* (1954), the Supreme Court ruled unanimously that separate schools were inherently unequal, establishing a precedent that applied directly to the South.[29]

Integrating schools proved difficult in western cities sharply divided by race and class. Blacks, whites, and Mexican Americans lived apart due to intractable patterns of residential segregation. Consider the case of postwar southern California, where the African American population doubled the general growth rate, and the Mexican American numbers increased fourfold. Restrictive covenants barred "non-Caucasians" from an estimated 95 percent of all the housing constructed immediately after the war. In 1947 James Shifflett, a leader of the African-American community in Los Angeles, moved his family to a bungalow in an all-white district of the city. "I remember a marshal ringing our doorbell and handing my parents a notice to move out," his daughter Lynne recalled. Shifflett's neighbors had filed suit to enforce the white-only covenant. The case went to the Supreme Court, which ruled that such restrictions were "unenforceable as law and contrary to public policy"—yet the practice continued informally for many years. The California legislature in 1963 passed the Fair Housing Act prohibiting racial discrimination in selling, renting, or leasing property, but the following year California voters, by a margin of two to one, passed a ballot proposition nullifying the act.[30]

African American and Mexican American newcomers crowded into existing ghettos and barrios, which expanded into fringe neighborhoods as whites fled to outlying suburbs. A study of racial segregation in Los Angeles County during the 1960s found that although blacks and Latinos made up 30 percent of the population, fifty-three of eighty-two suburban communities were 99 percent white, qualifying the county for the dubious distinction of being the most segregated in the nation. At about the same time, a California Department of Education survey found that 57 percent of the state's Hispanic students and 85 percent of the African Americans attended predominantly "minority schools." There was more school segregation by the 1970s, found historian Charles Wollenberg, than there had been in the 1940s.

As factory jobs moved to new industrial parks in the suburban fringe, unemployment rose among minorities trapped in the segregated urban core. Southern California was the most industrialized region in the country, yet, as historian Gerald Horne writes, "blacks were left without work, away from higher-wage union jobs." More than 40 percent of African American families in Los Angeles lived at or below the poverty level. On a hot, smoggy evening in 1965, a minor traffic accident and botched arrest in Watts, the most impoverished of L.A.'s black neighborhoods, ignited an uprising. For four successive days thirty thousand angry people fought with police and the National Guard, looting stores and burning hundreds of buildings within a forty-mile radius. Thirty-four people died in the Watts Riot. Over the next five years—one of the most tumultuous periods in American history—blacks rioted in major cities throughout the West and the nation.[31]

The uprisings were a national frontier phenomenon. Groups pushed to the geographic, economic, and social margins pushed back. The urban violence produced a militant political movement with a western mainspring—the Black Panthers of Oakland, California. Denouncing the strategy of the civil rights movement, they advocated political change by means of armed self-defense and violent revolution. The Panthers jumped from obscurity to infamy in 1967 when leaders Huey P. Newton and Bobby Seale, along with a small group of followers, entered the chamber of the California state assembly armed with automatic weapons and dressed in their standard-issue uniform of black leather jacket, black turtleneck, black slacks, and black berets. Membership skyrocketed after this successful media event, and soon Black Panther chapters blossomed in most western cities, with offshoots in the East. As with the American Indian Movement, a concerted assault by local

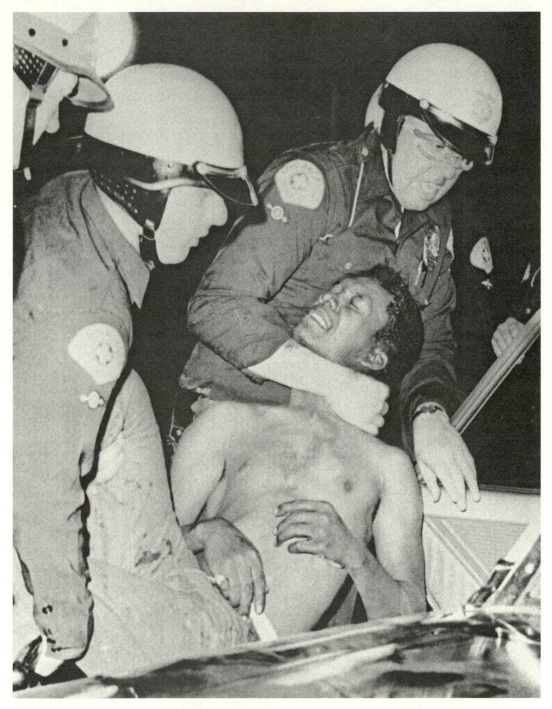

Los Angeles police make an arrest during the Watts Riot, 1965. Library of Congress.

Black Panther Party poster, Oakland, 1971. Author's collection.

police and the FBI eventually brought down the Panthers, but they contributed to their own demise by peddling in violence and drugs.

Although many Mexican Americans found employment in the booming industrial economy of the postwar West, thousands continued to labor in the fields as agricultural workers. Cesar Chavez joined the caravans of pickers following the ripening crops when his parents lost their small Arizona farm in the Great Depression. As a boy in the California desert town of Brawley, he and his brother were refused service at a diner, the waitress rejecting him with a laugh: "We don't sell to Mexicans." Incidents like these stung Chavez. The laugh, he remembered, "seemed to cut us out of the human race." A few years later he was arrested for refusing to move from the white-only section of a movie theater, his introduction to political activism. As a young married man in the barrio of San Jose, at the southern end of San Francisco Bay, Chavez went to work as an organizer for the Community Service Organization, a Hispanic rights group, then turned his attention to organizing farmworkers.[32]

The Mexican deportations of the 1930s and wartime mobilization had left growers short of farmworkers. Pressing the federal government for relief, they secured the passage of legislation permitting the entrance into the country of temporary Mexican farmworkers, or *braceros*. But the Bracero Program outlasted the war. In league with state and federal officials, growers used the program as a means of keeping a lid on wages and preventing strikes. As one grower candidly admitted, he preferred braceros to domestic workers because "they cannot protest [and] work at half the rate." The program also stimulated a huge increase in the number of migrants who came across the border illegally. By the early 1950s border patrols of the Immigration and Naturalization Service (INS) were apprehending more than half a million illegal border crossers each year, and estimates were that perhaps two or three times that many got across successfully. Chavez and other union organizers argued that the presence of a large pool of politically vulnerable noncitizens severely hampered efforts to unionize farmworkers. Mobilizing both Mexican Americans and liberals, Chavez's first success came when Congress eliminated the program in 1964.[33]

Chavez belonged to a vibrant group of young Mexican Americans seeking change in the United States, including Dolores Huerta, a labor organizer and civil rights activist from an old New Mexican family, and Luis Valdez, an actor and activist who created the theater troupe El Teatro Campesino. Chavez and his colleagues organized the United Farm Workers (UFW), the first independent farmworkers' organization since the 1930s, and in 1966 they launched their first strike ("Huelga!") against grape growers in California's Central Valley. To pressure growers, the UFW launched a nationwide table grape boycott. California governor Ronald Reagan was reduced to pleading with Americans to eat more grapes, while Richard Nixon ordered the Defense Department to buy tons more than they needed, sending planeloads off to the troops in Vietnam. But Chavez's charismatic and inspirational leadership proved stronger. In 1970 the growers relented and began signing union contracts. With the sympathetic support of Governor Jerry Brown, Reagan's successor, the UFW was able to raise the wages and living standards of its members. The historic achievement capped decades of struggle. But farmworkers lost ground in the conservative 1980s, and by the time Chavez died in 1993, the UFW was in disarray.

Chavez and the grape boycott raised national awareness of Mexican Americans in the Southwest, and activists and radicals generated more notice and notoriety. In New Mexico a wildcard leader named Reies Tijerina organized an *alianza* of twenty thousand Hispanics demanding an investigation of the wholesale theft of land that had taken place after the Mexican War. Frustrated at the inaction of authorities, he and his followers occupied federal lands at gunpoint in 1966, declaring an independent Hispanic nation. A confrontation with authorities ended in gunfire that wounded two officers, and Tijerina went to prison for two years. In south Texas farmworker organizing spilled into electoral politics and a new political group, El Partido Raza Unida, scored a series of impressive victories in local elections. Among young people throughout the urban Southwest there was a surge of enthusiasm for *mexicanismo*. Amid cries of "Viva la Raza!" activists celebrated the memory of pachucos and zoot-suiters. Activists began referring to themselves

Join the NON-VIOLENT STRIKE for JUSTICE

Walter Reuther (UAW) joins Cesar Chavez and the United Farm Workers in the
Delano Grape Strike picket line on December 16, 1965.

5TH YEAR OF STRIKE!
The Grape Strike is now in its fifth year. California and Arizona farm workers continue their strike against table grape growers who refuse to recognize their union and their right to live and work with dignity. The farm workers ask only the same rights and benefits which most American workers have enjoyed for decades.

FARM WORKERS NEED YOUR HELP
This is the third year of the table grape boycott and the struggle to bring table grape growers to the bargaining table. Most growers still refuse to recognize the farm workers' union and their workers' right to collective bargaining. Farm workers need your support of the grape boycott to bring these growers to the bargaining table. Only when growers and workers sit down together and sign a fair union contract can this dispute be ended. Only when farm workers enjoy the benefits and protections of the contract can they begin to free their lives of social and economic bondage.

DON'T BUY NON-UNION GRAPES

A few growers have recently signed the first table grape contracts with the United Farm Workers. These contracts provide some of the best wages and working conditions that field workers have ever enjoyed. They also afford protection from pesticides to workers and consumers alike.

Buy grapes only if you are sure they came out of a box with this emblem on it.

A BELL FOR DELANO — The "Delano Freedom Bell" is now traveling the country in a van provided by UAW to promote the grape boycott. The 300 pound bell, cast by the famous Whitechapel Bell Foundry of London, England, is a gift from friends of the Farm Workers. On April 17, 1970, Cesar Chavez asked mayor John Lindsay and Dean Francis Sayre to silence the bell with chains as a symbol of farm workers' enslavement to poverty and paternalism. The chains will be broken from the bell only when the grape workers of California and Arizona are free to bargain collectively for their wages and working conditions.

If you would like to help the cause or would like more information, contact your local boycott committee or people representing organized labor, or write to: United Farm Workers Organizing Committee AFL-CIO, P. O. Box 130, Delano, California 93215.

1

United Farm Workers Union leaflet, c. 1970. Beinecke Rare Book and Manuscript Library, Yale University.

as "Chicanos," embracing with pride a slang term that Mexican Americans had used for decades to denigrate Mexican newcomers. Being from Mexico, whether recently arrived or descended from the Aztecs, meant that you were more than American or Mexican—"Somos Uno Porque America Es Una" (We are one because America is one), "Somos un Pueblo sin Fronteras" (We are one people without borders).[34]

————

In 1965 Congress reformed the immigration laws, abolishing the system of quotas based on national origins enacted in 1924. Over the next three decades a massive new wave of immigration brought more than seven million Latino and five million Asian newcomers to the country. Most settled near the immigration gateways—Los Angeles, San Francisco, and Houston in the West, along with New York City and Chicago. LAX—L.A.'s international airport—became the new Ellis Island. From 1970 to 2010 the Hispanic or Latino population of the nation rose from nine million to more than fifty million and the Asian American population from less than a million to more than fourteen million, the majority of them in the West. Demographers project that western metro areas of the twenty-first century will attract another thirty million Latinos and seven million Asians.

The number of migrants entering the United States through unofficial gateways also increased enormously. During the last quarter of the twentieth century about half of the illegal migrants in the postwar period crossed into the country from Mexico. In the words of one commentator, they had "an economic gun to their backs"—the turmoil of the Mexican economy. For many other Latinos, the gun was all too real. Armed conflict in Central America created thousands of refugee Guatemalans, Salvadorans, and Nicaraguans. Tragedies proliferated at the border, where the desperate met a host of advantage-takers: corrupt Mexican national police, the *federales*, shaking down refugees; greedy middlemen, known as coyotes, extorting high fees for guiding illegals across; violent banditos lying in wait to rob vulnerable individuals of their possessions; and unknown hundreds, perhaps thousands, dying by drowning or exposure. On one California freeway near the Mexican border, traffic signs featured the silhouette of a fleeing family as a warning to drivers to watch out for illegals darting across traffic lanes. Federal authorities in the late 1990s estimated that more than 700,000 undocumented individuals crossed from Mexico to the United States each year. Ten years later, as the Mexican economy stabilized, that number had dropped to 150,000 per year.

But Latinos kept coming to work in textile factories and fruit orchards, suburban gardens and households. The rock-bottom wages employers paid for such work depressed the incomes of poor American citizens and made Latino migrants a convenient target for nativist anxiety and anger. In 1994 California voters approved

Proposition 187, an initiative that would have denied undocumented aliens or their children access to public services like education and health care, but a federal judge threw out the law as unconstitutional. Four years later California voters approved another ballot initiative that curtailed bilingual education programs. Other Americans argued for draconian measures at the border—electrified fences, minefields, or the creation of a no-man's-land between the United States and Mexico. Border militarization became a way to imagine a quick and clear solution to a problematic tangle of economic, racial, and social questions.

Ground zero for the new immigration was southern California, which became, in the words of historians Leonard and Dale Pitt, "the most ethnically diverse metropolitan area in the world." At the turn of the century the city of Los Angeles was home to immigrants from 140 countries, including the largest communities of Mexicans, Salvadorans, Guatemalans, Koreans, and Filipinos outside their homelands, as well as the country's largest concentrations of Japanese, Cambodians, and Iranians. In broad categories, the 2010 census found that the county was 48 percent Latino, 14 percent Asian American, 9 percent African American, and only 28 percent Anglo (defined as "non-Hispanic white").[35] "Our modern metropolis is returning to the enduring Puebla de Los Angeles of years past," declared California state senator Al Torres, who in 1998 became chairman of the state Democratic Party. Essayist Richard Rodriguez, reminding readers that Mexicans were a mestizo people, offered the observation that "Los Angeles has become the largest Indian city in the United States."[36]

In a great arc from the Gulf coast to the Pacific, the Southwest was in the process of turning "majority minority": New Mexico in 1996, California in 2000, Texas in 2005, and Arizona in 2010. According to Thomas Chan, an international lawyer from Hong Kong living in Los Angeles, the region was "moving rapidly from being a 'melting pot' of Europeans to a 'world city' with links to virtually every inhabitable part of the globe." The rise of foodie culture and fusion cuisine reflected this trend. Tortillas and ceviché joined egg rolls and fish paste on western plates and cooktops. The urban West would be unescapably and impressively "multi" in the

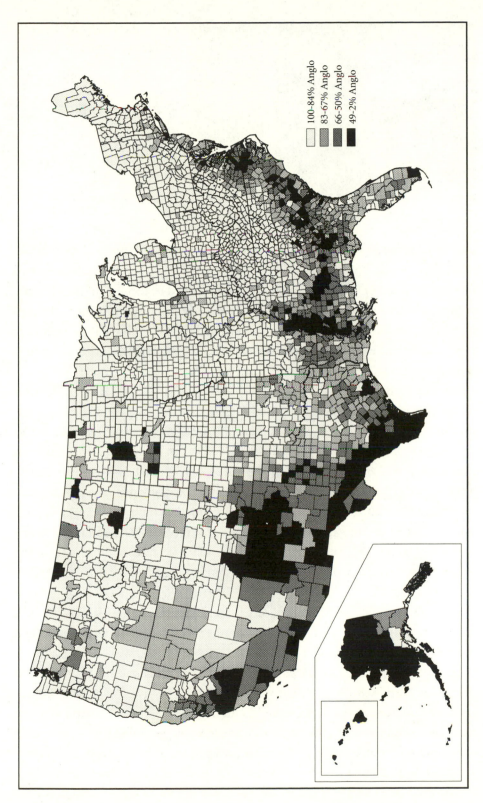

EMERGING MINORITY MAJORITIES

100-84% Anglo
83-67% Anglo
66-50% Anglo
49-2% Anglo

"Can we all get along?" Rodney King speaks to Los Angeles during the riots in 1992. Author's collection.

twenty-first century, achieving an epic mishmash of people and cultures. But adjustment to the new reality was slow. The West had always been multicultural, with uneven levels of contentment. Anglos made up a third of the Los Angeles County population but were 70 percent of the registered voters and 80 percent of the jury pool. They also controlled 90 percent of the fixed wealth. Although the economic gap between whites and minorities was narrowing nationally, in the Southwest it was growing.[37]

That contradiction broke open in the Los Angeles riots of 1992, demonstrating the intensity of popular anger that grew in the shadows of "world city" inequality. For decades the African American and Mexican American communities had complained of systematic brutality by the Los Angeles Police Department. When news outlets played an amateur videotape of four white officers brutally beating a black motorist named Rodney King, their guilt seemed obvious. The officers were indicted, but when a white suburban jury acquitted them of all but one charge, the city exploded. For three days rioters swept through black and Latino neighborhoods, looting and burning. At a news conference held at the height of the violence, Rodney King pleaded for calm. "People, I just want to say, can we all get along?" he said. "I mean, we're all stuck here for a while. Let's try to work it out." Before the National Guard restored order, at least fifty-one people died and the equivalent of several square miles was torched. More than twelve thousand people were arrested. The 1992 riots echoed the Watts uprising of 1965, but there were also differences. Not only was the later event deadlier and more destructive, but it was more multicultural. Forty-one percent of those arrested were African American, but 45 percent were Hispanic, and 12 percent were Anglo. And much of the violence was directed at the shops of Korean Americans, many of whom owned businesses in minority communities. Like its food and its population statistics, L.A.'s urban cataclysms had diversified.

The riots marked a turning point in the history of migration to California. Over the half-century from 1940 to 1990, the state's population expanded by

332 percent. But beginning in the 1990s California began losing more domestic migrants than it gained. Although the loss was counterbalanced by the flood of foreign migrants as well as natural increase—the state's population grew by 29 percent from 1990 to 2015—during that twenty-five-year period an estimated 3.4 million Californians left the state. Three-quarters were poor or low-wage individuals, leaving because they couldn't find work or pay the high cost of housing. There was a huge migration from Los Angeles east to the suburbs of Riverside and San Bernardino Counties. "People go on the freeway and drive until they can find a house they can afford," said Randall Lewis, head of a development company in San Bernardino. But thousands left the state for other locations in the West, for Phoenix, Las Vegas, or the metro complexes of Texas, Colorado, or Washington. California became the largest "sender" state in the nation, with a flow of out-migration greater than the eastern states of New York, Illinois, or Michigan. Often these transplants sparked resentment in their destination communities. A southern Californian who relocated to Idaho warned of the dangers. "I've seen it all happen on the coast," he declared, and "now it's happening here—trout streams dug up for freeways, the smog, the elk herd declining. It's the same old story of unplanned growth." Sentiments were capsulated in a Boise bumper sticker: "Don't Californicate Idaho!"[38]

FURTHER READING

Carl Abbott, *The Metropolitan Frontier: Cities in the Modern American West* (1993)

Peter A. Coates, *The Trans-Alaska Pipeline Controversy: Technology, Conservation, and the Frontier* (1991)

Lawrence Culver, *The Frontier of Leisure: Southern California and the Shaping of Modern America* (2010)

Mike Davis, *City of Quartz: Excavating the Future in Los Angeles* (1990)

Darren Dochuk, *From Bible Belt to Sunbelt: Plain-Folk Religion, Grassroots Politics, and the Rise of Evangelical Conservatism* (2010)

David G. Gutiérrez, *Walls and Mirrors: Mexican Americans, Mexican Immigrants, and the Politics of Ethnicity* (1995)

Gerald Horne, *Fire This Time: The Watts Uprising and the 1960s* (1995)

Kenneth T. Jackson, *Crabgrass Frontier: The Suburbanization of the United States* (1985)

Gretchen Lemke-Santangelo, *Abiding Courage: African American Migrant Women and the East Bay Community* (1996)

Patricia Nelson Limerick, *The Legacy of Conquest: The Unbroken Past of the American West* (1987)

Michelle M. Nickerson, *Mothers of Conservatism: Women and the Postwar Right* (2012)

Donald Worster, *Rivers of Empire: Water, Aridity, and the Growth of the American West* (1985)

12

"It Ain't Where You're From, It's Where You're At"

The vigilantes paid a visit to the Geffen spread to impart a lesson about the open range. The rambling manse blocked access to a key western resource: the southern California beach. In 1983 music and movie mogul David Geffen agreed to allow a "vertical easement" along his property to open a public access point to Malibu's coastline, trading the hypothetical walkway for state permits to install a swimming pool and other amenities on his property. Then he reconsidered, sued the California Coastal Commission to keep beachgoers from tramping past his place, and watched as the story went viral. Garry Trudeau, the cartoonist behind "Doonesbury," poked fun at "Lord Geffen" in a series of comic strips. Here was one of Hollywood's most famous liberals behaving like a spoiled monarch. Who did he think he was, stifling the American desire to bask in the sun? They might not have perfect cheekbones like movie star Charlize Theron or gaudy stock portfolios like Eli Broad, founder of two Fortune 500 companies and another Malibu homeowner, but ordinary people had just as much right to sink their toes in the wet sand as the rich and famous.[1]

Armed with maps and tape measures, the Los Angeles Urban Rangers rode out to Malibu to enforce their rights. A performance art collective founded in 2004, the rangers sponsored "safaris" to downtown's Bonaventure Hotel and the concrete-lined L.A. River, outings to Hollywood Boulevard, and reconnaissance missions to Malibu's public beaches. The rangers dressed in Stetsons and starched khaki shirts and pants and wore badges with a palm tree framed by an emblem of a looping freeway interchange. The costumes announced intent: they were public servants on hand to guide Angelenos through bewildering urban habitats. The rangers were dramatists—no state bureaucracy sanctioned their professional put-

428

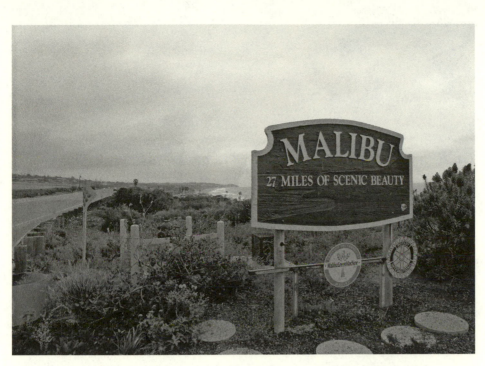

Malibu, California. Photograph by Pierre Andre LeClerq, 2012. Wikimedia Commons.

on—but their staged officialness underscored the revelatory potential of their art. The rangers instructed their audiences to see power as a show and perceive how performances of authority shaped their experiences of urban nature.[2]

Geffen and his neighbors made the rangers' point beautifully. For years homeowners in Malibu had been pretending that they owned the beach. California law declared the state's beaches public below the "median high tide line." But Malibu property owners used various props and techniques to discourage outsiders from reaching this space. They installed fences, built false-front garages to block street parking, posted official-looking "private beach" signs, and put out orange traffic cones each morning to close off public streets. The rangers countered these tactics with information and unbreakable facades of "scout-tastic chipperness." When homeowners cursed them out as "scumbags" and wrote emails asking for their addresses so that they could demonstrate the horrors of public access by coming over to "use your yard as a toilet and your porch as a garbage can," the rangers responded with humor and calm, quoting the law while encouraging their safari participants to continue to engage in "typical beach activities" like doing yoga, building sand castles, and reading trashy novels.[3]

The rangers, however, were careful not to push their amiability too far. They stopped leading tours to Malibu in 2010 and turned to high tech to continue the fight. In 2013 Jenny Price, a founding member of the Rangers, launched a Kickstarter campaign to finance a smartphone app that not only equipped would-be

The Los Angeles Urban Rangers using a narrow public-access pathway to Malibu beach. Photo-graph by Nicholas Brown, 2007. Creative Commons.

beachcombers with Malibu maps and tips for determining the median high tide line but encouraged them to share photos documenting blocked access points and misleading signs. The app was free for downloading. Self-anointed rangers could use their handhelds to exact justice at their leisure.

The Malibu beach conflict and the Los Angeles Urban Rangers' creative response to it demonstrated how much and how little had changed in the American West. People still fought over turf. Those with wealth and privilege fenced squatters out, turning public land into private real estate. Long-time residents rallied to protect their homes against invading hordes. Villainy and victimhood depended on where—and when—you stood. California Indians and Spanish-speaking Californios, whose domestic tranquillity had also been trampled by Americans touting a self-proclaimed right to go wherever they pleased, might sympathize with Geffen. Shift the perspective, and the battle resembled the struggles of the West's small producers against corporate goliaths that denied them access to water, grass, and timber. This particular fight over a patch of Malibu sand—with its smartphone apps and postmodern wryness—might seem very much a product of the twenty-first century. But the issues harkened back to the moment when Columbus breached the median high-tide line and engaged in the typical beach activities of a conqueror—planting crosses, unfurling flags, and reading proclamations—before the exasperated Taínos.

Still, this beach encounter was unique enough. Nothing proclaimed that times had changed more than the art collective's choice of roles. The Rangers and Regulators who prowled the eighteenth-century Carolinas and nineteenth-century Texas were not especially helpful. They were violent enforcers, the last people you would stop and ask for directions. The National Park Service played on that tradition when it dressed its field employees in boots and Stetsons. The costumes communicated power backed by violence. Not until female rangers put on these outfits in the 1920s did the ranger image move in a friendlier direction. Women smoothed the edges off the vigilante antecedents. They represented the values—knowledge, competence, hospitality—that came to define the modern ranger. The four women who founded the Urban Rangers imbued their characters with bold geniality borrowed from those pioneers. For their performance art, they had to act as if rangers had always been courteous. To fully grasp the political nuances of their outings, beachgoers needed not only a Malibu beach app, directing people to territory that swelled and receded with the tide. They needed a frontier history app—a book, perhaps—that could explain how bloody avengers became plucky service-industry professionals.

The West and its people connected with longer regional and frontier histories, even as they displayed the hallmarks of globalized existence. The proliferation of data and the speed of its transmission fractured the homogeneity of the Sun Belt suburbs. The West became the dominant region in the United States only to disappear into the trends it unleashed. The centripetal forces that unified the postwar period—Cold War politics, lavish government spending, manufacturing-based corporate capitalism, and broadcast entertainment and news—spun in reverse, flinging jobs, voting blocks, and cultural touchstones into unfamiliar orbits. The result was a society and a culture that lost the pretense of being a single society and a single culture. Multiplicity, the defining feature of American frontiers all along, staged a comeback.

Global networks of information connected human beings while reinforcing their isolation. Americans could still find the West, if they set their search preferences for regional content. But they could sift the same information through alternate filters. The Malibu beach conflict, for instance, might reach networked friends and followers as a celebrity Tweet, a real estate post, or a "Doonesbury" link. The same facts—the 1964 median-high tide law, Geffen's 1983 agreement, the 2013 beach access app—streamed through multiple channels. Networks spread the data to millions and splintered it into stories about nature, greed, privacy, bikinied actresses, and cheeky art collectives. Visitors, followers, friends, and internet surfers could locate the story in Los Angeles, California, or the West, or they could ignore the geographic coordinates altogether.

Regions, cities, houses, and beaches—actual places—existed in tandem with virtual locations. A person could buy the Malibu beach app and participate in the free-range fight without ever having to visit the ocean. At least since the ancient Greeks, the West had been an idea as well as a place. The internet revolution rendered the distinction moot. People once boarded ships and hopped trains to find the West in their heads (and were often let down by the reality they found). In the second decade of the twenty-first century, they repurposed actual places to decorate and enliven virtual creations like websites, feature films, television programs, and video clips. Regions, cities, neighborhoods, and stretches of sand might infiltrate Facebook posts or Twitter feeds without consumers noticing or even caring that they were corporeal things with complicated histories.

———

Quincy is an edgy place, not cool or hip like Berkeley or Brooklyn, just out there like Fargo. One resident described the central Washington town as "a farming community in the middle of a desert." In 2007 the Microsoft Corporation purchased seventy-five acres of bean fields and erected a giant shed to house hundreds of massive computers, a data center servicing various internet activities, including the Bing search engine and Hotmail. To run them, Microsoft tapped into the resources of the Grant County Public Utility District, owner and operator of two hydroelectric dams on the Columbia River. Soon other tech giants like Dell, Yahoo!, and Intuit built data centers of their own nearby. The energy needs of such high-tech server farms were enormous. In 2012 the cluster used nearly 42 million watts, four and a half times the usage of all the homes and businesses in Quincy. These numbers represent only a trickle of what's to come. The state of Washington has issued permits for the data centers in Quincy to use up to 337 megawatts, the equivalent of the output of a small nuclear power plant.[4]

Microsoft and the other tech firms touted their use of hydroelectric "green power." If users moved their applications and data to "the cloud," the company argued, their "carbon footprint" would be greatly reduced. But not all the juice to power the server farms came from the Columbia. The firms also installed dozens of mammoth diesel generators for backup power, and during a single year Microsoft ran its diesels an astonishing 3,615 hours, spewing deadly exhaust over the town, including a neighboring elementary school. The constant roar of the generators confounded officials of the power district. They were providing electricity at half the national rate in exchange for the software giant agreeing to purchase a specified amount of power. But instead of using all of its allocation of "green power," Microsoft regularly switched on the generators. Chagrined, the power district levied a substantial fine. Microsoft put the blame on the construction of

Quincy, Washington. Photograph by Ray Bouknight, 2013. Creative Commons.

new facilities, although an investigation revealed that the company was running generators at its other data centers as well. Whatever the rationale, the episode demonstrated the willingness of a sleek, modern, environmentally conscious corporation to gorge on energy, spew pollutants like a smokestack dinosaur, and act with an arrogant public-be-damned attitude. Microsoft bullied the power district into rescinding the fines, but the kerfuffle brought attention to the environmental costs of data storage. When Quincy's third-graders sucked in diesel fumes at recess, their inhalations confirmed the materiality of the cloud.

The Quincy server farms recall the many political struggles over industrialization, pollution, and idealized landscapes that stretch back at least as far as the gold rush. In a region defined by extractive industries that produced booms and busts, determining who or what would suffer during the fat times and who would clean up when the profits thinned was old sport. The Quincy example, however, supplied a new twist. Americans had a long tradition of expressing concern when industry blackened skies, fouled waters, and denuded hillsides. While air pollutants and waste figured in the case of Quincy as well, it wasn't the destruction of a local habitat that prompted the *New York Times* to send a reporter to the middle of

Washington. The story attracted the media because the diesel engines and corporate bullying soiled the image of the cloud. The internet itself was the ideal landscape under attack.

The information revolution prompted dreams of a New West. Instead of a cowboy, a miner, or a lumberjack, the new westerner was a telecommuter. The internet freed professionals from their urban workplaces. Instead of crawling through Los Angeles traffic to their cubicles, creative types could move to a cabin—or more likely a McMansion—in the Interior West and work from home. Dressed in pajamas, they could enjoy a spectacular view and sip a latté, the drink of choice in the New West, before journeying a few steps to the home office. Equipped with a laptop and broadband, workers could choose to live in places they only used to visit on vacation. But the telecommuter fantasy placed enormous pressure on western environments. While they spent many hours plugged into virtual worlds, the new migrants still needed to be hydrated and fed, heated and cooled. They needed services to carry away their waste and transport them to occasional flesh-and-blood conferences and meetings. These transplants brought lofty environmental expectations with their giant resource footprints.

───────

Americans cherished glorious western vistas and struggled to balance their desires to protect, enjoy, and exploit them. In the postwar period Congress created twenty-one new national parks, increasing the oversight of the National Park Service to eighty million acres, nine-tenths of it in the trans-Mississippi West and Alaska. The breathtaking scenery of the parks drew armies of tourists. The number of visits to national parks rose dramatically, from 30 million annually in 1941 to a record 292.8 million by 2014. During that period the nation's population increased by 150 percent, but the recreational use of federal lands increased ninefold. Federal parks earned millions of friends and followers, but popularity threatened to undercut the qualities that thrilled so many. The majesty of Yosemite Valley and the Grand Canyon was corroded by traffic jams and gift shops. The danger of Americans' loving the parks to death confronted National Park Service leaders with a fundamental dilemma they are still trying to resolve.

Historian Samuel P. Hayes argues that the enormous popularity of outdoor recreation in the postwar period was part of a broad change in values, from an obsession with production to a preoccupation with the "quality of life." New environmental values, he writes, "were an integral part of the continuous search for a better standard of living," which also explains the movement of millions to the suburbs. The wilderness acted as both an extension of and an antidote to the suburbanization of America. Expanses of "wild" nature provided Americans with geographic

Tourists at Old Faithful, Yellowstone National Park. Photograph by Acroterion, 2010. Creative Commons.

frontiers where they could regenerate. "Many of the attributes most distinctive of America and Americans" resulted from "the impress of the wilderness and the life that accompanied it," wrote naturalist Aldo Leopold in his *Sand County Almanac* (1949), a text that helped inspire the environmental movement. Robert O. Marshall, along with Leopold a founder of the Wilderness Society, wrote that only by setting aside wilderness areas could "the emotional values of the frontier be preserved." In the early 1960s the Wilderness Society and the Sierra Club lobbied Congress for legislation that would protect large areas of undeveloped country in the West. In 1964 Congress passed the Wilderness Act, initially setting aside 9 million acres of undeveloped federal land and gradually raising the allocation. By the early twenty-first century wilderness acreage stood at 110 million. The American, wrote novelist Wallace Stegner, "is a civilized man who has renewed himself in the wild." By preserving wilderness, "the hope and excitement can be passed on to newer Americans, Americans who never saw any phase of the frontier."[5]

The problem with Stegner's argument is that *frontier* can mean different things to different Americans. It can evoke the fantasy of lone men wrestling bears or shooting rapids in birchbarks. What was "characteristically American" about our civilization, insisted Senator Ernest Gruening of Alaska, was that it had been shaped "in a battle with nature." Alternately, it could stand for the process of development that had produced the powerful American economy, providing the standard of living that allowed Americans to live in suburban surroundings and spend their vacations at the Grand Canyon or Yellowstone. Indeed, most postwar encounters with nature involved families in automobiles trying to find a parking space. National parks became creatures of auto tourism. The windshield, not the eternal masculine struggle for supremacy, framed the wilderness experience.[6]

To escape the crowds and re-create the frontier dream of a lethal showdown with nature, some Americans upped the ante of their outdoor activities. In addition to beholding mountains, outdoor enthusiasts shimmied up rock faces and skied down hillsides. They risked injury or death to test the outer limits. Through acts of derring-do, outdoor athletes redefined the wilderness and the frontier into settings of extreme exertion. They adrenalized nature to escape the encroachments of tourism—roads, hotels, and amenities—that threatened to break the wilderness mood and the American frontier tradition.

For more than a century Americans had camped, hiked, climbed, skied, canoed, and hunted in remote places from Maine to Minnesota. In the West, outdoor enthusiasts in cities like Denver and San Francisco formed groups to teach and promote hiking, skiing, and mountain climbing. These early recreation clubs included both men and women. They undertook vigorous exercise in a social setting more like a picnic or ice-cream social than a hypermasculine throwdown with bristling nature. These coed voluntary associations and their middle-class values receded

Billy Kidd statue, Steamboat Springs, Colorado. Author's collection.

in importance after the war, when western outdoor recreation veered toward the extremes of corporatization and countercultural rebellion.

When Dwight D. Eisenhower signed the Federal Aid Highway Act in 1956, creating the interstate highway system, he redirected Colorado's future toward the mountainous backcountry. Cars streamed up I-70 from Denver and through the Eisenhower Tunnel to reach slopes heavy with several feet of powdery snow and traced by miles of tasty runs. Previously known for its ranching and mining, Colorado became synonymous with beautiful scenery and outdoor fun. Postwar ski towns like Winter Park, Vail, and Aspen created a Rocky Mountain high that many tourists chased when they visited and then purchased first or second homes in the Interior West.

With his cowboy hat, corporate ties, and skiing championships, William Winston "Billy" Kidd embodied the rise of the western tourist industry. Born in Vermont, Kidd learned to ski and take care of tourists in the resort town of Stowe, where his parents ran a motel. A gifted athlete, he rose through the ranks of American youth skiing. He competed in the 1964 Winter Olympics, winning a silver medal in the slalom. He skied on the World Cup Circuit until 1970, when he retired from amateur competition, moved to Steamboat Springs, Colorado, and began a forty-four-year association with the Steamboat ski corporation. Like a modern National Park Service ranger, Kidd took to wearing a Stetson to signal his western amiability. He had lucked into a name that recalled one of the West's most famous men—William "Billy the Kid" Bonney—but he and his corporate sponsors invented a persona for him and the ski town that synchronized skiing, resort development, and the American West. Billy Kidd made selling lift tickets and condo timeshares seem like stereotypical western behaviors. His hat turned an athletic pursuit, imported from the European Alps, into a home industry.

Steamboat Springs played up its cowboy chic. Yet the buckaroo turn was not the only move available to developers. Aspen exploited its mining town past, refurbishing its West End gingerbread Victorian mansions to house movie stars and its opera house to host comedy festivals. Vail borrowed its style from Bavaria, fashioning a village and a brand more lederhosen than chaps. Through these promotional performances, the Rocky Mountains came to service multiple consumer fantasies. Ski tourists could have their rib-eyes along with their schnitzels. They could imbibe the local histories of their resort destinations through walking tours or antique cocktails served in genuine western saloons complete with spittoons. Or they could strap on their Burton snowboards and ride a lift to a powdery bowl that required them to think only of the next carved turn. They could care deeply about the West, the frontier, the region, and the place. Or they could choose to care not a whit. Recreational tourism would seem the final step in dismantling the regional West. How could any place maintain coherence after global networks of entertainment and information chopped them into commodities and sold them piecemeal?

Still, many tourists proclaimed a devotion to western places that went beyond thoughtless consumption. They professed a love for the mountains, the rivers, and the oceans. Wine connoisseurs identified with the Napa Valley, surfers with the break at Mavericks south of San Francisco, backcountry skiers with Snodgrass Mountain near Crested Butte in the southern Rockies. They visited these places repeatedly and learned what they could about them. They swigged the terroir, acclimated to the terrain, and organized political associations to protect the sites they adored. They cultivated a sense of belonging and possession that ran counter to industrial tourism's casual consumption of western places.

Beginning in the 1950s a scraggly group of visitors to Yosemite National Park established a special relationship with the park's "Camp 4." It was not the most beautiful place to pitch a tent in Yosemite, but the site had several unique attractions. It had toilets and running water, it was secluded from the park's ranger headquarters, and it was surrounded by giant boulders. Young climbers flocked to Camp 4 to practice their moves on the rocks and party without harassment. Theirs was a rebellious subculture that combined a rejection of mainstream values with the pursuit of outdoor vigor and authentic experience. The congregation of "various risk-takers, oddballs, misfits, and other escapees from social convention" reeled off a series of epic climbs, scaling Half Dome's two thousand feet of vertical granite as well as El Capitan, the park's geographical jewel. Working to outdo one another, they climbed more difficult routes ever faster. The "dirt bags" of Camp

Tom Frost, Royal Robbins, Chuck Pratt, and Yvon Chouinard after their pioneering ascent of the North American Wall of El Capitan at Yosemite National Park. Photograph by Tom Frost, 1964. Wikimedia Commons.

4 revolutionized rock climbing, pushing the sport's athleticism and danger in the spirit of Teddy Roosevelt.[7]

Mountain climbers had debated the acceptable levels of risk for their sport since Europeans began topping peaks for fun in the nineteenth century. The denizens of Camp 4 enfolded these risk discussions into the postwar American context of suburban malaise and youth rebellion. Climbers argued over the purity of one another's ascents. To some, technology marred nature and diminished accomplishments. Critics denounced climbers who hammered dozens of pitons into rock walls to secure their ropes, who brought battery-powered drills to screw in anchors, or who used safety ropes as practice aids to retry difficult sections instead of as tethers of last resort. Violators of the climbing ethic might catch a beating in Camp 4. Fists flew because climbing meant more than reaching the tip of a spire or the rim of a vertical face. True climbers, those who used less gear, who left few traces on the rock, who risked their lives for their ideals, got closer to nature, and thus farther away from the stultifying orthodoxy of the American mainstream. The Yosemite daredevils—as much outsiders to the park as the tourists in Bermuda shorts they despised—laid claim to the audacious terrain through a sporting subculture that offered an authentic relationship with nature as long as you followed the prescribed code.

Yosemite climbers formed an elite subculture. Few climbers possessed the strength, dexterity, and skill, not to mention courage, to follow their routes and join their gang. But the influence of the Camp 4 subculture far exceeded their numbers who actually belonged to it. By the 1970s *ABC's Wide World of Sports* was televising Yosemite ascents. The best climbers soon became rock gods. They appeared on magazine covers, received endorsement deals, and founded fashion lines. A surprising number of popular outdoor apparel and gear companies emerged from the climbing subculture. Although the names and exploits of Yosemite climbers never reached the upper echelons of American sport, the gear companies were a different story. North Face, REI, Kelty, and Marmot sold the subculture to millions of Americans. Urban consumers purchased mountains of coats, sleeping bags, and hiking boots, buying into the fetish that connected these items to spectacular and genuine alpine environments. The elite climbing subculture manufactured an authentic relationship with western nature; the gear and apparel companies peddled it.

No climber or company better epitomized the welding of climbing subculture and outdoor fashion more than Yvon Chouinard and Patagonia. Chouinard's French Canadian father moved the family to southern California in 1947. While other boys surfed and built hot rods, Chouinard trained falcons and scrambled up rocks to investigate aeries. He joined the Sierra Club and fell in with the Yosemite climbers. In the 1960s he took part in several ascents, including the North American Wall and Muir Wall of El Capitan. Chouinard preached minimalism. His group climbed without fixed ropes. To do this and come back not only righteous but alive, climbers needed new technology—lighter and stronger pitons, anchors, wedges, and chocks that allowed them to fix fewer ropes and thereby hammer nature less. Chouinard advocated "clean climbing" and presented his gear as a technology for nature appreciation instead of conquest.

He began selling outdoor clothing and incorporated Patagonia in 1973. The company champions recycling, sources organic cotton, and funds environmental internships. Employees enjoy a vegan cafeteria and a flextime policy that gives them time to go climbing and surfing. The company has donated millions of dollars to groups seeking the protection and restoration of wild trout, the removal of dams, and a ban on petroleum drilling in the Arctic National Wildlife Refuge on Alaska's North Slope. Today Patagonia is as famous for its activism as for its fleeces and rain jackets. Patagonia contributes 1 percent of total sales or 10 percent of profits (whichever is bigger) to environmental groups.

With its high-priced clothing and accessory lines, the company marketed to a clientele with deep pockets and green politics. Their down vests and organic jeans sold in catalogs that featured magnificent coastlines and burbling mountain streams, suggesting that first-world consumers could enjoy and protect pristine nature while assembling a wardrobe fit for a walk-in closet. During the 2011 Christmas shopping season the company ran a marketing campaign that played off the contradictions of being Patagonia. "Don't Buy This Jacket," ads implored

Urban explorers, Chicago. Photograph by TheeErin, 2011. Creative Commons.

consumers. Think before you buy. A wealthy stratum was consuming more than their share of the planet's natural resources, a lavish indulgence that contributed to environmental problems from climate change to habitat destruction. These were Patagonia's people. Yet in the end, Patagonia sold more jackets by asking customers to "buy less."[8]

In truth, the new economies lean heavily on the earth. They extract energy and materials. They leave behind waste. The main difference between Microsoft, Patagonia, and U.S. Steel is packaging. Microsoft and Patagonia push the illusion that rich consumers can enjoy the digital content and the carabiner key fobs without worrying about the consequences of their privileged hoarding. Patagonia wears its hypocrisy more openly than most. Pointing out the company's flaws is easy. Patagonia retails state-of-the-art outdoor gear and apparel to a clientele that shuffles from houses to cars to cubicles. The top of El Capitan or the North Wall might as well be the surface of Mars to their average customers. Yet these couch-surfers buy into the purist climbing ethic when they consume Patagonia's products. Just as Chouinard and the purists at Camp 4 turned rock climbing into an ethical workout, the marketers at Patagonia turned shopping into a moral pursuit.

When a young urban professional hops off the Chicago Red Line, shoulders a Kelty backpack, and zips up a North Face fleece, when she wades through a puddle of slush in Keen boots and checks her email on a smartphone encased in a Patagonia sea lion shell, she radiates western material connections that probably go unnoticed by her and the crowd she joins on the street. Kelty (Boulder,

Colorado) and North Face (San Francisco) emerged from the same postwar stew of youth rebellion, sheer rock faces, and athletic performance that yielded Patagonia. Keen (Portland, Oregon) continued the tradition of western-based outdoor apparel companies that sold equipment for sports performed in trees, mountains, and rivers to subway riders. The Yuppie might know the regional derivation of her stuff, or she might enjoy the geographic dislocation of global consumer culture. She might worry about the damage her purchasing choices have on distant habitats, or she might feel herself cut off from nature, a city-dweller with no dog in far-off environmental fights. She could swerve in manifold directions, and that is the wonder of the information age. She could be a regionalist, a locavore, a huge fan of Yosemite, Portland, or even Quincy, or she could float above the earth in global streams of information, products, and affiliations. Perhaps she mingles both, living globally part of the time, locally at other moments. In an era of stupendous choice, locating people in cities, regions, and nations has become tricky. They might reside in a place, but that's no guarantee that they live there. Such is the world that tourism and extreme sports helped create.

––––––––––

The same freedom of immersion or oblivion flourishes in the entertainment industry. Westerns were the most popular story-telling genre of twentieth-century America. The dime novel tradition was continued with the "pulps," weekly or monthly story magazines printed on cheap paper made of wood pulp. The most successful writer of western pulp fiction was Zane Grey, a midwestern dentist who hit it big with his novel *Riders of the Purple Sage* (1912), in which the lightning-fast gunman hero rescues his lover from Mormon perfidy. Filled with violence, intrigue, cross-dressing, hard-riding women, and plenty of sex, the novel sold nearly two million copies. Over the next twenty years Grey published fifty-six westerns and sold at least seventeen million books. Between the world wars more than a hundred Hollywood films were based on Grey's novels.

The popularity of the western continued into the postwar period. In the 1950s westerns made up at least 10 percent of all the fiction titles published in the United States, and paperback westerns flew off the racks at the rate of thirty-five million a year. The unrivaled master of the postwar western was Louis L'Amour, a North Dakotan who spent years honing his Teddy Rooseveltian vigor, working as a ranch hand, miner, fruit picker, longshoreman, and professional boxer before enlisting as an officer in the tank corps during the war. He turned to writing after the fighting, scoring his first major success with the short story "The Gift of Cochise," which was the basis for the movie *Hondo* (1953), starring John Wayne. Before his death in 1988, L'Amour had sold two hundred million copies of more than a hundred westerns, at least thirty of which were adapted for motion pictures or television.

George Barnes aims at the audience. Frame from The Great Train Robbery *(1903). Wikimedia Commons.*

Churning out tough-guy plots featuring lone gunmen taking down Indians and bad guys with righteous violence, L'Amour dragged frontier stereotypes into the jet age and spread them to the recesses of the globe through mass-market fiction.

Hollywood had been making westerns since *The Great Train Robbery* (1903), the first motion picture to tell a complete story. Based on the holdup of the Union Pacific by an outlaw gang known as the Wild Bunch, the plot built on the Wild West formula pioneered by Buffalo Bill Cody. In the film's final sequence, one of the outlaws points his revolver directly at the audience and fires. People were thrilled. *The Great Train Robbery* marked the birth of the American motion picture industry, which from its beginnings was preoccupied with western stories. Over the next sixty years at least a third of all the films made in the United States were westerns.

Westerns became a primary source for twentieth-century images of American manhood. For sheer masculinity, probably no movie star before World War II was more powerful than Gary Cooper, who appeared in at least a dozen westerns by 1940. In the role that made him a star, Cooper played the nameless hero in *The Virginian* (1929), which faithfully followed Owen Wister's novel. Part of the appeal of westerns undoubtedly lies in the psychological realm. Feminist film critics argue persuasively that Hollywood pictures impose a male-oriented perspective— "the male gaze"—which encourages women as well as men to view women on the screen as the objects of male pleasure. But surely an actor like Cooper—lithe and sexually smoldering—was equally the object of an admiring "female gaze." The

Gary Cooper's breakout role in The Virginian *(1929). Wikimedia Commons.*

strong man with a gun has obvious sexual connotations, and as the roles of women
changed and broadened in the twentieth century there may have been women as
well as men who looked on images of male dominance with a shiver of nostalgia.
But there seems little doubt that the primary audience for westerns was male.

From 1945 through the mid-1960s, Hollywood produced an average of seventy-
five western features each year, a quarter of all films released in the United States.
Most were forgotten as soon as the house lights came up, but a few endured as
cinematic classics. John Ford had become the unrivaled master of the genre with
Stagecoach (1939), the most impressive and influential western of the late thirties. A
dangerous stagecoach journey through Apache country during Geronimo's uprising throws together a colorful cast of characters drawn directly from dime novels
and pulp fiction: a good-badman seeking revenge (John Wayne, in the role that
made him a star), a whore with a heart of gold, an alcoholic doctor, a respectable
army wife, an aristocratic southerner, and a venal banker. The film included scenes
shot in spectacular Monument Valley on the Navajo reservation, with its fantastic
buttes towering above the desert—a site fully worthy of Bierstadt's art. There is a
wonderful stunt sequence in which renegade Apaches (played by local Navajos)
chase the stagecoach through the desert until the day is saved by the last-minute
arrival of the cavalry. But Ford manipulates and recombines these conventional
elements into a film that amounts to considerably more than the sum of its parts.

Rio Grande *(1950), the third picture in director John Ford's "Cavalry Trilogy." Wikimedia Commons.*

He skillfully reveals the "civilized" members of the party as snobs, hypocrites, or crooks and recruits audience sympathy for the outcasts, who become the heroes of the melodrama. The film celebrates westering while it simultaneously debunks the civilization brought to the West by the East. In the end the good-badman and the whore ride off to spend their lives together on a ranch in Mexico, "saved from the blessings of civilization," as one of the characters puts it. *Stagecoach* is able to have it both ways, which is the way the western has always wanted to tell the story of America.

Ford returned to the genre after the hiatus of the war, taking up nearly all the major themes of postwar westerns. His "Cavalry Trilogy"—*Fort Apache* (1948), *She Wore a Yellow Ribbon* (1949), and *Rio Grande* (1950)—detailed the life of frontier troopers, encouraging viewers to identify with the war against the Indians, whom Ford presented as little more than terrorists. *Wagon Master* (1950) told the story of the Overland Trail and became the basis of a long-running television series. Perhaps most influential was Ford's lyrical *My Darling Clementine* (1946), in which Wyatt Earp (Henry Fonda) faces down a brutish family of outlaws, a black-and-white confrontation between "savagery and civilization."

Hollywood celebrated a particular vision of frontier justice—isolated men solving problems with bullets. *Shane* (1953), based on the range wars of the nineteenth century, featured a gunslinger (Alan Ladd) who reluctantly fights the ruthless cattlemen on behalf of wholesome homesteaders. Similarly in *High Noon* (1952), the sheriff (Gary Cooper) rejects the pleas of his Quaker bride (a reprise of a very similar scene in *The Virginian*) to stand alone against the outlaws. A remarkable series of films combining the talents of director Budd Boetticher, scriptwriter Burt Kennedy, and veteran actor Randolph Scott—*Seven Men from Now* (1956), *The Tall T* (1957), *Ride Lonesome* (1959), and *Comanche Station* (1960)—examined self-reliance and individual courage. As Scott asserts in a famous line: "There are some things a man can't ride around." Another series, directed by Anthony Mann and starring James Stewart—*Winchester '73* (1950), *Bend of the River* (1952), *The Naked Spur* (1953), *The Far Country* (1954), and *The Man from Laramie* (1955)—focused on characters driven by pathological rage but redeemed by their decision to act for the common good.[9]

Westerns also dominated television programming during the 1950s and 1960s. The first cowboy star to make the switch to the small screen was William Boyd, who played the good guy Hopalong Cassidy in a long series of B-westerns inaugurated in 1935. In 1948, with the series running out of steam, Boyd quietly acquired broadcast rights and leased the films to local television stations around the country. They proved so popular that NBC signed Boyd to star in a weekly program. *Hopalong Cassidy* was an immediate hit, with radio, comic book, and merchandising spinoffs adding to Boyd's estimated two-hundred-million-dollar take. In the wake of this success, westerns became the most popular children's television programs. Weekly series featured singing cowboys Gene Autry and Roy Rogers, the Lone Ranger and his faithful Indian companion Tonto, and the adventures of iconic frontier characters like Wild Bill Hickok, Kit Carson, and Annie Oakley. In 1954 Disney produced a Davy Crockett series that became a national sensation. Americans spent more than a hundred million dollars on coonskin caps and other Crockettabilia, including four million copies of the recording "The Ballad of Davy Crockett."

The next year westerns appeared on the prime-time network lineup for the first time. *Gunsmoke,* with fictional Dodge City marshal Matt Dillon (James Arness), was the number one show in the country by 1957. Suddenly the rush for western adult programming was on. In 1958 twenty-eight prime-time westerns provided more than seventeen hours of gunplay and Indian fighting each week, and according to the Neilson ratings, westerns captured eight of the nation's top ten program slots. The heroes were all men with access to firearms, tough sheriffs and bounty hunters, but unlike Hopalong Cassidy or Roy Rogers, they frequented saloons, drank whiskey, and cavorted with prostitutes. The regular violence brought criticism. "There must be dead bodies," the costar of the TV series *Wagon Train* angrily responded. "In the period of history we're dealing with, it's either kill or be killed. Anybody who studies history knows that." Television writers delivered retrograde

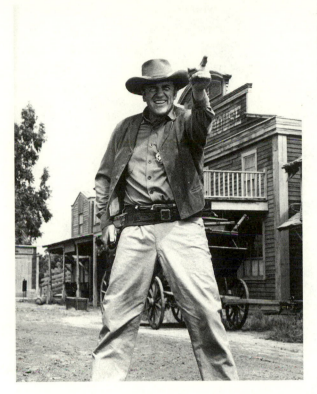

cartoons of western violence and justice. Guns settled disputes and legal questions. Lawyers and judges were rarely seen. The westerns trashed civil liberties.[10]

It was hard to miss the politics of most westerns. Most clearly, they served as a vehicle for promoting America's role in the Cold War. In *Rio Grande* (1950) the cavalry pursuit of Apaches provided an oblique commentary on the Korean War, and John Sturges's *The Magnificent Seven* (1960) offered a fantasy version of Third World counterinsurgency. Metaphors of western violence—showdowns, hired guns, last stands—permeated the language of postwar politics. "Would a Wyatt Earp stop at the 38th Parallel in Korea when the rustlers were escaping with his herd?" a conservative political commentator whined in 1958. "Would Marshal Dillon refuse to allow deputies to use shotguns for their own defense because of the terrible nature of the weapon itself? Ha!" The analogy continued into the Vietnam era. President Johnson told a reporter that "he had gone into Vietnam because, as at the Alamo, somebody had to get behind the log with those threatened people." And as a way of explaining the slow progress of political reform in American-controlled territory, ambassador to Vietnam Maxwell Taylor told a congressional committee that "it is very hard to plant corn outside a stockade when the Indians are still around." American troops carried these metaphors into battle. The primary object of the fighting, one veteran later recalled, was "the Indian idea: the

Clint Eastwood in A Fistful of Dollars *(1964), released in the United States in 1967. Wikimedia Commons.*

only good gook is a dead gook." Taking the ears of enemy dead was "like scalps, you know, like from the Indians. Some people were on an Indian trip over there." Reporter Michael Herr wrote of being invited to join an army company on a search and destroy mission. "'Come on,' hailed the captain, 'we'll take you out to play cowboys and Indians.'"[11]

The connection between westerns and political ideology is perhaps best evidenced by the precipitous demise of the genre amid the general cultural crisis of the 1960s and 1970s. Consider the case of filmmaker John Ford. Not since William Cody had an artist better assembled the components of frontier myth as popular entertainment. But in the final westerns of his career, Ford's vision of frontier history soured. *The Searchers* (1956), in which John Wayne plays an incorrigible racist, is an uncompromising study of the devastating effects of Indian hating, and *Sargent Rutledge* (1960) is a pathbreaking depiction of black Buffalo Soldiers in the frontier army. In *The Man Who Shot Liberty Valance* (1962), Ford called attention to the good things lost in the civilizing process, and in his final western, *Cheyenne Autumn* (1964), he finally presented a case for the Indians, exposing the American side of the frontier as murderous and corrupt.

By the mid-1960s doubt about the meaning of frontier history was evident in a flood of films that exploited the widening gap between old images and new ideas.

Sergio Leone's *A Fistful of Dollars* (1967)—Clint Eastwood's first star vehicle and the first of dozens of Italian spaghetti westerns—along with Sam Peckinpah's *The Wild Bunch* (1969) gloried in the amorality of violence. *Little Big Man* (1970), *Blazing Saddles* (1974), and *Buffalo Bill and the Indians, or Sitting Bull's History Lesson* (1976) lampooned the genre, subjecting the ideology of westering to devastating criticism. But soon even these antiwesterns wore thin. By the mid-1970s Hollywood studios were producing only a handful of westerns.

———

The Civil Rights Movement, the Vietnam War, the Watergate scandal, youth culture, and the conservative backlash against open sexuality, drug use, and racial and gender equality fractured the political and cultural consensus that flourished during the Cold War. Westerns joined the Democratic Party's New Deal coalition (African Americans, working-class immigrants, and southern whites), urban downtowns, and high-wage manufacturing jobs on the scrap heap. The occasional postmodern western appeared from time to time but mainly called attention to its own rebooting. Clint Eastwood's Oscar-winner *Unforgiven* (1992), for example, ruminated on the violence in his previous films as much as it commented on the West, the frontier, or the early 1990s political situation. *The Ballad of Little Jo* (1993), *Dead Man* (1995), *Lone Star* (1996), *Smoke Signals* (1998), *Brokeback Mountain* (2005), and *Django Unchained* (2012) took westerns into settings and subcultures never before seen on screen. These films took on the conventions of the genre— *Smoke Signals,* for instance, includes a devastating takedown of John Wayne—but they did more than counteract a master narrative. Some tried to wander free of gunslingers and righteous violence altogether and tell stories about western people rather than westering myths. Others kept the guns but transported their protagonists into geographies of weirdness. Quentin Tarantino's bloody ode to the spaghetti westerns, *Django Unchained,* is a train wreck of landscapes and regions. The Deep South and the Rocky Mountains overlap, as if peaks and plantations resided a fade-cut away from one another. The movie poked fun at the idea of coherent American regions. Do regions matter in an age when linked references lead users down rabbit holes of information? When attentions skitter ever sideways, what good are fixed coordinates?

Tarantino's hyperactive cutting and pasting was not the only reaction to the waning consensus. Other artists held onto place as the mainstream divided among countless channels. Regionalism staged something of an intellectual comeback. Native American writers like N. Scott Momaday, Leslie Marmon Silko, and Louise Erdrich set novels in the postwar West that expressed their characters' struggles to reconcile modern alienation and oppression with an enduring sense of tradition and connection to place. These writers often portrayed the bleakness of reservation life. They were realists with a political edge, not romantics looking for an escape in a mythic past. Still, the work of many native authors offered a spiritual understanding of the land as home, a source of sustenance and healing. Other regionalist writers followed this lead. Ivan Doig wrote about growing up in rural Montana, while Terry Tempest Williams chronicled her Mormon family's relationship to the natural environment in Utah, including the high incidences of cancer among her relatives living downwind from the Nevada Test Site where the federal government exploded nuclear weapons in the 1950s and 1960s. Many other western writers shared this sense of place and history. Rudolfo Anaya, James Welch, E. Annie Proulx, John Nichols, Jane Smiley, and Barbara Kingsolver contributed works to the regional movement.

Regional art flourished amid the fragmentation of American culture. Yet the disintegration that ate at the frontier myth also gnawed at regions. The internet scattered users, friends, and followers across information networks. Choices piled upon choices. People could use the internet to root themselves in a region: they could shop for western real estate, purchase western art and jewelry, and converse with locals via email and Twitter. Or they could use the internet to stream anime cartoons and compile antique cocktail recipes. The West entered the new millennium one obsession among many.

———

Yet the West didn't disappear as much as hide in plain sight. Hollywood stopped making westerns, but filmmakers continued to use the West. The 2004 comedy *Napoleon Dynamite*—a huge underground hit which was made for a pittance but grossed forty-five million dollars—epitomized the West's supporting role in post-internet cinema. Directed by Jared Hess, a Mormon from the Interior West, the film told the story of a goofy teenager who manages to overcome his misfit status, win the attention of a girl, and prove his worth with the cool kids. The plot resembled the hackneyed high school dramas made by director John Hughes in the 1980s, which take place in nondescript suburbs. Most viewers have no idea where *Napoleon Dynamite* is set, but location plays a central role in the picture.

Hess shot the film in his hometown of Preston, Idaho, a prosperous farming community in the Cache valley, north of the Utah border, where Mormon farmers grow sugar beets and potatoes in irrigated fields and Mexican American farmworkers harvest the crops. This social inequality is represented in the film by the character of Pedro Sanchez, Napoleon's friend and an underdog candidate for student-body president. Once the movie went viral, "Vote for Pedro" T-shirts became hot merchandise, although few fans realized that the message was a comment on a real political situation. Voting for Pedro in Preston meant overturning the local power structure. The film is laced with dozens of similar inside jokes.

U.S. 91, approaching Preston, Idaho. Photograph by Ken Lund, 2007. Creative Commons.

Mormonism is never mentioned, but as historian Nicolaas Mink points out, the film refers to Mormon culture "through symbolism, cultural imagery, and some clever phrasing." Napoleon feeds his pet llama a casserole; Mormons themselves joke about their fondness for casseroles. Hess applied Hughes's formula to a small Mormon community in the Interior West, and the mixture ignited across the information networks, entering most users' awareness as a weird assortment of fashion choices and left-field one-liners. "Vote for me," says Pedro, "and all your wildest dreams will come true."[12]

Napoleon Dynamite demonstrated how the local might translate into the global in the internet age. Other artists used the universality of the high school drama to bring very different western settings to broader publics, as Sherman Alexie did in *The Absolutely True Diary of a Part-Time Indian* (2007). A writer, standup comic, movie producer, poet, and songwriter, Alexie wrote the young adult novel, illustrated with comic-book-style graphics, to reach a set of readers his previous work had not. He reintroduces Junior, a character who appears in many of his novels (and the film adaptation of one of them, *Smoke Signals*). Junior lives on the Spokane Indian Reservation. Small and weak, debilitated from a childhood bout with "water on the brain," Junior doesn't quite fit in on the reservation. He

Spokane Indian Reservation in eastern Washington State. Photograph by Greg Goebel, 2013. Creative Commons.

is friends with Rowdy, a strong and fearless athlete who protects him. Like American Indian authors of the 1970s, Alexie does not shrink from the problems of the reservation. Most of his characters are poor. They drink heavily, and prospects look dark for most everybody. In a desperate act of rebellion and self-preservation, Junior throws an outdated textbook at one of his teachers at the reservation high school. Instead of being angry, the white teacher interprets Junior's defiance as hope. He advises the young man to leave the reservation school to attend the white school in the town of Reardon.[13]

At Reardon, Junior drops into a plot setup redolent with John Hughes flourishes. A flagrant outsider, he eventually befriends the prettiest girl in school, becomes a star on the basketball team, and runs with the cool crowd. He finds his confidence, learns that rich white kids have problems too, and in a triumphant moment beats Rowdy and the reservation high school team in a basketball game. Junior's victory, however, proves far more wrenching than anything experienced by Molly Ringwald or Ferris Bueller. All teenagers have problems, but Alexie shows that Indian kids from poor reservations have tragically dire ones. Junior's life is filled with death. His sister dies in a fire, too drunk to save herself or her husband; his beloved grandmother is killed by an intoxicated driver. The undertow of desperation prompts Junior's flight to Reardon, but this decision, with all its wonderful consequences, exiles him from the reservation. To survive and thrive, Junior has to risk his friendship with Rowdy and his membership in the Indian community.

Sherman Alexie. Photograph by Larry D. Moore, 2007. Creative Commons.

Alexie ends on a hopeful note. Junior seems to be headed toward a future where being Indian and being safe, happy, and successful are not mutually exclusive experiences. Still, unlike most high school dramas, Junior does not ride off into the sunset with his true love after vanquishing the cliques. Alexie uses the conventions of the genre to underscore the seriousness of American Indian poverty and racial exclusion, bringing the harsh reality of the Spokane Indian Reservation to the attention of young adult fiction devotees more accustomed to reading about boy wizards and human and vampire love affairs than chronic alcoholism and rural stagnation.

Junior and Napoleon are both unavoidably and unrecognizably western. The products of specific places—the Spokane reservation and Preston, Idaho—the characters' localisms, the ways they talk and dress, and their family and community lives make them strange and endearing to movie and reading audiences. They could represent "the new kids," the iconic protagonists in teenage high school dramas, because they parachute in from the rural West, the geographic and socioeconomic peripheries. Mainstream audiences no longer recognize Napoleon's casseroles or Junior's fry-bread as western, but they eat up the idiosyncrasies even if they haven't a clue about the historical forces that hatched them—U.S. Indian policy, the Mormon exodus to Utah, and the politics of irrigation.

At 10:07 p.m. on Friday, January 24, 2014, sports reporter Mike Pesca tweeted: "I figured out Napoleon Dynamite. It was just a series of gifs, memes and image macros before those things existed." Twelve of Pesca's followers retweeted his assessment, hardly a landslide of attention but a testament nonetheless to *Dynamite*'s staying power and inscrutability. The film continues to deliver non sequiturs to those uninitiated in Mormon culture or western history. Viewers could deploy their search engines to find out more about Jared Hess and his pocket of the Interior West. Or they could revel in the outlandishness of Napoleon and his family and click on another link. Viewers like Pesca don't need to solve the puzzle of *Napoleon Dynamite*. They can consume the movie's delightfully off-kilter sensibility without questioning whether anyone actually considers dancing in moonboots to Jamiroquai kilter.[14]

Neither Junior nor Napoleon can ignore their marginality. They know where they stand in regard to the mainstream culture. They are fodder for the entertainment of others. Both Alexie and Hess push against this exploitation. Alexie includes a very funny scene in which a megarich, New Age "friend of the Indians" known as Billionaire Ted descends on the Spokanes during the funeral of Junior's grandmother. He tries to return a powwow dance costume that he mistakenly thinks belonged to her. The dress is from another tribe, and it represents the earnest obliviousness of a man of privilege who used his wealth to gather Indian content—artifacts, archives, libraries—without bothering to get to know native people. He leaves the funeral in a huff after the mourners break into laughter.

The representative from the outside world who shows up in *Napoleon Dynamite* is LaFawnduh Lucas. An African American woman from Detroit, LaFawnduh befriends Napoleon's brother Kip over the internet. They fall in love and marry near the end of the movie. LaFawnduh, says Nicolaas Mink, represents "the cultural gap between rural western life and mainstream America." LaFawnduh wears stylish clothes, she listens to hip-hop, and she is urban. Kip and Napoleon catch glimpses of this mainstream over "cyberspace." A digital conduit brings Detroit to them. Unlike Billionaire Ted, who dropped in uninvited on the Spokanes, LaFawnduh leaps from one periphery to another. A convergence of backwaters, her union with Kip suggests the merging of economic, racial, and geographic frontiers. Because their connection seems to empower both LaFawnduh and Kip, it plays much sweeter than Ted's imposition.[15]

LaFawnduh puts a bow on this book. LaFawndah and Kip represent the twin poles of American frontier history and hip-hop culture: the historical, social, and economic forces that root people in place and the transmittable ideas, values, and art forms that connect people across space. The rappers Eric B. & Rakim expressed this push and pull in a lyric from their 1987 song "I Know You Got Soul." "It ain't where you're from," growled Rakim, "it's where you're at." Like regional artists, rappers in the 1980s and 1990s often proclaimed their allegiance to place. Where you were from—East Coast versus West Coast, Bronx versus Brooklyn, Compton versus Long Beach—meant a great deal. Region, city, and neighborhood separated friends from enemies; geographic coordinates underwrote an artist's authenticity.

Being from a rough place signaled your ability to speak the truth of the streets. But other ideas in hip-hop pulled against the notion that where you were from determined who you were and who you weren't. Some of the earliest rappers, artists like Afrika Bambaataa, preached universal ideologies of "Zulu" religion, anti-racism, and free thought. For Bambaataa and the rappers of his generation, "at" outshone "from." Hip-hop was not geographically fixed but open to anyone who believed.[16]

Hip-hop has wavered back and forth between the poles of at and from; so too the scholarship of the American West. The proponents of at and from, process and place, continue to argue and represent. The vitality of the debate seems to be tied to the inability of the participants to settle the question. The information revolution heightened the standoff by allowing imaginative acts like LaFawnduh Lucas. Both at and from, LaFawnduh offers hope that digital conduits linking disparate frontiers like Detroit and Preston, Idaho, might rearrange the places and processes that define and inspire us. Instead of eroding our common ground, the interwebs might bring peripheries and centers together in new configurations, breeding new frontiers, filled with magical absurdities, that tell us where we came from and help us better understand where we might end up at.

FURTHER READING

Jeff Chang, *Can't Stop Won't Stop: A History of the Hip-Hop Generation* (2005)
Annie Gilbert Coleman, *Ski Style: Sport and Culture in the Rockies* (2004)
Philip J. Deloria, *Indians in Unexpected Places* (2004)
Matthew Klingle, *Emerald City: An Environmental History of Seattle* (2007)
J. Fred MacDonald, *Who Shot the Sheriff? The Rise and Fall of the Television Western* (1987)
William Philpott, *Vacationland: Tourism and Environment in the Colorado High Country* (2013)
Daniel T. Rodgers, *Age of Fracture* (2011)
Richard Slotkin, *Gunfighter Nation: The Myth of the Frontier in Twentieth-Century America* (1992)
Joseph E. Taylor III, *Pilgrims of the Vertical: Yosemite Rock Climbers and Nature at Risk* (2010)
Jon Tuska, *The Filming of the West* (1976)

Notes

Introduction

1. Woodrow Wilson, "The Proper Perspective of American History," *Forum* 19 (July 1895): 544–59.
2. Loren Baritz, "The Idea of the West," *American Historical Review* 66 (1961): 628; Felipe Fernández-Armesto, *Columbus on Himself* (Indianapolis, Ind., 2010), 32.
3. Baritz, "Idea of the West," 621.
4. "Emergence Song," in *The Portable North American Indian Reader,* ed. Frederick W. Turner III (New York, 1974), 239.
5. Carl Ortwin Sauer, *Sixteenth Century North America: The Land and the People as Seen by the Europeans* (Berkeley, Calif., 1971), 203.
6. James Axtell, *After Columbus: Essays in the Ethnohistory of Colonial North America* (New York, 1988), 142.
7. Genesis 1:28.
8. John Mack Faragher, ed., *Rereading Frederick Jackson Turner: "The Significance of the Frontier in American History" and Other Essays* (New Haven, 1999), 31–60.
9. Robert G. Athearn, *The Mythic West in Twentieth-Century America* (Lawrence, Kans., 1986), 15.

Chapter 1: A New World Begins

1. *The Journal of Christopher Columbus,* trans. Cecil Jane (London, 1950), 57, 101–2.
2. Ibid., 194; Crióbal Colón, *Textos y documentos completos,* ed. Consuelo Valera (Madrid, 1982), 302; Francisco López de Gómara, *La conquista de Mexico,* ed. José Luis Rojas (Madrid, 1987), 87.
3. Peter Martyr, *De Orbe Novo,* trans. F. A. MacNutt, 2 vols. (London, 1912), 1:400; Bernal Díaz, *The Conquest of New Spain,* trans. J. M. Cohen (New York, 1963), 33.
4. Miguel León-Portilla, ed., *The Broken Spears: The Aztec Account of the Conquest of Mexico* (Boston, 1962; rev. ed., 1992), 6; John Bierhorst, *Four Masterworks of American Indian Literature* (New York, 1974), 37.
5. León-Portilla, *Broken Spears,* 51.
6. Díaz, *Conquest of New Spain,* 87.
7. Hugh Thomas, *Conquest: Moctezuma, Cortés, and the Fall of Old Mexico* (New York, 1963), 301, 433.

8. Ronald Wright, *Stolen Continents: The Americas through Indian Eyes since 1492* (Boston, 1992), 45.

9. Bartolomé de Las Casas, *In Defense of the Indians,* ed. Stafford Poole (Dekalb, Ill., 1974), 201–2.

10. Ibid., 237.

11. Thomas, *Conquest,* 74.

12. Nicolás Sánchez-Albornoz, *The Population of Latin America: A History,* trans. W. A. R. Richardson (Berkeley, Calif., 1974), 76.

13. David J. Weber, *The Spanish Frontier in North America* (New Haven, 1992), 51.

14. Herbert E. Bolton, *The Spanish Borderlands* (New Haven, 1921), 148–49.

15. Carl Ortwin Sauer, *Sixteenth Century North America: The Land and the People as Seen by Europeans* (Berkeley, Calif., 1971), 131.

16. Ramón A. Gutiérrez, *When Jesus Came, the Corn Mothers Went Away: Marriage, Sexuality, and Power in New Mexico, 1500–1816* (Stanford, Calif., 1991), 15, 12.

17. Ibid., 15.

18. Ibid., 73–74.

19. Tom Lea, *The King Ranch,* 2 vols. (Boston, 1957), 1:112.

20. Quintard Taylor, *In Search of the Racial Frontier: African Americans in the American West, 1528–1990* (New York, 1998), 36.

21. Charles W. Hackett, ed., *Historical Documents Relating to New Mexico,* 3 vols. (Washington, D.C., 1923–37), 1:435.

Chapter 2: Contest of Cultures

1. Carl Ortwin Sauer, *Sixteenth Century North America: The Land and the People as Seen by the Europeans* (Berkeley, Calif., 1971), 59–60.

2. John Bartlett Brebner, *Explorers of North America, 1492–1806* (New York, 1955), 90.

3. Sauer, *Sixteenth Century North America,* 88.

4. Ibid.

5. Reuben Gold Thwaites, ed., *The Jesuit Relations and Allied Documents, 1610–1791,* 73 vols. (Cleveland, 1896–1901), 54:280–81; Steven Mintz, ed., *Native American Voices: A History and Anthology* (Saint James, N.Y., 1995), 58.

6. Sauer, *Sixteenth Century North America,* 80, 88.

7. Ibid., 88.

8. Walter O'Meara, *Daughters of the Country: The Women of the Fur Traders and Mountain Men* (New York, 1968), 70, 140.

9. Olive Dickason, "From 'One Nation' in the Northeast to 'New Nation' in the Northwest: A Look at the Emergence of the Metis," *American Indian Culture and Research Journal* 6 (1982): 7.

10. Thwaites, *Jesuit Relations,* 5:113.

11. Sophie White, *Wild Frenchmen and Frenchified Indians: Material Culture and Race in Colonial Louisiana* (Philadelphia, 2013), 81.

12. Mintz, *Native American Voices,* 52–53.

13. James Axtell, *The Invasion Within: The Conquest of Cultures in Colonial North America* (New York, 1985), 107; W. J. Eccles, *The Canadian Frontier, 1534–1760,* rev. ed. (Albuquerque, N.Mex., 1986), 48.

14. Richard Hakluyt, *Discourse on Western Planting,* facsimile ed. (London, 1993), 123.

15. Thomas Hariot, *A Briefe and True Report of the New Found Land of Virginia,* facsimile ed. (New York, 1972), 28.

16. Lyon Gardiner Tyler, ed., *Narratives of Early Virginia, 1606–1626* (New York, 1907), 36; Samuel G. Drake, *Biography and History of the Indians of North America* (Boston, 1841), 352.

17. Drake, *Biography and History,* 353.

18. *Two Broad-sides against Tobacco . . .* (London, 1676), 6.

19. Neal Salisbury, *Manitou and Providence: Indians, Europeans, and the Making of New England, 1500–1643* (New York, 1982), 103; Francis Jennings, *The Invasion of America: Indians, Colonialism, and the Cant of Conquest* (New York, 1975), 24.

20. William Cronon, *Changes in the Land: Indians, Colonists, and the Ecology of New England* (New York, 1983), 88.

21. Salisbury, *Manitou and Providence,* 124; Alfred A. Cave, *The Pequot War* (Amherst, Mass., 1996), 46.

22. Cronon, *Changes in the Land,* 56.

23. Salisbury, *Manitou and Providence,* 191.

24. Jennings, *Invasion of America,* 223.

25. Edmund S. Morgan, *Roger Williams: The Church and the State* (New York, 1967), 122.

26. Richard Drinnon, *Facing West: The Metaphysics of Indian-Hating and Empire-Building* (Minneapolis, Minn., 1980), 50.

27. Jill Lepore, *The Name of War: King Philip's War and the Origins of American Identity* (New York, 1998), 94.

28. Richard Slotkin, *Regeneration through Violence: The Mythology of the American Frontier, 1600–1860* (Middletown, Conn., 1973), 101.

29. Ibid., 173.

30. Daniel K. Richter, *The Ordeal of the Longhouse: The Peoples of the Iroquois League in the Era of European Colonization* (Chapel Hill, N.C., 1992), 61.

31. Ibid., 118.

32. Ibid., 153, 155.

33. Ibid., 184.

Chapter 3: The Struggle of Empires

1. Terry Jordan and Matti Kaups, *The American Backwoods Frontier: An Ethnic and Ecological Interpretation* (Baltimore, 1989), 2.

2. Albert Cook Myers, ed., *Narratives of Early Pennsylvania, West New Jersey, and Delaware, 1630–1701* (New York, 1912), 235.

3. Benjamin Franklin, *Writings* (New York, 1987), 367; Thomas Malthus, *Essay on the Principle of Population,* ed. Michael P. Fogarty, 2 vols. (New York, 1958), 1:305–6.

4. Jacqueline Peterson, "Prelude to Red River: A Social Portrait of the Great Lakes Métis," *Ethnohistory* 25 (1978): 41–67.

5. W. J. Eccles, *The Canadian Frontier, 1534–1760,* rev. ed. (Albuquerque, N.Mex., 1974), 132.

6. Daniel K. Richter, *The Ordeal of the Longhouse: The Peoples of the Iroquois League in the Era of European Colonization* (Chapel Hill, N.C., 1992), 155, 206.

7. Ronald Wright, *Stolen Continents: The New World through Indian Eyes since 1492* (Boston, 1992), 130.

8. Richter, *Ordeal of the Longhouse,* 268.

9. Ibid., 263, 266.

10. Francis Jennings, *Empire of Fortune: Crowns, Colonies, and Tribes in the Seven Years War in America* (New York, 1988), 402; Richard White, *The Middle Ground: Indians, Empires, and Republics in the Great Lakes Region, 1650–1815* (Cambridge, 1991), 248–49.

11. White, *Middle Ground,* 269.

12. Gregory Dowd, *A Spirited Resistance: The North American Indian Struggle for Unity, 1745–1815* (Baltimore, 1992), 34–35.

13. Jennings, *Empire of Fortune,* 447.

14. Ibid., 463n.; John C. Fitzpatrick, ed., *The Writings of George Washington,* 39 vols. (Washington, D.C., 1931–44), 2:458.

15. Hector Chevigny, *Russian America: The Great Alaskan Venture, 1741–1867* (Portland, Oreg., 1965), 50.

16. Philip L. Fradkin, *The Seven States of California: A Natural and Human History* (New York, 1995), 276; George H. Phillips, *The Enduring Struggle: Indians in California* (San Francisco, 1981), 24.

17. Carey McWilliams, *Southern California Country* (New York, 1946), 29; *The First French Expedition to California: Lapérouse in 1786,* trans. Charles N. Rudkin (Los Angeles, 1959), 75.

18. Wilbur R. Jacobs, ed., *The Paxton Riots and the Frontier Theory* (Chicago, 1967), 27.

19. Richard Maxwell Brown, *The South Carolina Regulators* (Cambridge, Mass., 1963), 135.

Chapter 4: The Land and Its Markers

1. Colin G. Calloway, *The World Turned Upside Down: Indian Voices from Early America* (Boston, 1994), 149.

2. Ronald Wright, *Stolen Continents: The Americas through Indian Eyes since 1492* (Boston, 1992), 139.

3. Richard W. Van Alstyne, *The Rising American Empire* (New York, 1960), 72.

4. Wright, *Stolen Continents,* 227.

5. Henry Steele Commager, *Documents of American History* (New York, 1949), 120.

6. Ibid., 123.

7. Thomas Jefferson, *Writings,* ed. Merrill D. Peterson (New York, 1984), 752–53.

8. Henry Nash Smith, *Virgin Land: The American West as Symbol and Myth* (1950; reprint ed., Cambridge, Mass., 1969), 127–28, 206.

9. R. Douglas Hurt, *The Ohio Frontier: Crucible of the Old Northwest, 1720–1830* (Bloomington, Ind., 1996), 147.

10. Richard Henry Lee, *The Letters of Richard Henry Lee,* ed. James Ballagh, 2 vols. (New York, 1914), 2:425.

11. Don E. Fehrenbacher, *The Slaveholding Republic: An Account of the United States Government's Relations to Slavery* (New York, 2001), 256.

12. John Mack Faragher, *Daniel Boone: The Life and Legend of an American Pioneer* (New York, 1992), 70.

13. Ibid., 5, 60, 326; Harriet Louisa Arnow, *Seed Time on the Cumberland* (New York, 1960), 169.

14. Richard White, *The Middle Ground: Indians, Empires, and Republics in the Great Lakes Region, 1650–1815* (Cambridge, 1991), 441.

15. Francis Paul Prucha, ed., *Documents of United States Indian Policy* (Lincoln, Nebr., 1990), 10.

16. Ibid., 14.

17. Wilcomb E. Washburn, ed., *The American Indian and the United States: A Documentary History*, 4 vols. (Westport, Conn., 1973), 4:2286–90.

18. Prucha, *Documents of United States Indian Policy*, 19; Philip Weeks, ed., *The American Indian Experience* (Arlington Heights, Ill., 1988), 104.

19. Clyde A. Milner II, Carol A. O'Connor, and Martha Sandweiss, eds., *The Oxford History of the American West* (New York, 1994), 125–26.

20. Faragher, *Daniel Boone*, 250.

21. Anthony F. C. Wallace, *The Death and Rebirth of the Seneca* (New York, 1969), 197.

22. Ibid., 203, 206.

23. R. David Edmunds, *The Shawnee Prophet* (Lincoln, Nebr., 1984), 131, 31–32.

24. Alvin M. Josephy Jr., *The Patriot Chiefs: A Chronicle of Indian Resistance* (New York, 1969), 159; Robert V. Remini, *Andrew Jackson and the Course of American Empire, 1767–1821* (New York, 1977), 188.

25. R. David Edmunds, *Tecumseh and the Quest for Indian Leadership* (Boston, 1984), 131, 145; John Mack Faragher, *Sugar Creek: Life on the Illinois Prairie* (New Haven, 1986), 31–32.

26. Wright, *Stolen Continents*, 210.

27. Ibid., 213.

28. Ibid., 217.

Chapter 5: Finding Purchase

1. John Mack Faragher, *Daniel Boone: The Life and Legend of an American Pioneer* (New York, 1992), 7, 298.

2. Ibid., 277, 299–300.

3. Ibid., 300–301; Faragher, "They May Say What They Please: Daniel Boone and the Evidence," *Register of the Kentucky Historical Society* 88 (Autumn 1990): 391.

4. William Appleman Williams, *The Roots of the Modern American Empire: A Study of the Growth and Shaping of Social Consciousness in a Marketplace Society* (New York, 1969), 50; Lloyd C. Gardner, Walter F. LaFeber, and Thomas J. McCormick, *Creation of the American Empire* (Chicago, 1973), 31; Richard W. Van Alstyne, *The Rising American Empire* (New York, 1960), 78, 69.

5. Francis Wrigley Hirst, *The Life and Letters of Thomas Jefferson* (New York, 1926), 390.

6. E. Wilson Lyon, *Louisiana in French Diplomacy* (Norman, Okla., 1934), 225–26; Bobby Lee, "The Price of Purchase" (unpublished ms., 2015).

7. Bernard DeVoto, *The Journals of Lewis and Clark* (Boston, 1953), 60, 256–57.

8. Ibid., 90.

9. Donald Jackson, ed., *The Journals of Zebulon Pike*, 2 vols. (Norman, Okla., 1966), 1:442.

10. Edwin James, *Account of an Expedition from Pittsburgh to the Rocky Mountains*, 3 vols. (Philadelphia, 1823), 2:361.

11. John Ewers, *Artists of the Old West* (New York, 1965), 26.

12. George Catlin, *Letters and Notes on the Manners, Customs and Conditions of the North American Indian*, 2 vols. (1841; reprint ed., New York, 1973), 1:xiv, 3, 13; Jules David Prown et al., *Discovered Lands, Invented Pasts: Transforming Visions of the American West* (New Haven, 1992), 6.

13. Catlin, *Letters and Notes*, 1:16.

14. Laura L. Mielke, *Moving Encounters: Sympathy and the Indian Question in Antebellum Literature* (Amherst, Mass., 2008), 128.

15. Bernard DeVoto, *The Course of Empire* (Boston, 1952).

16. Charles Frances Adams, ed., *Memoirs of John Quincy Adams*, 12 vols. (Philadelphia, 1874–77), 4:438–39.

17. Fred W. Powell, ed., *Hall J. Kelley on Oregon* (Princeton, N.J., 1932), 60.

18. Julie Roy Jeffrey, *Converting the West: A Biography of Narcissa Whitman* (Norman, Okla., 1991), 53.

19. Jeffrey, *Converting the West*, 108, 164, 168.

20. Ibid., 182.

21. Anne F. Hyde, *Empires, Nations, and Families: A New History of the North American West, 1800–1860* (Lincoln, Nebr., 2011), 109.

22. James Fenimore Cooper, *The Leatherstocking Tales*, 2 vols. (New York, 1985), 1:250–324.

23. Martin Ridge and Ray Allen Billington, eds., *America's Frontier Story: A Documentary History of Westward Expansion* (New York, 1969), 453–54.

24. William H. Goetzmann and Glyndwr Williams, *The Atlas of North American Exploration: From the Norse Voyages to the Race to the Pole* (New York, 1992), 159.

Chapter 6: War and Destiny

1. Frederick Merk, *Manifest Destiny and Mission in American History: A Reinterpretation* (New York, 1963), 28; Julian P. Boyd et al., *The Papers of Thomas Jefferson*, 41 vols. (Princeton, N.J., 1950–2014), 4:237–38.

2. Merk, *Manifest Destiny*, 29; Robert Sampson, *John L. O'Sullivan and His Times* (Kent, Ohio, 2002), 193.

3. James D. Richardson, ed., *A Compilation of Messages and Papers of the Presidents*, 10 vols. (Washington, D.C., 1900), 3:1252.

4. Francis Paul Prucha, ed., *Documents of United States Indian Policy* (Lincoln, Nebr., 1990), 61.

5. William G. McLoughlin, *Cherokees and Missionaries, 1789–1839* (New Haven, 1984), 135–36; "The Diaries of John Quincy Adams: A Digital Collection," June 30, 1841, www.masshist.org/jqadiaries.

6. Donald Jackson, ed., *Black Hawk: An Autobiography* (Urbana, Ill., 1964), 101, 108.

7. William C. Davis, *A Way through the Wilderness: The Natchez Trace and the Civilization of the Southern Frontier* (New York, 1995), 73–74.

8. Joan E. Cashin, *A Family Venture: Men and Women on the Southern Frontier* (New York, 1991), 103, 114.

9. Thomas D. Clark and John D. W. Guice, *The Old Southwest, 1795–1830: Frontiers in Conflict* (Norman, Okla., 1996), 322–23.

10. Quintard Taylor, *In Search of the Racial Frontier: African Americans in the American West, 1528–1990* (New York, 1998), 37.

11. Andrew J. Torget, *Seeds of Empire: Cotton, Slavery, and the Transformation of the Texas Borderlands, 1800–1850* (Chapel Hill: University of North Carolina Press, 2015), 144.

12. Susan Prendergast Schoelwer, *Alamo Images: Changing Perceptions of a Texas Experience* (Dallas, Tex., 1985), 108.

13. Paul D. Lack, *The Texas Revolutionary Experience: A Political and Social History, 1835–1836* (College Station, Tex., 1992), 168.

14. Taylor, *In Search of the Racial Frontier*, 42; Torget, *Seeds of Empire*, 204.

15. *Speech of the Honorable John Quincy Adams . . . May 25, 1836* (New York, 1836), 12.

16. Sean Wilentz, ed., *Major Problems in the Early Republic, 1787–1848* (Lexington, Mass., 1992), 379.

17. Merk, *Manifest Destiny*, 31.

18. Richard White, *"It's Your Misfortune and None of My Own": A New History of the American West* (Norman, Okla., 1991), 78.

19. William MacDonald, ed., *Select Documents Illustrative of the History of the United States, 1776–1861* (New York, 1898), 352.

20. Wilentz, *Major Problems*, 543; William S. McFeely, *Grant: A Biography* (New York, 1981), 30.

21. Wilentz, *Major Problems*, 532–33.

22. Leonard Pitt, *The Decline of the Californios: A Social History of the Spanish-Speaking Californians, 1846–1890* (Berkeley, Calif., 1970), 28–30.

23. Carey McWilliams, *North from Mexico: The Spanish-Speaking People of the United States* (1948; reprint ed., New York, 1968), 102–3.

24. Merk, *Manifest Destiny*, 28.

25. Ibid., 162.

26. Wilentz, *Major Problems*, 538; John H. Schroeder, *Mr. Polk's War: American Opposition and Dissent, 1846–1848* (Madison, Wis., 1973), 116, 144.

27. David G. Gutiérrez, *Walls and Mirrors: Mexican Americans, Mexican Immigrants, and the Politics of Ethnicity* (Berkeley, Calif., 1995), 17; MacDonald, *Select Documents*, 369.

28. Howard R. Lamar, ed., *The New Encyclopedia of the American West* (New Haven, 1998), 748; Carlos G. Vélez-Ibáñez, *Border Visions: Mexican Cultures in the Southwest United States* (Tucson, Ariz., 1996), 292; James W. Parins, *John Rollin Ridge: His Life and Works* (Lincoln, Nebr., 1991), 99.

29. W. Eugene Hollon, *Frontier Violence: Another Look* (New York, 1974), 41.

30. Jerry D. Thompson, ed., *Juan Cortina and the Texas-Mexico Frontier, 1859–1877* (El Paso, Tex., 1994), 15, 25, 27.

31. D. Michael Quinn, ed., *The New Mormon History: Revisionist Essays on the Past* (Salt Lake City, Utah, 1992), 61, 67.

32. Francis Paul Prucha, *The Great Father: The United States Government and the American Indians*, 2 vols. (Lincoln, Nebr., 1984), 1:346.

33. White, *"It's Your Misfortune and None of My Own,"* 58–59.

34. James M. McPherson, *Battle Cry of Freedom: The Civil War Era* (New York, 1988), 55.

35. Ibid., 292, 784, 786.

36. Donald S. Frazier, *Blood and Treasure: Confederate Empire in the Southwest* (College Station, Tex., 1995), 5.

37. Alvin M. Josephy Jr., *The Civil War in the American West* (New York, 1991), 80.

38. McPherson, *Battle Cry of Freedom*, 292, 784, 786.

39. William G. McLoughlin, *After the Trail of Tears: The Cherokees' Struggle for Sovereignty, 1839–1880* (Chapel Hill, N.C., 1993), 210–11.

40. Prucha, *Great Father*, 1:324, 352.

41. Ibid., 1:439; Gary Clayton Anderson and Alan R. Woolworth, eds., *Through Dakota Eyes: Narrative Accounts of the Minnesota Indian War of 1862* (Saint Paul, Minn., 1988), 23.

42. Josephy, *Civil War in the West*, 109; Robert M. Utley, *The Indian Frontier of the American West, 1846–1890* (Albuquerque, N.Mex., 1984), 76.

43. Josephy, *Civil War in the West*, 277.

44. Ibid., 286.

45. Dee Brown, *Bury My Heart at Wounded Knee: An Indian History of the American West* (New York, 1970), 79; George E. Hyde, *Life of George Bent: Written from His Letters*, ed. Savoie Lottinville (Norman, Okla., 1968), 147.

46. Josephy, *Civil War in the West*, 307; David Svaldi, *Sand Creek and the Rhetoric of Extermination: A Case Study in Indian-White Relations* (New York, 1989), 291.

47. Hyde, *Life of George Bent*, 152.

48. Sol Lewis, ed., *The Sand Creek Massacre: A Documentary History* (New York, 1973), 280; Richard Drinnon, *Facing West: The Metaphysics of Indian-Hating and Empire-Building* (Minneapolis, Minn., 1980), 539.

49. Hyde, *Life of George Bent*, 181.

Chapter 7: Machine

1. Richard White, *Railroaded: The Transcontinentals and the Making of Modern America* (New York, 2011), xxxii.

2. Rodman Wilson Paul, *Mining Frontiers of the Far West, 1848–1880* (New York, 1963), 13–14; Cheryl Elizabeth Wright, "Life in Topsy-Turvy-Dom: Women and Men in Gold Rush California" (senior thesis, Mount Holyoke College, 1987), 3.

3. Malcom J. Rohrbough, *Days of Gold: The California Gold Rush and the American Nation* (Berkeley, Calif., 1997), 126.

4. Norris Hundley Jr., *The Great Thirst: Californians and Water, 1770s–1990s* (Berkeley, Calif., 1992), 75; Rohrbough, *Days of Gold*, 197.

5. Louisa Amelia Knapp Clappe, *The Shirley Letters from the California Mines, 1851–1852*, ed. Carl I. Wheat (New York, 1949), 121.

6. Richard H. Peterson, *Manifest Destiny in the Mines: A Cultural Interpretation of Anti-Mexican Nativism in California, 1848–1853* (San Francisco, 1975), 9, 33, 38.

7. Peterson, *Manifest Destiny in the Mines*, 36; Edwin Beilharz and Carlos Lopez, eds., *We Were Forty-Niners! Chilean Accounts of the California Gold Rush* (Pasadena, Calif., 1976), 119–20.

8. Ronald Takaki, *A Different Mirror: A History of Multicultural America* (New York, 1993), 193.

9. Ibid., 195.

10. Robert F. Heizer and Alan F. Almquist, *The Other Californians: Prejudice and Discrimination under Spain, Mexico, and the United States to 1920* (Berkeley, Calif., 1976), 230, 233.

11. Liping Zhu, *A Chinaman's Chance: The Chinese on the Rocky Mountain Mining Frontier* (Niwot, Colo., 1997), 150.

12. Carlos Arnaldo Schwantes, *Hard Traveling: A Portrait of Work Life in the New Northwest* (Lincoln, Nebr., 1994), 6.

13. John Hoyt Williams, *A Great and Shining Road: The Epic Story of the Transcontinental Railroad* (New York, 1988), 40.

14. Ibid., 275.

15. Dee Brown, *Hear That Lonesome Whistle Blow: Railroads in the West* (New York, 1977), 45.

16. Howard R. Lamar, ed., *The New Encyclopedia of the American West* (New Haven, 1998), 37.

17. Stuart Daggett, *Chapters in the History of the Southern Pacific* (New York, 1920), 211; David Lavender, *The Great Persuader* (New York, 1970), 128–29.

18. J. C. Mutchler, "Ranching in the Magdalena, New Mexico Area: The Last Cowboys" (MA thesis, University of New Mexico, 1992), 22.

19. Henry Nash Smith, *Virgin Land: The American West as Symbol and Myth* (Cambridge, Mass., 1950), 173; Roy M. Robbins, *Our Landed Heritage: The Public Domain, 1776–1936* (Lincoln, Nebr., 1962), 177, 182.

20. Henry Steele Commager, ed., *Documents of American History* (New York, 1949), 410.

21. Fred A. Shannon, *The Farmer's Last Frontier: Agriculture, 1860–1897* (New York, 1945), 74–75.

22. Ibid., 62.

23. Smith, *Virgin Land*, 192.

24. Lamar, *New Encyclopedia of the American West*, 37; Williams, *Great and Shining Road*, 122.

25. Williams, *Great and Shining Road*, 96; Takaki, *Different Mirror*, 197; William F. Deverell, *Railroad Crossing: Californians and the Railroad, 1850–1910* (Berkeley, Calif., 1994), 184.

26. Brown, *Hear That Lonesome Whistle Blow*, 132.

27. Deverell, *Railroad Crossing*, 15.

28. Richard White, *"It's Your Misfortune and None of My Own": A New History of the American West* (Norman, Okla., 1991), 260.

29. Frederick Hale, ed., *Danes in North America* (Seattle, Wash., 1984), 73–74.

30. Kenneth N. Owens, ed., *John Sutter and a Wider West* (Lincoln, Nebr., 1994), 67; Rohrbough, *Days of Gold*, 13; Albert Hurtado, *Indian Survival on the California Frontier* (New Haven, 1988), 104, 112.

31. Heizer and Almquist, *Other Californians*, 86.

32. Ibid., 28.

33. George Harwood Phillips, *Indians and Indian Agents: The Origins of the Reservation System in California, 1849–1852* (Norman, Okla., 1997), 167; Heizer and Almquist, *Other Californians*, 26.

34. Hurtado, *Indian Survival*, 131; Heizer and Almquist, *Other Californians*, 40, 46, 57.

35. David D. Smits, "The Frontier Army and the Destruction of the Buffalo, 1865–1883," *Western Historical Quarterly* 25 (1994): 337.

36. Ibid., 330, 337; John G. Neihardt, *Black Elk Speaks* (New York, 1961), 181.

37. Deverell, *Railroad Crossing*, 39.

38. Ibid., 49–50; Lucy E. Salyer, *Laws Harsh as Tigers: Chinese Immigrants and the Shaping of Modern Immigration Law* (Chapel Hill, N.C., 1995), 7.

39. Deverell, *Railroad Crossing*, 74–75, 80–81.

40. James C. Olson, *Red Cloud and the Sioux Problem* (Lincoln, Nebr., 1965), 32.

41. Wilcomb E. Washburn, ed., *The American Indian and the United States: A Documentary History*, 4 vols. (Westport, Conn., 1973), 4:2519.

42. Robert M. Utley, *The Lance and the Shield: The Life and Times of Sitting Bull* (New York, 1993), 73.

43. Ibid., 116.

44. Louise Barnett, *Touched by Fire: The Life, Death, and Mythic Afterlife of George Armstrong Custer* (New York, 1996), 346.

45. Peter Nabokov, ed., *Native American Testimony: A Chronicle of Indian-White Relations from Prophecy to the Present, 1492–1992* (New York, 1991), 108.

46. Ibid., 108.

47. Wayne Moquin, ed., *Great Documents in American Indian History* (New York, 1973), 228; Utley, *Lance and Shield*, 179.

48. Arrel Morgan Gibson, *The American Indian: Prehistory to the Present* (Lexington, Mass., 1980), 392.

49. David Roberts, *Once They Moved Like the Wind: Cochise, Geronimo, and the Apache Wars* (New York, 1993), 111, 113, 260, 263, 300.

50. "Old Apache Chief Geronimo Is Dead," *New York Times*, February 1909.

Chapter 8: A Search for Community

1. John Mack Faragher, *Sugar Creek: Life on the Illinois Prairie* (New Haven, 1986), 50.

2. Ibid., 51–52.

3. Hamlin Garland, *Son of the Middle Border* (New York, 1920), 402.

4. Sandra L. Myres, *Westering Women and the Frontier Experience, 1800–1915* (Albuquerque, N.Mex., 1982), 168; Sigmund Diamond, ed., *The Nation Transformed: The Creation of an Industrial Society* (New York, 1963), 333; Everett Dick, *The Sod-House Frontier, 1854–1890* (New York, 1937), 235.

5. Kathleen Underwood, "Schoolmarms on the Upper Missouri," *Great Plains Quarterly* 11 (1991): 228.

6. David L. Kimbrough, *Reverend Joseph Tarkington, Methodist Circuit* (Knoxville, Tenn., 1997), 17; Faragher, *Sugar Creek*, 160–61; T. Scott Miyakawa, *Protestants and Pioneers: Individualism and Conformity on the American Frontier* (Chicago, 1964), 201.

7. Faragher, *Sugar Creek*, 163.

8. Dean L. May, *Three Frontiers: Family, Land, and Society in the American West, 1850–1900* (Cambridge, 1994), 197.

9. Sarah Barringer Gordon, "'The Liberty of Self-Degradation': Polygamy, Woman Suffrage, and Consent in Nineteenth-Century America," *Journal of American History* 83 (1996): 823, 828.

10. Eric Foner, *Reconstruction: America's Unfinished Revolution, 1863–1877* (New York, 1988), 600; Nell Irvin Painter, *Exodusters: Black Migration to Kansas after Reconstruction* (New York, 1977), 158–59, 231.

11. Jane Anne Staw and Mary Swander, *Parsnips in the Snow: Talks with Midwestern Gardeners* (Iowa City, Iowa, 1990), 195, 201.

12. Nupur Chaudhuri, "'We All Seem Like Brothers and Sisters': The African-American Community in Manhattan, Kansas, 1865–1940," *Kansas History* 14 (1991–92): 276, 277, 282, 283.

13. Gordon Parks, *Voices in the Mirror: An Autobiography* (New York, 1990), 1–2, 4.

14. Ibid., 331–33; *Gordon Parks: A Poet and His Camera* (London, 1969), n.p.

15. Francis Paul Prucha, *The Great Father: The United States Government and the American Indians*, 2 vols. (Lincoln, Nebr., 1984), 1:439.

16. Ibid., 1:528–29.

17. Philip Weeks, ed., *The American Indian Experience: A Profile, 1524 to the Present* (Arlington Heights, Ill., 1988), 196.

18. Prucha, *Great Father,* 2:647; Fred Hoxie, ed., *Indians in American History: An Introduction* (Arlington Heights, Ill., 1988), 247–48.

19. Prucha, *Great Father,* 2:691.

20. John H. Bodley, *Victims of Progress* (Palo Alto, Calif., 1982), 108.

21. Prucha, *Great Father,* 1:342, 441.

22. Weeks, *American Indian Experience,* 196.

23. Prucha, *Great Father,* 2:629, 666.

24. Weeks, *American Indian Experience,* 170.

25. James Mooney, *The Ghost-Dance Religion and the Sioux Outbreak of 1890* (1896; reprint ed., Chicago, 1965), 307; Prucha, *Great Father,* 2:728.

26. Virgil J. Vogel, *This Country Was Ours: A Documentary History of the American Indian* (New York, 1972), 182.

27. John G. Neihardt, *Black Elk Speaks: Being the Life Story of a Holy Man of the Oglala Sioux* (1932; reprint ed., New York, 1972), 217, 220–21.

28. Frederick C. Luebke, ed., *European Immigrants in the American West: Community Histories* (Albuquerque, N.Mex., 1998), vii; Luebke, ed., *Ethnicity on the Great Plains* (Lincoln, Nebr., 1980), 7; Dorothy Burton Skardahl, *The Divided Heart: Scandinavian Immigrant Experience through Literary Sources* (Lincoln, Nebr., 1974), 239.

29. Luebke, *European Immigrants in the West,* 61.

30. Steven Hahn and Jonathan Prude, eds., *The Countryside in the Age of Capitalist Transformation: Essays in the Social History of Rural America* (Chapel Hill, N.C., 1985), 276.

31. Robert C. Ostergren, *A Community Transplanted: The Trans-Atlantic Experience of a Swedish Immigrant Settlement in the Upper Middle West, 1835–1915* (Madison, Wis., 1988), 230.

32. April R. Schultz, *Ethnicity on Parade: Inventing the Norwegian American through Celebration* (Amherst, Mass., 1994), 29, 37, 58, 117.

33. Sinclair Lewis, *Main Street* (New York, 1920), 26–27.

34. Zona Gale, *Friendship Village* (New York, 1920).

35. Frederick Russel Burnham, *Scouting on Two Continents* (Los Angeles, Calif., 1934), 10.

36. Vachel Lindsay, *Collected Poems* (New York, 1927).

37. Sucheng Chan, *This Bittersweet Soil: The Chinese in California Agriculture, 1860–1910* (Berkeley, Calif., 1986), 185–87, 335.

38. Ibid., 332; Lucy E. Salyer, *Laws Harsh as Tigers: Chinese Immigrants and the Shaping of Modern Immigration Law* (Chapel Hill, N.C., 1995), 15; Carey McWilliams, *Southern California Country: An Island on the Land* (New York, 1947), 90.

39. Brian Masaru Hayashi, *"For the Sake of Our Japanese Brethren": Assimilation, Nationalism, and Protestantism among the Japanese of Los Angeles, 1895–1942* (Stanford, Calif., 1995), 31–32; Carey McWilliams, *Factories in the Field: The Story of Migratory Farm Labor in California* (Boston, 1939).

40. Sayler, *Laws Harsh as Tigers,* 126; Gilbert G. González, *Labor and Community: Mexican Citrus Worker Villages in a Southern California County, 1900–1950* (Urbana, Ill., 1994), 49.

41. David Mas Masumoto, *Country Voices: The Oral History of a Japanese American Family Farm Community* (Del Ray, Calif., 1987), 12; Valerie J. Matsumoto, *Farming the Home*

Place: A Japanese American Community in California, 1919–1982 (Ithaca, N.Y., 1993), 31–32.

42. Masumoto, *Country Voices*, 2.

43. Matsumoto, *Farming the Home Place*, 52–53; Masumoto, *Country Voices*, 65–66, 97, 124.

44. Thomas H. Heuterman, *The Burning Horse: Japanese-American Experience in the Yakima Valley, 1920–1942* (Cheney, Wash., 1995), 26, 49, 98; Philip L. Fradkin, *The Seven States of California: A Natural and Human History* (New York, 1995), 145.

45. Masakazu Iwata, *Planted in Good Soil: The History of Issei in United States Agriculture*, 2 vols. (New York, 1992), 2:686–87, 690–91.

46. David Montejano, *Anglos and Mexicans in the Making of Texas, 1836–1986* (Austin, Tex., 1987), 112.

47. Ibid., 127.

48. Mario T. García, *Desert Immigrants: The Mexicans of El Paso, 1880–1920* (New Haven, 1981), 51.

49. Devra Weber, *Dark Sweat, White Gold: California Farm Workers, Cotton, and the New Deal* (Berkeley, Calif., 1994), 61; George Sánchez, *Becoming Mexican American: Ethnicity, Culture, and Identity in Chicano Los Angeles, 1900–1945* (Berkeley, Calif., 1993), 15.

50. David G. Gutiérrez, *Walls and Mirrors: Mexican Americans, Mexican Immigrants, and the Politics of Ethnicity* (Berkeley, Calif., 1995), 49; Don Mitchell, *The Lie of the Land: Migrant Workers and the California Landscape* (Minneapolis, Minn., 1996), 91; Ronald Takaki, *A Different Mirror: A History of Multicultural America* (New York, 1993), 315; Weber, *Dark Sweat, White Gold*, 94.

51. Weber, *Dark Sweat, White Gold*, 74; Mitchell, *Lie of the Land*, 129, 135, 163.

52. Carey McWilliams, *The Education of Carey McWilliams* (New York, 1978), 75.

53. González, *Labor and Community*, 189.

Chapter 9: The Urban Frontier

1. John Mack Faragher, ed., *Rereading Frederick Jackson Turner: "Significance of the Frontier in American History" and Other Essays* (New Haven, 1999), 31, 34; Adna F. Weber, *The Growth of Cities in the Nineteenth Century* (New York, 1899), 20, 27.

2. David Hamer, *New Towns in the New World: Images and Perceptions of the Nineteenth-Century Frontier* (New York, 1990), 97, 118, 185.

3. Richard Wade, *The Urban Frontier: The Rise of Western Cities, 1790–1830* (Cambridge, Mass., 1959), 322.

4. R. Douglas Hurt, *The Ohio Frontier: Crucible of the Old Northwest, 1720–1830* (Bloomington, Ind., 1996), 239.

5. Carl Abbott, *Boosters and Businessmen: Popular Economic Thought and Urban Growth in the Antebellum Middle West* (Westport, Conn., 1981), 45; Hurt, *Ohio Frontier*, 247–48.

6. Timothy R. Mahoney, *River Towns in the Great West: The Structure of Provincial Urbanization in the American Midwest, 1820–1870* (New York, 1990), 124–25.

7. Hamer, *New Towns in the New World*, 182; Charles N. Glaab, "Visions of Metropolis: William Gilpin and Theories of City Growth in the American West," *Wisconsin Magazine of History* 45 (1961): 26.

8. J. Christopher Schnell and Katherine B. Clinton, "The New West: Themes in Nineteenth-Century Urban Promotion, 1815–1880," *Bulletin of the Missouri Historical Society* 30 (Jan-

uary 1974): 77–78, 80; Jeffrey S. Adler, *Yankee Merchants and the Making of the Urban West: The Rise and Fall of Antebellum Saint Louis* (Cambridge, 1991), 56.

9. Adler, *Yankee Merchants,* 130, 134.

10. William Cronon, *Nature's Metropolis: Chicago and the Great West* (New York, 1991), 297, 299, 309.

11. Ibid., 297, 299, 309.

12. Weber, *Growth of Cities,* 228; Gilbert Stelter, "The City and Westward Expansion: A Western Case Study," *Western Historical Quarterly* 3 (1973): 189.

13. Richard O'Conner, *Iron Wheels and Broken Men: The Railroad Barons and the Plunder of the West* (New York, 1973), 101.

14. Earl Pomeroy, *The Pacific Slope: A History of California, Oregon, Washington, Idaho, Utah, and Nevada* (Seattle, Wash., 1965), 134.

15. Bascom N. Timmons, *Jesse H. Jones: The Man and the Statesmen* (New York, 1956), 81; David G. McComb, *Houston: The Bayou City* (Austin, Tex., 1969), 112, 116–17.

16. Rodman Paul, *Mining Frontiers of the Far West, 1848–1880* (New York, 1963), 86.

17. Pomeroy, *Pacific Slope,* 125.

18. Carey McWilliams, *Southern California Country: An Island on the Land* (New York, 1946), 98, 100.

19. Robert M. Fogelson, *The Fragmented Metropolis: Los Angeles, 1850–1930* (Cambridge, Mass., 1967), 67.

20. Raymond Dasmann, *The Destruction of California* (New York, 1966), 129.

21. Fogelson, *Fragmented Metropolis,* 110; Marc Reisner, *Cadillac Desert: The American West and Its Disappearing Water* (New York, 1986), 77.

22. Fogelson, *Fragmented Metropolis,* 85; Kenneth T. Jackson, *Crabgrass Frontier: The Suburbanization of the United States* (New York, 1985), 122.

23. McWilliams, *Southern California Country,* 235.

24. Ibid., 212, 237; James M. Cain, *The Postman Always Rings Twice* (New York, 1934), 150.

25. Bengt Ankerloo, "Agriculture and Women's Work: Directions of Change in the West, 1700–1900," *Journal of Family History* 4 (1979): 118.

26. Hamlin Garland, *Main-Travelled Roads* (New York, 1899), 118–19; *The Needs of Farm Women,* U.S. Department of Agriculture Reports, 103 (Washington, D.C., 1915), 12–14.

27. David Peterson del Mar, *What Trouble I Have Seen: A History of Violence against Wives* (Cambridge, Mass., 1996), 1, 24, 25, 31; Susan Armitage and Elizabeth Jameson, eds., *The Women's West* (Norman, Okla., 1987), 113.

28. Joanne J. Meyerowitz, *Women Adrift: Independent Wage Earners in Chicago, 1880–1930* (Chicago, 1988), 17–18.

29. Ibid., 18; Mary Murphy, *Mining Cultures: Men, Women, and Leisure in Butte, 1914–41* (Urbana, Ill., 1997), 99.

30. Bradford Luckingham, "Immigrant Life in Emergent San Francisco," *Journal of the West* 12 (1973): 600.

31. Pomeroy, *Pacific Slope,* 127; Ronald Takaki, *A Different Mirror: A History of Multicultural America* (New York, 1993), 215.

32. Charles Wollenberg, "Mendez v. Westminster: Race, Nationality and Segregation in California Schools," *California Historical Quarterly* 53 (1974): 318; Judy Yung, *Unbound Feet: A Social History of Chinese Women in San Francisco* (Berkeley, Calif., 1995), 207; Victor G.

and Bred de Bary Nee, *Longtime Californ': A Documentary Study of an American China-town* (New York, 1972), 44.

33. Yung, *Unbound Feet,* 49, 129.

34. McWilliams, *Southern California Country,* 160.

35. Ibid., 232.

36. Ibid., 135.

37. Fogelson, *Fragmented Metropolis,* 200; Martha Menchaca, *The Mexican Outsiders: A Community History of Marginalization and Discrimination in California* (Austin, Tex., 1995), 53; Mike Davis, *City of Quartz: Excavating the Future in Los Angeles* (New York, 1990), 163.

38. Gerald Horne, *Fire This Time: The Watts Uprising and the 1960s* (Charlottesville, Va., 1995), 26, 27.

39. Ibid., 249, 257; Fogelson, *Fragmented Metropolis,* 204.

40. George Sánchez, *Becoming Mexican American: Ethnicity, Culture and Identity in Chicano Los Angeles, 1900–1945* (New York, 1993), 200.

41. Sánchez, *Becoming Mexican American,* 213; Francisco E. Balderrama and Raymond Rodríguez, *Decade of Betrayal: Mexican Repatriation in the 1930s* (Albuquerque, N.Mex., 1995), 56.

42. Sánchez, *Becoming Mexican American,* 141, 144–45, 225.

43. Horne, *Fire This Time,* 257; Sánchez, *Becoming Mexican American,* 253.

44. Harry H. L. Kitano, *Japanese Americans: The Evolution of a Subculture* (Englewood Cliffs, N.J., 1969), 3; Brian Masaru Hayashi, *"For the Sake of Our Japanese Brethren": Assimilation, Nationalism, and Protestantism among the Japanese of Los Angeles, 1895–1942* (Stanford, Calif., 1995), 41, 136.

45. Monica Sone, *Nisei Daughter* (Boston, 1953), 42; Hayashi, *"For the Sake of Our Japanese Brethren,"* 85, 93.

46. Valerie J. Matsumoto, *Farming the Home Place: A Japanese Community in California, 1919–1982* (Ithaca, N.Y., 1993), 94; *New York Times,* June 20, 1998.

47. Richard Drinnon, *Keeper of Concentration Camps: Dillon S. Myer and American Racism* (Berkeley, Calif., 1987), vii, 31, 39.

Chapter 10: New Frontiers

1. U.S. Census Office, *Compendium of the Eleventh Census: 1890. Part I. Population* (Washington, D.C.: Government Printing Office, 1892), xlviii; John Mack Faragher, ed., *Rereading Frederick Jackson Turner: "The Significance of the Frontier in American History" and Other Essays* (New Haven, 1999), 31, 60.

2. Frank Popper, "The Strange Case of the Contemporary American Frontier," *Yale Review* 76 (Autumn 1986): 101–21.

3. Edgar W. Nye, *Remarks by Bill Nye* (New York, 1887), 467.

4. Elliott West, "Reconstructing Race," *Western Historical Quarterly* 34 (2003): 23–26.

5. William Appleman Williams, *History as a Way of Learning* (New York, 1973), 148; Fred Hoxie, ed., *Indians in American History: An Introduction* (Arlington Heights, Ill., 1988), 244.

6. Williams, *History as a Way of Learning,* 145; Faragher, *Rereading Frederick Jackson Turner,* 144, 149.

7. L. G. Moses, *Wild West Shows and the Images of American Indians, 1883–1933* (Albuquerque, N.Mex., 1996), 272; John G. Neihardt, *Black Elk Speaks: Being the Life Story of a Holy Man of the Oglala Sioux* (1932; reprint ed., New York, 1972), 193.

8. Richard Slotkin, *Gunfighter Nation: The Myth of the Frontier in Twentieth-Century America* (New York, 1992), 81–82.

9. G. Edward White, *The Eastern Establishment and the Western Experience: The West of Frederic Remington, Theodore Roosevelt, and Owen Wister* (New Haven, 1968), 80, 85, 91.

10. Slotkin, *Gunfighter Nation*, 171.

11. Owen Wister, *The Virginian: A Horseman of the Plains* (New York, 1903), 29, 474, 503.

12. White, *Eastern Establishment and Western Experience*, 58, 59, 100, 106, 107, 121.

13. Jules David Prown et al., *Discovered Lands, Invented Pasts: Transforming Visions of the American West* (New Haven, 1992), 106.

14. White, *Eastern Establishment and Western Experience*, 57, 109.

15. Donald Worster, *An Unsettled Country: Changing Landscapes of the American West* (Albuquerque, N.Mex., 1994), 71.

16. Roy M. Robbins, *Our Landed Heritage: The Public Domain, 1776–1936* (Lincoln, Nebr., 1962), 246.

17. Patricia Trenton and Peter H. Hassrick, *The Rocky Mountains: A Vision for Artists in the Nineteenth Century* (Norman, Okla., 1983), 121, 128.

18. Ibid., 128; Prown et al., *Discovered Lands, Invented Pasts*, 12–13, 15.

19. Worster, *Unsettled Country*, 76; Howard R. Lamar, ed., *The New Encyclopedia of the American West* (New Haven, 1998), 118; David M. Wrobel, *The End of American Exceptionalism: Frontier Anxiety from the Old West to the New Deal* (Lawrence, Kans., 1993), 66.

20. Joseph M. Petulla, *American Environmental History: The Exploitation and Conservation of Natural Resources* (San Francisco, 1977), 230; Roderick Nash, *Wilderness and the American Mind*, 3rd ed. (New Haven, 1982), 107, 110.

21. Nash, *Wilderness and the American Mind*, 111.

22. Ibid., 113, 114.

23. Ibid., 126, 128.

24. Richard West Sellars, *Preserving Nature in the National Parks: A History* (New Haven, 1997), 119.

25. Nash, *Wilderness and the American Mind*, 128, 130.

26. Roderick Nash, ed., *American Environmentalism: Readings in Conservation History*, 3rd ed. (New York, 1990), 60.

27. Ibid., 44; John Perlin, *A Forest Journey: The Role of Wood in the Development of Civilization* (New York, 1989), 361.

28. William G. Robbins, *Hard Times in Paradise: Coos Bay, Oregon, 1850–1986* (Seattle, Wash., 1988), 18, 20.

29. Nash, *Wilderness and the American Mind*, 137.

30. Wrobel, *End of American Exceptionalism*, 96–97.

31. Charles F. Wilkinson, *Crossing the Next Meridian: Land, Water, and the Future of the West* (Washington, D.C., 1992), 128; Samuel P. Hays, *Conservation and the Gospel of Efficiency: The Progressive Conservation Movement, 1890–1920* (Cambridge, Mass., 1959), 1.

32. Nash, *Wilderness and the American Mind*, 128, 135, 138–39; Hays, *Conservation and the Gospel of Efficiency*, 1.

33. William Robbins, *Lumberjacks and Legislators: Political Economy of the U.S. Lumber Industry, 1890–1941* (College Station, Tex., 1982), 10; Sandy Marvinney, "Theodore Roosevelt, Conservationist," *New York State Conservationist* 50 (June 1996): 77.

34. Marvinney, "Theodore Roosevelt, Conservationist."

35. Timothy Cochrane, "Early Forest Service Rangers' Fire Stories," *Forest and Conservation History* 35 (1991): 18; White, *Eastern Establishment and Western Experience*, 197.

36. Polly Welts Kaufman, *National Parks and the Woman's Voice: A History* (Albuquerque, N.Mex., 1996), 65.

37. Ibid., 80–82.

38. Ibid., 87.

39. Wilkinson, *Crossing the Next Meridian*, 20.

40. Ibid., 246.

41. Donald Worster, *Rivers of Empire: Water, Aridity, and the Growth of the American West* (New York, 1985), 167.

42. *Oxford English Dictionary*, s.v. "Reclamation" (compact ed., 1987).

43. John Muir, *The Yosemite* (New York, 1962), 197; Norris Hundley Jr., *The Great Thirst: Californians and Water, 1770s–1990s* (Berkeley, Calif., 1992), 172–73, 175; Nash, *American Environmentalism*, 97; Hays, *Conservation and the Gospel of Efficiency*, 194.

44. Donald Worster, *Dust Bowl: The Southern Plains in the 1930s* (New York, 1979), 58; Marsha L. Weisiger, *Land of Plenty: Oklahomans in the Cotton Fields of Arizona, 1933–1942* (Norman, Okla., 1995), 14.

45. John Steinbeck, *The Grapes of Wrath* (New York, 1939), 126.

46. Worster, *Dust Bowl*, 17.

47. Thomas R. Cox et al., *This Well-Wooded Land: Americans and Their Forests from Colonial Times to the Present* (Lincoln, Nebr., 1985), 217; Wrobel, *End of American Exceptionalism*, 135.

48. Worster, *Unsettled Country*, 103; Richard Hofstader, *The Progressive Historians: Turner, Beard, Parrington* (New York, 1969), 90.

49. Jordan A. Schwarz, *The New Dealers: Power Politics in the Age of Roosevelt* (New York, 1993), 298; Robert G. Athearn, *The Mythic West in the Twentieth-Century America* (Lawrence, Kans., 1986), 114.

50. Ibid., 256, 299.

51. Ibid., 316–17.

52. Philip Weeks, ed., *The American Indian Experience: A Profile, 1524 to the Present* (Arlington Heights, Ill., 1988), 240.

53. Horace M. Kallen, *Culture and Democracy in the United States* (New York, 1924), 116.

54. Meghan Fraze, "Legislating Divisions: The Failure of the Indian Reorganization Act on Pine Ridge" (senior essay, Yale College, 1997), 15, 20.

55. Kenneth R. Philip, *Indian Self Rule: First-Hand Accounts of Indian-White Relations from Roosevelt to Reagan* (Salt Lake City, Utah, 1986), 54.

56. Peter Iverson, *When Indians Became Cowboys: Native Peoples and Cattle Ranching in the American West* (Norman, Okla., 1994), 119–20, 181.

57. Weeks, *American Indian Experience*, 254.

58. Richard White, *The Roots of Dependency: Subsistence, Environment, and Social Change among the Choctaws, Pawnees, and Navajos* (Lincoln, Nebr., 1983), 258, 259.

Chapter 11: As the West Goes . . .

1. Neil Morgan, *Westward Tilt: The American West Today* (New York, 1961), vii.
2. Gerald Nash, *The American West Transformed: The Impact of the Second World War* (Bloomington, Ind., 1985), 157.
3. James L. Clayton, *The Economic Impact of the Cold War: Sources and Readings* (New York, 1970), 70.
4. Gerald D. Nash, *The American West in the Twentieth Century: A Short History of an Urban Oasis* (Englewood Cliffs, N.J., 1973), 6.
5. John R. Borchert, "America's Changing Metropolitan Regions," *Annals of the Association of American Geographers* 62 (1972): 352–73.
6. Kenneth T. Jackson, *Crabgrass Frontier: The Suburbanization of the United States* (New York, 1985), 265.
7. Greg Hise, *Magnetic Los Angeles: Planning the Twentieth-Century Metropolis* (Baltimore, 1997), 10.
8. Larry Gordon and Tom Gorman, "Inland Empire Leads in Fatal Road Rage," *Los Angeles Times*, March 9, 1999.
9. Timothy Egan, "Drawing a Hard Line against Urban Sprawl," *New York Times*, December 30, 1996.
10. Gilbert Townsend and J. Ralph Dalzell, *How to Plan a House* (1942; reprint ed., Chicago, 1953), 2–4; Thomas Hine, *Populuxe* (New York, 1987), 49.
11. Michael L. Johnson, *New Westers: The West in Contemporary American Culture* (Lincoln, Nebr., 1996), 45.
12. Howell Raines, "From Film Star to Candidate," *New York Times*, July 17, 1980.
13. "Transcript of Campaign's First Presidential Debate, with Reagan vs. Anderson," *New York Times*, September 22, 1980, "Transcript of Second Inaugural Address by Reagan," January 22, 1985.
14. Dan Frost, "American Indians in the 1990s," *American Demographics* 13 (December 1991): 28.
15. *Bergen Record*, March 17, 1991.
16. D'Arcy McNickle, *Native American Tribalism: Indian Survivals and Renewals* (New York, 1973), 107–8.
17. Joan Weibel-Orlando, *Indian Country, L.A.: Maintaining Ethnic Community in Complex Society* (Urbana, Ill., 1991), 104.
18. Peter Matthiessen, *In the Spirit of Crazy Horse* (New York, 1983), 35; Steven Mintz, ed., *Native American Voices: A History and Anthology* (St. James, N.Y., 1995), 175.
19. W. John Moore, "Tribal Imperatives," *National Journal*, June 9, 1990, 1396.
20. Frost, "American Indians in the 1990s," 26.
21. William Plummer, "Hearing His Own Drum: Activist Russell Means Dances with Hollywood," *People*, October 12, 1992.
22. Quintard Taylor, *In Search of the Racial Frontier: African Americans in the American West, 1528–1990* (New York, 1998), 261.
23. Gretchen Lemke-Santangelo, *Abiding Courage: African American Migrant Women and the East Bay Community* (Chapel Hill, N.C., 1996), 1, 65.
24. Lemke-Santangelo, *Abiding Courage*, 67; Taylor, *In Search of a Racial Frontier*, 257, 265.
25. Taylor, *In Search of the Racial Frontier*, 261.

26. Stan Steiner, *La Raza: The Mexican Americans* (New York, 1969), 180–81; "Roybal Recalls Prejudice inside Council, Congress," *Los Angeles Times*, July 27, 1987; Manuel Jimenez, "For 43 Years, Roybal Has 'Fought for His People,'" *Los Angeles Times*, January 28, 1993.

27. Augustus F. Hawkins, "Chilling a Quarter Century of Civil-Rights Progress Is No Mere Technicality," *Los Angeles Times*, July 11, 1989.

28. Charles Wollenberg, "Mendez v. Westminister: Race, Nationality, and Segregation in California Schools," *California Historical Quarterly* 53 (1974): 318.

29. Taylor, *In Search of a Racial Frontier*, 280.

30. Peter Y. Hong, "West Adams: A Home for Dreamers," *Los Angeles Times*, January 10, 1995.

31. Gerald Horne, *Fire This Time: The Watts Uprising and the 1960s* (Charlottesville, Va., 1995), 249.

32. Richard Griswold del Castillo, *Cesar Chávez: A Triumph of Spirit* (Norman, Okla., 1995), 13.

33. Gerald Nash and Richard Etulain, eds., *The Twentieth-Century West: Historical Interpretations* (Albuquerque, N.Mex., 1989), 134.

34. Griswold del Castillo, *Cesar Chávez*, 48–49; David G. Gutiérrez, *Walls and Mirrors: Mexican Americans, Mexican Immigrants, and the Politics of Ethnicity* (Berkeley, Calif., 1991), 88.

35. *Los Angeles Almanac*, http://www.laalmanac.com/population/po13.htm.

36. Leonard Pitt and Dale Pitt, *Los Angeles A to Z: An Encyclopedia of the City and County* (Berkeley, Calif., 1997), 140; David Rieff, *Los Angeles: Capital of the Third World* (New York, 1991), 151; Richard Rodriguez, "Go North, Young Man," *Mother Jones*, July–August 1995.

37. Rieff, *Los Angeles*, 192.

38. Neil Nisperos, "Why 42,000 People Moved from Los Angeles County to San Bernardino County from 2007-2-11," *Inland Valley Daily Bulletin*, February 5, 2014; Timothy Egan, "Eastward, Ho! The Great Move Reverses," *New York Times*, May 30, 1993.

Chapter 12: "It Ain't Where You're From, It's Where You're At"

1. David Ng, "The Los Angeles Urban Rangers Go on 'Safari' in the City," *Los Angeles Times*, August 16, 2009.

2. Sophie Duvernoy, "Westin Bonaventure Hotel Tour with the L.A. Urban Rangers: Great Adventure or Postmodern Dystopia," *LA Weekly*, July 12, 2011.

3. Ibid.

4. James Glanz, "Data Barns in a Farm Town, Gobbling Power and Flexing Muscle," *New York Times*, September 24, 2012.

5. Samuel P. Hays, *Beauty, Health, and Permanence: Environmental Politics in the United States, 1955–1985* (New York, 1987), 34; Roderick Nash, *Wilderness and the American Mind*, 3rd ed. (New Haven, 1982), 188, 288; Nash, ed., *American Environmentalism: Readings in Conservation History*, 3rd ed. (New York, 1990), 77; Richard West Sellars, *Preserving Nature in the National Parks: A History* (New Haven, 1997), 194.

6. Peter A. Coates, *The Trans-Alaska Pipeline Controversy: Technology, Conservation, and the Frontier* (Washington, D.C., 1992), 91.

7. Joseph E. Taylor, *Pilgrims of the Vertical: Yosemite Rock Climbers and Nature at Risk* (Cambridge, Mass., 2010), 137.

8. Kyle Stock, "Patagonia's 'Buy Less' Plea Spurs More Buying," *Bloomberg Businessweek,* August 28, 2013.

9. Edward Buscombe, ed., *The BFI Companion to the Western* (New York, 1988), 321.

10. J. Fred MacDonald, *Who Shot the Sheriff? The Rise and Fall of the Television Western* (New York, 1987), 103.

11. Ibid., 108; Richard Slotkin, *The Fatal Environment: The Myth of the Frontier in the Age of Industrialization, 1800–1890* (Middletown, Conn., 1985), 16; Slotkin, *Gunfighter Nation: The Myth of the Frontier in Twentieth-Century America* (New York, 1992), 495–96.

12. Nicolaas Mink, "A (Napoleon) Dynamite Identity: Rural Idaho, the Politics of Place, and the Creation of New Western Film," *Western Historical Quarterly* 39 (2008): 164; *Napoleon Dynamite,* directed by Jared Hess (Fox Searchlight, 2004), DVD.

13. Sherman Alexie, *The Absolutely True Diary of a Part-Time Indian* (New York, 2009), 1.

14. Mike Pesca, "I figured out Napoleon Dynamite," January 24, 2014, 10:16 p.m., Tweet.

15. Mink, "(Napoleon) Dynamite Identity," 161.

16. "I Know You Got Soul," *Paid in Full,* 4th and B'way Records, 1987.

Index

Abbott, Carl, 312

Abenakis, 65

Absolutely True Diary of a Part-Time Indian, The (Alexie), 451–54

Accault, Michel, 49

Acomas, 32, 34–35

Act for the Government and Protection of Indians (Cal.), 251

activism, pan-Indian, 409–11

Adamic, Louis, 330

Adams, John Quincy, 156–57, 179, 182–83, 191

Adams, Mildred, 331

aerospace industry, 389–90, 391–93. *See also* Hughes, Howard

African Americans: Black Panthers, 418–20; Buffalo Soldiers, 220–21, 448; in Congress, 416; migration to Kansas, 279–82; in southern California, 331–33, 417–18; Southern Homestead Act and, 279; and Texan independence, 186–87, 189; unemployment, 418; urban riots, 418, *419*; during and after World War II, 413. *See also* Africans, enslaved; segregation; slavery

African Methodist Episcopal Church, 280–81

Africans, enslaved: in the British colonies, 80–81, 139; in the Caribbean, 27; harsh treatment of, 185; and Texan independence, 186–87, 189; western slavery, 143. *See also* slavery

Agricultural Adjustment Act (1932), 373–74

agriculture: 20th-century transformation in, 369–70; Asian workers, 298–300, 302–3; bonanza farms, 247–48; citrus fruit, 298, 324; Depression-era migration of workers, 374; and the Dust Bowl, 374–76; and federal irrigation projects, 371, 372–73; mechanization of, 246–48, 369–70; Mexican farmworkers, 306–9, 420–22; native practices, 6; new Deal reforms, 373–74; surplus and falling prices, 370, 373; in Texas, 304. *See also* farming

Agriculture Department, 325, 364

AIM (American Indian Movement), 409–11

aircraft construction, 389–90, 391–92

Alabama, 132, 166, 185, *200*, 425

Alamo, the, 98, 188

Alaska, 96–98, 228, *425*

Albright, Horace, 367–69

Alcatraz Island, AIM occupation of, 410

alcohol, 88–89, 124

Aleutian Islands, 96–98

Aleuts, 96–98

Alexie, Sherman, 451–54

Algonquians: Christian converts, 65, 66; and French traders and colonists, 48–49, 61; hunting methods, 74–75; vs. Iroquois, 41; Lakotas driven west by, 145; log cabins adopted, 75–76; New England colonists' relations with, 62–69; Rowlandson held captive, 67–68; and the Virginia colonists, 54–56, 57–61. *See also* Delawares (Lenni-Lenapes); Narragansetts; Pequots; Wampanoags

Allen, Paul, 393

allotment of reservation lands, 287–88, 380–82

Alpine, Utah, 276–77

Alta California. *See* California

Alton, Illinois, 313

American Forestry Association, 361

American G.I. Forum, 416

American Indian Defense Association, 381

American Railway Union, 259–60

American Revolution, 106–10; land claims following, 110–12

Ames, Oakes, 236

Amherst, Jeffrey, Gen., 92–94

Annawon (Wampanoag warrior), 68–69

Anthony, Susan B., 278

anti-Catholicism, 201, 204

Apaches: Comanche raids on, 81–82; federal campaign against, 216–17; herds, and raids on Pueblos, 37; horses acquired, 81; and the Indian Removal Act, *180*; move to reservations resisted, 266–68; name, 3; San Carlos Apaches, 266–67, 383–84

Appalachian Mountains, settlement of, 79–80, 95

Apple, 393

Arapahos: at Fort Laramie conference, 208; Ghost Dancers, *289*; and the Indian Removal Act, *180*; at Little Bighorn, 263–65; move onto Plains, 165–66; and the Sand Creek Massacre, 219–20; treaties with, 217

Arikaras, 164, 208

Arizona: Apache reservation, 266–67, 383–84; arrival of the Spaniards, *32*; during the Civil War, 212; cotton production, 212; emerging majority minority (map), *425*; Geronimo's raids in, 267–68; Japanese farmers in, 302–3; mining in, 228, *232*; school segregation ended, 417; statehood, *200*; U.S. acquisition of, 200–201. *See also* Apaches; Navajos; New Mexico (Spanish/Mexican); Phoenix

Arkansas, 166, 185, 191, *200*, 374, *425*

Arkansas River, 162

Armstrong, John, 116

Arness, James, 446, *447*

Arroyo de la Cuesta, Fr. Felipe, 100

art of the West, 148–53, 346–48, 351–54, 357. *See also specific artists*

Asbury, Francis, Bishop, 274

Ashley, William, 163–65

Asian Americans, 423–24, 426. *See also* Chinese immigrants and Chinese Americans; Japanese immigrants and Japanese Americans

Asisara, Lorenzo, 101

Aspen, Colorado, 437

assimilation policies, 285–87, 380

Assiniboines, 208, 371

Astor, John Jacob, 155

Astoria, 155–56

Atchison, David Rice, 210

Athearn, Robert, 10

atomic bomb, 392

Austin, Moses, 167–69, 313

Austin, Stephen F., *167*, 168–69, 187, 188

automobiles, 324, 399, 401, 436

Autry, Gene, 446

Aztecs, 15–20, *21*, 24, 29, 31

Bacon's Rebellion, 60–61

Baker, Ross, 405

Balderrama, Francisco E., 335

Ballinger, Richard, 366

Bambaataa, Afrika, 455

Bank of America, 390, 391

Banks, Dennis, 409

Bartlett, John Russell, 200

Bassett, Isabel, 367

Battle of Fallen Timbers, 107, 125–26

Battle of Horseshoe Bend, 132, 179

Battle of Little Bighorn, 263–65, 344

Battle of the Blue Licks, 110

Battle of the Thames, 131

Battle of Tippecanoe, 130

beach access, 428–30

Bear Dance, The (Catlin, c. 1844), *152*

Bear Flag Republic, 195–96

bears, 349

Beaumont, Texas, 414

beaver, 43–44, 69, 153, 163–65, 349

Beaver Wars, 69

Bechtel, Stephen, 391

Benedict, Ruth, 381

Bent, Charles, 165, 194, 220

Bent, George, 219–20

Bent, William, 165, 219

Benton, Thomas Hart, 172–73, 174

Bering, Vitus, 96

Berkeley, George, 3

Berkeley, Sir William, 60

BIA. *See* Bureau of Indian Affairs

Bidwell, John, 298

Bierstadt, Albert, 351–53, 357

Big Eagle (Sioux chief), 215, 287

Big Foot (Sioux chief), 288, 290–91

Biloxi, Mississippi, 51

Bird, John, 186

bison: decline and disappearance, 251–53,
   254, 348–49, 356; hide trade, 143–44;
   Indian hunting and use of, 81, 143–44,
   165–66, 252–53

Black Elk (Sioux), 290, 295, 344

Black Hawk, 183, *186*

Black Hawk and his lieutenants in chains
   (Catlin), *186*

Black Hills: Great Sioux Reservation,
   260–63, 265 (*see also* Battle of Little Bighorn); Indian conflicts over, 145; mining
   in, 228, 245

Black Kettle (Cheyenne chief), 217–20, 263

Black Panthers, 418–20

Blackfeet Indian Reservation, 356

Blackfoot Indians, *382*

BLM (Bureau of Land Management). *See*
   Bureau of Land Management

Blue Lake (New Mexico), 411

Boas, Franz, 381

Bodmer, Karl, 148–49, *150*, 152, 153

Boeing, William, 391–92

Boeing Aircraft, 392, 393

Boetticher, Budd, 446

Bontemps, Arna, 333

Boone, Daniel, 78–79, 119–21, 135–37, 138,
   141

Boone, Rebecca Bryan, 78–79, 119

Boone and Crockett Club, 345, 356, 363

Boonesborough, 119

Borchert, John, 394–95

Bosque Redondo reservation, 216–17

Boudinot, Elias, 133–34

Bowie, James (Jim), 160, 187, 188

Boyd, William, 446

Bracero Program, 420–21

Brackenridge, Henry Marie, 120

Braddock, Edward, Gen., 90

Brant, Joseph (Mohawk leader), 107–9, 110,
   111, 121

Brisbin, James, 237

British colonies, *50*. *See also specific colonies*

Brown, Jerry, 421

Brown, John, 210

Brown v. Board of Education of Topeka
   (1954), 417

Browne, J. Ross, 249

Bryant, William Cullen, 314

Bryce, James, 321–22

Buchanan, James, 278

buffalo. *See* bison

Buffalo Bill, the King of Border Men (Buntline), 342

"Buffalo Bill's Wild West" show, 342–44.
   See also Cody, William

Buffalo Soldiers, 220–21, 448

Bureau of Indian Affairs (BIA), 207, 215, 285,
   381–86. *See also* reservations

Bureau of Land Management (BLM), 376.
   See also land policy, federal

Bureau of Reclamation, 371, 372–73

Burlingame Treaty (1868), 258, 297

Burnett, Peter H., 170, 249

Burnham, Frederick Russell, 297

Bury My Heart at Wounded Knee (Brown),
   410–11

Bush, George H. W., 402

Bush, George W., 402

Butler, Doris Elder, 273

Butte, Montana, 245–46, 291–92

Cabeza de Vaca, Álvar Núñez, 22–23

Cain, James M., 324

Calamity Jane, 160, *161*

Calhoun, John C., 199

California: 20th-century population boom, 394, *395*; aerospace industry, 389–90, 393; African American population (WWII), 413; agriculture, 247–48, 298–99, 324; beach access, 428–30; Bear Flag rebellion, 195–96; Chinese in, 231–33, 298–300; cotton production, 212; Depression-era migration to, 374; environmental impact of mining in, 227, 350–51; ethnic diversity, 229; farm-labor strikes (1930s), 307–9; Gold Rush (1848–55), 225–30, 232, 235, 248–49; and the Greater California economic region, 395–96; high-tech industry, 393; hydroelectric projects, 378; illegal immigration, 423–24; Indians in, 99–102, 248–51; Japanese in, 300–303, 331–32, 336–38; logging in, 361–62; majority minority in, 424, *425*; Mexican-American political participation, 415–16; migration from (1990–present), 426–27; oil fields, 331, 351; petrochemical industry, 392; property tax revolt, 403; racial/ethnic conflict in, 229–30, 249–51; segregation in, 332–33, 417–18; Spanish colonization of, 98–102; statehood, *200*; suburban development, 322, 324, 397–99; U.S. acquisition of, 193, 194–96, 198–200; WWII-era industrialization, 380. *See also* Mexican Americans; Mexican immigrants; Mexicans; *and specific cities and locations*

California Battalion of Mounted Volunteers, 196

California Institute of Technology (Caltech), 392

California Redwood Company, 240

Camp 4 climbers, 438–40

camp meetings, 275

Canada: border with U.S., 157, 171, 192, *200*; British supremacy over the French, 91–92; Sitting Bull refused asylum, 265; westward expansion, 166 (*see also* Pacific Northwest). *See also* Great Britain; New France; *and specific provinces, territories, cities, tribes, and individuals*

Canasatego (Iroquois leader), 87

Cane Ridge revival meeting, 275

captivity narratives, 22–23, 67–69

Caribbean islands, 12–15, 27, 85, 91, 92, 139. *See also specific islands*

Caribs, 15

Carlisle Indian Industrial School, 285, *286*

Carlton, James H., 216–17

Carson, Kit, 160, 174, 176, 216–17, 446

Carter, Jimmy, 401, 403

Cartier, Jacques, 41–44

Cartwright, Peter, 274–75

Casement, Jack and Dan, 242, 243

Cashin, Joan E., 185

casinos, Indian, 411–12

Catherine the Great, Tsarina, 97

Catholic missionaries: and the Aztecs, 20; in California, 98–102; and the Cayuse, 158; conversion of Indians in New France, 49, 51–53; and the Iroquois, 69–71; and the Pueblos, 31, 33–37; and Spanish treatment of Indians, 23 (*see also* Las Casas, Bartolomé de); Spanish vs. French approach, 52, 53

Catlin, George, 150–52, *186*

cattle: bison supplanted, 251–52, 254; cattle trails and drives, 254–55, *256*; Chicago meatpacking industry, 316–17; in colonial New Mexico, 34; Indian cattle ranching, 383–84; land granted by Austin for, 169; large-scale ranching, 237–38, 256–57; Texas longhorns, 253–54. *See also* ranching

Cayugas, 45, 69, 107–9. *See also* Iroquois Confederacy (Haudenosaunee; Five Nations; Six nations); Iroquois peoples

Cayuse tribe, 158–59

Central Pacific Railroad, 234–36, 237, 242–45, 257–58

Chae Chan Ping v. United States (1889), 304

Champlain, Samuel de, 44, 45–46

Chan, Thomas, 424

Charbonneau, Toussaint, 142

Charles I, King (Spain), 24

Charleston, South Carolina, 85

Chavez, Cesar, 420–21

Cherokee Nation v. Georgia (1831), 181

Cherokees: acculturation vs. traditionalism among, 131–34; alliance with the French, 84; and the American Revolution, 131; casino, *412*; and the Civil War, 212, 213; enrollment queries, 405; and the French and Indian War, 91; and the Indian Removal Act, 179–83; land ceded to British, 95; land lost through allotment, 380; population, 81; written language and literacy of, 132–34, 180

Cheyenne Autumn (1964 film), 448

Cheyennes: Bents' alliance with, 165; Dog Soldiers, 217, 220; and the Indian Removal Act, *180*; migration and inter-tribal conflicts, 145; Plains travel treaties, 208–9; Sand Creek Massacre, 217–20; strength of, 175; wars with the U.S., 263–65

Chicago, 315–17, 339, 350

Chicago and Rock Island Railroad, 236, 315–16

Chicanos (term), 423. *See also* Mexican Americans; Mexican immigrants

Chickasaws, 29, 84, 94, 179–80, 212

Chief Joseph (Nez Perce leader), 283

China, treaties with, 297

Chinese Exclusion Act (1882), 258, 304, 330

Chinese immigrants and Chinese Americans: Chinatowns, 232, 258, 300, 328–30; citizenship of, 298, 304; legal cases, 233–34, 304, 329–30; miners, 231–34; railroad workers, 242–44, 258; violence against, 258, *259*, 298–300

Chinooks, 159

Chisum, John, 238

Chivington, John M., 212, 217, 219–20

Choctaws, 84, 94, 179–80, 212

Chouinard, Yvon, 440

Chouteau, Jean Pierre, 162

Chouteau family, 162

Christianity, and the European worldview, 8–9. *See also* Catholic missionaries; churches

Chrysler ads, ix, xi, xii–xiii

Church, Benjamin, 68–69, 388

Church of Jesus Christ of Latter-Day Saints. *See* Mormons

churches: African American, 280–81; of immigrants, 291, 294; in settler communities, 273–76, 280–81, 291. *See also* Catholic missionaries; Mormons; Society of Friends (Quakers)

Cincinnati, Ohio, 311–13

circuit riders, Methodist, 274–75

cities: 20th-century population boom, 394, *395*; city planning, 397; economic relationships between, 394–95; failure vs. success of, 313–14; female migration to, 325, 327; immigrant populations, 327–28 (*see also specific groups*); Indian migration to, 409; metropolitan regions and dependent hinterlands, 395–96; riots, 418, *419*; role in westward expansion, 310–11; suburban development, 324, 396–400; traffic, 399; as urban jungles, 387–88. *See also specific cities*

Civil Rights Act (1870), 232

Civil War, 209, 211–13, 254

Civilian Conservation Corps (CCC), 376

Clappe, Louisa Amelia, 229

Clark, George Rogers, 109–10, *122*

Clark, William, Capt., 138, 140–43, 145–47. *See also* Lewis and Clark expedition

Clay, Henry, 191

Clayton, James L., 393

Cleveland, Grover, 363

Clinton, Bill, 401, 405

Clinton, George, Gov., 109

clothing: Levi's, 227, 401, 403; outdoor apparel companies, 440–42; Western, 401, 403 (*see also* Stetson hats)

Clovis culture, 4

coastal resources, native peoples and, 5–6

code talkers, 405–6

Cody, William ("Buffalo Bill"), 317–18, 342–44

Cold War, xi–xii, 447

colleges, Indian, 412–13

Collier, John, 381–86

colonial wars, 84–87. *See also specific wars*

conservation. *See* environmental movement; national forests (forest reserves); national parks

conservative politics (1945–present), 402. *See also* Reagan, Ronald

Constitution of the United States, 123

Conzen, Kathleen Niels, 291

Cook, James, Capt., 155

Cooke, Jay, 209, 223–24, 357

Coolidge, Calvin, 373

Cooper, Gary, 443, *444*, 446

Cooper, James Fenimore, 159–60, 348

copper mines, 245–46

Cornplanter (Seneca chief), 126

Cornwallis, Charles, Gen., 110

Coronado, Francisco Vásquez de, *28*, 31

corporations: graft by, 236–37; power of, 224–25. *See also* industrial capitalism; *and individual corporations*

Corps of Discovery. *See* Lewis and Clark expedition

Cortés, Hernán, 14, 16–20, *28*, 29

Cortez Colony, 302

Cortina, Juan, 203–4

cotton, 131, 169, 179, 212

cotton gin, 131, *179*

country and western music, 401

Covenant Chain, 71–72, 85

covenants, housing. *See* restrictive covenants

cowboys, *256*; in Buffalo Bill's Wild West show, 342; in fiction and film, 446 (*see also* fictional depictions of the West); Indian cowboys, 383–84; Mexican vaqueros, 254. *See also* cattle; ranching; Reagan, Ronald; Roosevelt, Theodore

Crazy Horse (Oglala leader), 260–63, 265

Creeks: alliance with English settlers, 84; and the Civil War, 212; and the Indian Removal Act, 180; population, 81; resettlement in Florida, 85; smallpox among, 94; Tecumseh and, 130; U.S. treaty with, 123; war with the U.S., 132. *See also* Seminoles

Crees, 145

Creoles (Russian-Aleuts), 98

Crèvecoeur, J. Hector St. John de, 115

Crocker, Charles, 234–36, 242–43

Crockett, David (Davy), 160, 186, 188, 446

Cronon, William, 316

Crook, George, Gen., 263, 266

Crows, 145, 208

cultural pluralism, 381, 382

Cushinberry, Grant, 280–81

Custer, George Armstrong, Gen., 125, 263–65, 344

Cutler, Manasseh, 116

Dakota Territory, 228, *232*, *246*, 247–48. *See also* Black Hills; North Dakota; South Dakota

Dallas-Fort Worth, *395*, 395

Dalrymple, Oliver, 247

Daly, Marcus, 291

dams, 371, 378–80, 390, 392, 432

Dare, Ananias and Eleanor White, 56

Dare, Virginia, 56

Dasmann, Raymond, 322

data centers, 432–34

Davis, Jefferson, 212

Dawes, Henry, 287

De Smet, Pierre-Jean, 158

de Soto, Hernando, *28*, 29

Deadwood Dick (fictional character), 160, *161*

Death of General Wolfe, The (West painting), 91, *92*

Debs, Eugene, 259

del Mar, David Peterson, 326

Del Rey, California, 301–2

Delaware valley, European settlement of, 73–76. *See also* Pennsylvania

Delawares (Lenni-Lenapes): and the American Revolution, 109; Delaware Prophet (Neolin), 94; gender roles, 73–74; Gnadenhutten massacre, 110; Haudenosaunee and, 86; and the Indian Removal Act, *180*; in the Ohio country, 90, 94, 121; Penn's treaty with, 76–77, 87; and the Walking Purchase, 87, *88*

Denver, 318, 319, 354–55, 392–93, *395*, 396

Denver Pacific Railroad, 318

fur trade, 43–44; and beaver, 43–44, 69, 153, 163–65; Beaver Wars, 69; dependent on Indian labor, 153; and disease, 44–45, 166; ecological impacts, 165–66, 349; French and, 43–46, 47; and the Mandans, 141; in the Pacific Northwest, 154–56; Rocky Mountain fur trade, 163–65; Russians and, 96; Saint Louis and, 162–65; trading companies, 153–55. *See also* bison; Hudson's Bay Company
Fur traders in camp (Miller), *164*

Gadsden, James, 200
Gadsden Purchase, 200–201
Galbraith, Thomas J., 283–84
Gale, Zona, 295
Galveston, Texas, 318
gaming, Indian, 67, 411–12
Garland, Hamlin, 272, 296, 325
Garokontié, Daniel (Onondaga leader), 70
Gates, Bill, 393
Geffen, David, 428
gender roles, European vs. Indian, 42–43. *See also* women
General Land Office, 207, 240
Gentlemen's Agreement, 300–301
George, Henry, 321
Georgia, 80, 112–13, 117, 181, *200, 425*
German Americans, loyalty of, 337
German immigrants, 79, 292, 328
Geronimo (Apache leader), 266–68
Ghost Dancers, 288–91
Giannini, Amadeo Peter, 328, 390, 391
Glacier National Park, 356, 360
Glorieta Pass, battle of, 212
Goff, Seldon, 227
gold: in the Black Hills, 260; in California, 225–30, 232, 248 (*see also* Gold Rush); discovered in the Rockies, 212, 260; Spanish desire for, 13–14, 17–18
Gold Rush (California, 1848–55), 225–31, *232, 235,* 248–49
Goldwater, Barry, 402, 403
Goliad, battle of, 188
Gonzalez, Alfredo Guerra, 335–36

González, Gilbert G., 309
González, Henry B., 416
Goodnight, Charles, 223–24, 237
Gore, Al, 401
Gracon, Ruth, 414
Grand Canyon of the Yellowstone (Moran, 1872), 353, *354*
Grand Coulee Dam, 380
Grant, Ulysses S., 193–94, 197
grape boycott, 421–22, *422*
Grapes of Wrath, The (Steinbeck), 374
Great Britain: 49th parallel treaty, 192; and the American Revolution, 107–10; hunting restricted to upper classes, 74; Indian Country established, 94–95; Indians in, 54; Seven Years War, 90–92; Spanish galleons raided, 53–54; and U.S. westward expansion, 110, 121, 122, 124–26; War of 1812, 130–31, 156. *See also* Canada; *and specific colonies and individuals*
Great Depression, 333–35, 374, 378
Great Lakes, French colonization of, 47, 50–51, 83. *See also* New France
Great Migration of 1843, 170
Great Plains: conservation programs, 376; cyclical droughts, 256–57, 374–76; native way of life on, 143–45; travel across, 207–9 (*see also* railroads); as wasteland, 148. *See also* bison; Plains Indians; *and specific territories, states, and tribes*
Great Sioux Reservation, 260–63, 265. *See also* Battle of Little Bighorn
Great Swamp Fight, 66
Great Train Robbery, The (1903 film), 443
Greater California (economic region), 395–96
Green Bay, French settlement at, *83*
Grey, Zane, 442
Grinnell, George Bird, 356
Gros Ventre tribe, 371
Gruening, Ernest, 436
Guerrero, Vicente, 187
guns and firearms, 213, *214*
Gunsmoke (television show), 446, *447*

Kennedy, John F., 388, 409

Kent, Henry, 227

Kentucky: Battle of the Blue Licks, 110; Boone and the settlement of, 119–20; land ceded by Virginia to, *112*; minority population (map), *425*; population, 121; statehood, 121, 166, *200*

Kidd, William Winston (Billy), 437

King, Richard, 238

King, Rodney, 426

King Philip's War, 65–67

King William's War, 85, 86

Kiowa people, *180*, 208–9

Knox, Henry, 122, 123

Ku Klux Klan, 281, 331

La Salle, René-Robert Cavelier, Sieur de, 50–51

La Vérendrye, Pierre de Varennes, Sieur de, 141–42

labor movements, 257–60, 307–9, 330

Laguna Pueblo, 411

Lakewood, California, 397

Lakotas. *See* Sioux

L'Amour, Louis, 442–43

Lancaster, Pennsylvania, 87

Land Ordinance (1785), 113–15

land policy, federal: dispersal of public lands halted, 376–77; Homestead Act (1862), 115, 211, 238–41; map of federal lands, *377*; national parks and, 358–59; sale of public lands, 115–17, 239–40, 356, 361; survey system, 113–15. *See also* national forests; national parks; reservations

land scams, 116–17, 240

land speculation, 117, 323

Lapérouse, Jean- François de Galaup, Comte de, 101

Larkin, Thomas O., 248

Las Casas, Bartolomé de, 23–26

Lawrence, Kansas, 210, 213

Lawton, Henry W., 268

lead mines, 313

Leadville, Colorado, 228, *232*

League of United Latin American Citizens (LULAC), 416–17

Leatherstocking Tales (Cooper), 159–60, 348

Leavenworth, Kansas, 318

Lee, Jason, Rev., 157, 169

Lee, John D., 278

Lee, Richard Henry, 117

Lee, Robert E., 204

Lenni-Lenapes. *See* Delawares

Leopold, Aldo, 436

Letters from an American Farmer (Crève-coeur), 115

Levi's (jeans), 227, 401, 403

Levittown, 399–400, 401

Lewis, Meriwether, 138, 140–43, 145–47, 153

Lewis, Randall, 427

Lewis, Sinclair, 295

Lewis and Clark expedition, 138, 140–43, 145–47, 153

Lincoln, Abraham, 211, 316, 401

Lindsay, Vachel, 297

Lindsley, Marguerite, 367–78

Lisa, Manuel, 163

Little Bighorn, Battle of, 263–65, 344

Little Crow (Sioux chief), 215

Little Turtle (Miami chief), 124–25, 126, 129

log cabins, 73, *74*, 75–76, 78, 89

Logan, Greenbury, 189

logging, 350, 360–63, 364–66, 408–9. *See also* timber industry

Lone Ranger, 446

Long, Stephen H., 148

Long Island Sound, 63–64

Longhouse Religion, 128

longhouses, 41–42

Longoria, Felix, 416

Los Alamos National Laboratory, 392

Los Angeles: airport, 423; ethnic diversity, 424–26; founding of, 100; Japanese residents interned, 337–38; migration to, 330–33; minorities in, 331–37, 416, 417–18, 426; movie industry, 331; oil fields, 331; population (1990), *395*; post–WWII era, 387–88; riots, 418, *419*, 426; rise of metropolis, 322; suburban development, 324, 397–99; urban flight, 427; water supply, 322–23, 371; Watts area, 333, 418, *419*

Mexican immigrants: cross-border migration patterns, 306–7; deportation of, 333–35; in the early 20th century, 304, 306–7; farmworkers, 306, 307–9, 420–22; in Los Angeles, 331–32, 333–36

Mexican War, 192–200, 209, 210

Mexicans: and the California Gold Rush, 225, 229–30; vaqueros, 254. *See also* Mexican Americans; Mexican immigrants; Tejanos

Mexico: and Austin's Texas land grants, 168–69; boundary with the U.S., 200–201; economy, and illegal migration, 423; independence, 166; and Mexican migrant worker strikes, 309; native population, 26; Revolution, 304, 306, 307; social and racial equality in, 186–87; and Texan independence, 187–89; war with the U.S., 192–200. *See also* New Spain

Mexico City, 28–29; American campaign for, 196–97, *198*. *See also* Tenochtitlán

Meyerowitz, Joanne, 326–27

Miami Indians, 109, 121, 124–25, *180*. *See also* Little Turtle (Miami chief)

Michigan, 166, *200*, 425

Micmacs, 39–40, 52

Microsoft, 393, 432–34, 441

migration: of African Americans, 279–81, 413–14; from California (1990–present), 426–27; and community, 270–72; during the Depression, 374; Great Migration of 1843, 170; of the Iroquois, 111; to Los Angeles, 330–33; post–WWII boom, 394; from reservations to cities, 409; right of, 297–98; of women, to cities, 325–27. *See also* immigrants; removal of Indians; *and specific states, tribes, and immigrant groups*

Miller, Alfred Jacob, 149–50, *151*, 153, *164*

Miller, Joaquin, 174

miners: Chinese, 231–34; Indian, 248–49; Irish, 291–92; Mexican, 225, 229–30. *See also* Gold Rush; mining

Mingo Indians, 109, 121

mining: 20th-century decline, 393–94; copper, 245–46; Denver and, 319; impact on Indians, 248–49, 260; industrial techniques, 227, *228*, 350; lead, 313; map of mining areas, *232*; mercury, 350–51; mine owners, 245, 320–21; placer mining, 225, 248; and the settlement of the West, 227–28. *See also* Gold Rush; miners

Mink, Nicholaas, 451, 454

Minneapolis and Saint Paul, 319

Minnesota: Eastern Sioux reservation and uprising, 215, *216*; European immigrants in, 292, *293*, 294–95; logging in, 350; minority population (map), *425*; statehood, *200*

Minnetarees, 141

Miriam Report, 380–81

Mississippi, 166, 185, *200*, 425

Mississippi River: as beginning of the West, 10; French claims ceded to Britain, Spain, 91; French exploration and colonization, 47, 50–51; Saint Louis and, 313, *314*, 315–16; Spanish control of, 91, 139

Missouri: Boone's land grant in, 135; during the Civil War, 212–13; Kansas invaded by proslavery militias from, 210; minority population (map), *425*; Mormons in, 205; statehood, 166, 178, *200*

Missouri Compromise, 178, 210

Missouri Fur Company, 163

Missouri River: as beginning of the West, 10; and the fur trade, 162–64; Great Sioux Reservation bounded by, 260; Kansas City and, 318; Lewis and Clark's exploration of, *140*, 141, 145, 153; Saint Louis and, 162–63, 313

Miwoks, 248

mob violence, 104. *See also* Paxton Boys; vigilantes

Moctezuma, 16, 17–18, 20. *See also* Aztecs

Mohawks: and the American Revolution, 107–9; Christian converts among, 70–71; and the Dutch, 61; and the Iroquois Confederacy, 45, 69–70; and King Philip's War, 66, 69; and King William's War, 85. *See also* Brant, Joseph; Iroquois Confederacy; Iroquois peoples

Mohegan casino, 67, 412

Momaday, N. Scott, 449–50

Monroe, James, 179

Montana: mining in, 228, *232*, 245–46; minority population (map), *425*; ranches in, 254; Sioux resistance in, 260; statehood, *200*, 358

Montcalm, Marquis de, 91

Montreal, 46, 47

Mooney, James, 288

Moran, Thomas, 353–54, *357*

Morgan, Edward, 65

Mormons: *Book of Mormon*, 204–5; driven West, 200, 205, 206–7; isolationism vs. industrial development, 318–19; missionaries, 276; Mormon culture in *Napoleon Dynamite*, 451; polygamy among, 205–6, 278–79; settlement of Utah, 276–78

Morse, Jedidiah, 137–38

mountain climbing, 436, 438–40

movie industry (Hollywood), 331, 390–91

movies, Western, 442–49. *See also specific titles*

Muir, John, 359–60, 363, 364, *365*, 371, 372

Murphy, Mary, 327

Murrieta, Joaquin, 201, *202*

music, country and western, 401

Mutchler, J. C., 237

My Darling Clementine (1946), 445

Myer, Dillon S., 338, 406

Nacogdoches, Texas, 167, *168*

Napoleon Bonaparte, 169

Napoleon Dynamite (2004 film), 450–51, 453–54

Narragansetts, 39, 40, 64–67

Narváez, Panfilo de, 21–22

Nash, Gerald, 393

Natchez Indians, 84

National Council of American Indians, 406

National Forest Service, 364, 366–67, 368, 382

national forests (forest reserves), 363, 364–66

national monuments, 364

National Park Service, 367–69, 431

national parks, 356–60, 364, 367–69, 431, 434–36. *See also specific parks*

Native Americans. *See* Indians; *specific tribes; and headings beginning with* Indian

natural resources, 351, 360–61, 411. *See also* Dust Bowl; environmental movement; logging; mining; national parks; wildlife, decline and disappearance of

Nauvoo, Illinois, 205–7

Navajos: enforced submission of, 217; herds, 35, 37, *385*, 385–86; name, 3; Pueblos raided, *37*; reorganization rejected by, 385–86; in *Stagecoach*, 444

Navarro, Ramon Jil, 230

Nebraska, *200*, 210, 292, 374, *425*

Neolin (Indian leader), 94

Nevada, 200, 228, *232*, *425*

New Deal, 373–74, 376–80, 389; Indian New Deal, 381–86

New England, 68–69; coastal Indians, 39–40 (*see also specific tribes*); colonial population growth, 78–79, 80; colonists' relations with Indians, 62–69; land distribution and settlement, 113. *See also* Pilgrims; Puritans; *and specific colonies, localities, tribes, individuals, and events*

New France: culture and social structure, 46–50, 82–84; earliest trading expeditions to, 41–45; establishment of, 44, 45–46; French and Indian War (1754–63), 90–92; missionaries and conversion of Indians in, 49, 51–53; and the Ohio country, 89–90; population growth, 82; territory claimed, 50–51; trade with the Mandans, 141–42. *See also* Canada

New Mexico (Spanish/Mexican): Comanches and, 81, 98; northern settlement strategy, 166; Pike and, 147–48; Pueblo Revolt, 36–37, 81; sheep and cattle, 34;

New Mexico (Spanish/Mexican)
(*continued*)
Spanish invasion and colonization,
31–37; U.S. acquisition of, 193, 194,
195, 198–99, 200–201. *See also* Pueblo
peoples
New Mexico (U.S.): acquisition of, 193, 194,
195, 198–99, 200–201; atomic bomb
developed, 392; Civil War and, 212;
Elephant Butte Dam, 371; federal campaigns against Apaches and Navajos,
216–17; majority minority in, 424, *425*;
Mexican-American activism in, 421; and
slavery, 210; statehood, *200. See also* New
Mexico (Spanish/Mexican); Pueblo
peoples
New Netherlands, 71. *See also* Dutch traders
and colonists
New Orleans, 51, 92, 124, 139–40. *See also
headings beginning with* Louisiana
New Spain: governance, 29; intermarriage
in, 27–28; Mexican independence, 166;
mining, 31; native population, 26, 27;
Pike and, 147–48; Spanish conquest,
15–20, *21*; Texas settlements, 98. *See
also* Mexico; Mexico City; New Mexico
(Spanish/Mexican)
New Sweden, 73
New York, 71; English-Iroquois alliance
(Covenant Chain), 71–72; and the
French and Indian War, 90; German
settlers in, 79; minority population
(map), *425*; Mormon church founded
in, 204–5; settlement of western New
York, 95; statehood, *200*; western lands
claimed/ceded, 112–13
newspapers, 198, 234–36
Newton, Huey P., 418
Nez Perce tribe, 283
Nicodemus, Kansas, 280–81
Nisei. *See* Japanese immigrants and
Japanese-Americans
Nixon, Richard, 402, 409, 421
North Carolina, 80, 112–13, *200*, *425*.
North Dakota, *200*, 374, *425. See also* Dakota
Territory

North West Company, 153–55
Northern Pacific Railroad, 247
Northwest Ordinance of 1787, 117–19, 122,
178
Northwest Passage, search for, 41, 44
Northwest Territory, *112*, 113–19, *118. See also*
Ohio country; *and specific territories and
states*
Norwegian immigrants, *293*, 294–95
Nueces Strip, 193
Nye, Bill, 340

Oakley, Annie, 342–44, 446
Obama, Barack, 401
Oglala Sioux, 260–65, 412. *See also* Pine
Ridge Reservation; Sioux
Ohio (state), 166, *200*, 205, *425. See also*
Cincinnati, Ohio
Ohio Associates, 116–17
Ohio Company, 90, 95
Ohio country, 89–91, 92–96, *114*, 124–26
Ohio Indians: and the American Revolu-
tion, 109, 110, 111; and British sover-
eignty, 92–94; composition of, 90, 121;
and the French and Indian War, 90–91;
land ceded to U.S., 126; Tecumseh and,
129–31; uprising, 94; U.S. battles against,
124–26
Ohio Indians meet with the British in 1764
(West engraving), *93*
oil, 320, 331, 351. *See also* petrochemical
industries
Ojibwas, 145, 380
Oklahoma, *200*, 374, 380, 395, *425. See also*
Dust Bowl
Old Faithful geyser, *435*
Old Jules (Sandoz), 326
Olmsted, Frederick Law, 313, 357
Omaha, Nebraska, 327, *395*
Oñate, Juan de, 31–33
Oneida utopian community, 206
Oneidas, 45, 69, 107, 111. *See also* Iroquois
Confederacy; Iroquois peoples
Onondagas, 45, 69, 70, 72, 107–9. *See also*
Iroquois Confederacy; Iroquois peoples;
Otreouti (Onondaga leader)

Pocahontas, *58*, 59

police brutality, 426

Polk, James K., 191, 192–95, 198–200, 226

polygamy, 205–6, 278–79

Ponce de León, Juan, 21, *28*

Pontiac (Ottawa leader), 94

Popé (Pueblo leader), 36–37

popular culture: 19th-century depictions of the West, 159–61, 170; 21st-century depictions of the West, 450–54; frontier life in, 342–48; hip-hop music and culture, ix, x–xi, 454–55; outdoor gear and apparel, 440–42; popularity of western styles, 388, 400–401 (*see also* Levi's; Stetson hats); Western art, 346–48, 351–54; Western brand, 388; Western movies and television, 442–49. *See also* fictional depictions of the West

popular sovereignty, 210

population growth: 1776–1850, 166; colonial era, 78–79, 80, 82; emerging majority minorities, *425*; Latino/a immigration and (1965–present), 423–24; Native American (1950–2010), 405; urban (20th century), 394–96, 413

pork-packing industry, 311–12

Portland, Oregon, 327, *395*, 399, 413

Portolá, Gaspar de, 98

Postman Always Rings Twice, The (Cain), 324

postmodern westerns, 449

Pottawatomies, 121, *180*

Powhatan (Wahunsenecawh), 57–59

powwows, 409

Pratt, Richard Henry, 285

Presbyterians, 157–58, 273–74

presidents, western, 401–5. *See also specific presidents*

Preston, Idaho, 450–51. See also *Napoleon Dynamite*

Price, Jenny, 429–30

property rights, native vs. European traditions of, 8, 123, 183. *See also* allotment of reservation lands

property taxes, 403

Proposition 187 (Cal.), 423–24

prostitution, 47–48, 232

Protestant missionaries, 157–59, 273–75

public lands. *See* land policy, federal; national forests; national parks

Pueblo peoples: architecture, 31, *33*; culture, 33–35; name origin, 3; Navajo and Apache raids on, 216, 217; Pueblo Revolt, 36–37, 81; religion, 34–37, 285; resistance by, 194, 381; Spanish conquest and colonization, 31–37. *See also* Hopis; Taos tribe; Zunis

Puerto Rico, 15

Pulaski, Edward, 367

Puritans, 63–65, 67. *See also* Massachusetts Bay Colony; New England

Quakers. *See* Society of Friends

Quantrill, William, 213

Quebec City, 44, 45, 47, 91

Queen Anne's War, 85

Quincy, Washington, 432–34

racism: among the French, 49; in the armed services, 414–15; class solidarity eroded, 259–60; in Kansas, 281–82; racialization of politics, 121–22; vs. Western ideas of individual rights, 303–4. *See also* Indian policy, federal; segregation; slavery; *and specific racial and ethnic groups*

railroads: Apache territory encircled, 266; and bison's disappearance, 252; and bonanza farming, 247; federal land subsidies, 240; graft, 236–37; labor unrest, 257–60; map, *224*; and the national parks, 357, 359, 360; transcontinental, 209, 211, 224, 234–37, 241–45; and urban development, 315–19, 322

Rakim (rapper), 454

Raleigh, Sir Walter, 54, 56. *See also* Roanoke colony

Ralston, William, 245

ranch houses, 400–401

ranching, 169, 237–38, 256–57, 383–84, 393–94. *See also* cattle

range lands, public, 376

can settlement of, 167–69, 186–87; annexation of, 191–92, *200*; cattle-ranching in, 237–38, 253–54; and the Civil War, 212; Depression-era migration from, 374; German immigrants in, 292; and the Imperial Texas economic region, 395; majority minority in, 424, *425*; Mexican-American activism in, 421–23; oil fields, 320; petrochemical industry, 392; Pike on, 148; racial and ethnic conflicts, 189, 203–4, 304–6, 414; revolution and independence, 187–91; segregation in, 414–15, 416; slavery in, 186–87, 189; under the Spanish, 22, *50*, 98, 166–67, *168*; Texas-Mexico border dispute, 193–94. *See also* Tejanos; *and specific cities*

Texas Rangers, 203, 305–6, 366, 431

Thayendanega (Mohawk leader). *See* Brant, Joseph

Thoreau, Henry David, 199

Tijerina, Reies, 421

Timber Cutting Act (1878), 232

timber industry, 240, 350, 361–62, 364–66. *See also* forests; logging

timing, early colonization and, 40–41

Timucuas (Florida), 5, 30–31

Tippecanoe, 129–30

Tishcohan (Delaware chief), *88*

Tlaxcalans (Mexico), 20, 31

tobacco, 59–60

Tocqueville, Alexis de, 310–11

Tohono O'odham tribe, 384

Toledo, Preston and Frank, *406*

Tombstone, Arizona, 228, *232*

Tonto, 446

Topographical Engineers, Army Corps of, 172, 173–74, 195, 196

Torres, Al, 424

tourist industry, 391, 437–38. *See also* national parks; outdoor recreation

Toussaint, François-Dominique, 139

Townes, Samuel, 185

tract construction, 397

trade, 44–45, 88. *See also* fur trade

trading posts, federal, 123–24

traffic, 399

Trail of Tears, 181–82. *See also* Cherokees

transportation: air transport and Denver's growth, 396; commercial connections redirected to New York City, 211; Overland Trails, *175*, 207–8, 271, 276, 445; Pacific Electric interurban rail system, 324; rivers and, 311–13, *314*, 316; road congestion, 399; wagon trains, 207–8. *See also* railroads

Trans-World Airlines (TWA), 390

Travis, William Barret ("Buck"), 187–88

Treaty of Fort Atkinson, 208–9

Treaty of Fort Laramie (1868), 260, 262

Treaty of Guadalupe Hidalgo (1848), 200–201, 204

Treaty of Nanking (1842), 297

Treaty of New Echota (1835), 181

Treaty of Paris (1763), 91–92

treaty system, 123–24, 284–85. *See also specific Indian treaties and tribes*

Trist, Nicholas, 199–200, 201

Trudeau, Garry, 428

Truman, Harry, 401

Tsali (Cherokee visionary), 131

Tsosie, Nathan, 411

Turner, Frederick Jackson, frontier thesis of, 9–10, 310, 339–42, 405

Tuscaloosas, 29

Tuscaroras, 107, 111

Twain, Mark, 352–53

Two Moons (Cheyenne chief), 264

Tyler, John, 191–92

unemployment, 333, 412, 418

Unforgiven (1992 film), 449

Union Pacific Railroad, 236, 242–45, 257, 258, 318

United Farm Workers (UFW), 421, *422*

United States v. Wong Kim Ark (1898), 304

urban sprawl. *See* suburban development

Utah: copper mine, 245; minority population (map), *425*; Mormon settlement of, 276–78; and slavery, 210; statehood, *200*, 279; territory created, 277; U.S. acquisition of, 200; women's suffrage in, 278–79. *See also* Mormons; Salt Lake City

Willamette River valley, 171. *See also* Oregon
    Country
William of Orange, 85
Williams, Roger, 65
Williams, Terry Tempest, 450
Williams, William Appleman, 342
Wilmot, David, 210
Wilmot Proviso, 210
Wilson, Woodrow, 1, 306, 341
Wingina (Roanoke Algonquian chief), 54,
    55
Winnebagos, 183
Winthrop, John, 63
Wisconsin: German immigrants in, 292;
    Indians massacred, 183; minority popu-
    lation (map), *425*; Peshtigo fire, 350;
    Saint Louis trade and, 313; statehood,
    200. See also Green Bay; Menominees;
    Winnebagos
Wister, Olan, 382
Wister, Owen, 344, 345–46
Witherspoon, John, Rev., 3
Wolfe, James, Gen., 91
Wollenberg, Charles, 418
wolves, 348–49
women: Chinese immigrants, 231–32;
    Delaware women, 73–74; domestic
    violence against, 326–27; as forest and
    park rangers, 367–69, 431; frontier
    hardships, 272; hat plumes, 356; Indian
    women and sexuality, 34, 47–48, 53; In-
    dian women as intermediaries, 142–43;
    Iroquois women, 42; Japanese women,
    301; Miller's paintings of Indian women,
    149–50; Plains women, 153; Pueblo
    women, 34–35; Scandinavian women,
    74; schoolteachers, 273, *274*; urban mi-
    gration of, 325–27; voting rights, 278–79
Wong, Esther, 330
Wood, Leonard, 268
Wooden Leg (Cheyenne warrior), 263–64
Woods, John, 270
Worcester v. Georgia (1832), 181, 284

World Trade Organization protests (1999),
    xii
World War I, 306
World War II: African Americans during,
    413–14; defense spending, 389–90,
    392–93; Japanese internment, 337–38;
    minorities in military service, 389–90,
    405–6; ship and aircraft construction,
    380, 389–90, 413
World's Colombian Exhibition (1893), 339
Worster, Donald, 349, 376
Wounded Knee: massacre (1890), 290–91;
    occupation (1973), 409–10
Wovoka (Paiute shaman), 288. *See also*
    Ghost Dancers
Wozniak, Stephen, 393
writers, Native American, 449–50, 451–54
Wyeth, Nathaniel, 157
Wyoming: anti-Chinese violence in, 258,
    259; minority population (map), *425*;
    railroad construction in, *242*, 258;
    ranches in, *254*; statehood, *200*, 358

Yazoo Act (Georgia), 117
Yellowstone National Park: created, 356,
    357–59; environmental policy in, 358,
    360; Moran's paintings of, 353; Old
    Faithful geyser, *435*; park rangers,
    367–69. *See also* national parks
York (slave of M. Lewis), 141
Yosemite National Park: Camp 4 climbers
    at, 438–40; Hetch Hetchy valley, 371–72;
    Muir at, 359–60, *365*; preservation of,
    357; tourism, 434
Young, Brigham, 206–7, 276–78, 318
Yucatán peninsula, 15

Zhu, Liping, 234
Zimmerman telegram, 306
Zook, Dwight, 333
Zoot-Suit Riots, 335–36
Zunis, 31, *33*, 34–35. *See also* Pueblo peoples